MANAGEMENT INFORMATION SYSTEMS

MANAGING THE DIGITAL FIRM

SIXTEENTH EDITION

Kenneth C. Laudon
New York University

Jane P. Laudon
Azimuth Information Systems

 Pearson

Vice President of Courseware Portfolio Management: Andrew Gilfillan

Executive Portfolio Manager: Samantha Lewis
Team Lead, Content Production: Laura Burgess
Content Producer: Faraz Sharique Ali
Development Editor: Rachael Mann, Laura Town
Portfolio Management Assistant: Bridget Daly
Director of Product Marketing: Brad Parkins
Director of Field Marketing: Jonathan Cottrell
Product Marketing Manager: Heather Taylor
Field Marketing Manager: Bob Nisbet
Product Marketing Assistant: Liz Bennett
Field Marketing Assistant: Derrica Moser
Senior Operations Specialist: Diane Peirano

Senior Art Director: Mary Seiner
Interior and Cover Design: Pearson CSC
Cover Photo: Titima Ongkantong/Shutterstock
Senior Product Model Manager: Eric Hakanson
Manager, Digital Studio: Heather Darby
Course Producer, MyLab MIS: Jaimie Noy
Digital Studio Producer: Tanika Henderson
Full-Service Project Manager: Gowthaman Sadhanandham
Full Service Vendor: Integra Software Service Pvt. Ltd.
Manufacturing Buyer: LSC Communications, Maura Zaldivar-Garcia
Text Printer/Bindery: LSC Communications
Cover Printer: LSC Communications

Microsoft and/or its respective suppliers make no representations about the suitability of the information contained in the documents and related graphics published as part of the services for any purpose. All such documents and related graphics are provided "as is" without warranty of any kind. Microsoft and/or its respective suppliers hereby disclaim all warranties and conditions with regard to this information, including all warranties and conditions of merchantability, whether express, implied or statutory, fitness for a particular purpose, title and non-infringement. In no event shall Microsoft and/or its respective suppliers be liable for any special, indirect or consequential damages or any damages whatsoever resulting from loss of use, data or profits, whether in an action of contract, negligence or other tortious action, arising out of or in connection with the use or performance of information available from the services.

The documents and related graphics contained herein could include technical inaccuracies or typographical errors. Changes are periodically added to the information herein. Microsoft and/or its respective suppliers may make improvements and/or changes in the product(s) and/or the program(s) described herein at any time. Partial screen shots may be viewed in full within the software version specified.

Microsoft® Windows® and Microsoft Office® are registered trademarks of Microsoft Corporation in the U.S.A. and other countries. This book is not sponsored or endorsed by or affiliated with the Microsoft Corporation.

Library of Congress Cataloging-in-Publication Data

Names: Laudon, Kenneth C., author. | Laudon, Jane P. (Jane Price), author.
Title: Management information systems: managing the digital firm / Kenneth C. Laudon, New York University, Jane P. Laudon, Azimuth Information Systems.
Description: Sixteenth edition. | New York, NY: Pearson, [2020] | Includes bibliographical references and index.
Identifiers: LCCN 2018053013| ISBN 9780135191798 | ISBN 0135191793
Subjects: LCSH: Management information systems.
Classification: LCC T58.6 .L376 2020 | DDC 658.4/038011--dc23
LC record available at https://lccn.loc.gov/2018053013

ISBN 10:   0-13-519179-3
ISBN 13: 978-0-13-519179-8

BRIEF CONTENTS

Kenneth C. Laudon is a Professor of Information Systems at New York University's Stern School of Business. He holds a B.A. in Economics from Stanford and a Ph.D. from Columbia University. He has authored 12 books dealing with electronic commerce, information systems, organizations, and society. Professor Laudon has also written more than 40 articles concerned with the social, organizational, and management impacts of information systems, privacy, ethics, and multimedia technology.

Professor Laudon's current research is on the planning and management of large-scale information systems and multimedia information technology. He has received grants from the National Science Foundation to study the evolution of national information systems at the Social Security Administration, the IRS, and the FBI. Ken's research focuses on enterprise system implementation, computer-related organizational and occupational changes in large organizations, changes in management ideology, changes in public policy, and understanding productivity change in the knowledge sector.

Ken Laudon has testified as an expert before the United States Congress. He has been a researcher and consultant to the Office of Technology Assessment (United States Congress), the Department of Homeland Security, and the Office of the President, several executive branch agencies, and Congressional Committees. Professor Laudon also acts as an in-house educator for several consulting firms and as a consultant on systems planning and strategy to several Fortune 500 firms.

At NYU's Stern School of Business, Ken Laudon teaches courses on Managing the Digital Firm, Information Technology and Corporate Strategy, Professional Responsibility (Ethics), and Electronic Commerce and Digital Markets. Ken Laudon's hobby is sailing.

Jane Price Laudon is a management consultant in the information systems area and the author of seven books. Her special interests include systems analysis, data management, MIS auditing, software evaluation, and teaching business professionals how to design and use information systems.

Jane received her Ph.D. from Columbia University, her M.A. from Harvard University, and her B.A. from Barnard College. She has taught at Columbia University and the New York University Graduate School of Business. She maintains a lifelong interest in the languages and civilizations of East Asia.

The Laudons have two daughters, Erica and Elisabeth, to whom this book is dedicated.

Chapter 4   Ethical and Social Issues in Information Systems   120

PART TWO   Information Technology Infrastructure   161

Chapter 5   IT Infrastructure and Emerging Technologies   162

PART **THREE** Key System Applications for the Digital Age 337

Chapter 10

Chapter 11

Managing Knowledge and Artificial Intelligence 418

Chapter 14   Managing Projects   532

BUSINESS CASES AND INTERACTIVE SESSIONS

Here are some of the business firms you will find described in the cases and Interactive Sessions of this book:

Chapter 1: Information Systems in Global Business Today
PCL Construction: The New Digital Firm
Can You Run the Company with Your iPhone?
UPS Competes Globally with Information Technology
Did Information Systems Cause Deutsche Bank to Stumble?

Chapter 2: Global E-business and Collaboration
Enterprise Social Networking Helps Sanofi Pasteur Innovate and Improve Quality
Data Changes How NFL Teams Play the Game and How Fans See It
Videoconferencing: Something for Everyone
Should Companies Embrace Social Business?

Chapter 3: Information Systems, Organizations, and Strategy
Technology Helps Starbucks Find Better Ways to Compete
Digital Technology Helps Crayola Brighten Its Brand
Smart Products—Coming Your Way
Grocery Wars

Chapter 4: Ethical and Social Issues in Information Systems
Are Cars Becoming Big Brother on Wheels?
Will Automation Kill Jobs?
How Harmful Are Smartphones?
Facebook Privacy: Your Life for Sale

Chapter 5: IT Infrastructure and Emerging Technologies
PeroxyChem's Cloud Computing Formula for Success
Is Business Ready for Wearable Computers?
Look to the Cloud
Is BYOD Good for Business?

Chapter 6: Foundations of Business Intelligence: Databases and Information Management
Data Management Helps the Charlotte Hornets Learn More About Their Fans
Kraft Heinz Finds a New Recipe for Analyzing Its Data
Databases Where the Data Aren't There
How Reliable Is Big Data?

Chapter 7: Telecommunications, the Internet, and Wireless Technology
Tour de France Wins with Wireless Technology
Net Neutrality: The Battle Rages On
Monitoring Employees on Networks: Unethical or Good Business?
Google, Apple, and Facebook Battle for Your Internet Experience

New To This Edition

Management Information Systems, 16th edition has new features and content to make your MIS course more exciting, current, and relevant.

New Features

- **New Career Opportunities** section in each chapter, identified by , shows students specifically how this book can help them find a job and build their careers. The last major section of each chapter presents a description of an entry-level job for a recent college graduate based on a real-world job description. The job requirements are related to the topics covered in that chapter. The job description shows the required educational background and skills, lists business-related questions that might arise during the job interview, and provides author tips for answering the questions and preparing for the interview.

- **New Conceptual Videos** collection includes 45 conceptual videos of 3 to 5 minutes in length. Ken Laudon walks students through three of the most important concepts in each chapter using a contemporary animation platform. Available only in the MyLab MIS digital edition.

- **New Video Cases** collection: 36 video cases (two or more per chapter) and 10 additional instructional videos covering key concepts and experiences in the MIS world. The video cases illustrate how real-world corporations and managers are using information technology and systems. Video Cases are listed at the beginning of each chapter.

- **Learning Tracks:** 49 Learning Tracks in MyLab MIS for additional coverage of selected topics. This edition includes new Learning Tracks for case-based reasoning and fuzzy logic.

New Topics

The 16th edition features all new opening, closing, and Interactive Session cases. The text, figures, tables, and cases have been updated through September 2018 with the latest sources from industry and MIS research. New topics and coverage include:

- **Updated coverage of artificial intelligence (AI):** Chapter 11 has been rewritten to include new coverage of machine learning, "deep learning," natural language systems, computer vision systems, and robotics, reflecting the surging interest in business uses of AI and "intelligent" techniques.

- **Big Data and the Internet of Things:** In-depth coverage of big data, big data analytics, and the Internet of Things (IoT) in Chapters 1, 6, 7, and 12. Includes big data analytics, analyzing IoT data streams, Hadoop, in-memory computing, nonrelational databases, data lakes, and analytic platforms.

- **Cloud Computing:** Updated and expanded coverage of cloud computing in Chapter 5 (IT infrastructure) with more detail on types of cloud services, private and public clouds, hybrid clouds, managing cloud services, and a new Interactive Session on using cloud services. Cloud computing also covered in Chapter 6 (databases in the cloud), Chapter 8 (cloud security), Chapter 9 (cloud-based CRM and ERP), Chapter 10 (e-commerce), and Chapter 13 (cloud-based systems development).

- **Social, Mobile, Local:** New e-commerce content in Chapter 10 describing how social tools, mobile technology, and location-based services are transforming marketing and advertising.

- **Social Business:** Expanded coverage of social business, introduced in Chapter 2 and discussed throughout the text. Detailed discussions of enterprise (internal corporate) social networking as well as social networking in e-commerce.

  - Machine learning
  - Natural language processing
  - Computer vision systems
  - Robotics
  - "Deep learning"
  - Supervised learning
  - Unsupervised learning
  - Edge computing
  - 5G networks
  - General Data Protection Regulation (GDPR)
  - Mobile device management (MDM)
  - Office 365
  - Blockchain
  - Data lake
  - Distributed database
  - FinTech

The CORE Laudon text and MyLab MIS provide the most up-to-date and comprehensive overview of information systems used by business firms today. After reading this book, we expect students will be able to participate in, and even lead, management discussions of information systems for their firms and understand how to use information technology in their jobs to achieve bottom-line business results. Regardless of whether students are accounting, finance, management, operations management, marketing, or information systems majors, the knowledge and information in this book will be valuable throughout their business careers.

The MyLab MIS platform provides an interactive digital environment that supports the unique strengths of our work. Our goal with *Management Information Systems: Managing the Digital Firm* is to provide students with an introduction to the MIS field that is authoritative, up-to-date, interactive, and engaging for students and professors. The MyLab MIS edition extends these features to a digital platform that emphasizes videos, animations, interactive quizzes, and student comprehension of concepts, theories, and issues. The MyLab MIS environment reflects the new learning styles of students, which are more social, interactive, and usable on digital devices such as smartphones and tablets.

Reach Every Student with MyLab MIS

MyLab is the teaching and learning platform that empowers you to reach every student. By combining trusted authors' content with digital tools and a flexible platform, MyLab MIS personalizes the learning experience and improves results for each student. And with MIS Decision-Making Sims and auto-graded Excel and Access Projects, students understand how MIS concepts will help them succeed in their future careers.

Solving Teaching and Learning Challenges

The Laudon learning package is more current, real-world, and authoritative than competitors. Laudon MIS16 and MyLab MIS help students understand MIS concepts and issues through extensive use of examples of real-world companies, a wide variety of short and long text and video cases based on real-world organizations, and numerous line art illustrations, interactive animations, and hands-on software projects.

The Laudons are known for their outstanding real-world case studies, which describe how well-known business firms are using IT to solve problems and achieve objectives. Students are often asked to analyze the business problem and propose alternative solutions. The Laudons also provide hands-on MIS software and management decision-making problems in each chapter that are based on real-world companies and business scenarios.

The Laudon text and learning package now has a very strong career focus, which incentivizes students to learn by showing exactly how each chapter will help them prepare for future jobs. In addition to Career Opportunities, MyLab MIS features Career Resources, including how to incorporate MIS knowledge into resumes, cover letters, and job interviews.

The MyLab MIS edition offers unique digital interactive features that hold student attention spans longer and make learning more effective, including 45 animated conceptual learning modules that walk students through key concepts in each chapter; 36 online video cases, and interactive quizzes. All of this is available anytime, anywhere, on any digital device. The result is a comprehensive learning environment that will heighten student engagement and learning in the MIS course.

The Core Text

The core text provides an overview of fundamental MIS concepts using an integrated framework for describing and analyzing information systems. This framework shows information systems composed of management, organization, and technology elements and is reinforced in student projects and case studies. The core text consists of 15 chapters with hands-on projects covering the most essential topics in MIS. An important part of the core text is the Video

Case Study and Instructional Video Package: 36 video case studies (two to three per chapter) plus 10 instructional videos that illustrate business uses of information systems, explain new technologies, and explore concepts. Videos are keyed to the topics of each chapter.

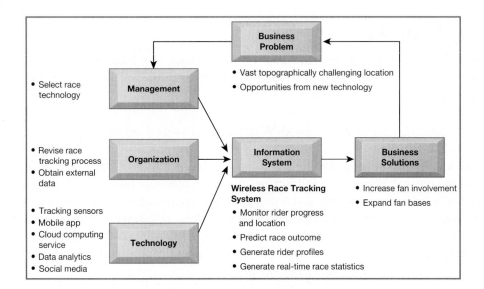

◀ A diagram accompanying each chapter-opening case graphically illustrates how management, organization, and technology elements work together to create an information system solution to the business challenges discussed in the case.

Chapter Organization

Each chapter contains the following elements:

- A Chapter Outline based on Learning Objectives
- Lists of all the Case Studies and Video Cases for each chapter
- A chapter-opening case describing a real-world organization to establish the theme and importance of the chapter
- A diagram analyzing the opening case in terms of the management, organization, and technology model used throughout the text
- Two Interactive Sessions with Case Study Questions
- A Career Opportunities section showing students how to use the text for job hunting and career preparation
- A Review Summary keyed to the Student Learning Objectives
- A list of Key Terms that students can use to review concepts
- Review questions for students to test their comprehension of chapter material
- Discussion questions raised by the broader themes of the chapter
- A series of Hands-on MIS Projects consisting of two Management Decision Problems, a hands-on application software project, and a project to develop Internet skills
- A Collaboration and Teamwork Project to develop teamwork and presentation skills with options for using open source collaboration tools
- A chapter-ending case study for students to apply chapter concepts
- Two assisted-graded writing questions with prebuilt grading rubrics
- Chapter references

Student Learning-Focused

Student Learning Objectives are organized around a set of study questions to focus student attention. Each chapter concludes with a Review Summary and Review Questions organized around these study questions, and each major chapter section is based on a Learning Objective.

Key Features

We have enhanced the text to make it more interactive, leading edge, and appealing to both students and instructors. The features and learning tools are described in the following sections.

Business-Driven with Real-World Business Cases and Examples

The text helps students see the direct connection between information systems and business performance. It describes the main business objectives driving the use of information systems and technologies in corporations all over the world: operational excellence, new products and services, customer and supplier intimacy, improved decision making, competitive advantage, and survival. In-text examples and case studies show students how specific companies use information systems to achieve these objectives.

We use current (2018) examples from business and public organizations throughout the text to illustrate the important concepts in each chapter. All the case studies describe companies or organizations that are familiar to students, such as Uber, the NFL, Facebook, Crayola, Walmart, Amazon, Google, Starbucks, and GE.

Interactivity

There's no better way to learn about MIS than by doing MIS! We provide different kinds of hands-on projects where students can work with real-world business scenarios and data and learn firsthand what MIS is all about. These projects heighten student involvement in this exciting subject.

- **MyLab MIS Online Video Case Package.** Students can watch short videos online, either in-class or at home, and then apply the concepts of the book to the analysis of the video. Every chapter contains at least two business video cases that explain how business firms and managers are using information systems and explore concepts discussed in the chapter. Each video case consists of one or more videos about a real-world company, a background text case, and case study questions. These video cases enhance students' understanding of MIS topics and the relevance of MIS to the business world. In addition, there are 10 Instructional Videos that describe developments and concepts in MIS keyed to respective chapters.

- **MyLab MIS Online Conceptual Videos.** Forty-five video animations where the authors walk students through three concepts from each chapter.

- **Interactive Sessions.** Two short cases in each chapter have been redesigned as Interactive Sessions to be used in the classroom (or on Internet discussion boards) to stimulate student interest and active learning. Each case concludes with case study questions. The case study questions provide topics for class discussion, Internet discussion, or written assignments.

INTERACTIVE SESSION ORGANIZATIONS

Digital Technology Helps Crayola Brighten Its Brand

Crayola is one of the world's most beloved brands for children and their parents. The Easton, Pennsylvania–based company has been noted for high-quality, non-toxic crayons, markers, pencils, modeling clay, creative toys, and innovative art tools that have inspired artistic creativity in children for more than one hundred years. You can find Crayola products nearly everywhere, including schools, offices, supermarkets, drug stores, hospitals, theme parks, airports, gas stations, and restaurants.

The Crayola crayon box became part of the collective history and experiences of generations of Americans, and a symbol of the color and fun of childhood. But today, that Crayola crayon box is not as iconic as in the past. The popularity of Crayola crayons is under assault—not by Crayola's traditional competitors (Faber-Castelli, DixonTiconderoga, and MEGA Brands), but by changing times.

There has been a profound technological and cultural shift in how children play. Children and their families are being bombarded with increasingly sophisticated forms of entertainment, many of them digitally based. Digital products are starting to supplant physical ones in the world of children's play as well as in other areas of work and everyday life. With the advent of computers and web-based learning, children are leaving behind hand-held art supplies at an increasingly younger age. The phenomenon is called KGOY, standing for "Kids Growing Older Younger." As children reach the age of 4 or 5, when they become old enough to play with a computer, they become less interested in toys and crayons and prefer electronics

help children learn and play in colorful ways. The question they asked was not, how can we sell more crayons? Instead they asked, what kinds of experiences and technologies should Crayola embrace? Crayola has reframed its business model, introduced a new innovation process for product development, and created new products and revenue streams. The company has been transformed from a manufacturer of crayons and art tools into a trusted source of tools and experiences for creative play.

Crayola is using digital technology, but not to replace its core crayon business. Instead, it's integrating the old and the new. The company now offers a new range of products like the iMarker, an all-in-one digital pen, crayon, and pencil, designed for use with the Color Studio HD iPad app. It's like a traditional coloring book, but includes new interactive sounds and motion. Lights, Camera, Color! is another digital application that allows kids to turn their favorite photos into digital coloring book pages. Tech toys such as the Digital Light Designer, a 360-degree domed drawing surface, encourage imaginations to run wild with colored LED lights. Children can play updated versions of their favorite games or animate and save up to 50 pieces of their own artwork. Crayola found that parents are looking for toys that are less messy than traditional markers or fingerpaints. These digital toys are "100 percent mess-proof," and technology has helped Crayola make its other products less messy as well.

In designing new digital products and experiences, Crayola has drawn on its extensive knowledge of child development. It understands how digital tech-

◀ Each chapter contains two Interactive Sessions on Management, Organizations, and Technology using real-world companies to illustrate chapter concepts and issues.

CASE STUDY QUESTIONS

1. Analyze Crayola's problem. What management, organization, and technology factors contributed to the problem?

2. What competitive strategies is Crayola pursuing? How does digital technology support those strategies?

3. What people issues did Crayola have to address in designing its new technology-based products?

4. How has digital technology changed Crayola's business model and the way it runs its business?

◀ Case Study Questions encourage students to apply chapter concepts to real-world companies in class discussions, student presentations, or writing assignments.

- **Hands-On MIS Projects.** Every chapter concludes with a Hands-On MIS Projects section containing three types of projects: two Management Decision Problems; a hands-on application software exercise using Microsoft Excel, Access, or web page and blog creation tools; and a project that develops Internet business skills. A Dirt Bikes USA running case in MyLab MIS provides additional hands-on projects for each chapter.

- **Collaboration and Teamwork Projects.** Each chapter features a collaborative project that encourages students working in teams to use Google Drive, Google Docs, or other open source collaboration tools. The first team project in Chapter 1 asks students to build a collaborative Google site.

▶ Students practice using software in real-world settings for achieving operational excellence and enhancing decision making.

▶ Each chapter features a project to develop Internet skills for accessing information, conducting research, and performing online calculations and analysis.

Improving Decision Making: Using Web Tools to Configure and Price an Automobile

Software skills: Internet-based software
Business skills: Researching product information and pricing

3-11 In this exercise, you will use software at car websites to find product information about a car of your choice and use that information to make an important purchase decision. You will also evaluate two of these sites as selling tools.

You are interested in purchasing a new Ford Escape (or some other car of your choice). Go to the website of CarsDirect (www.carsdirect.com) and begin your investigation. Locate the Ford Escape. Research the various Escape models, and choose one you prefer in terms of price, features, and safety ratings. Locate and read at least two reviews. Surf the website of the manufacturer, in this case Ford (www.ford.com). Compare the information available on Ford's website with that of CarsDirect for the Ford Escape. Try to locate the lowest price for the car you want in a local dealer's inventory. Suggest improvements for CarsDirect.com and Ford.com.

Customization and Flexibility

Our Learning Tracks and Video Cases in MyLab MIS give instructors the flexibility to provide in-depth coverage of the topics and additional cases they choose. Video Cases and Instructional Videos are listed at the beginning of each chapter as well as in the Preface.

Learning Tracks

There are 49 Learning Tracks in MyLab MIS available to instructors and students. This supplementary content takes students deeper into MIS topics, concepts, and debates and reviews basic technology concepts in hardware, software, database design, telecommunications, and other areas.

Chapter	Learning Tracks
Chapter 1: Information Systems in Global Business Today	How Much Does IT Matter? Information Systems and Your Career The Mobile Digital Platform
Chapter 2: Global E-business and Collaboration	Systems from a Functional Perspective IT Enables Collaboration and Teamwork Challenges of Using Business Information Systems Organizing the Information Systems Function Occupational and Career Outlook for Information Systems Majors 2014–2020
Chapter 3: Information Systems, Organizations, and Strategy	The Changing Business Environment for IT
Chapter 4: Ethical and Social Issues in Information Systems	Developing a Corporate Code of Ethics for IT
Chapter 5: IT Infrastructure and Emerging Technologies	How Computer Hardware Works How Computer Software Works Service Level Agreements The Open Source Software Initiative Comparing Stages in IT Infrastructure Evolution Cloud Computing

Chapter	Learning Tracks
Chapter 6: Foundations of Business Intelligence: Databases and Information Management	Database Design, Normalization, and Entity-Relationship Diagramming Introduction to SQL Hierarchical and Network Data Models
Chapter 7: Telecommunications, the Internet, and Wireless Technology	Broadband Network Services and Technologies Cellular System Generations Wireless Applications for Customer Relationship Management, Supply Chain Management, and Healthcare Introduction to Web 2.0 LAN Topologies
Chapter 8: Securing Information Systems	The Booming Job Market in IT Security The Sarbanes-Oxley Act Computer Forensics General and Application Controls for Information Systems Management Challenges of Security and Control Software Vulnerability and Reliability
Chapter 9: Achieving Operational Excellence and Customer Intimacy: Enterprise Applications	SAP Business Process Map Business Processes in Supply Chain Management and Supply Chain Metrics Best-Practice Business Processes in CRM Software
Chapter 10: E-commerce: Digital Markets, Digital Goods	E-commerce Challenges: The Story of Online Groceries Build an E-commerce Business Plan Hot New Careers in E-Commerce E-commerce Payment Systems Building an E-commerce Website
Chapter 11: Managing Knowledge and Artificial Intelligence	Challenges of Knowledge Management Systems Case-Based Reasoning Fuzzy Logic
Chapter 12: Enhancing Decision Making	Building and Using Pivot Tables
Chapter 13: Building Information Systems	Unified Modeling Language Primer on Business Process Design and Documentation Primer on Business Process Management Fourth-Generation Languages
Chapter 14: Managing Projects	Capital Budgeting Methods for Information Systems Investments Enterprise Analysis (Business Systems Planning) and Critical Success Factors Information Technology Investments and Productivity

Video Cases and Instructional Videos

Instructors can download step-by-step instructions for accessing the video cases from the Instructor Resources Center.

Chapter	Video
Chapter 1: Information Systems in Global Business Today	Business in the Cloud: Facebook, Google, and eBay Data Centers UPS Global Operations with the DIAD and Worldport Instructional Video: Tour IBM's Raleigh Data Center
Chapter 2: Global E-business and Collaboration	Walmart's Retail Link Supply Chain CEMEX: Becoming a Social Business Instructional Video: US Foodservice Grows Market with Oracle CRM on Demand
Chapter 3: Information Systems, Organizations, and Strategy	GE Becomes a Digital Firm: The Emerging Industrial Internet National Basketball Association: Competing on Global Delivery with Akamai OS Streaming
Chapter 4: Ethical and Social Issues in Information Systems	What Net Neutrality Means for You Facebook and Google Privacy: What Privacy? The United States vs. Terrorism: Data Mining for Terrorists and Innocents Instructional Video: Viktor Mayer Schönberger on the Right to Be Forgotten
Chapter 5: IT Infrastructure and Emerging Technologies	Rockwell Automation Fuels the Oil and Gas Industry with the Internet of Things (IoT) ESPN.com: The Future of Sports Coverage in the Cloud Netflix: Building a Business in the Cloud

Video Cases and Instructional Videos (Continued)

Chapter	Video
Chapter 6: Foundations of Business Intelligence: Databases and Information Management	Dubuque Uses Cloud Computing and Sensors to Build a Smarter City Brooks Brothers Closes in on Omnichannel Retail Maruti Suzuki Business Intelligence and Enterprise Databases
Chapter 7: Telecommunications, the Internet, and Wireless Technology	Telepresence Moves out of the Boardroom and into the Field Virtual Collaboration with IBM Sametime
Chapter 8: Securing Information Systems	Stuxnet and Cyberwarfare Cyberespionage: The Chinese Threat Instructional Video: Sony PlayStation Hacked; Data Stolen from 77 Million Users Instructional Video: Meet the Hackers: Anonymous Statement on Hacking SONY
Chapter 9: Achieving Operational Excellence and Customer Intimacy: Enterprise Applications	Life Time Fitness Gets in Shape with Salesforce CRM Instructional Video: GSMS Protects Products and Patients by Serializing Every Bottle of Drugs
Chapter 10: E-commerce: Digital Markets, Digital Goods	Walmart Takes on Amazon: A Battle of IT and Management Systems Groupon: Deals Galore Etsy: A Marketplace and Community Instructional Video: Walmart's eCommerce Fulfillment Center Network Instructional Video: Behind the Scenes of an Amazon Warehouse
Chapter 11: Managing Knowledge and Artificial Intelligence	How IBM's Watson Became a Jeopardy Champion Alfresco: Open Source Document Management and Collaboration
Chapter 12: Enhancing Decision Making	PSEG Leverages Big Data and Business Analytics Using GE's Predix Platform FreshDirect Uses Business Intelligence to Manage Its Online Grocery Business Intelligence Helps the Cincinnati Zoo Work Smarter
Chapter 13: Building Information Systems	IBM: Business Process Management in a SaaS Environment IBM Helps the City of Madrid with Real-Time BPM Software Instructional Video: Workflow Management Visualized Instructional Video: BPM: Business Process Management Customer Story
Chapter 14: Managing Projects	Blue Cross Blue Shield Smarter Computing Project NASA Project Management Challenges
Chapter 15: Managing Global Systems	Daum Runs Oracle Apps on Linux Lean Manufacturing and Global ERP: Humanetics and Global Shop

Developing Career Skills

For students to succeed in a rapidly changing job market, they should be aware of their career options and how to go about developing a variety of skills. With MyLab MIS and Management Information Systems: Managing the Digital Firm, we focus on developing these skills in the following ways.

Career Opportunities and Resources

Every student who reads this text wants to know: How will this book help my career? Our new Career Opportunities feature shows how to use this text and MyLab MIS as tools for job-hunting and career-building. Job interviewers will typically ask about why you want the job, along with your ability to communicate, multitask, work in a team, show leadership, solve problems, and meet goals. These are general skills and behaviors you'll need to succeed in any job, and you should be prepared to provide examples from your course work and job experiences that demonstrate these skills. But there are also business knowledge and professional skills that employers will ask you about. Career Opportunities will show you how to use what you have learned in this text to demonstrate these skills.

The Career Opportunities section, identified by this icon ✿ is the last major section of each chapter under the heading "How will MIS help my career?". There you will find a description of an entry-level job for a recent college graduate based on a real-world job description from major online job sites related to the topics covered in that chapter. The name of the company offering the job and its location have been changed. Each chapter's job posting describes the required educational background and specific job skills, and suggests some of the business-related questions that might arise during the job interview. The authors provide tips for answering the questions and preparing for the interview. Career Opportunities also show where students can find out more information about the technical and business knowledge required for the job in this text and on the web and social media.

Below are the job descriptions used in this edition based on postings from both large and small businesses. A few of these jobs call for an MIS major, others for MIS course work, but many postings are not that specific. Some require some previous internship or job experience, but many are entry-level positions suitable for new college graduates, and some of these positions provide on-the-job training. However, all require knowledge of business information systems and applications and the ability to work in a digital environment.

Chapter	Career Opportunity Job Description
1. Business Information Systems in Your Career	Financial Client Support and Sales Assistant
2. Global E-business and Collaboration	Entry Level Sales Support Specialist
3. Information Systems, Organizations, and Strategy	Entry Level Business Development Representative
4. Ethical and Social Issues in Information Systems	Junior Privacy Analyst
5. IT Infrastructure and Emerging Technologies	Entry Level IT Consultant
6. Foundations of Business Intelligence: Databases and Information Management	Entry Level Data Analyst
7. Telecommunications, the Internet, and Wireless Technology	Automotive Digital Advisor
8. Securing Information Systems	Entry Level Identity Access and Management Support Specialist
9. Achieving Operational Excellence and Customer Intimacy: Enterprise Applications	Manufacturing Management Trainee
10. E-Commerce: Digital Markets, Digital Goods	Junior E-Commerce Data Analyst
11. Managing Knowledge and Artificial Intelligence	AI Technology Sales Assistant
12. Improving Decision Making	Entry Level Data Analyst
13. Building Information Systems	Entry Level Junior Business Systems Analyst
14. Managing Projects	IT Project Management Assistant
15. Managing Global Systems	Global Data Services Sales and Marketing Trainee

Students can use Career Opportunities to shape their resumes and career plans as well as to prepare for interviews. For instructors, Career Opportunities are potential projects for student research and in-class discussion.

In MyLab MIS we have provided additional Career Resources, including job-hunting guides and instructions on how to build a Digital Portfolio demonstrating the business knowledge, application software proficiency, and Internet skills acquired from using the text. The portfolio can be included in a resume or job application or used as a learning assessment tool for instructors.

Table of Contents Overview

Instructor Teaching Resources

Supplements available to instructors at www.pearsonhighered.com/laudon	Features of the Supplement
Instructor's Manual	• Chapter-by-chapter summaries • Examples and activities not in the main book • Teaching outlines • Teaching tips • Solutions to all questions and problems in the book
Test Bank authored by Professor Kenneth Laudon, New York University	The authors have worked closely with skilled test item writers to ensure that higher-level cognitive skills are tested. Test bank multiple-choice questions include questions on content but also include many questions that require analysis, synthesis, and evaluation skills. **AACSB Assessment Guidelines** As a part of its accreditation activities, the AACSB has developed an Assurance of Learning Program designed to ensure that schools do in fact teach students what they promise. Schools are required to state a clear mission, develop a coherent business program, identify student learning objectives, and then prove that students do in fact achieve the objectives. We have attempted in this book to support AACSB efforts to encourage assessment-based education. The end papers of this edition identify student learning objectives and anticipated outcomes for our Hands-On MIS projects. The authors will provide custom advice on how to use this text in colleges with different missions and assessment needs. Please e-mail the authors or contact your local Pearson representative for contact information.
Computerized TestGen	TestGen allows instructors to: • Customize, save, and generate classroom tests • Edit, add, or delete questions from the Test Item Files • Analyze test results • Organize a database of tests and student results

Supplements available to instructors at www.pearsonhighered.com/laudon	Features of the Supplement
PowerPoints authored by Professor Kenneth Laudon, New York University	The authors have prepared a comprehensive collection of 50 PowerPoint slides for each chapter to be used in your lectures. Many of these slides are the same as used by Ken Laudon in his MIS classes and executive education presentations. Each of the slides is annotated with teaching suggestions for asking students questions, developing in-class lists that illustrate key concepts, and recommending other firms as examples in addition to those provided in the text. The annotations are like an Instructor's Manual built into the slides and make it easier to teach the course effectively. PowerPoints meet accessibility standards for students with disabilities. Features include but are not limited to: • Keyboard and Screen Reader access • Alternative text for images • High color contrast between background and foreground colors

Acknowledgments

The production of any book involves valued contributions from a number of persons. We would like to thank all of our editors for encouragement, insight, and strong support for many years. We thank our editor, Samantha McAfee Lewis and Content Producer, Faraz Sharique Ali for their role in managing the project.

Our special thanks go to our supplement authors for their work, including the following MyLab MIS content contributors: Roberta M. Roth, University of Northern Iowa; Gipsi Sera, Indiana University; Robert J. Mills, Utah State University; and John Hupp, Columbus State University. We are indebted to Erica Laudon for her contributions to Career Opportunities and to Megan Miller for her help during production.

Special thanks to colleagues at the Stern School of Business at New York University; to Professor Werner Schenk, Simon School of Business, University of Rochester; to Professor Mark Gillenson, Fogelman College of Business and Economics, University of Memphis; to Robert Kostrubanic, Indiana-Purdue University Fort Wayne; to Professor Ethné Swartz, Department of Information Management and Business Analytics, Feliciano School of Business; to Professor Detlef Schoder of the University of Cologne; to Professor Walter Brenner of the University of St. Gallen; to Professor Lutz Kolbe of the University of Gottingen; and to Professor Donald Marchand of the International Institute for Management Development who provided additional suggestions for improvement. Thank you to Professor Ken Kraemer, University of California at Irvine, and Professor John King, University of Michigan, for more than a decade-long discussion of information systems and organizations. And a special remembrance and dedication to Professor Rob Kling, University of Indiana, for being our friend and colleague over so many years.

We also want to especially thank all our reviewers whose suggestions helped improve our texts. Reviewers for recent editions include:

Brad Allen, Plymouth State University
Wanda Curtsinger, Texas A&M University
Dawit Demissie, University of Albany
Anne Formalarie, Plymouth State University
Bin Gu,University of Texas–Austin

Essia Hamouda, University of California–Riverside
Linda Lau, Longwood University
Kimberly L. Merritt, Oklahoma Christian University
James W. Miller, Dominican University
Fiona Nah, University of Nebraska–Lincoln
M. K. Raja, University of Texas Arlington
Thomas Schambach, Illinois State University
Shawn Weisfeld, Florida Institute of Technology

Organizations, Management, and the Networked Enterprise

PART ONE introduces the major themes of this book, raising a series of important questions: What is an information system, and what are its management, organization, and technology dimensions? Why are information systems so essential in businesses today? Why are systems for collaboration and social business so important? How can information systems help businesses become more competitive? What broader ethical and social issues are raised by widespread use of information systems?

Information Systems in Global Business Today

LEARNING OBJECTIVES

After reading this chapter, you will be able to answer the following questions:

1-1 How are information systems transforming business, and why are they so essential for running and managing a business today?

1-2 What is an information system? How does it work? What are its management, organization, and technology components? Why are complementary assets essential for ensuring that information systems provide genuine value for organizations?

1-3 What academic disciplines are used to study information systems, and how does each contribute to an understanding of information systems?

1-4 How will MIS help my career?

CHAPTER CASES

PCL Construction: The New Digital Firm
Can You Run the Company with Your iPhone?
UPS Competes Globally with Information Technology
Did Information Systems Cause Deutsche Bank to Stumble?

VIDEO CASES

Business in the Cloud: Facebook, Google, and eBay Data Centers
UPS Global Operations with the DIAD and Worldport

Instructional Video:
Tour IBM's Raleigh Data Center

MyLab MIS
Discussion Questions: 1-4, 1-5, 1-6; **Hands-on MIS Projects:** 1-7, 1-8, 1-9, 1-10;
Writing Assignments: 1-16, 1-17; **eText with Conceptual Animations**

PCL Construction: The New Digital Firm

Many people think the most widely used tool in a construction project is a hammer, but it is more likely a filing cabinet or fax machine. The construction industry has traditionally been very paper-intensive and manual. A complex project such as a large building requires hundreds of architectural drawings and design documents, which can change daily. Costly delays because of difficulty locating and accessing the documents and other project information could make or break a project. Now that's changing, and PCL Construction is at the forefront. Information technology has transformed the way this business works, and it is a prime example of the new digital firm.

PCL is a group of independent general contracting construction companies, with over 4,400 employees in the United States, Canada, and Australia. The organization is active in the commercial, institutional, multifamily residential, renewable energy, heavy industrial, historical restoration, and civil construction sectors. PCL has corporate headquarters in Edmonton, Alberta, Canada and a United States head office in Denver, Colorado.

At a PCL job site, you'll now see employees using mobile devices, including smartphones, tablets, and laptops, to access important information from PCL systems or input data. Electronic touch-screen kiosks throughout the job site and electronic plan rooms provide access to digitized, updated blueprints so team members don't have to waste time tracking down paper versions.

In the past, on-site trailers used to house large paper blueprints for a project. Each time a project team member wanted to view plans, that person

© Ndoeljindoel/123RF

had to visit a trailer. With up to 800 active construction projects running simultaneously, PCL had trouble keeping project documentation up to date. Information on paper forms to track small changes to project specifications or work requirements might not reach project decision makers until 30–40 days from the time it was recorded. By then, it was too late—decisions were made "from the gut" rather than based on facts.

PCL Construction plans are now in digital form, or the paper versions are scanned for digital storage. Digitized plans can be revised much more rapidly. By performing much of the design and planning work on the computer, PCL is able to identify and resolve conflicts and constructability issues early in the construction process to help keep projects ahead of schedule and within budget.

PCL implemented Project Document Controls (PDC) to facilitate collaboration among project team members. A secure project-based website provides real-time storage and management of information in a single shared accessible location. Construction contractors, subcontractors, consultants, suppliers, and clients can work from the same documents wherever they are. PCL uses its own proprietary project management system for budgeting, costing, forecasting, subcontractor tracking, production, and reporting. The project management system is linked to other PCL systems, including the People and Projects database, client management and accounting systems, and the BEST Estimating system. BEST Estimating is PCL's in-house estimating program for creating lump sum and unit price estimates and providing accurate resource and cost information.

PCL started moving its computing work to Microsoft Azure Cloud, which hosts the hardware and software for running some of PCL's applications in remote computing centers managed by Microsoft. Staff working on PCL projects can access information from cloud-based systems at any time and location using mobile devices as well as conventional desktop machines and an Internet connection. PCL saves 80 percent of the cost of backing up its corporate data by using the Azure platform. Azure Cloud also hosts a real-time analytics dashboard to monitor project performance in terms of quality, safety, schedule, and cost. The data are displayed visually as bar graphs or pie charts to construction field staff, project managers, and executives, and colors ranging from red to orange to green display performance ratings.

Sources: "Technology and Innovation," pcl.com, accessed February 9, 2018; "PCL: Capitalizing on the Cloud," itworldcanada.com, accessed February 9, 2018; Brian Jackson, "PCL Constructors Reach New Heights with Real-time Analytics Solution in the Cloud," *IT World Canada*, November 9, 2017.

PCL Construction's experience shows how essential information systems are today. PCL operates construction projects in numerous distributed locations in an industry that has been traditionally very paper-intensive. Processing and accessing the large number of documents and other information required by construction projects was excessively costly and time-consuming, driving up costs. PCL used leading-edge information technology to digitize documents and streamline business processes for documenting, tracking, and analyzing projects. The information flows that drive PCL's business have become largely digital, making use of mobile tools and a cloud computing infrastructure. PCL Construction has become a leading example of a digital firm.

The chapter-opening diagram calls attention to important points raised by this case and this chapter. To reduce time and costs and improve customer service in a heavily paper-based industry, PCL management chose to use information technology to increase the precision and efficiency of key business activities for designing, costing, budgeting, and monitoring a construction project. These technologies include mobile devices (phones, tablets, laptops), touch screen kiosks, cloud computing services, the Internet, and software for creating models, managing documents, monitoring project progress, budgeting, estimating costs, and

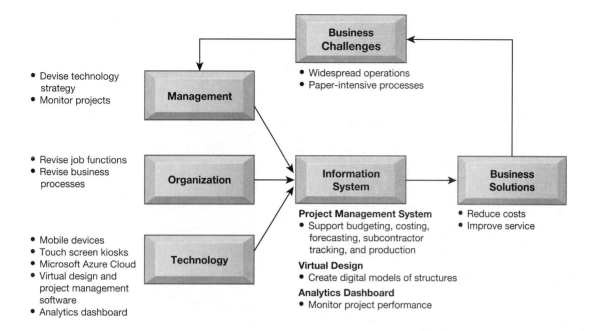

Devise technology strategy
- Monitor projects

- Revise job functions
- Revise business processes

- Mobile devices
- Touch screen kiosks
- Microsoft Azure Cloud
- Virtual design and project management software
- Analytics dashboard

Business Challenges
- Widespread operations
- Paper-intensive processes

Management

Organization

Technology

Information System

Business Solutions
- Reduce costs
- Improve service

Project Management System
- Support budgeting, costing, forecasting, subcontractor tracking, and production

Virtual Design
- Create digital models of structures

Analytics Dashboard
- Monitor project performance

displaying key project performance indicators on a digital dashboard. The use of leading-edge digital technologies to drive business operations and management decisions is a key topic today in the MIS world and will be discussed throughout this text.

It is also important to note that deploying information technology has changed the way PCL Construction runs its business. To effectively use all of its new digital tools, PCL had to redesign jobs and procedures for gathering, inputting, and accessing information, for designing, budgeting, and calculating costs, and for monitoring project progress. These changes had to be carefully planned to make sure they enhanced efficiency, service, and profitability.

Here are some questions to think about: How did information technology change operations at PCL construction? What was the role of mobile technology and cloud computing?

1-1 How are information systems transforming business, and why are they so essential for running and managing a business today?

It's not business as usual in the United States or the rest of the global economy anymore. In 2017, American businesses spent nearly $1 trillion on information systems hardware, software, and telecommunications equipment. In addition, they spent another $143 billion on business and management consulting and services—much of which involves redesigning firms' business operations to take advantage of these new technologies. In fact, most of the business value of IT investment derives from these organizational, management, and cultural changes inside firms (Saunders and Brynjolfsson, 2016). Figure 1.1 shows that between 1999 and 2017, private business investment in information technology consisting of hardware, software, and communications equipment grew from 21 to 33 percent of all invested capital.

> **FIGURE 1.1   INFORMATION TECHNOLOGY CAPITAL INVESTMENT**
>
> Information technology capital investment, defined as hardware, software, and communications equipment, grew from 21 to 33 percent of all invested capital between 1999 and 2017.
>
> Source: Based on data in U.S. Department of Commerce, Bureau of Economic Analysis, *National Income and Product Accounts*, Table 5.3.6. Real Private Fixed Investment by Type, Chained Dollars (2018).

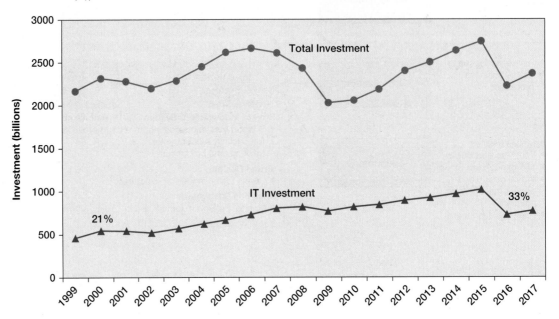

As managers, most of you will work for firms that are intensively using information systems and making large investments in information technology. You will certainly want to know how to invest this money wisely. If you make wise choices, your firm can outperform competitors. If you make poor choices, you will be wasting valuable capital. This book is dedicated to helping you make wise decisions about information technology and information systems.

How Information Systems Are Transforming Business

You can see the results of this large-scale spending around you every day by observing how people conduct business. Changes in technology and new innovative business models have transformed social life and business practices. More than 269 million Americans have mobile phones (81 percent of the population), and 230 million of these people access the Internet using smartphones and tablets. Fifty-five percent of the entire population now uses tablet computers, whose sales have soared. Two hundred million Americans use online social networks; 175 million use Facebook, while 54 million use Twitter. Smartphones, social networking, texting, e-mailing, and webinars have all become essential tools of business because that's where your customers, suppliers, and colleagues can be found (eMarketer, 2018).

By June 2017, more than 140 million businesses worldwide had dot-com Internet sites registered. Today, 220 million Americans shop online, and 190 million will purchase online. In 2017, FedEx moved about 16 million packages daily in 220 countries and territories around the world, mostly overnight, and the United Parcel Service (UPS) moved more than 28 million packages daily. Businesses are using information technology to sense and respond to rapidly changing customer demand, reduce inventories to the lowest possible levels, and achieve higher levels of operational efficiency. Supply chains have become more fast-paced, with companies of all sizes depending on just-in-time inventory to reduce their overhead costs and get to market faster.

As newspaper print readership continues to decline, in 2017 more than 180 million people read a newspaper online, and millions more read other news sites. Online digital newspaper readership is growing at 10 percent annually, about twice as fast as the Internet itself. About 128 million people watch a video online every day, 85 million read a blog, and 30 million post to blogs, creating an explosion of new writers and new forms of customer feedback that did not exist five years ago (eMarketer, 2018). Social networking site Facebook attracted 214 million monthly visitors in 2018 in the United States and more than 2 billion worldwide. Businesses are using social networking tools to connect their employees, customers, and managers worldwide. Most *Fortune* 500 companies now have Facebook pages, Twitter accounts, and Tumblr sites.

E-commerce and Internet advertising continue to expand. Google's U.S. online ad revenues surpassed $32 billion in 2017, and Internet advertising continues to grow at more than 20 percent a year in the United States, reaching more than $107 billion in revenues in 2018 (eMarketer, 2018).

New federal security and accounting laws requiring many businesses to keep e-mail messages for five years, coupled with existing occupational and health laws requiring firms to store employee chemical exposure data for up to 60 years, are spurring the annual growth of digital information at the estimated rate of 5 exabytes annually, equivalent to 37,000 new Libraries of Congress.

What's New in Management Information Systems?

Plenty. In fact, there's a whole new world of doing business using new technologies for managing and organizing. What makes the MIS field the most exciting area of study in schools of business is the continuous change in technology, management, and business processes. Five changes are of paramount importance.

IT Innovations. A continuing stream of information technology innovations is transforming the traditional business world. Examples include the emergence of cloud computing, the growth of a mobile digital business platform based on smartphones and tablet computers, big data and the Internet of Things (IoT), business analytics, machine learning systems, and the use of social networks by managers to achieve business objectives. Most of these changes have occurred in the past few years. These innovations are enabling entrepreneurs and innovative traditional firms to create new products and services, develop new business models, and transform the day-to-day conduct of business. In the process, some old businesses, even industries, are being destroyed while new businesses are springing up.

New Business Models. For instance, the emergence of online video services for streaming or downloading, such as Netflix, Apple iTunes, and Amazon, has forever changed how premium video is distributed and even created. Netflix in 2018 attracted more than 125 million subscribers worldwide to what it calls the "Internet TV revolution." Netflix has moved into premium TV show production with nearly 1,000 original shows such as *American Vandal, Suburra, The Crown, Friends From College, No Country For Old Men, House of Cards*, and *Orange Is the New Black*, challenging cable and broadcast producers of TV shows, and potentially disrupting cable network dominance of TV show production. Apple's iTunes now accounts for 67 percent of movie and TV show downloads and has struck deals with major Hollywood studios for recent movies and TV shows. A growing trickle of viewers are unplugging from cable and using only the Internet for entertainment.

E-commerce Expansion. E-commerce generated about $700 billion in revenues in 2017 and is estimated to grow to nearly $950 billion by 2020. E-commerce is changing how firms design, produce, and deliver their products and services. E-commerce has reinvented itself again, disrupting the traditional marketing and advertising industry and putting major media and content firms in jeopardy. Facebook and other social networking sites such as YouTube, Twitter, and Tumblr, along with Netflix, Apple Music, and many other media firms, exemplify the new face of e-commerce in the twenty-first century. They sell services. When we think of e-commerce, we tend to think of selling physical products. While this iconic vision of e-commerce is still very powerful and the fastest-growing form of retail in the United States, growing up alongside is a whole new value stream based on selling services, not goods. It's a services model of e-commerce. Growth in social commerce is spurred by powerful growth of the mobile platform: 85 percent of Facebook's users access the service from mobile phones and tablets. Information systems and technologies are the foundation of this new services-based e-commerce. Mobile e-commerce hit $229 billion in 2017 and is growing at 30 percent a year.

Management Changes. The management of business firms has changed: With new mobile smartphones, high-speed wireless Wi-Fi networks, and tablets, remote salespeople on the road are only seconds away from their managers' questions and oversight. Management is going mobile. Managers on the move are in direct, continuous contact with their employees. The growth of enterprise-wide information systems with extraordinarily rich data means that managers no longer operate in a fog of confusion but instead have online, nearly instant access to the really important information they need for accurate and timely decisions. In addition to their public uses on the web, social networking tools, wikis, and blogs are becoming important corporate tools for communication, collaboration, and information sharing.

Changes in Firms and Organizations. Compared to industrial organizations of the previous century, new fast-growing twenty-first-century business firms put less emphasis on hierarchy and structure and more emphasis on employees taking on multiple roles and tasks and collaborating with others on a team. They put greater emphasis on competency and skills rather than position in the hierarchy. They emphasize higher-speed and more-accurate decision making based on data and analysis. They are more aware of changes in technology, consumer attitudes, and culture. They use social media to enter into conversations with consumers and demonstrate a greater willingness to listen to consumers, in part because they have no choice. They show better understanding of the importance of information technology in creating and managing business firms and other organizations. To the extent organizations and business firms demonstrate these characteristics, they are twenty-first-century digital firms.

You can see some of these trends at work in the Interactive Session on Management. Millions of managers rely heavily on the mobile digital platform to coordinate suppliers and shipments, satisfy customers, and manage their employees. A business day without these mobile devices or Internet access would be unthinkable.

INTERACTIVE SESSION MANAGEMENT

Can You Run the Company with Your iPhone?

Can you run the company just by using your iPhone? Perhaps not entirely, but there are many business functions today that can be performed using an iPhone, iPad, or Android mobile device. Smartphones and tablets have become all-in-one tools that help managers and employees work more efficiently, packing a powerful, networked computer into a pocket-size device. With a tap or flick of a finger, these mobile devices can access the Internet or serve as a telephone, camera, music or video player, an e-mail and messaging machine, and, increasingly, a gateway into corporate systems. New software applications for document sharing, collaboration, sales, order processing, inventory management, scheduling, and production monitoring make these devices even more versatile business tools.

Network Rail runs, maintains, and develops the rail tracks, signaling, bridges, tunnels, level crossings, and many key stations for most of the rail network in England, Scotland, and Wales. Keeping trains running on time is one of its top priorities. To maintain 20,000 miles of track safely and efficiently, skilled workers must be equipped with appropriate tools and work across thousands of sites throughout the rail network, 24 hours a day. Network Rail uses a group of custom apps for its 22,000 iPhone and iPad devices to streamline maintenance operations, quickly capture incident data, and immediately share critical information.

Several apps help Network Rail improve railway performance and safety. The Close Call app helps employees report hazards as they are found so problems can be addressed quickly. The MyWork app gives maintenance teams all the information they need to start and complete repair tasks. The Sentinel app allows field managers to electronically scan ID cards to verify that workers are qualified to perform specific tasks.

The iPhone and iPad apps provide maintenance technicians with current technical data, GPS locations, and streamlined reports, replacing cumbersome reference books and rain-soaked paperwork that slowed the repair process. Many service calls start with hazardous conditions reported by Network Rail employees themselves. Rather than waiting hours to fill out a report at the depot, workers can take pictures of dangerous situations right away,

using the Close Call app to describe situations and upload photos to the call center. Once provided with the hazard's GPS coordinates, the call center will usually schedule repairs within 24 hours.

MyWork gives maintenance workers a simple overview of all of the jobs each team needs to complete during a specific shift. This mobile app clusters jobs by location, skills required, and opening and closing times. Using precise map coordinates, workers can find sites easily and finish jobs more quickly. By electronically delivering daily job schedules to over 14,000 maintenance staff members, MyWork has enabled them to complete over a half a million work orders to date while minimizing interruptions.

British Airways is the largest airline in the United Kingdom, with operations in more than 200 airports worldwide. The airline has found many ways to use the iPad to improve customer service and operational efficiency. The airline has created more than 40 custom apps for over 17,000 iPads for its workforce that have transformed the way it does business.

Unforeseen disruptions can create long lines of passengers seeking flight information and rebooking. The FlightReact app used by British Airways mobilizes agents to scan a boarding pass, review the customer's booking, look up alternate flight options, and rebook and reticket passengers—all within four minutes. iBanner allows agents to identify passengers transferring onto a specific flight, while iTranslate enables staff to communicate easily with travelers speaking any language.

Inside the airport, iPads and iPhones communicate with low-energy wireless Bluetooth signals from iBeacon, notifying customers of Wi-Fi access, gate locations, and flight updates. Beyond the terminal, mobile apps are helping British Airways to improve the aircraft turnaround process. British Airways has more than 70 planes at London Heathrow Terminal, five turning around at once, and each requiring a team of around 30 people. To shorten and streamline this process can generate huge business benefits.

Loading luggage and cargo onto an aircraft is one of the most complex parts of the turnaround process, requiring detailed communications between the turnaround manager (TRM), who coordinates and manages the services around the aircraft during departure and arrival, the offsite Centralized Load Control (CLC) team, and the pilot. With iPads running the iLoad Direct app, turnaround managers are able to monitor the aircraft loading process and share data with pilots and back-office staff in real time. TRMs can receive and input real-time data about the aircraft load's contents, weight, and distribution. These data are essential to help the pilot calculate the right amount of fuel and position the plane for take-off. By streamlining communications between the ground crew, the CLC team, and the pilot, iLoad Direct and iPad speed up the pace at which aircraft become airborne. These mobile tools have helped British Airways achieve an industry-leading benchmark for aircraft turnaround.

In addition to facilitating managerial work, mobile devices are helping rank-and-file employees manage their work lives more effectively. Shyft is one of several smartphone apps that allow workers to share information, make schedule changes, and report labor violations. Thousands of employees at chains like Starbucks and Old Navy are using these apps to view their schedules and swap shifts when they've got a scheduling conflict or need extra work.

Sources: "British Airways: Transforming the Travel Experience from Start to Finish," *Apple at Work*, www.apple.com, accessed February 7, 2018; www.networkrail.co.uk,accessed September 2, 2018; "Network Rail," *iPhone in Business*, www.apple.com, accessed January 4, 2017; and Lauren Weber, "Apps Empower Employees, Ease Scheduling," *Wall Street Journal*, January 3, 2017.

CASE STUDY QUESTIONS

1. What kinds of applications are described here? What business functions do they support? How do they improve operational efficiency and decision making?

2. Identify the problems that the business in this case study solved by using mobile digital devices.

3. What kinds of businesses are most likely to benefit from equipping their employees with mobile digital devices such as iPhones and iPads?

4. One company deploying iPhones has stated, "The iPhone is not a game changer, it's an industry changer. It changes the way that you can interact with your customers" and "with your suppliers." Discuss the implications of this statement.

iPhone and iPad
Applications for Business

1. Salesforce
2. Cisco WebEx Meetings
3. SAP Business One
4. iWork
5. Evernote
6. Adobe Acrobat Reader
7. Oracle Business Intelligence Mobile
8. Dropbox

© Mama_mia/Shutterstock

Whether it's attending an online meeting, checking orders, working with files and documents, or obtaining business intelligence, Apple's iPhone and iPad offer unlimited possibilities for business users. A stunning multitouch display, full Internet browsing, and capabilities for messaging, video and audio transmission, and document management make each an all-purpose platform for mobile computing.

Globalization Challenges and Opportunities: A Flattened World

In 1492, Columbus reaffirmed what astronomers were long saying: the world was round and the seas could be safely sailed. As it turned out, the world was populated by peoples and languages living in isolation from one another, with great disparities in economic and scientific development. The world trade that ensued after Columbus's voyages has brought these peoples and cultures closer. The "industrial revolution" was really a worldwide phenomenon energized by expansion of trade among nations and the emergence of the first global economy.

In 2005, journalist Thomas Friedman wrote an influential book declaring the world was now "flat," by which he meant that the Internet and global communications had greatly reduced the economic and cultural advantages of developed countries. Friedman argued that the United States and European countries were in a fight for their economic lives, competing for jobs, markets, resources, and even ideas with highly educated, motivated populations in low-wage areas in the less-developed world (Friedman, 2007). This "globalization" presents both challenges and opportunities for business firms.

A significant percentage of the economy of the United States and other advanced industrial countries in Europe and Asia depends on imports and exports. In 2017, about 30 percent of the $20 trillion U.S. economy resulted from foreign trade, both imports and exports. In Europe and Asia, the number exceeded 50 percent. Many Fortune 500 U.S. firms derive more than half their revenues from foreign operations. Tech companies are particularly dependent on offshore revenue: 80 percent of Intel's revenues in 2017 came from overseas sales of its microprocessors, while Apple got 60 percent of its revenue outside of the United States. Eighty percent of the toys sold in the United States are manufactured in China, while about 90 percent of the PCs manufactured in China use American-made Intel or Advanced Micro Design (AMD) chips. The microprocessor chips are shipped from the United States to China for assembly into devices.

It's not just goods that move across borders. So too do jobs, some of them high-level jobs that pay well and require a college degree. In the past decade, the United States lost 7 million manufacturing jobs to offshore, low-wage producers. But manufacturing is now a very small part of U.S. employment (less than 12 percent of the labor force and declining). In a normal year, about 300,000 service jobs move offshore to lower-wage countries. Many of the jobs are in less-skilled information system occupations, but some are "tradable service" jobs in architecture, financial services, customer call centers, consulting, engineering, and even radiology. Yet at the same time the United States has lost so many jobs, it has added 33 million new service jobs.

The U.S. economy creates more than 3.5 million new jobs in a normal, non-recessionary year. Although only 1.1 million private sector jobs were created in 2011 due to slow economic recovery, by 2017, the U.S. economy was adding more than 2 million new jobs annually for the third straight year. Employment in information systems and the other service occupations is expanding rapidly, and wages are stable. Outsourcing may have accelerated the development of new systems worldwide, as these systems could be maintained and developed in low-wage countries. In part this explains why the job market for MIS and computer science graduates is growing rapidly in the United States.

The challenge for you as a business student is to develop high-level skills through education and on-the-job experience that cannot be outsourced.

The challenge for your business is to avoid markets for goods and services that can be produced offshore much less expensively. The opportunities are equally immense. Throughout this book you will find examples of companies and individuals who either failed or succeeded in using information systems to adapt to this new global environment.

What does globalization have to do with management information systems? That's simple: everything. The emergence of the Internet into a full-blown international communications system has drastically reduced the costs of operating and transacting on a global scale. Communication between a factory floor in Shanghai and a distribution center in Rapid City, South Dakota, is now instant and virtually free. Customers can now shop in a worldwide marketplace, obtaining price and quality information reliably 24 hours a day. Firms producing goods and services on a global scale achieve extraordinary cost reductions by finding low-cost suppliers and managing production facilities in other countries. Internet service firms, such as Google and eBay, are able to replicate their business models and services in multiple countries without having to redesign their expensive fixed-cost information systems infrastructure. Briefly, information systems enable globalization.

The Emerging Digital Firm

All of the changes we have just described, coupled with equally significant organizational redesign, have created the conditions for a fully digital firm. A digital firm can be defined along several dimensions. A **digital firm** is one in which nearly all of the organization's *significant business relationships* with customers, suppliers, and employees are digitally enabled and mediated. *Core business processes* are accomplished through digital networks spanning the entire organization or linking multiple organizations.

Business processes refer to the set of logically related tasks and behaviors that organizations develop over time to produce specific business results and the unique manner in which these activities are organized and coordinated. Developing a new product, generating and fulfilling an order, creating a marketing plan, and hiring an employee are examples of business processes, and the ways organizations accomplish their business processes can be a source of competitive strength. (A detailed discussion of business processes can be found in Chapter 2.)

Key corporate assets—intellectual property, core competencies, and financial and human assets—are managed through digital means. In a digital firm, any piece of information required to support key business decisions is available at any time and anywhere in the firm.

Digital firms sense and respond to their environments far more rapidly than traditional firms, giving them more flexibility to survive in turbulent times. Digital firms offer extraordinary opportunities for more-flexible global organization and management. In digital firms, both time shifting and space shifting are the norm. *Time shifting* refers to business being conducted continuously, 24/7, rather than in narrow "work day" time bands of 9 a.m. to 5 p.m. *Space shifting* means that work takes place in a global workshop as well as within national boundaries. Work is accomplished physically wherever in the world it is best accomplished.

Many firms, such as Cisco Systems, 3M, and GE (see the Chapter 12 ending case), are close to becoming digital firms, using the Internet to drive every aspect of their business. Most other companies are not fully digital, but they are moving toward close digital integration with suppliers, customers, and employees.

Strategic Business Objectives of Information Systems

What makes information systems so essential today? Why are businesses investing so much in information systems and technologies? In the United States, more than 25 million business and financial managers, and 36 million professional workers in the labor force rely on information systems to conduct business. Information systems are essential for conducting day-to-day business in the United States and most other advanced countries as well as achieving strategic business objectives.

Entire sectors of the economy are nearly inconceivable without substantial investments in information systems. E-commerce firms such as Amazon, eBay, Google, and E*Trade simply would not exist. Today's service industries—finance, insurance, and real estate as well as personal services such as travel, medicine, and education—could not operate without information systems. Similarly, retail firms such as Walmart and Target and manufacturing firms such as General Motors and GE require information systems to survive and prosper. Just as offices, telephones, filing cabinets, and efficient tall buildings with elevators were once the foundations of business in the twentieth century, information technology is a foundation for business in the twenty-first century.

There is a growing interdependence between a firm's ability to use information technology and its ability to implement corporate strategies and achieve corporate goals (see Figure 1.2). What a business would like to do in five years often depends on what its systems will be able to do. Increasing market share, becoming the high-quality or low-cost producer, developing new products, and increasing employee productivity depend more and more on the kinds and quality of information systems in the organization. The more you understand about this relationship, the more valuable you will be as a manager.

Specifically, business firms invest heavily in information systems to achieve six strategic business objectives: operational excellence; new products, services,

FIGURE 1.2   THE INTERDEPENDENCE BETWEEN ORGANIZATIONS AND INFORMATION SYSTEMS

In contemporary systems, there is a growing interdependence between a firm's information systems and its business capabilities. Changes in strategy, rules, and business processes increasingly require changes in hardware, software, databases, and telecommunications. Often, what the organization would like to do depends on what its systems will permit it to do.

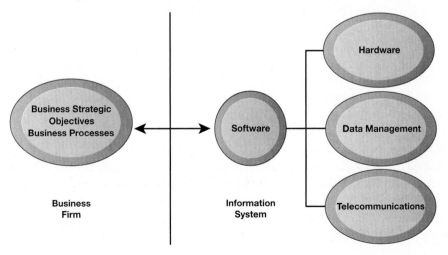

and business models; customer and supplier intimacy; improved decision making; competitive advantage; and survival.

Operational Excellence

Businesses continuously seek to improve the efficiency of their operations in order to achieve higher profitability. Information systems and technologies are some of the most important tools available to managers for achieving higher levels of efficiency and productivity in business operations, especially when coupled with changes in business practices and management behavior.

Walmart, the largest retailer on earth, exemplifies the power of information systems coupled with state-of-the-art business practices and supportive management to achieve world-class operational efficiency. In fiscal year 2018, Walmart achieved over $500 billion in sales—nearly one-tenth of retail sales in the United States—in large part because of its Retail Link system, which digitally links its suppliers to every one of Walmart's stores. As soon as a customer purchases an item, the supplier monitoring the item knows to ship a replacement to the shelf. Walmart is the most efficient retail store in the industry, achieving sales of more than $600 per square foot, compared with its closest competitor, Target, at $425 per square foot and other large general merchandise retail firms producing less than $200 per square foot.

New Products, Services, and Business Models

Information systems and technologies are a major enabling tool for firms to create new products and services as well as entirely new business models. A **business model** describes how a company produces, delivers, and sells a product or service to create wealth.

Today's music industry is vastly different from the industry a decade ago. Apple Inc. transformed an old business model of music distribution based on vinyl records, tapes, and CDs into an online, legal distribution model based on its own iPod technology platform. Apple has prospered from a continuing stream of innovations, including the iTunes music service, the iPad, and the iPhone.

Customer and Supplier Intimacy

When a business really knows its customers and serves them well, the customers generally respond by returning and purchasing more. This raises revenues and profits. Likewise with suppliers, the more a business engages its suppliers, the better the suppliers can provide vital inputs. This lowers costs. How to really know your customers or suppliers is a central problem for businesses with millions of offline and online customers.

The Mandarin Oriental in Manhattan and other high-end hotels exemplify the use of information systems and technologies to achieve customer intimacy. These hotels use computers to keep track of guests' preferences, such as their preferred room temperature, check-in time, frequently dialed telephone numbers, and television programs, and store these data in a large data repository. Individual rooms in the hotels are networked to a central network server computer so that they can be remotely monitored and controlled. When a customer arrives at one of these hotels, the system automatically changes the room conditions, such as dimming the lights, setting the room temperature, or selecting appropriate music, based on the customer's digital profile. The hotels also analyze their customer data to identify their best customers and to develop individualized marketing campaigns based on customers' preferences.

JCPenney exemplifies the benefits of information systems–enabled supplier intimacy. Every time a dress shirt is bought at a JCPenney store in the

United States, the record of the sale appears immediately on computers in Hong Kong at the TAL Apparel Ltd. supplier, a contract manufacturer that produces one in eight dress shirts sold in the United States. TAL runs the numbers through a computer model it developed and then decides how many replacement shirts to make and in what styles, colors, and sizes. TAL then sends the shirts to each JCPenney store, bypassing completely the retailer's warehouses. In other words, JCPenney's shirt inventory is near zero, as is the cost of storing it.

Improved Decision Making

Many business managers operate in an information fog bank, never really having the right information at the right time to make an informed decision. Instead, managers rely on forecasts, best guesses, and luck. The result is over- or under-production of goods and services, misallocation of resources, and poor response times. These poor outcomes raise costs and lose customers. In the past decade, information systems and technologies have made it possible for managers to use real-time data from the marketplace when making decisions.

For instance, Verizon Corporation, one of the largest telecommunications companies in the United States, uses a web-based digital dashboard to provide managers with precise real-time information on customer complaints, network performance for each locality served, and line outages or storm-damaged lines. Using this information, managers can immediately allocate repair resources to affected areas, inform consumers of repair efforts, and restore service fast.

Competitive Advantage

When firms achieve one or more of these business objectives—operational excellence; new products, services, and business models; customer/supplier intimacy; and improved decision making—chances are they have already achieved a competitive advantage. Doing things better than your competitors, charging less for superior products, and responding to customers and suppliers in real time all add up to higher sales and higher profits that your competitors cannot match. Apple Inc., Walmart, and UPS, described later in this chapter, are industry leaders because they know how to use information systems for this purpose.

Survival

Business firms also invest in information systems and technologies because they are necessities of doing business. Sometimes these "necessities" are driven by industry-level changes. For instance, after Citibank introduced the first automated teller machines (ATMs) in the New York region in 1977 to attract customers through higher service levels, its competitors rushed to provide ATMs to their customers to keep up with Citibank. Today, virtually all banks in the United States have regional ATMs and link to national and international ATM networks, such as CIRRUS. Providing ATM services to retail banking customers is simply a requirement of being in and surviving in the retail banking business.

There are many federal and state statutes and regulations that create a legal duty for companies and their employees to retain records, including digital records. For instance, the Toxic Substances Control Act (1976), which regulates the exposure of U.S. workers to more than 75,000 toxic chemicals, requires firms to retain records on employee exposure for 30 years. The Sarbanes-Oxley Act (2002), which was intended to improve the accountability of public firms and their auditors, requires certified public accounting firms that audit public companies to retain audit working papers and records, including all e-mails, for five years. The Dodd-Frank Wall Street Reform and Consumer Protection Act (2010), which was intended to strengthen regulation of the banking industry, requires firms to retain all records for 10 years. Many other pieces of federal and state legislation in health care, financial services, education, and privacy protection impose significant information retention and reporting requirements on U.S. businesses. Firms turn to information systems and technologies to provide the capability to respond to these challenges.

1-2 What is an information system? How does it work? What are its management, organization, and technology components? Why are complementary assets essential for ensuring that information systems provide genuine value for organizations?

So far we've used *information systems* and *technologies* informally without defining the terms. **Information technology (IT)** consists of all the hardware and software that a firm needs to use in order to achieve its business objectives. This includes not only computer machines, storage devices, and handheld mobile devices but also software, such as the Windows or Linux operating systems, the Microsoft Office desktop productivity suite, and the many thousands of computer programs that can be found in a typical large firm. "Information systems" are more complex and can be best understood by looking at them from both a technology and a business perspective.

What Is an Information System?

An **information system** can be defined technically as a set of interrelated components that collect (or retrieve), process, store, and distribute information to support decision making and control in an organization. In addition to supporting decision making, coordination, and control, information systems may also help managers and workers analyze problems, visualize complex subjects, and create new products.

Information systems contain information about significant people, places, and things within the organization or in the environment surrounding it. By **information** we mean data that have been shaped into a form that is meaningful and useful to human beings. **Data**, in contrast, are streams of raw facts representing events occurring in organizations or the physical environment before they have been organized and arranged into a form that people can understand and use.

A brief example contrasting information and data may prove useful. Supermarket checkout counters scan millions of pieces of data from bar codes, which describe each product. Such pieces of data can be totaled and analyzed to provide meaningful information, such as the total number of bottles of dish detergent sold at a particular store, which brands of dish detergent were selling the most rapidly at that store or sales territory, or the total amount spent on that brand of dish detergent at that store or sales region (see Figure 1.3).

Three activities in an information system produce the information that organizations need to make decisions, control operations, analyze problems, and

FIGURE 1.3   DATA AND INFORMATION

Raw data from a supermarket checkout counter can be processed and organized to produce meaningful information, such as the total unit sales of dish detergent or the total sales revenue from dish detergent for a specific store or sales territory.

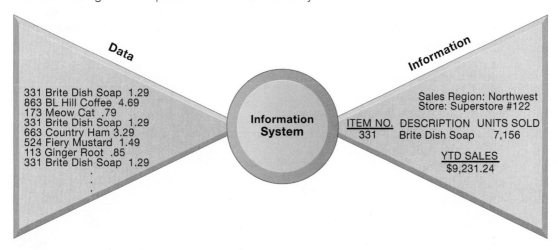

create new products or services. These activities are input, processing, and output (see Figure 1.4). **Input** captures or collects raw data from within the organization or from its external environment. **Processing** converts this raw input into a meaningful form. **Output** transfers the processed information to the people who will use it or to the activities for which it will be used. Information systems also require **feedback**, which is output that is returned to appropriate members of the organization to help them evaluate or correct the input stage.

In PCL's project management system, input includes the names and addresses of contractors and subcontractors, project names and identification numbers, project activities, labor costs, materials costs, and start and completion dates for project activities. Computers store these data and process them to calculate how much each project activity and the entire project will cost and estimated completion time. The system provides meaningful information such as the size, cost, and duration of all projects under PCL management, projects over and under budget, and projects and project activities that are late or on time.

Although computer-based information systems use computer technology to process raw data into meaningful information, there is a sharp distinction between a computer and a computer program on the one hand and an information system on the other. Computers and related software programs are the technical foundation, the tools and materials, of modern information systems. Computers provide the equipment for storing and processing information. Computer programs, or software, are sets of operating instructions that direct and control computer processing. Knowing how computers and computer programs work is important in designing solutions to organizational problems, but computers are only part of an information system.

A house is an appropriate analogy. Houses are built with hammers, nails, and wood, but these do not make a house. The architecture, design, setting, landscaping, and all of the decisions that lead to the creation of these features are part of the house and are crucial for solving the problem of putting a roof over one's head. Computers and programs are the hammers, nails, and lumber of computer-based information systems, but alone they cannot produce the information a particular organization needs. To understand information systems, you

FIGURE 1.4   FUNCTIONS OF AN INFORMATION SYSTEM

An information system contains information about an organization and its surrounding environment. Three basic activities—input, processing, and output—produce the information organizations need. Feedback is output returned to appropriate people or activities in the organization to evaluate and refine the input. Environmental actors, such as customers, suppliers, competitors, stockholders, and regulatory agencies, interact with the organization and its information systems.

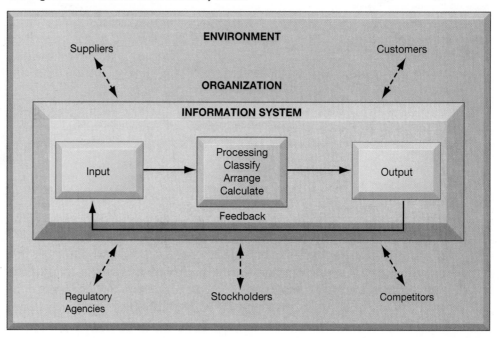

must understand the problems they are designed to solve, their architectural and design elements, and the organizational processes that lead to the solutions.

Dimensions of Information Systems

To fully understand information systems, you must understand the broader organization, management, and information technology dimensions of systems (see Figure 1.5) and their power to provide solutions to challenges and problems in the business environment. We refer to this broader understanding of information systems, which encompasses an understanding of the management and organizational dimensions of systems as well as the technical dimensions of systems, as **information systems literacy**. **Computer literacy**, in contrast, focuses primarily on knowledge of information technology.

The field of **management information systems (MIS)** tries to achieve this broader information systems literacy. MIS deals with behavioral issues as well as technical issues surrounding the development, use, and impact of information systems used by managers and employees in the firm.

Let's examine each of the dimensions of information systems—organizations, management, and information technology.

Organizations

Information systems are an integral part of organizations. Indeed, for some companies, such as credit reporting firms, there would be no business without an information system. The key elements of an organization are its people, structure,

FIGURE 1.5   INFORMATION SYSTEMS ARE MORE THAN COMPUTERS

Using information systems effectively requires an understanding of the organization, management, and information technology shaping the systems. An information system creates value for the firm as an organizational and management solution to challenges posed by the environment.

business processes, politics, and culture. We introduce these components of organizations here and describe them in greater detail in Chapters 2 and 3.

Organizations have a structure that is composed of different levels and specialties. Their structures reveal a clear-cut division of labor. Authority and responsibility in a business firm are organized as a hierarchy, or a pyramid structure. The upper levels of the hierarchy consist of managerial, professional, and technical employees, whereas the lower levels consist of operational personnel.

Senior management makes long-range strategic decisions about products and services as well as ensures financial performance of the firm. **Middle management** carries out the programs and plans of senior management, and **operational management** is responsible for monitoring the daily activities of the business. **Knowledge workers**, such as engineers, scientists, or architects, design products or services and create new knowledge for the firm, whereas **data workers**, such as secretaries or clerks, assist with scheduling and communications at all levels of the firm. **Production or service workers** actually produce the product and deliver the service (see Figure 1.6).

Experts are employed and trained for different business functions. The major **business functions**, or specialized tasks performed by business organizations, consist of sales and marketing, manufacturing and production, finance and accounting, and human resources (see Table 1.1). Chapter 2 provides more detail on these business functions and the ways in which they are supported by information systems.

An organization coordinates work through its hierarchy and through its *business processes*. Most organizations' business processes include formal rules that have been developed over a long time for accomplishing tasks. These rules guide employees in a variety of procedures, from writing an invoice to responding to customer complaints. Some of these business processes have been written down, but others are informal work practices, such as a requirement to return telephone calls from coworkers or customers, that are not formally documented. Information systems automate many business processes. For instance, how a

FIGURE 1.6   LEVELS IN A FIRM

Business organizations are hierarchies consisting of three principal levels: senior management, middle management, and operational management. Information systems serve each of these levels. Scientists and knowledge workers often work with middle management.

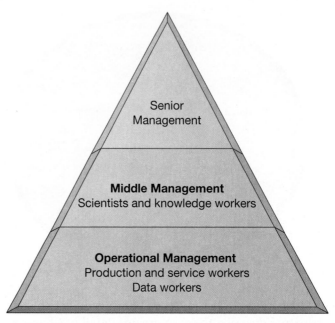

customer receives credit or how a customer is billed is often determined by an information system that incorporates a set of formal business processes.

Each organization has a unique **culture**, or fundamental set of assumptions, values, and ways of doing things, that has been accepted by most of its members. You can see organizational culture at work by looking around your university or college. Some bedrock assumptions of university life are that professors know more than students, that the reason students attend college is to learn, and that classes follow a regular schedule.

Parts of an organization's culture can always be found embedded in its information systems. For instance, UPS's first priority is customer service, which is an aspect of its organizational culture that can be found in the company's package tracking systems, which we describe in this section.

Different levels and specialties in an organization create different interests and points of view. These views often conflict over how the company should be run and how resources and rewards should be distributed. Conflict is the basis for organizational politics. Information systems come out of this cauldron of differing perspectives, conflicts, compromises, and agreements that are a

TABLE 1.1   MAJOR BUSINESS FUNCTIONS

FUNCTION	PURPOSE
Sales and marketing	Selling the organization's products and services
Manufacturing and production	Producing and delivering products and services
Finance and accounting	Managing the organization's financial assets and maintaining the organization's financial records
Human resources	Attracting, developing, and maintaining the organization's labor force; maintaining employee records

natural part of all organizations. In Chapter 3, we examine these features of organizations and their role in the development of information systems in greater detail.

Management

Management's job is to make sense out of the many situations faced by organizations, make decisions, and formulate action plans to solve organizational problems. Managers perceive business challenges in the environment, they set the organizational strategy for responding to those challenges, and they allocate the human and financial resources to coordinate the work and achieve success. Throughout, they must exercise responsible leadership. The business information systems described in this book reflect the hopes, dreams, and realities of real-world managers.

But managers must do more than manage what already exists. They must also create new products and services and even re-create the organization from time to time. A substantial part of management responsibility is creative work driven by new knowledge and information. Information technology can play a powerful role in helping managers design and deliver new products and services and redirecting and redesigning their organizations. Chapter 12 treats management decision making in detail.

Information Technology

Information technology is one of many tools managers use to cope with change. **Computer hardware** is the physical equipment used for input, processing, and output activities in an information system. It consists of the following: computers of various sizes and shapes (including mobile handheld devices); various input, output, and storage devices; and telecommunications devices that link computers together.

Computer software consists of the detailed, preprogrammed instructions that control and coordinate the computer hardware components in an information system. Chapter 5 describes the contemporary software and hardware platforms used by firms today in greater detail.

Data management technology consists of the software governing the organization of data on physical storage media. More detail on data organization and access methods can be found in Chapter 6.

Networking and telecommunications technology, consisting of both physical devices and software, links the various pieces of hardware and transfers data from one physical location to another. Computers and communications equipment can be connected in networks for sharing voice, data, images, sound, and video. A **network** links two or more computers to share data or resources, such as a printer.

The world's largest and most widely used network is the **Internet**. The Internet is a global "network of networks" that uses universal standards (described in Chapter 7) to connect millions of networks in more than 230 countries around the world.

The Internet has created a new "universal" technology platform on which to build new products, services, strategies, and business models. This same technology platform has internal uses, providing the connectivity to link different systems and networks within the firm. Internal corporate networks based on Internet technology are called **intranets**. Private intranets extended to authorized users outside the organization are called **extranets**, and firms use such networks to coordinate their activities with other firms for making purchases, collaborating on design, and other interorganizational work. For most business firms today, using Internet technology is both a business necessity and a competitive advantage.

The **World Wide Web** is a service provided by the Internet that uses universally accepted standards for storing, retrieving, formatting, and displaying information in a page format on the Internet. Web pages contain text, graphics, animations, sound, and video and are linked to other web pages. By clicking on highlighted words or buttons on a web page, you can link to related pages to find additional information and links to other locations on the web. The web can serve as the foundation for new kinds of information systems such as UPS's web-based package tracking system described in the Interactive Session.

All of these technologies, along with the people required to run and manage them, represent resources that can be shared throughout the organization and constitute the firm's **information technology (IT) infrastructure**. The IT infrastructure provides the foundation, or *platform*, on which the firm can build its specific information systems. Each organization must carefully design and manage its IT infrastructure so that it has the set of technology services it needs for the work it wants to accomplish with information systems. Chapters 5 through 8 of this book examine each major technology component of information technology infrastructure and show how they all work together to create the technology platform for the organization.

The Interactive Session on Technology describes some of the typical technologies used in computer-based information systems today. UPS invests heavily in information systems technology to make its business more efficient and customer oriented. It uses an array of information technologies, including bar code scanning systems, wireless networks, large mainframe computers, handheld computers, the Internet, and many different pieces of software for tracking packages, calculating fees, maintaining customer accounts, and managing logistics.

Let's identify the organization, management, and technology elements in the UPS package tracking system we have just described. The organization element anchors the package tracking system in UPS's sales and production functions (the main product of UPS is a service—package delivery). It specifies the required procedures for identifying packages with both sender and recipient information, taking inventory, tracking the packages en route, and providing package status reports for UPS customers and customer service representatives.

The system must also provide information to satisfy the needs of managers and workers. UPS drivers need to be trained in both package pickup and delivery procedures and in how to use the package tracking system so that they can work efficiently and effectively. UPS customers may need some training to use UPS in-house package tracking software or the UPS website.

UPS's management is responsible for monitoring service levels and costs and for promoting the company's strategy of combining low cost and superior service. Management decided to use computer systems to increase the ease of sending a package using UPS and of checking its delivery status, thereby reducing delivery costs and increasing sales revenues.

The technology supporting this system consists of handheld computers, bar code scanners, desktop computers, wired and wireless communications networks, UPS's data center, storage technology for the package delivery data, UPS in-house package tracking software, and software to access the World Wide Web. The result is an information system solution to the business challenge

UPS Competes Globally with Information Technology

United Parcel Service (UPS) started out in 1907 in a closet-sized basement office. Jim Casey and Claude Ryan—two teenagers from Seattle with two bicycles and one phone—promised the "best service and lowest rates." UPS has used this formula successfully for more than a century to become the world's largest ground and air package-delivery company. It's a global enterprise with more than 454,000 employees, over 112,000 vehicles, and the world's ninth-largest airline.

Today, UPS delivers 5.1 billion packages and documents in more than 220 countries and territories. The firm has been able to maintain leadership in small-package delivery services despite stiff competition from FedEx and the U.S. Postal Service by investing heavily in advanced information technology. UPS spends more than $1 billion each year to maintain a high level of customer service while keeping costs low and streamlining its overall operations.

It all starts with the scannable bar-coded label attached to a package, which contains detailed information about the sender, the destination, and when the package should arrive. Customers can download and print their own labels using special software provided by UPS or by accessing the UPS website. Before the package is even picked up, information from the "smart" label is transmitted to one of UPS's computer centers in Mahwah, New Jersey, or Alpharetta, Georgia, and sent to the distribution center nearest its final destination.

Dispatchers at this center download the label data and use special routing software called ORION to create the most efficient delivery route for each driver that considers traffic, weather conditions, and the location of each stop. Each UPS driver makes an average of 100 stops per day. In a network with 55,000 routes in the United States alone, shaving even one mile off each driver's daily route translates into big savings: $50 million per year. These savings are critical as UPS tries to boost earnings growth as more of its business shifts to less-profitable e-commerce deliveries. UPS drivers who used to drop off several heavy packages a day at one retailer now make many stops scattered across residential neighborhoods, delivering one lightweight package per household. The shift requires more fuel and more time, increasing the cost to deliver each package.

The first thing a UPS driver picks up each day is a handheld computer called a Delivery Information Acquisition Device (DIAD), which can access a wireless cell phone network. As soon as the driver logs on, his or her day's route is downloaded onto the handheld. The DIAD also automatically captures customers' signatures along with pickup and delivery information. Package tracking information is then transmitted to UPS's computer network for storage and processing. From there, the information can be accessed worldwide to provide proof of delivery to customers or to respond to customer queries. It usually takes less than 60 seconds from the time a driver presses "complete" on the DIAD for the new information to be available on the web.

Through its automated package tracking system, UPS can monitor and even reroute packages throughout the delivery process. At various points along the route from sender to receiver, bar code devices scan shipping information on the package label and feed data about the progress of the package into the central computer. Customer service representatives are able to check the status of any package from desktop computers linked to the central computers and respond immediately to inquiries from customers. UPS customers can also access this information from the company's website using their own computers or mobile phones. UPS now has mobile apps and a mobile website for iPhone, BlackBerry, and Android smartphone users.

Anyone with a package to ship can access the UPS website to track packages, check delivery routes, calculate shipping rates, determine time in transit, print labels, and schedule a pickup. The data collected at the UPS website are transmitted to the UPS central computer and then back to the customer after processing. UPS also provides tools that enable customers, such Cisco Systems, to embed UPS functions, such as tracking and cost calculations, into their own websites so that they can track shipments without visiting the UPS site.

UPS is now leveraging its decades of expertise managing its own global delivery network to manage logistics and supply chain activities for other companies. It created a UPS Supply Chain Solutions division that provides a complete bundle of standardized services to subscribing companies at a fraction of what it would cost to build their own systems and infrastructure. These services include supply chain design and management, freight forwarding, customs brokerage, mail services, multimodal transportation, and financial services in addition to logistics services. CandleScience, based in Durham, North Carolina, is an industry leader in the candle and soap supply industry, providing raw materials such as waxes, wicks, and fragrances to candle makers around the world. UPS worked with CandleScience to accurately model shipping rates for the company and its customers and to add a freight shipping option capability to its website. UPS also helped CandleScience identify the optimal location for a new warehouse for its West Coast customers. The new West Coast warehouse in Sparks, Nevada lets the company reach some of its largest customers faster, more efficiently and less expensively.

UPS provides both financial and shipping advice and services to Flags of Valor, a small business based in Ashton, Virginia, which sells hundreds of hand-crafted wooden flags each day to online customers. Using UPS Quantum View Manage® technology, the staff can view and monitor outbound packages and immediately respond to customer questions about order status. UPS Capital®, the financial service division of UPS, showed the company how to protect its cash flow and assets by moving to a comprehensive insurance plan.

Sources: Paul Ziobro, "UPS's $20 Billion Problem: Operations Stuck in the 20th Century," *Wall Street Journal*, June 15, 2018; www.ups.com, accessed February 7, 2018; "Igniting Growth with CandleScience," *UPS Compass*, May 2017; and "Stars and Stripes Flying High," *UPS Compass*, December 2017.

CASE STUDY QUESTIONS

1. What are the inputs, processing, and outputs of UPS's package tracking system?

2. What technologies are used by UPS? How are these technologies related to UPS's business strategy?

3. What strategic business objectives do UPS's information systems address?

4. What would happen if UPS's information systems were not available?

of providing a high level of service with low prices in the face of mounting competition.

It Isn't Just Technology: A Business Perspective on Information Systems

Managers and business firms invest in information technology and systems because they provide real economic value to the business. The decision to build or maintain an information system assumes that the returns on this investment will be superior to other investments in buildings, machines, or other assets. These superior returns will be expressed as increases in productivity, as increases in revenues (which will increase the firm's stock market value), or perhaps as superior long-term strategic positioning of the firm in certain markets (which will produce superior revenues in the future).

We can see that from a business perspective, an information system is an important instrument for creating value for the firm. Information systems enable the firm to increase its revenue or decrease its costs by providing information that helps managers make better decisions or that improves the execution of business processes. For example, the information system for analyzing supermarket checkout data illustrated in Figure 1.3 can increase firm profitability by helping managers make better decisions as to which products to stock and promote in retail supermarkets.

Every business has an information value chain, illustrated in Figure 1.7, in which raw information is systematically acquired and then transformed

FIGURE 1.7   THE BUSINESS INFORMATION VALUE CHAIN

From a business perspective, information systems are part of a series of value-adding activities for acquiring, transforming, and distributing information that managers can use to improve decision making, enhance organizational performance, and, ultimately, increase firm profitability.

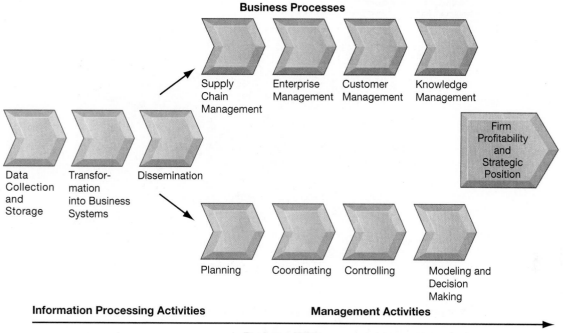

through various stages that add value to that information. The value of an information system to a business, as well as the decision to invest in any new information system, is, in large part, determined by the extent to which the system will lead to better management decisions, more efficient business processes, and higher firm profitability. Although there are other reasons why systems are built, their primary purpose is to contribute to corporate value.

The business perspective calls attention to the organizational and managerial nature of information systems. An information system represents an organizational and management solution, based on information technology, to a challenge or problem posed by the environment. Every chapter in this book begins with a short case study that illustrates this concept. A diagram at the beginning of each chapter illustrates the relationship between a business challenge and resulting management and organizational decisions to use IT as a solution to challenges generated by the business environment. You can use this diagram as a starting point for analyzing any information system or information system problem you encounter.

Review the diagram at the beginning of this chapter. The diagram shows how PCL's systems solved the business problem of inefficiencies created by a far-flung, highly paper-intensive business. These systems provided a solution that takes advantage of opportunities provided by new wireless digital technology and the Internet. PCL digitally enabled its key business processes for planning, designing, and monitoring its construction projects. These systems have been essential in improving PCL's overall business performance. The diagram also illustrates how management, technology, and organizational elements work together to create the systems.

> **FIGURE 1.8** **VARIATION IN RETURNS ON INFORMATION TECHNOLOGY INVESTMENT**
>
> Although, on average, investments in information technology produce returns far above those returned by other investments, there is considerable variation across firms.
>
> Source: Brynjolfsson, Erik and Lorin M. Hitt. "Beyond Computation: Information Technology, Organizational Transformation, and Business Performance." Journal of Economic Perspectives 14, No. 4 (2000).

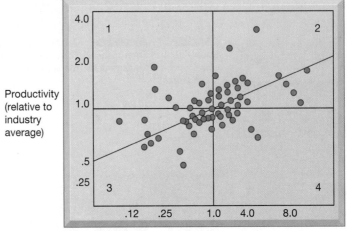

IT Capital Stock (relative to industry average)

Complementary Assets: Organizational Capital and the Right Business Model

Awareness of the organizational and managerial dimensions of information systems can help us understand why some firms achieve better results from their information systems than others. Studies of returns from information technology investments show that there is considerable variation in the returns firms receive (see Figure 1.8). Some firms invest a great deal and receive a great deal (quadrant 2); others invest an equal amount and receive few returns (quadrant 4). Still other firms invest little and receive much (quadrant 1), whereas others invest little and receive little (quadrant 3). This suggests that investing in information technology does not by itself guarantee good returns. What accounts for this variation among firms?

The answer lies in the concept of complementary assets. Information technology investments alone cannot make organizations and managers more effective unless they are accompanied by supportive values, structures, and behavior patterns in the organization and other complementary assets. Business firms need to change how they do business before they can really reap the advantages of new information technologies.

Complementary assets are those assets required to derive value from a primary investment (Teece, 1998). For instance, to realize value from automobiles requires substantial complementary investments in highways, roads, gasoline stations, repair facilities, and a legal regulatory structure to set standards and control drivers.

Research indicates that firms that support their technology investments with investments in complementary assets, such as new business models, new business processes, management behavior, organizational culture, or training, receive superior returns, whereas those firms failing to make these complementary investments receive less or no returns on their information technology investments (Brynjolfsson, 2005; Brynjolfsson and Hitt, 2000; Laudon, 1974). These investments in organization and management are also known as **organizational and management capital**.

TABLE 1.2 COMPLEMENTARY SOCIAL, MANAGERIAL, AND ORGANIZATIONAL ASSETS REQUIRED TO OPTIMIZE RETURNS FROM INFORMATION TECHNOLOGY INVESTMENTS

Organizational assets	Supportive organizational culture that values efficiency and effectiveness
	Appropriate business model
	Efficient business processes
	Decentralized authority
	Distributed decision-making rights
	Strong IS development team
Managerial assets	Strong senior management support for technology investment and change
	Incentives for management innovation
	Teamwork and collaborative work environments
	Training programs to enhance management decision skills
	Management culture that values flexibility and knowledge-based decision making.
Social assets	The Internet and telecommunications infrastructure
	IT-enriched educational programs raising labor force computer literacy
	Standards (both government and private sector)
	Laws and regulations creating fair, stable market environments
	Technology and service firms in adjacent markets to assist implementation

Table 1.2 lists the major complementary investments that firms need to make to realize value from their information technology investments. Some of this investment involves tangible assets, such as buildings, machinery, and tools. However, the value of investments in information technology depends to a large extent on complementary investments in management and organization.

Key organizational complementary investments are a supportive business culture that values efficiency and effectiveness, an appropriate business model, efficient business processes, decentralization of authority, highly distributed decision rights, and a strong information system (IS) development team.

Important managerial complementary assets are strong senior management support for change, incentive systems that monitor and reward individual innovation, an emphasis on teamwork and collaboration, training programs, and a management culture that values flexibility and knowledge.

Important social investments (not made by the firm but by the society at large, other firms, governments, and other key market actors) are the Internet and the supporting Internet culture, educational systems, network and computing standards, regulations and laws, and the presence of technology and service firms.

Throughout the book, we emphasize a framework of analysis that considers technology, management, and organizational assets and their interactions. Perhaps the single most important theme in the book, reflected in case studies and exercises, is that managers need to consider the broader organization and management dimensions of information systems to understand current problems as well as to derive substantial above-average returns from their information technology investments. As you will see throughout the text, firms that can address these related dimensions of the IT investment are, on average, richly rewarded.

1-3 What academic disciplines are used to study information systems, and how does each contribute to an understanding of information systems?

The study of information systems is a multidisciplinary field. No single theory or perspective dominates. Figure 1.9 illustrates the major disciplines that contribute problems, issues, and solutions in the study of information systems. In general, the field can be divided into technical and behavioral approaches. Information systems are sociotechnical systems. Though they are composed of machines, devices, and "hard" physical technology, they require substantial social, organizational, and intellectual investments to make them work properly.

Technical Approach

The technical approach to information systems emphasizes mathematically based models to study information systems as well as the physical technology and formal capabilities of these systems. The disciplines that contribute to the technical approach are computer science, management science, and operations research.

Computer science is concerned with establishing theories of computability, methods of computation, and methods of efficient data storage and access. Management science emphasizes the development of models for decision-making and management practices. Operations research focuses on mathematical techniques for optimizing selected parameters of organizations, such as transportation, inventory control, and transaction costs.

FIGURE 1.9   **CONTEMPORARY APPROACHES TO INFORMATION SYSTEMS**

The study of information systems deals with issues and insights contributed from technical and behavioral disciplines.

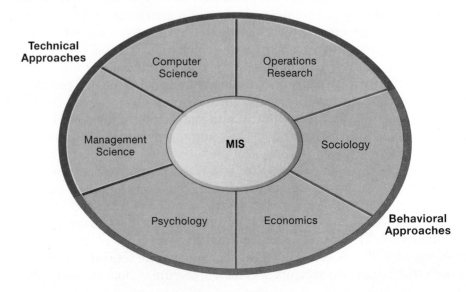

Behavioral Approach

An important part of the information systems field is concerned with behavioral issues that arise in the development and long-term maintenance of information systems. Issues such as strategic business integration, design, implementation, utilization, and management cannot be explored usefully with the models used in the technical approach. Other behavioral disciplines contribute important concepts and methods.

For instance, sociologists study information systems with an eye toward how groups and organizations shape the development of systems and also how systems affect individuals, groups, and organizations. Psychologists study information systems with an interest in how human decision makers perceive and use formal information. Economists study information systems with an interest in understanding the production of digital goods, the dynamics of digital markets, and how new information systems change the control and cost structures within the firm.

The behavioral approach does not ignore technology. Indeed, information systems technology is often the stimulus for a behavioral problem or issue. But the focus of this approach is generally not on technical solutions. Instead, it concentrates on changes in attitudes, management and organizational policy, and behavior.

Approach of This Text: Sociotechnical Systems

Throughout this book, you will find a rich story with four main actors: suppliers of hardware and software (the technologists); business firms making investments and seeking to obtain value from the technology; managers and employees seeking to achieve business value (and other goals); and the contemporary legal, social, and cultural context (the firm's environment). Together these actors produce what we call *management information systems*.

The study of management information systems (MIS) arose to focus on the use of computer-based information systems in business firms and government agencies. MIS combines the work of computer science, management science, and operations research with a practical orientation toward developing system solutions to real-world problems and managing information technology resources. It is also concerned with behavioral issues surrounding the development, use, and impact of information systems, which are typically discussed in the fields of sociology, economics, and psychology.

Our experience as academics and practitioners leads us to believe that no single approach effectively captures the reality of information systems. The successes and failures of information systems are rarely all technical or all behavioral. Our best advice to students is to understand the perspectives of many disciplines. Indeed, the challenge and excitement of the information systems field are that it requires an appreciation and tolerance of many different approaches.

The view we adopt in this book is best characterized as the **sociotechnical view** of systems. In this view, optimal organizational performance is achieved by jointly optimizing both the social and technical systems used in production.

Adopting a sociotechnical systems perspective helps to avoid a purely technological approach to information systems. For instance, the fact that information technology is rapidly declining in cost and growing in power does not

> **FIGURE 1.10** A SOCIOTECHNICAL PERSPECTIVE ON INFORMATION SYSTEMS
>
> In a sociotechnical perspective, the performance of a system is optimized when both the technology and the organization mutually adjust to one another until a satisfactory fit is obtained.

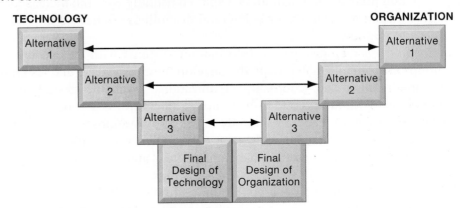

necessarily or easily translate into productivity enhancement or bottom-line profits. The fact that a firm has recently installed an enterprise-wide financial reporting system does not necessarily mean that it will be used, or used effectively. Likewise, the fact that a firm has recently introduced new business procedures and processes does not necessarily mean employees will be more productive in the absence of investments in new information systems to enable those processes.

In this book, we stress the need to optimize the firm's performance as a whole. Both the technical and behavioral components need attention. This means that technology must be changed and designed in such a way as to fit organizational and individual needs. Sometimes, the technology may have to be "de-optimized" to accomplish this fit. For instance, mobile phone users adapt this technology to their personal needs, and as a result manufacturers quickly seek to adjust the technology to conform to user expectations. Organizations and individuals must also be changed through training, learning, and planned organizational change to allow the technology to operate and prosper. Figure 1.10 illustrates this process of mutual adjustment in a sociotechnical system.

1-4 How will MIS help my career?

Here is how Chapter 1 and this text can help you find an entry-level job as a financial client support and sales assistant.

The Company

Power Financial Analytics Data Services, a data and software company serving the financial industry with offices in New York City, Atlanta, Los Angeles, and Chicago, is looking to fill an entry-level position for a financial client support and sales assistant. The company has 1,600 employees, many of whom are consultants showing clients how to work with its powerful financial analytics software and data products.

Position Description

The financial client support and sales assistant will be part of a team in the company's consulting services. Consulting teams combine a thorough understanding of finance and technology with specific expertise in Power Financial Analytics Data Services software and assist clients in a variety of ways. The company provides on-the-job training in its software and consulting methods. Job responsibilities include:

- Supporting Financial Analytics Data Services applications.
- Helping the team create custom models and screens.
- Training clients in their offices and at seminars.
- Providing expert consultation to clients by telephone and on-site.

Job Requirements

- Recent college graduate or investment professional with one to two years of experience. Applicants with backgrounds in finance, MIS, economics, accounting, business administration, and mathematics are preferred
- Knowledge of or interest in learning about financial markets
- Sound working knowledge of spreadsheets
- Very strong communication and interpersonal skills
- Strong desire to learn in rapidly changing environment

Interview Questions

1. What is your background in finance? What courses did you take? Have you ever worked in the financial industry? What did you do there?
2. What is your proficiency level with spreadsheet software? What work have you done with Excel spreadsheets? Can you show examples of your work?
3. Are you able to discuss current trends in the financial industry and how they impact Power Financial's business model and client base?
4. Did you ever work with clients? Can you give examples of how you provided client service or support?
5. Can you give us an example of a finance-related problem or other business problem that you helped solve? Did you do any writing and analysis? Can you provide examples?

Author Tips

1. Use the web to learn about financial markets and the financial industry.
2. Use the web to research the company, its financial products, and the tools and services it offers customers. Learn what you can about its consulting services. Additionally, examine the company's social medial channels, such as LinkedIn and Facebook, for trends and themes.
3. Inquire exactly how you would be using spreadsheets for this job. Provide examples of how you used spreadsheets to solve problems in the classroom or for a job assignment. Show the spreadsheet work you did in finance.
4. Bring examples of your writing (including some from your Digital Portfolio described in MyLab MIS) demonstrating your analytical skills and project experience. Be prepared to discuss how you helped customers solve a business problem or the business problem solving you did for your courses.

REVIEW **SUMMARY**

1-1 **How are information systems transforming business, and why are they so essential for running and managing a business today?**

E-mail, online conferencing, smartphones, and tablet computers have become essential tools for conducting business. Information systems are the foundation of fast-paced supply chains. The Internet allows many businesses to buy, sell, advertise, and solicit customer feedback online. Organizations are trying to become more competitive and efficient by digitally enabling their core business processes and evolving into digital firms. The Internet has stimulated globalization by dramatically reducing the costs of producing, buying, and selling goods on a global scale. New information system trends include the emerging mobile digital platform, big data, and cloud computing.

Information systems are a foundation for conducting business today. In many industries, survival and the ability to achieve strategic business goals are difficult without extensive use of information technology. Businesses today use information systems to achieve six major objectives: operational excellence; new products, services, and business models; customer/supplier intimacy; improved decision making; competitive advantage; and day-to-day survival.

1-2 **What is an information system? How does it work? What are its management, organization, and technology components? Why are complementary assets essential for ensuring that information systems provide genuine value for organizations?**

From a technical perspective, an information system collects, stores, and disseminates information from an organization's environment and internal operations to support organizational functions and decision making, communication, coordination, control, analysis, and visualization. Information systems transform raw data into useful information through three basic activities: input, processing, and output.

From a business perspective, an information system provides a solution to a problem or challenge facing a firm and represents a combination of management, organization, and technology elements. The management dimension of information systems involves issues such as leadership, strategy, and management behavior. The technology dimension consists of computer hardware, software, data management technology, and networking/telecommunications technology (including the Internet). The organization dimension of information systems involves issues such as the organization's hierarchy, functional specialties, business processes, culture, and political interest groups.

In order to obtain meaningful value from information systems, organizations must support their technology investments with appropriate complementary investments in organizations and management. These complementary assets include new business models and business processes, supportive organizational culture and management behavior, and appropriate technology standards, regulations, and laws. New information technology investments are unlikely to produce high returns unless businesses make the appropriate managerial and organizational changes to support the technology.

1-3 **What academic disciplines are used to study information systems, and how does each contribute to an understanding of information systems?**

The study of information systems deals with issues and insights contributed from technical and behavioral disciplines. The disciplines that contribute to the technical approach focusing on formal models and capabilities of systems are computer science, management science, and operations research. The disciplines contributing to the behavioral approach focusing on the design, implementation, management, and business impact of systems are psychology, sociology, and economics. A sociotechnical view of systems considers both technical and social features of systems and solutions that represent the best fit between them.

Key Terms

MyLab MIS

To complete the problems with MyLab MIS, go to the EOC Discussion Questions in MyLab MIS.

Review Questions

1-1 How are information systems transforming business, and why are they so essential for running and managing a business today?

- Describe how information systems have changed the way businesses operate and their products and services.
- Identify three major new information system trends.
- Describe the characteristics of a digital firm.
- Describe the challenges and opportunities of globalization in a "flattened" world.
- List and describe six reasons why information systems are so important for business today.

1-2 What is an information system? How does it work? What are its management, organization, and technology components? Why are complementary assets essential for ensuring that information systems provide genuine value for organizations?

- Define an information system and describe the activities it performs.
- List and describe the organizational, management, and technology dimensions of information systems.

- Distinguish between data and information and between information systems literacy and computer literacy.
- Explain how the Internet and the World Wide Web are related to the other technology components of information systems.
- Define complementary assets and describe their relationship to information technology.
- Describe the complementary social, managerial, and organizational assets required to optimize returns from information technology investments.

1-3 What academic disciplines are used to study information systems, and how does each contribute to an understanding of information systems?

- List and describe each discipline that contributes to a technical approach to information systems.
- List and describe each discipline that contributes to a behavioral approach to information systems.
- Describe the sociotechnical perspective on information systems.

Discussion Questions

1-4
MyLab MIS
Information systems are too important to be left to computer specialists. Do you agree? Why or why not?

1-5
MyLab MIS
If you were setting up the website for a Major League Baseball team, what management, organization, and technology issues might you encounter?

1-6
MyLab MIS
What are some of the organizational, managerial, and social complementary assets that help make UPS's information systems so successful?

Hands-On MIS Projects

The projects in this section give you hands-on experience in analyzing financial reporting and inventory management problems, using data management software to improve management decision making about increasing sales, and using Internet software for researching job requirements. Visit MyLab MIS to access this chapter's Hands-On MIS Projects.

Management Decision Problems

1-7 Snyders of Hanover, which sells about 80 million bags of pretzels, snack chips, and organic snack items each year, had its financial department use spreadsheets and manual processes for much of its data gathering and reporting. Snyder's financial analyst would spend the entire final week of every month collecting spreadsheets from the heads of more than 50 departments worldwide. She would then consolidate and reenter all the data into another spreadsheet, which would serve as the company's monthly profit-and-loss statement. If a department needed to update its data after submitting the spreadsheet to the main office, the analyst had to return the original spreadsheet, then wait for the department to resubmit its data before finally submitting the updated data in the consolidated document. Assess the impact of this situation on business performance and management decision making.

1-8 Dollar General Corporation operates deep-discount stores offering housewares, cleaning supplies, clothing, health and beauty aids, and packaged food, with most items selling for $1. Its business model calls for keeping costs as low as possible. The company has no automated method for keeping track of inventory at each store. Managers know approximately how many cases of a particular product the store is supposed to receive when a delivery truck arrives, but the stores lack technology for scanning the cases or verifying the item count inside the cases. Merchandise losses from theft or other mishaps have been rising and now represent more than 3 percent of total sales. What decisions have to be made before investing in an information system solution?

Improving Decision Making: Using Databases to Analyze Sales Trends

Software skills: Database querying and reporting
Business skills: Sales trend analysis

1-9 In this project, you will start out with raw transactional sales data and use Microsoft Access database software to develop queries and reports that help managers make better decisions about product pricing, sales promotions, and inventory replenishment. In MyLab MIS, you can find a Store and Regional Sales Database developed in Microsoft Access. The database contains raw data on weekly store sales of computer equipment in various sales regions. The database includes fields for store identification number, sales region, item number, item description, unit price, units sold, and the weekly sales period when the sales were made. Use Access to develop some reports and queries to make this information more useful for running the business. Sales and production managers want answers to the following questions:

- Which products should be restocked?
- Which stores and sales regions would benefit from a promotional campaign and additional marketing?
- When (what time of year) should products be offered at full price, and when should discounts be used?

You can easily modify the database table to find and report your answers. Print your reports and results of queries.

Improving Decision Making: Using the Internet to Locate Jobs Requiring Information Systems Knowledge

Software skills: Internet-based software
Business skills: Job searching

1-10 Visit a job-posting website such as Monster.com. Spend some time at the site examining jobs for accounting, finance, sales, marketing, and human resources. Find two or three descriptions of jobs that require some information systems knowledge. What information systems knowledge do these jobs require? What do you need to do to prepare for these jobs? Write a one- to two-page report summarizing your findings.

Collaboration and Teamwork Project

Selecting Team Collaboration Tools

1-11 Form a team with three or four classmates and review the capabilities of Google Drive and Google Sites for your team collaboration work. Compare the capabilities of these two tools for storing team documents, project announcements, source materials, work assignments, illustrations, electronic presentations, and web pages of interest. Learn how each works with Google Docs. Explain why Google Drive or Google Sites is more appropriate for your team. If possible, use Google Docs to brainstorm and develop a presentation of your findings for the class. Organize and store your presentation using the Google tool you have selected.

Did Information Systems Cause Deutsche Bank to Stumble?

CASE STUDY

Deutsche Bank AG, founded in 1870, is one of the world's top financial companies, with 2,425 branches worldwide. It offers a range of financial products and services, including retail and commercial banking, foreign exchange, and services for mergers and acquisitions. The bank provides products for mortgages, consumer finance, credit cards, life insurance, and corporate pension plans; financing for international trade; and customized wealth management services for wealthy private clients. Deutsche Bank is also the largest bank in Germany, and plays a central role in German economic life. In many ways, Deutsche Bank is the embodiment of the global financial system.

Deutsche Bank has the world's largest portfolio of derivatives, valued at about $46 trillion. A financial derivative is a contract between two or more parties whose value is dependent upon or derived from one or more underlying assets, such as stocks, bonds, commodities, currencies, and interest rates. Although Deutsche Bank had survived the 2008 banking crisis, which was partly triggered by flawed derivatives, it is now struggling with seismic changes in the banking industry, including recent regulatory change. The bank was forced to pay $7.2 billion to resolve U.S. regulator complaints about its sale of toxic mortgage securities that contributed to the 2008 financial crisis.

In addition, the Commodity Futures Trading Commission (CFTC) charged that Deutsche Bank submitted incomplete and untimely credit default swap data, failed to properly supervise employees responsible for swap data reporting, and lacked an adequate business continuity and disaster recovery plan. (A credit default swap is a type of credit insurance contract in which an insurer promises to compensate an insured party [such as a bank] for losses incurred when a debtor [such as a corporation] defaults on a debt and that can be purchased or sold by either party on the financial market. Credit default swaps are very complex financial instruments.)

The CFTC complained that on April 16, 2016, Deutsche Bank's swap data reporting system experienced a system outage that prevented Deutsche Bank from reporting any swap data for multiple asset classes for approximately five days. Deutsche Bank's subsequent efforts to end the system outage repeatedly exacerbated existing reporting problems and led to the discovery and creation of new reporting problems.

For example, Deutsche Bank's swap data reported before and after the system outage revealed persistent problems with the integrity of certain data fields, including numerous invalid legal entity identifiers. (A legal entity identifier [LEI] is an identification code to uniquely identify all legal entities that are parties to financial transactions.) The CFTC complaint alleged that a number of these reporting problems persist today, affecting market data that is made available to the public as well as data that is used by the CFTC to evaluate systemic risk throughout the swaps markets. The CFTC complaint also alleged that Deutsche Bank's system outage and subsequent reporting problems occurred in part because Deutsche Bank failed to have an adequate business continuity and disaster recovery plan and other appropriate supervisory systems in place.

In addition to incurring high costs associated with coping with regulators and paying fines, Deutsche Bank was a very unwieldy and expensive bank to operate. U.S. regulators have identified Deutsche Bank's antiquated technology as one reason why the bank was not always able to provide the correct information for running its business properly and responding to regulators. Poor information systems may have even contributed to the 2008 financial crisis. Banks often had trouble untangling the complex financial products they had bought and sold to determine their underlying value.

Banks, including Deutsche Bank, are intensive users of information technology, and they rely on technology to spot misconduct. If Deutsche Bank was such an important player in the German and world financial systems, why were its systems not up to the job?

It turns out that Deutsche Bank, like other leading global financial companies, had undergone decades of mergers and expansion. When these banks merged or acquired other financial companies, they often did not make the requisite (and often far-reaching) changes to integrate their information systems with those of their acquisitions. The effort and costs required for this integration, including coordination across many management teams, were too great. So the banks left many old systems in place to handle the workload for each of their businesses. This created what experts call "spaghetti balls" of overlapping and often incompatible technology platforms and software programs. These antiquated legacy systems were designed to handle large numbers of transactions and sums of money, but they were not well suited to managing large bank operations. They often did not allow information to be shared easily among departments or provide senior management with a coherent overview of bank operations.

Deutsche Bank had more than 100 different booking systems for trades in London alone and no common set of codes for identifying clients in each of these systems. Each of these systems might use a different number or code for identifying the same client, so it would be extremely difficult or impossible to show how the same client was treated in all of these systems. Individual teams and traders each had their own incompatible platforms. The bank had employed a deliberate strategy of pitting teams against each other to spur them on, but this further encouraged the use of different systems because competing traders and teams were reluctant to share their data. Yet the bank ultimately had to reconcile the data from these disparate systems, often by hand, before trades could be processed and recorded.

This situation has made it very difficult for banks to undertake ambitious technology projects for the systems that they need today or to comply with regulatory requirements. U.S. regulators criticized Deutsche Bank for its inability to provide essential information because of its antiquated technology. Regulators are demanding that financial institutions improve the way they manage risk. The banks are under pressure to make their aging computer systems comply, but the IT infrastructures at many traditional financial institutions are failing to keep up with these regulatory pressures or with changing consumer expectations. Deutsche Bank and its peers must also adapt to new innovative technology competitors such as Apple that are muscling into banking services.

In July 2015, John Cryan became Deutsche Bank's CEO. He tried to reduce costs and improve efficiency, laying off thousands of employees. He focused on overhauling Deutsche Bank's fragmented, antiquated information systems, which are a major impediment to controlling costs and finding new sources of profit and growth. Cryan noted that the bank's cost base was swollen by poor and ineffective business processes, inadequate technology, and too many tasks being handled manually. He has called for standardizing the bank's systems and procedures, eliminating legacy software, standardizing and enhancing data, and improving reporting.

Cryan appointed technology specialist Kim Hammonds as chief operating officer to oversee reengineering the bank's information systems and operations. Hammonds had been Deutsche Bank's global chief information officer and, before that, chief information officer at Boeing. Hammonds observed that Deutsche Bank's information systems operated by trial and error, as if her former employer Boeing launched aircraft into the sky, watched them crash, and then tried to learn from the mistakes.

In February 2015, Deutsche Bank announced a 10-year, multibillion-dollar deal with Hewlett-Packard (HP) to standardize and simplify its IT infrastructure, reduce costs, and create a more modern and agile technology platform for launching new products and services. Deutsche Bank would migrate to a cloud computing infrastructure where it would run its information systems in HP's remote computer centers. HP would provide computing services, hosting, and storage. Deutsche Bank would still be in charge of application development and information security technologies, which it considers as proprietary and crucial for competitive differentiation.

Deutsche Bank is withdrawing from high-risk client relationships, improving its control framework, and automating manual reconciliations. To modernize its IT infrastructure, the bank is reducing the number of its individual operating systems that control the way a computer works from 45 to four, replacing scores of outdated computers, and replacing antiquated software applications. Thousands of applications and functions will be shifted from Deutsche Bank's mainframes to HP's cloud computing services. Automating manual processes will promote efficiency and better control. These improvements are expected to reduce "run the bank" costs by 800 million euros. Eliminating 6,000 contractors will create total savings of 1 billion euros. Deutsche Bank has also opened four technology centers to work with financial technology startups to improve its technology.

Despite all of these efforts, Deutsche Bank has struggled to regain profitability and stability. In early April 2018 the bank's supervisory board replaced Cryan with Christian Sewing, a longtime insider who had been in charge of the bank's wealth management division and its branch network in Germany. During his tenure, Cryan was unable to restore profitability. In February 2018 the bank reported a loss of €735 million, or about $900 million, for 2017, which represented its third consecutive annual loss.

Deutsche Bank has not been the only major bank to be hampered by system problems. IT shortcomings were one reason Banco Santander's U.S. unit in 2016 failed the U.S. Federal Reserve's annual "stress tests," which gauge how big banks would fare in a new financial crisis. A 2015 Accenture consultants' report found that only 6 percent of board of director members and 3 percent of CEOs at the world's largest banks had professional technology experience. Financial technology innovations, security, IT resilience, and technology implications of regulatory changes are now all critical issues for bank boards of directors, but many lack the knowledge to assess these issues and make informed decisions about strategy, investment, and how best to allocate technology resources.

Sources: Jack Ewing, "Deutsche Bank Replaces CEO Amid Losses and Lack of Direction," *New York Times*, April 8, 2018; Charles Riley, "Deutsche Bank Hasn't Made a Profit in Three Years," *CNN Money*, February 2, 2018; Anna Irrera, "Deutsche Bank Launches Tech Startup Lab in New York City," *Reuters*, March 21, 2017; Geoffrey Smith, "Things You Should Know About the Deutsche Bank Train Wreck," *Fortune*, September 28, 2016; Hayley McDowell, "System Outage Sees Deutsche Bank Charged over Reporting Failures," *The Trade News*, August 19, 2016; Derek du Preez, "US Regulator Charges Deutsche Bank over Multiple Systems Failures," *Diginomica*, August 19, 2016; Kat Hall, "Deutsche Bank's Creaking IT Systems Nervously Eyeing Bins," *The Register*, October 27, 2015; Martin Arnold and Tom Braithwaite, "Banks' Ageing IT Systems Buckle Under Strain," *Financial Times*, June 18, 2015; Martin Arnold, "Deutsche Bank to Rip Out IT Systems Blamed for Problems," *Financial Times*, October 26, 2015; Ben Moshinsky, "Deutsche Bank Has a Technology Problem," *Business Insider*, October 20, 2015; Edward Robinson and Nicholas Comfort, "Cryan's Shakeup at Deutsche Bank Sees Tech Restart," *Bloomberg*, December 20, 2015; and Accenture, "Bank Boardrooms Lack Technology Experience, Accenture Global Research Finds," October 28, 2015.

CASE STUDY QUESTIONS

1-12 Identify the problem described in this case study. What management, organization, and technology factors contributed to this problem?

1-13 What was the role of information technology at Deutsche Bank? How was IT related to the bank's operational efficiency, decision-making capability, and business strategy?

1-14 Was Deutsche Bank using technology effectively to pursue its business strategy? Explain your answer.

1-15 What solution for Deutsche Bank was proposed? How effective do you think it will be? Explain your answer.

MyLab MIS

Go to the Assignments section of MyLab MIS to complete these writing exercises.

1-16 What are the strategic objectives that firms try to achieve by investing in information systems and technologies? For each strategic objective, give an example of how a firm could use information systems to achieve that objective.

1-17 Describe the complementary assets that firms need in order to optimize returns from their information system investments. For each type of complementary asset, give an example of a specific asset a firm should have.

Chapter 1 References

Baldwin, Richard. *The Great Convergence: Information Technology and the New Globalization.* Cambridge, MA: Harvard University Press (2016.)

Brynjolfsson, Erik. "VII Pillars of IT Productivity." *Optimize* (May 2005).

Brynjolfsson, Erik, and Lorin M. Hitt. "Beyond Computation: Information Technology, Organizational Transformation, and Business Performance." *Journal of Economic Perspectives* 14, No. 4 (2000).

Bureau of Economic Analysis. *National Income and Product Accounts.* www.bea.gov, accessed June 19, 2018.

Chae, Ho-Chang, Chang E. Koh, and Victor Prybutok. "Information Technology Capability and Firm Performance: Contradictory Findings and Their Possible Causes." *MIS Quarterly* 38, No. 1 (March 2014).

Dedrick, Jason, Vijay Gurbaxani, and Kenneth L. Kraemer. "Information Technology and Economic Performance: A Critical Review of the Empirical Evidence." Center for Research on Information Technology and Organizations, University of California, Irvine (December 2001).

eMarketer. "Number of Bloggers in the United States from 2014 to 2020 (in Millions)." *eMarketer* (2018).

_____. "Average Daily Time Spent with Media According to US Internet Users, 2012 & 2017 (Hours)," March 14, 2018.

eMarketer Chart. "US Digital Ad Spending, by Format, 2014–2020 (billions and % change)," June 17, 2018.

FedEx Corporation. "SEC Form 10-K for the Fiscal Year Ended May 31, 2018."

Friedman, Thomas. *The World Is Flat.* New York: Picador (2007).

Gartner Inc. "Gartner Identifies the Top 10 Strategic Technology Trends for 2018." (October 4, 2017).

Hughes, Alan, and Michael S. Scott Morton. "The Transforming Power of Complementary Assets." *MIT Sloan Management Review* 47, No. 4 (Summer 2006).

Lamb, Roberta, Steve Sawyer, and Rob Kling. "A Social Informatics Perspective of Socio-Technical Networks." http://lamb.cba.hawaii.edu/pubs (2004).

Laudon, Kenneth C. *Computers and Bureaucratic Reform.* New York: Wiley (1974).

Lev, Baruch. "Intangibles: Management, Measurement, and Reporting." The Brookings Institution Press (2001).

McKinsey Global Institute. "Digital America: A Tale of the Haves and Have-Mores" (December 2015).

Mithas, Sunil, and Roland T. Rust. "How Information Technology Strategy and Investments Influence Firm Performance: Conjecture and Empirical Evidence." *MIS Quarterly* (March 2016).

Morris, Betsy. "From Music to Maps: How Apple's IPhone Changed Business." *Wall Street Journal* (June 27, 2017).

Nevo, Saggi, and Michael R. Wade. "The Formation and Value of IT-Enabled Resources: Antecedents and Consequences of Synergistic Relationships." *MIS Quarterly* 34, No. 1 (March 2010).

Otim, Samuel, Kevin E. Dow, Varun Grover, and Jeffrey A. Wong. "The Impact of Information Technology Investments on Downside Risk of the Firm: Alternative Measurement of the Business Value of IT." *Journal of Management Information Systems* 29, No. 1 (Summer 2012).

Ren, Fei, and Sanjeev Dewan. "Industry-Level Analysis of Information Technology Return and Risk: What Explains the Variation?" *Journal of Management Information Systems* 21, No. 2 (2015).

Ross, Jeanne W., and Peter Weill. "Four Questions Every CEO Should Ask About IT." *Wall Street Journal* (April 25, 2011).

Sabherwal, Rajiv, and Anand Jeyaraj. "Information Technology Impacts on Firm Performance: An Extension of Kohli and Devaraj (2003)." *MIS Quarterly* (December 2015).

Sampler, Jeffrey L., and Michael J. Earl. "What's Your Information Footprint?" *MIT Sloan Management Review* (Winter 2014).

Saunders, Adam, and Erik Brynjolfsson. "Valuing Information Technology Related Intangible Assets." *MIS Quarterly* (March 2016).

Shanks, Ryan, Sunit Sinha, and Robert J. Thomas. "Managers and Machines, Unite!" *Accenture* (2015).

Teece, David. *Economic Performance and Theory of the Firm*: *The Selected Papers of David Teece.* London: Edward Elgar Publishing (1998).

U.S. Bureau of Labor Statistics. *Occupational Outlook Handbook.* 2018–2019 (April 19, 2018).

2

Global E-business and Collaboration

LEARNING OBJECTIVES

After reading this chapter, you will be able to answer the following questions:

2-1 What are business processes? How are they related to information systems?

2-2 How do systems serve the different management groups in a business, and how do systems that link the enterprise improve organizational performance?

2-3 Why are systems for collaboration and social business so important, and what technologies do they use?

2-4 What is the role of the information systems function in a business?

2-5 How will MIS help my career?

CHAPTER CASES

Enterprise Social Networking Helps Sanofi Pasteur Innovate and Improve Quality

Data Changes How NFL Teams Play the Game and How Fans See It

Videoconferencing: Something for Everyone

Should Companies Embrace Social Business?

VIDEO CASES

Walmart's Retail Link Supply Chain

CEMEX: Becoming a Social Business

Instructional Video:

U.S. Foodservice Grows Market with Oracle CRM on Demand

MyLab MIS

Discussion Questions: 2-5, 2-6, 2-7; **Hands-on MIS Projects:** 2-8, 2-9, 2-10, 2-11;
Writing Assignments: 2-16, 2-17; **eText with Conceptual Animations**

Enterprise Social Networking Helps Sanofi Pasteur Innovate and Improve Quality

Sanofi Pasteur is the vaccines division of the multinational pharmaceutical company Sanofi and the largest company in the world devoted entirely to vaccines. It is headquartered in Lyon, France, has nearly 15,000 employees worldwide, and produces more than 1 billion doses of vaccine per year to inoculate more than 500 million people around the globe. Sanofi Pasteur's corporate vision is to work toward a world where no one suffers or dies from a vaccine-preventable disease. Every day the company invests more than € 1 million in research and development. Collaboration, sharing information, ongoing innovation, and rigorous pursuit of quality are essential for Sanofi Pasteur's business success and commitment to improving the health of the world's population.

Until recently, the company lacked appropriate tools to encourage staff to have dialogues, share ideas, and work with other members of the company, including people that they might not know. As a large, centralized firm with a traditional hierarchical culture, initiatives were primarily driven from the top down. The company wanted to give employees more opportunities to experiment and innovate on their own, and adopted Microsoft Yammer as the platform for this change. Ideas for improvement can come from anywhere in the organization and through Yammer can be shared everywhere.

© Rawpixel.com/Shutterstock

Microsoft Yammer is an enterprise social networking platform for internal business uses, although it can also create external networks linking to suppliers, customers, and others outside the organization. Yammer enables employees to create groups to collaborate on projects and share and edit documents, and includes a news feed to find out what's happening within the company. A People Directory provides a searchable database of contact information, skills, and expertise. Yammer can be accessed through the web using desktop and mobile devices, and can be integrated with other Microsoft tools such as SharePoint and Office 365, to make other applications more "social." (SharePoint is Microsoft's platform for collaboration, document sharing, and document management. Office 365 is Microsoft's online service for its desktop productivity applications such as word processing, spreadsheet, electronic presentations, and data management.)

How has Sanofi Pasteur benefited from becoming more "social"? Employees are using Yammer to share updates, ask for feedback, and connect volunteers to improvement initiatives. A recent project involving Yammer resulted in a 60 percent simplification of a key quality process at one manufacturing site, saving the company thousands of Euros, and reducing overall end-to-end process time. Through Yammer, employees spread the word about this improvement to other locations around the globe.

Using Yammer, Sanofi employees set up activist networks for change in large manufacturing sites. Each group has attracted more than 1,000 people. These networks help create a more collegial, personal culture that helps people feel comfortable about making suggestions for improvements and working with other groups across the globe. They also provide management with observations about policies and procedures across departments and hierarchies that can be used to redesign the firm's manufacturing and business processes to increase quality and cost-effectiveness. For example, a building operator shared his ideas about how to reduce waste when managing a specific material in his production facility. The new procedure for handling the material saved his facility more than 100,000 Euros per year and became a global best practice at all Sanofi Pasteur production sites. Yammer-powered communities raised awareness of health, safety, and attention to detail, and more attention to these issues helped reduce human errors by 91 percent.

Sources: "Yammer Collaboration Helps Sanofi Pasteur Improve Quality, Make More Life-Saving Vaccines," www.microsoft.com, January 24, 2017; www.sanofipasteur.us, accessed February 4, 2018; and Jacob Morgan, "Three Ways Sanofi Pasteur Encourages Collaboration," *Forbes,* October 20, 2015.

Sanofi Pasteur's experience illustrates how much organizations today rely on information systems to improve their performance and remain competitive. It also shows how much systems supporting collaboration and teamwork make a difference in an organization's ability to innovate, execute, grow profits, and, in this case, provide important social benefits.

The chapter-opening diagram calls attention to important points raised by this case and this chapter. Sanofi Pasteur is a knowledge-intensive company that prizes innovation, but it was hampered by hierarchical top-down processes that prevented employees and managers from freely sharing information and innovating. This impacted the company's ability to create and deliver new leading-edge products and maintain its high quality standards.

Sanofi Pasteur management found that the best solution was to deploy new technology to move from a hierarchical corporate knowledge and work environment to one that actively engaged employees and enabled them to obtain more knowledge from colleagues. The company took advantage of Microsoft Yammer's social tools to increase employee collaboration and engagement. There is more effective sharing of employee knowledge, and the company has become more innovative and cost-efficient.

New technology alone would not have solved Sanofi Pasteur's problem. To make the solution effective, Sanofi Pasteur had to change its organizational culture and business processes for knowledge dissemination and collaborative work, and the new technology made these changes possible.

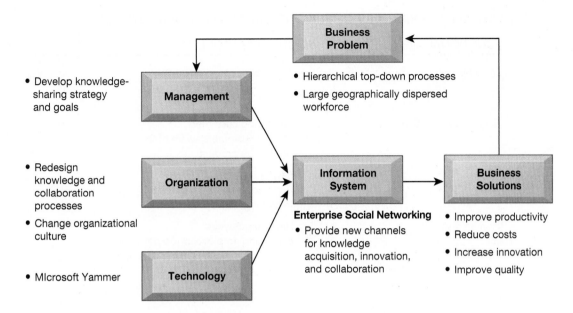

- Develop knowledge-sharing strategy and goals

Management

- Hierarchical top-down processes
- Large geographically dispersed workforce

Business Problem

- Redesign knowledge and collaboration processes
- Change organizational culture

Organization

Information System

Enterprise Social Networking

- Provide new channels for knowledge acquisition, innovation, and collaboration

Business Solutions

- Improve productivity
- Reduce costs
- Increase innovation
- Improve quality

- MIcrosoft Yammer

Technology

Here are some questions to think about: How are collaboration and employee engagement keeping Sanofi Pasteur competitive and quality-conscious? How did using Yammer change the way work was performed at Sanofi Pasteur?

2-1 What are business processes? How are they related to information systems?

In order to operate, businesses must deal with many different pieces of information about suppliers, customers, employees, invoices, and payments, and of course their products and services. They must organize work activities that use this information to operate efficiently and enhance the overall performance of the firm. Information systems make it possible for firms to manage all their information, make better decisions, and improve the execution of their business processes.

Business Processes

Business processes, which we introduced in Chapter 1, refer to the manner in which work is organized, coordinated, and focused to produce a valuable product or service. Business processes are the collection of activities required to produce a product or service. These activities are supported by flows of material, information, and knowledge among the participants in business processes. Business processes also refer to the unique ways in which organizations coordinate work, information, and knowledge, and the ways in which management chooses to coordinate work.

To a large extent, the performance of a business firm depends on how well its business processes are designed and coordinated. A company's business processes can be a source of competitive strength if they enable the company to innovate or to execute better than its rivals. Business processes can also be liabilities if they are based on inefficient ways of working that impede organizational responsiveness and efficiency. The chapter-opening case describing Sanofi Pasteur's improvements in knowledge-sharing processes clearly illustrates these points, as do many of the other cases in this text.

TABLE 2.1 EXAMPLES OF FUNCTIONAL BUSINESS PROCESSES

FUNCTIONAL AREA	BUSINESS PROCESS
Manufacturing and production	Assembling the product Checking for quality Producing bills of materials
Sales and marketing	Identifying customers Making customers aware of the product Selling the product
Finance and accounting	Paying creditors Creating financial statements Managing cash accounts
Human resources	Hiring employees Evaluating employees' job performance Enrolling employees in benefits plans

Every business can be seen as a collection of business processes, some of which are part of larger encompassing processes. For instance, uses of mentoring, wikis, blogs, and videos are all part of the overall knowledge management process. Many business processes are tied to a specific functional area. For example, the sales and marketing function is responsible for identifying customers, and the human resources function is responsible for hiring employees. Table 2.1 describes some typical business processes for each of the functional areas of business.

Other business processes cross many different functional areas and require coordination across departments. For instance, consider the seemingly simple business process of fulfilling a customer order (see Figure 2.1). Initially, the sales department receives a sales order. The order passes first to accounting to ensure the customer can pay for the order either by a credit verification or request for immediate payment prior to shipping. Once the customer credit is

FIGURE 2.1 THE ORDER FULFILLMENT PROCESS

Fulfilling a customer order involves a complex set of steps that requires the close coordination of the sales, accounting, and manufacturing functions.

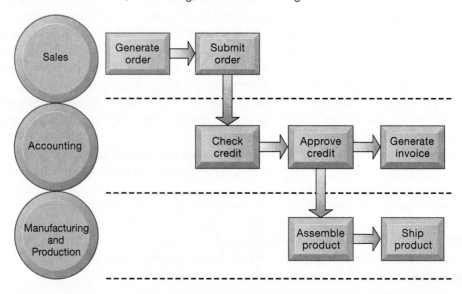

established, the production department pulls the product from inventory or produces the product. Then the product is shipped (and this may require working with a logistics firm, such as UPS or FedEx). A bill or invoice is generated by the accounting department, and a notice is sent to the customer indicating that the product has shipped. The sales department is notified of the shipment and prepares to support the customer by answering calls or fulfilling warranty claims.

What at first appears to be a simple process, fulfilling an order, turns out to be a very complicated series of business processes that require the close coordination of major functional groups in a firm. Moreover, to efficiently perform all these steps in the order fulfillment process requires a great deal of information. The required information must flow rapidly within the firm from one decision maker to another; with business partners, such as delivery firms; and with the customer. Computer-based information systems make this possible.

How Information Technology Improves Business Processes

Exactly how do information systems improve business processes? Information systems automate many steps in business processes that were formerly performed manually, such as checking a client's credit or generating an invoice and shipping order. But today, information technology can do much more. New technology can actually change the flow of information, making it possible for many more people to access and share information, replacing sequential steps with tasks that can be performed simultaneously, and eliminating delays in decision making. New information technology frequently changes the way a business works and supports entirely new business models. Downloading a Kindle e-book from Amazon, buying a computer online at Best Buy, and downloading a music track from iTunes are entirely new business processes based on new business models that would be inconceivable without today's information technology.

That's why it's so important to pay close attention to business processes, both in your information systems course and in your future career. By analyzing business processes, you can achieve a very clear understanding of how a business actually works. Moreover, by conducting a business process analysis, you will also begin to understand how to change the business by improving its processes to make it more efficient or effective. Throughout this book, we examine business processes with a view to understanding how they might be improved by using information technology to achieve greater efficiency, innovation, and customer service.

2-2 How do systems serve the different management groups in a business, and how do systems that link the enterprise improve organizational performance?

Now that you understand business processes, it is time to look more closely at how information systems support the business processes of a firm. Because there are different interests, specialties, and levels in an organization, there are different kinds of systems. No single system can provide all the information an organization needs.

A typical business organization has systems supporting processes for each of the major business functions—sales and marketing, manufacturing and production, finance and accounting, and human resources. You can find examples of systems for each of these business functions in the Learning Tracks for this chapter. Functional systems that operate independently of each other are becoming a thing of the past because they cannot easily share information to support cross-functional business processes. Many have been replaced with large-scale cross-functional systems that integrate the activities of related business processes and organizational units. We describe these integrated cross-functional applications later in this section.

A typical firm also has different systems supporting the decision-making needs of each of the main management groups we described in Chapter 1. Operational management, middle management, and senior management each use systems to support the decisions they must make to run the company. Let's look at these systems and the types of decisions they support.

Systems for Different Management Groups

A business firm has systems to support different groups or levels of management. These systems include transaction processing systems and systems for business intelligence.

Transaction Processing Systems

Operational managers need systems that keep track of the elementary activities and transactions of the organization, such as sales, receipts, cash deposits, payroll, credit decisions, and the flow of materials in a factory. **Transaction processing systems (TPS)** provide this kind of information. A transaction processing system is a computerized system that performs and records the daily routine transactions necessary to conduct business, such as sales order entry, hotel reservations, payroll, employee record keeping, and shipping.

The principal purpose of systems at this level is to answer routine questions and to track the flow of transactions through the organization. How many parts are in inventory? What happened to Mr. Smith's payment? To answer these kinds of questions, information generally must be easily available, current, and accurate.

At the operational level, tasks, resources, and goals are predefined and highly structured. The decision to grant credit to a customer, for instance, is made by a lower-level supervisor according to predefined criteria. All that must be determined is whether the customer meets the criteria.

Figure 2.2 illustrates a TPS for payroll processing. A payroll system keeps track of money paid to employees. An employee time sheet with the employee's name, social security number, and number of hours worked per week represents a single transaction for this system. Once this transaction is input into the system, it updates the system's master file (or database—see Chapter 6) that permanently maintains employee information for the organization. The data in the system are combined in different ways to create reports of interest to management and government agencies and to send paychecks to employees.

Managers need TPS to monitor the status of internal operations and the firm's relations with the external environment. TPS are also major producers of information for the other systems and business functions. For example, the payroll system illustrated in Figure 2.2, along with other accounting TPS, supplies data to the company's general ledger system, which is responsible for maintaining records of the firm's income and expenses and for producing

FIGURE 2.2 A PAYROLL TPS

A TPS for payroll processing captures employee payment transaction data (such as a time card). System outputs include online and hard-copy reports for management and employee paychecks.

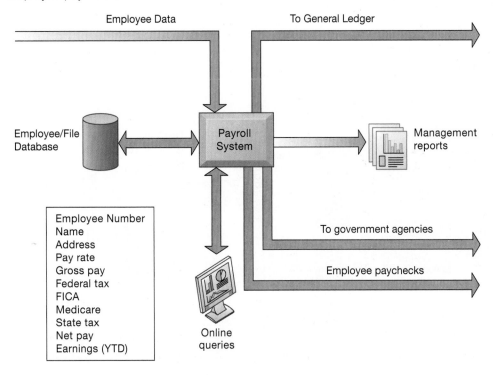

Employee Data

To General Ledger

Employee/File Database

Payroll System

Management reports

Employee Number
Name
Address
Pay rate
Gross pay
Federal tax
FICA
Medicare
State tax
Net pay
Earnings (YTD)

To government agencies

Employee paychecks

Online queries

Payroll data on master file

reports such as income statements and balance sheets. It also supplies employee payment history data for insurance, pension, and other benefits calculations to the firm's human resources function and employee payment data to government agencies such as the U.S. Internal Revenue Service and Social Security Administration.

Transaction processing systems are often so central to a business that TPS failure for a few hours can lead to a firm's demise and perhaps that of other firms linked to it. Imagine what would happen to UPS if its package tracking system was not working! What would the airlines do without their computerized reservation systems?

Systems for Business Intelligence

Firms also have business intelligence systems that focus on delivering information to support management decision making. **Business intelligence** is a contemporary term for data and software tools for organizing, analyzing, and providing access to data to help managers and other enterprise users make more informed decisions. Business intelligence addresses the decision-making needs of all levels of management. This section provides a brief introduction to business intelligence. You'll learn more about this topic in Chapters 6 and 12.

Business intelligence systems for middle management help with monitoring, controlling, decision-making, and administrative activities. In Chapter 1, we defined management information systems as the study of information systems in business and management. The term **management information systems (MIS)** also designates a specific category of information systems serving middle

FIGURE 2.3 HOW MANAGEMENT INFORMATION SYSTEMS OBTAIN THEIR DATA FROM THE ORGANIZATION'S TPS

In the system illustrated by this diagram, three TPS supply summarized transaction data to the MIS reporting system at the end of the time period. Managers gain access to the organizational data through the MIS, which provides them with the appropriate reports.

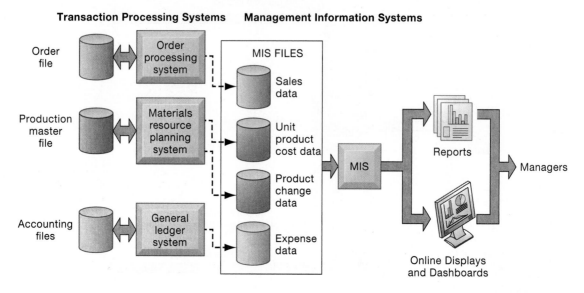

management. MIS provide middle managers with reports on the organization's current performance. This information is used to monitor and control the business and predict future performance.

MIS summarize and report on the company's basic operations using data supplied by transaction processing systems. The basic transaction data from TPS are compressed and usually presented in reports that are produced on a regular schedule. Today, many of these reports are delivered online. Figure 2.3 shows how a typical MIS transforms transaction-level data from inventory, production, and accounting into MIS files that are used to provide managers with reports. Figure 2.4 shows a sample report from this system.

FIGURE 2.4 SAMPLE MIS REPORT

This report, showing summarized annual sales data, was produced by the MIS in Figure 2.3.

Consolidated Consumer Products Corporation Sales by Product and Sales Region: 2019

PRODUCT CODE	PRODUCT DESCRIPTION	SALES REGION	ACTUAL SALES	PLANNED	ACTUAL versus PLANNED
4469	Carpet Cleaner	Northeast	4,066,700	4,800,000	0.85
		South	3,778,112	3,750,000	1.01
		Midwest	4,867,001	4,600,000	1.06
		West	4,003,440	4,400,000	0.91
	TOTAL		16,715,253	17,550,000	0.95
5674	Room Freshener	Northeast	3,676,700	3,900,000	0.94
		South	5,608,112	4,700,000	1.19
		Midwest	4,711,001	4,200,000	1.12
		West	4,563,440	4,900,000	0.93
	TOTAL		18,559,253	17,700,000	1.05

MIS typically provide answers to routine questions that have been specified in advance and have a predefined procedure for answering them. For instance, MIS reports might list the total pounds of lettuce used this quarter by a fast-food chain or, as illustrated in Figure 2.4, compare total annual sales figures for specific products to planned targets. These systems generally are not flexible and have little analytical capability. Most MIS use simple routines, such as summaries and comparisons, as opposed to sophisticated mathematical models or statistical techniques.

Other types of business intelligence systems support more non-routine decision making. **Decision-support systems (DSS)** focus on problems that are unique and rapidly changing, for which the procedure for arriving at a solution may not be fully predefined in advance. They try to answer questions such as these: What would be the impact on production schedules if we were to double sales in the month of December? What would happen to our return on investment if a factory schedule were delayed for six months?

Although DSS use internal information from TPS and MIS, they often bring in information from external sources, such as current stock prices or product prices of competitors. These systems are employed by "super-user" managers and business analysts who want to use sophisticated analytics and models to analyze data.

An interesting, small, but powerful DSS is the voyage-estimating system of a large global shipping company that transports bulk cargoes of coal, oil, ores, and finished products. The firm owns some vessels, charters others, and bids for shipping contracts in the open market to carry general cargo. A voyage-estimating system calculates financial and technical voyage details. Financial calculations include ship/time costs (fuel, labor, capital), freight rates for various types of cargo, and port expenses. Technical details include myriad factors, such as ship cargo capacity, speed, port distances, fuel and water consumption, and loading patterns (location of cargo for different ports).

The system can answer questions such as the following: Given a customer delivery schedule and an offered freight rate, which vessel should be assigned at what rate to maximize profits? What is the optimal speed at which a particular vessel can optimize its profit and still meet its delivery schedule? What is the optimal loading pattern for a ship bound for the U.S. West Coast from Malaysia? Figure 2.5 illustrates the DSS built for this company. The system operates on a powerful desktop personal computer, providing a system of menus that makes it easy for users to enter data or obtain information.

The voyage-estimating DSS we have just described draws heavily on models. Other business intelligence systems are more data-driven, focusing instead on extracting useful information from very large quantities of data. For example, large ski resort companies such as Intrawest and Vail Resorts collect and store large amounts of customer data from call centers, lodging and dining reservations, ski schools, and ski equipment rental stores. They use special software to analyze these data to determine the value, revenue potential, and loyalty of each customer to help managers make better decisions about how to target their marketing programs.

Business intelligence systems also address the decision-making needs of senior management. Senior managers need systems that focus on strategic issues and long-term trends, both in the firm and in the external environment. They are concerned with questions such as: What will employment levels be in five years? What are the long-term industry cost trends? What products should we be making in five years?

FIGURE 2.5 VOYAGE-ESTIMATING DECISION-SUPPORT SYSTEM

This DSS operates on a powerful PC. It is used daily by managers who must develop bids on shipping contracts.

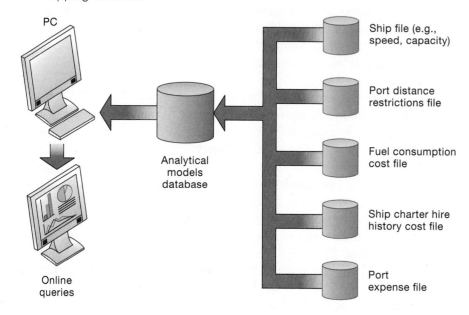

Executive support systems (ESS) help senior management make these decisions. They address nonroutine decisions requiring judgment, evaluation, and insight because there is no agreed-on procedure for arriving at a solution. ESS present graphs and data from many sources through an interface that is easy for senior managers to use. Often the information is delivered to senior executives through a **portal**, which uses a web interface to present integrated personalized business content.

ESS are designed to incorporate data about external events, such as new tax laws or competitors, but they also draw summarized information from internal MIS and DSS. They filter, compress, and track critical data, displaying the data of greatest importance to senior managers. Increasingly, such systems include business intelligence analytics for analyzing trends, forecasting, and "drilling down" to data at greater levels of detail.

For example, the chief operating officer (COO) and plant managers at Valero, the world's largest independent petroleum refiner, use a Refining Dashboard to display real-time data related to plant and equipment reliability, inventory management, safety, and energy consumption. With the displayed information, the COO and his team can review the performance of each Valero refinery in the United States and Canada in terms of how each plant is performing compared to the production plan of the firm. The headquarters group can drill down from executive level to refinery level and individual system-operator level displays of performance. Valero's Refining Dashboard is an example of a **digital dashboard**, which displays on a single screen graphs and charts of key performance indicators for managing a company. Digital dashboards are becoming an increasingly popular tool for management decision makers.

The Interactive Session on Organizations describes examples of several of these types of systems that the NFL (National Football League) and its teams use. Note the types of systems illustrated by this case and the role they play in improving both operations and decision making.

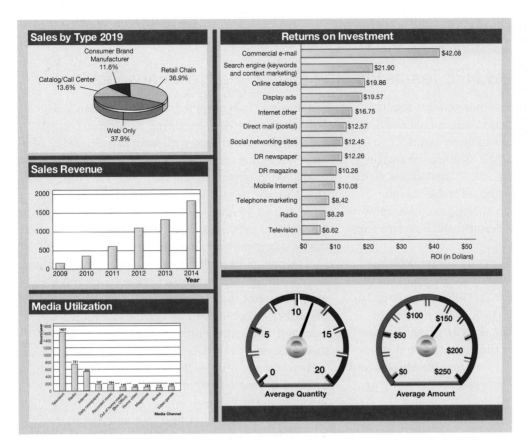

A digital dashboard delivers comprehensive and accurate information for decision making, often using a single screen. The graphical overview of key performance indicators helps managers quickly spot areas that need attention.

Systems for Linking the Enterprise

Reviewing all the different types of systems we have just described, you might wonder how a business can manage all the information in these different systems. You might also wonder how costly it is to maintain so many different systems. And you might wonder how all these different systems can share information and how managers and employees are able to coordinate their work. In fact, these are all important questions for businesses today.

Enterprise Applications

Getting all the different kinds of systems in a company to work together has proven a major challenge. Typically, corporations are put together both through normal "organic" growth and through acquisition of smaller firms. Over a period of time, corporations end up with a collection of systems, most of them older, and face the challenge of getting them all to "talk" with one another and work together as one corporate system. There are several solutions to this problem.

One solution is to implement **enterprise applications**, which are systems that span functional areas, focus on executing business processes across the firm, and include all levels of management. Enterprise applications help businesses become more flexible and productive by coordinating their business processes more closely and integrating groups of processes so they focus on efficient management of resources and customer service.

There are four major enterprise applications: enterprise systems, supply chain management systems, customer relationship management systems, and knowledge management systems. Each of these enterprise applications integrates a related set of functions and business processes to enhance the

Data Changes How NFL Teams Play the Game and How Fans See It

All professional sports teams today collect detailed data on player and team performance, fan behavior, and sales, and increasingly use these data to drive decisions about every aspect of the business—marketing, ticketing, player evaluation, and TV and digital media deals. This includes the National Football League (NFL), which is increasingly turning to data to improve how its players and teams perform and how fans experience the game.

Since 2014 the NFL has been capturing player movement data on the field by putting nickel-sized radio frequency identification (RFID) tags beneath players' shoulder pads to track every move they make. The information the sensors gather is used by NFL teams to improve their training and strategy, by commentators on live game broadcasts, and by fans attending games or using the NFL app on the Xbox One.

The NFL's player tracking system is based on the Zebra Sports Solution developed by Zebra Technologies, a Chicago-based firm specializing in tracking technology that includes the bar codes on groceries and other consumer goods and radio frequency identification (RFID) technology. The Zebra Sports Solution system records players' speed, direction, location on the field, how far they ran on a play, and how long they were sprinting, jogging, or walking. The system can also determine what formation a team was in and how players' speed or acceleration affects their on-field performance. Want to know how hard Eli Manning is throwing passes or the force with which a ball arrives in the hands of receiver Odell Beckham? The system knows how to do all that.

NFL players have RFID chips in their left and right shoulder pads that transmit data to 20 radio receivers strategically located in the lower and upper levels of stadiums to collect data about how each player moves, using metrics such as velocity, speed in miles per hour, and distance traveled. From there the data are transmitted to an on-site server computer, where Zebra's software matches an RFID tag to the correct player or official. The football also has a sensor transmitting location data. The data are generated in real-time as the game is being played. Each sensor transmits its location about 25 times per player.

It takes just two seconds for data to be received by the motion sensors, analyzed, and pushed out to remote cloud computers run by Amazon Web Services for the NFL. From the NFL cloud computers, the data are shared with fans, broadcasters, and NFL teams. The data captured by the NFL are displayed to fans using the NFL Next Gen Stats website, NFL social media channels, and the NFL app on Windows 10 and the Xbox One. The data are also transmitted to the giant display screens in the arena to show fans during the game.

The data have multiple uses. NFL teams use them to evaluate player and team performance and to analyze tactics, such as whether it might be better to press forward or to punt in a particular fourth-down situation. Data transmitted to broadcasters, to stadium screens, to Next Gen Stats, and to the Next Gen Stats feature of Microsoft's Xbox One NFL app help create a deeper fan experience that gets fans more involved in the game.

Some of the statistics fans can now see on Next Gen Stats include Fastest Ball Carriers, Longest Tackles, Longest Plays, Passing Leaders, Rushing Leaders, and Receiving Leaders. Next Gen Stats also features charts for individual players and videos that explain the differences and similarities between players, teams, and games based on the data.

While the data may be entertaining for fans, they could prove strategic for the teams. Data markers for each play are recorded, including type of offense, type of defense, whether there was a huddle, all movement during the play, and the yard line where the ball was stopped. The NFL runs custom-created analytics to deliver visualizations of the data to each team within 24 hours of the game, via a custom-built web portal. The system displays charts and graphs as well as tabular data to let teams have more insight. Each NFL team may also hire its own data analyst to wring even more value from the data. The data are giving NFL fans, teams, coaches, and players a deeper look into the game they love.

Sources: Jason Hiner, "How the NFL and Amazon Unleashed 'Next Gen Stats' to Grok Football Games," *TechRepublic,* February 2, 2018; Teena Maddox, "Super Bowl 52: How the NFL and US Bank Stadium Are Ready to Make Digital History," *TechRepublic,* February 1, 2018; Brian McDonough, "How the NFL's Data Operation Tracks Every Move on the Field," *Information Management,* December 7, 2016; www.zebra.com, accessed March 15, 2017; and Mark J. Burns, "Zebra Technologies, NFL Revamp Partnership For Third Season," *SportTechie,* September 6, 2016.

CASE STUDY QUESTIONS

1. What kinds of systems are illustrated in this case study? Where do they obtain their data? What do they do with the data? Describe some of the inputs and outputs of these systems.

2. What business functions do these systems support? Explain your answer.

3. How do the data about teams and players captured by the NFL help NFL football teams and the NFL itself make better decisions? Give examples of two decisions that were improved by the systems described in this case.

4. How did using data help the NFL and its teams improve the way they run their business?

performance of the organization as a whole. Figure 2.6 shows that the architecture for these enterprise applications encompasses processes spanning the entire organization and, in some cases, extending beyond the organization to customers, suppliers, and other key business partners.

Enterprise Systems Firms use **enterprise systems**, also known as enterprise resource planning (ERP) systems, to integrate business processes in manufacturing and production, finance and accounting, sales and marketing, and human resources into a single software system. Information that was previously

FIGURE 2.6 ENTERPRISE APPLICATION ARCHITECTURE

Enterprise applications automate processes that span multiple business functions and organizational levels and may extend outside the organization.

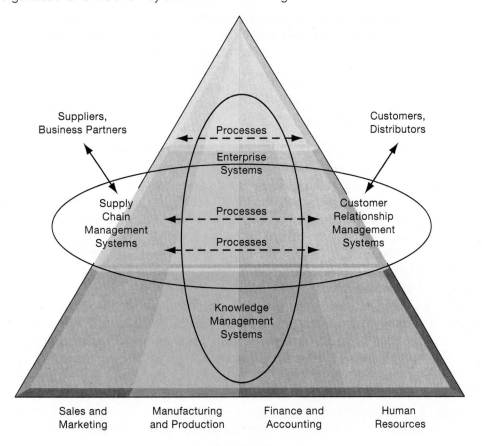

FUNCTIONAL AREAS

fragmented in many different systems is stored in a single comprehensive data repository where it can be used by many different parts of the business.

For example, when a customer places an order, the order data flow automatically to other parts of the company that are affected by them. The order transaction triggers the warehouse to pick the ordered products and schedule shipment. The warehouse informs the factory to replenish whatever has been depleted. The accounting department is notified to send the customer an invoice. Customer service representatives track the progress of the order through every step to inform customers about the status of their orders. Managers are able to use firmwide information to make more-precise and timely decisions about daily operations and longer-term planning.

Supply Chain Management Systems   Firms use **supply chain management (SCM) systems** to help manage relationships with their suppliers. These systems help suppliers, purchasing firms, distributors, and logistics companies share information about orders, production, inventory levels, and delivery of products and services so they can source, produce, and deliver goods and services efficiently. The ultimate objective is to get the right amount of their products from their source to their point of consumption in the least amount of time and at the lowest cost. These systems increase firm profitability by lowering the costs of moving and making products and by enabling managers to make better decisions about how to organize and schedule sourcing, production, and distribution.

Supply chain management systems are one type of **interorganizational system** because they automate the flow of information across organizational boundaries. You will find examples of other types of interorganizational information systems throughout this text because such systems make it possible for firms to link digitally to customers and to outsource their work to other companies.

Customer Relationship Management Systems   Firms use **customer relationship management (CRM) systems** to help manage their relationships with their customers. CRM systems provide information to coordinate all of the business processes that deal with customers in sales, marketing, and service to optimize revenue, customer satisfaction, and customer retention. This information helps firms identify, attract, and retain the most profitable customers; provide better service to existing customers; and increase sales.

Knowledge Management Systems   Some firms perform better than others because they have better knowledge about how to create, produce, and deliver products and services. This firm knowledge is unique, is difficult to imitate, and can be leveraged into long-term strategic benefits. **Knowledge management systems (KMS)** enable organizations to better manage processes for capturing and applying knowledge and expertise. These systems collect all relevant knowledge and experience in the firm and make it available wherever and whenever it is needed to improve business processes and management decisions. They also link the firm to external sources of knowledge.

We examine enterprise systems and systems for supply chain management and customer relationship management in greater detail in Chapter 9. We discuss collaboration systems that support knowledge management in this chapter and cover other types of knowledge management applications in Chapter 11.

Intranets and Extranets

Enterprise applications create deep-seated changes in the way the firm conducts its business, offering many opportunities to integrate important business data into a single system. They are often costly and difficult to implement. Intranets and extranets deserve mention here as alternative tools for increasing integration and expediting the flow of information within the firm and with customers and suppliers.

Intranets are simply internal company websites that are accessible only by employees. The term *intranet* refers to an internal network, in contrast to the Internet, which is a public network linking organizations and other external networks. Intranets use the same technologies and techniques as the larger Internet, and they often are simply a private access area in a larger company website. Likewise with extranets, which are company websites that are accessible to authorized vendors and suppliers and are often used to coordinate the movement of supplies to the firm's production apparatus.

For example, Six Flags, which operates 18 theme parks throughout North America, maintains an intranet for its 1900 full-time employees that provides company-related news and information on each park's day-to-day operations, including weather forecasts, performance schedules, and details about groups and celebrities visiting the parks. The company also uses an extranet to broadcast information about schedule changes and park events to its 30,000 seasonal employees. We describe the technology for intranets and extranets in more detail in Chapter 7.

E-business, E-commerce, and E-government

The systems and technologies we have just described are transforming firms' relationships with customers, employees, suppliers, and logistic partners into digital relationships using networks and the Internet. So much business is now enabled by or based upon digital networks that we use the terms *electronic business* and *electronic commerce* frequently throughout this text.

Electronic business, or e-business, refers to the use of digital technology and the Internet to execute the major business processes in the enterprise. E-business includes activities for the internal management of the firm and for coordination with suppliers and other business partners. It also includes **electronic commerce, or e-commerce**.

E-commerce is the part of e-business that deals with the buying and selling of goods and services over the Internet. It also encompasses activities supporting those market transactions, such as advertising, marketing, customer support, security, delivery, and payment.

The technologies associated with e-business have also brought about similar changes in the public sector. Governments on all levels are using Internet technology to deliver information and services to citizens, employees, and businesses with which they work. **E-government** refers to the application of the Internet and networking technologies to digitally enable government and public sector agencies' relationships with citizens, businesses, and other arms of government.

In addition to improving delivery of government services, e-government makes government operations more efficient and also empowers citizens by giving them easier access to information and the ability to network electronically with other citizens. For example, citizens in some states can renew their driver's licenses or apply for unemployment benefits online, and the Internet has become a powerful tool for instantly mobilizing interest groups for political action and fundraising.

2-3 Why are systems for collaboration and social business so important, and what technologies do they use?

With all these systems and information, you might wonder how it is possible to make sense of them. How do people working in firms pull it all together, work toward common goals, and coordinate plans and actions? In addition to the types of systems we have just described, businesses need special systems to support collaboration and teamwork.

What Is Collaboration?

Collaboration is working with others to achieve shared and explicit goals. Collaboration focuses on task or mission accomplishment and usually takes place in a business or other organization and between businesses. You collaborate with a colleague in Tokyo who has expertise on a topic about which you know nothing. You collaborate with many colleagues in publishing a company blog. If you're in a law firm, you collaborate with accountants in an accounting firm in servicing the needs of a client with tax problems.

Collaboration can be short-lived, lasting a few minutes, or longer term, depending on the nature of the task and the relationship among participants. Collaboration can be one-to-one or many-to-many.

Employees may collaborate in informal groups that are not a formal part of the business firm's organizational structure, or they may be organized into formal teams. **Teams** have a specific mission that someone in the business assigned to them. Team members need to collaborate on the accomplishment of specific tasks and collectively achieve the team mission. The team mission might be to "win the game" or "increase online sales by 10 percent." Teams are often short-lived, depending on the problems they tackle and the length of time needed to find a solution and accomplish the mission.

Collaboration and teamwork are more important today than ever for a variety of reasons.

- *Changing nature of work.* The nature of work has changed from factory manufacturing and pre-computer office work where each stage in the production process occurred independently of one another and was coordinated by supervisors. Work was organized into silos. Within a silo, work passed from one machine tool station to another, from one desktop to another, until the finished product was completed. Today, jobs require much closer coordination and interaction among the parties involved in producing the service or product. A report from the consulting firm McKinsey & Company estimated that 41 percent of the U.S. labor force is now composed of jobs where interaction (talking, e-mailing, presenting, and persuading) is the primary value-adding activity (McKinsey, 2012). Even in factories, workers today often work in production groups, or pods.

- *Growth of professional work.* "Interaction" jobs tend to be professional jobs in the service sector that require close coordination and collaboration. Professional jobs require substantial education and the sharing of information and opinions to get work done. Each actor on the job brings specialized expertise to the problem, and all the actors need to take one another into account in order to accomplish the job.

- *Changing organization of the firm.* For most of the industrial age, managers organized work in a hierarchical fashion. Orders came down the hierarchy, and responses moved back up the hierarchy. Today, work is organized into groups and teams, and the members are expected to develop their own methods for accomplishing the task. Senior managers observe and measure results but are much less likely to issue detailed orders or operating procedures. In part, this is because expertise and decision-making power have been pushed down in organizations.

- *Changing scope of the firm.* The work of the firm has changed from a single location to multiple locations—offices or factories throughout a region, a nation, or even around the globe. For instance, Henry Ford developed the first mass-production automobile plant at a single Dearborn, Michigan factory. In 2017, Ford employed 202,000 people at about 67 locations worldwide. With this kind of global presence, the need for close coordination of design, production, marketing, distribution, and service obviously takes on new importance and scale. Large global companies need to have teams working on a global basis.

- *Emphasis on innovation.* Although we tend to attribute innovations in business and science to great individuals, these great individuals are most likely working with a team of brilliant colleagues. Think of Bill Gates and Steve Jobs (founders of Microsoft and Apple), both of whom are highly regarded innovators and both of whom built strong collaborative teams to nurture and support innovation in their firms. Their initial innovations derived from close collaboration with colleagues and partners. Innovation, in other words, is a group and social process, and most innovations derive from collaboration among individuals in a lab, a business, or government agencies. Strong collaborative practices and technologies are believed to increase the rate and quality of innovation.

- *Changing culture of work and business.* Most research on collaboration supports the notion that diverse teams produce better outputs faster than individuals working on their own. Popular notions of the crowd ("crowdsourcing" and the "wisdom of crowds") also provide cultural support for collaboration and teamwork.

What Is Social Business?

Many firms today enhance collaboration by embracing **social business**—the use of social networking platforms, including Facebook, Twitter, and internal corporate social tools—to engage their employees, customers, and suppliers. These tools enable workers to set up profiles, form groups, and "follow" each other's status updates. The goal of social business is to deepen interactions with groups inside and outside the firm to expedite and enhance information sharing, innovation, and decision making.

A key word in social business is *conversations*. Customers, suppliers, employees, managers, and even oversight agencies continually have conversations about firms, often without the knowledge of the firm or its key actors (employees and managers).

Supporters of social business argue that if firms could tune in to these conversations, they would strengthen their bonds with consumers, suppliers, and employees, increasing their emotional involvement in the firm.

All of this requires a great deal of information transparency. People need to share opinions and facts with others quite directly, without intervention from executives or others. Employees get to know directly what customers and other employees think, suppliers will learn very directly the opinions of supply chain partners, and even managers presumably will learn more directly from their employees how well they are doing. Nearly everyone involved in the creation of value will know much more about everyone else.

TABLE 2.2	APPLICATIONS OF SOCIAL BUSINESS
SOCIAL BUSINESS APPLICATION	**DESCRIPTION**
Social networks	Connect through personal and business profiles
Crowdsourcing	Harness collective knowledge to generate new ideas and solutions
Shared workspaces	Coordinate projects and tasks; co-create content
Blogs and wikis	Publish and rapidly access knowledge; discuss opinions and experiences
Social commerce	Share opinions about purchasing on social platforms
File sharing	Upload, share, and comment on photos, videos, audio, text documents
Social marketing	Use social media to interact with customers; derive customer insights
Communities	Discuss topics in open forums; share expertise

If such an environment could be created, it is likely to drive operational efficiencies, spur innovation, and accelerate decision making. If product designers can learn directly about how their products are doing in the market in real time, based on consumer feedback, they can speed up the redesign process. If employees can use social connections inside and outside the company to capture new knowledge and insights, they will be able to work more efficiently and solve more business problems.

Table 2.2 describes important applications of social business inside and outside the firm. This chapter focuses on enterprise social business—its internal corporate uses. Chapters 7 and 10 describe social business applications relating to customers and suppliers outside the company.

Business Benefits of Collaboration and Social Business

Much of the research on collaboration has been anecdotal, but there is a general belief among both business and academic communities that the more a business firm is "collaborative," the more successful it will be, and that collaboration within and among firms is more essential than in the past. *MIT Sloan Management Review*'s research found that a focus on collaboration is central to how digitally advanced companies create business value and establish competitive advantage (Kiron, 2017). A global survey of business and information systems managers found that investments in collaboration technology produced organizational improvements that returned more than four times the amount of the investment, with the greatest benefits for sales, marketing, and research and development functions (Frost and Sullivan, 2009). McKinsey & Company consultants predict that social technologies used within and across enterprises could potentially raise the productivity of interaction workers by 20 to 25 percent (McKinsey Global Institute, 2012).

Table 2.3 summarizes some of the benefits of collaboration and social business that have been identified. Figure 2.7 graphically illustrates how collaboration is believed to affect business performance.

TABLE 2.3 BUSINESS BENEFITS OF COLLABORATION AND SOCIAL BUSINESS

BENEFIT	RATIONALE
Productivity	People interacting and working together can capture expert knowledge and solve problems more rapidly than the same number of people working in isolation from one another. There will be fewer errors.
Quality	People working collaboratively can communicate errors and corrective actions faster than if they work in isolation. Collaborative and social technologies help reduce time delays in design and production.
Innovation	People working collaboratively can come up with more innovative ideas for products, services, and administration than the same number working in isolation from one another. There are advantages to diversity and the "wisdom of crowds."
Customer service	People working together using collaboration and social tools can solve customer complaints and issues faster and more effectively than if they were working in isolation from one another.
Financial performance (profitability, sales, and sales growth)	As a result of all of the above, collaborative firms have superior sales, sales growth, and financial performance.

FIGURE 2.7 REQUIREMENTS FOR COLLABORATION

Successful collaboration requires an appropriate organizational structure and culture along with appropriate collaboration technology.

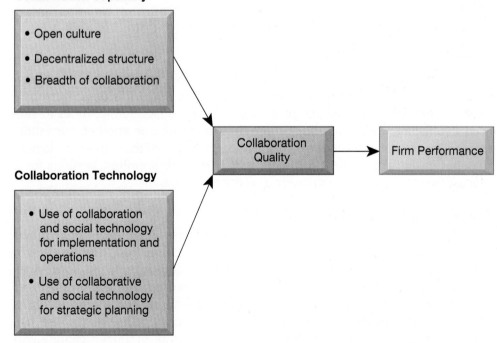

Building a Collaborative Culture and Business Processes

Collaboration won't take place spontaneously in a business firm, especially in the absence of supportive culture or business processes. Business firms, especially large firms, had a reputation in the past for being "command and control" organizations where the top leaders thought up all the really important matters and then ordered lower-level employees to execute senior management plans. The job of middle management supposedly was to pass messages back and forth, up and down the hierarchy.

Command and control firms required lower-level employees to carry out orders without asking too many questions, with no responsibility to improve processes, and with no rewards for teamwork or team performance. If your work group needed help from another work group, that was something for the bosses to figure out. You never communicated horizontally, always vertically, so management could control the process. Together, the expectations of management and employees formed a culture, a set of assumptions about common goals and how people should behave. Many business firms still operate this way.

A collaborative business culture and business processes are very different. Senior managers are responsible for achieving results but rely on teams of employees to achieve and implement the results. Policies, products, designs, processes, and systems are much more dependent on teams at all levels of the organization to devise, to create, and to build. Teams are rewarded for their performance, and individuals are rewarded for their performance in a team. The function of middle managers is to build the teams, coordinate their work, and monitor their performance. The business culture and business processes are more "social." In a collaborative culture, senior management establishes collaboration and teamwork as vital to the organization, and it actually implements collaboration for the senior ranks of the business as well.

Tools and Technologies for Collaboration and Social Business

A collaborative, team-oriented culture won't produce benefits without information systems in place to enable collaboration and social business. Currently there are hundreds of tools designed to deal with the fact that, in order to succeed in our jobs, we are all much more dependent on one another, our fellow employees, customers, suppliers, and managers. Some of these tools are expensive, but others are available online for free (or with premium versions for a modest fee). Let's look more closely at some of these tools.

E-mail and Instant Messaging (IM)

E-mail and instant messaging (including text messaging) have been major communication and collaboration tools for interaction jobs. Their software operates on computers, mobile phones, tablets, and other wireless devices and includes features for sharing files as well as transmitting messages. Many instant messaging systems allow users to engage in real-time conversations with multiple participants simultaneously. In recent years, e-mail use has declined, with messaging and social media becoming preferred channels of communication.

Wikis

Wikis are a type of website that makes it easy for users to contribute and edit text content and graphics without any knowledge of web page development or programming techniques. The most well-known wiki is Wikipedia, the largest collaboratively edited reference project in the world. It relies on volunteers, makes no money, and accepts no advertising.

Wikis are very useful tools for storing and sharing corporate knowledge and insights. Enterprise software vendor SAP AG has a wiki that acts as a base of information for people outside the company, such as customers and software developers who build programs that interact with SAP software. In the past, those people asked and sometimes answered questions in an informal way on SAP online forums, but that was an inefficient system, with people asking and answering the same questions over and over.

Virtual Worlds

Virtual worlds, such as Second Life, are online 3-D environments populated by "residents" who have built graphical representations of themselves known as avatars. Companies like IBM, Cisco, and Intel Corporations use the online world for meetings, interviews, guest speaker events, and employee training. Real-world people represented by avatars meet, interact, and exchange ideas at these virtual locations using gestures, chat box conversations, and voice communication.

Collaboration and Social Business Platforms

There are now suites of software products providing multifunction platforms for collaboration and social business among teams of employees who work together from many different locations. The most widely used are Internet-based audio conferencing and video conferencing systems, cloud collaboration services such as Google's online services and tools, corporate collaboration systems such as Microsoft SharePoint and IBM Notes, and enterprise social networking tools such as Salesforce Chatter, Microsoft Yammer, Jive, Facebook Workplace, and IBM Connections.

Virtual Meeting Systems   In an effort to reduce travel expenses and enable people in different locations to meet and collaborate, many companies, both large and small, are adopting videoconferencing and web conferencing technologies. Companies such as Heinz, GE, and PepsiCo are using virtual meeting systems for product briefings, training courses, and strategy sessions.

A videoconference allows individuals at two or more locations to communicate simultaneously through two-way video and audio transmissions. High-end videoconferencing systems feature **telepresence** technology, an integrated audio and visual environment that allows a person to give the appearance of being present at a remote location (see the Interactive Session on Technology). Free or low-cost Internet-based systems such as Skype group videoconferencing, Amazon Chime, and Zoom are of lower quality, but still useful for smaller companies. Apple's FaceTime is useful for one-to-one videoconferencing. Some of these tools are available on mobile devices.

Companies of all sizes are finding web-based online meeting tools such as Cisco WebEx, Skype for Business, GoTo Meeting, and Adobe Connect especially helpful for training and sales presentations. These products enable participants to share documents and presentations in conjunction with audioconferencing and live video.

Videoconferencing: Something for Everyone

When it comes to collaboration, videoconferencing is becoming a tool of choice for organizations of all sizes. In the past, videoconferencing was limited to the very largest companies that could afford dedicated videoconference rooms and expensive networking and software for this purpose. Today, videoconferencing has been democratized. There's something for everyone.

The cost of the technology has radically fallen; global Internet and desktop transmission of video and audio data is affordable. There are inexpensive mobile and desktop tools as well as high-end videoconferencing and telepresence systems to manage business processes and to connect and collaborate with others—even customers—around the globe.

The current generation of telepresence platforms provide much more than video collaboration, with the ability to coordinate multiple rich data streams that integrate digital information from mobile, desktop, and video, create a collaborative environment, and move the information to where managers and professionals are making decisions. Cisco's IX5000 immersive telepresence system is an example. It offers leading-edge telepresence, but it's much more affordable and easier to use than in the past. Three 4K ultra high-definition cameras clustered discreetly above three 70-inch LCD screens provide crisp, high-definition video. Theater-quality sound emanates from 18 custom speakers and one powerful sub-woofer, creating a high-quality lifelike collaboration experience for 8 to 18 people. The camera and graphic processors are able to capture the whole room in fine detail, so you can stand up and move around or go the whiteboard. Images can be cropped to show participants seated behind their tables, but when someone stands up, the crop is removed to show both standing and sitting participants.

Installing the IX500 system requires no special changes to a room, and it needs only half the power, installation time, and data transmission capacity (bandwidth) as previous telepresence systems. A 6-seat IX5000 studio lists for $299,000, while the 18-seat studio costs $339,000.

Produban, Grupo Santander's technology company specializing in the continuous design and operation of IT infrastructures, adopted the IX5000 system to bring people together to make better decisions faster.

Grupo Santander is a Spanish banking group and one of the largest banks in the world, with over 188,000 employees serving more than 125 million customers and operations across Europe, Latin America, North America, Africa, and Asia. Produban is responsible for the entire IT infrastructure of this sprawling global company and also provides expertise to 120 other companies in IT infrastructure design and services. Produban has over 5,500 employees working in 9 different countries.

With 50 percent less power usage, 50 percent less data transmission capacity and half the installation time of earlier systems (only 8 hours), the IX5000 has reduced the total cost of purchasing and operating the telepresence system by 30 percent over 3 years. Lower overall costs enable Produban to set up video rooms in more locations, so more teams can benefit. Produban is intent on using videoconferencing throughout the entire corporation.

King County, Washington, which includes the city of Seattle and has 14,000 employees, opted for a less-sophisticated but more-affordable solution. In 2016 it started using Logitech's SmartDock audio and video videoconferencing and collaboration system to hold meetings, interview job candidates, and handle other tasks. SmartDock is a user-friendly touch-screen control console to launch and manage audio and video calls in any meeting space, large or small. It has an embedded Microsoft Surface Pro tablet running a special version of Skype for Business, called Skype Room System, and works with Office for Business productivity tools and qualified devices, including Logitech ConferenceCams. With Logitech SmartDock, people can start meetings with a single touch, then instantly project to the display in the room and share with remote participants via their Skype for Business clients on a smartphone or laptop. Participants can share content in a meeting and view and edit documents in real time. An embedded motion sensor activates the system when anyone is in the room. Prices range from $1,999 to $3,999, depending on the size of the meeting room and the need for webcams.

In the past, King County had used a variety of systems and technologies for videoconferencing and collaboration. They were time consuming for the county's IT staff to administer and had limited capabilities and features. Teams couldn't connect remotely and establish multipoint connections with smartphones and tablets. King County's IT staff might spend 20 minutes or more setting up a videoconferencing system, which often relied on legacy technology from multiple vendors along with computer monitors and outdated VGA-quality TV sets. King County received multiple requests to use these systems daily in its 30 on-site conference rooms and needed to standardize the technology and make it more supportive of collaboration.

The King County IT staff was able to handle installation and implementation of the Logitech SmartDock system on its own. Employees are using the videoconferencing and collaboration systems without IT involvement. Being able to share presentations and co-edit documents in Word, Excel, and other formats has made working much more collaborative.

Sources: "'Less Is More' as Cisco Completely Reimagines Flagship Three-Screen Video Conferencing Technology" and "Cisco Telepresence IX5000 Series," www.cisco.com, accessed February 5, 2018; www.produban.com, accessed February 5, 2018; www.santander.com, accessed February 5, 2018; www.logitech.com, accessed February 5, 2018; and Samuel Greengard, "King County Focuses on Collaboration," *CIO Insight*, December 20, 2017.

CASE STUDY QUESTIONS

1. Compare the capabilities of Cisco's IX5000 telepresence and the Logitech SmartDock systems. How do they promote collaboration and innovation?

2. Why would a company like Produban want to invest in a high-end telepresence system such as Cisco's IX5000? How is videoconferencing technology and telepresence related to Produban's business model and business strategy?

3. Why would King County, Washington want to implement the Logitech SmartDock system? What business benefits did it obtain from using this technology?

Cloud Collaboration Services   Google offers many online tools and services, and some are suitable for collaboration. They include Google Drive, Google Docs, G Suites, and Google Sites. Most are free of charge.

Google Drive is a file storage and synchronization service for cloud storage, file sharing, and collaborative editing. Such web-based online file-sharing services allow users to upload files to secure online storage sites from which the files can be shared with others. Microsoft OneDrive and Dropbox are other leading cloud storage services. They feature both free and paid services, depending on the amount of storage space and administration required. Users are able to synchronize their files stored online with their local PCs and other kinds of devices, with options for making the files private or public and for sharing them with designated contacts.

Google Drive and Microsoft OneDrive are integrated with tools for document creation and sharing. OneDrive provides online storage for Microsoft Office documents and other files and works with Microsoft Office apps, both installed and on the web. It can share to Facebook as well. Google Drive is integrated with Google Docs, Sheets, and Slides, a suite of productivity applications that offer collaborative editing on documents, spreadsheets, and presentations. Google's cloud-based productivity suite for businesses, called G Suite, also works with Google Drive. Google Sites allows users to quickly create online team-oriented sites where multiple people can collaborate and share files.

Microsoft SharePoint and IBM Notes   Microsoft SharePoint is a browser-based collaboration and document management platform, combined with a powerful search engine, that is installed on corporate servers. SharePoint has a web-based interface and close integration with productivity tools such as Microsoft Office.

SharePoint software makes it possible for employees to share their documents and collaborate on projects using Office documents as the foundation.

SharePoint can be used to host internal websites that organize and store information in one central workspace to enable teams to coordinate work activities, collaborate on and publish documents, maintain task lists, implement workflows, and share information via wikis and blogs. Users are able to control versions of documents and document security. Because SharePoint stores and organizes information in one place, users can find relevant information quickly and efficiently while working closely together on tasks, projects, and documents. Enterprise search tools help locate people, expertise, and content. SharePoint now features social tools.

IBM Notes (formerly Lotus Notes) is a collaborative software system with capabilities for sharing calendars, e-mail, messaging, collective writing and editing, shared database access, and online meetings. Notes software installed on desktop or laptop computers obtains applications stored on an IBM Domino server. Notes is web-enabled and offers an application development environment so that users can build custom applications to suit their unique needs. Notes has also added capabilities for blogs, microblogs, wikis, online content aggregators, help desk systems, voice and video conferencing, and online meetings. IBM Notes promises high levels of security and reliability and the ability to retain control over sensitive corporate information.

Enterprise Social Networking Tools   The tools we have just described include capabilities for supporting social business, but there are also more specialized social tools for this purpose, such as Salesforce Chatter, Microsoft Yammer, Jive, Facebook Workplace, and IBM Connections. Enterprise social networking tools create business value by connecting the members of an organization through profiles, updates, and notifications similar to Facebook features but tailored to internal corporate uses. Table 2.4 provides more detail about these internal social capabilities.

TABLE 2.4   ENTERPRISE SOCIAL NETWORKING SOFTWARE CAPABILITIES

SOCIAL SOFTWARE CAPABILITY	DESCRIPTION
Profiles	Ability to set up member profiles describing who individuals are, educational background, interests. Includes work-related associations and expertise (skills, projects, teams).
Content sharing	Share, store, and manage content including documents, presentations, images, and videos.
Feeds and notifications	Real-time information streams, status updates, and announcements from designated individuals and groups.
Groups and team workspaces	Establish groups to share information, collaborate on documents, and work on projects with the ability to set up private and public groups and to archive conversations to preserve team knowledge.
Tagging and social bookmarking	Indicate preferences for specific pieces of content, similar to the Facebook Like button. Tagging lets people add keywords to identify content they like.
Permissions and privacy	Ability to make sure private information stays within the right circles, as determined by the nature of relationships. In enterprise social networks, there is a need to establish who in the company has permission to see what information.

Although companies have benefited from enterprise social networking, internal social networking has not always been easy to implement. The chapter-ending case study addresses this topic.

Checklist for Managers: Evaluating and Selecting Collaboration and Social Software Tools

With so many collaboration and social business tools and services available, how do you choose the right collaboration technology for your firm? To answer this question, you need a framework for understanding just what problems these tools are designed to solve. One framework that has been helpful for us to talk about collaboration tools is the time/space collaboration and social tool matrix developed in the early 1990s by a number of collaborative work scholars (Figure 2.8).

The time/space matrix focuses on two dimensions of the collaboration problem: time and space. For instance, you need to collaborate with people in different time zones, and you cannot all meet at the same time. Midnight in New York is noon in Mumbai, so this makes it difficult to have a videoconference (the people in New York are too tired). Time is clearly an obstacle to collaboration on a global scale.

Place (location) also inhibits collaboration in large global or even national and regional firms. Assembling people for a physical meeting is made difficult by the physical dispersion of distributed firms (firms with more than one location), the cost of travel, and the time limitations of managers.

The collaboration and social technologies we have just described are ways of overcoming the limitations of time and space. Using this time/space framework will help you to choose the most appropriate collaboration and teamwork tools for your firm. Note that some tools are applicable in more than one time/place scenario. For example, Internet collaboration suites such as IBM Notes have capabilities for both synchronous (instant messaging, meeting tools) and asynchronous (e-mail, wikis, document editing) interactions.

FIGURE 2.8 **THE TIME/SPACE COLLABORATION AND SOCIAL TOOL MATRIX**

Collaboration and social technologies can be classified in terms of whether they support interactions at the same or different times or places, and whether these interactions are remote or colocated.

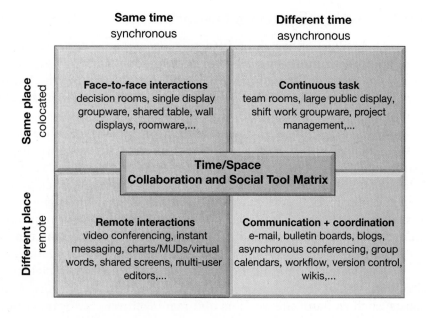

Here's a "to-do" list to get started. If you follow these six steps, you should be led to investing in the correct collaboration software for your firm at a price you can afford and within your risk tolerance.

1. What are the collaboration challenges facing the firm in terms of time and space? Locate your firm in the time/space matrix. Your firm can occupy more than one cell in the matrix. Different collaboration tools will be needed for each situation.

2. Within each cell of the matrix where your firm faces challenges, exactly what kinds of solutions are available? Make a list of vendor products.

3. Analyze each of the products in terms of its cost and benefits to your firm. Be sure to include the costs of training in your cost estimates and the costs of involving the information systems department, if needed.

4. Identify the risks to security and vulnerability involved with each of the products. Is your firm willing to put proprietary information into the hands of external service providers over the Internet? Is your firm willing to expose its important operations to systems controlled by other firms? What are the financial risks facing your vendors? Will they be here in three to five years? What would be the cost of making a switch to another vendor in the event the vendor firm fails?

5. Seek the help of potential users to identify implementation and training issues. Some of these tools are easier to use than others.

6. Make your selection of candidate tools, and invite the vendors to make presentations.

2-4 What is the role of the information systems function in a business?

We've seen that businesses need information systems to operate today and that they use many different kinds of systems. But who is responsible for running these systems? Who is responsible for making sure the hardware, software, and other technologies used by these systems are running properly and are up to date? End users manage their systems from a business standpoint, but managing the technology requires a special information systems function.

The Information Systems Department

In all but the smallest of firms, the **information systems department** is the formal organizational unit responsible for information technology services. The information systems department is responsible for maintaining the hardware, software, data storage, and networks that comprise the firm's IT infrastructure. We describe IT infrastructure in detail in Chapter 5.

The information systems department consists of specialists, such as programmers, systems analysts, project leaders, and information systems managers. **Programmers** are highly trained technical specialists who write the software instructions for computers. **Systems analysts** constitute the principal liaisons between the information systems groups and the rest of the organization. It is the systems analyst's job to translate business problems and requirements into information requirements and systems. **Information systems managers** are leaders of teams of programmers and analysts, project managers, physical facility managers, telecommunications managers, or database specialists. They are also managers of computer operations and data entry staff. Also, external specialists, such as hardware vendors and manufacturers, software firms, and consultants, frequently participate in the day-to-day operations and long-term planning of information systems.

In many companies, the information systems department is headed by a **chief information officer (CIO)**. The CIO is a senior manager who oversees the use of information technology in the firm. Today's CIOs are expected to have a strong business background as well as information systems expertise and to play a leadership role in exploring new technologies and integrating technology into the firm's business strategy. Large firms today also have positions for a chief security officer, chief knowledge officer, chief data officer, and chief privacy officer, all of whom work closely with the CIO.

The **chief security officer (CSO)** is in charge of information systems security for the firm and is responsible for enforcing the firm's information security policy (see Chapter 8). (Sometimes this position is called the chief information security officer [CISO] where information systems security is separated from physical security.) The CSO is responsible for educating and training users and information systems specialists about security, keeping management aware of security threats and breakdowns, and maintaining the tools and policies chosen to implement security.

Information systems security and the need to safeguard personal data have become so important that corporations collecting vast quantities of personal data have established positions for a **chief privacy officer (CPO)**. The CPO is responsible for ensuring that the company complies with existing data privacy laws.

The **chief knowledge officer (CKO)** is responsible for the firm's knowledge management program. The CKO helps design programs and systems to find new sources of knowledge or to make better use of existing knowledge in organizational and management processes.

The **chief data officer (CDO)** is responsible for enterprise-wide governance and utilization of information to maximize the value the organization can realize from its data. The CDO ensures that the firm is collecting the appropriate data to serve its needs, deploying appropriate technologies for analyzing the data, and using the results to support business decisions. This position arose to deal with the very large amounts of data organizations are now generating and collecting (see Chapter 6).

End users are representatives of departments outside of the information systems group for whom applications are developed. These users are playing an increasingly large role in the design and development of information systems.

In the early years of computing, the information systems group was composed mostly of programmers who performed highly specialized but limited technical functions. Today, a growing proportion of staff members are systems analysts and network specialists, with the information systems department acting as a powerful change agent in the organization. The information systems department suggests new business strategies and new information-based products and services and coordinates both the development of the technology and the planned changes in the organization.

In 2019 there are about 4.5 million information system managers and employees in the United States, with an estimated growth rate of 13 percent through 2026, expanding the number of new jobs by more than 550,000. Although all IT/IS occupations show above-average growth, the fastest-growing occupations are information security analysts (28 percent), software developers (24 percent), computer scientists (19 percent), web developers (15 percent), IS/IT managers (12 percent), computer support specialists (11 percent), database administrators (11 percent), systems analysts (9 percent), computer network architects (6 percent), and network and system administrators (6 percent) (Bureau of Labor Statistics, 2018). The number of computer programmers will decline 7 percent in this period, in part because the process of creating computer programs is becoming increasingly efficient with the growth of online software services, cloud computing, and outsourcing of coding to low-wage countries. In general, the management of IT occupations is showing faster expansion than the technical occupations in IT. System and network security management positions are especially in demand. See the Learning Track for this chapter titled "Occupational and Career Outlook for Information Systems Majors 2016–2026" for more details on IS job opportunities.

Organizing the Information Systems Function

There are many types of business firms, and there are many ways in which the IT function is organized within the firm. A very small company will not have a formal information systems group. It might have one employee who is responsible for keeping its networks and applications running, or it might use consultants for these services. Larger companies will have a separate information systems department, which may be organized along several different lines, depending on the nature and interests of the firm. Our Learning Track describes alternative ways of organizing the information systems function within the business.

The question of how the information systems department should be organized is part of the larger issue of IT governance. **IT governance** includes the strategy and policies for using information technology within an organization. It specifies the decision rights and framework for accountability to ensure that the use of information technology supports the organization's strategies and objectives. How much should the information systems function be centralized? What decisions must be made to ensure effective management and use of information technology, including the return on IT investments? Who should make these decisions? How will these decisions be made and monitored? Firms with superior IT governance will have clearly thought out the answers.

2-5 How will MIS help my career?

Here is how Chapter 2 and this book can help you find a job as a sales support specialist.

The Company

Comprehensive Supplemental Insurance USA is a leading provider of individual supplemental accident, disability, health, and life insurance products. It is headquartered in Minneapolis and has an open position for an entry-level sales support specialist. The company offers supplemental insurance to complement existing employer benefits programs, maintaining a field sales force and corporate staff of over 5,000 people worldwide. It is known for investing in its employees and their career development.

Position Description

This position will provide overall systems, administrative, and data management support to the national sales organization for the company's division that markets to small businesses. Job responsibilities include:

- Daily administration and support of the firm's Salesforce.com customer relationship management system, including managing user setup, profiles and roles, and validating data.

- Assisting with data management and providing system training and ongoing support to the field.
- Preparing routine weekly, monthly, and quarterly sales and key performance indicator reports for sales management.
- Preparing agent commission reports and creating new reports as requested.
- Supporting various projects related to agent licensing and agent compensation.

Job Requirements

- Strong Excel skills plus some knowledge of data management
- Strong customer service skills
- Strong analytical, critical thinking, and communication skills
- Ability to multitask in a fast-paced environment
- College degree or 2 years equivalent experience

Interview Questions

1. What do you know about customer relationship management? Have you ever worked with Salesforce.com? If so, what have you used the system for?
2. What do you know about data management? Have you ever worked with data management software? If so, what exactly have you done with it?
3. Tell us what you can do with Excel. What kinds of problems have you used Excel to solve? Did you take courses in Excel?
4. Have you ever worked in customer service? What exactly did you do? What do you think is required to take on a successful client-oriented role for this company's agents and customers?
5. Can you give an example of a client service challenge you had to face? How did you approach this challenge?

Author Tips

1. Review the section of this chapter on enterprise applications, the Chapter 9 discussion of customer relationship management, and Chapter 6 on data management.
2. Use the web and the professional networking site LinkedIn to find out more about the company, its insurance products and services, and the way it operates. Think about what it needs to do to support its agents and its customers and why customer relationship management and data management are so important. You might inquire about your responsibilities for data management in this job position.
3. Learn what you can about Salesforce.com, especially how to set up user profiles and roles and how to validate data. Indicate you want to learn more about Salesforce and work with this tool.
4. Inquire how you would be using Excel; for example, calculating agent commissions. If you've never done that before, show some of the Excel work you have done (and perhaps bring examples with you to the interview). Show that you would be eager to learn what you don't know in Excel to fulfill your job assignments.

REVIEW **SUMMARY**

2-1 What are business processes? How are they related to information systems?

A business process is a logically related set of activities that defines how specific business tasks are performed, and it represents a unique way in which an organization coordinates work, information, and knowledge. Managers need to pay attention to business processes because they determine how well the organization can execute its business, and they may be a source of strategic advantage. There are business processes specific to each of the major business functions, but many business processes are cross-functional. Information systems automate parts of business processes, and they can help organizations redesign and streamline these processes.

2-2 How do systems serve the different management groups in a business, and how do systems that link the enterprise improve organizational performance?

Systems serving operational management are transaction processing systems (TPS), such as payroll or order processing, that track the flow of the daily routine transactions necessary to conduct business. Management information systems (MIS) produce reports serving middle management by condensing information from TPS, and these are not highly analytical. Decision-support systems (DSS) support management decisions that are unique and rapidly changing using advanced analytical models. All of these types of systems provide business intelligence that helps managers and enterprise employees make more-informed decisions. These systems for business intelligence serve multiple levels of management and include executive support systems (ESS) for senior management that provide data in the form of graphs, charts, and dashboards delivered via portals using many sources of internal and external information.

Enterprise applications are designed to coordinate multiple functions and business processes. Enterprise systems integrate the key internal business processes of a firm into a single software system to improve coordination and decision making. Supply chain management systems help the firm manage its relationship with suppliers to optimize the planning, sourcing, manufacturing, and delivery of products and services. Customer relationship management (CRM) systems coordinate the business processes surrounding the firm's customers. Knowledge management systems enable firms to optimize the creation, sharing, and distribution of knowledge. Intranets and extranets are private corporate networks based on Internet technology that assemble information from disparate systems. Extranets make portions of private corporate intranets available to outsiders.

2-3 Why are systems for collaboration and social business so important, and what technologies do they use?

Collaboration is working with others to achieve shared and explicit goals. Social business is the use of internal and external social networking platforms to engage employees, customers, and suppliers, and it can enhance collaborative work. Collaboration and social business have become increasingly important in business because of globalization, the decentralization of decision making, and growth in jobs where interaction is the primary value-adding activity. Collaboration and social business enhance innovation, productivity, quality, and customer service. Tools for collaboration and social business include e-mail and instant messaging, wikis, virtual meeting systems, virtual worlds, cloud-based file-sharing services, corporate collaboration systems such as Microsoft SharePoint and IBM Notes, and enterprise social networking tools such as Chatter, Yammer, Jive, and IBM Connections.

2-4 What is the role of the information systems function in a business?

The information systems department is the formal organizational unit responsible for information technology services. It is responsible for maintaining the hardware, software, data storage, and networks that comprise the firm's IT infrastructure. The department consists of specialists, such as programmers, systems analysts, project leaders, and information systems managers, and is often headed by a CIO.

Key Terms

Business intelligence, 47
Chief data officer (CDO), 67
Chief information officer (CIO), 67
Chief knowledge officer (CKO), 67
Chief privacy officer (CPO), 67
Chief security officer (CSO), 67
Collaboration, 56
Customer relationship management (CRM) systems, 54
Decision-support systems (DSS), 49
Digital dashboard, 50
Electronic business (e-business), 55
Electronic commerce (e-commerce), 55
E-government, 55
End users, 67
Enterprise applications, 51
Enterprise systems, 53

Executive support systems (ESS), 50
Information systems department, 66
Information systems managers, 66
Interorganizational system, 54
IT governance, 68
Knowledge management systems (KMS), 54
Management information systems (MIS), 47
Portal, 50
Programmers, 66
Social business, 57
Supply chain management (SCM) systems, 54
Systems analysts, 66
Teams, 56
Telepresence, 61
Transaction processing systems (TPS), 46

MyLab MIS

To complete the problems marked with MyLab MIS, go to the EOC Discussion Questions in MyLab MIS.

Review Questions

2-1 What are business processes? How are they related to information systems?

- Define business processes and describe the role they play in organizations.

- Describe the relationship between information systems and business processes.

2-2 How do systems serve the different management groups in a business, and how do systems that link the enterprise improve organizational performance?

- Describe the characteristics of transaction processing systems (TPS) and the roles they play in a business.

- Describe the characteristics of management information systems (MIS) and explain how MIS differ from TPS and from DSS.

- Describe the characteristics of decision-support systems (DSS) and how they benefit businesses.

- Describe the characteristics of executive support systems (ESS) and explain how these systems differ from DSS.

- Explain how enterprise applications improve organizational performance.

- Define enterprise systems, supply chain management systems, customer relationship management systems, and knowledge

management systems and describe their business benefits.

- Explain how intranets and extranets help firms integrate information and business processes.

2-3 Why are systems for collaboration and social business so important, and what technologies do they use?

- Define collaboration and social business and explain why they have become so important in business today.

- List and describe the business benefits of collaboration and social business.

- Describe a supportive organizational culture and business processes for collaboration.

- List and describe the various types of collaboration and social business tools.

2-4 What is the role of the information systems function in a business?

- Describe how the information systems function supports a business.

- Compare the roles played by programmers, systems analysts, information systems managers, the chief information officer (CIO), the chief security officer (CSO), the chief data officer (CDO), and the chief knowledge officer (CKO).

Discussion Questions

2-5
MyLab MIS
How could information systems be used to support the order fulfillment process illustrated in Figure 2.1? What are the most important pieces of information these systems should capture? Explain your answer.

2-6
MyLab MIS
Identify the steps that are performed in the process of selecting and checking out a book from your college library and the information that flows among these activities. Diagram the process. Are there any ways this process could be changed to improve the performance of your library or your school? Diagram the improved process.

2-7
MyLab MIS
Use the time/space collaboration and social tool matrix to classify the collaboration and social technologies used by Sanofi Pasteur.

Hands-On MIS Projects

The projects in this section give you hands-on experience analyzing opportunities to improve business processes with new information system applications, using a spreadsheet to improve decision making about suppliers, and using Internet software to plan efficient transportation routes. Visit MyLab MIS to access this chapter's Hands-On MIS Projects.

Management Decision Problems

2-8 Don's Lumber Company on the Hudson River features a large selection of materials for flooring, decks, moldings, windows, siding, and roofing. The prices of lumber and other building materials are constantly changing. When a customer inquires about the price on prefinished wood flooring, sales representatives consult a manual price sheet and then call the supplier for the most recent price. The supplier in turn uses a manual price sheet, which has been updated each day. Often, the supplier must call back Don's sales reps because the company does not have the newest pricing information immediately on hand. Assess the business impact of this situation, describe how this process could be improved with information technology, and identify the decisions that would have to be made to implement a solution.

2-9 Henry's Hardware is a small family business in Sacramento, California. The owners, Henry and Kathleen, must use every square foot of store space as profitably as possible. They have never kept detailed inventory or sales records. As soon as a shipment of goods arrives, the items are immediately placed on store shelves. Invoices from suppliers are only kept for tax purposes. When an item is sold, the item number and price are rung up at the cash register. The owners use their own judgment in identifying items that need to be reordered. What is the business impact of this situation? How could information systems help Henry and Kathleen run their business? What data should these systems capture? What decisions could the systems improve?

Improving Decision Making: Using a Spreadsheet to Select Suppliers

Software skills: Spreadsheet date functions, data filtering, DAVERAGE function
Business skills: Analyzing supplier performance and pricing

2-10 In this exercise, you will learn how to use spreadsheet software to improve management decisions about selecting suppliers. You will filter transactional data on suppliers based on several different criteria to select the best suppliers for your company.

You run a company that manufactures aircraft components. You have many competitors who are trying to offer lower prices and better service to customers, and you are trying to determine whether you can benefit from better supply chain management. In MyLab MIS, you will find a spreadsheet file that contains a list of all of the items that your firm has ordered from its suppliers during the past three months. The fields in the spreadsheet file include vendor name, vendor identification number, purchaser's order number, item identification number and item description (for each item ordered from the vendor), cost per item, number of units of the item ordered (quantity), total cost of each order, vendor's accounts payable terms, order date, and actual arrival date for each order.

Prepare a recommendation of how you can use the data in this spreadsheet database to improve your decisions about selecting suppliers. Some criteria to consider for identifying preferred suppliers include the supplier's track record for on-time deliveries, suppliers offering the best accounts payable terms, and suppliers offering lower pricing when the same item can be provided by multiple suppliers. Use your spreadsheet software to prepare reports to support your recommendations.

Achieving Operational Excellence: Using Internet Software to Plan Efficient Transportation Routes

Software skills: Internet-based software
Business skills: Transportation planning

2-11 In this exercise, you will use Google Maps to map out transportation routes for a business and select the most efficient route.

You have just started working as a dispatcher for Cross-Country Transport, a new trucking and delivery service based in Cleveland, Ohio. Your first assignment is to plan a delivery of office equipment and furniture from Elkhart, Indiana (at the corner of E. Indiana Ave. and Prairie Street), to Hagerstown, Maryland (at the corner of Eastern Blvd. N. and Potomac Ave.). To guide your trucker, you need to know the most efficient route between the two cities. Use Google Maps to find the route that is the shortest distance between the two cities. Use Google Maps again to find the route that takes the least time. Compare the results. Which route should Cross-Country use?

Collaboration and Teamwork Project

Identifying Management Decisions and Systems

2-12 With a team of three or four other students, find a description of a manager in a corporation in *Business Week, Forbes, Fortune*, the *Wall Street Journal*, or another business publication, or do your research on the web. Gather information about what the manager does and the role he or she plays in the company. Identify the organizational level and business function where this manager works. Make a list of the kinds of decisions this manager has to make and the kind of information the manager would need for those decisions. Suggest how information systems could supply this information. If possible, use Google Docs and Google Drive or Google Sites to brainstorm, organize, and develop a presentation of your findings for the class.

Should Companies Embrace Social Business?
CASE STUDY

As companies become more dispersed in the global marketplace, businesses are turning increasingly to workplace collaboration technology, including tools for internal social networking. These tools can promote employee collaboration and knowledge sharing, and help employees make faster decisions, develop more innovative ideas for products and services, and become more engaged in their work and their companies.

Adoption of internal enterprise social networking is also being driven by the flood of email that employees typically receive each day and are increasingly unable to handle. Hundreds of email messages must be opened, read, answered, forwarded, or deleted. For example, too much email is what drove Hawk Ridge Systems to adopt a Glip, a cloud-based social tool for its 200 employees located in 15 offices in the United States and Canada. Glip features real-time messaging, group chat, videoconferencing, shared calendars, task management, and file sharing all in one place. Glip helped Hawk Ridge operations manager Samuel Eakin go from 200 to around 30 emails per day. Another driver of enterprise social networking is "app fatigue." In order to collaborate, many employees have to log on to numerous apps, creating additional work. Contemporary enterprise social networking systems often integrate multiple capabilities in one place.

A recent survey of 421 professionals conducted by Harvard Business Review Analytics Services found that collaboration tools could be effective in boosting efficiency and productivity, while enabling users to make better business decisions. The products also expanded the potential for innovation. However, not all companies are successfully using them. Implementation and adoption of enterprise social networking depend not only on the capabilities of the technology but on the organization's culture and the compatibility of these tools with the firm's business processes.

When firms introduce new social media technology (as well as other technologies), a sizable number of employees resist the new tools, clinging to old ways of working, including email, because these methods are more familiar and comfortable. There are companies where employees have duplicated communication on both social media and email, increasing the time and cost of performing their jobs. BASF, the world's largest chemical producer with subsidiaries and joint ventures in more than 80 countries, prohibited some project teams from using e-mail to encourage employees to use new social media tools.

Social business requires a change in thinking, including the ability to view the organization more democratically in a flatter and more horizontal way. A social business is much more open to everyone's ideas. A secretary, assembly line worker, or sales clerk might be the source of the next big idea. As a result, getting people to espouse social business tools requires a more of a "pull" approach, one that engages workers and offers them a significantly better way to work. In most cases, they can't be forced to use social business apps.

Enterprise capabilities for managing social networks and sharing digital content can help or hurt an organization. Social networks can provide rich and diverse sources of information that enhance organizational productivity, efficiency, and innovation, or they can be used to support pre-existing groups of like-minded people that are reluctant to communicate and exchange knowledge with outsiders. Productivity and morale will fall if employees use internal social networks to criticize others or pursue personal agendas.

Social business applications modeled on consumer-facing platforms such as Facebook and Twitter will not necessarily work well in an organization or organizational department that has incompatible objectives. Will the firm use social business for operations, human resources, or innovation? The social media platform that will work best depends on its specific business purpose. Additionally, employees who have actively used Facebook and Twitter in their personal lives are often hesitant to use similar social tools for work purposes because they see social media primarily as an informal, personal means of self-expression and communication with friends and family. Most managers want employees to use internal social tools to communicate informally about work, but not to discuss personal matters. Employees accustomed to Facebook and Twitter may have trouble imagining how they could use social tools without getting personal.

This means that instead of focusing on the technology, businesses should first identify how social initiatives will actually improve work practices for employees and managers. They need a detailed understanding of social networks: how people are currently working, with whom they are working, what their needs are, and measures for overcoming employee biases and resistance.

A successful social business strategy requires leadership and behavioral changes. Just sponsoring a social project is not enough—managers need to demonstrate their commitment to a more open, transparent work style. Employees who are used to collaborating and doing business in more traditional ways need an incentive to use social software. Changing an organization to work in a different way requires enlisting those most engaged and interested to help design and build the right workplace environment for using social technologies.

Management needs to ensure that the internal and external social networking efforts of the company are providing genuine value to the business. Content on the networks needs to be relevant, up to date, and easy to access; users need to be able to connect to people that have the information they need and that would otherwise be difficult or impossible to reach. Social business tools should be appropriate for the tasks on hand and the organization's business processes, and users need to understand how and why to use them.

For example, NASA's Goddard Space Flight Center had to abandon a custom-built enterprise social network called Spacebook because no one knew how its social tools would help people do their jobs. Spacebook had been designed and developed without taking into consideration the organization's culture and politics. This is not an isolated phenomenon. Dimension Data found that one-fourth of the 900 enterprises it surveyed focused more on the successful implementation of collaboration technology, rather than how it's used and adopted.

Despite the challenges associated with launching an internal social network, there are companies using these networks successfully. For example, Covestro, a leading global supplier of coatings and adhesives, polyurethanes, and highly impact-resistant plastics, made social collaboration a success by making the tools more accessible; demonstrating the value of these tools in pilot projects; employing a reverse mentoring

program for senior executives; and training employee experts to spread know-how of the new social tools and approaches within the company, and demonstrate their usefulness. Using IBM Connections as the social business toolset, Covestro's efforts are now paying off: 50 percent of employees are now routinely active in the company's enterprise social network. Although ROI on social business initiatives has been difficult to measure, Covestro has benefited from faster knowledge flows, increased efficiency, and lower operating costs.

Another company that has made social business work is ModCloth, a popular online apparel, accessories, and home décor retailer noted for its fun and engaging customer shopping experience. The company's business is based on strong social media ties with customers, with 134,000 Twitter followers and 1,600,000 Facebook "likes." Because social networks played such a large role in ModCloth's growth and development, the company was eager to adopt social networking tools for internal communication. ModCloth adopted Microsoft's Yammer as its social business tool.

ModCloth started piloting Yammer with a small test group, and used a People Team to promote the tool. Yammer caught on quickly with employees, and was soon being used by over 250 employees across four offices in the United States. Every new ModCloth employee is introduced to Yammer on his or her first day of work. Yammer helps new hires learn their coworkers' names and feel they are part of the company.

Yammer has proved very useful for connecting people and ideas, saving ModCloth considerable time and money. For example, Scott Hernandez, ModCloth Head of Talent Acquisition, has used Yammer to identify promising hires for engineering through referrals from ModCloth employees. Yammer has helped save teams from duplicating work that has already been done. ModCloth's User Experience group began designing a research campaign to find out what users wanted in mobile applications for the company, posting news of the project to Yammer. Within hours, a member of ModCloth's Social Team posted the results of a large user survey on mobile expectations, including a detailed spreadsheet with customer feedback data that it had already completed. The User Experience team was able to save two weeks of work.

The Esquel Group, based in Hong Kong, is a supplier of cotton textiles and apparel, doing everything from cotton farming and fabric production to garment manufacturing and finishing. Its core business is making cotton tops for fashion brands such as Lacoste, Ralph Lauren, and Nike. This company was attracted to internal social networking as a way to unite its different lines of business in various locations. Esquel chose Microsoft Yammer as its enterprise social networking tool. Esquel employees communicate in a variety of languages, so it especially appreciated Yammer's translation capabilities.

Management sees many benefits in being able to "listen" to its workforce. When people post complaints on the network, it is able to find innovative solutions and new ideas. For example, workers in Esquel's garment operation posted a complaint on Yammer about having to wait in a long line to recharge their cards for purchasing meals in the company cafeteria. Four months later, the company had a solution—a kiosk that instantly transferred funds from payroll to the meal card.

Ideas posted on Yammer were used to improve Esquel's quality control process. Instead of using measuring tape to ensure that sleeves and collars matched specifications, an employee in the quality control department used Yammer to float the idea of an electric ruler. The concept was refined through more Yammer discussion. Instead of taking measurements and writing numbers down, staff can capture measurements faster and more accurately electronically.

Yammer also helps Esquel replicate innovation- and efficiency-promoting solutions throughout the company. Traditionally, an innovation at one site often is not rolled out to other locations. Yammer provides a channel for news of innovations and better practices to spread more easily throughout the organization.

Esquel's industry is one where companies often move to lower-wage countries as labor costs rise. Rather than relocating operations, Esquel prefers to achieve savings through improvements in productivity. By helping employees work more efficiently and effectively, business social networking has helped Esquel save approximately $2 million each year.

Sources: "Top Four Social Collaboration Software Fails," search-mobilecoputing.techtarget.com, accessed February 7, 2018; "ModCloth: Keeping Employees Engaged While Scaling Up," and "Esquel Group: Social Technology Weaves an Enterprise Together," blogs.office.com, accessed February 7, 2018; Margaret Jones and Cordelia Kroob, "The Growth of an Enterprise Social Network at BASF," www.simply-communicate.com, accessed March 12, 2018; Paul Leonardi and Tsedal Neeley, "What Managers Need to Know About Social Tools," *Harvard Business Review*, November-December 2017; Sue Hildreth, "What's Next for Workplace Collaboration?" searchcontentmanagement.com, March 2, 2017; Arunima Majumdar, "3 Reasons Why Collaboration Tools Fail to Make the intended Impact," *eLearning Industry*, January 20, 2017; Harvard Business Review Analytic Services, "Collaboration Technology Boosts Organizations," Insight Enterprises Inc. (February 13, 2017); and Dimension Data, "2016 Connected Enterprise Report," 2016.

CASE STUDY QUESTIONS

2-13 Identify the management, organization, and technology factors affecting adoption of internal corporate social networks.

2-14 Compare the experiences implementing internal social networks of the organizations described in this case. Why were some successful? What role did management play in this process?

2-15 Should all companies implement internal enterprise social networks? Why or why not?

MyLab MIS

Go to the Assignments section of MyLab MIS to complete these writing exercises.

2-16 Identify and describe the capabilities of enterprise social networking software. Describe how a firm could use each of these capabilities.

2-17 Describe the systems used by various management groups within the firm in terms of the information they use, their outputs, and groups served.

Chapter 2 References

Aral, Sinan, Erik Brynjolfsson, and Marshall Van Alstyne. "Productivity Effects of Information Diffusion in Networks." MIT Center for Digital Business (July 2007).

Arena, Michael, Rob Cross, Jonathan Sims, and Mary Uhl-Bie. "How to Catalyze Innovation in Your Organization." *MIT Sloan Management Review* (Summer 2017).

Bala, Hillol, Anne P. Massey, and Mitzi M. Montoya. "The Effects of Process Orientations on Collaboration Technology Use and Outcomes in Product Development." *Journal of Management Information Systems* 34 No. (2017).

Banker, Rajiv D., Nan Hu, Paul A. Pavlou, and Jerry Luftman. "CIO Reporting Structure, Strategic Positioning, and Firm Performance." *MIS Quarterly* 35, No. 2 (June 2011).

Boughzala, Imed, and Gert-Jan De Vreede. "Evaluating Team Collaboration Quality: The Development and Field Application of a Collaboration Maturity Model." *Journal of Management Information Systems* 32 No. 3 (2015).

Bughin, Jacques, Michael Chui, and Martin Harrysson. "How Social Tools Can Reshape the Organization." McKinsey Global Institute (May 2016).

Bureau of Labor Statistics. "Occupational Outlook Handbook 2018–2019." Bernan Press (January 9. 2018).

Colony, George F. "CIOs and the Future of IT." *MIT Sloan Management Review* (Spring 2018).

Cummings, Jeff, and Alan Dennis. "Virtual First Impressions Matter: The Effect of Enterprise Social Networking on Impression Formation in Virtual Teams." *MIS Quarterly* 42, No. 3 (September 2018).

Forrester Research. "Social Business: Delivering Critical Business Value." (April 2012).

Frost and Sullivan. "Meetings Around the World II: Charting the Course of Advanced Collaboration." (October 14, 2009).

Gast, Arne, and Raul Lansink. "Digital Hives: Creating a Surge Around Change." *McKinsey Quarterly* (April 2015).

Greengard, Samuel. "Collaboration: At the Center of Effective Business." *Baseline* (January 24, 2014).

_____. "The Social Business Gets Results." *Baseline* (June 19, 2014).

Guillemette, Manon G., and Guy Pare. "Toward a New Theory of the Contribution of the IT Function in Organizations." *MIS Quarterly* 36, No. 2 (June 2012).

Haffke, Ingmar, Bradley Kalgovas, and Alexander Benloan. "Options for Transforming the IT Function Using Bimodal IT." *MIS Quarterly Executive* (June 2017).

Harvard Business Review Analytic Services. "Collaboration Technology Boosts Organizations." Insight Enterprises Inc. (February 13, 2017).

Johnson, Bradford, James Manyika, and Lareina Yee. "The Next Revolution in Interactions." *McKinsey Quarterly* No. 4 (2005).

Kane, Gerald C. "Enterprise Social Media: Current Capabilities and Future Possibilities." *MIS Quarterly Executive* 14, No. 1 (2015).

Kane, Gerald C., Doug Palmer, Anh Nguyen Phillips, and David Kiron. "Finding the Value in Social Business." *MIT Sloan Management Review* 55, No. 3 (Spring 2014).

Kiron, David. "Why Your Company Needs More Collaboration," *MIT Sloan Management Review* (Fall 2017).

Kiron, David, Doug Palmer, Anh Nguyen Phillips, and Nina Kruschwitz. "What Managers Really Think About Social Business." *MIT Sloan Management Review* 53, No. 4 (Summer 2012).

Kolfschoten, Gwendolyn L., Fred Niederman, Robert O. Briggs, and Gert-Jan De Vreede. "Facilitation Roles and Responsibilities for Sustained Collaboration Support in Organizations." *Journal of Management Information Systems* 28, No. 4 (Spring 2012).

Leonardi, Paul and Tsedal Neeley. "What Managers Need to Know About Social Tools." *Harvard Business Review* (November–December 2017).

Li, Charlene. "Making the Business Case for Enterprise Social Networks." Altimeter Group (February 22, 2012).

Malone, Thomas M., Kevin Crowston, Jintae Lee, and Brian Pentland. "Tools for Inventing Organizations: Toward a Handbook of Organizational Processes." *Management Science* 45, No. 3 (March 1999).

Maruping, Likoebe M., and Massimo Magni. "Motivating Employees to Explore Collaboration Technology in Team Contexts." *MIS Quarterly* 39, No.1 (March 2015).

McKinsey & Company. "Transforming the Business Through Social Tools." (2015).

McKinsey Global Institute. "The Social Economy: Unlocking Value and Productivity Through Social Technologies." McKinsey & Company (July 2012).

Miller, Claire Cain. "Tech's Damaging Myth of the Loner Genius Nerd." *New York Times* (August 12, 2017).

Mortensen, Mark. "Technology Alone Won't Solve Our Collaboration Problems." *Harvard Business Review* (March 26, 2015).

Poltrock, Steven, and Mark Handel. "Models of Collaboration as the Foundation for Collaboration Technologies." *Journal of Management Information Systems* 27, No. 1 (Summer 2010).

Ricards, Tuck, Kate Smaje, and Vik Sohoni. "'Transformer in Chief': The New Chief Digital Officer." *McKinsey Digital* (September 2015).

Ross, Jeanne. "Architect Your Company for Agility." *MIT Sloan Management Review* (January 10, 2018).

Saunders, Carol, A. F. Rutkowski, Michiel van Genuchten, Doug Vogel, and Julio Molina Orrego. "Virtual Space and Place: Theory and Test." *MIS Quarterly* 35, No. 4 (December 2011).

Srivastava, Shirish, and Shalini Chandra. "Social Presence in Virtual World Collaboration: An Uncertainty Reduction Perspective Using a Mixed Methods Approach." *MIS Quarterly* 42, No. 3 (September 2018).

Tallon, Paul P., Ronald V. Ramirez, and James E. Short. "The Information Artifact in IT Governance: Toward a Theory of Information Governance." *Journal of Management Information Systems* 30, No. 3 (Winter 2014).

Weill, Peter, and Jeanne W. Ross. *IT Governance*. Boston: Harvard Business School Press (2004).

3

Information Systems, Organizations, and Strategy

LEARNING OBJECTIVES

After reading this chapter, you will be able to answer the following questions:

3-1 Which features of organizations do managers need to know about to build and use information systems successfully?

3-2 What is the impact of information systems on organizations?

3-3 How do Porter's competitive forces model, the value chain model, synergies, core competencies, and network economics help companies develop competitive strategies using information systems?

3-4 What are the challenges posed by strategic information systems, and how should they be addressed?

3-5 How will MIS help my career?

CHAPTER CASES

Technology Helps Starbucks Find Better Ways to Compete

Digital Technology Helps Crayola Brighten Its Brand

Smart Products—Coming Your Way

Grocery Wars

VIDEO CASES

GE Becomes a Digital Firm: The Emerging Industrial Internet

National Basketball Association: Competing on Global Delivery with Akamai OS Streaming

---

MyLab MIS

Discussion Questions: 3-5, 3-6, 3-7; **Hands-on MIS Projects:** 3-8, 3-9, 3-10, 3-11;
Writing Assignments: 3-17, 3-18; **eText with Conceptual Animations**

Technology Helps Starbucks Find Better Ways to Compete

Starbucks is the world's largest specialty coffee retailer, with over 24,000 shops in 75 markets. Starbucks's reputation rests on its high-end specialty coffees and beverages, friendly and knowledgeable servers, and customer-friendly coffee shops. This was a winning formula for many years and has enabled Starbucks to charge premium prices for many of its items. But Starbucks has competitors, and must constantly fine-tune its business model and business strategy to keep pace with the competitive environment.

Starbucks tried online retailing and it didn't work out. If you go to the Starbucks.com website, you'll see coffee, branded mugs, espresso machines, and brewing accessories described online, but you will need to purchase these items from Starbucks stores, supermarkets, or Starbucks-designated retailers. Starbucks stopped selling online in August of 2017. Starbucks management believes there has been a "seismic shift" in retailing, and merchants need to create unique and immersive in-store experiences to survive. For Starbucks, products and services, for the most part, should not be sold online.

© Atstock Productions/Shutterstock

Instead, Starbucks is focusing on improving the in-store experience. The company rolled out a new Mercato menu of freshly-made sandwiches and salads to more than 1,000 stores in 2018 and plans to expand its line of caffeinated fruit juices (Starbucks Refreshers) and nitro-brew cold drinks. Management hopes to double food sales by 2021. Starbucks is also building high-end cafes around the world under the "Reserve" brand to draw customers willing to pay more for premium coffee and pastries.

Starbucks continues to enhance the customer's in-store experience through information technology. Each Starbucks store has a Wi-Fi network providing free wireless Internet access for customers. Many Starbucks customers are active users of smartphones. Starbucks launched a mobile ordering app for the iPhone and Android mobile devices in September 2015. The Starbucks Mobile Order & Pay app makes it fast and easy to pay for drinks and food.

Customers can place their orders on the way to Starbucks stores with Mobile Order & Pay and also tip the barista. Those ordering are told the time when their beverage will be ready. There's no need to wait in line. The mobile app can also identify the songs playing in Starbucks stores and save them to a playlist on Spotify. The app helps Starbucks target products to customers more effectively, which could be especially important as the chain also adds more lunch items and cold drinks to its menu to draw in more customers after the morning coffee rush. Cold drinks now represent half of Starbucks' beverage sales.

Starbucks wants U.S. customers who use its in-store Wi-Fi network to enter their email address in the first store where they get connected. The company's software remembers the customer's device and connects it automatically thereafter. That would give Starbucks additional email addresses that it could target with more promotions.

Sources: Julie Jargon, "Starbucks Aims for More Mobile Orders," Wall Street Journal, March 21, 2018; Stacy Cowley, "Starbucks Closes Online Store to Focus on In-Person Experience," *New York Times*, October 1, 2017; "Starbucks' Mobile Order Push Meets Resistance From Ritual Seekers," Reuters, March 21, 2018; and www.starbucks.com, accessed March 28, 2018.

Starbucks illustrates some of the ways that information systems help businesses compete, as well as the challenges of finding the right business strategy and how to use technology in that strategy. Retailing today is an extremely crowded and competitive playing field, both online and in physical brick-and-mortar stores. Even though Starbucks is the world's leading specialty coffee retailer, it has many competitors, and it is searching for ways to keep growing its business. Customers are increasingly doing more retail shopping online, but Starbucks products do not sell well on the web. They are meant for an in-person experience. They are too experiential.

The chapter-opening diagram calls attention to important points raised by this case and this chapter. Starbucks' business model is based on an aggressive product differentiation strategy, intended to emphasize the high quality of its beverages and foods, efficient and helpful customer service, and the pleasures of purchasing and consuming these items in a Starbucks store. Starbucks is using information technology to improve its in-store customer experience. Its Mobile Order & Pay app expedites order and payment for Starbucks beverages and food, and Starbucks had to redesign its payment process to take advantage of mobile technology. The free Wi-Fi network makes Starbucks stores more inviting to visit, linger, and consume food and beverages. The mobile app enables stores to serve more customers, and enrollment in the Wi-Fi service provides additional e-mail addresses for promotional campaigns.

Here are some questions to think about: What is Starbucks' business strategy? How much has technology helped Starbucks compete? Explain your answer.

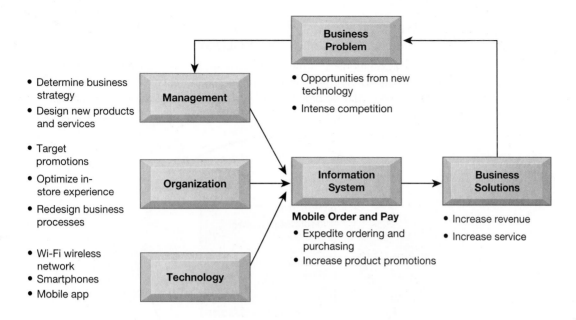

- Determine business strategy
- Design new products and services

- Target promotions
- Optimize in-store experience
- Redesign business processes

- Wi-Fi wireless network
- Smartphones
- Mobile app

Business Problem

- Opportunities from new technology
- Intense competition

Management

Organization

Technology

Information System

Mobile Order and Pay

- Expedite ordering and purchasing
- Increase product promotions

Business Solutions

- Increase revenue
- Increase service

3-1 Which features of organizations do managers need to know about to build and use information systems successfully?

Information systems and organizations influence one another. Information systems are built by managers to serve the interests of the business firm. At the same time, the organization must be aware of and open to the influences of information systems to benefit from new technologies.

The interaction between information technology and organizations is complex and is influenced by many mediating factors, including the organization's structure, business processes, politics, culture, surrounding environment, and management decisions (see Figure 3.1). You will need to understand how information systems can change social and work life in your firm. You will not be able to design new systems successfully or understand existing systems without understanding your own business organization.

As a manager, you will be the one to decide which systems will be built, what they will do, and how they will be implemented. You may not be able to anticipate all of the consequences of these decisions. Some of the changes that occur in business firms because of new information technology (IT) investments cannot be foreseen and have results that may or may not meet your expectations. Who would have imagined 15 years ago, for instance, that e-mail and instant messaging would become a dominant form of business communication and that many managers would be inundated with more than 200 e-mail messages each day?

What Is an Organization?

An **organization** is a stable, formal social structure that takes resources from the environment and processes them to produce outputs. This technical definition focuses on three elements of an organization. Capital and labor are primary production factors provided by the environment. The organization (the firm)

FIGURE 3.1 THE TWO-WAY RELATIONSHIP BETWEEN ORGANIZATIONS
AND INFORMATION TECHNOLOGY

This complex two-way relationship is mediated by many factors, not the least of which
are the decisions made—or not made—by managers. Other factors mediating the
relationship include the organizational culture, structure, politics, business processes,
and environment.

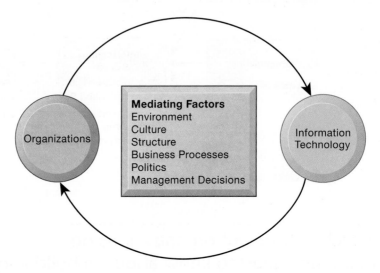

transforms these inputs into products and services in a production function.
The products and services are consumed by environments in return for supply
inputs (see Figure 3.2).

An organization is more stable than an informal group (such as a group of
friends that meets every Friday for lunch) in terms of longevity and routine-
ness. Organizations are formal legal entities with internal rules and procedures
that must abide by laws. Organizations are also social structures because they
are collections of social elements, much as a machine has a structure—a particular arrangement of valves, cams, shafts, and other parts.

This definition of organizations is powerful and simple, but it is not very de-
scriptive or even predictive of real-world organizations. A more realistic behavioral definition of an organization is a collection of rights, privileges, obligations,

FIGURE 3.2 THE TECHNICAL MICROECONOMIC DEFINITION OF THE
ORGANIZATION

In the microeconomic definition of organizations, capital and labor (the primary production factors provided by the environment) are transformed by the firm through the production process into products and services (outputs to the environment). The products
and services are consumed by the environment, which supplies additional capital and
labor as inputs in the feedback loop.

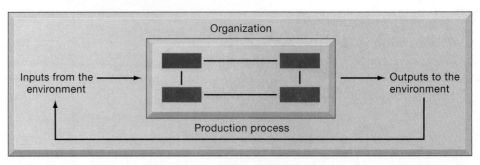

FIGURE 3.3   THE BEHAVIORAL VIEW OF ORGANIZATIONS

The behavioral view of organizations emphasizes group relationships, values, and structures.

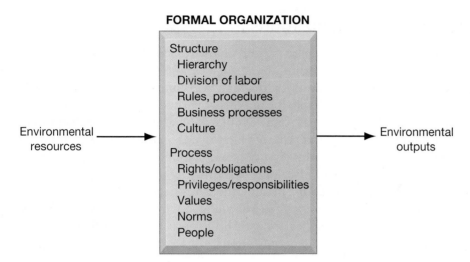

FORMAL ORGANIZATION

Environmental resources → Structure / Hierarchy / Division of labor / Rules, procedures / Business processes / Culture / Process / Rights/obligations / Privileges/responsibilities / Values / Norms / People → Environmental outputs

and responsibilities delicately balanced over a period of time through conflict and conflict resolution (see Figure 3.3).

In this behavioral view of the firm, people who work in organizations develop customary ways of working; they gain attachments to existing relationships; and they make arrangements with subordinates and superiors about how work will be done, the amount of work that will be done, and under what conditions work will be done. Most of these arrangements and feelings are not discussed in any formal rulebook.

How do these definitions of organizations relate to information systems technology? A technical view of organizations encourages us to focus on how inputs are combined to create outputs when technology changes are introduced into the company. The firm is seen as infinitely malleable, with capital and labor substituting for each other quite easily. But the more realistic behavioral definition of an organization suggests that building new information systems, or rebuilding old ones, involves much more than a technical rearrangement of machines or workers—that some information systems change the organizational balance of rights, privileges, obligations, responsibilities, and feelings that have been established over a long period of time.

Changing these elements can take a long time, be very disruptive, and requires more resources to support training and learning. For instance, the length of time required to implement a new information system effectively is much longer than usually anticipated simply because there is a lag between implementing a technical system and teaching employees and managers how to use the system.

Technological change requires changes in who owns and controls information, who has the right to access and update that information, and who makes decisions about whom, when, and how. This more complex view forces us to look at the way work is designed and the procedures used to achieve outputs.

The technical and behavioral definitions of organizations are not contradictory. Indeed, they complement each other: The technical definition tells us how thousands of firms in competitive markets combine capital, labor, and information technology, whereas the behavioral model takes us inside the individual firm to see how that technology affects the organization's inner workings. Section 3-2 describes how each of these definitions of organizations can help explain the relationships between information systems and organizations.

Features of Organizations

All modern organizations share certain characteristics. They are bureaucracies with clear-cut divisions of labor and specialization. Organizations arrange specialists in a hierarchy of authority in which everyone is accountable to someone and authority is limited to specific actions governed by abstract rules or procedures. These rules create a system of impartial and universal decision making. Organizations try to hire and promote employees on the basis of technical qualifications and professionalism (not personal connections). The organization is devoted to the principle of efficiency: maximizing output using limited inputs. Other features of organizations include their business processes, organizational culture, organizational politics, surrounding environments, structure, goals, constituencies, and leadership styles. All of these features affect the kinds of information systems used by organizations.

Routines and Business Processes

All organizations, including business firms, become very efficient over time because individuals in the firm develop **routines** for producing goods and services. Routines—sometimes called *standard operating procedures*—are precise rules, procedures, and practices that have been developed to cope with virtually all expected situations. As employees learn these routines, they become highly productive and efficient, and the firm is able to reduce its costs over time as efficiency increases. For instance, when you visit a doctor's office, receptionists have a well-developed set of routines for gathering basic information from you, nurses have a different set of routines for preparing you for an interview with a doctor, and the doctor has a well-developed set of routines for diagnosing you. *Business processes*, which we introduced in Chapters 1 and 2, are collections of such routines. A business firm, in turn, is a collection of business processes (Figure 3.4).

Organizational Politics

People in organizations occupy different positions with different specialties, concerns, and perspectives. As a result, they naturally have divergent viewpoints about how resources, rewards, and punishments should be distributed. These differences matter to both managers and employees, and they result in political struggles for resources, competition, and conflict within every organization. Political resistance is one of the great difficulties of bringing about organizational change—especially the development of new information systems. Virtually all large information systems investments by a firm that bring about significant changes in strategy, business objectives, business processes, and procedures become politically charged events. Managers who know how to work with the politics of an organization will be more successful than less-skilled managers in implementing new information systems. Throughout this book, you will find many examples where internal politics defeated the best-laid plans for an information system.

Organizational Culture

All organizations have bedrock, unassailable, unquestioned (by the members) assumptions that define their goals and products. Organizational culture encompasses this set of assumptions about what products the

FIGURE 3.4   ROUTINES, BUSINESS PROCESSES, AND FIRMS

All organizations are composed of individual routines and behaviors, a collection of which make up a business process. A collection of business processes make up the business firm. New information system applications require that individual routines and business processes change to achieve high levels of organizational performance.

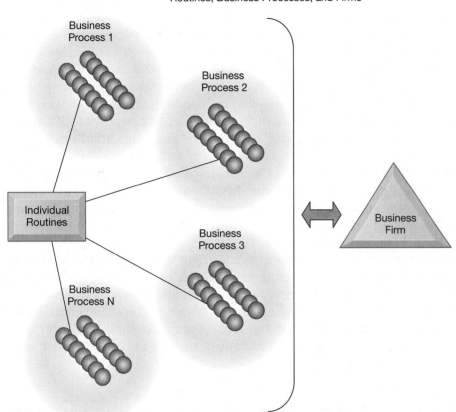

Routines, Business Processes, and Firms

organization should produce, how it should produce them, where, and for whom. Generally, these cultural assumptions are taken totally for granted and are rarely publicly announced or discussed. Business processes—the actual way business firms produce value—are usually ensconced in the organization's culture.

You can see organizational culture at work by looking around your university or college. Some bedrock assumptions of university life are that professors know more than students, the reason students attend college is to learn, and classes follow a regular schedule. Organizational culture is a powerful unifying force that restrains political conflict and promotes common understanding, agreement on procedures, and common practices. If we all share the same basic cultural assumptions, agreement on other matters is more likely.

At the same time, organizational culture is a powerful restraint on change, especially technological change. Most organizations will do almost anything to avoid making changes in basic assumptions. Any technological change that threatens commonly held cultural assumptions usually meets a great deal of resistance. However, there are times when the only sensible way for a firm to move forward is to employ a new technology that directly opposes an existing organizational culture. When this occurs, the technology is often stalled while the culture slowly adjusts.

Organizational Environments

Organizations reside in environments from which they draw resources and to which they supply goods and services. Organizations and environments have a reciprocal relationship. On the one hand, organizations are open to and dependent on the social and physical environment that surrounds them. Without financial and human resources—people willing to work reliably and consistently for a set wage or revenue from customers—organizations could not exist. Organizations must respond to legislative and other requirements imposed by government as well as the actions of customers and competitors. On the other hand, organizations can influence their environments. For example, business firms form alliances with other businesses to influence the political process; they advertise to influence customer acceptance of their products.

Figure 3.5 illustrates the role of information systems in helping organizations perceive changes in their environments and also in helping organizations act on their environments. Information systems are key instruments for *environmental scanning*, helping managers identify external changes that might require an organizational response.

Environments generally change much faster than organizations. New technologies, new products, and changing public tastes and values (many of which result in new government regulations) put strains on any organization's culture, politics, and people. Most organizations are unable to adapt to a rapidly changing environment. Inertia built into an organization's standard operating procedures, the political conflict raised by changes to the existing order, and the

FIGURE 3.5   ENVIRONMENTS AND ORGANIZATIONS HAVE A RECIPROCAL RELATIONSHIP

Environments shape what organizations can do, but organizations can influence their environments and decide to change environments altogether. Information technology plays a critical role in helping organizations perceive environmental change and in helping organizations act on their environment.

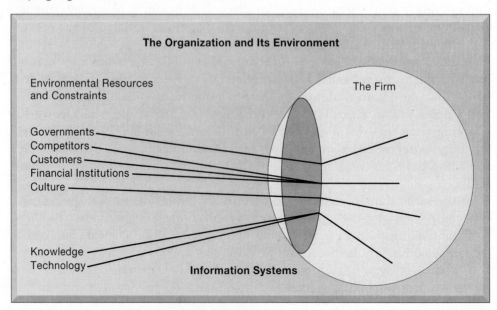

threat to closely held cultural values inhibit organizations from making significant changes. Young firms typically lack resources to sustain even short periods of troubled times. It is not surprising that only 10 percent of the *Fortune* 500 companies in 1919 still exist today.

Disruptive Technologies: Riding the Wave Sometimes a technology and resulting business innovation come along to radically change the business landscape and environment. These innovations are loosely called "disruptive" (Christensen, 2003; Christensen, Raynor, and McDonald, 2015). What makes a technology disruptive? In some cases, **disruptive technologies** are substitute products that perform as well as or better (often much better) than anything currently produced. The car substituted for the horse-drawn carriage, the word processor for typewriters, the Apple iPod and streaming music service for portable CD players, and digital photography for process film photography. Table 3.1 describes just a few disruptive technologies from the past.

In these cases, entire industries were put out of business. In other cases, disruptive technologies simply extend the market, usually with less functionality and much less cost than existing products. Eventually they turn into low-cost competitors for whatever was sold before. Disk drives are an example: Small hard disk drives used in PCs extended the market for disk drives by offering cheap digital storage for small files. Eventually, small PC hard disk drives became the largest segment of the disk drive marketplace.

TABLE 3.1 DISRUPTIVE TECHNOLOGIES: WINNERS AND LOSERS

TECHNOLOGY	DESCRIPTION	WINNERS AND LOSERS
Microprocessor chips (1971)	Thousands and eventually millions of transistors on a silicon chip	Microprocessor firms win (Intel, Texas Instruments), while transistor firms (GE) decline.
Personal computers (1975)	Small, inexpensive, but fully functional desktop computers	PC manufacturers (HP, Apple, IBM) and chip manufacturers prosper (Intel), while mainframe (IBM) and minicomputer (DEC) firms lose.
Digital photography (1975)	Using CCD (charge-coupled device) image sensor chips to record images	CCD manufacturers and traditional camera companies win; manufacturers of film products lose.
World Wide Web (1989)	A global database of digital files and "pages" instantly available	Owners of online content and news benefit, while traditional publishers (newspapers, magazines, and broadcast television) lose.
Internet music, video, TV services (1998)	Repositories of downloadable music, video, and TV broadcasts on the web	Owners of Internet platforms, telecommunications providers owning Internet backbone (ATT, Verizon), and local Internet service providers win, while content owners and physical retailers (Tower Records, Blockbuster) lose.
PageRank algorithm	A method for ranking web pages in terms of their popularity to supplement web search by key terms	Google is the winner (it owns the patent), while traditional key word search engines (Alta Vista) lose.
Software as web service	Using the Internet to provide remote access to online software	Online software services companies (Salesforce.com) win, while traditional "boxed" software companies (Microsoft, SAP, Oracle) lose.

Some firms are able to create these technologies and ride the wave to profits; others learn quickly and adapt their business; still others are obliterated because their products, services, and business models become obsolete. They may be very efficient at doing what no longer needs to be done! There are also cases where no firms benefit and all the gains go to consumers (firms fail to capture any profits). Moreover, not all change or technology is disruptive (King and Baatartogtokh, 2015). Managers of older businesses often do make the right decisions and find ways to continue competing. Disruptive technologies are tricky. Firms that invent disruptive technologies as "first movers" do not always benefit if they lack the resources to exploit the technology or fail to see the opportunity. The MITS Altair 8800 is widely regarded as the first PC, but its inventors did not take advantage of their first mover status. Second movers, so-called "fast followers," such as IBM and Microsoft, reaped the rewards. Citibank's ATMs revolutionized retail banking, but they were copied by other banks. Now all banks use ATMs, with the benefits going mostly to the consumers.

Organizational Structure

All organizations have a structure or shape. Mintzberg's classification, described in Table 3.2, identifies five basic kinds of organizational structure (Mintzberg, 1971).

The kind of information systems you find in a business firm—and the nature of problems with these systems—often reflects the type of organizational structure. For instance, in a professional bureaucracy such as a hospital, it is not unusual to find parallel patient record systems operated by the administration, another by doctors, and another by other professional staff such as nurses and social workers. In small entrepreneurial firms, you will often find poorly designed systems developed in a rush that quickly outgrow their usefulness. In huge multidivisional firms operating in hundreds of locations,

TABLE 3.2 ORGANIZATIONAL STRUCTURES

ORGANIZATIONAL TYPE	DESCRIPTION	EXAMPLES
Entrepreneurial structure	Young, small firm in a fast-changing environment. It has a simple structure and is managed by an entrepreneur serving as its single chief executive officer.	Small start-up business
Machine bureaucracy	Large bureaucracy existing in a slowly changing environment, producing standard products. It is dominated by a centralized management team and centralized decision making.	Midsize manufacturing firm
Divisionalized bureaucracy	Combination of multiple machine bureaucracies, each producing a different product or service, all topped by one central headquarters.	*Fortune* 500 firms, such as General Motors
Professional bureaucracy	Knowledge-based organization where goods and services depend on the expertise and knowledge of professionals. Dominated by department heads with weak centralized authority.	Law firms, school systems, hospitals
Adhocracy	Task force organization that must respond to rapidly changing environments. Consists of large groups of specialists organized into short-lived multidisciplinary teams and has weak central management.	Consulting firms, such as the Rand Corporation

you will frequently find there is not a single integrating information system, but instead each locale or each division has its own set of information systems.

Other Organizational Features

Organizations have goals and use different means to achieve them. Some organizations have coercive goals (e.g., prisons); others have utilitarian goals (e.g., businesses). Still others have normative goals (universities, religious groups). Organizations also serve different groups or have different constituencies, some primarily benefiting their members, others benefiting clients, stockholders, or the public. The nature of leadership differs greatly from one organization to another—some organizations may be more democratic or authoritarian than others. Another way organizations differ is by the tasks they perform and the technology they use. Some organizations perform primarily routine tasks that can be reduced to formal rules that require little judgment (such as manufacturing auto parts), whereas others (such as consulting firms) work primarily with nonroutine tasks.

3-2 What is the impact of information systems on organizations?

Information systems have become integral, online, interactive tools deeply involved in the minute-to-minute operations and decision making of large organizations. Over the past decade, information systems have fundamentally altered the economics of organizations and greatly increased the possibilities for organizing work. Theories and concepts from economics and sociology help us understand the changes brought about by IT.

Economic Impacts

From the point of view of economics, IT changes both the relative costs of capital and the costs of information. Information systems technology can be viewed as a factor of production that can be substituted for traditional capital and labor. As the cost of information technology decreases, it is substituted for labor, which historically has been a rising cost. Hence, information technology should result in a decline in the number of middle managers and clerical workers as information technology substitutes for their labor.

As the cost of information technology decreases, it also substitutes for other forms of capital such as buildings and machinery, which remain relatively expensive. Hence, over time we should expect managers to increase their investments in IT because of its declining cost relative to other capital investments.

IT also affects the cost and quality of information and changes the economics of information. Information technology helps firms contract in size because it can reduce transaction costs—the costs incurred when a firm buys on the marketplace what it cannot make itself. According to **transaction cost theory**, firms and individuals seek to economize on transaction costs, much as they do on production costs. Using markets is expensive because of costs such as locating and communicating with distant suppliers, monitoring contract compliance, buying insurance, obtaining information on products, and so forth (Coase, 1937; Williamson, 1985). Traditionally, firms have tried to reduce transaction costs through vertical integration, by getting bigger, hiring more employees, and buying their own suppliers and distributors, as both General Motors and Ford used to do.

Information technology, especially the use of networks, can help firms lower the cost of market participation (transaction costs), making it worthwhile for firms to contract with external suppliers instead of using internal sources. As a result, firms can shrink in size (numbers of employees) because it is far less expensive to outsource work to a competitive marketplace rather than hire employees.

For instance, by using computer links to external suppliers, automakers such as Chrysler, Toyota, and Honda can achieve economies by obtaining more than 70 percent of their parts from the outside. Information systems make it possible for companies such as Apple Cisco Systems and Dell Inc. to outsource assembly of iPhones to contract manufacturers such as Foxconn instead of making their products themselves.

As transaction costs decrease, firm size (the number of employees) should shrink because it becomes easier and cheaper for the firm to contract for the purchase of goods and services in the marketplace rather than to make the product or offer the service itself. Firm size can stay constant or contract even as the company increases its revenues. For example, when Eastman Chemical Company split off from Kodak in 1994, it had $3.3 billion in revenue and 24,000 full-time employees. In 2017, it generated $9.5 billion in revenue with only 14,500 employees.

Information technology also can reduce internal management costs. According to **agency theory**, the firm is viewed as a "nexus of contracts" among self-interested individuals rather than as a unified, profit-maximizing entity (Jensen and Meckling, 1976). A principal (owner) employs "agents" (employees) to perform work on his or her behalf. However, agents need constant supervision and management; otherwise, they will tend to pursue their own interests rather than those of the owners. As firms grow in size and scope, agency costs or coordination costs rise because owners must expend more and more effort supervising and managing employees.

Information technology, by reducing the costs of acquiring and analyzing information, permits organizations to reduce agency costs because it becomes easier for managers to oversee a greater number of employees. By reducing overall management costs, information technology enables firms to increase revenues while shrinking the number of middle managers and clerical workers. We have seen examples in earlier chapters where information technology expanded the power and scope of small organizations by enabling them to perform coordinated activities such as processing orders or keeping track of inventory with very few clerks and managers.

Because IT reduces both agency and transaction costs for firms, we should expect firm size to shrink over time as more capital is invested in IT. Firms should have fewer managers, and we expect to see revenue per employee increase over time.

Organizational and Behavioral Impacts

Theories based in the sociology of complex organizations also provide some understanding about how and why firms change with the implementation of new IT applications.

IT Flattens Organizations

Large, bureaucratic organizations, which primarily developed before the computer age, are often inefficient, slow to change, and less competitive than newly created organizations. Some of these large organizations have downsized, reducing the number of employees and the number of levels in their organizational hierarchies.

Behavioral researchers have theorized that information technology facilitates flattening of hierarchies by broadening the distribution of information to empower lower-level employees and increase management efficiency (see Figure 3.6). IT pushes decision-making rights lower in the organization because lower-level employees receive the information they need to make decisions without supervision. (This empowerment is also possible because of higher educational levels among the workforce, which give employees more capabilities to make intelligent decisions.) Because managers now receive so much more accurate information on time, they become much faster at making decisions, so fewer managers are required. Management costs decline as a percentage of revenues, and the hierarchy becomes much more efficient.

These changes mean that the management span of control has also been broadened, enabling high-level managers to manage and control more workers spread over greater distances. Many companies have eliminated thousands of middle managers as a result of these changes.

Postindustrial Organizations

Postindustrial theories based more on history and sociology than economics also support the notion that IT should flatten hierarchies. In postindustrial societies, authority increasingly relies on knowledge and competence and not merely on formal positions. Hence, the shape of organizations flattens because professional workers tend to be self-managing, and decision making should become

---

FIGURE 3.6 FLATTENING ORGANIZATIONS

Information systems can reduce the number of levels in an organization by providing managers with information to supervise larger numbers of workers and by giving lower-level employees more decision-making authority.

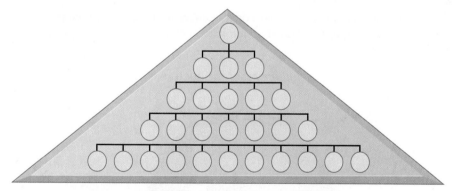

A traditional hierarchical organization with many levels of management

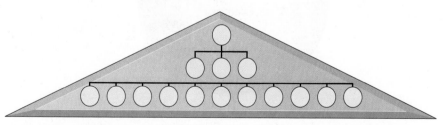

An organization that has been "flattened" by removing layers of management

more decentralized as knowledge and information become more widespread throughout the firm.

Information technology may encourage task force–networked organizations in which groups of professionals come together—face-to-face or electronically—for short periods of time to accomplish a specific task (e.g., designing a new automobile); once the task is accomplished, the individuals join other task forces. The global consulting service Accenture is an example. Many of its 373,000 employees move from location to location to work on projects at client locations in more than 56 different countries.

Who makes sure that self-managed teams do not head off in the wrong direction? Who decides which person works on which team and for how long? How can managers evaluate the performance of someone who is constantly rotating from team to team? How do people know where their careers are headed? New approaches for evaluating, organizing, and informing workers are required, and not all companies can make virtual work effective.

Understanding Organizational Resistance to Change

Information systems inevitably become bound up in organizational politics because they influence access to a key resource—namely, information. Information systems can affect who does what to whom, when, where, and how in an organization. Many new information systems require changes in personal, individual routines that can be painful for those involved and require retraining and additional effort that may or may not be compensated. Because information systems potentially change an organization's structure, culture, business processes, and strategy, there is often considerable resistance to them when they are introduced.

There are several ways to visualize organizational resistance. Research on organizational resistance to innovation suggests that four factors are paramount: the nature of the IT innovation, the organization's structure, the culture of people in the organization, and the tasks affected by the innovation (see Figure 3.7).

FIGURE 3.7   **ORGANIZATIONAL RESISTANCE TO INFORMATION SYSTEM INNOVATIONS**

Implementing information systems has consequences for task arrangements, structures, and people. According to this model, to implement change, all four components must be changed simultaneously.

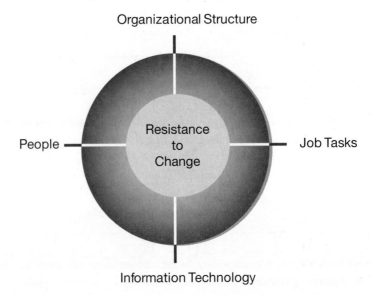

Here, changes in technology are absorbed, interpreted, deflected, and defeated by organizational task arrangements, structures, and people. In this model, the only way to bring about change is to change the technology, tasks, structure, and people simultaneously. Other authors have spoken about the need to "unfreeze" organizations before introducing an innovation, quickly implementing it, and "refreezing" or institutionalizing the change (Kolb and Frohman, 1970).

Because organizational resistance to change is so powerful, many information technology investments flounder and do not increase productivity. Indeed, research on project implementation failures demonstrates that the most common reason for failure of large projects to reach their objectives is not the failure of the technology but organizational and political resistance to change. Chapter 14 treats this issue in detail. Therefore, as a manager involved in future IT investments, your ability to work with people and organizations is just as important as your technical awareness and knowledge.

The Internet and Organizations

The Internet, especially the World Wide Web, has an important impact on the relationships between many firms and external entities and even on the organization of business processes inside a firm. The Internet increases the accessibility, storage, and distribution of information and knowledge for organizations. In essence, the Internet is capable of dramatically lowering the transaction and agency costs facing most organizations. For instance, a global sales force can receive nearly instant product price information updates using the web or instructions from management sent by e-mail or text messaging on smartphones or mobile laptops. Vendors of some large retailers can access retailers' internal websites directly to find up-to-the-minute sales information and to initiate replenishment orders instantly.

Businesses are rapidly rebuilding some of their key business processes based on Internet technology and making this technology a key component of their IT infrastructures. If prior networking is any guide, one result will be simpler business processes, fewer employees, and flatter organizations than in the past.

Implications for the Design and Understanding of Information Systems

To deliver genuine benefits, information systems must be built with a clear understanding of the organization in which they will be used. In our experience, the central organizational factors to consider when planning a new system are the following:

- The environment in which the organization must function
- The structure of the organization: hierarchy, specialization, routines, and business processes
- The organization's culture and politics
- The type of organization and its style of leadership
- The principal interest groups affected by the system and the attitudes of workers who will be using the system
- The kinds of tasks, decisions, and business processes that the information system is designed to assist

3-3 How do Porter's competitive forces model, the value chain model, synergies, core competencies, and network economics help companies develop competitive strategies using information systems?

In almost every industry you examine, you will find that some firms do better than most others. There's almost always a standout firm. In the automotive industry, Toyota is considered a superior performer. In pure online retail, Amazon is the leader; in off-line retail, Walmart, the largest retailer on earth, is the leader. In online music, Apple's iTunes is considered the leader with more than 60 percent of the downloaded music market. In web search, Google is considered the leader.

Firms that "do better" than others are said to have a competitive advantage over others: They either have access to special resources that others do not, or they are able to use commonly available resources more efficiently—usually because of superior knowledge and information assets. In any event, they do better in terms of revenue growth, profitability, or productivity growth (efficiency), all of which ultimately in the long run translate into higher stock market valuations than their competitors.

But why do some firms do better than others, and how do they achieve competitive advantage? How can you analyze a business and identify its strategic advantages? How can you develop a strategic advantage for your own business? And how do information systems contribute to strategic advantages? One answer to that question is Michael Porter's competitive forces model.

Porter's Competitive Forces Model

Arguably, the most widely used model for understanding competitive advantage is Michael Porter's **competitive forces model** (see Figure 3.8). This model provides a general view of the firm, its competitors, and the firm's environment. Earlier in this chapter, we described the importance of a firm's environment and the dependence of firms on environments. Porter's model is all about the firm's general business environment. In this model, five competitive forces shape the fate of the firm.

FIGURE 3.8 PORTER'S COMPETITIVE FORCES MODEL

In Porter's competitive forces model, the strategic position of the firm and its strategies are determined not only by competition with its traditional direct competitors but also by four other forces in the industry's environment: new market entrants, substitute products, customers, and suppliers.

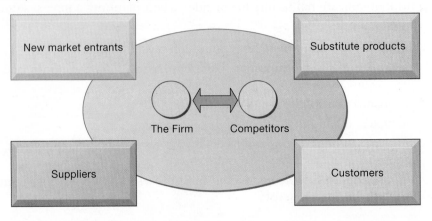

Traditional Competitors

All firms share market space with other competitors who are continuously devising new, more-efficient ways to produce by introducing new products and services, and attempting to attract customers by developing their brands and imposing switching costs on their customers.

New Market Entrants

In a free economy with mobile labor and financial resources, new companies are always entering the marketplace. In some industries, there are very low barriers to entry, whereas in other industries, entry is very difficult. For instance, it is fairly easy to start a pizza business or just about any small retail business, but it is much more expensive and difficult to enter the computer chip business, which has very high capital costs and requires significant expertise and knowledge that are hard to obtain. New companies have several possible advantages: They are not locked into old plants and equipment, they often hire younger workers who are less expensive and perhaps more innovative, they are not encumbered by old worn-out brand names, and they are "more hungry" (more highly motivated) than traditional occupants of an industry. These advantages are also their weaknesses: They depend on outside financing for new plants and equipment, which can be expensive; they have a less-experienced workforce; and they have little brand recognition.

Substitute Products and Services

In just about every industry, there are substitutes that your customers might use if your prices become too high. New technologies create new substitutes all the time. Ethanol can substitute for gasoline in cars; vegetable oil for diesel fuel in trucks; and wind, solar, coal, and hydro power for industrial electricity generation. Likewise, Internet and wireless telephone service can substitute for traditional telephone service. And, of course, an Internet music service that allows you to download music tracks to an iPad or smartphone has become a substitute for CD-based music stores. The more substitute products and services in your industry, the less you can control pricing and the lower your profit margins.

Customers

A profitable company depends in large measure on its ability to attract and retain customers (while denying them to competitors) and charge high prices. The power of customers grows if they can easily switch to a competitor's products and services or if they can force a business and its competitors to compete on price alone in a transparent marketplace where there is little **product differentiation** and all prices are known instantly (such as on the Internet). For instance, in the used college textbook market on the Internet, students (customers) can find multiple suppliers of just about any current college textbook. In this case, online customers have extraordinary power over used-book firms.

Suppliers

The market power of suppliers can have a significant impact on firm profits, especially when the firm cannot raise prices as fast as can suppliers. The more different suppliers a firm has, the greater control it can exercise over suppliers in terms of price, quality, and delivery schedules. For instance, manufacturers of laptop PCs almost always have multiple competing suppliers of key components, such as keyboards, hard drives, and display screens.

Supermarkets and large retail stores such as Walmart use sales data captured at the checkout counter to determine which items have sold and need to be reordered. Walmart's continuous replenishment system transmits orders to restock directly to its suppliers. The system enables Walmart to keep costs low while fine-tuning its merchandise to meet customer demands.

© Betty LaRue/Alamy Stock Photo

Information System Strategies for Dealing with Competitive Forces

What is a firm to do when it is faced with all these competitive forces? And how can the firm use information systems to counteract some of these forces? How do you prevent substitutes and inhibit new market entrants? There are four generic strategies, each of which often is enabled by using information technology and systems: low-cost leadership, product differentiation, focus on market niche, and strengthening customer and supplier intimacy.

Low-Cost Leadership

Use information systems to achieve the lowest operational costs and the lowest prices. The classic example is Walmart. By keeping prices low and shelves well stocked using a legendary inventory replenishment system, Walmart became the leading retail business in the United States. Walmart's continuous replenishment system sends orders for new merchandise directly to suppliers as soon as consumers pay for their purchases at the cash register. Point-of-sale terminals record the bar code of each item passing the checkout counter and send a purchase transaction directly to a central computer at Walmart headquarters. The computer collects the orders from all Walmart stores and transmits them to suppliers. Suppliers can also access Walmart's sales and inventory data using web technology.

Because the system replenishes inventory with lightning speed, Walmart does not need to spend much money on maintaining large inventories of goods in its own warehouses. The system also enables Walmart to adjust purchases of store items to meet customer demands. Competitors, such as Sears, have been spending 24.9 percent of sales on overhead. But by using systems to keep operating costs low, Walmart pays only 16.6 percent of sales revenue for overhead. (Operating costs average 20.7 percent of sales in the retail industry.)

Walmart's continuous replenishment system is also an example of an **efficient customer response system**. An efficient customer response system directly links consumer behavior to distribution and production and supply chains. Walmart's continuous replenishment system provides such an efficient customer response.

Product Differentiation

Use information systems to enable new products and services or greatly change the customer convenience in using your existing products and services. Big Tech firms like Google, Facebook, Amazon, Apple, and others are pouring billions of dollars into research and deployment of new services, and enhancements to their most valuable services and products in order to differentiate them from potential competitors. For instance, in 2018 Google updated its Google Assistant to enable more natural continuous conversations and smart displays that can display the output of Assistant to screens. Google added Assistant support to its core Google Maps service to make interaction with Maps more natural, and released a Machine Language Kit for developers that supports text recognition, face detection, image labeling, and landmark recognition. The continual stream of innovations flowing from Big Tech companies ensures their products are unique, and difficult to copy.

Crayola, not known as a tech company, is another firm that is creating new technology-based products and services to inspire children, parents, and educators, and differentiate their products from competitors. (See the Interactive Session on Organizations.)

Manufacturers and retailers are using information systems to create products and services that are customized and personalized to fit the precise specifications of individual customers. For example, Nike sells customized sneakers through its NIKEiD program on its website. Customers are able to select the type of shoe, colors, material, outsoles, and even a logo of up to eight characters. Nike transmits the orders via computers to specially equipped plants in China and Korea. The sneakers take about three weeks to reach the customer. This ability to offer individually tailored products or services using the same production resources as mass production is called **mass customization**.

Table 3.3 lists a number of companies that have developed IT-based products and services that other firms have found difficult to copy—or at least taken a long time to copy.

Focus on Market Niche

Use information systems to enable a specific market focus and serve this narrow target market better than competitors. Information systems support this strategy by producing and analyzing data for finely tuned sales and marketing techniques. Information systems enable companies to analyze customer buying patterns, tastes, and preferences closely so that they efficiently pitch advertising and marketing campaigns to smaller and smaller target markets.

The data come from a range of sources—credit card transactions, demographic data, purchase data from checkout counter scanners at supermarkets

TABLE 3.3	IT-ENABLED NEW PRODUCTS AND SERVICES PROVIDING COMPETITIVE ADVANTAGE
Amazon: One-click shopping	Amazon holds a patent on one-click shopping that it licenses to other online retailers.
Online music: Apple iTunes	Apple sells music from an online library of more than 45 million songs.
Golf club customization: Ping	Customers can select from more than 1 million different golf club options; a build-to-order system ships their customized clubs within 48 hours.
Online person-to-person payment: PayPal	PayPal enables the transfer of money between individual bank accounts and between bank accounts and credit card accounts.

Digital Technology Helps Crayola Brighten Its Brand

Crayola is one of the world's most beloved brands for children and their parents. The Easton, Pennsylvania–based company has been noted for high-quality, non-toxic crayons, markers, pencils, modeling clay, creative toys, and innovative art tools that have inspired artistic creativity in children for more than one hundred years. You can find Crayola products nearly everywhere, including schools, offices, supermarkets, drug stores, hospitals, theme parks, airports, gas stations, and restaurants.

The Crayola crayon box became part of the collective history and experiences of generations of Americans, and a symbol of the color and fun of childhood. But today, that Crayola crayon box is not as iconic as in the past. The popularity of Crayola crayons is under assault—not by Crayola's traditional competitors (Faber-Castelli, DixonTiconderoga, and MEGA Brands), but by changing times.

There has been a profound technological and cultural shift in how children play. Children and their families are being bombarded with increasingly sophisticated forms of entertainment, many of them digitally based. Digital products are starting to supplant physical ones in the world of children's play as well as in other areas of work and everyday life. With the advent of computers and web-based learning, children are leaving behind hand-held art supplies at an increasingly younger age. The phenomenon is called KGOY, standing for "Kids Growing Older Younger." As children reach the age of 4 or 5, when they become old enough to play with a computer, they become less interested in toys and crayons and prefer electronics such as video games and digital tablets and smartphones. Crayola is not immune to this problem.

Will Crayola become a dinosaur from a different era? Not likely, thanks to the company's forward-looking management, which embarked over a decade ago on far-reaching changes in leadership, organizational culture, and the product development function. The organization restructured around consumer insights and needs rather than specific product lines.

Vicky Lozano, Crayola's VP of Corporate Strategy and her team recognized that Crayola's purpose has always been to nourish originality and to help parents and teachers raise creative and inspired children. Crayola's broader mission is not just to put crayons and art materials in children's hands but to help children learn and play in colorful ways. The question they asked was not, how can we sell more crayons? Instead they asked, what kinds of experiences and technologies should Crayola embrace? Crayola has reframed its business model, introduced a new innovation process for product development, and created new products and revenue streams. The company has been transformed from a manufacturer of crayons and art tools into a trusted source of tools and experiences for creative play.

Crayola is using digital technology, but not to replace its core crayon business. Instead, it's integrating the old and the new. The company now offers a new range of products like the iMarker, an all-in-one digital pen, crayon, and pencil, designed for use with the Color Studio HD iPad app. It's like a traditional coloring book, but includes new interactive sounds and motion. Lights, Camera, Color! is another digital application that allows kids to turn their favorite photos into digital coloring book pages. Tech toys such as the Digital Light Designer, a 360-degree domed drawing surface, encourage imaginations to run wild with colored LED lights. Children can play updated versions of their favorite games or animate and save up to 50 pieces of their own artwork. Crayola found that parents are looking for toys that are less messy than traditional markers or fingerpaints. These digital toys are "100 percent mess-proof," and technology has helped Crayola make its other products less messy as well.

In designing new digital products and experiences, Crayola has drawn on its extensive knowledge of child development. It understands how digital technology can play a part at different ages. For instance, the My First Crayola line is targeted specifically at one-year-olds; while Crayola Catwalk Creations is designed for "tween" girls who like expressing themselves through fashion.

Crayola also understood that it had to change the way it markets its products as well as the products themselves and has been investing more and more in digital marketing. These initiatives include online advertising, promotions, social media pushes, and other digital activation programs that allow Crayola to connect with parents and educators invested in raising children's creativity level. Social media has proven especially effective and Crayola has a presence on Facebook, YouTube, Pinterest, Twitter, and Instagram.

Crayola's YouTube channel features colorful videos on Crayola products and instructions for creative projects where they can be used. The company's Facebook presence features a live chat series with experts and creative celebrities called "Inside the Crayon Box." Crayola wants to stimulate conversations around creativity so parents can learn from each other and understand how to build creativity in their children.

Crayola's core parent audience is turning to the web for gift and usage ideas, comparing prices, and reading reviews before making purchases. Crayola wants to be first in mind as a source of $20 artsy toys and mess-proof gifts. The company focuses heavily on search, social media, and digital display, to help parents find the Crayola products needed for their children's school supplies or gifts. Crayola closely tracks activity on its online channels through Google Analytics to make sure it is getting the most out of its marketing and ad campaigns.

Crayola's website has been thoughtfully designed for children, parents, and educators. It features free ideas for crafts, printable coloring pages, and even advice on how to remove stains. The website also can be used for ordering Crayola products online. Thanks to its new array of products and services, Crayola has experienced better growth, and its future looks as bright as the vibrant colors of its iconic crayons.

Sources: www.crayola.com, accessed March 28, 2018; "Crayola SWOT," www.marketingteacher.com, accessed March 29, 2018; and Jon Coen, "Crayola's Colorful Evolution," *Think Play*, July 2012.

CASE STUDY QUESTIONS

1. Analyze Crayola's problem. What management, organization, and technology factors contributed to the problem?

2. What competitive strategies is Crayola pursuing? How does digital technology support those strategies?

3. What people issues did Crayola have to address in designing its new technology-based products?

4. How has digital technology changed Crayola's business model and the way it runs its business?

and retail stores, and data collected when people access and interact with websites. Sophisticated software tools find patterns in these large pools of data and infer rules from them to guide decision making. Analysis of such data drives one-to-one marketing that creates personal messages based on individualized preferences. For example, Hilton Hotels' OnQ system analyzes detailed data collected on active guests in all of its properties to determine the preferences of each guest and each guest's profitability. Hilton uses this information to give its most profitable customers additional privileges, such as late checkouts. Contemporary customer relationship management (CRM) systems feature analytical capabilities for this type of intensive data analysis (see Chapters 2 and 9).

Credit card companies are able to use this strategy to predict their most profitable cardholders. The companies gather vast quantities of data about consumer purchases and other behaviors and mine these data to construct detailed profiles that identify cardholders who might be good or bad credit risks. We discuss the tools and technologies for data analysis in Chapters 6 and 12.

Strengthen Customer and Supplier Intimacy

Use information systems to tighten linkages with suppliers and develop intimacy with customers. Toyota, Ford, and other automobile manufacturers use information systems to facilitate direct access by suppliers to production schedules and even permit suppliers to decide how and when to ship supplies to their factories. This allows suppliers more lead time in producing goods.

TABLE 3.4 FOUR BASIC COMPETITIVE STRATEGIES

STRATEGY	DESCRIPTION	EXAMPLE
Low-cost leadership	Use information systems to produce products and services at a lower price than competitors while enhancing quality and level of service	Walmart
Product differentiation	Use information systems to differentiate products, and enable new services and products	Uber, Nike, Apple
Focus on market niche	Use information systems to enable a focused strategy on a single market niche; specialize	Hilton Hotels, Harrah's
Customer and supplier intimacy	Use information systems to develop strong ties and loyalty with customers and suppliers	Toyota Corporation, Amazon

On the customer side, Amazon keeps track of user preferences for book and CD purchases and can recommend titles purchased by others to its customers. Strong linkages to customers and suppliers increase **switching costs** (the cost of switching from one product to a competing product) and loyalty to your firm.

Table 3.4 summarizes the competitive strategies we have just described. Some companies focus on one of these strategies, but you will often see companies pursuing several of them simultaneously. For example, Starbucks, the world's largest specialty coffee retailer, offers unique high-end specialty coffees and beverages but is also trying to compete by more targeted marketing.

The Internet's Impact on Competitive Advantage

Because of the Internet, the traditional competitive forces are still at work, but competitive rivalry has become much more intense (Porter, 2001). Internet technology is based on universal standards that any company can use, making it easy for rivals to compete on price alone and for new competitors to enter the market. Because information is available to everyone, the Internet raises the bargaining power of customers, who can quickly find the lowest-cost provider on the web. Profits have been dampened. Table 3.5 summarizes some of the potentially negative impacts of the Internet on business firms identified by Porter.

The Internet has nearly destroyed some industries and has severely threatened more. For instance, the printed encyclopedia industry and the travel

TABLE 3.5 IMPACT OF THE INTERNET ON COMPETITIVE FORCES AND INDUSTRY STRUCTURE

COMPETITIVE FORCE	IMPACT OF THE INTERNET
Substitute products or services	Enables substitutes to emerge with new approaches to meeting needs and performing functions
Customers' bargaining power	Availability of global price and product information shifts bargaining power to customers
Suppliers' bargaining power	Procurement over the Internet tends to raise bargaining power over suppliers; suppliers can also benefit from reduced barriers to entry and from the elimination of distributors and other intermediaries standing between them and their users
Threat of new entrants	Reduces barriers to entry, such as the need for a sales force, access to channels, and physical assets; provides a technology for driving business processes that makes other things easier to do
Positioning and rivalry among existing competitors	Widens the geographic market, increasing the number of competitors and reducing differences among competitors; makes it more difficult to sustain operational advantages; puts pressure to compete on price

agency industry have been nearly decimated by the availability of substitutes over the Internet. Likewise, the Internet has had a significant impact on the retail, music, book, retail brokerage, software, telecommunications, and newspaper industries.

However, the Internet has also created entirely new markets; formed the basis for thousands of new products, services, and business models; and provided new opportunities for building brands with very large and loyal customer bases. Amazon, eBay, iTunes, YouTube, Facebook, Travelocity, and Google are examples. In this sense, the Internet is "transforming" entire industries, forcing firms to change how they do business.

Smart Products and the Internet of Things

The growing use of sensors in industrial and consumer products, often called the Internet of Things (IoT), is an excellent example of how the Internet is changing competition within industries and creating new products and services. Under Armour and other sports and fitness companies are pouring money into wearable health trackers and fitness equipment that use sensors to report users' activities to remote corporate computing centers where the data can be analyzed (see the Interactive Session on Technology). John Deere tractors are loaded with field radar, GPS transceivers, and hundreds of sensors keeping track of the equipment, as described in the Chapter 12 opening case. GE is creating a new business helping its aircraft and wind turbine clients improve operations by examining the data generated from the many thousands of sensors in the equipment. The result is what are referred to as "smart products"—products that are a part of a larger set of information-intensive services sold by firms (Gandhi and Gervet, 2016; Porter and Heppelmann, 2014; Iansiti and Lakhani, 2014).

The impact of smart, Internet-connected products is just now being understood. Smart products offer new functionality, greater reliability, and more intense use of products while providing detailed information that can be used to improve both the products and the customer experience. They expand opportunities for product and service differentiation. When you buy a wearable digital health product, you not only get the product itself, you also get a host of services available from the manufacturer's cloud servers. Smart products increase rivalry among firms that will either innovate or lose customers to competitors. Smart products generally raise switching costs and inhibit new entrants to a market because existing customers are trapped in the dominant firm's software environment. Finally, smart products may decrease the power of suppliers of industrial components if, as many believe, the physical product becomes less important than the software and hardware that make it run.

The Business Value Chain Model

Although the Porter model is very helpful for identifying competitive forces and suggesting generic strategies, it is not very specific about what exactly to do, and it does not provide a methodology to follow for achieving competitive advantages. If your goal is to achieve operational excellence, where do you start? Here's where the business value chain model is helpful.

The **value chain model** highlights specific activities in the business where competitive strategies can best be applied (Porter, 1985) and where information systems are most likely to have a strategic impact. This model identifies specific, critical leverage points where a firm can use information technology most effectively to enhance its competitive position. The value chain model views the firm as a series or chain of basic activities that add a margin of value

INTERACTIVE SESSION TECHNOLOGY

Smart Products—Coming Your Way

If you don't use a smart product yet, you soon will. Your shoes, your clothing, your watch, your water bottle, and even your toothbrush are being redesigned to incorporate sensors and metering devices connected to the Internet so that their performance can be monitored and analyzed. Your home will increasingly use smart devices such as smart thermostats, smart electrical meters, smart security systems, and smart lighting systems.

Under Armour, noted for performance clothing, spent $710 million to scoop up mobile apps such as MyFitnessPal, Map My Fitness, and Endomondo, which enable it to tap into the world's largest digital health and fitness community, with more than 225 million registered users. According to company data, Under Armour's connected fitness users have logged more than 500 million workouts and taken 7 trillion steps since the company started tracking the data. Analyzing these data has provided insights such as 3.1 miles being the average distance for a run and that May is the most active month for exercise.

Under Armour is trying to enhance its performance clothing with digital technology. The company now sells connected running shoes. The shoes come in several models and feature a built-in wireless Bluetooth sensor that tracks cadence, distance, pace, stride length, and steps, even if the runner does not bring a smartphone along. The data are stored on the shoe until they can sync wirelessly to Under Armour's Map My Run app for iPhone, iPad, and Android devices. Users can also connect to the app on third-party devices such as AppleWatch, Garmin, or Fitbit, to incorporate metrics such as heart rate that can't be tracked by the shoes. The shoe's analytics will let users know when it's time to purchase new shoes and sensor batteries have to be charged.

Under Armour has recently added a digital coaching feature for the connected running shoes and Map My Run app. Runners will be able to monitor their gait and stride length mile after mile, and see how that impacts their pace and cadence. By analyzing these data, along with data about the runner's gender, age, weight, and height, Map My Run will be able to provide a runner with tips on how to improve his or her pace and splits, by taking shorter or longer strides while running, for instance.

Under Armour can generate revenue from in-app ads, including ads from other companies, and purchases from app users referred to its products. The platform delivers unprecedented depth of information and insight about fitness- and health-oriented consumers, creating numerous opportunities for Under Armour and other brands to engage with potential and existing customers. For example, Map My Fitness collects data about a user's name, e-mail address, birth date, location, performance, and profile if the user connects to the app using social media. Under Armour does not sell identifiable personal data about individuals to third parties but does provide advertisers with aggregate information about app users. Under Armour is hoping that daily use of its smartphone apps will build stronger ties to customers that will lead to stronger sales of its own apparel, footwear, and other athletic gear. The company is clearly benefiting from bringing the power of software to its physical products.

Smart products are also finding their way into people's homes. Between 2017 and 2022, Con Edison, which supplies electrical power and natural gas to the New York City metropolitan area, is installing 3.6 million new electric smart meters and 1.2 million new gas smart meters in all its customers' homes and businesses. A smart meter is a digital meter that communicates between a residence or business and Con Edison through a secure wireless communication network. The smart meter records and transmits each customer's energy consumption regularly throughout the day. The smart meter transmits data to a system of access points on utility poles, which send the usage information to Con Edison.

The smart meter will let the company know when a customer loses service, resulting in faster repairs, and will also provide real-time billing information to customers based on energy usage, enabling them to pinpoint areas for energy savings. They will also permit more definitive voltage regulation, enhancing electric distribution-system efficiency, reducing costs, and providing savings that ultimately get reflected in lower customer bills. Data from the new meters will let Con Ed set prices based on customers' time and level of use. Rates might jump during summer hours when hot weather makes people turn on their air conditioners, or drop overnight when power use is lowest.

Con Ed customers can use an online My Account dashboard with tools to track their daily energy consumption down to 15-minute increments. They can analyze their usage by comparing hour to hour, weekday versus weekend, or day versus evening use to see where they can save, and they can receive high bill alerts if they are using more energy than usual. Con Ed also offers a mobile app for iPhone

and Android smartphone users so that they can track their detailed energy usage while they are on the go.

Sources: Jen Booton, "Under Armour's New HOVR Smart Shoe Will Automatically Track Your Run," *SportTechie*, January 26, 2018; Edgar Alvarez, "Under Armour's HOVR smart running shoes are more than just a gimmick," *Engadget*, February 9, 2018; www.coned.com, accessed March 28, 2018; Edward C. Baig, "Under Armour and HTC Team Up on Connected Fitness," *USA Today*, January 5, 2016; www.underarmour.com, accessed April 20, 2018; and John Kell, "Why Under Armour Is Making a Costly Bet on Connected Fitness," *Fortune*, April 21, 2016.

CASE STUDY QUESTIONS

1. Describe the role of information technology in the products described in this case. How is it adding value to these products? How is it transforming these products?

2. How are these smart products changing operations and decision making for these organizations?

How are they changing the behavior of their users?

3. Are there any ethical issues raised by these smart products, such as their impact on consumer privacy? Explain your answer.

to a firm's products or services. These activities can be categorized as either primary activities or support activities (see Figure 3.9).

Primary activities are most directly related to the production and distribution of the firm's products and services, which create value for the customer. Primary activities include inbound logistics, operations, outbound logistics, sales and marketing, and service. Inbound logistics includes receiving and storing materials for distribution to production. Operations transforms inputs into finished products. Outbound logistics entails storing and distributing finished products. Sales and marketing includes promoting and selling the firm's products. The service activity includes maintenance and repair of the firm's goods and services.

Support activities make the delivery of the primary activities possible and consist of organization infrastructure (administration and management), human resources (employee recruiting, hiring, and training), technology (improving products and the production process), and procurement (purchasing input).

Now you can ask at each stage of the value chain, "How can we use information systems to improve operational efficiency and improve customer and supplier intimacy?" This will force you to critically examine how you perform value-adding activities at each stage and how the business processes might be improved. You can also begin to ask how information systems can be used to improve the relationship with customers and with suppliers who lie outside the firm's value chain but belong to the firm's extended value chain where they are absolutely critical to your success. Here, supply chain management systems that coordinate the flow of resources into your firm and customer relationship management systems that coordinate your sales and support employees with customers are two of the most common system applications that result from a business value chain analysis. We discuss these enterprise applications in detail later in Chapter 9.

Using the business value chain model will also cause you to consider benchmarking your business processes against your competitors or others in related industries and identifying industry best practices. **Benchmarking** involves

FIGURE 3.9 THE VALUE CHAIN MODEL

This figure provides examples of systems for both primary and support activities of a firm and of its value partners that can add a margin of value to a firm's products or services.

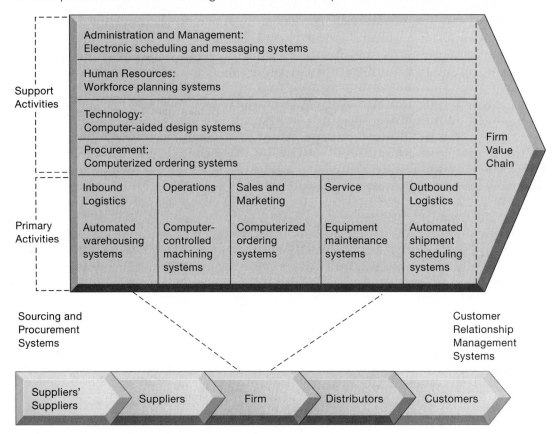

comparing the efficiency and effectiveness of your business processes against strict standards and then measuring performance against those standards. Industry **best practices** are usually identified by consulting companies, research organizations, government agencies, and industry associations as the most successful solutions or problem-solving methods for consistently and effectively achieving a business objective.

Once you have analyzed the various stages in the value chain at your business, you can come up with candidate applications of information systems. Then, once you have a list of candidate applications, you can decide which to develop first. By making improvements in your own business value chain that your competitors might miss, you can achieve competitive advantage by attaining operational excellence, lowering costs, improving profit margins, and forging a closer relationship with customers and suppliers. If your competitors are making similar improvements, then at least you will not be at a competitive disadvantage—the worst of all cases!

Extending the Value Chain: The Value Web

Figure 3.9 shows that a firm's value chain is linked to the value chains of its suppliers, distributors, and customers. After all, the performance of most firms depends not only on what goes on inside a firm but also on how well the firm coordinates with direct and indirect suppliers, delivery firms (logistics partners, such as FedEx or UPS), and, of course, customers.

How can information systems be used to achieve strategic advantage at the industry level? By working with other firms, industry participants can use information technology to develop industrywide standards for exchanging information or business transactions electronically, which force all market participants to subscribe to similar standards. Such efforts increase efficiency, making product substitution less likely and perhaps raising entry costs—thus discouraging new entrants. Also, industry members can build industrywide, IT-supported consortia, symposia, and communications networks to coordinate activities concerning government agencies, foreign competition, and competing industries.

Looking at the industry value chain encourages you to think about how to use information systems to link up more efficiently with your suppliers, strategic partners, and customers. Strategic advantage derives from your ability to relate your value chain to the value chains of other partners in the process. For instance, if you are Amazon.com, you want to build systems that:

- Make it easy for suppliers to display goods and open stores on the Amazon site
- Make it easy for customers to pay for goods
- Develop systems that coordinate the shipment of goods to customers
- Develop shipment tracking systems for customers

Internet technology has made it possible to create highly synchronized industry value chains called value webs. A **value web** is a collection of independent firms that use information technology to coordinate their value chains to produce a product or service for a market collectively. It is more customer driven and operates in a less linear fashion than the traditional value chain.

Figure 3.10 shows that this value web synchronizes the business processes of customers, suppliers, and trading partners among different companies in an industry or in related industries. These value webs are flexible and adaptive to changes in supply and demand. Relationships can be bundled or unbundled in response to changing market conditions. Firms will accelerate time to market and to customers by optimizing their value web relationships to make quick decisions on who can deliver the required products or services at the right price and location.

Synergies, Core Competencies, and Network-Based Strategies

A large corporation is typically a collection of businesses. Often, the firm is organized financially as a collection of strategic business units and the returns to the firm are directly tied to the performance of all the strategic business units. Information systems can improve the overall performance of these business units by promoting synergies and core competencies.

Synergies

The idea of synergies is that when the output of some units can be used as inputs to other units or two organizations pool markets and expertise, these relationships lower costs and generate profits. Bank and financial firm mergers such as the merger of JPMorgan Chase and Bank of New York as well as Bank of America and Countrywide Financial Corporation occurred precisely for this purpose.

One use of information technology in these synergy situations is to tie together the operations of disparate business units so that they can act as a whole. For example, acquiring Countrywide Financial enabled Bank of America to extend its mortgage lending business and to tap into a large pool of new customers

FIGURE 3.10 THE VALUE WEB

The value web is a networked system that can synchronize the value chains of business partners within an industry to respond rapidly to changes in supply and demand.

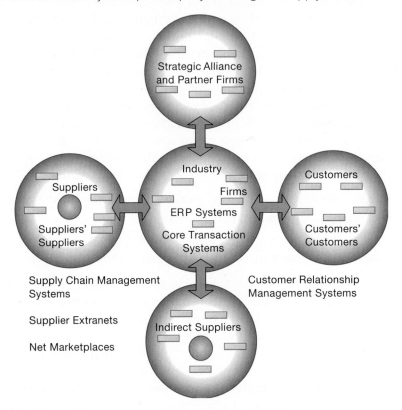

who might be interested in its credit card, consumer banking, and other financial products. Information systems would help the merged companies consolidate operations, lower retailing costs, and increase cross-marketing of financial products.

Enhancing Core Competencies

Yet another way to use information systems for competitive advantage is to think about ways that systems can enhance core competencies. The argument is that the performance of all business units will increase insofar as these business units develop, or create, a central core of competencies. A **core competency** is an activity for which a firm is a world-class leader. Core competencies may involve being the world's best miniature parts designer, the best package delivery service, or the best thin-film manufacturer. In general, a core competency relies on knowledge that is gained over many years of practical field experience with a technology. This practical knowledge is typically supplemented with a long-term research effort and committed employees.

Any information system that encourages the sharing of knowledge across business units enhances competency. Such systems might encourage or enhance existing competencies and help employees become aware of new external knowledge; such systems might also help a business leverage existing competencies to related markets. For example, Procter & Gamble, a world leader in brand management and consumer product innovation, uses a series of systems to enhance its core competencies by helping people working on similar problems share ideas and expertise. Employees working in research and development (R&D), engineering, purchasing, marketing, legal affairs, and business information systems around the world can share documents, reports, charts, videos, and other data from various sources online and locate employees with special expertise. P&G systems also can link to research scientists and entrepreneurs outside the company who are searching for new, innovative products worldwide.

Network-Based Strategies

Internet and networking technology have inspired strategies that take advantage of firms' abilities to create networks or network with each other. Network-based strategies include the use of network economics, a virtual company model, and business ecosystems.

Network Economics **Network economics** refers to market situations where the economic value being produced depends on the number of people using a product. For certain products and markets, the real economic value comes from the fact that other people use the product. In these situations, "network effects" are at work. For instance, what's the value of a telephone if it is not connected to millions of others? Email has value because it allows us to communicate with millions of others. Business models that are based on network effects have been highly successful on the Internet, including social networks, software, messaging apps, and on-demand companies like Uber and Airbnb.

In traditional economics—the economics of factories and agriculture—production experiences diminishing returns. The more any given resource is applied to production, the lower the marginal gain in output, until a point is reached where the additional inputs produce no additional outputs. This is the law of diminishing returns, and it is the foundation for most of modern economics.

In some situations, the law of diminishing returns does not work. For instance, in a network, the marginal costs of adding another participant are about zero, whereas the marginal gain is much larger. The larger the number of subscribers in a telephone system or the Internet, the greater the value to all participants because each user can interact with more people. It is not much more expensive to operate a television station with 1,000 subscribers than with 10 million subscribers. The value of a community of people grows with size, whereas the cost of adding new members is inconsequential. The value of Facebook to users increases greatly as more people use the social network.

From this network economics perspective, information technology can be strategically useful. Internet sites can be used by firms to build communities of users—like-minded customers who want to share their experiences. This builds customer loyalty and enjoyment and builds unique ties to customers. eBay, the giant online auction site, is an example. This business is based on a network of millions of users, and has built an online community by using the Internet. The more people offering products on eBay, the more valuable the eBay site is to everyone because more products are listed, and more competition among suppliers lowers prices. Network economics also provides strategic benefits to commercial software vendors. The value of their software and complementary software products increases as more people use them, and there is a larger installed base to justify continued use of the product and vendor support.

Virtual Company Model Another network-based strategy uses the model of a virtual company to create a competitive business. A **virtual company**, also known as a virtual organization, uses networks to link people, assets, and ideas, enabling it to ally with other companies to create and distribute products and services without being limited by traditional organizational boundaries or physical locations. One company can use the capabilities of another company without being organizationally tied to that company. The virtual company model is useful when a company finds it cheaper to acquire products, services, or capabilities from an external vendor or when it needs to move quickly to exploit new market opportunities and lacks the time and resources to respond on its own.

Fashion companies, such as GUESS, Ann Taylor, Levi Strauss, and Reebok, enlist Hong Kong–based Li & Fung to manage production and shipment of their garments. Li & Fung handles product development, raw material sourcing, production planning, quality assurance, and shipping. Li & Fung does not own any fabric, factories, or machines, outsourcing all of its work to a network of more than 15,000 suppliers in 40 countries all over the world. Customers place orders with Li & Fung over its private extranet. Li & Fung then sends instructions to appropriate raw material suppliers and factories where the clothing is produced. The Li & Fung extranet tracks the entire production process for each order. Working as a virtual company keeps Li & Fung flexible and adaptable so that it can design and produce the products ordered by its clients in short order to keep pace with rapidly changing fashion trends.

Business Ecosystems and Platforms The Internet and the emergence of digital firms call for some modification of the industry competitive forces model. The traditional Porter model assumes a relatively static industry environment; relatively clear-cut industry boundaries; and a relatively stable set of suppliers, substitutes, and customers. Instead of participating in a single industry, some of today's firms participate in industry sets—collections of industries that provide related services and products that deliver value to the customer (see Figure 3.11). **Business ecosystem** is another term for these loosely coupled but interdependent networks of suppliers, distributors, outsourcing firms, transportation service firms, and technology manufacturers (Iansiti and Levien, 2004).

An example of a business ecosystem is the mobile Internet platform. In this ecosystem there are four industries: device makers (Apple iPhone, Samsung, LG, and others), wireless telecommunication firms (AT&T, Verizon, T-Mobile, Sprint, and others), independent software applications providers (generally

FIGURE 3.11 AN ECOSYSTEM STRATEGIC MODEL

The digital firm era requires a more dynamic view of the boundaries among industries, firms, customers, and suppliers, with competition occurring among industry sets in a business ecosystem. In the ecosystem model, multiple industries work together to deliver value to the customer. IT plays an important role in enabling a dense network of interactions among the participating firms.

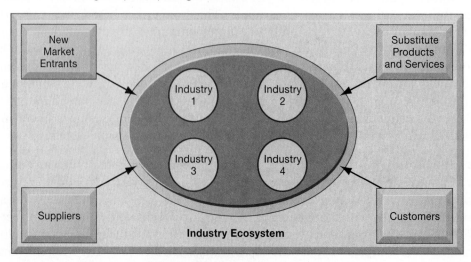

small firms selling games, applications, and ring tones), and Internet service providers (who participate as providers of Internet service to the mobile platform). Each of these industries has its own history, interests, and driving forces. But these elements come together in a sometimes cooperative and sometimes competitive new mobile digital platform ecosystem, creating value for consumers that none of them could achieve acting alone.

Business ecosystems typically have one or only a few keystone firms that dominate the ecosystem and create the **platforms** used by other niche firms. For instance, both Microsoft and Facebook provide platforms composed of information systems, technologies, and services that thousands of other firms in different industries use to enhance their own capabilities (Van Alstyne et. al, 2016). Facebook is a platform used by billions of people and millions of businesses to interact and share information as well as to buy, market, and sell numerous products and services. More firms are trying to use information systems to develop into keystone firms by building IT-based platforms that other firms can use. Alternatively, firms should consider how their information systems will enable them to become profitable niche players in the larger ecosystems created by keystone firms.

3-4 What are the challenges posed by strategic information systems, and how should they be addressed?

Strategic information systems often change the organization as well as its products, services, and operating procedures, driving the organization into new behavioral patterns. Successfully using information systems to achieve a competitive advantage is challenging and requires precise coordination of technology, organizations, and management.

Sustaining Competitive Advantage

The competitive advantages that strategic systems confer do not necessarily last long enough to ensure long-term profitability. Because competitors can retaliate and copy strategic systems, competitive advantage is not always sustainable. Markets, customer expectations, and technology change; globalization has made these changes even more rapid and unpredictable. The Internet can make competitive advantages disappear very quickly because virtually all companies can use this technology. Classic strategic systems, such as American Airlines's SABRE computerized reservation system, Citibank's ATM system, and FedEx's package tracking system, benefited by being the first in their industries. Then rival systems emerged. Amazon was an e-commerce leader but now faces competition from eBay, Walmart, and Google. Information systems alone cannot provide an enduring business advantage. Systems originally intended to be strategic frequently become tools for survival, required by every firm to stay in business, or they may inhibit organizations from making the strategic changes essential for future success.

Aligning IT with Business Objectives

The research on IT and business performance has found that (a) the more successfully a firm can align information technology with its business goals, the more profitable it will be, and (b) only one-quarter of firms achieve alignment of IT with the business. About half of a business firm's profits can be explained by alignment of IT with business (Luftman, 2003).

Most businesses get it wrong: Information technology takes on a life of its own and does not serve management and shareholder interests very well. Instead of businesspeople taking an active role in shaping IT to the enterprise, they ignore it, claim not to understand IT, and tolerate failure in the IT area as just a nuisance to work around. Such firms pay a hefty price in poor performance. Successful firms and managers understand what IT can do and how it works, take an active role in shaping its use, and measure its impact on revenues and profits.

Management Checklist: Performing a Strategic Systems Analysis

To align IT with the business and use information systems effectively for competitive advantage, managers need to perform a strategic systems analysis. To identify the types of systems that provide a strategic advantage to their firms, managers should ask the following questions:

1. What is the structure of the industry in which the firm is located?
   - What are some of the competitive forces at work in the industry? Are there new entrants to the industry? What is the relative power of suppliers, customers, and substitute products and services over prices?
   - Is the basis of competition quality, price, or brand?
   - What are the direction and nature of change within the industry? From where are the momentum and change coming?
   - How is the industry currently using information technology? Is the organization behind or ahead of the industry in its application of information systems?

2. What are the business, firm, and industry value chains for this particular firm?
   - How is the company creating value for the customer—through lower prices and transaction costs or higher quality? Are there any places in the value chain where the business could create more value for the customer and additional profit for the company?
   - Does the firm understand and manage its business processes using the best practices available? Is it taking maximum advantage of supply chain management, customer relationship management, and enterprise systems?
   - Does the firm leverage its core competencies?
   - Is the industry supply chain and customer base changing in ways that benefit or harm the firm?
   - Can the firm benefit from strategic partnerships, value webs, ecosystems, or platforms?
   - Where in the value chain will information systems provide the greatest value to the firm?

3. Have we aligned IT with our business strategy and goals?
   - Have we correctly articulated our business strategy and goals?
   - Is IT improving the right business processes and activities to promote this strategy?
   - Are we using the right metrics to measure progress toward those goals?

Managing Strategic Transitions

Adopting the kinds of strategic systems described in this chapter generally requires changes in business goals, relationships with customers and suppliers, and business processes. These sociotechnical changes, affecting both social and technical elements of the organization, can be considered **strategic transitions**—a movement between levels of sociotechnical systems.

Such changes often entail blurring of organizational boundaries, both external and internal. Suppliers and customers must become intimately linked and may share each other's responsibilities. Managers will need to devise new business processes for coordinating their firms' activities with those of customers, suppliers, and other organizations. The organizational change requirements surrounding new information systems are so important that they merit attention throughout this text. Chapter 14 examines organizational change issues in more detail.

3-5 How will MIS help my career?

Here is how Chapter 3 and this book can help you find a job as an entry-level business development representative.

The Company

Superior Data Quality, a fast-growing Los Angeles–based company providing software and services to help large companies manage their data and data quality, is looking for an entry-level business development representative. The company's data quality and data management tools and services help firms correct, standardize, and enhance customer data by capturing accurate address, email, and phone information; removing duplicate data in corporate systems; analyzing data to discover relationships; restructuring and standardizing data; and monitoring data to ensure ongoing quality control and standardization. The company has 12,000 clients worldwide, 450 employees, and offices throughout the United States, Europe, and Asia.

Position Description

The business development representative will help the company's sales team meet aggressive growth targets. The company provides classroom and on-the-job training on how to communicate with prospects and customers, how to identify appropriate markets for its solutions, how to write a sales plan, and how to use tools such as Salesforce.com. Job responsibilities include:

- Researching targeted accounts to generate potential business opportunities.
- Supporting customer acquisition and sales strategies.
- Implementing tactics for successful execution of marketing campaigns.
- Building and managing a pipeline of sales leads through prospecting and qualifying marketing-generated leads.
- Reporting on the success of campaigns and lead generation activities.

Job Requirements

- Bachelor's degree
- Strong interest in a sales career
- Exceptional communication, interpersonal, analytical, and problem-solving skills
- Ability to multitask in fast-paced environment

Interview Questions

1. What do you know about data quality and data management? Have you any work experience in these areas? Have you ever encountered a data quality problem? If so, can you describe how the problem was solved?

2. Have you ever worked with Salesforce.com? What do you know about it? How have you used the software?

3. Can you give us an example of a marketing or sales-related problem or other business problem that you helped solve? Do you have any examples of your writing and analysis work?

4. Have you had much face-to-face contact with customers? Can you describe what work you did with customers?

Author Tips

1. Review the discussion of IT and business strategy in Chapter 3 and also the section on data management, including data quality, in Chapter 6.

2. Use the web to find out more about tools and services for promoting data quality and data management and research the company's specific offerings in this area.

3. Review the company's LinkedIn profile and posts in addition to other social media channels. Are there consistent themes across these channels on which the company seems to focus? Be prepared to show that you understand the kinds of business challenges facing this company.

4. Learn what you can about Salesforce.com related to the responsibilities outlined for this job. Inquire about exactly how you would be using Salesforce.com in your work.

5. Consider inquiring what kinds of problems with customers' data quality you would be most likely to encounter on the job.

REVIEW **SUMMARY**

3-1 Which features of organizations do managers need to know about to build and use information systems successfully?

All modern organizations are hierarchical, specialized, and impartial, using explicit routines to maximize efficiency. All organizations have their own cultures and politics arising from differences in interest groups, and they are affected by their surrounding environment. Organizations differ in goals, groups served, social roles, leadership styles, incentives, types of tasks performed, and type of structure. These features help explain differences in organizations' use of information systems. Information systems and the organizations in which they are used interact with and influence each other.

3-2 What is the impact of information systems on organizations?

The introduction of a new information system will affect organizational structure, goals, work design, values, competition between interest groups, decision making, and day-to-day behavior. At the same time, information systems must be designed to serve the needs of important organizational groups and will be shaped by the organization's structure, business processes, goals, culture, politics, and management. Information technology can reduce transaction and agency costs, and such changes have been accentuated in organizations using the Internet. New systems disrupt established patterns of work and power relationships, so there is often considerable resistance to them when they are introduced.

3-3 How do Porter's competitive forces model, the value chain model, synergies, core competencies, and network economics help companies develop competitive strategies using information systems?

In Porter's competitive forces model, the strategic position of the firm and its strategies are determined by competition with its traditional direct competitors, but they are also greatly affected by new market entrants, substitute products and services, suppliers, and customers. Information systems help companies compete by maintaining low costs, differentiating products or services, focusing on market niche, strengthening ties with customers and suppliers, and increasing barriers to market entry with high levels of operational excellence.

The value chain model highlights specific activities in the business where competitive strategies and information systems will have the greatest impact. The model views the firm as a series of primary and support activities that add value to a firm's products or services. Primary activities are directly related to production and distribution, whereas support activities make the delivery of primary activities possible. A firm's value chain can be linked to the value chains of its suppliers, distributors, and customers. A value web consists of information systems that enhance competitiveness at the industry level by promoting the use of standards and industrywide consortia and by enabling businesses to work more efficiently with their value partners.

Because firms consist of multiple business units, information systems achieve additional efficiencies or enhance services by tying together the operations of disparate business units. Information systems help businesses leverage their core competencies by promoting the sharing of knowledge across business units. Information systems facilitate business models based on large networks of users or subscribers that take advantage of network economics. A virtual company strategy uses networks to link to other firms so that a company can use the capabilities of other companies to build, market, and distribute products and services. In business ecosystems, multiple industries work together to deliver value to the customer. Information systems support a dense network of interactions among the participating firms.

3-4 **What are the challenges posed by strategic information systems, and how should they be addressed?**

Implementing strategic systems often requires extensive organizational change and a transition from one sociotechnical level to another. Such changes are called strategic transitions and are often difficult and painful to achieve. Moreover, not all strategic systems are profitable, and they can be expensive to build. Many strategic information systems are easily copied by other firms, so that strategic advantage is not always sustainable.

Key Terms

Agency theory, 90
Benchmarking, 103
Best practices, 104
Business ecosystem, 108
Competitive forces model, 94
Core competency, 106
Disruptive technologies, 87
Efficient customer response system, 96
Mass customization, 97
Network economics, 107
Organization, 81

Platforms, 109
Primary activities, 103
Product differentiation, 95
Routines, 84
Strategic transitions, 111
Support activities, 103
Switching costs, 100
Transaction cost theory, 89
Value chain model, 101
Value web, 105
Virtual company, 107

MyLab MIS

To complete the problems with MyLab MIS, go to the EOC Discussion Questions in MyLab MIS.

Review Questions

3-1 Which features of organizations do managers need to know about to build and use information systems successfully?

- Define an organization and compare the technical definition of organizations with the behavioral definition.

- Identify and describe the features of organizations that help explain differences in organizations' use of information systems.

3-2 What is the impact of information systems on organizations?

- Describe the major economic theories that help explain how information systems affect organizations.

- Describe the major behavioral theories that help explain how information systems affect organizations.

- Explain why there is considerable organizational resistance to the introduction of information systems.
- Describe the impact of the Internet and disruptive technologies on organizations.

3-3 How do Porter's competitive forces model, the value chain model, synergies, core competencies, and network economics help companies develop competitive strategies using information systems?

- Define Porter's competitive forces model and explain how it works.
- Describe what the competitive forces model explains about competitive advantage.
- List and describe four competitive strategies enabled by information systems that firms can pursue.
- Describe how information systems can support each of these competitive strategies and give examples.
- Explain why aligning IT with business objectives is essential for strategic use of systems.
- Define and describe the value chain model.
- Explain how the value chain model can be used to identify opportunities for information systems.

- Define the value web and show how it is related to the value chain.
- Explain how the value web helps businesses identify opportunities for strategic information systems.
- Describe how the Internet has changed competitive forces and competitive advantage.
- Explain how information systems promote synergies and core competencies.
- Describe how promoting synergies and core competencies enhances competitive advantage.
- Explain how businesses benefit by using network economics and ecosystems.
- Define and describe a virtual company and the benefits of pursuing a virtual company strategy.

3-4 What are the challenges posed by strategic information systems, and how should they be addressed?

- List and describe the management challenges posed by strategic information systems.
- Explain how to perform a strategic systems analysis.

Discussion Questions

3-5
MyLab MIS
It has been said that there is no such thing as a sustainable strategic advantage. Do you agree? Why or why not?

3-6
MyLab MIS
It has been said that the advantage that leading-edge retailers such as Dell and Walmart have over their competition isn't

technology; it's their management. Do you agree? Why or why not?

3-7
MyLab MIS
What are some of the issues to consider in determining whether the Internet would provide your business with a competitive advantage?

Hands-On MIS Projects

The projects in this section give you hands-on experience identifying information systems to support a business strategy and to solve a customer retention problem, using a database to improve decision making about business strategy, and using web tools to configure and price an automobile. Visit MyLab MIS to access this chapter's Hands-On MIS Projects.

Management Decision Problems

3-8 Macy's, Inc., through its subsidiaries, operates approximately 840 department stores in the United States. Its retail stores sell a range of merchandise, including apparel, home furnishings, and housewares. Senior management has decided that Macy's needs to tailor merchandise more to local tastes and that the colors, sizes, brands, and styles of clothing and other merchandise should be based on the sales patterns in each individual Macy's store. How could information systems help Macy's management implement this new strategy? What pieces of data should these systems collect to help management make merchandising decisions that support this strategy?

3-9 T-Mobile has launched aggressive campaigns to attract customers with lower mobile phone prices, and it has added to its customer base. However, management wants to know if there are other ways of luring and keeping customers. Are customers concerned about the level of customer service, uneven network coverage, or data plans? How can the company use information systems to help find the answer? What management decisions could be made using information from these systems?

Improving Decision Making: Using a Database to Clarify Business Strategy

Software skills: Database querying and reporting; database design
Business skills: Reservation systems; customer analysis

3-10 In this exercise, you will use database software to analyze the reservation transactions for a hotel and use that information to fine-tune the hotel's business strategy and marketing activities.

In MyLab MIS, you will find a database for hotel reservation transactions developed in Microsoft Access with information about the President's Inn in Cape May, New Jersey. At the Inn, 10 rooms overlook side streets, 10 rooms have bay windows that offer limited views of the ocean, and the remaining 10 rooms in the front of the hotel face the ocean. Room rates are based on room choice, length of stay, and number of guests per room. Room rates are the same for one to four guests. Fifth and sixth guests must pay an additional $20 charge each per person per day. Guests staying for seven days or more receive a 10 percent discount on their daily room rates.

The owners currently use a manual reservation and bookkeeping system, which has caused many problems. Use the database to develop reports on average length of stay, average visitors per room, base revenue per room (i.e., length of visit multiplied by the daily rate), and strongest customer base. After answering these questions, write a brief report about the Inn's current business situation and suggest future strategies.

Improving Decision Making: Using Web Tools to Configure and Price an Automobile

Software skills: Internet-based software
Business skills: Researching product information and pricing

3-11 In this exercise, you will use software at car websites to find product information about a car of your choice and use that information to make an important purchase decision. You will also evaluate two of these sites as selling tools.

You are interested in purchasing a new Ford Escape (or some other car of your choice). Go to the website of CarsDirect (www.carsdirect.com) and begin your investigation. Locate the Ford Escape. Research the various Escape models, and choose one you prefer in terms of price, features, and safety ratings. Locate and read at least two reviews. Surf the website of the manufacturer, in this case Ford (www.ford.com). Compare the information available on Ford's website with that of CarsDirect for the Ford Escape. Try to locate the lowest price for the car you want in a local dealer's inventory. Suggest improvements for CarsDirect.com and Ford.com.

Collaboration and Teamwork Project

Identifying Opportunities for Strategic Information Systems

3-12 With your team of three or four other students, select a company described in the *Wall Street Journal, Fortune, Forbes*, or another business publication or do your research on the web. Visit the company's website to find additional information about that company and to see how the firm is using the web. On the basis of this information, analyze the business. Include a description of the organization's features, such as important business processes, culture, structure, and environment as well as its business strategy. Suggest strategic information systems appropriate for that particular business, including those based on Internet technology, if appropriate. If possible, use Google Docs and Google Drive or Google Sites to brainstorm, organize, and develop a presentation of your findings for the class.

Grocery Wars
CASE STUDY

On June 16, 2017 Amazon announced that it was purchasing the upscale food market chain Whole Foods for $13.7 billion. The acquisition, completed in August of that year, was Amazon's largest, and sent shock waves throughout the grocery industry. The purchase has profound implications for the future of groceries, the entire food industry, and perhaps the future of shopping itself.

Even before acquiring Whole Foods, Amazon had been expanding into groceries and physical locations, including bookstores, two Seattle drive-through grocery stores where customers can pick up online orders, and a convenience store called Amazon Go that uses sensors and software to let shoppers pay for purchases without waiting in line to check out. Amazon has also acquired experience with online grocery sales through its Amazon Fresh program. However, Amazon hadn't quite achieved the success with online groceries as it had with books and media. Whole Foods gives Amazon new ways to enhance its online business while establishing a presence in physical retail outlets.

The grocery business is notoriously competitive and low-margin, with profits of 1–2 cents on the dollar. Although Amazon is skilled at competing on low price, why take on this challenge? From Amazon's standpoint, there are several reasons why Whole Foods might turn out to be a very good investment. Groceries are an important purchase category, representing $800 billion in U.S. sales. A recent report by the Food Marketing Institute found that U.S. grocery sales could grow fivefold over the next decade. Purchasing Whole Foods helps Amazon become a major player in the grocery industry. Whole Foods takes Amazon's physical presence to a new level, with more than 460 stores in the United States, Canada, and Britain and sales of $16 billion in fiscal 2017. It will be within an hour or 30 minutes of as many people as possible.

Amazon could use its $119-a-year Prime membership service, which gives customers free, two-day shipping and other benefits, to offer Whole Foods customers a better price on groceries, as it does for books in its bookstores. The stores could also serve as an advertisement to get more customers to sign up for Prime. As of September 2017, Prime had 49 million subscribers in the United States, representing about 44 percent of households.

Amazon is a master at providing what's known as "consumer convenience." E-commerce is soaring and food-delivery businesses are taking off because people are too busy or otherwise occupied to leave their homes to go out and shop. Americans are ordering more of their groceries and meals online. A study commissioned by the market-research firm Euromonitor projects that the online market is projected to grow 15 times faster than the rest of the restaurant business through the end of the decade. Amazon can continue to sell groceries online but it can also provide the customer experience of shopping for food in person.

Whole Foods can also be used as a delivery network for Amazon's other non-grocery products. Amazon has been trying to open warehouses closer to customers so it can deliver orders in as little as two hours, and Whole Foods stores will bring Amazon physically closer to its shoppers. The stores could become locations for returning online orders of all kinds. Amazon could also use them to cut delivery times for online orders.

Several analysts have observed that Whole Foods' urban and suburban locations are so valuable for Amazon's delivery business that the deal could be worthwhile even if Whole Foods pretty much stopped selling food. When Amazon bought Whole Foods, it acquired 431 U.S. upper-income, prime-location distribution points for everything it does. With Whole Foods' footprint in affluent areas and Amazon's expertise in supply chain and delivery, it could upend both food retailing and food delivery.

One expert has called Amazon a "life bundle," particularly for affluent Americans. Amazon Prime could become the cable bundle of the future—an annual subscription to a group of diverse services that give Amazon a dependable revenue stream and a growing, loyal customer base. More than half of American households with incomes over $100,000 are already Prime subscribers, and they spend more than $1,000 a year using this service. Affluent families regularly spend $500 a month at Whole Foods. Once Amazon owns Whole Foods, its richest customers could be expected to spend thousands of dollars a year through Amazon. As Whole Foods customers are urged to sign up for Amazon Prime—and as Prime customers get enticing deals at Whole Foods—Amazon's penetration of the upscale market should grow, even as it offers discounts to lower-income Americans.

Amazon started making changes to Whole Foods as soon as the acquisition was completed in August 2017. The day the acquisition went through, prices of many Whole Foods staples dropped. Prices of some items decreased by up to 40 percent. An identical basket of items from a Whole Foods location in Brooklyn went from $97.76 pre-acquisition to $75.85 post-acquisition. In November 2017, Whole Foods announced another round of price cuts, with a focus on holiday staples and best-sellers as well as Whole Foods' private-label 365 line of products.

In February 2018, Amazon and Whole Foods launched a test to deliver groceries and other goods directly from Whole Foods in four cities across the United States. Whole Foods was basically used as an Amazon depot. Customers can order fresh produce, seafood, meat, flowers, baked goods, and dairy products for delivery, with items arriving at their doorstep within two hours. The company plans to roll out the service through Prime Now to more cities. Later in February, Amazon extended its 5 percent cash-back benefit to Prime members shopping at Whole Foods with the Amazon Prime Rewards Visa Card. Selected Whole Foods stores have begun selling Amazon technology products, including the Amazon Echo voice-controlled speaker system, Echo Dots, Fire TV, Kindle e-readers, and Fire tablets.

Whole Foods announced that Amazon Prime would replace Whole Foods' loyalty program. And Whole Foods goods are now available on Amazon. com, AmazonFresh (Amazon's grocery delivery service), Prime Pantry, and Prime Now. Some Whole Foods stores have added Amazon Lockers, allowing customers to have their Amazon.com orders delivered to a secure location inside certain Whole Foods stores until it's time to pick them up. Customers can also use lockers to return Amazon items. Amazon and Whole Foods are integrating their point-of-sale systems to enable more of Amazon's brands to be available at Whole Foods, and vice versa.

Buying Whole Foods represents an escalation of Amazon's long-running battle with Walmart. Walmart is the world's largest and most successful physical retailer, while Amazon dominates the online commerce space. Each wants to move into the other's turf: Amazon would like to have a more formidable physical presence as well as online, while Walmart is making a big push to expand in e-commerce.

Walmart is the largest seller of groceries in the United States, and with Sam's Club, accounts for about 18 percent of the grocery market. Grocery accounts for 56 percent of Walmart's total sales, and grocery shopping is a major driver of store traffic and customer loyalty. The company is intent on maintaining its position as the leading U.S. grocer. Walmart has invested and tested in click-and-collect programs, stand-alone grocery pick-up sites, and scanning and paying for items with smartphones. Grocery is where Walmart really shines. If Walmart loses the grocery battle to Amazon, it has no chance of ever overtaking Amazon as the world's largest e-commerce player.

Online grocery sales were a key part of Walmart's e-commerce sales growth in 2017, and management expects online grocery expansion to be the main driver of Walmart's sales growth going forward. But if Walmart wants to meet their goal of 40 percent growth in online sales in 2018, it will have to do even more. Management rolled out same-day grocery delivery to 100 markets by the end of 2018, covering 40 percent of U.S. households. Deliveries are handled by Uber Technologies and other providers, with a $9.95 service fee for a minimum $30 purchase. Walmart's online order and pickup service was available at 2,000 stores by the end of 2018. Management is hoping growth will continue to increase year over year with rollout of new stores into the online order and pickup program.

The move into home delivery will help get more of Walmart's in-store shoppers to start buying online as well, where they typically spend twice as much. It also complements Walmart's rollout of curbside grocery pickup, now available in 1,200 stores and adding an additional 1,000 this year.

Walmart will compete against Amazon's Prime Now service, which offers free two-hour delivery to members of its loyalty program. Both companies have also introduced services that allow delivery people to enter homes and leave packages inside.

How will the rest of the grocery industry fare as a result of these developments? Amazon terrifies competitors because it can offer such low prices on so many different categories of items. If Whole Foods follows this playbook, shoppers can expect prices to fall, and other grocery industry players will suffer. Stocks for Kroger, Costco, and Dollar General all fell more than six percent when Amazon announced the Whole Foods acquisition. The merger might be even worse news for Instacart, the grocery-delivery service that has had a close relationship with Whole Foods.

There are other forces at work affecting Amazon-Whole Foods, Walmart, and the grocery industry's competitive landscape. Money spent on dining out has surpassed grocery sales. Instead of shopping weekly at the supermarket for groceries to prepare meals at home, consumers are increasingly snacking and using prepared foods. Companies in the $1.5 billion meal kit industry (such as Blue Apron) have moved into the market, though grocery chains are creating their own pre-packaged food kits as well.

Grocers are also adapting to surging consumer demand for fresher items, personalized options, and use of technology to improve the food-buying experience. Deloitte researchers found an overwhelming majority of shoppers are deploying digital devices to research the groceries they intend to buy. Deloitte also found that shoppers spend more when using digital tools.

Despite the growth of online food shopping and these other shifts in the competitive landscape, experts believe the market for supermarkets is strong. According to brokerage and advisory firm Marcus & Millichap, there will be a wave of grocery store openings consuming 25 million square feet of commercial space over the next five years. Domestic chains and German discount supermarkets Aldi and Lidl are opening U.S. locations and smaller-format stores are likely to be part of the mix.

Sources: Kate Taylor, "Here Are the Changes Amazon Is Making to Whole Foods," *Business Insider*, March 2, 2018; Adam Levy, "Walmart's Grocery Efforts Probably Aren't Enough to Overcome Amazon," *The Motley Fool*, March 17, 2018; Matthew Boyle, "Walmart to Expand Grocery Delivery as Amazon Battle Rages," *Bloomberg*, March 14, 2018; John Cook, "Walmart Counterpunches Amazon with Plan to Expand Grocery Delivery Service to 100 U.S. Markets," *GeekWire*, March 14, 2018; Toby Clarence-Smith, "Amazon vs. Walmart: Bezos Goes for the Jugular with Whole Foods Acquisition," www.Toptal.com, accessed March 21, 2018; Tom McGee," Perspective for the Grocery Wars: Shoppers Crave Experience," *Forbes*, September 13, 2017; Derek Thompson, "Why Amazon Bought Whole Foods," *The Atlantic*, June 16, 2017; and Nick Wingfield and Michael J. de la Merced, "Amazon to Buy Whole Foods for $13.4 Billion," *New York Times*, June 16, 2017.

CASE STUDY QUESTIONS

3-13 Analyze Amazon.com and Walmart using the value chain and competitive forces models.

3-14 Compare the role of grocery sales in Amazon and Walmart's business strategies.

3-15 What role does information technology play in these strategies?

3-16 Which company is more likely to dominate grocery retailing? Explain your answer.

MyLab MIS

Go to the Assignments section of MyLab MIS to complete these writing exercises.

3-17 Describe the impact of the Internet on each of the five competitive forces.

3-18 What are the main factors that mediate the relationship between information technology and organizations and that managers need to take into account when developing new information systems? Give a business example of how each factor would influence the development of new information systems.

Chapter 3 References

Amladi, Pradip. "The Digital Economy: How It Will Transform Your Products and Your Future." *Big Data Quarterly* (March 25, 2016).

Andriole, Stephen J. "Five Myths About Digital Transformation," *MIT Sloan Management Review* 58, No. 3 (Spring 2017).

Bernstein, Ethan, John Bunch, Niko Canner, and Michael Lee. "Beyond the Holocracy Hype." *Harvard Business Review* (July–August 2016).

Bresnahan, Timothy F., Erik Brynjolfsson, and Lorin M. Hitt, "Information Technology, Workplace Organization, and the Demand for Skilled Labor." *Quarterly Journal of Economics* 117 (February 2002).

Ceccagnoli, Marco, Chris Forman, Peng Huang, and D. J. Wu. "Cocreation of Value in a Platform Ecosystem: The Case of Enterprise Software." *MIS Quarterly* 36, No. 1 (March 2012).

Christensen, Clayton M. *The Innovator's Dilemma: The Revolutionary Book That Will Change the Way You Do Business*. New York: HarperCollins (2003).

_____. "The Past and Future of Competitive Advantage." *Sloan Management Review* 42, No. 2 (Winter 2001).

Christensen, Clayton M., Michael E. Raynor, and Rory McDonald. "What Is Disruptive Innovation?" *Harvard Business Review* (December 2015).

Coase, Ronald H. "The Nature of the Firm." (1937). In Putterman, Louis and Randall Kroszner. *The Economic Nature of the Firm: A Reader*. Cambridge University Press, 1995.

Cohen, Daniel, and Joshua S. Gans. "Warding Off the Threat of Digital Disruption." *MIT Sloan Management Review* 58, No. 2 (Winter 2017).

Davenport, Thomas H., and Stephan Kudyba. "Designing and Developing Analytics-Based Data Products." *MIT Sloan Management Review* 58, No. 1 (Winter 2016).

Downes, Larry, and Paul Nunes. "Finding Your Company's Second Act." *Harvard Business Review* (January–February 2018).

Drucker, Peter. "The Coming of the New Organization." *Harvard Business Review* (January–February 1988).

Gandhi, Suketo, and Eric Gervet. "Now That Your Products Can Talk, What Will They Tell You?" *MIT Sloan Management Review* (Spring 2016).

Gurbaxani, V., and S. Whang, "The Impact of Information Systems on Organizations and Markets." *Communications of the ACM* 34, No. 1 (January 1991).

Hagiu, Andrei, and Elizabeth J. Altman. "Finding the Platform in Your Product." Harvard Business Review (July–August 2017).

Hagiu, Andrei, and Simon Rothman. "Network Effects Aren't Enough." *Harvard Business Review* (April 2016).

Hitt, Lorin M., and Erik Brynjolfsson. "Information Technology and Internal Firm Organization: An Exploratory Analysis." *Journal of Management Information Systems* 14, No. 2 (Fall 1997).

Iansiti, Marco, and Karim R. "Digital Ubiquity: How Connections, Sensors, and Data Are Revolutionizing Business." *Harvard Business Review* (November 2014).

_____. "Managing Our Hub Economy." *Harvard Business Review* (September–October 2017).

Iansiti, Marco, and Roy Levien. "Strategy as Ecology." *Harvard Business Review* (March 2004).

Jensen, M. C., and W. H. Meckling. "Specific and General Knowledge and Organizational Science." In *Contract Economics*, edited by L. Wetin and J. Wijkander. Oxford: Basil Blackwell (1992).

Jensen, Michael C., and William H. Meckling. "Theory of the Firm: Managerial Behavior, Agency Costs, and Ownership Structure." *Journal of Financial Economics* 3 (1976).

Kapur, Rahul, and Thomas Klueter. "Organizing for New Technologies." *MIT Sloan Management Review* 58, No. 2 (Winter 2017).

Kauffman, Robert J., and Yu-Ming Wang. "The Network Externalities Hypothesis and Competitive Network Growth." *Journal of Organizational Computing and Electronic Commerce* 12, No. 1 (2002).

King, Andrew A., and Baljir Baatartogtokh. "How Useful Is the Theory of Disruptive Innovation?" *MIT Sloan Management Review* (Fall 2015).

King, J. L., V. Gurbaxani, K. L. Kraemer, F. W. McFarlan, K. S. Raman, and C. S. Yap. "Institutional Factors in Information Technology Innovation." *Information Systems Research* 5, No. 2 (June 1994).

Kling, Rob. "Social Analyses of Computing: Theoretical Perspectives in Recent Empirical Research." *Computing Survey* 12, No. 1 (March 1980).

Kolb, D. A., and A. L. Frohman. "An Organization Development Approach to Consulting." *Sloan Management Review* 12, No. 1 (Fall 1970).

Lamb, Roberta, and Rob Kling. "Reconceptualizing Users as Social Actors in Information Systems Research." *MIS Quarterly* 27, No. 2 (June 2003).

Laudon, Kenneth C. "A General Model of the Relationship Between Information Technology and Organizations." Center for Research on Information Systems, New York University. Working paper, National Science Foundation (1989).

_____. "Environmental and Institutional Models of Systems Development." *Communications of the ACM* 28, No. 7 (July 1985).

_____. *Dossier Society: Value Choices in the Design of National Information Systems*. New York: Columbia University Press (1986).

Laudon, Kenneth C., and Kenneth L. Marr. "Information Technology and Occupational Structure." (April 1995).

Leavitt, Harold J., and Thomas L. Whisler. "Management in the 1980s." *Harvard Business Review* (November–December 1958).

Luftman, Jerry. *Competing in the Information Age: Align in the Sand* (2nd ed.). Oxford University Press USA (August 6, 2003).

March, James G., and Herbert A. Simon. *Organizations*. New York: Wiley (1958).

McAfee, Andrew, and Erik Brynjolfsson. "Investing in the IT That Makes a Competitive Difference." *Harvard Business Review* (July–August 2008).

McLaren, Tim S., Milena M. Head, Yufei Yuan, and Yolande E. Chan. "A Multilevel Model for Measuring Fit Between a Firm's Competitive Strategies and Information Systems Capabilities." *MIS Quarterly* 35, No. 4 (December 2011).

Mintzberg, Henry. "Managerial Work: Analysis from Observation." *Management Science* 18 (October 1971).

Nan, Ning, and Hüseyin Tanriverdi. "Unifying the Role of IT in Hyperturbulence and Competitive Advantage Via a Multilevel Perspective of IS Strategy." *MIS Quarterly* 41 No. 3 (September 2017).

Parker, Geoffrey, Marshall Van Alstyne, and Xiaoyue Jiang. "Platform Ecosystems: How Developers Invert the Firm," *MIS Quarterly* 41, No. 1 (March 2017).

Porter, Michael E. *Competitive Advantage*. New York: Free Press (1985).

_____. *Competitive Strategy*. New York: Free Press (1980).

_____. "Strategy and the Internet." *Harvard Business Review* (March 2001).

_____. "The Five Competitive Forces That Shape Strategy." *Harvard Business Review* (January 2008).

Porter, Michael E., and James E. Heppelmann. "How Smart, Connected Products Are Transforming Competition." *Harvard Business Review* (November 2014).

Porter, Michael E., and Scott Stern. "Location Matters." *Sloan Management Review* 42, No. 4 (Summer 2001).

Ross, Jeanne W., Ina M. Sebastian, and Cynthia M. Beath. "How to Develop a Great Digital Strategy." *MIT Sloan Management Review* 58, No. 2 (Winter 2017).

Shapiro, Carl, and Hal R. Varian. *Information Rules*. Boston, MA: Harvard Business School Press (1999).

Song, Peijian, Ling Xue, Arun Rai, and Cheng Zhang. "The Ecosystem of Software Platform: A Study of Asymmetric Cross-Side Network Effects and Platform Governance." *MIS Quarterly* 42 No. 1 (March 2018).

Suarez, Fernando Fl, James Utterback, Paul Von Gruben, and Hye Young Kang. "The Hybrid Trap: Why Most Efforts to Bridge Old and New Technology Miss the Mark." *MIT Sloan Management Review* 59, No. 3 (Spring 2018).

Svahn, Fredrik, Lars Mathiassen, and Rikard Lindgren. "Embracing Digital Innovation in Incumbent Firms: How Volvo Cars Managed Competing Concerns," *MIS Quarterly* 41, No. 1 (March 2017).

Taneja, Hemant, and Kevin Maney. "The End of Scale." *MIT Sloan Management Review* (Spring 2018).

Tushman, Michael L., and Philip Anderson. "Technological Discontinuities and Organizational Environments." *Administrative Science Quarterly* 31 (September 1986).

Van Alstyne, Marshall W., Geoffrey G. Parer, and Sangeet Paul Choudary. "Pipelines, Platforms, and the New Rules of Strategy." *Harvard Business Review* (April 2016).

Weber, Max. *The Theory of Social and Economic Organization*. Translated by Talcott Parsons. New York: Free Press (1947).

Williamson, Oliver E. *The Economic Institutions of Capitalism*. New York: Free Press, (1985).

Wixom, Barbara H., and Jeanne W. Ross. "How to Monetize Your Data." *MIT Sloan Management Review* 58, No. 3 (Spring 2017).

Zhu, Feng, and Nathan Furr. "Products to Platforms: Making the Leap." *Harvard Business Review* (April 2016).

4

Ethical and Social Issues in Information Systems

LEARNING OBJECTIVES

After reading this chapter, you will be able to answer the following questions:

4-1 What ethical, social, and political issues are raised by information systems?

4-2 What specific principles for conduct can be used to guide ethical decisions?

4-3 Why do contemporary information systems technology and the Internet pose challenges to the protection of individual privacy and intellectual property?

4-4 How have information systems affected laws for establishing accountability and liability and the quality of everyday life?

4-5 How will MIS help my career?

CHAPTER CASES

Are Cars Becoming Big Brother on Wheels?
Will Automation Kill Jobs?
How Harmful Are Smartphones?
Facebook Privacy: Your Life for Sale

VIDEO CASES

What Net Neutrality Means for You
Facebook and Google Privacy: What Privacy?
United States v. Terrorism: Data Mining for Terrorists and Innocents

Instructional Video:
Viktor Mayer-Schönberger on the Right to Be Forgotten

MyLab MIS

Discussion Questions: 4-5, 4-6, 4-7; **Hands-on MIS Projects:** 4-8, 4-9, 4-10, 4-11; **Writing Assignments:** 4-17, 4-18; **eText with Conceptual Animations**

Are Cars Becoming Big Brother on Wheels?

Cars today have become sophisticated listening posts on wheels. They can track phone calls and texts, record what radio stations you listen to, monitor the speed at which you drive and your braking actions, and even tell when you are breaking the speed limit, often without your knowledge.

Tens of millions of drivers in the United States are currently being monitored, with that number rising every time a new vehicle is sold or leased. There are 78 million cars on the road with an embedded cyber connection that can be used for monitoring drivers. According to research firm Gartner Inc., 98 percent of new cars sold in the United States and Europe will be connected by 2021.

Since 2014, every new car in the United States comes with an event data recorder (EDR), which records and stores over a dozen data points, including vehicle speed, seat belt use, and braking activation. EDR data are available to any auto maker as well as to insurance companies, which use these stored EDR data to help establish responsibility for an accident or to detect fraud.

EDRs are mandated and regulated by the U.S. government, but other data-gathering software in today's cars is not. Such software underlies numerous sensors, diagnostic systems, in-dash navigation systems, and built-in cellular connections, as well as driver-assistance systems to help drivers park, stay in their lane, avoid rear-ending another car, and steer for short time periods. All of this software keeps track of what drivers are doing. Newer cars may record driver eye movements, the weight of people in the front seats, and whether the driver's hands are on the wheel. Smartphones, whether connected to the car or not, can also track your activities, including any texting while driving. Auto makers are able to mine all this information, as are app developers and companies such as Google or Spotify.

© Metamorworks/Shutterstock

With the exception of medical information, the United States has few regulations governing what data companies can gather and how they can use the data. Companies generally are not required to conceal names or other personal details. In most cases the driver must consent to allowing his or her personal information to be tracked or monitored. Many people unwittingly provide this consent when they check off a box on one of the lengthy service agreement forms required to register a car's in-dash system or navigation app.

Collecting such large amounts of personal data generated by drivers has raised concerns about whether automakers and others are doing enough to protect people's privacy. Drivers may welcome the use of information to relay helpful diagnostic information or updates on nearby traffic jams. But they do not necessarily endorse other uses, and automakers have refrained from commenting on future data collection plans and policies.

Automakers argue that the data are valuable for improving vehicle performance and vehicle safety and soon will be able to reduce traffic accidents and fatalities. Amassing detailed data about human driving behavior is also essential for the development of self-driving cars. But privacy experts believe the practice is dangerous. With enough data about driver behavior, individual profiles as unique as fingerprints could be developed. Trips to businesses reveal buying habits and relationships that could be valuable to corporations, government agencies, or law enforcement. For example, frequent visits to a liquor store or mental health clinic could reveal information about someone's drinking habits or health problems. People obviously would not want such confidential data shared with others.

Sources: Peter Holley, "Big Brother on Wheels: Why Your Car Company May Know More About You Than Your Spouse." *Washington Post*, January 15, 2018; Christina Rogers, "What Your Car Knows about You," *Wall Street Journal*, August 18, 2018; John R. Quain, "Cars Suck Up Data About You. Where Does It All Go?" *New York Times*, July 27, 2017; and Russ Heaps, "Data Collection for Self-Driving Cars Could Be Risking Your Privacy," *Autotrader*, September 2016.

The challenges that connected vehicles and big data pose to privacy, described in the chapter-opening case, show that technology can be a double-edged sword. It can be the source of many benefits, including the capability to make driving safer and more efficient. At the same time, digital technology creates new opportunities for invading privacy and using information that could cause harm.

The chapter-opening diagram calls attention to important points this case and this chapter raise. Developments in data management technology, the Internet of Things (IoT), and analytics have created opportunities for organizations to use big data to improve operations and decision making. Big data analytics are now being applied to all the data generated by motor vehicles, especially those with Internet connections. The auto makers and other organizations described here are benefiting from using big data to monitor vehicle performance and driver behavior and to provide drivers with helpful tools for driving safely and caring for their cars. However, the use of big data from motor vehicles is also taking benefits away from individuals. Individuals might be subject to job discrimination or higher insurance rates because organizations have new tools to assemble and analyze huge quantities of data about their driving behavior. There are very few privacy protections for all the personal data gathered from car driving. New privacy protection laws and policies need to be developed to keep up with the technologies for assembling and analyzing big data.

This case illustrates an ethical dilemma because it shows two sets of interests at work, the interests of organizations that have raised profits or even helped many people with the data generated by connected vehicles and those who fervently believe that businesses and public organizations should not use big data analysis to invade privacy or harm individuals. As a manager, you will need to be sensitive to both the positive and negative impacts of information systems for your firm, employees, and customers. You will need to learn how to resolve ethical dilemmas involving information systems.

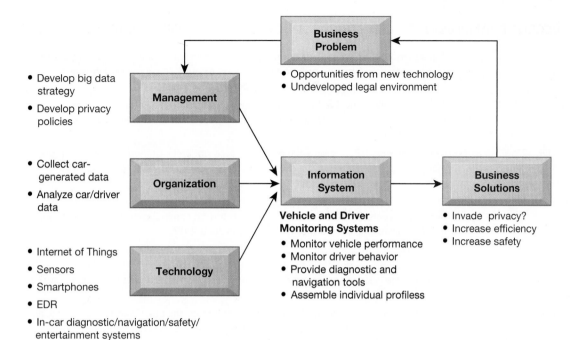

- Develop big data strategy
- Develop privacy policies

- Collect car-generated data
- Analyze car/driver data

- Internet of Things
- Sensors
- Smartphones
- EDR
- In-car diagnostic/navigation/safety/ entertainment systems

Business Problem
- Opportunities from new technology
- Undeveloped legal environment

Management

Organization

Technology

Information System

Vehicle and Driver Monitoring Systems
- Monitor vehicle performance
- Monitor driver behavior
- Provide diagnostic and navigation tools
- Assemble individual profiless

Business Solutions
- Invade privacy?
- Increase efficiency
- Increase safety

Here are some questions to think about: Does analyzing big data from motor vehicles create an ethical dilemma? Why or why not? Should there be new privacy laws to protect personal data collected from cars? Why or why not?

4-1 What ethical, social, and political issues are raised by information systems?

In the past 20 years, we have witnessed, arguably, one of the most ethically challenging periods for U.S. and global business. Table 4.1 provides a small sample of recent cases demonstrating failed ethical judgment by senior and middle managers. These lapses in ethical and business judgment occurred across a broad spectrum of industries.

In today's new legal environment, managers who violate the law and are convicted will most likely spend time in prison. U.S. federal sentencing guidelines adopted in 1987 mandate that federal judges impose stiff sentences on business executives based on the monetary value of the crime, the presence of a conspiracy to prevent discovery of the crime, the use of structured financial transactions to hide the crime, and failure to cooperate with prosecutors (U.S. Sentencing Commission, 2004).

Although business firms would, in the past, often pay for the legal defense of their employees enmeshed in civil charges and criminal investigations, firms are now encouraged to cooperate with prosecutors to reduce charges against the entire firm for obstructing investigations. More than ever, as a manager or an employee, you will have to decide for yourself what constitutes proper legal and ethical conduct.

These major instances of failed ethical and legal judgment were not masterminded by information systems departments, but information systems were instrumental in many of these frauds. In many cases, the perpetrators of these crimes artfully used financial reporting information systems to bury their decisions from public scrutiny.

TABLE 4.1 RECENT EXAMPLES OF FAILED ETHICAL JUDGMENT BY SENIOR MANAGERS	
Wells Fargo (2018)	Wells Fargo bank admitted to opening millions of false accounts, manipulating terms of mortgages, and forcing auto loan customers to purchase unneeded insurance. The bank was fined $2.5 billion by the federal government.
Deerfield Management (2017)	Washington, D.C., hedge fund indicted for using confidential information about government financing to trade shares in healthcare companies that would be affected by the changes.
General Motors, Inc. (2015)	General Motors CEO admitted the firm covered up faulty ignition switches for more than a decade, resulting in the deaths of at least 114 customers. More than 100 million vehicles worldwide were affected.
Takata Corporation (2015)	Takata executives admitted they covered up faulty airbags used in millions of cars over many years. Three executives were indicted on criminal charges and Takata was fined $1 billion. Takata filed for bankruptcy in June 2017.
GlaxoSmithKline LLC (2012)	The global healthcare giant admitted to unlawful and criminal promotion of certain prescription drugs, its failure to report certain safety data, and its civil liability for alleged false price reporting practices. Fined $3 billion, the largest healthcare fraud settlement in U.S. history.
Bank of America (2012)	Federal prosecutors charged Bank of America and its affiliate, Countrywide Financial, with defrauding government-backed mortgage agencies by churning out loans at a rapid pace without proper controls. Prosecutors sought $1 billion in penalties from the bank.

We deal with the issue of control in information systems in Chapter 8. In this chapter, we will talk about the ethical dimensions of these and other actions based on the use of information systems.

Ethics refers to the principles of right and wrong that individuals, acting as free moral agents, use to make choices to guide their behavior. Information systems raise new ethical questions for both individuals and societies because they create opportunities for intense social change and, thus, threaten existing distributions of power, money, rights, and obligations. Like other technologies, such as steam engines, electricity, and the telephone, information technology can be used to achieve social progress, but it can also be used to commit crimes and threaten cherished social values. The development of information technology will produce benefits for many and costs for others.

Ethical issues in information systems have been given new urgency by the rise of the Internet and e-commerce. Internet and digital technologies make it easier than ever to assemble, integrate, and distribute information, unleashing new concerns about the appropriate use of customer information, the protection of personal privacy, and the protection of intellectual property.

Other pressing ethical issues that information systems raise include establishing accountability for the consequences of information systems, setting standards to safeguard system quality that protects the safety of the individual and society, and preserving values and institutions considered essential to the quality of life in an information society. When using information systems, it is essential to ask, "What is the ethical and socially responsible course of action?"

A Model for Thinking about Ethical, Social, and Political Issues

Ethical, social, and political issues are closely linked. The ethical dilemma you may face as a manager of information systems typically is reflected in social and political debate. One way to think about these relationships is

---

FIGURE 4.1 THE RELATIONSHIP BETWEEN ETHICAL, SOCIAL, AND POLITICAL ISSUES IN AN INFORMATION SOCIETY

The introduction of new information technology has a ripple effect, raising new ethical, social, and political issues that must be dealt with on the individual, social, and political levels. These issues have five moral dimensions: information rights and obligations, property rights and obligations, system quality, quality of life, and accountability and control.

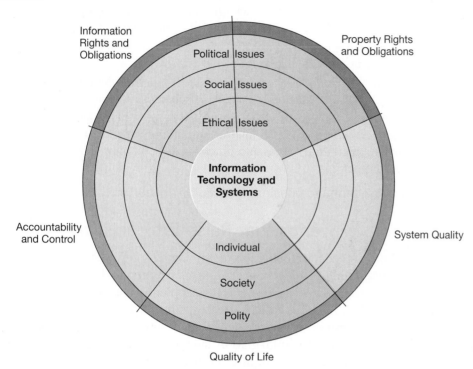

shown in Figure 4.1. Imagine society as a more or less calm pond on a summer day, a delicate ecosystem in partial equilibrium with individuals and with social and political institutions. Individuals know how to act in this pond because social institutions (family, education, organizations) have developed well-honed rules of behavior, and these are supported by laws developed in the political sector that prescribe behavior and promise sanctions for violations. Now toss a rock into the center of the pond. What happens? Ripples, of course.

Imagine instead that the disturbing force is a powerful shock of new information technology and systems hitting a society more or less at rest. Suddenly, individual actors are confronted with new situations often not covered by the old rules. Social institutions cannot respond overnight to these ripples—it may take years to develop etiquette, expectations, social responsibility, politically correct attitudes, or approved rules. Political institutions also require time before developing new laws and often require the demonstration of real harm before they act. In the meantime, you may have to act. You may be forced to act in a legal gray area.

We can use this model to illustrate the dynamics that connect ethical, social, and political issues. This model is also useful for identifying the main moral dimensions of the information society, which cut across various levels of action—individual, social, and political.

Five Moral Dimensions of the Information Age

The major ethical, social, and political issues that information systems raise include the following moral dimensions.

- *Information rights and obligations* What **information rights** do individuals and organizations possess with respect to themselves? What can they protect?

- *Property rights and obligations* How will traditional intellectual property rights be protected in a digital society in which tracing and accounting for ownership are difficult, and ignoring such property rights is so easy?

- *Accountability and control* Who can and will be held accountable and liable for the harm done to individual and collective information and property rights?

- *System quality* What standards of data and system quality should we demand to protect individual rights and the safety of society?

- *Quality of life* What values should be preserved in an information- and knowledge-based society? Which institutions should we protect from violation? Which cultural values and practices does the new information technology support?

We explore these moral dimensions in detail in Section 4-3.

Key Technology Trends that Raise Ethical Issues

Ethical issues long preceded information technology. Nevertheless, information technology has heightened ethical concerns, taxed existing social arrangements, and made some laws obsolete or severely crippled. Five key technological trends are responsible for these ethical stresses, summarized in Table 4.2.

The doubling of computing power every 18 months has made it possible for most organizations to use information systems for their core production processes. As a result, our dependence on systems and our vulnerability to system errors and poor data quality have increased. Social rules and laws have not yet adjusted to this dependence. Standards for ensuring the accuracy and reliability of information systems (see Chapter 8) are not universally accepted or enforced.

Advances in data storage techniques and rapidly declining storage costs have been responsible for the proliferation of databases on individuals—employees, customers, and potential customers—maintained by private and public organizations. These advances in data storage have made the routine violation of individual privacy both inexpensive and effective. Enormous data storage systems

TABLE 4.2   TECHNOLOGY TRENDS THAT RAISE ETHICAL ISSUES

TREND	IMPACT
Computing power doubles every 18 months	More organizations depend on computer systems for critical operations and become more vulnerable to system failures.
Data storage costs rapidly decline	Organizations can easily maintain detailed databases on individuals. There are no limits on the data collected about you.
Data analysis advances	Companies can analyze vast quantities of data gathered on individuals to develop detailed profiles of individual behavior. Large-scale population surveillance is enabled.
Networking advances	The cost of moving data and making data accessible from anywhere falls exponentially. Access to data becomes more difficult to control.
Mobile device growth impact	Individual cell phones may be tracked without user consent or knowledge. The always-on device becomes a tether.

© Dedivan1923/123RF

Credit card purchases can make personal information available to market researchers, telemarketers, and direct mail companies. Advances in information technology facilitate the invasion of privacy.

for terabytes and petabytes of data are now available on-site or as online services for firms of all sizes to use in identifying customers.

Advances in data analysis techniques for large pools of data are another technological trend that heightens ethical concerns because companies and government agencies can find out highly detailed personal information about individuals. With contemporary data management tools (see Chapter 6), companies can assemble and combine myriad pieces of information about you stored on computers much more easily than in the past.

Think of all the ways you generate digital information about yourself—credit card purchases; telephone calls; magazine subscriptions; video rentals; mail-order purchases; banking records; local, state, and federal government records (including court and police records); and visits to websites. Put together and mined properly, this information could reveal not only your credit information but also your driving habits, your tastes, your associations, what you read and watch, and your political interests.

Companies purchase relevant personal information from these sources to help them more finely target their marketing campaigns. Chapters 6 and 12 describe how companies can analyze large pools of data from multiple sources to identify buying patterns of customers rapidly and make individualized recommendations. The use of computers to combine data from multiple sources and create digital dossiers of detailed information on individuals is called **profiling**.

For example, several thousand of the most popular websites allow DoubleClick (owned by Google), an Internet advertising broker, to track the activities of their visitors in exchange for revenue from advertisements based on visitor information DoubleClick gathers. DoubleClick uses this information to create a profile of each online visitor, adding more detail to the profile as the visitor accesses an associated DoubleClick site. Over time, DoubleClick can create a detailed dossier of a person's spending and computing habits on the web that is sold to companies to help them target their web ads more precisely. Advertisers can combine online consumer information with offline information, such as credit card purchases at stores.

LexisNexis Risk Solutions (formerly ChoicePoint) gathers data from police, criminal, and motor vehicle records, credit and employment histories, current and previous addresses, professional licenses, and insurance claims to assemble and maintain dossiers on almost every adult in the United States. The company sells this personal information to businesses and government agencies. Demand for personal data is so enormous that data broker businesses, such as Risk Solutions, Acxiom, Nielsen, Experian, Equifax, and CoreLogic, are flourishing. The two largest credit card networks, Visa Inc. and Mastercard Inc., have agreed to link credit card purchase information with consumer social network and other information to create customer profiles that could be sold to advertising firms.

A data analysis technology called **nonobvious relationship awareness (NORA)** has given both the government and the private sector even more powerful profiling capabilities. NORA can take information about people from many disparate sources, such as employment applications, telephone records, customer listings, and wanted lists, and correlate relationships to find obscure connections that might help identify criminals or terrorists (see Figure 4.2).

NORA technology scans data and extracts information as the data are being generated so that it could, for example, instantly discover a man at an airline ticket counter who shares a phone number with a known terrorist before that person boards an airplane. The technology is considered a valuable tool for homeland security but does have privacy implications because it can provide such a detailed picture of the activities and associations of a single individual.

FIGURE 4.2 NONOBVIOUS RELATIONSHIP AWARENESS (NORA)

NORA technology can take information about people from disparate sources and find obscure, nonobvious relationships. It might discover, for example, that an applicant for a job at a casino shares a telephone number with a known criminal and issue an alert to the hiring manager.

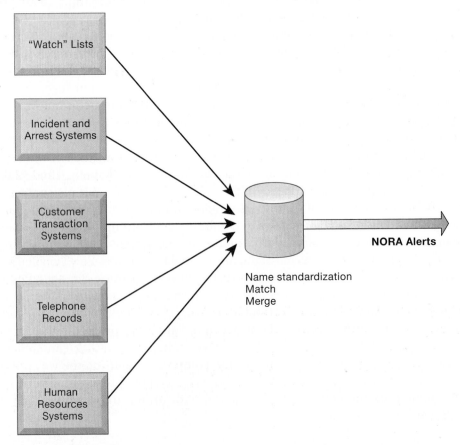

Finally, advances in networking, including the Internet, promise to reduce greatly the costs of moving and accessing large quantities of data and open the possibility of mining large pools of data remotely by using small desktop machines, mobile devices, and cloud servers, permitting an invasion of privacy on a scale and with a precision heretofore unimaginable.

4-2 What specific principles for conduct can be used to guide ethical decisions?

Ethics is a concern of humans who have freedom of choice. Ethics is about individual choice: When faced with alternative courses of action, what is the correct moral choice? What are the main features of ethical choice?

Basic Concepts: Responsibility, Accountability, and Liability

Ethical choices are decisions made by individuals who are responsible for the consequences of their actions. **Responsibility** is a key element of ethical action. Responsibility means that you accept the potential costs, duties, and obligations for the decisions you make. **Accountability** is a feature of systems and social institutions; it means that mechanisms are in place to determine who took action and who is responsible. Systems and institutions in which it is impossible to find out who took what action are inherently incapable of ethical analysis or ethical action. **Liability** extends the concept of responsibility further to the area of laws. Liability is a feature of political systems in which a body of laws is in place that permits individuals to recover the damages done to them by other actors, systems, or organizations. **Due process** is a related feature of law-governed societies and is a process in which laws are known and understood, and ability exists to appeal to higher authorities to ensure that the laws are applied correctly.

These basic concepts form the underpinning of an ethical analysis of information systems and those who manage them. First, information technologies are filtered through social institutions, organizations, and individuals. Systems do not have impacts by themselves. Whatever information system effects exist are products of institutional, organizational, and individual actions and behaviors. Second, responsibility for the consequences of technology falls clearly on the institutions, organizations, and individual managers who choose to use the technology. Using information technology in a socially responsible manner means that you can and will be held accountable for the consequences of your actions. Third, in an ethical, political society, individuals and others can recover damages done to them through a set of laws characterized by due process.

Ethical Analysis

When confronted with a situation that seems to present ethical issues, how should you analyze it? The following five-step process should help:

1. *Identify and describe the facts clearly* Find out who did what to whom and where, when, and how. In many instances, you will be surprised at the errors in the initially reported facts, and often you will find that simply getting the facts straight helps define the solution. It also helps to get the opposing parties involved in an ethical dilemma to agree on the facts.

2. *Define the conflict or dilemma and identify the higher-order values involved* Ethical, social, and political issues always reference higher values. The parties to a dispute all claim to be pursuing higher values (e.g., freedom, privacy, protection of property, or the free enterprise system). Typically, an ethical issue involves a dilemma: two diametrically opposed courses of action that support worthwhile values. For example, the chapter-opening case study illustrates two competing values: the need to make organizations more efficient and cost-effective and the need to respect individual privacy.

3. *Identify the stakeholders* Every ethical, social, and political issue has stakeholders: players in the game who have an interest in the outcome, who have invested in the situation, and usually who have vocal opinions. Find out the identity of these groups and what they want. This will be useful later when designing a solution.

4. *Identify the options that you can reasonably take* You may find that none of the options satisfy all the interests involved but that some options do a better job than others. Sometimes arriving at a good or ethical solution may not always be a balancing of consequences to stakeholders.

5. *Identify the potential consequences of your options* Some options may be ethically correct but disastrous from other points of view. Other options may work in one instance but not in similar instances. Always ask yourself, "What if I choose this option consistently over time?"

Candidate Ethical Principles

Once your analysis is complete, what ethical principles or rules should you use to make a decision? What higher-order values should inform your judgment? Although you are the only one who can decide which among many ethical principles you will follow, and how you will prioritize them, it is helpful to consider some ethical principles with deep roots in many cultures that have survived throughout recorded history:

1. Do unto others as you would have them do unto you (the **Golden Rule**). Putting yourself in the place of others, and thinking of yourself as the object of the decision, can help you think about fairness in decision making.

2. If an action is not right for everyone to take, it is not right for anyone (**Immanuel Kant's categorical imperative**). Ask yourself, "If everyone did this, could the organization, or society, survive?"

3. If an action cannot be taken repeatedly, it is not right to take at all. This is the **slippery slope rule**: An action may bring about a small change now that is acceptable, but if it is repeated, it would bring unacceptable changes in the long run. In the vernacular, it might be stated as "once started down a slippery path, you may not be able to stop."

4. Take the action that achieves the higher or greater value (**utilitarian principle**). This rule assumes you can prioritize values in a rank order and understand the consequences of various courses of action.

5. Take the action that produces the least harm or the least potential cost (**risk aversion principle**). Some actions have extremely high failure costs of very low probability (e.g., building a nuclear generating facility in an urban area) or extremely high failure costs of moderate probability (speeding and automobile accidents). Avoid actions that have extremely high failure costs; focus on reducing the probability of accidents occurring.

6. Assume that virtually all tangible and intangible objects are owned by someone else unless there is a specific declaration otherwise. (This is the **ethical no-free-lunch rule**.) If something someone else has created is useful to you, it has value, and you should assume the creator wants compensation for this work.

Actions that do not easily pass these rules deserve close attention and a great deal of caution. The appearance of unethical behavior may do as much harm to you and your company as actual unethical behavior.

Professional Codes of Conduct

When groups of people claim to be professionals, they take on special rights and obligations because of their special claims to knowledge, wisdom, and respect. Professional codes of conduct are promulgated by associations of professionals such as the American Medical Association (AMA), the American Bar Association (ABA), the Association of Information Technology Professionals (AITP), and the Association for Computing Machinery (ACM). These professional groups take responsibility for the partial regulation of their professions by determining entrance qualifications and competence. Codes of ethics are promises by professions to regulate themselves in the general interest of society. For example, avoiding harm to others, honoring property rights (including intellectual property), and respecting privacy are among the General Moral Imperatives of the ACM's Code of Ethics and Professional Conduct.

Some Real-World Ethical Dilemmas

Information systems have created new ethical dilemmas in which one set of interests is pitted against another. For example, many companies use voice recognition software to reduce the size of their customer support staff by enabling computers to recognize a customer's responses to a series of computerized questions. Many companies monitor what their employees are doing on the Internet to prevent them from wasting company resources on nonbusiness activities (see the Chapter 7 Interactive Session on Management).

In each instance, you can find competing values at work, with groups lined up on either side of a debate. A company may argue, for example, that it has a right to use information systems to increase productivity and reduce the size of its workforce to lower costs and stay in business. Employees displaced by information systems may argue that employers have some responsibility for their welfare. Business owners might feel obligated to monitor employee email and Internet use to minimize drains on productivity. Employees might believe they should be able to use the Internet for short personal tasks in place of the telephone. A close analysis of the facts can sometimes produce compromised solutions that give each side half a loaf. Try to apply some of the principles of ethical analysis described to each of these cases. What is the right thing to do?

4-3 Why do contemporary information systems technology and the Internet pose challenges to the protection of individual privacy and intellectual property?

In this section, we take a closer look at the five moral dimensions of information systems first described in Figure 4.1. In each dimension, we identify the ethical, social, and political levels of analysis and use real-world examples to illustrate the values involved, the stakeholders, and the options chosen.

TABLE 4.3 FEDERAL PRIVACY LAWS IN THE UNITED STATES

GENERAL FEDERAL PRIVACY LAWS	PRIVACY LAWS AFFECTING PRIVATE INSTITUTIONS
Freedom of Information Act of 1966 as Amended (5 USC 552)	Fair Credit Reporting Act of 1970
Privacy Act of 1974 as Amended (5 USC 552a)	Family Educational Rights and Privacy Act of 1974
Electronic Communications Privacy Act of 1986	Right to Financial Privacy Act of 1978
Computer Matching and Privacy Protection Act of 1988	Privacy Protection Act of 1980
Computer Security Act of 1987	Cable Communications Policy Act of 1984
Federal Managers Financial Integrity Act of 1982	Electronic Communications Privacy Act of 1986
Driver's Privacy Protection Act of 1994	Video Privacy Protection Act of 1988
E-Government Act of 2002	The Health Insurance Portability and Accountability Act (HIPAA) of 1996
	Children's Online Privacy Protection Act (COPPA) of 1998
	Financial Modernization Act (Gramm-Leach-Bliley Act) of 1999

Information Rights: Privacy and Freedom in the Internet Age

Privacy is the claim of individuals to be left alone, free from surveillance or interference from other individuals or organizations, including the state. Claims to privacy are also involved at the workplace. Millions of employees are subject to digital and other forms of high-tech surveillance. Information technology and systems threaten individual claims to privacy by making the invasion of privacy cheap, profitable, and effective.

The claim to privacy is protected in the United States, Canadian, and German constitutions in a variety of ways and in other countries through various statutes. In the United States, the claim to privacy is protected primarily by the First Amendment guarantees of freedom of speech and association, the Fourth Amendment protections against unreasonable search and seizure of one's personal documents or home, and the guarantee of due process.

Table 4.3 describes the major U.S. federal statutes that set forth the conditions for handling information about individuals in such areas as credit reporting, education, financial records, newspaper records, and electronic and digital communications. The Privacy Act of 1974 has been the most important of these laws, regulating the federal government's collection, use, and disclosure of information. At present, most U.S. federal privacy laws apply only to the federal government and regulate very few areas of the private sector.

Most American and European privacy law is based on a regime called **Fair Information Practices (FIP)**, first set forth in a report written in 1973 by a federal government advisory committee and updated in 2010 to take into account new privacy-invading technology (U.S. Department of Health, Education, and Welfare, 1973). FIP is a set of principles governing the collection and use of information about individuals. FIP principles are based on the notion of a mutuality of interest between the record holder and the individual. The individual has an interest in engaging in a transaction, and the record keeper—usually a business or government agency—requires information about the individual to support the transaction. After information is gathered, the individual maintains an interest in the record, and the record may not be used to support other activities without the individual's consent. In 1998, the Federal Trade

TABLE 4.4 FEDERAL TRADE COMMISSION FAIR INFORMATION PRACTICE PRINCIPLES

Notice/awareness (core principle). Websites must disclose their information practices before collecting data. Includes identification of collector; uses of data; other recipients of data; nature of collection (active/inactive); voluntary or required status; consequences of refusal; and steps taken to protect confidentiality, integrity, and quality of the data.

Choice/consent (core principle). A choice regime must be in place allowing consumers to choose how their information will be used for secondary purposes other than supporting the transaction, including internal use and transfer to third parties.

Access/participation. Consumers should be able to review and contest the accuracy and completeness of data collected about them in a timely, inexpensive process.

Security. Data collectors must take responsible steps to ensure that consumer information is accurate and secure from unauthorized use.

Enforcement. A mechanism must be in place to enforce FIP principles. This can involve self-regulation, legislation giving consumers legal remedies for violations, or federal statutes and regulations.

Commission (FTC) restated and extended the original FIP to provide guidelines for protecting online privacy. Table 4.4 describes the FTC's FIP principles.

The FTC's FIP principles are being used as guidelines to drive changes in privacy legislation. In July 1998, the U.S. Congress passed the Children's Online Privacy Protection Act (COPPA), requiring websites to obtain parental permission before collecting information on children under the age of 13. The FTC has recommended additional legislation to protect online consumer privacy in advertising networks that collect records of consumer web activity to develop detailed profiles, which other companies then use to target online ads. In 2010, the FTC added three practices to its framework for privacy. Firms should adopt privacy by design, building products and services that protect privacy; firms should increase the transparency of their data practices; and firms should require consumer consent and provide clear options to opt out of data collection schemes (Federal Trade Commission, 2012). Other proposed Internet privacy legislation focuses on protecting the online use of personal identification numbers, such as social security numbers; protecting personal information collected on the Internet from individuals not covered by COPPA; and limiting the use of data mining for homeland security. In 2015 the FTC was researching new guidance for the protection of privacy and the Internet of Things (IoT), and mobile health apps (Federal Trade Commission, 2015).

In 2012, the FTC extended its FIP doctrine to address the issue of behavioral targeting. However, the government, privacy groups, and the online ad industry are still at loggerheads over two issues. Privacy advocates want both an opt-in policy at all sites and a national Do Not Track list. The online industry opposes these moves and continues to insist that an opt-out capability is the only way to avoid tracking. Nevertheless, there is an emerging consensus among all parties that greater transparency and user control (especially making opting out of tracking the default option) is required to deal with behavioral tracking. Public opinion polls show an ongoing distrust of online marketers. Although there are many studies of privacy issues at the federal level, there has been no significant legislation in recent years. A 2016 survey by the Pew Research Center found that 91 percent of Americans feel consumers have lost control of their personal information online and 86 percent have taken steps to protect their information online.

Privacy protections have also been added to recent laws deregulating financial services and safeguarding the maintenance and transmission of health information about individuals. The Gramm-Leach-Bliley Act of 1999, which repeals earlier restrictions on affiliations among banks, securities firms, and insurance companies, includes some privacy protection for consumers of financial services. All financial institutions are required to disclose their policies and practices for protecting the privacy of nonpublic personal information and to allow customers to opt out of information-sharing arrangements with nonaffiliated third parties.

The Health Insurance Portability and Accountability Act (HIPAA) of 1996, which took effect on April 14, 2003, includes privacy protection for medical records. The law gives patients access to their personal medical records that healthcare providers, hospitals, and health insurers maintain and the right to authorize how protected information about themselves can be used or disclosed. Doctors, hospitals, and other healthcare providers must limit the disclosure of personal information about patients to the minimum amount necessary to achieve a given purpose.

The European Directive on Data Protection

In Europe, privacy protection is much more stringent than in the United States. Unlike the United States, European countries do not allow businesses to use personally identifiable information without consumers' prior consent. In 1998, the European Commission's Data Protection Directive went into effect, requiring companies in European Union (EU) nations to inform people when they collect information about them and disclose how it will be stored and used. Customers must provide their **informed consent** before any company can legally use data about them, and they have the right to access that information, correct it, and request that no further data be collected. Informed consent can be defined as consent given with knowledge of all the facts needed to make a rational decision. Individual EU member nations translated these principles into their own laws and prohibited the transfer of personal data to countries, such as the United States, that do not have similar privacy protection regulations. In 2009, the European Parliament passed new rules governing the use of third-party cookies for behavioral tracking purposes. These new rules require website visitors to give explicit consent to be tracked by cookies and websites to have highly visible warnings on their pages if third-party cookies are being used (European Parliament, 2009).

In 2012, the EU changed its data protection rules to apply to all companies providing services in Europe and required Internet companies, such as Amazon, Facebook, Apple, Google, and others, to obtain explicit consent from consumers about the use of their personal data, delete information at the user's request, and retain information only as long as absolutely necessary. In 2014, the European Parliament extended greater control to Internet users by establishing the "right to be forgotten," which gives EU citizens the right to ask Google and social network sites to remove their personal information. Although the privacy policies of U.S. firms (in contrast to the government's) are largely voluntary, in Europe, corporate privacy policies are mandated and more consistent across jurisdictions.

The European Commission and the U.S. Department of Commerce developed a safe harbor framework for U.S. firms. A **safe harbor** is a private, self-regulating policy and enforcement mechanism that meets the objectives of government regulators and legislation but does not involve government regulation or enforcement. U.S. businesses would be allowed to use personal data from EU countries if the firms developed privacy protection policies that met EU standards. Enforcement would occur in the United States by using self-policing, regulation, and government enforcement of fair trade statutes.

By 2015 the EU started taking steps to replace safe harbor and the Data Protection Directive with a more stringent **General Data Protection**

Regulation (GDPR). The GDPR applies to any firm operating in any EU country, requires unambiguous consent to use personal data for purposes like tracking individuals across the web, and limits the use of data for purposes other than those for which it was collected (such as constructing user profiles). It also strengthens the right to be forgotten by allowing individuals to remove personal data from social platforms like Facebook and to prevent such companies from collecting any new information. Companies operating in the EU are required to delete personal information once it no longer serves the purpose for which it was collected (European Commission, 2016).

Following the revelation that U.S. government intelligence agencies had access to personal information on EU citizens, and a growing sense that Facebook and Google were not complying with EU policies, the EU GDPR was revised in 2016 to further strengthen users' ability to control what information is collected and retained, with whom it is shared, and how and where it is processed. Fines for failure to comply were increased to up to 4 percent of a firm's global revenue (about $1.6 billion for Facebook). GDPR also created a single EU privacy policy that governed all 28 nations in the Union. One result in Europe, but not in the United States, is that ad targeting will be reduced, along with the likelihood that ads will follow users around the Internet. The GDPR went into effect in May 2018. Facebook, Google, and Microsoft are building major data centers in Europe, and are planning to implement the GDPR regulations worldwide.

Internet Challenges to Privacy

Internet technology has posed new challenges for the protection of individual privacy. Websites track searches that have been conducted, the websites and web pages visited, the online content a person has accessed, and what items that person has inspected or purchased over the web. This monitoring and tracking of website visitors occurs in the background without the visitor's knowledge. It is conducted not just by individual websites but by advertising networks such as Microsoft Advertising, Yahoo, and Google's DoubleClick that are capable of tracking personal browsing behavior across thousands of websites. Both website publishers and the advertising industry defend tracking of individuals across the web because doing so allows more relevant ads to be targeted to users, and this pays for the cost of publishing websites. In this sense, it's like broadcast television: advertiser-supported content that is free to the user. The commercial demand for this personal information is virtually insatiable. However, these practices also impinge on individual privacy.

Cookies are small text files deposited on a computer hard drive when a user visits websites. Cookies identify the visitor's web browser software and track visits to the website. When the visitor returns to a site that has stored a cookie, the website software searches the visitor's computer, finds the cookie, and knows what that person has done in the past. It may also update the cookie, depending on the activity during the visit. In this way, the site can customize its content for each visitor's interests. For example, if you purchase a book on Amazon.com and return later from the same browser, the site will welcome you by name and recommend other books of interest based on your past purchases. DoubleClick, described earlier in this chapter, uses cookies to build its dossiers with details of online purchases and examine the behavior of website visitors. Figure 4.3 illustrates how cookies work.

Websites using cookie technology cannot directly obtain visitors' names and addresses. However, if a person has registered at a site, that information can be combined with cookie data to identify the visitor. Website owners can also combine the data they have gathered from cookies and other website monitoring

FIGURE 4.3 HOW COOKIES IDENTIFY WEB VISITORS

Cookies are written by a website on a visitor's computer. When the visitor returns to that website, the web server requests the ID number from the cookie and uses it to access the data stored by that server on that visitor. The website can then use these data to display personalized information.

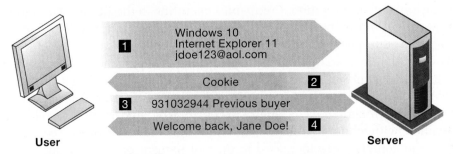

1. The web server reads the user's web browser and determines the operating system, browser name, version number, Internet address, and other information.
2. The server transmits a tiny text file with user identification information called a cookie, which the user's browser receives and stores on the user's computer hard drive.
3. When the user returns to the website, the server requests the contents of any cookie it deposited previously in the user's computer.
4. The web server reads the cookie, identifies the visitor, and calls up data on the user.

tools with personal data from other sources, such as offline data collected from surveys or paper catalog purchases, to develop very detailed profiles of their visitors.

There are now even more subtle and surreptitious tools for surveillance of Internet users. **Web beacons**, also called *web bugs* (or simply tracking files), are tiny software programs that keep a record of users' online clickstreams. They report this data back to whomever owns the tracking file, which is invisibly embedded in email messages and web pages to monitor the behavior of the user visiting a website or sending email. Web beacons are placed on popular websites by third-party firms who pay the websites a fee for access to their audience. So how common is web tracking? In a path-breaking series of articles in the *Wall Street Journal*, researchers examined the tracking files on 50 of the most popular U.S. websites. What they found revealed a very widespread surveillance system. On the 50 sites, they discovered 3,180 tracking files installed on visitor computers. Only one site, Wikipedia, had no tracking files. Two-thirds of the tracking files came from 131 companies whose primary business is identifying and tracking Internet users to create consumer profiles that can be sold to advertising firms looking for specific types of customers. The biggest trackers were Google, Microsoft, and Quantcast, all of whom are in the business of selling ads to advertising firms and marketers. A follow-up study found tracking on the 50 most popular sites had risen nearly fivefold due to the growth of online ad auctions where advertisers buy the data about users' web-browsing behavior.

Other **spyware** can secretly install itself on an Internet user's computer by piggybacking on larger applications. Once installed, the spyware calls out to websites to send banner ads and other unsolicited material to the user, and it can report the user's movements on the Internet to other computers. More information is available about intrusive software in Chapter 8.

Nearly 80 percent of global Internet users use Google Search and other Google services, making Google the world's largest collector of online user data. Whatever Google does with its data has an enormous impact on online privacy. Most experts believe that Google possesses the largest collection of personal information in the world—more data on more people than any government agency. The nearest competitor is Facebook.

After Google acquired the advertising network DoubleClick in 2007, it began using behavioral targeting to help display more relevant ads based on users' search activities and to target individuals as they move from one site to another to show them display or banner ads. Google allows tracking software on its search pages, and using DoubleClick, it can track users across the Internet. One of its programs enables advertisers to target ads based on the search histories of Google users, along with any other information the user submits to Google such as age, demographics, region, and web activities (such as blogging). Google's AdSense program enables Google to help advertisers select keywords and design ads for various market segments based on search histories such as helping a clothing website create and test ads targeted at teenage females. Google now displays targeted ads on YouTube and Google mobile applications, and its DoubleClick ad network serves up targeted banner ads.

The United States has allowed businesses to gather transaction information generated in the marketplace and then use that information for other marketing purposes without obtaining the informed consent of the individual whose information is being used. These firms argue that when users agree to the sites' terms of service, they are also agreeing to allow the site to collect information about their online activities. An **opt-out** model of informed consent permits the collection of personal information until the consumer specifically requests the data not to be collected. Privacy advocates would like to see wider use of an **opt-in** model of informed consent in which a business is prohibited from collecting any personal information unless the consumer specifically takes action to approve information collection and use. Here, the default option is no collection of user information.

The online industry has preferred self-regulation to privacy legislation for protecting consumers. Members of the advertising network industry, including Google's DoubleClick, have created an industry association called the Network Advertising Initiative (NAI) to develop its own privacy policies to help consumers opt out of advertising network programs and provide consumers redress from abuses.

Individual firms such as Microsoft, Mozilla Foundation, Yahoo, and Google have recently adopted policies on their own in an effort to address public concern about tracking people online. Microsoft's Internet Explorer 11 web browser was released in 2015 with the opt-out option as the default, but this was changed to opt-in by default because most websites ignored the request to opt out. Other browsers have opt-out options, but users need to turn them on, and most users fail to do this. AOL established an opt-out policy that allows users of its site to choose not to be tracked. Yahoo follows NAI guidelines and allows opt-out for tracking and web beacons (web bugs). Google has reduced retention time for tracking data.

In general, most Internet businesses do little to protect the privacy of their customers, and consumers do not do as much as they should to protect themselves. For commercial websites that depend on advertising to support themselves, most revenue derives from selling access to customer information. Of the companies that do post privacy policies on their websites, about half do not monitor their sites to ensure that they adhere to these policies. The vast majority of online customers claim they are concerned about online privacy, but fewer than half read the privacy statements on websites. In general, website privacy policies require a law degree to understand and are ambiguous about key terms (Laudon and Traver, 2019). Today, what firms such as Facebook and

Google call a privacy policy is in fact a data use policy. The concept of privacy is associated with consumer rights, which firms do not wish to recognize. A data use policy simply tells customers how the information will be used without any mention of rights.

A group of students at the University of California at Berkeley conducted surveys of online users and of complaints filed with the FTC involving privacy issues. Some results showed that people feel they have no control over the information collected about them, and they don't know to whom to complain. Websites collect all this information but do not let users have access, their policies are unclear, and they share data with affiliates but never identify who the affiliates are and how many there are. Web bug trackers are ubiquitous, and users are not informed of trackers on the pages they visit. The results of this study and others suggest that consumers want some controls on what personal information can be collected, what is done with the information, and the ability to opt out of the entire tracking enterprise. (The full report is available at knowprivacy.org.)

Technical Solutions

In addition to legislation, there are a few technologies that can protect user privacy during interactions with websites. Many of these tools are used for encrypting email, for making email or surfing activities appear anonymous, for preventing client computers from accepting cookies, or for detecting and eliminating spyware. For the most part, technical solutions have failed to protect users from being tracked as they move from one site to another.

Many browsers have Do Not Track options. For users who have selected the Do Not Track browser option, their browser will send a request to websites that the user's behavior not be tracked, but websites are not obligated to honor these requests. There is no online advertising industry agreement on how to respond to Do Not Track requests nor, currently, any legislation requiring websites to stop tracking. Private browser encryption software or apps on mobile devices provide consumers a powerful opportunity to at least keep their messages private.

Property Rights: Intellectual Property

Contemporary information systems have severely challenged existing laws and social practices that protect **intellectual property**. Intellectual property is defined as tangible and intangible products of the mind created by individuals or corporations. Information technology has made it difficult to protect intellectual property because computerized information can be so easily copied or distributed on networks. Intellectual property is subject to a variety of protections under four legal traditions: copyright, patents, trademarks, and trade secrets.

Copyright

Copyright is a statutory grant that protects creators of intellectual property from having their work copied by others for any purpose during the life of the author plus an additional 70 years after the author's death. For corporate-owned works, copyright protection lasts for 95 years after their initial creation. Congress has extended copyright protection to books, periodicals, lectures, dramas, musical compositions, maps, drawings, artwork of any kind, and motion pictures. The intent behind copyright laws has been to encourage creativity and authorship by ensuring that creative people receive the financial and other benefits of their work. Most industrial nations have their own copyright laws, and there are several international conventions and bilateral agreements through which nations coordinate and enforce their laws.

In the mid-1960s, the Copyright Office began registering software programs, and in 1980, Congress passed the Computer Software Copyright Act, which clearly provides protection for software program code and copies of the original sold in commerce; it sets forth the rights of the purchaser to use the software while the creator retains legal title.

Copyright protects against copying entire programs or their parts. Damages and relief are readily obtained for infringement. The drawback to copyright protection is that the underlying ideas behind a work are not protected, only their manifestation in a work. A competitor can use your software, understand how it works, and build new software that follows the same concepts without infringing on a copyright.

Look-and-feel copyright infringement lawsuits are precisely about the distinction between an idea and its expression. For instance, in the early 1990s, Apple Computer sued Microsoft Corporation and Hewlett-Packard for infringement of the expression of Apple's Macintosh interface, claiming that the defendants copied the expression of overlapping windows. The defendants countered that the idea of overlapping windows can be expressed only in a single way and, therefore, was not protectable under the merger doctrine of copyright law. When ideas and their expression merge, the expression cannot be copyrighted.

In general, courts appear to be following the reasoning of a 1989 case—*Brown Bag Software v. Symantec Corp*—in which the court dissected the elements of software alleged to be infringing. The court found that similar concept, function, general functional features (e.g., drop-down menus), and colors are not protectable by copyright law (*Brown Bag Software v. Symantec Corp.*, 1992).

Patents

A **patent** grants the owner an exclusive monopoly on the ideas behind an invention for 20 years. The congressional intent behind patent law was to ensure that inventors of new machines, devices, or methods receive the full financial and other rewards of their labor and yet make widespread use of the invention possible by providing detailed diagrams for those wishing to use the idea under license from the patent's owner. The granting of a patent is determined by the United States Patent and Trademark Office and relies on court rulings.

The key concepts in patent law are originality, novelty, and invention. The Patent Office did not accept applications for software patents routinely until a 1981 Supreme Court decision held that computer programs could be part of a patentable process. Since that time, hundreds of patents have been granted, and thousands await consideration.

The strength of patent protection is that it grants a monopoly on the underlying concepts and ideas of software. The difficulty is passing stringent criteria of nonobviousness (e.g., the work must reflect some special understanding and contribution), originality, and novelty as well as years of waiting to receive protection.

In what some call the patent trial of the century, in 2011, Apple sued Samsung for violating its patents for iPhones, iPads, and iPods. On August 24, 2012, a California jury in federal district court awarded Apple $1 billion in damages and prohibited Samsung from selling its new Galaxy 10 tablet computer in the United States. The decision established criteria for determining just how close a competitor can come to an industry-leading and standard-setting product like Apple's iPhone before it violates the design and utility patents of the leading firm. Samsung subsequently won a patent infringement case against Apple that banned a handful of older iPhone and iPad devices. In 2014, Apple sued Samsung again, claiming infringement of five patents covering hardware and software techniques for handling photos, videos, and lists used on the Samsung Galaxy 5. In 2015, the U.S. Court of Appeals reaffirmed that Samsung had copied specific design patents, but reduced the damages asked by Apple from $2 billion to $930 million. This lawsuit returned to court in May 2018 to consider how to calculate the damages caused by Samsung's infringement.

To make matters more complicated, Apple has been one of Samsung's largest customers for flash memory processors, graphic chips, solid-state drives, and display parts that are used in Apple's iPhones, iPads, iPod Touch devices, and MacBooks. The Samsung and Apple patent cases are indicative of the complex relationships among the leading computer firms.

Trademarks

Trademarks are the marks, symbols, and images used to distinguish products in the marketplace. Trademark laws protect consumers by ensuring they receive what they paid for. These laws also protect the investments that firms have made to bring products to market. Typical trademark infringement violations occur when one firm appropriates or pirates the marks of a competing firm. Infringement also occurs when firms dilute the value of another firm's marks by weakening the connection between a mark and the product. For instance, if a search engine firm copies the trademarked Google icon, colors, and images, it would be infringing on Google's trademarks. It would also be diluting the connection between the Google search service and its trademarks, potentially creating confusion in the marketplace.

Trade Secrets

Any intellectual work product—a formula, device, pattern, or compilation of data—used for a business purpose can be classified as a **trade secret**, provided it is not based on information in the public domain. Protections for trade secrets vary from state to state. In general, trade secret laws grant a monopoly on the ideas behind a work product, but it can be a very tenuous monopoly.

Software that contains novel or unique elements, procedures, or compilations can be considered a trade secret. Trade secret law protects the actual ideas in a work product, not only their manifestation. To make this claim, the creator or owner must take care to bind employees and customers with nondisclosure agreements and prevent the secret from falling into the public domain.

The limitation of trade secret protection is that, although virtually all software programs of any complexity contain unique elements of some sort, it is difficult to prevent the ideas in the work from falling into the public domain when the software is widely distributed.

Challenges to Intellectual Property Rights

Contemporary information technologies, especially software, pose severe challenges to existing intellectual property regimes and, therefore, create significant ethical, social, and political issues. Digital media differ from books, periodicals, and other media in terms of ease of replication; ease of transmission; ease of alteration; compactness, making theft easy; and difficulties in establishing uniqueness.

The proliferation of digital networks, including the Internet, has made it even more difficult to protect intellectual property. Before widespread use of networks, copies of software, books, magazine articles, or films had to be stored on physical media, such as paper, computer disks, or videotape, creating some hurdles to distribution. Using networks, information can be more widely reproduced and distributed. The BSA Global Software Survey conducted by International Data Corporation and The Software Alliance (also known as BSA) reported that 37 percent of the software installed on personal computers was unlicensed in 2018 (The Software Alliance, 2018).

The Internet was designed to transmit information freely around the world, including copyrighted information. You can easily copy and distribute virtually anything to millions of people worldwide, even if they are using different types of computer systems. Information can be illicitly copied from one place and distributed through other systems and networks even though these parties do not willingly participate in the infringement.

Individuals have been illegally copying and distributing digitized music files on the Internet for several decades. File-sharing services such as Napster and, later, Grokster, Kazaa, Morpheus, Megaupload, and The Pirate Bay sprang up to help users locate and swap digital music and video files, including those protected by copyright. Illegal file sharing became so widespread that it threatened the viability of the music recording industry and, at one point, consumed 20 percent of Internet bandwidth. The recording industry won several legal battles for shutting these services down, but it has not been able to halt illegal file sharing entirely. The motion picture and cable television industries are waging similar battles. Several European nations have worked with U.S. authorities to shut down illegal sharing sites, with mixed results.

As legitimate online music stores such as iTunes and streaming services such as Pandora expanded, illegal file sharing significantly declined. The Apple iTunes Store legitimized paying for music and entertainment and created a closed environment from which music and videos could not be easily copied and widely distributed unless played on Apple devices. Amazon's Kindle also protects the rights of publishers and writers because its books cannot be copied to the Internet and distributed. Streaming of Internet radio, on services such as Pandora and Spotify, and Hollywood movies (at sites such as Hulu and Netflix) also inhibit piracy because the streams cannot be easily recorded on separate devices and videos cannot be downloaded so easily. Despite these gains in legitimate online music platforms, artists and record labels have experienced a 50 percent decline in revenues and the loss of thousands of jobs since 2000.

The **Digital Millennium Copyright Act (DMCA)** of 1998 also provides some copyright protection. The DMCA implemented a World Intellectual Property Organization Treaty that makes it illegal to circumvent technology-based protections of copyrighted materials. Internet service providers (ISPs) are required to take down sites of copyright infringers they are hosting when the ISPs are notified of the problem. Microsoft and other major software and information content firms are represented by the Software and Information Industry Association (SIIA), which lobbies for new laws and enforcement of existing laws to protect intellectual property around the world. The SIIA runs an antipiracy hotline for individuals to report piracy activities, offers educational programs to help organizations combat software piracy, and has published guidelines for employee use of software.

4-4 How have information systems affected laws for establishing accountability and liability and the quality of everyday life?

Along with privacy and property laws, new information technologies are challenging existing liability laws and social practices for holding individuals and institutions accountable. If a person is injured by a machine controlled, in part, by software, who should be held accountable and, therefore, held liable? Should a social network site like Facebook or Twitter be held liable and accountable for the posting of pornographic material or racial insults, or should it be held harmless against any liability for what users post (as is true of common carriers, such as the telephone system)? What about the Internet? If you outsource your information processing to the cloud, and the cloud provider fails to provide adequate service, what can you do? Cloud providers often claim the software you are using is the problem, not the cloud servers.

Computer-Related Liability Problems

In late 2013 hackers obtained credit card, debit card, and additional personal information about 70 to 110 million customers of Target, one of the largest U.S. retailers. Target's sales and reputation took an immediate hit from which it has still not completely recovered. Target says it has spent over $60 million to strengthen its systems. In 2015, Target agreed to pay $10 million to customers and $19 million to Mastercard. It has paid an even greater price through the loss of sales and trust.

Who is liable for any economic harm caused to individuals or businesses whose credit cards were compromised? Is Target responsible for allowing the breach to occur despite efforts it did make to secure the information? Or is this just a cost of doing business in a credit card world where customers and businesses have insurance policies to protect them against losses? Customers, for instance, have a maximum liability of $50 for credit card theft under federal banking law.

Are information system managers responsible for the harm that corporate systems can do? Beyond IT managers, insofar as computer software is part of a machine, and the machine injures someone physically or economically, the producer of the software and the operator can be held liable for damages. Insofar as the software acts like a book, storing and displaying information, courts have been reluctant to hold authors, publishers, and booksellers liable for contents (the exception being instances of fraud or defamation); hence, courts have been wary of holding software authors liable.

In general, it is very difficult (if not impossible) to hold software producers liable for their software products that are considered to be like books, regardless of the physical or economic harm that results. Historically, print publishers of books and periodicals have not been held liable because of fears that liability claims would interfere with First Amendment rights guaranteeing freedom of expression. The kind of harm software failures cause is rarely fatal and typically inconveniences users but does not physically harm them (the exception being medical devices).

What about software as a service? ATMs are a service provided to bank customers. If this service fails, customers will be inconvenienced and perhaps harmed economically if they cannot access their funds in a timely manner. Should liability protections be extended to software publishers and operators of defective financial, accounting, simulation, or marketing systems?

Software is very different from books. Software users may develop expectations of infallibility about software; software is less easily inspected than a book, and it is more difficult to compare with other software products for quality; software claims to perform a task rather than describe a task, as a book does; and people come to depend on services essentially based on software. Given the centrality of software to everyday life, the chances are excellent that liability law will extend its reach to include software even when the software merely provides an information service.

Telephone systems have not been held liable for the messages transmitted because they are regulated common carriers. In return for their right to provide telephone service, they must provide access to all, at reasonable rates, and achieve acceptable reliability. Likewise, cable networks are considered private networks not subject to regulation, but broadcasters using the public airwaves are subject to a wide variety of federal and local constraints on content and facilities. In the United States, with few exceptions, websites are not held liable for content posted on their sites regardless of whether it was placed there by the website owners or users.

System Quality: Data Quality and System Errors

White Christmas turned into a blackout for millions of Netflix customers and social network users on December 24, 2012. The blackout was caused by the failure of Amazon's cloud computing service (AWS), which provides storage and computing power for many websites and services, including Netflix. The loss of service lasted for a day. Amazon blamed it on elastic load balancing, a software program that balances the loads on all its cloud servers to prevent overload. Amazon's cloud computing services have had several subsequent outages, although none as long-lasting as the Christmas Eve outage. In September 2016, AWS experienced a five-hour outage. Outages at cloud computing services are rare but recur. These outages have called into question the reliability and quality of cloud services. Are these outages acceptable?

The debate over liability and accountability for unintentional consequences of system use raises a related but independent moral dimension: What is an acceptable, technologically feasible level of system quality? At what point should system managers say, "Stop testing, we've done all we can to perfect this software. Ship it!" Individuals and organizations may be held responsible for avoidable and foreseeable consequences, which they have a duty to perceive and correct. The gray area is that some system errors are foreseeable and correctable only at very great expense, expense so great that pursuing this level of perfection is not feasible economically—no one could afford the product.

For example, although software companies try to debug their products before releasing them to the marketplace, they knowingly ship buggy products because the time and cost of fixing all minor errors would prevent these products from ever being released. What if the product was not offered on the marketplace? Would social welfare as a whole falter and perhaps even decline? Carrying this further, just what is the responsibility of a producer of computer services—should it withdraw the product that can never be perfect, warn the user, or forget about the risk (let the buyer beware)?

Three principal sources of poor system performance are (1) software bugs and errors, (2) hardware or facility failures caused by natural or other causes, and (3) poor input data quality. The Chapter 8 Learning Track discusses why zero defects in software code of any complexity cannot be achieved and why the seriousness of remaining bugs cannot be estimated. Hence, there is a technological barrier to perfect software, and users must be aware of the potential for catastrophic failure. The software industry has not yet arrived at testing standards for producing software of acceptable but imperfect performance.

Although software bugs and facility catastrophes are likely to be widely reported in the press, by far the most common source of business system failure is data quality (see Chapter 6). Few companies routinely measure the quality of their data, but individual organizations report data error rates ranging from 0.5 to 30 percent.

Quality of Life: Equity, Access, and Boundaries

The negative social costs of introducing information technologies and systems are beginning to mount along with the power of the technology. Many of these negative social consequences are not violations of individual rights or property crimes. Nevertheless, they can be extremely harmful to individuals, societies, and political institutions. Computers and information technologies potentially can destroy valuable elements of our culture and society even while they bring us benefits. If there is a balance of good and bad consequences of using information systems, whom do we hold responsible for the bad consequences? Next, we briefly examine some of the negative social consequences of systems, considering individual, social, and political responses.

Balancing Power: Center Versus Periphery

An early fear of the computer age was that huge, centralized mainframe computers would centralize power in the nation's capital, resulting in a Big Brother society, as was suggested in George Orwell's novel *1984*. The shift toward highly decentralized client–server computing, coupled with an ideology of empowerment of Twitter and social media users, and the decentralization of decision making to lower organizational levels, until recently reduced the fears of power centralization in government institutions. Yet much of the empowerment described in popular business magazines is trivial. Lower-level employees may be empowered to make minor decisions, but the key policy decisions can be as centralized as in the past. At the same time, corporate Internet behemoths such as Google, Apple, Yahoo, Amazon, and Microsoft have come to dominate the collection and analysis of personal private information of all citizens. Since the terrorist attacks against the United States on September 11, 2001, the federal government has greatly expanded its use of this private sector information under the authority of the Patriot Act of 2001, and subsequent and secret executive orders. In this sense, the power of information has become more centralized in the hands of a few private oligopolies and large government agencies.

Rapidity of Change: Reduced Response Time to Competition

Information systems have helped to create much more efficient national and international markets. Today's rapid-moving global marketplace has reduced the normal social buffers that permitted businesses many years to adjust to competition. Time-based competition has an ugly side; the business you work for may not have enough time to respond to global competitors and may be wiped out in a year along with your job. We stand the risk of developing a just-in-time society with just-in-time jobs and just-in-time workplaces, families, and vacations. One impact of Uber (see Chapter 10) and other on-demand services firms is to create just-in-time jobs with no benefits or insurance for employees.

Maintaining Boundaries: Family, Work, and Leisure

The danger of ubiquitous computing, telecommuting, nomad computing, mobile computing, and the do-anything-anywhere computing environment is that it is actually coming true. The traditional boundaries that separate work from family and just plain leisure have been weakened.

© David Pereiras Villagrá/123RF

Although some people enjoy the convenience of working at home, the do-anything-anywhere computing environment can blur the traditional boundaries between work and family time.

Although writers have traditionally worked just about anywhere, the advent of information systems, coupled with the growth of knowledge-work occupations, means that more and more people are working when traditionally they would have been playing or communicating with family and friends. The work umbrella now extends far beyond the eight-hour day into commuting time, vacation time, and leisure time. The explosive growth and use of smartphones have only heightened the sense of many employees that they are never away from work.

Even leisure time spent on the computer threatens these close social relationships. Extensive Internet and cell phone use, even for entertainment or recreational purposes, takes people away from their family and friends. Among middle school and teenage children, it can lead to harmful antisocial behavior, such as the recent upsurge in cyberbullying.

Weakening these institutions poses clear-cut risks. Family and friends historically have provided powerful support mechanisms for individuals, and they act as balance points in a society by preserving private life, providing a place for people to collect their thoughts, think in ways contrary to their employer, and dream.

Dependence and Vulnerability

Today, our businesses, governments, schools, and private associations, such as churches, are incredibly dependent on information systems and are, therefore, highly vulnerable if these systems fail. Think of what would happen if the nation's electric power grid shut down, with no backup structure to make up for the loss of the system. With systems now as ubiquitous as the telephone system, it is startling to remember that there are no regulatory or standard-setting forces in place that are similar to telephone, electrical, radio, television, or other public utility technologies. The absence of standards and the criticality of some system applications will probably call forth demands for national standards and perhaps regulatory oversight.

Computer Crime and Abuse

New technologies, including computers, create new opportunities for committing crime by creating new, valuable items to steal, new ways to steal them, and new ways to harm others. **Computer crime** is the commission of illegal acts by using a computer or against a computer system. Simply accessing a computer system without authorization or with intent to do harm, even by accident, is now a federal crime. The most frequent types of incidents comprise a greatest hits list of cybercrime: malware, phishing, network interruption, spyware, and denial of service attacks (PwC, 2016). The true cost of all computer crime is unknown, but it is estimated to be in the billions of dollars. You can find a more detailed discussion of computer crime in Chapter 8.

Computer abuse is the commission of acts involving a computer that may not be illegal but are considered unethical. The popularity of the Internet, email, and mobile phones has turned one form of computer abuse—spamming—into a serious problem for both individuals and businesses. Originally, **spam** was junk email an organization or individual sent to a mass audience of Internet users who had expressed no interest in the product or service being marketed. Spammers tend to market pornography, fraudulent deals and services, outright scams, and other products not widely approved in most civilized societies. Some countries have passed laws to outlaw spamming or restrict its use. In the United States, it is still legal if it does not involve fraud and the sender and subject of the email are properly identified.

Spamming has mushroomed because it costs only a few cents to send thousands of messages advertising wares to Internet users. The percentage of all email that is spam was estimated at around 60 percent in 2017 (Symantec, 2018). Most spam originates from bot networks, which consist of thousands of captured PCs that can initiate and relay spam messages. Spam costs for businesses are very high (estimated at more than $50 billion per year) because of the computing and network resources and the time required to deal with billions of unwanted email messages.

Identity and financial-theft cybercriminals are targeting smartphones as users check email, do online banking, pay bills, and reveal personal information. Cell phone spam usually comes in the form of SMS text messages, but increasingly, users are receiving spam in their Facebook News feed and messaging service as well.

ISPs and individuals can combat spam by using spam filtering software to block suspicious email before it enters a recipient's email inbox. However, spam filters may block legitimate messages. Spammers know how to skirt filters by continually changing their email accounts, by incorporating spam messages in images, by embedding spam in email attachments and digital greeting cards, and by using other people's computers that have been hijacked by botnets (see Chapter 8). Many spam messages are sent from one country although another country hosts the spam website.

Spamming is more tightly regulated in Europe than in the United States. In 2002, the European Parliament passed a ban on unsolicited commercial messaging. Digital marketing can be targeted only to people who have given prior consent.

The U.S. CAN-SPAM Act of 2003, which went into effect in 2004, does not outlaw spamming but does ban deceptive email practices by requiring commercial email messages to display accurate subject lines, identify the true senders, and offer recipients an easy way to remove their names from email lists. It also prohibits the use of fake return addresses. A few people have been prosecuted under this law, but it has had a negligible impact on spamming, in large part because of the Internet's exceptionally poor security and the use of offshore servers and botnets. Most large-scale spamming has moved offshore to Russia and Eastern Europe, where hackers control global botnets capable of generating billions of spam messages. One of the largest spam networks in recent years was the Russian network Festi, based in St. Petersburg. Festi is best known as the spam generator behind the global Viagra-spam industry.

Employment: Trickle-Down Technology and Reengineering Job Loss

Reengineering work is typically hailed in the information systems community as a major benefit of new information technology. It is much less frequently noted that redesigning business processes has caused millions of mid-level factory managers and clerical workers to lose their jobs. Some economists have sounded new alarms about information and computer technology threatening middle-class, white-collar jobs (in addition to blue-collar factory jobs). Erik Brynjolfsson and Andrew P. McAfee argue that the pace of automation has picked up in recent years because of a combination of technologies, including robotics, numerically controlled machines, computerized inventory control, pattern recognition, voice recognition, and online commerce. One result is that machines can now do a great many jobs heretofore reserved for humans, including tech support, call center work, X-ray examination, and even legal document review (Brynjolfsson and McAfee, 2011).

These views contrast with other economists' assessments that new technologies created as many or more new jobs than they destroyed. In some cases, employment has grown or remained unchanged in industries like finance, where investment in IT capital is highest. For instance, the growth of e-commerce has led to a decline in retail sales jobs but an increase in jobs for warehouse workers, supervisors, and delivery work. These economists also believe that bright, educated workers who are displaced by technology will move to better jobs in fast-growth industries. Missing from this equation are unskilled, blue-collar workers and older, less–well-educated middle managers. It is not clear that these groups can be retrained easily for high-quality, high-paying jobs. The Interactive Session on Organizations explores this issue.

Equity and Access: Increasing Racial and Social Class Cleavages

Does everyone have an equal opportunity to participate in the digital age? Will the social, economic, and cultural gaps that exist in the United States and other societies be reduced by information systems technology? Or will the cleavages be increased, permitting the better-off to become even more better-off relative to others?

These questions have not yet been fully answered because the impact of systems technology on various groups in society has not been thoroughly studied. What is known is that information, knowledge, computers, and access to these resources through educational institutions and public libraries are inequitably distributed along ethnic and social class lines, as are many other information resources. Several studies have found that low-income groups in the United States are less likely to have computers or online Internet access even though computer ownership and Internet access have soared in the past five years. Although the gap in computer access is narrowing, higher-income families in each ethnic group are still more likely to have home computers and broadband Internet access than lower-income families in the same group. Moreover, the children of higher-income families are far more likely to use their Internet access to pursue educational goals, whereas lower-income children are much more likely to spend time on entertainment and games. This is called the "time-wasting" gap.

Left uncorrected, this **digital divide** could lead to a society of information haves, who are computer literate and skilled, versus a large group of information have-nots, who are computer illiterate and unskilled. Public interest groups want to narrow this digital divide by making digital information services—including the Internet—available to virtually everyone, just as basic telephone service is now.

INTERACTIVE SESSION   ORGANIZATIONS

Will Automation Kill Jobs?

Dennis Kriebal of Youngstown, Ohio, had been a supervisor at an aluminum extrusion factory, where he punched out parts for cars and tractors. Six years ago, he lost his job to a robot, and since then has been doing odd jobs to keep afloat. Sherry Johnson used to work for the local newspaper in Marietta, Georgia, feeding paper into printing machines and laying out pages. She lost this job as well as others making medical equipment and working in inventory and filing to automation.

These situations illustrate the negative impact of computer technology on jobs. Far more U.S. jobs have been lost to robots and automation than to trade with China, Mexico, or any other country. According to a study by the Center for Business and Economic Research at Ball State University, about 87 percent of manufacturing job losses between 2000 and 2010 stemmed from factories becoming more efficient through automation and better technology. Only 13 percent of job losses were due to trade. For example, the U.S. steel industry lost 400,000 jobs between 1962 and 2005. A study by the American Economic Review found that steel shipments did not decline, but fewer people were needed to do the same amount of work as before, with major productivity gains from using mini mills (small plants that make specialty steel from scrap iron).

A November 2015 McKinsey Global Institute report by Michael Chui, James Manyika, and Mehdi Miremadi examined 2,000 distinct types of work activities in 800 occupations. The authors found that 45 percent of these work activities could be automated by 2055 using technologies that currently exist. About 51 percent of the work activities Americans perform involve predictable and routine physical work, data collection, and data processing. All of these tasks are ripe for some degree of automation. No one knows exactly how many U.S. jobs will be lost or how soon, but the researchers estimate that from 9 to 47 percent of jobs could eventually be affected and perhaps 5 percent of jobs eliminated entirely. These changes shouldn't lead to mass unemployment because automation could increase global productivity by 0.8 percent to 1.4 percent annually over the next 50 years and create many new jobs.

According to a study by MIT labor economist David Autor, automation advances up to this point have not eliminated most jobs. Sometimes machines do replace humans, as in agriculture and manufacturing, but not across an entire economy. Productivity gains from workforce automation have increased the demand for goods and services, in turn increasing the demand for new forms of labor. Jobs that have not been eliminated by automation are often enhanced by it. For example, since BMW's Spartanburg, South Carolina, plant automated many routine production tasks over the past decade, it has more than doubled its annual car production to more than 400,000 units. The Spartanburg labor force has grown from 4,200 workers to 10,000, and they handle vastly more complex autos. (Cars that once had 3,000 parts now have 15,000.)

The positive and negative impacts of technology are not delivered in an equal way. All the new jobs created by automation are not necessarily better jobs. There have been increases in high-paying jobs (such as accountants) but also in low-paying jobs such as food service workers and home health aides. Disappearing factory jobs have been largely replaced by new jobs in the service sector but often at lower wages.

Manufacturing jobs have been the hardest hit by robots and automation. There are more than 5 million fewer jobs in manufacturing today than in 2000. According to a study by economists Daron Acemoglu of MIT and Pascual Restrepo of Boston University, for every robot per thousand workers, up to six workers lost their jobs and wages fell as much as 0.75 percent. Acemoglu and Restrepo found very little employment increase in other occupations to offset job losses in manufacturing. That increase could eventually happen, but right now there are large numbers of people out of work in the United States, especially blue-collar men and women without college degrees. These researchers also found industrial robots were to blame for as many as 670,000 manufacturing jobs lost between 1990 and 2007, and this number will rise going forward because the number of industrial robots is predicted to quadruple. Acemoglu and Restrepo noted that a specific local economy, such as Detroit, could be especially hard-hit, although nationally the effects of robots are smaller because jobs were created in other places. The new jobs created by technology are not necessarily in the places losing jobs, such as the Rust Belt. Those forced out of a job by robots generally do not have the skills or mobility to assume the new jobs created by automation.

Automation is not just affecting manual labor and factory jobs. Computers are now capable of taking over certain kinds of white collar and service-sector work, including X-ray analysis and sifting through documents. Job opportunities are shrinking slightly for medical technicians, supervisors, and even lawyers. Work that requires creativity, management, information technology skills, or personal caregiving is least at risk.

According to Boston University economist James Bessen, the problem is not mass unemployment; it's transitioning people from one job to another. People need to learn new skills to work in the new economy. When the United States moved from an agrarian to an industrialized economy, high school education

expanded rapidly. By 1951 the average American had 6.2 more years of education than someone born 75 years earlier. Additional education enabled people to do new kinds of jobs in factories, hospitals, and schools.

Sources: William Wilkes, "How the World's Biggest Companies Are Fine-Tuning the Robot Revolution," *Wall Street Journal*, May 14, 2018; James Manyika and Michael Spence, "The False Choice Between Automation and Jobs," *Harvard Business Review*, February 5, 2018; Andrew Hobbs, "Automation Will Replace 9 Percent of U.S. Jobs in 2018," *Internet of Business*, February 16, 2018; Patrick Gillespie, "Rise of the Machines: Fear Robots, Not China or Mexico," *CNN Money*, January 30, 2017; Claire Cain Miller, "Evidence That Robots Are Winning the Race for American Jobs," *New York Times*, March 28, 2017; "The Long-Term Jobs Killer Is Not China, It's Automation," *New York Times*, December 21, 2016; "A Darker Theme in Obama's Farewell: Automation Can Divide Us," *New York Times*, January 12, 2017; Steve Lohr, "Robots Will Take Jobs, But Not as Fast as Some Fear," *New York Times*, January 12, 2017; Michael Chui, James Manyika, and Mehdi Miremadi, "Where Machines Could Replace Humans—and Where They Can't (Yet)," *McKinsey Quarterly*, July 2016; Stephen Gold, "The Future of Automation—and Your Job," *Industry Week*, January 18, 2016; and Christopher Mims, "Automation Can Actually Create More Jobs," *Wall Street Journal*, December 11, 2016.

CASE STUDY QUESTIONS

1. How does automating jobs pose an ethical dilemma? Who are the stakeholders? Identify the options that can be taken and the potential consequences of each.

2. If you were the owner of a factory deciding on whether to acquire robots to perform certain tasks, what people, organization, and technology factors would you consider?

Health Risks: RSI, CVS, and Cognitive Decline

A common occupational disease today is **repetitive stress injury (RSI)**. RSI occurs when muscle groups are forced through repetitive actions often with high-impact loads (such as tennis) or tens of thousands of repetitions under low-impact loads (such as working at a computer keyboard). The incidence of RSI is estimated to affect as much as one-third of the labor force and accounts for one-third of all disability cases.

The single largest source of RSI is computer keyboards. The most common kind of computer-related RSI is **carpal tunnel syndrome (CTS)**, in which pressure on the median nerve through the wrist's bony structure, called a carpal tunnel, produces pain. The pressure is caused by constant repetition of keystrokes: In a single shift, a word processor may perform 23,000 keystrokes. Symptoms of CTS include numbness, shooting pain, inability to grasp objects, and tingling. Millions of workers have been diagnosed with CTS. It affects an estimated 3 to 6 percent of the workforce (LeBlanc and Cestia, 2011).

Repetitive stress injury (RSI) is a leading occupational disease today. The single largest cause of RSI is computer keyboard work.

© Ian Allenden/123RF

RSI is avoidable. Designing workstations for a neutral wrist position (using a wrist rest to support the wrist), proper monitor stands, and footrests all contribute to proper posture and reduced RSI. Ergonomically correct keyboards are also an option. These measures should be supported by frequent rest breaks and rotation of employees to different jobs.

RSI is not the only occupational illness computers cause. Back and neck pain, leg stress, and foot pain also result from poor ergonomic designs of workstations. **Computer vision syndrome (CVS)** refers to any eyestrain condition related to display screen use in desktop computers, laptops, e-readers, smartphones, and handheld video games. CVS affects about 90 percent of people who spend three hours or more per day at a computer. Its symptoms, which are usually temporary, include headaches, blurred vision, and dry and irritated eyes.

In addition to these maladies, computer technology may be harming our cognitive functions or at least changing how we think and solve problems. Although the Internet has made it much easier for people to access, create, and use information, some experts believe that it is also preventing people from focusing and thinking clearly on their own. They argue that excessive use of computers (and smartphones—see the Interactive Session on Technology) reduces intelligence. One MIT scholar believes exposure to computers encourages looking up answers rather than engaging in real problem solving. Students, in this view, don't learn much surfing the web or answering email when compared to listening, drawing, arguing, looking, and exploring (Henry, 2011).

The computer has become part of our lives—personally as well as socially, culturally, and politically. It is unlikely that the issues and our choices will become easier as information technology continues to transform our world. The growth of the Internet and the information economy suggests that all the ethical and social issues we have described will be heightened further as we move further into the first digital century.

INTERACTIVE SESSION TECHNOLOGY

How Harmful Are Smartphones?

For many of us, smartphones have become indispensable, but they have also come under fire for their impact on the way we think and behave, especially among children. Two of the largest investors in Apple Inc. are urging the iPhone maker to take action against smartphone addiction among children over growing concerns about the negative effects of technology.

An open letter to Apple on January 6, 2018 from New York-based JANA Partners and the California State Teachers' Retirement System (CalSTRS) stated that the firm must do more to help children fight smartphone addiction. These two shareholders together control about $2 billion in Apple stock.

The investors' letter urged Apple to offer tools to prevent smartphone addiction and to provide more parental options for monitoring children's smartphone usage. The iOS operating system for Apple smartphones and tablets already has limited parental controls for restricting apps, features such as location sharing, and access to certain types of content. The investors felt Apple needs to do more—for example, enable parents to specify the age of the user of the phone during setup, establish limits on screen time, select hours of the day the phone can be used, and block social media services.

The average American teenager who uses a smartphone receives his or her first phone at age 10 and spends over 4.5 hours a day on it (excluding texting and talking). Seventy-eight percent of teens check their phones at least hourly and 50 percent report feeling "addicted" to their phones. The investors' letter cited a number of studies on the negative effects of heavy smartphone and social media use on the mental and physical health of children whose brains are still developing. These range from distractions in the classroom to a higher risk of suicide and depression.

A recent survey of over 2,300 teachers by the Center on Media and Child Health and the University of Alberta found that 67 percent of the teachers reported that the number of students who are negatively distracted by digital technologies in the classroom is growing. Seventy-five percent of these teachers think students' ability to focus on educational tasks has decreased. Research by psychology professor Jean Twenge of San Diego State University found that U.S. teenagers who spend 3 hours a day or more on electronic devices are 35 percent more likely, and those who spend 5 hours or more are 71 percent more

likely, to have a risk factor for suicide than those who spend less than 1 hour. This research also showed that eighth-graders who are heavy users of social media have a 27 percent higher risk of depression. Those who spend more than the average time playing sports, hanging out with friends in person, or doing homework have a significantly lower risk. Additionally, teens who spend 5 or more hours a day on electronic devices are 51 percent more likely to get less than 7 hours of sleep per night (versus the recommended 9).

Nicholas Carr, who has studied the impact of technology on business and culture, shares these concerns. He has been highly critical of the Internet's effect on cognition, and these cognitive effects extend to smartphone use. Carr worries that excessive use of mobile devices diminishes the capacity for concentration and contemplation.

Carr recognizes that smartphones provide many useful functions in a very handy form. However, this extraordinary usefulness gives them too much influence on our attention, thinking, and behavior. Smartphones shape our thoughts in deep and complicated ways, and their effects persist even when we aren't using the devices. Research suggests that the intellect weakens as the brain grows dependent on the technology.

Carr points to the work of Adrian Ward, a cognitive psychologist and marketing professor at the University of Texas at Austin, who for a decade has been studying how smartphones and the Internet affect people's thoughts and judgment. Ward has observed that using a smartphone, or even hearing one ring or vibrate, produces distractions that make it harder to concentrate on a difficult problem or job. Divided attention impedes reasoning and performance.

A study published in Applied Cognitive Psychology in April 2017 examined how smartphones affected learning in a lecture class with 160 students at the University of Arkansas at Monticello. It found that students who didn't bring their phones to the classroom scored a full letter-grade higher on a test of the material presented than those who brought their phones. It didn't matter whether students who brought their phones used them or not. A study of 91 U.K. secondary schools, published in 2016 in the journal *Labour Economics*, found that when schools ban smartphones, students' examination scores go up substantially, and the weakest students benefit the most.

Carr also observes that using smartphones extensively can be detrimental to social skills and relationships. Connecting with "friends" electronically via smartphones is not a substitute for genuine person-to-person relationships and face-to-face conversations.

Sources: "Letter from JANA Partners & CalSTRS to Apple, Inc.," posted by Anne Sheehan, California State Teachers' Retirement System, Harvard Law School Forum on Corporate Governance and Financial Regulation, January 19, 2018; Samuel Gibbs, "Apple Investors Call for Action over iPhone 'Addiction' among Children," *The Guardian*, January 8, 2018; David Benoit, "iPhones and Children Are a Toxic Pair, Say Two Big Apple Investors," *Wall Street Journal*, January 7, 2018; and Nicholas Carr, "How Smartphones Hijack Our Minds," *Wall Street Journal*, October 7, 2017.

CASE STUDY QUESTIONS

1. Identify the problem described in this case study. In what sense is it an ethical dilemma?

2. Should restrictions be placed on children's and teenagers' smartphone use? Why or why not?

3. Can the problem of smartphones reducing cognitive skills be solved? Why or why not? Explain your answer.

4-5 How will MIS help my career?

Here is how Chapter 4 and this book can help you find a job as a junior privacy analyst.

The Company

Pinnacle Air Force Base in Texas has an open entry-level position for a junior privacy analyst in its human resources office. The office maintains detailed personnel records, including work history, compensation, healthcare, and retirement benefits, on more than 6,800 military members and their families and 1,250 civilian employees.

Position Description

The junior privacy analyst will assist with employee recordkeeping and help ensure compliance with all federal and state privacy regulations. Job responsibilities include:

- Analyzing and developing policy and procedures related to privacy office functions.
- Logging and tracking Privacy Act requests, assistance with review, redaction and preparation of responsive records, and tracking all privacy office correspondence.
- Monitoring and responding to written, verbal, and electronic correspondence and inquiries directed to the government privacy office, including sensitive beneficiary/personnel correspondence.
- Coordinating privacy office meetings.
- Reviewing and analyzing data and documents and assessing options, issues, and positions for a variety of program planning, reporting, and execution activities.

Job Requirements

- Bachelor's degree in liberal arts or business
- Strong communication and organizational skills
- Experience with recordkeeping and file systems desirable

Interview Questions

1. What background or job experience do you have in the privacy protection field?
2. What do you know about the Privacy Act?
3. What do you know about privacy protection practices for both written and electronic correspondence?
4. If you were asked to improve privacy protection for our organization, how would you proceed?
5. Have you ever dealt with a problem involving privacy protection? What role did you play in its solution?

Author Tips

1. Review this chapter, with special attention to the sections dealing with information systems and privacy.
2. Use the web to find out more about the Privacy Act and privacy protection procedures and policies for personnel records.
3. Try to find out more about employee recordkeeping and privacy protection at U.S. military bases or other organizations.
4. If you do not have any hands-on experience in the privacy area, explain what you do know about privacy and why it is so important to protect sensitive personal data, and indicate you would be very interested in learning more and doing privacy-related work.

REVIEW **SUMMARY**

4-1 What ethical, social, and political issues are raised by information systems?

Information technology is introducing changes for which laws and rules of acceptable conduct have not yet been developed. Increasing computing power, storage, and networking capabilities—including the Internet—expand the reach of individual and organizational actions and magnify their impacts. The ease and anonymity with which information is now communicated, copied, and manipulated in online environments pose new challenges to the protection of privacy and intellectual property. The main ethical, social, and political issues information systems raise center on information rights and obligations, property rights and obligations, accountability and control, system quality, and quality of life.

4-2 What specific principles for conduct can be used to guide ethical decisions?

Six ethical principles for judging conduct include the Golden Rule, Immanuel Kant's categorical imperative, the slippery slope rule, the utilitarian principle, the risk aversion principle, and the ethical no-free-lunch rule. These principles should be used in conjunction with an ethical analysis.

4-3 Why do contemporary information systems technology and the Internet pose challenges to the protection of individual privacy and intellectual property?

Contemporary data storage and data analysis technology enable companies to gather personal data from many sources easily about individuals and analyze these data to create detailed digital profiles about individuals and their behaviors. Data flowing over the Internet can be monitored at many points. Cookies and other web monitoring tools closely track the activities of website visitors. Not all websites have strong privacy protection policies, and they do not always allow for informed consent regarding the use of personal information. Traditional copyright laws are insufficient to protect against software piracy because digital material can be copied so easily and transmitted to many locations simultaneously over the Internet.

4-4 How have information systems affected laws for establishing accountability and liability and the quality of everyday life?

New information technologies are challenging existing liability laws and social practices for holding individuals and institutions accountable for harm done to others. Although computer systems have been sources of efficiency and wealth, they have some negative impacts. Computer errors can cause serious harm to individuals and organizations. Poor data quality is also responsible for disruptions and losses for businesses. Jobs can be lost when computers replace workers or tasks become unnecessary in reengineered business processes. The ability to own and use a computer may be exacerbating socio-economic disparities among different ethnic groups and social classes. Widespread use of computers increases opportunities for computer crime and computer abuse. Computers can also create health and cognitive problems such as repetitive stress injury, computer vision syndrome, and the inability to think clearly and perform complex tasks.

Key Terms

Accountability, 129
Carpal tunnel syndrome (CTS), 149
Computer abuse, 146
Computer crime, 145
Computer vision syndrome (CVS), 150
Cookies, 135
Copyright, 138
Digital divide, 147
Digital Millennium Copyright Act (DMCA), 141
Due process, 129
Ethical no-free-lunch rule, 130
Ethics, 124
Fair Information Practices (FIP), 132
General Data Protection Regulation (GDPR), 134
Golden Rule, 130
Immanuel Kant's categorical imperative, 130
Information rights, 126
Informed consent, 134
Intellectual property, 138

Liability, 129
Nonobvious relationship awareness (NORA), 128
Opt-in, 137
Opt-out, 137
Patent, 139
Privacy, 132
Profiling, 127
Repetitive stress injury (RSI), 149
Responsibility, 129
Risk aversion principle, 130
Safe harbor, 134
Slippery slope rule, 130
Spam, 146
Spyware, 136
Trade secret, 140
Trademarks, 140
Utilitarian principle, 130
Web beacons, 136

MyLab MIS

To complete the problems with MyLab MIS, go to the EOC Discussion Questions in MyLab MIS.

Review Questions

4-1 What ethical, social, and political issues are raised by information systems?

- Explain how ethical, social, and political issues are connected and give some examples.

- List and describe the key technological trends that heighten ethical concerns.

- Differentiate between responsibility, accountability, and liability.

4-2 What specific principles for conduct can be used to guide ethical decisions?

- List and describe the five steps in an ethical analysis.

- Identify and describe six ethical principles.

4-3 Why do contemporary information systems technology and the Internet pose challenges to the protection of individual privacy and intellectual property?

- Define privacy and Fair Information Practices.

- Explain how the Internet challenges the protection of individual privacy and intellectual property.

- Explain how informed consent, legislation, industry self-regulation, and technology tools help protect the individual privacy of Internet users.

- List and define the three regimes that protect intellectual property rights.

4-4 How have information systems affected laws for establishing accountability and liability and the quality of everyday life?

- Explain why it is so difficult to hold software services liable for failure or injury.
- List and describe the principal causes of system quality problems.

- Name and describe four quality of life impacts of computers and information systems.
- Define and describe computer vision syndrome and repetitive stress injury (RSI) and explain their relationship to information technology.

Discussion Questions

4-5
MyLab MIS
Should producers of software-based services, such as ATMs, be held liable for economic injuries suffered when their systems fail?

4-6
MyLab MIS
Should companies be responsible for unemployment their information systems cause? Why or why not?

4-7
MyLab MIS
Discuss the pros and cons of allowing companies to amass personal data for behavioral targeting.

Hands-On MIS Projects

The projects in this section give you hands-on experience in analyzing the privacy implications of using online data brokers, developing a corporate policy for employee web usage, using blog creation tools to create a simple blog, and analyzing web browser privacy. Visit MyLab MIS to access this chapter's Hands-On MIS Projects.

Management Decision Problems

4-8 InfoFree's website is linked to massive databases that consolidate personal data on millions of people. Users can purchase marketing lists of consumers broken down by location, age, gender, income level, home value, and interests. One could use this capability to obtain a list, for example, of everyone in Peekskill, New York, making $150,000 or more per year. Do data brokers such as InfoFree raise privacy issues? Why or why not? If your name and other personal information were in this database, what limitations on access would you want to preserve your privacy? Consider the following data users: government agencies, your employer, private business firms, other individuals.

4-9 As the head of a small insurance company with six employees, you are concerned about how effectively your company is using its networking and human resources. Budgets are tight, and you are struggling to meet payrolls because employees are reporting many overtime hours. You do not believe that the employees have a sufficiently heavy workload to warrant working longer hours and are looking into the amount of time they spend on the Internet.

Each employee uses a computer with Internet access on the job. Review a sample of your company's weekly report of employee web usage, which can be found in MyLab MIS.

- Calculate the total amount of time each employee spent on the web for the week and the total amount of time that company computers were used for this purpose. Rank the employees in the order of the amount of time each spent online.
- Do your findings and the contents of the report indicate any ethical problems employees are creating? Is the company creating an ethical problem by monitoring its employees' use of the Internet?
- Use the guidelines for ethical analysis presented in this chapter to develop a solution to the problems you have identified.

Achieving Operational Excellence: Creating a Simple Blog

Software skills: Blog creation
Business skills: Blog and web page design

4-10 In this project, you'll learn how to build a simple blog of your own design using the online blog creation software available at Blogger.com. Pick a sport, hobby, or topic of interest as the theme for your blog. Name the blog, give it a title, and choose a template for the blog. Post at least four entries to the blog, adding a label for each posting. Edit your posts if necessary. Upload an image, such as a photo from your computer, or the web, to your blog. Add capabilities for other registered users, such as team members, to comment on your blog. Briefly describe how your blog could be useful to a company selling products or services related to the theme of your blog. List the tools available to Blogger that would make your blog more useful for business and describe the business uses of each. Save your blog and show it to your instructor.

Improving Decision Making: Analyzing Web Browser Privacy

Software Skills: Web browser software
Business Skills: Analyzing web browser privacy protection features

4-11 This project will help develop your Internet skills for using the privacy protection features of leading web browser software.

Examine the privacy protection features and settings for two leading web browsers such as Internet Explorer, Mozilla Firefox, or Google Chrome. Make a table comparing the features of two of these browsers in terms of functions provided and ease of use.

- How do these privacy protection features protect individuals?
- How do these privacy protection features affect what businesses can do on the Internet?
- Which browser does the best job of protecting privacy? Why?

Collaboration and Teamwork Project

Developing a Corporate Code of Ethics

4-12 With three or four of your classmates, develop a corporate ethics code on privacy that addresses both employee privacy and the privacy of customers and users of the corporate website. Be sure to consider email privacy and employer monitoring of worksites as well as corporate use of information about employees concerning their off-the-job behavior (e.g., lifestyle, marital arrangements, and so forth). If possible, use Google Docs and Google Drive or Google Sites to brainstorm, organize, and develop a presentation of your findings for the class.

Facebook Privacy: Your Life for Sale

CASE STUDY

Facebook describes its corporate mission as giving people the power to build community and bring the world closer together. In 2017 and 2018 these lofty objectives took a serious blow when it became known that Facebook had lost control of the personal information users share on the site. Facebook had allowed its platform to be exploited by Russian intelligence and political consultants with the intention of intensifying existing political cleavages, driving people away from community and from one another during the U.S. presidential election of 2016.

In January 2018, a founder and former employee of a political consulting and voter profiling company called Cambridge Analytica revealed that his firm had harvested the personal information of as many as 87 million users of Facebook, and used this information in an effort to influence the U.S. presidential election of 2016. Facebook does not sell the personal information of its users, but it did allow third-party apps to obtain the personal information of Facebook users. In this case, a U.K. researcher was granted access to 50,000 Facebook users for the purpose of research. He developed an app quiz that claimed to measure users' personality traits. Facebook's design allowed this app to not only collect the personal information of people who agreed to take the survey, but also the personal information of all the people in those users' Facebook social network. The researcher sold the data to Cambridge Analytica, who in turn used it to send targeted political ads in the presidential election.

In a Senate hearing in October 2017, Facebook testified that Russian operatives had exploited Facebook's social network in an effort to influence the 2016 presidential election. More than 130,000 fake messages and stories had been sent to Facebook users in the United States using an army of automated software bots, built and operated by several thousand Russian-based hackers working for a Russian intelligence agency, the Internet Research Agency. (A bot is a software program that performs an automated task, and is often on the Internet for malicious purposes—see Chapter 8.) Using 75,000 fake Facebook accounts, and 230,000 bots, the Russian messages were sent to an estimated 146 million people on Facebook. The messages targeted people based on their personal information collected by Facebook in the normal course of business, including users' religion, race, ethnicity, personal interests, and political views. The ads targeted groups who had opposing political views, with the intention of intensifying social conflict among them.

How could all this happen? As it turns out, it was quite easy and inexpensive, given the design and management of Facebook. Once Facebook grants access to advertisers, app developers, or researchers, it has a very limited capability to control how that information is used. Third-party agreements and policies are rarely reviewed by Facebook to check for compliance. Facebook executives claimed they were as shocked as others that 87 million Facebook users had their personal information harvested by Russian intelligence agencies and used by Cambridge Analytica to target political ads.

It gets worse: In early June 2018, several months after Facebook was forced to explain its privacy measures and pledge reforms in the wake of the Cambridge Analytica scandal, the *New York Times* reported that Facebook had data-sharing partnerships with at least 60 device makers. Facebook allowed Apple, Samsung, Amazon, and other companies that sell mobile phones, tablets, TVs, and video game consoles to gain access not only to data about Facebook users but also personal data about their friends—without their explicit consent. As of 2015, Facebook had supposedly prohibited app software developers from collecting information about customers' friends. Apparently, these restrictions did not extend to device makers.

Shortly thereafter, it was also revealed that Facebook had struck customized data-sharing deals that gave select companies such as Royal Bank of Canada and Nissan Motor Co. special access to user records, even though Facebook claimed it had it walled off that information in 2015. Certain companies were also allowed access to additional information about a user's Facebook friends.

Facebook again came under attack from the press, privacy advocates, and government authorities for pleading ignorance and for allowing uncontrolled data sharing to happen. For the first time since its founding, Facebook is facing a serious existential crisis, and potentially a threat to its business model. Facebook's current crisis follows from a history of privacy abuses in its short 14-year life. Facebook has quickly morphed from a small, niche networking site for mostly Ivy League college students into a publicly traded company with a market worth of $534 billion in 2018. Facebook boasts that it is free to join and always will be, so where's the money coming from to service 2.1 billion worldwide subscribers? Just like its fellow tech titan and rival Google, Facebook's revenue comes almost entirely from advertising (97 percent of $40.6 billion in revenue in 2017). Facebook watches what you do on Facebook and then sells that information and information about your friends to advertisers, not just on Facebook but all over the web. As Tim Cook, CEO of Apple, noted, at Facebook, the product they sell is you.

More than ever, companies such as Facebook and Google, which made approximately $110 billion in advertising revenue in 2017, are using your online activity to develop a frighteningly accurate digital picture of your life, and then selling access to their platform of personal information to advertisers. Facebook's goal is to serve advertisements that are more relevant to you than anywhere else on the web, but the personal information it gathers about you both with and without your consent can also be used against you in other ways.

Facebook has a diverse array of compelling and useful features. It has helped families find lost pets and allows active-duty soldiers to stay in touch with their families; it gives smaller companies a chance to further their e-commerce efforts and larger companies a chance to solidify their brands; and, perhaps most obviously, Facebook makes it easier for you to keep in touch with your friends, relatives, local restaurants, and, in short, just about all the things you are interested in. These are the reasons so many people use Facebook—it provides real value to users. The cost of participating in the Facebook platform is that your personal information is shared with advertisers and with others you may not know.

Facebook has a checkered past of privacy violations and missteps that raise doubts about whether it should be responsible for the personal data of billions of people. There are no laws in the United States that give consumers the right to know what data companies like Facebook have compiled. You can challenge information in credit reports because of the Fair Credit Reporting Act, but until recently, you could not obtain what data Facebook has gathered about you. It's been different in Europe: for several years, users had the right to demand that Facebook turn over a report of all the information it had collected on individuals. In 2018, Facebook allowed users to download all the information they had collected on a person, even though users had no legal right to demand that information.

Think you own your face? Not on Facebook, thanks to its facial recognition software for photo tagging of users. This "tag suggestions" feature is automatically on when you sign up, and there is no user consent. A federal court in 2016 allowed a lawsuit to go forward contesting Facebook's right to photo tag without user consent. This feature is in violation of several state laws that seek to secure the privacy of biometric data.

A *Consumer Reports* study found that among 150 million Americans on Facebook every day, at least 4.8 million were willingly sharing information that could be used against them in some way. That includes plans to travel on a particular day, which burglars could use to time robberies, or Liking a page about a particular health condition or treatment, which might prompt insurers to deny coverage. Credit card companies and similar organizations have begun engaging in weblining, taken from the term *redlining*, by altering their treatment of you based on the actions of other people with profiles similar to yours. Employers can assess your personality and behavior by using your Facebook Likes. Thirteen million users have never adjusted Facebook's privacy controls, which allow friends using Facebook applications to transfer your data unwittingly to a third party without your knowledge.

Why, then, do so many people share sensitive details of their life on Facebook? Often, it's because users do not realize that their data are being collected and transmitted in this way. A Facebook user's friends are not notified if information about them is collected by that user's applications. Many of Facebook's features and services are enabled by default when they are launched without notifying users, and a study by Siegel + Gale found that Facebook's privacy policy is more difficult to comprehend than government notices or typical bank credit card agreements, which are notoriously dense. Did you know that whenever you log into a website using Facebook, Facebook shares some personal information with that site and can track your movements in that site? Next time you visit Facebook, click Privacy Settings and see whether you can understand your options.

However, there are some signs that Facebook might become more responsible with its data collection processes, whether by its own volition or because it is forced to do so. As a publicly traded company, Facebook now invites more scrutiny from investors and regulators. In 2018, in response to a maelstrom of criticism in the United States, and Europe's new General Data Protection Regulation (GDPR), Facebook changed its privacy policy to make it easier for users to select their privacy preferences; to know exactly what they are consenting to; to download users' personal archives and the information that Facebook collects and shares, including facial images; to restrict click bait and spam in newsfeeds; to more closely monitor app developers' use of personal information; and to increase efforts to eliminate millions of fake accounts. Facebook hired 10,000 new employees and several hundred fact-checking firms to identify and eliminate fake news. For the first time in its history, Facebook is being forced to apply editorial controls to the content posted by users and, in that sense, become more like a traditional publisher and news outlet that takes responsibility for its content. Unfortunately, as researchers have long known, and Facebook executives understand, very few users—estimated to be less than 12 percent—take the time to understand and adjust their privacy preferences. In reality, user choice is not a powerful check on Facebook's use of personal information.

Although U.S. Facebook users have little recourse to access data that Facebook has collected on them, users from other countries have done better. In Europe, over 100,000 Facebook users have already requested their data, and European law requires Facebook to respond to these requests within 40 days. Government privacy regulators from France, Spain, Italy, Germany, Belgium, and the Netherlands have been actively investigating Facebook's privacy controls as the European Union pursues more stringent privacy protection legislation.

While Facebook has shut down several of its more egregious privacy-invading features, and enhanced its consent process, the company's data use policies make it very clear that, as a condition of using the service, users grant the company wide latitude in using their personal information in advertising. The default option for users is "opt-in"; most users do not know how to control use of their information; and they cannot "opt out" of all sharing if they want to use Facebook. This is called the "control paradox" by researchers: even when users are given controls over the use of their personal information, they typically choose not to use those controls. Although users can limit some uses of their information, an advanced degree in Facebook data features is required. Facebook shows you ads not only on Facebook but across the

web through its Facebook Audience Network, which keeps track of what its users do on other websites and then targets ads to those users on those websites.

Critics have asked Facebook why it doesn't offer an ad-free service—like music streaming sites—for a monthly fee. Others want to know why Facebook does not allow users just to opt out of tracking. But these kinds of changes would be very difficult for Facebook because its business model depends entirely on the largely unfettered use of its users' personal private information, just as it declares in its data use policy. That policy states very openly that if you use Facebook you agree to their terms of service, which enable it to share your information with third parties.

Sources: Deepa Seetharaman and Kirsten Grind, "Facebook Gave Some Companies Access to Additional Data About Users' Friends," *Wall Street Journal*, June 8, 2018; Natalia Drozdiak, Sam Schechner, and Valentina Pop, "Mark Zuckerberg Apologizes to EU Lawmakers for Facebook's Fake-News Failures," *Wall Street Journal*, May 22, 2018; Cecilia Kang and Sheera Frenkel, "Facebook Says Cambridge Analytica Harvested Data of Up to 87 Million Users," *New York Times*, April 24, 2018; Eduardo Porter, "The Facebook Fallacy: Privacy Is Up to You," *New York Times*, April 24, 2018; Jack Nicas, "Facebook to Require Verified Identities for Future Political Ads," *New York Times*, April 6, 2018; Sheera Frenkel and Natasha Singer, "Facebook Introduces Central Page for Privacy and Security Settings," *New York Times*, March 28, 2018; David Mayer, "Facebook Is Giving You New Privacy Options, But It's Clear What It Wants You to Choose," *Fortune*, March 19, 2018; Matthew Rosenberg, Nicholas Confessore, and Carole Cadwalladr, "How Trump Consultants Exploited the Facebook Data of Millions," *New York Times*, March 17, 2018; Sheera Frenkel, **"**Tech Giants Brace for Europe's New Data Privacy Rules," *New York Times*, January 28, 2018; Georgia Wells and Deepa Seetharaman, "New Facebook Data Shows Russians Targeted Users by Education, Religion, Politics," *Wall Street Journal*, November 1, 2017; Hunt Allcott and Matthew Gentzkow, "Social Media and Fake News in the 2016 Election," *Journal of Economic Perspectives*, March, 2017; Samuel Gibbs, "Facebook Facing Privacy Actions Across Europe as France Fines Firm €150k," *The Guardian*, May 16, 2017; and Katie Collins, "Facebook's Newest Privacy Problem: 'Faceprint' Data," *CNET*, May 16, 2016.

CASE STUDY QUESTIONS

4-13 Perform an ethical analysis of Facebook. What is the ethical dilemma presented by this case?

4-14 What is the relationship of privacy to Facebook's business model?

4-15 Describe the weaknesses of Facebook's privacy policies and features. What management, organization, and technology factors have contributed to those weaknesses?

4-16 Will Facebook be able to have a successful business model without invading privacy? Explain your answer. Could Facebook take any measures to make this possible?

MyLab MIS

Go to the Assignments section of MyLab MIS to complete these writing exercises.

4-17 What are the five principles of Fair Information Practices? For each principle, describe a business situation in which the principle comes into play and how you think managers should react.

4-18 What are five digital technology trends in business today that raise ethical issues for business firms and managers? Provide an example from business or personal experience when an ethical issue resulted from each of these trends.

Chapter 4 References

Adjerid, Idris, Eyal Peer, and Alessandro Acquisti. "Beyond the Privacy Paradox: Objective Versus Relative Risk in Privacy Decision Making." *MIS Quarterly* 42, No. 2 (June 2018).

Anderson, Chad, Richard L. Baskerville, and Mala Kaul. "Information Security Control Theory: Achieving a Sustainable Reconciliation Between Sharing and Protecting the Privacy of Information." *Journal of Management Information Systems* 34, No. 4 (2017).

Belanger, France, and Robert E. Crossler. "Privacy in the Digital Age: A Review of Information Privacy Research in Information Systems." *MIS Quarterly* 35, No. 4 (December 2011).

Bernstein, Amy, and Anand Raman. "The Great Decoupling: An Interview with Erik Brynjolfsson and Andrew McAfee." *Harvard Business Review* (June 2015).

Bernstein, Ethan, Saravanan Kesavan, and Bradley Staats. "How to Manage Scheduling Software Fairly." *Harvard Business Review* (December 2014).

Bilski v. Kappos, 561 US (2010).

Brown Bag Software vs. Symantec Corp. 960 F2D 1465 (Ninth Circuit, 1992).

Brynjolfsson, Erik, and Andrew McAfee. *Race Against the Machine.* (Digital Frontier Press, 2011).

Chan, Jason, Anindya Ghose, and Robert Seamans. "The Internet and Racial Hate Crimes: Offline Spillovers from Online Access." *MIS Quarterly* 40, No. 2 (June 2016).

Clemons, Eric K., and Joshua S. Wilson. "Family Preferences Concerning Online Privacy, Data Mining, and Targeted Ads: Regulatory Implications." *Journal of Management Information Systems* 32, No. 2 (2015).

Culnan, Mary J., and Cynthia Clark Williams. "How Ethics Can Enhance Organizational Privacy." *MIS Quarterly* 33, No. 4 (December 2009).

Davenport, Thomas H., and Julia Kirby. "Beyond Automation." *Harvard Business Review* (June 2015).

European Commission. "The EU-U.S. Privacy Shield Factsheet." July 2016. http://ec.europa.eu, accessed June 15, 2017.

European Parliament. "Directive 2009/136/EC of the European Parliament and of the Council of November 25, 2009." European Parliament (2009).

Federal Trade Commission. "Protecting Consumer Privacy in an Era of Rapid Change." (Washington, DC, 2012).

_____. "Internet of Things (IoT): Privacy & Security in a Connected World." (January 2015).

Goelmarch, Vindu. "One Billion Yahoo Accounts Still for Sale, Despite Hacking Indictments." *New York Times* (March 17, 2017).

Goldfarb, Avi, and Catherine Tucker. "Why Managing Consumer Privacy Can Be an Opportunity." *MIT Sloan Management Review* 54, No. 3 (Spring 2013).

Gopal, Ram D., Hooman Hidaji, Raymond A. Patterson, Erik Rolland, and Dmitry Zhdanov. "How Much to Share with Third Parties? User Privacy Concerns and Website Dilemmas." *MIS Quarterly* 42, No. 1 (March 2018).

Groysberg, Boris, Eric Lin, George Serafeim, and Robin Abrahams. "The Scandal Effect." *Harvard Business Review* (September 2016).

Henry, Patrick. "Why Computers Make Us Stupid." *Slice of MIT* (March 6, 2011).

Hsieh, J. J. Po-An, Arun Rai, and Mark Keil. "Understanding Digital Inequality: Comparing Continued Use Behavioral Models of the Socio-Economically Advantaged and Disadvantaged." *MIS Quarterly* 32, No. 1 (March 2008).

Hutter, Katja, Johann Fuller, Julia Hautz, Volker Bilgram, and Kurt Matzler. "Machiavellianism or Morality: Which Behavior Pays Off In Online Innovation Contests?" *Journal of Management Information Systems* 32, No. 3 (2015).

Laudon, Kenneth C. *Dossier Society: Value Choices in the Design of National Information Systems.* (New York: Columbia University Press, 1986).

Laudon, Kenneth C., and Carol Guercio Traver. *E-Commerce 2018: Business, Technology, Society,* 13th ed. (Upper Saddle River, NJ: Prentice-Hall, 2019).

LeBlanc, K. E., and W. Cestia. "Carpal Tunnel Syndrome." *American Family Physician* 83, No. 8 (2011).

Lee, Dong-Joo, Jae-Hyeon Ahn, and Youngsok Bang. "Managing Consumer Privacy Concerns in Personalization: A Strategic Analysis of Privacy Protection." *MIS Quarterly* 35, No. 2 (June 2011).

Lowry, Paul Benjamin, Gregory D. Moody, and Sutirtha Chatterjee. "Using IT Design to Prevent Cyberbullying." *Journal of Management Information Systems* 34, No. 3 (2017).

MacCrory, Frank, George Westerman, Erik Brynjolfsson, and Yousef Alhammadi. "Racing with and Against the Machine: Changes in Occupational Skill Composition in an Era of Rapid Technological Advance." (2014).

Manyika, James, and Michael Spence. "The False Choice Between Automation and Jobs." *Harvard Business Review* (February 5, 2018).

Pew Research Center. "The State of Privacy in America." (January 20, 2016).

PwC. "US State of Cybercrime Survey 2015." (June 2016).

Saunders, Carol, Martin Wiener, Sabrina Klett, and Sebastian Sprenger. "The Impact of Mental Representations on ICT-Related Overload in the Use of Mobile Phones." *Journal of Management Information Systems* 34, No. 3 (2017).

The Software Alliance. "BSA Global Software Survey 2018." (June 2018).

Sojer, Manuel, Oliver Alexy, Sven Kleinknecht, and Joachim Henkel. "Understanding the Drivers of Unethical Programming Behavior: The Inappropriate Reuse of Internet-Accessible Code." *Journal of Management Information Systems* 31, No. 3 (Winter 2014).

Symantec. "2018 Internet Security Threat Report." (2018).

Tarafdar, Monideepa, John D'Arcy, Ofir Turel, and Ashish Gupta. "The Dark Side of Information Technology." *MIT Sloan Management Review* 56, No. 2 (Winter 2015).

U.S. Department of Health, Education, and Welfare. *Records, Computers, and the Rights of Citizens.* (Cambridge: MIT Press, 1973).

U.S. Senate. "Do-Not-Track Online Act of 2011." Senate 913 (May 9, 2011).

U.S. Sentencing Commission. "Sentencing Commission Toughens Requirements for Corporate Compliance Programs." (April 13, 2004).

Wolcott, Robert C. "How Automation Will Change Work, Purpose, and Meaning." *Harvard Business Review* (January 11, 2018).

Information Technology Infrastructure

PART TWO provides the technical foundation for understanding information systems by examining hardware, software, database, and networking technologies along with tools and techniques for security and control. This part answers questions such as: What technologies do businesses today need to accomplish their work? What do I need to know about these technologies to make sure they enhance the performance of the firm? How are these technologies likely to change in the future? What technologies and procedures are required to ensure that systems are reliable and secure?

5 IT Infrastructure and Emerging Technologies

LEARNING OBJECTIVES

After reading this chapter, you will be able to answer the following questions:

5-1 What is IT infrastructure, and what are the stages and drivers of IT infrastructure evolution?

5-2 What are the components of IT infrastructure?

5-3 What are the current trends in computer hardware platforms?

5-4 What are the current computer software platforms and trends?

5-5 What are the challenges of managing IT infrastructure and management solutions?

5-6 How will MIS help my career?

CHAPTER CASES

PeroxyChem's Cloud Computing Formula for Success

Is Business Ready for Wearable Computers?

Look to the Cloud

Is BYOD Good for Business?

VIDEO CASES

Rockwell Automation Fuels the Oil and Gas Industry with the Internet of Things (IoT)

ESPN.com: The Future of Sports Coverage in the Cloud

Netflix: Building a Business in the Cloud

MyLab MIS

Discussion Questions: 5-6, 5-7, 5-8; **Hands-on MIS Projects:** 5-9, 5-10, 5-11, 5-12; **Writing Assignments:** 5-18, 5-19; **eText with Conceptual Animations**

PeroxyChem's Cloud Computing Formula for Success

Peroxychem is a leading global supplier of hydrogen peroxide and related substances for electronics, paper production, and household medical products. The company is headquartered in Philadelphia, Pennsylvania and has about 500 employees; generates over $400 million in revenue; and operates research, sales, and manufacturing facilities in North America, Europe, and Asia.

In February 2014 PeroxyChem was divested from its parent company and had just one year to take over management of its business systems. It would have to create its own IT infrastructure and IT department, all while keeping day-to-day business systems and operations running smoothly. As part of a large corporation, PeroxyChem had not been responsible for maintaining and managing its own IT systems but suddenly had to become self-sufficient. The company was understandably reluctant at that point to take on the cost or risk of procuring its own hardware, setting up a data center on premises, and maintaining a large in-house IT department, nor did it have the in-house expertise to do so.

© Olegdudko/123RF

According to PeroxyChem CIO Jim Curley, management didn't want to change any of its applications, but it did want to transition to a cloud infrastructure where the computer hardware and software for running a firm's systems are available as on-demand services in remote computing centers accessed via the Internet. The goal was for PeroxyChem IT personnel to spend only 40 percent of their time on operational tasks to keep the company running and 60 percent on strategic projects designed to grow the business. PeroxyChem also lacked the time and resources to hire and train new personnel to run day-to-day operations.

PeroxyChem worked with IBM to migrate its existing systems to IBM's SoftLayer cloud computing infrastructure. This is a managed cloud infrastructure in which IBM, as a trusted and experienced third party, manages the organization's cloud computing activities, freeing the organization to focus on its core competencies. IBM also helped implement enterprise and business intelligence applications from SAP, configuring the systems to meet PeroxyChem's business requirements. The new infrastructure was rigorously tested and was able to go live in four and a half months with no disruptions to PeroxyChem's existing IT operations.

PeroxyChem can run and extend its enterprise business systems with a lean in-house team. The managed IBM Cloud hosting solution has made it possible for PeroxyChem's IT staff to spend less time on routine maintenance and more time on leveraging its core competencies and developing innovative products for specialty industries such as food safety and electronics.

Using a cloud infrastructure has reduced costs and risk by avoiding large up-front capital investment for new hardware, software, and a data center, as well as the expense of maintaining a large in-house IT team. The infrastructure is scalable and can expand computing capacity if the company grows or has peaking workloads, or reduce computing resources (and expenses) if the company has fewer users or less computing work. The company can easily add more users without purchasing additional computing, storage, and networking resources of its own. PeroxyChem's cloud infrastructure is operational around the clock, making it easier to for this global company to do business.

Sources: David Slovensky, "PeroxyChem Builds a Whole New IT Infrastructure in Less Than Five Months," www.ibm.com, January 17, 2017; "PeroxyChem LLC." www.03-ibm.com, accessed February 20, 2018; Ken Murphy, "PeroxyChem Starts a Cloud Reaction," *SAP Insider Profiles*, December 12, 2016; and www.peroxychem.com, accessed February 20, 2018.

The experience of PeroxyChem illustrates the importance of information technology infrastructure in running a business today. The right technology at the right price will improve organizational performance. After divestiture from its parent corporation, PeroxyChem was left to manage its own information systems. The company would have been overwhelmed with setting up its own IT department and learning how to run its own systems, with no time for developing systems to support its strategy and future growth. PeroxyChem would be prevented from operating as efficiently and effectively as it could have.

The chapter-opening case diagram calls attention to important points raised by this case and this chapter. Divestiture left PeroxyChem with limited resources and a short time frame to set up and run its essential business information systems and data center. Using cloud computing for its IT infrastructure enabled PeroxyChem to quickly delegate the operation and management of its IT systems to outside specialists, to maintain a very small in-house IT staff, and to use that staff to support innovation rather than day-to-day operations. The company pays for only the computing capacity it actually uses on an as-needed basis, and did not have to make extensive and costly up-front IT investments.

Here are some questions to think about: What were the business benefits for PeroxyChem of using a cloud computing infrastructure? What role did divestiture play in PeroxyChem's choice of a solution?

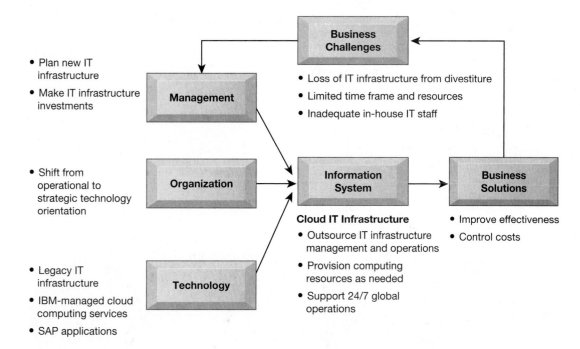

- Plan new IT infrastructure
- Make IT infrastructure investments

- Shift from operational to strategic technology orientation

- Legacy IT infrastructure
- IBM-managed cloud computing services
- SAP applications

Management

Organization

Technology

Business Challenges

- Loss of IT infrastructure from divestiture
- Limited time frame and resources
- Inadequate in-house IT staff

Information System

Cloud IT Infrastructure

- Outsource IT infrastructure management and operations
- Provision computing resources as needed
- Support 24/7 global operations

Business Solutions

- Improve effectiveness
- Control costs

5-1 What is IT infrastructure, and what are the stages and drivers of IT infrastructure evolution?

In Chapter 1, we defined *information technology (IT) infrastructure* as the shared technology resources that provide the platform for the firm's specific information system applications. An IT infrastructure includes investment in hardware, software, and services—such as consulting, education, and training—that are shared across the entire firm or across entire business units in the firm. A firm's IT infrastructure provides the foundation for serving customers, working with vendors, and managing internal firm business processes (see Figure 5.1).

Supplying firms worldwide with IT infrastructure (hardware, software, networking, and IT services) in 2018 was estimated to be a $3.7 trillion industry (Gartner, 2018). Investments in infrastructure account for between 25 and 50 percent of information technology expenditures in large firms, led by financial services firms where IT investment is well over half of all capital investment.

Defining IT Infrastructure

An IT infrastructure consists of a set of physical devices and software applications that are required to operate the entire enterprise. But IT infrastructure also includes a set of firmwide services budgeted by management and composed of both human and technical capabilities. These services include the following:

- Computing platforms used to provide computing services that connect employees, customers, and suppliers into a coherent digital environment, including large mainframes, midrange computers, desktop and laptop computers, and mobile handheld and remote cloud computing services

FIGURE 5.1 CONNECTION BETWEEN THE FIRM, IT INFRASTRUCTURE, AND BUSINESS CAPABILITIES

The services a firm is capable of providing to its customers, suppliers, and employees are a direct function of its IT infrastructure. Ideally, this infrastructure should support the firm's business and information systems strategy. New information technologies have a powerful impact on business and IT strategies as well as the services that can be provided to customers.

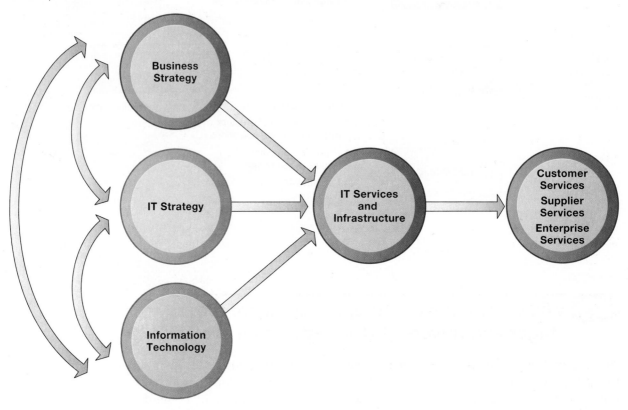

- Telecommunications services that provide data, voice, and video connectivity to employees, customers, and suppliers

- Data management services that store and manage corporate data and provide capabilities for analyzing the data

- Application software services, including online software services, that provide enterprise-wide capabilities such as enterprise resource planning, customer relationship management, supply chain management, and knowledge management systems that are shared by all business units

- Physical facilities management services that develop and manage the physical installations required for computing, telecommunications, and data management services

- IT management services that plan and develop the infrastructure, coordinate with the business units for IT services, manage accounting for the IT expenditure, and provide project management services

- IT standards services that provide the firm and its business units with policies that determine which information technology will be used, when, and how

- IT education services that provide training in system use to employees and offer managers training in how to plan for and manage IT investments

- IT research and development services that provide the firm with research on potential future IT projects and investments that could help the firm differentiate itself in the marketplace

This "service platform" perspective makes it easier to understand the business value provided by infrastructure investments. For instance, the real business value of a fully loaded personal computer operating at 3.5 gigahertz that costs about $1,000 and a high-speed Internet connection is hard to understand without knowing who will use it and how it will be used. When we look at the services provided by these tools, however, their value becomes more apparent: The new PC makes it possible for a high-cost employee making $100,000 a year to connect to all the company's major systems and the public Internet. The high-speed Internet service saves this employee about an hour per day in reduced wait time for Internet information. Without this PC and Internet connection, the value of this one employee to the firm might be cut in half.

Evolution of IT Infrastructure

The IT infrastructure in organizations today is an outgrowth of more than 50 years of evolution in computing platforms. There have been five stages in this evolution, each representing a different configuration of computing power and infrastructure elements (see Figure 5.2). The five eras are general-purpose mainframe and minicomputer computing, personal computers, client/server networks, enterprise computing, and cloud and mobile computing.

Technologies that characterize one era may also be used in another time period for other purposes. For example, some companies still run traditional mainframe systems or use mainframe computers as servers supporting large websites and corporate enterprise applications.

General-Purpose Mainframe and Minicomputer Era (1959 to Present)

The introduction of the IBM 1401 and 7090 transistorized machines in 1959 marked the beginning of widespread commercial use of **mainframe** computers. In 1965, the mainframe computer truly came into its own with the introduction of the IBM 360 series. The 360 was the first commercial computer that could provide time sharing, multitasking, and virtual memory in more advanced models. IBM has dominated mainframe computing from this point on. Mainframe computers became powerful enough to support thousands of online remote terminals connected to the centralized mainframe using proprietary communication protocols and proprietary data lines.

The mainframe era was a period of highly centralized computing under the control of professional programmers and systems operators (usually in a corporate data center), with most elements of infrastructure provided by a single vendor, the manufacturer of the hardware and the software.

This pattern began to change with the introduction of **minicomputers**, produced by Digital Equipment Corporation (DEC) in 1965. DEC minicomputers (PDP-11 and later the VAX machines) offered powerful machines at far lower prices than IBM mainframes, making possible decentralized computing, customized to the specific needs of individual departments or business units rather than time sharing on a single huge mainframe. In recent years, the minicomputer has evolved into a midrange computer or midrange server and is part of a network.

FIGURE 5.2   **ERAS IN IT INFRASTRUCTURE EVOLUTION**

Illustrated here are the typical computing configurations characterizing each of the five eras of IT infrastructure evolution.

Stages in IT Infrastructure Evolution

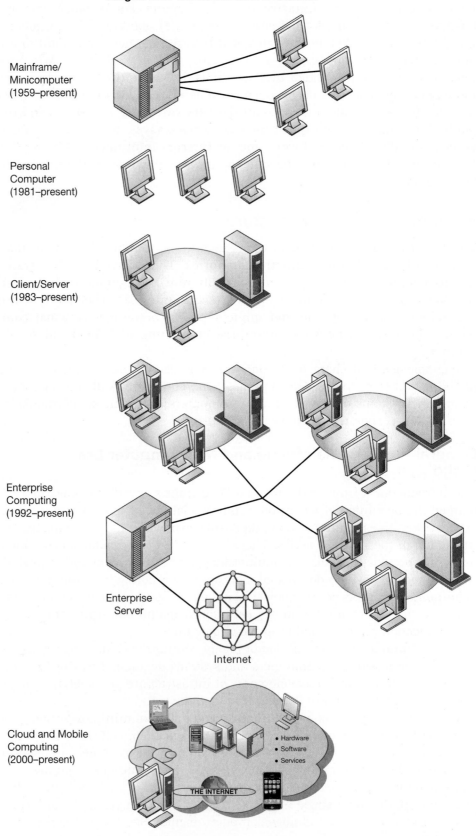

Mainframe/
Minicomputer
(1959–present)

Personal
Computer
(1981–present)

Client/Server
(1983–present)

Enterprise
Computing
(1992–present)

Enterprise
Server

Internet

Cloud and Mobile
Computing
(2000–present)

- Hardware
- Software
- Services

THE INTERNET

Personal Computer Era (1981 to Present)

Although the first truly personal computers (PCs) appeared in the 1970s (the Xerox Alto, the MITS Altair 8800, and the Apple I and II, to name a few), these machines had only limited distribution to computer enthusiasts. The appearance of the IBM PC in 1981 is usually considered the beginning of the PC era because this machine was the first to be widely adopted by businesses. At first using the DOS operating system, a text-based command language, and later the Microsoft Windows operating system, the **Wintel PC** computer (Windows operating system software on a computer with an Intel microprocessor) became the standard desktop personal computer. Worldwide PC sales have declined because of the popularity of tablets and smartphones, but the PC is still a popular tool for business. Approximately 88 percent of desktop PCs are thought to run a version of Windows, and about 8 percent run a version of MacOS. Wintel dominance as a computing platform is receding as iPhone and Android device sales increase.

Proliferation of PCs in the 1980s and early 1990s launched a spate of personal desktop productivity software tools—word processors, spreadsheets, electronic presentation software, and small data management programs—that were very valuable to both home and corporate users. These PCs were stand-alone systems until PC operating system software in the 1990s made it possible to link them into networks.

Client/Server Era (1983 to Present)

In **client/server computing**, desktop or laptop computers called **clients** are networked to powerful **server** computers that provide the client computers with a variety of services and capabilities. Computer processing work is split between these two types of machines. The client is the user point of entry, whereas the server typically processes and stores shared data, serves up web pages, or manages network activities. The term *server* refers to both the software application and the physical computer on which the network software runs. The server could be a mainframe, but today, server computers typically are more powerful versions of personal computers, based on inexpensive chips and often using multiple processors in a single computer box or in server racks.

The simplest client/server network consists of a client computer networked to a server computer, with processing split between the two types of machines. This is called a *two-tiered client/server architecture*. Whereas simple client/server networks can be found in small businesses, most corporations have more complex, **multitiered client/server architectures** (often called *N-tier client/server architectures*) in which the work of the entire network is balanced over several different levels of servers, depending on the kind of service being requested (see Figure 5.3).

For instance, at the first level, a **web server** will serve a web page to a client in response to a request for service. Web server software is responsible for locating and managing stored web pages. If the client requests access to a corporate system (a product list or price information, for instance), the request is passed along to an **application server**. Application server software handles all application operations between a user and an organization's back-end business systems. The application server may reside on the same computer as the web server or on its own dedicated computer. Chapters 6 and 7 provide more detail on other pieces of software that are used in multitiered client/server architectures for e-commerce and e-business.

FIGURE 5.3   A MULTITIERED (N-TIER) CLIENT/SERVER NETWORK

In a multitiered client/server network, client requests for service are handled by different levels of servers.

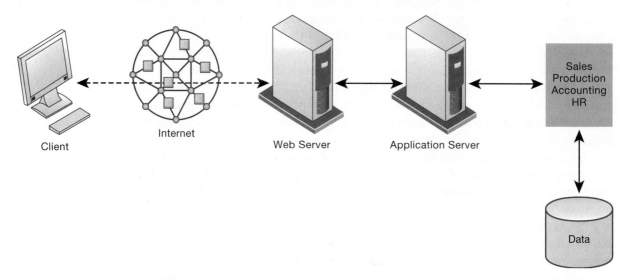

Client/server computing enables businesses to distribute computing work across a series of smaller, inexpensive machines that cost much less than centralized mainframe systems. The result is an explosion in computing power and applications throughout the firm.

Novell NetWare was the leading technology for client/server networking at the beginning of the client/server era. Today, Microsoft is the market leader with its **Windows** operating systems (Windows Server, Windows 10, Windows 8, and Windows 7).

Enterprise Computing Era (1992 to Present)

In the early 1990s, firms turned to networking standards and software tools that could integrate disparate networks and applications throughout the firm into an enterprise-wide infrastructure. As the Internet developed into a trusted communications environment after 1995, business firms began seriously using the *Transmission Control Protocol/Internet Protocol (TCP/IP)* networking standard to tie their disparate networks together. We discuss TCP/IP in detail in Chapter 7.

The resulting IT infrastructure links different pieces of computer hardware and smaller networks into an enterprise-wide network so that information can flow freely across the organization and between the firm and other organizations. It can link different types of computer hardware, including mainframes, servers, PCs, and mobile devices, and it includes public infrastructures such as the telephone system, the Internet, and public network services. The enterprise infrastructure also requires software to link disparate applications and enable data to flow freely among different parts of the business, such as enterprise applications (see Chapters 2 and 9) and web services (discussed in Section 5-4).

Cloud and Mobile Computing Era (2000 to Present)

The growing bandwidth power of the Internet has pushed the client/server model one step further, toward what is called the "cloud computing model." **Cloud computing** refers to a model of computing that provides access to a shared pool of computing resources (computers, storage, applications, and services) over the network, often the Internet. These "clouds" of computing resources can be accessed on an as-needed basis from any connected device and location.

Cloud computing bas become the fastest-growing form of computing, with worldwide public cloud spending to reach $411 billion by 2020. Cisco Systems predicts that 94 percent of all computer workloads will run in some type of cloud environment by 2021 (Gartner, 2017; Cisco 2018).

Thousands or even hundreds of thousands of computers are located in cloud data centers, where they can be accessed by desktop computers, laptop computers, tablets, entertainment centers, smartphones, and other client machines linked to the Internet. Amazon, Google, IBM, and Microsoft operate huge, scalable cloud computing centers that provide computing power, data storage, application development tools, and high-speed Internet connections to firms that want to maintain their IT infrastructures remotely. Firms such as Google, Microsoft, SAP, Oracle, and Salesforce.com sell software applications as services delivered over the Internet.

We discuss cloud and mobile computing in more detail in Section 5-3. The Learning Tracks include a table titled "Comparing Stages in IT Infrastructure Evolution," which compares each era on the infrastructure dimensions introduced.

Technology Drivers of Infrastructure Evolution

The changes in IT infrastructure we have just described have resulted from developments in computer processing, memory chips, storage devices, networking hardware and software, and software design that have exponentially increased computing power while exponentially reducing costs. Let's look at the most important developments.

Moore's Law and Microprocessing Power

In 1965, Gordon Moore, the director of Fairchild Semiconductor's Research and Development Laboratories, wrote in *Electronics* magazine that since the first microprocessor chip was introduced in 1959, the number of components on a chip with the smallest manufacturing costs per component (generally transistors) had doubled each year. This assertion became the foundation of **Moore's Law**. Moore later reduced the rate of growth to a doubling every two years.

There are at least three variations of Moore's Law, none of which Moore ever stated: (1) the power of microprocessors doubles every 18 months, (2) computing power doubles every 18 months, and (3) the price of computing falls by half every 18 months.

Figure 5.4 illustrates the relationship between number of transistors on a microprocessor and millions of instructions per second (MIPS), a common measure of processor power. Figure 5.5 shows the exponential decline in the cost of transistors and rise in computing power. For instance, in 2018, you could buy an Intel i7 processor chip with 2.5 billion transistors for about one ten-millionth of a dollar per transistor.

Exponential growth in the number of transistors and the power of processors coupled with an exponential decline in computing costs may not be able to continue much longer. In the last five years, the cost improvement rate has fallen to single digits from 30 percent annual reductions. Chip manufacturers continue to miniaturize components. Today's transistors are 14 nanometers in size, and should no longer be compared to the size of a human hair (80 thousand nanometers) but rather to the size of a virus (400 nanometers). Within the next five years or so, chip makers may reach the physical limits

FIGURE 5.4 MOORE'S LAW AND MICROPROCESSOR PERFORMANCE

Packing 5 billion transistors into a tiny microprocessor has exponentially increased processing power. Processing power has increased to more than 250,000 MIPS (about 2.6 billion instructions per second).

Source: Authors' estimate.

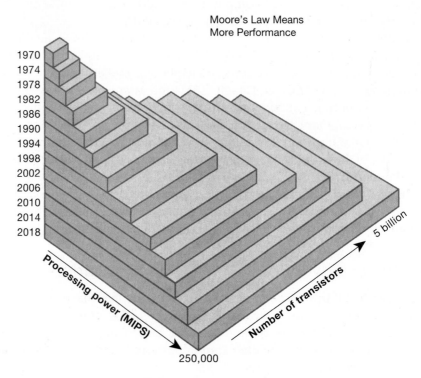

FIGURE 5.5 FALLING COST OF CHIPS

Changes in production technology, and very-large-scale production runs, have driven dramatic declines in the cost of chips, and the products that use them.

Source: Authors' estimate.

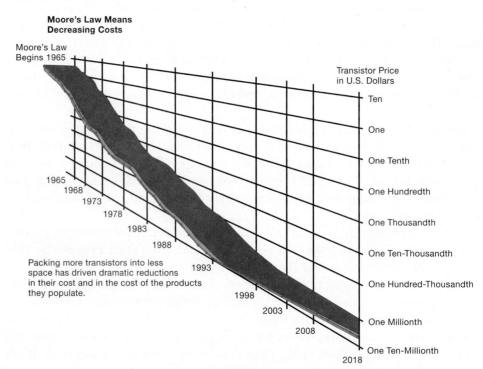

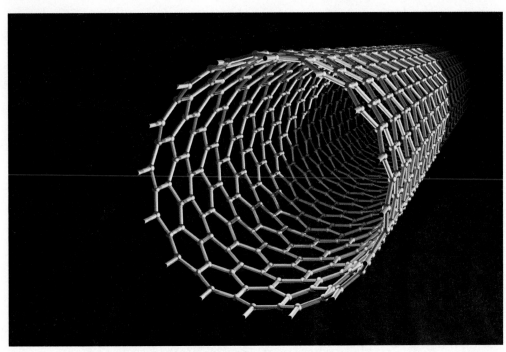

Nanotubes are tiny tubes about 10,000 times thinner than a human hair. They consist of rolled-up sheets of carbon hexagons, have potential use as minuscule wires or in ultrasmall electronic devices, and are very powerful conductors of electrical current.

© Forance/123RF

of semiconductor size. At that point they may need to use alternatives to fashioning chips from silicon or find other ways to make computers more powerful.

Chip manufacturers can shrink the size of transistors down to the width of several atoms by using nanotechnology. **Nanotechnology** uses individual atoms and molecules to create computer chips and other devices that are thousands of times smaller than current technologies permit. Chip manufacturers are trying to develop a manufacturing process to produce nanotube processors economically. Stanford University scientists have built a nanotube computer.

The Law of Mass Digital Storage

A second technology driver of IT infrastructure change is the Law of Mass Digital Storage. The amount of digital information is roughly doubling every year (Lyman and Varian, 2003). Fortunately, the cost of storing digital information is falling at an exponential rate of 100 percent a year. Figure 5.6 shows that the number of megabytes that can be stored on magnetic media for $1 from 1950 to the present roughly doubled every 15 months. In 2018, a 1 terabyte hard disk drive sells at retail for about $50.

Metcalfe's Law and Network Economics

Moore's Law and the Law of Mass Digital Storage help us understand why computing resources are now so readily available. But why do people want more computing and storage power? The economics of networks and the growth of the Internet provide some answers.

Robert Metcalfe—inventor of Ethernet local area network technology—claimed in 1970 that the value or power of a network grows exponentially as a function of the number of network members. Metcalfe and others point to the *increasing returns to scale* that network members receive as more and more people join the network. As the number of members in a network grows

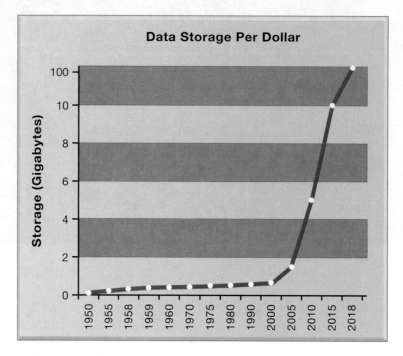

FIGURE 5.6 THE AMOUNT OF STORAGE PER DOLLAR RISES EXPONENTIALLY, 1950–2018

Cloud storage services like Google Drive provide 100 gigabytes of storage for $1.99 per month.

Source: Authors' estimates.

linearly, the value of the entire system grows exponentially and continues to grow as members increase. Demand for information technology has been driven by the social and business value of digital networks, which rapidly multiply the number of actual and potential links among network members.

Declining Communications Costs and the Internet

A fourth technology driver transforming IT infrastructure is the rapid decline in the costs of communication and the exponential growth in the size of the Internet. Today there are 4.2 billion Internet users worldwide (Internetworldstats.com, 2018). Figure 5.7 illustrates the exponentially declining cost of communication both over the Internet and over telephone networks (which increasingly are based on the Internet). As communication costs fall toward a very small number and approach zero, utilization of communication and computing facilities explode. In 2018, one megabit of Internet access costs about $2.60. In 2000, the cost was over $300 if available. In this same time frame, average household Internet speeds have risen from .2 Mbps to 18 Mbps.

To take advantage of the business value associated with the Internet, firms must greatly expand their Internet connections, including wireless connectivity, and greatly expand the power of their client/server networks, desktop clients, and mobile computing devices. There is every reason to believe these trends will continue.

Standards and Network Effects

Today's enterprise infrastructure and Internet computing would be impossible—both now and in the future—without agreements among manufacturers and

FIGURE 5.7 EXPONENTIAL DECLINES IN INTERNET COMMUNICATIONS
COSTS ($/MBPS)

The cost of communication over the Internet and over telephone networks has declined exponentially, fueling the explosive growth of communication and computing worldwide.

Sources: 2007–2018: "Average Internet Connection Speed in the United States from 2007 to 2017 (in Mbps), by Quarter" Statista, 2018; 2006 Home Broadband Adoption 2006 BY John B. Horrigan PEW Research 2007; Internet speeds: How Fast Does Internet Speed grow?By Xah Lee. Date: 2006-12-30. Last updated: 2017-01-22,http://xahlee.info/comp/bandwidth.html

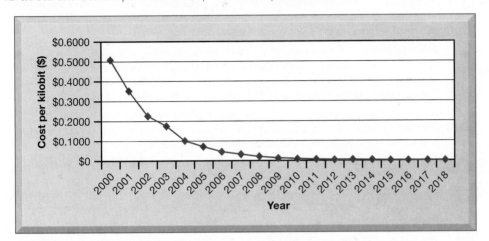

widespread consumer acceptance of **technology standards**. Technology standards are specifications that establish the compatibility of products and the ability to communicate in a network.

Technology standards unleash powerful economies of scale and result in price declines as manufacturers focus on the products built to a single standard. Without these economies of scale, computing of any sort would be far more expensive than is currently the case. Table 5.1 describes important standards that have shaped IT infrastructure.

In the 1990s, corporations started moving toward standard computing and communications platforms. The Wintel PC with the Windows operating system and Microsoft Office desktop productivity applications became the standard desktop and mobile client computing platform. (It now shares the spotlight with other standards, such as Apple's iOS and Macintosh operating systems and the Android operating system.) Widespread adoption of Unix-Linux as the enterprise server operating system of choice made possible the replacement of proprietary and expensive mainframe infrastructures. In networking, the Ethernet standard enabled PCs to connect together in small local area networks (LANs; see Chapter 7), and the TCP/IP standard enabled these LANs to be connected into firmwide networks, and ultimately, to the Internet.

5-2 What are the components of IT infrastructure?

IT infrastructure today is composed of seven major components. Figure 5.8 illustrates these infrastructure components and the major vendors within each component category. These components constitute investments that must be coordinated with one another to provide the firm with a coherent infrastructure.

TABLE 5.1 SOME IMPORTANT STANDARDS IN COMPUTING

STANDARD	SIGNIFICANCE
American Standard Code for Information Interchange (ASCII) (1958)	Made it possible for computer machines from different manufacturers to exchange data; later used as the universal language linking input and output devices such as keyboards and mice to computers. Adopted by the American National Standards Institute in 1963.
Common Business Oriented Language (COBOL) (1959)	An easy-to-use software language that greatly expanded the ability of programmers to write business-related programs and reduced the cost of software. Sponsored by the Defense Department in 1959.
Unix (1969–1975)	A powerful multitasking, multiuser, portable operating system initially developed at Bell Labs (1969) and later released for use by others (1975). It operates on a wide variety of computers from different manufacturers. Adopted by Sun, IBM, HP, and others in the 1980s, it became the most widely used enterprise-level operating system.
Ethernet (1973)	A network standard for connecting desktop computers into local area networks that enabled the widespread adoption of client/server computing and local area networks and further stimulated the adoption of personal computers.
Transmission Control Protocol/Internet Protocol (TCP/IP) (1974)	Suite of communications protocols and a common addressing scheme that enables millions of computers to connect together in one giant global network (the Internet). Later, it was used as the default networking protocol suite for local area networks and intranets. Developed in the early 1970s for the U.S. Department of Defense.
IBM/Microsoft/Intel Personal Computer (1981)	The standard Wintel design for personal desktop computing based on standard Intel processors and other standard devices, Microsoft DOS, and later Windows software. The emergence of this standard, low-cost product laid the foundation for a 25-year period of explosive growth in computing throughout all organizations around the globe. Today, more than 1 billion PCs power business and government activities every day.
World Wide Web (1989–1993)	Standards for storing, retrieving, formatting, and displaying information as a worldwide web of electronic pages incorporating text, graphics, audio, and video enables creation of a global repository of billions of web pages.

In the past, technology vendors supplying these components offered purchasing firms a mixture of incompatible, proprietary, partial solutions that could not work with other vendor products. Increasingly, vendor firms have been forced to cooperate in strategic partnerships with one another in order to keep their customers. For instance, a hardware and services provider such as IBM cooperates with all the major enterprise software providers, has strategic relationships with system integrators, and promises to work with whichever data management products its client firms wish to use (even though it sells its own database management software called DB2).

Another big change is that companies are moving more of their IT infrastructure to the cloud or to outside services, owning and managing much less on their premises. Firms' IT infrastructure will increasingly be an amalgam of components and services that are partially owned, partially rented or licensed, partially located on site, and partially supplied by external vendors or cloud services.

Computer Hardware Platforms

Firms worldwide are expected to spend $704 billion on computer hardware devices in 2018, including mainframes, servers, PCs, tablets, and smartphones. All these devices constitute the computer hardware platform for corporate (and personal) computing worldwide.

FIGURE 5.8 THE IT INFRASTRUCTURE ECOSYSTEM

There are seven major components that must be coordinated to provide the firm with a coherent IT infrastructure. Listed here are major technologies and suppliers for each component.

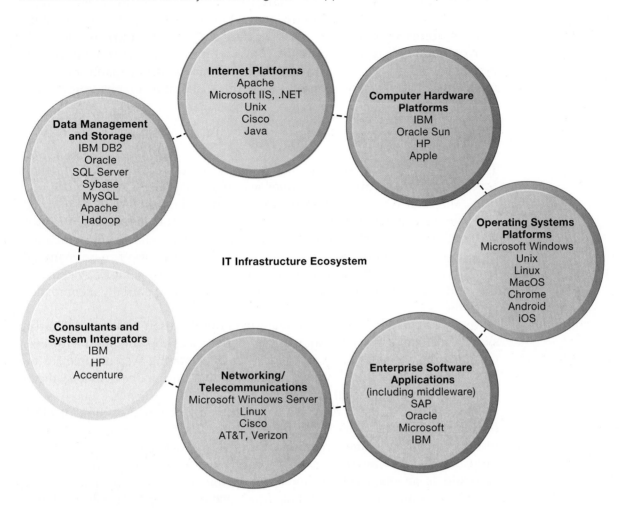

Most business computing has taken place using microprocessor chips manufactured or designed by Intel Corporation and, to a lesser extent, AMD Corporation. Intel and AMD processors are often referred to as "i86" processors because the original IBM PCs used an Intel 8086 processor and all the Intel (and AMD) chips that followed are downward compatible with this processor. (For instance, you should be able to run a software application designed 10 years ago on a new PC you bought yesterday.)

The computer platform changed dramatically with the introduction of mobile computing devices, from the iPod in 2001 to the iPhone in 2007 and the iPad in 2010. Worldwide, 2 billion people use smartphones. You can think of these devices as a second computer hardware platform, one that is consumer device–driven.

Mobile devices are not required to perform as many tasks as computers in the first computer hardware platform, so they consume less power, and generate less heat. Processors for mobile devices are manufactured by a wide range of firms, including Apple, Samsung, and Qualcomm, using an architecture designed by ARM Holdings.

Mainframes have not disappeared. They continue to be used to reliably and securely handle huge volumes of transactions, for analyzing very large quantities of data, and for handling large workloads in cloud computing centers. The mainframe is still the digital workhorse for banking and telecommunications networks that are often running software programs that are older and require a specific hardware platform. However, the number of providers has dwindled to one: IBM. IBM has also repurposed its mainframe systems so they can be used as giant servers for enterprise networks and corporate websites. A single IBM mainframe can run thousands of instances of Linux or Windows Server software and is capable of replacing thousands of smaller servers (see the discussion of virtualization in Section 5-3).

Operating System Platforms

The leading operating systems for corporate servers are Microsoft Windows Server, **Unix**, and **Linux**, an inexpensive and robust open source relative of Unix. Microsoft Windows Server is capable of providing enterprise-wide operating system and network services and appeals to organizations seeking Windows-based IT infrastructures. Unix and Linux are scalable, reliable, and much less expensive than mainframe operating systems. They can also run on many different types of processors. The major providers of Unix operating systems are IBM, HP, and Oracle-Sun, each with slightly different and partially incompatible versions.

Nearly 90 percent of PCs use some form of the Microsoft Windows **operating system** for managing the resources and activities of the computer. However, there is now a much greater variety of client operating systems than in the past, with new operating systems for computing on handheld mobile digital devices or cloud-connected computers.

Google's **Chrome OS** provides a lightweight operating system for cloud computing using a web-connected computer. Programs are not stored on the user's computer but are used over the Internet and accessed through the Chrome web browser. User data reside on servers across the Internet. **Android** is an open source operating system for mobile devices such as smartphones and tablet computers, developed by the Open Handset Alliance led by Google. It has become the most popular smartphone platform worldwide, competing with iOS, Apple's mobile operating system for the iPhone, iPad, and iPod Touch. Conventional client operating system software is designed around the mouse and keyboard but increasingly is becoming more natural and intuitive by using touch technology. **iOS**, the operating system for the phenomenally popular Apple iPad and iPhone, features a **multitouch** interface, where users employ one or more fingers to manipulate objects on a screen without a mouse or keyboard. Microsoft's **Windows 10** and Windows 8, which run on tablets as well as PCs, have multitouch capabilities, as do many Android devices.

Enterprise Software Applications

Firms worldwide are expected to spend about $389 billion in 2018 on software for enterprise applications that are treated as components of IT infrastructure. We introduced the various types of enterprise applications in Chapter 2, and Chapter 9 provides a more detailed discussion of each.

The largest providers of enterprise application software are SAP and Oracle. Also included in this category is middleware software supplied by vendors such as IBM and Oracle for achieving firmwide integration by linking the firm's existing application systems. Microsoft is attempting to move into the lower ends of this market by focusing on small and medium-sized businesses.

Data Management and Storage

Enterprise database management software is responsible for organizing and managing the firm's data so that they can be efficiently accessed and used. Chapter 6 describes this software in detail. The leading database software providers are IBM (DB2), Oracle, Microsoft (SQL Server), and SAP Sybase (Adaptive Server Enterprise). MySQL is a Linux open source relational database product now owned by Oracle Corporation, and Apache Hadoop is an open source software framework for managing very large data sets (see Chapter 6).

Networking/Telecommunications Platforms

Companies worldwide are expected to spend $1.43 trillion for telecommunications services in 2018 (Gartner, Inc., 2018). Windows Server is predominantly used as a local area network operating system, followed by Linux and Unix. Large, enterprise-wide area networks use some variant of Unix. Most local area networks, as well as wide area enterprise networks, use the TCP/IP protocol suite as a standard (see Chapter 7).

Cisco and Juniper Networks are leading networking hardware providers. Telecommunications platforms are typically provided by telecommunications/ telephone services companies that offer voice and data connectivity, wide area networking, wireless services, and Internet access. Leading telecommunications service vendors include AT&T and Verizon. This market is exploding with new providers of cellular wireless, high-speed Internet, and Internet telephone services.

Internet Platforms

Internet platforms include hardware, software, and management services to support a firm's website, including web hosting services, routers, and cabling or wireless equipment. A **web hosting service** maintains a large web server, or series of servers, and provides fee-paying subscribers with space to maintain their websites.

The Internet revolution created a veritable explosion in server computers, with many firms collecting thousands of small servers to run their Internet operations. There has been a steady push to reduce the number of server computers by increasing the size and power of each and by using software tools that make it possible to run more applications on a single server. Use of stand-alone server computers is decreasing as organizations transition to cloud computing services. The Internet hardware server market has become increasingly concentrated in the hands of IBM, Dell, Oracle, and HP, as prices have fallen dramatically.

The major web software application development tools and suites are supplied by Microsoft (Microsoft Visual Studio and the Microsoft .NET development platform), Oracle-Sun, and a host of independent software developers, including Adobe. Chapter 7 describes the components of the firm's Internet platform in greater detail.

Consulting and System Integration Services

Today, even a large firm does not have the staff, the skills, the budget, or the necessary experience to deploy and maintain its entire IT infrastructure. Implementing a new infrastructure requires (as noted in Chapters 13 and 14) significant changes in business processes and procedures, training and education, and software integration. Leading consulting firms providing this expertise include Accenture, IBM Services, HP, Infosys, and Wipro.

Software integration means ensuring the new infrastructure works with the firm's older, so-called legacy systems and ensuring the new elements of the infrastructure work with one another. **Legacy systems** are generally older transaction processing systems created for mainframe computers that continue to be used to avoid the high cost of replacing or redesigning them. Replacing these systems is cost prohibitive and generally not necessary if these older systems can be integrated into a contemporary infrastructure.

5-3 What are the current trends in computer hardware platforms?

The exploding power of computer hardware and networking technology has dramatically changed how businesses organize their computing power, putting more of this power on networks and mobile handheld devices and obtaining more of their computing capabilities in the form of services. We look at eight hardware trends: the mobile digital platform, consumerization of IT and BYOD, quantum computing, virtualization, cloud computing, edge computing, green computing, and high-performance/power-saving processors.

The Mobile Digital Platform

Chapter 1 pointed out that new mobile digital computing platforms have emerged as alternatives to PCs and larger computers. The iPhone and Android smartphones have taken on many functions of PCs, including transmitting data, surfing the web, transmitting e-mail and instant messages, displaying digital content, and exchanging data with internal corporate systems. The new mobile platform also includes small, lightweight netbooks optimized for wireless communication and Internet access, **tablet computers** such as the iPad, and digital e-book readers such as Amazon's Kindle with some web access capabilities.

Smartphones and tablets are becoming the primary means of accessing the Internet and are increasingly used for business computing as well as for consumer applications. For example, senior executives at General Motors are using smartphone applications that drill down into vehicle sales information, financial performance, manufacturing metrics, and project management status.

Wearable computing devices are a recent addition to the mobile digital platform. These include smartwatches, smart glasses, smart ID badges, and activity trackers. Wearable computing technology has many business uses, and it is changing the way firms work, as described in the Interactive Session on Technology.

Consumerization of IT and BYOD

The popularity, ease of use, and rich array of useful applications for smartphones and tablet computers have created a groundswell of interest in allowing employees to use their personal mobile devices in the workplace, a phenomenon

INTERACTIVE SESSION TECHNOLOGY

Is Business Ready for Wearable Computers?

Wearable computing is starting to take off. Smartwatches, smart glasses, smart ID badges, and activity trackers promise to change how we go about each day and the way we do our jobs. According to Gartner Inc., sales of wearables will increase from 275 million units in 2016 to 477 million units by 2020. Although smartwatches such as the Apple Watch and fitness trackers have been successful consumer products, business uses for wearables appear to be advancing more rapidly. A report from research firm Tractica projects that worldwide sales for enterprise wearables will increase exponentially to 66.4 million units by 2021.

Doctors and nurses are using smart eyewear for hands-free access to patients' medical records. Oil rig workers sport smart helmets to connect with land-based experts, who can view their work remotely and communicate instructions. Warehouse managers are able to capture real-time performance data using a smartwatch to better manage distribution and fulfillment operations. Wearable computing devices improve productivity by delivering information to workers without requiring them to interrupt their tasks, which in turn empowers employees to make more-informed decisions more quickly.

Wearable devices are helping businesses learn more about employees and the everyday workplace than ever before. New insights and information can be uncovered as IoT sensor data is correlated to actual human behavior. Information on task duration and the proximity of one device or employee to another, when combined with demographic data, can shed light on previously unidentified workflow inefficiencies. Technologically sophisticated firms will understand things they never could before about workers and customers; what they do every day, how healthy they are, where they go, and even how well they feel. This obviously has implications for protecting individual privacy, raising potential employee (and customer) fears that businesses are collecting sensitive data about them. Businesses will need to tread carefully.

Global logistics company DHL worked with Ricoh, the imaging and electronics company, and Ubimax, a wearable computing services and solutions company, to implement "vision picking" in its warehouse operations. Location graphics are displayed on smart glasses guiding staffers through the warehouse to both speed the process of finding items and reduce errors. The company says the technology delivered a 25 percent increase in efficiency. Vision picking gives workers locational information about the items they need to retrieve and allows them to automatically scan retrieved items. Future enhancements will enable the system to plot optimal routes through the warehouse, provide pictures of items to be retrieved (a key aid in case an item has been misplaced on the warehouse shelves), and instruct workers on loading carts and pallets more efficiently.

Google has developed Glass Enterprise Edition smart glasses for business use, with its development partners creating applications for specific industries such as manufacturing and healthcare. Glass Enterprise Edition is being touted as a tool for easing workflows by removing distractions that prevent employees from remaining engaged and focused on tasks. More than 50 businesses including Dignity Health, The Boeing Company, and Volkswagen have been using Glass to complete their work more rapidly and efficiently.

Duke Energy has been piloting the use of smart glasses, and sees multiple uses for them. According to Aleksandar Vukojevic, technology development manager for Duke Energy's Emerging Technologies Office, smart glasses can enable employees working in the field to access training or instructional videos to help with equipment repairs or upgrades. The glasses also allow remote management, enabling managers to capture what a line or transformer worker sees, annotate images and video with instructions, and send them back out to workers in the field. Duke also tried out the smart glasses in its warehouses for stock inventory. As a worker looks at an item code, it's automatically recorded against an existing database.

There are some challenges. Locking down data that's accessed with smart glasses is essential, as with any other mobile device used in the enterprise. Today's smart glasses haven't been designed with security in mind. The sensors in the smart glasses are also not as accurate as other products. A field worker using smart glasses to locate a breaker or other device might be off by 10 or 15 feet using Google's GPS instead of a military-grade solution more common to the energy industry, which can locate equipment to within one centimeter. Additionally, smart glasses don't necessarily allow safety glasses to be worn over them. Integrating data from smart glasses with Duke's internal databases could prove difficult.

Smart glasses are like smartphones. Without integration with internal content and the right applications, they would not be so useful. The value of wearable computing devices isn't from transferring the same information from a laptop or smartphone to a smartwatch or eyeglass display. Rather, it's about finding ways to use wearables to augment and enhance business processes. Successful adoption of wearable computing depends not only on cost effectiveness but on the development of new and better apps and integration with existing IT infrastructure and the organization's tools for managing and securing mobile devices (see the chapter-ending case study).

Sources: George Thangadurai, "Wearables at Work: Why Enterprise Usage Is Outshining Consumer Usage," *IoT Agenda*, March 8, 2018; Josh Garrett, "Wearables: The Next Wave of Enterprise IoT?" *IoT Agenda*, February 1, 2018; and Lucas Mearian, "Is Google Glass Really Ready for the Enterprise?" *Computerworld*, August 1, 2017.

CASE STUDY QUESTIONS

1. Wearables have the potential to change the way organizations and workers conduct business. Discuss the implications of this statement.

2. What management, organization, and technology issues would have to be addressed if a company was thinking of equipping its workers with a wearable computing device?

3. What kinds of businesses are most likely to benefit from wearable computers? Select a business and describe how a wearable computing device could help that business improve operations or decision making.

popularly called *"bring your own device" (BYOD)*. **BYOD** is one aspect of the **consumerization of IT**, in which new information technology that first emerges in the consumer market spreads into business organizations. Consumerization of IT includes not only mobile personal devices but also business uses of software services that originated in the consumer marketplace as well, such as Google and Yahoo search, Gmail, Google Maps, Dropbox, and even Facebook and Twitter.

Consumerization of IT is forcing businesses to rethink the way they obtain and manage information technology equipment and services. Historically, at least in large firms, the IT department was responsible for selecting and managing the information technology and applications used by the firm and its employees. It furnished employees with desktops or laptops that were able to access corporate systems securely. The IT department maintained control over the firm's hardware and software to ensure that the business was being protected and that information systems served the purposes of the firm and its management. Today, employees and business departments are playing a much larger role in technology selection, in many cases demanding that employees be able to use their own personal computers, smartphones, and tablets to access the corporate network. It is more difficult for the firm to manage and control these consumer technologies and make sure they serve the needs of the business. The chapter-ending case study explores some of these management challenges created by BYOD and IT consumerization.

Quantum Computing

Quantum computing uses the principles of quantum physics to represent data and perform operations on these data. While conventional computers handle bits of data as either 0 or 1 but not both, quantum computing can process units of data as 0, 1, or both simultaneously. A quantum computer would gain enormous processing power through this ability to be in multiple states at once, allowing it to solve some scientific and business problems millions of times faster than can be done today. IBM has made quantum computing available to the general public through IBM Cloud. Google's Alphabet, Microsoft, Intel, and NASA and are also working on quantum computing platforms. Quantum computing is still an emerging technology, but its real-world applications are growing.

Virtualization

Virtualization is the process of presenting a set of computing resources (such as computing power or data storage) so that they can all be accessed in ways that are not restricted by physical configuration or geographic location. Virtualization enables a single physical resource (such as a server or a storage device) to appear to the user as multiple logical resources. For example, a server or mainframe can be configured to run many instances of an operating system (or different operating systems) so that it acts like many different machines. Each virtual server "looks" like a real physical server to software programs, and multiple virtual servers can run in parallel on a single machine. VMware is the leading virtualization software vendor for Windows and Linux servers.

Server virtualization is a common method of reducing technology costs by providing the ability to host multiple systems on a single physical machine. Most servers run at just 15 to 20 percent of capacity, and virtualization can boost server utilization rates to 70 percent or higher. Higher utilization rates translate into fewer computers required to process the same amount of work, reduced data center space to house machines, and lower energy usage. Virtualization also facilitates centralization and consolidation of hardware administration.

Virtualization also enables multiple physical resources (such as storage devices or servers) to appear as a single logical resource, as in **software-defined storage (SDS)**, which separates the software for managing data storage from storage hardware. Using software, firms can pool and arrange multiple storage infrastructure resources and efficiently allocate them to meet specific application needs. SDS enables firms to replace expensive storage hardware with lower-cost commodity hardware and cloud storage hardware. There is less under- or over-utilization of storage resources (Letschin, 2016).

Cloud Computing

It is now possible for companies and individuals to perform all of their computing work using a virtualized IT infrastructure in a remote location, as is the case with cloud computing. Cloud computing is a model of computing in which computer processing, storage, software, and other services are provided as a shared pool of virtualized resources over a network, primarily the Internet. These "clouds" of computing resources can be accessed on an as-needed basis from any connected device and location. Figure 5.9 illustrates the cloud computing concept.

FIGURE 5.9 CLOUD COMPUTING PLATFORM

In cloud computing, hardware and software capabilities are a pool of virtualized resources provided over a network, often the Internet. Businesses and employees have access to applications and IT infrastructure anywhere, at any time, and on any device.

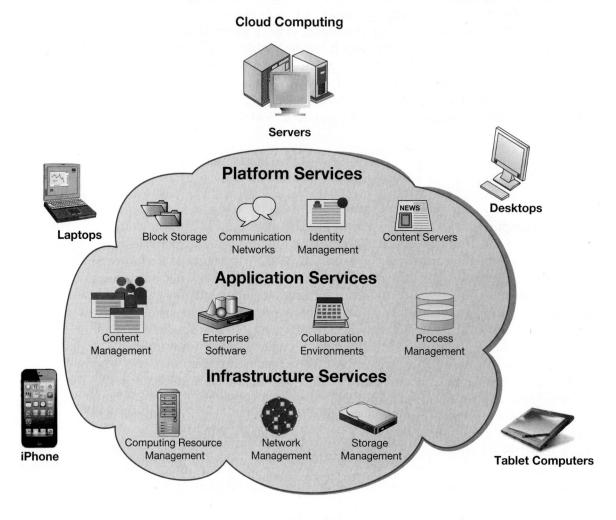

The U.S. National Institute of Standards and Technology (NIST) defines cloud computing as having the following essential characteristics (Mell and Grance, 2009):

- **On-demand self-service:** Consumers can obtain computing capabilities such as server time or network storage as needed automatically on their own.

- **Ubiquitous network access:** Cloud resources can be accessed using standard network and Internet devices, including mobile platforms.

- **Location-independent resource pooling:** Computing resources are pooled to serve multiple users, with different virtual resources dynamically assigned according to user demand. The user generally does not know where the computing resources are located.

- **Rapid elasticity:** Computing resources can be rapidly provisioned, increased, or decreased to meet changing user demand.

- **Measured service:** Charges for cloud resources are based on amount of resources actually used.

Cloud computing consists of three different types of services:

- **Infrastructure as a service (IaaS):** Customers use processing, storage, networking, and other computing resources from cloud service providers to run their information systems. For example, Amazon uses the spare capacity of its IT infrastructure to provide a broadly based cloud environment selling IT infrastructure services. These include its Simple Storage Service (S3) for storing customers' data and its Elastic Compute Cloud (EC2) service for running their applications. Users pay only for the amount of computing and storage capacity they actually use. (See the Interactive Session on Organizations). Figure 5.10 shows the range of services Amazon Web Services offers.

- **Software as a service (SaaS):** Customers use software hosted by the vendor on the vendor's cloud infrastructure and delivered as a service over a network. Leading **software as a service (SaaS)** examples are Google's G Suite, which provides common business applications online, and Salesforce.com, which leases customer relationship management and related software services over the Internet. Both charge users an annual subscription fee, although Google has a pared-down free version. Users access these applications from a web browser, and the data and software are maintained on the providers' remote servers.

- **Platform as a service (PaaS):** Customers use infrastructure and programming tools supported by the cloud service provider to develop their own applications. For example, Microsoft offers PaaS tools and services for software development and testing among its Azure cloud services. Another example is Salesforce.com's Salesforce Platform.

Chapter 2 discussed Google Docs, Microsoft Office 365, and related software services for desktop productivity and collaboration. These are among

---

FIGURE 5.10 AMAZON WEB SERVICES

Amazon Web Services (AWS) is a collection of web services that Amazon provides to users of its cloud platform. AWS is the largest provider of cloud computing services in the United States.

INTERACTIVE SESSION   ORGANIZATIONS

Look to the Cloud

If you want to see where computing is taking place, look to the cloud. Cloud computing is now the fastest-growing form of computing. According to Cisco Systems, 94 percent of all computing workloads will run in some form of cloud environment by 2021. This includes both public and private cloud platforms. Dedicated servers will be a distinct minority.

Cloud computing has become an affordable and sensible option for companies of all sizes, ranging from tiny Internet startups to established companies like Netflix and FedEx. For example, Amazon Web Services (AWS) provides subscribing companies with flexible computing power and data storage as well as data management, messaging, payment, and other services that can be used together or individually, as the business requires. Anyone with an Internet connection and a little bit of money can harness the same computing systems that Amazon itself uses to run its retail business. If customers provide specifications on the amount of server space, bandwidth, storage, and any other services they require, AWS can automatically allocate those resources. You don't pay a monthly or yearly fee to use Amazon's computing resources—instead, you pay for exactly what you use. Economies of scale keep costs astonishingly low, and AWS has been able to keep reducing prices. To remain competitive, other cloud computing vendors have had to follow suit.

Cloud computing also appeals to many businesses because the cloud services provider will handle all of the maintenance and upkeep of their IT infrastructures, allowing these businesses to spend more time on higher-value work. Start-up companies and smaller companies are finding that they no longer need to build their own data center. With cloud infrastructures like Amazon's readily available, they have access to technical capability that was formerly available to only much larger businesses. Hi-Media is the Internet publisher of the Fotolog photo blogging website. Hi-Media rebuilt the site and moved it to AWS where it can easily scale computing capacity to meet the demands of Fotolog's 32 million global users who have collectively posted 1 billion photos and 10 billion comments.

Although cloud computing has been touted as a cheap and more flexible alternative to buying and owning information technology, this isn't always the case. For large companies, paying a public cloud provider a monthly service fee for 10,000 or more employees may actually be more expensive than having the company maintain its own IT infrastructure and staff. Companies also worry about unexpected "runaway costs" from using a pay-per-use model. Integrating cloud services with existing IT infrastructures, errors, mismanagement, or unusually high volumes of web traffic will run up the bill for cloud service users.

A major barrier to widespread cloud adoption has been concerns about cloud reliability and security. Problems with Amazon Web Services' Direct Connect service took down several large customers on the morning of March 2, 2018, including enterprise software tool provider Atalassian, Capital One, and Amazon's own Alexa personal assistant. (AWS Direct Connect is used by hybrid cloud customers to set up a secure connection between AWS infrastructure and the customer's on-premises infrastructure.) Amazon's S3 cloud storage service experienced a four-hour outage February 28, 2017, shutting down thousands of websites across the Internet. There were also significant Amazon cloud outages in the preceding five years. As cloud computing continues to mature and the major cloud infrastructure providers gain more experience, cloud service and reliability have steadily improved. Experts recommend that companies for whom an outage would be a major risk consider using another computing service as a backup.

In February 2016 Netflix completed a decade-long project to shut down its own data centers and use Amazon's cloud exclusively to run its business. Management liked not having to guess months beforehand what the firm's hardware, storage, and networking needs would be. AWS would provide whatever Netflix needed at the moment. Netflix also maintains a content-delivery network through Internet service providers and other third parties to speed up the delivery of movies and web traffic between Netflix and its customers. Netflix competes with Amazon in the video-streaming business, and it wanted to retain control of its own content delivery network.

Dropbox, on the other hand, did the opposite. The online file hosting company saved nearly

$75 million in infrastructure costs over two years following a cloud data migration off AWS. Dropbox had been an early AWS success story, but it had never run all of its systems on AWS. Dropbox had originally split its architecture to host metadata that provides information about other data in private data centers and to host file content on the AWS Simple Storage Service (S3). Dropbox subsequently built systems better suited to its needs, which so far has produced big savings following its cloud data migration off AWS. However, that transition was costly. The company spent more than $53 million for custom architectures in three colocation facilities to accommodate exabytes of storage. Dropbox stores the remaining 10 percent of user data on AWS, in part to localize data in the United States and Europe, and it uses Amazon's public cloud to help deliver its services. Experts believe that Dropbox's experience with AWS is not representative of most companies. Dropbox's strategy to build one of the largest data stores in the world depended on owning its computing resources.

Many large companies are moving more of their computing to the cloud but are unable to migrate completely. Legacy systems are the most difficult to switch over. Most midsized and large companies will gravitate toward a hybrid approach. The top cloud providers themselves—Amazon, Google, Microsoft, and IBM—use their own public cloud services for some purposes, but they continue to keep certain functions on private servers. Worries about reliability, security, and risks of change have made it difficult for them to move critical computing tasks to the public cloud.

Honda UK implemented the hybrid cloud model to enable its IT infrastructure to handle sudden spikes in usage of its websites. The company had experienced sudden web server crashes due to bandwidth limitations. Honda UK had initially moved to a private cloud model, which was used during the launch of the Accord Tourer model to handle heavy user demand for its website. Honda UK then started using the public cloud during the launch of the Honda CR-Z. Honda UK had to pay for the cloud service only when the company used it. The pay-as-you-go model helped keep costs in check while ensuring optimum scalability.

Sources: Trevor Jones, "Dropbox Is Likely an Outlier with its Successful Cloud Data Migration off AWS," searchaws.com, February 28, 2018; Andy Patrizio, "Cisco Says Almost All Workloads Will Be Cloud-Based Within 3 Years," *Network World,* February 5, 2018; Tom Krazit, "Widespread Outage at Amazon Web Services' U.S. East Region Takes down Alexa, Atlassian Developer Tools," *GeekWire,* March 2, 2018; DasGupta, "A Case Study: How Hybrid Clouds Should Be Done," Cloudwards.net, January 21, 2018; Robert McMillan, "Amazon Grapples with Outage at AWS Cloud Service," *Wall Street Journal,* March 1, 2017; "AWS Case Study: Hi-Media," www.aws.amazon.com, accessed May 14, 2017; and Kelly Bit, "The $10 Hedge Fund Supercomputer That's Sweeping Wall Street," *Bloomberg Business Week,* May 20, 2015.

CASE STUDY QUESTIONS

1. What business benefits do cloud computing services provide? What problems do they solve?

2. What are the disadvantages of cloud computing?

3. What kinds of businesses are most likely to benefit from using cloud computing? Why?

the most popular software services for consumers, although they are increasingly used in business. Salesforce.com is a leading software service for business. Salesforce.com provides customer relationship management (CRM) and other application software solutions as software services leased over the Internet. Its sales and service clouds offer applications for improving sales and customer service. A marketing cloud enables companies to engage in digital marketing interactions with customers through email, mobile, social, web, and connected products. Salesforce.com also provides a community cloud platform for online collaboration and engagement and an analytics cloud platform to deploy sales, service, marketing, and custom analytics apps.

Salesforce.com is also a leading example of platform as a service (PaaS). Its Salesforce Platform gives users the ability to develop, launch, and manage applications without having to deal with the infrastructure required for creating new software. The Salesforce Platform provides a set of development tools and IT services that enable users to build new applications and run them in the cloud on Salesforce.com's data center infrastructure. Salesforce.com also lists software from other independent developers on its AppExchange, an online marketplace for third-party applications that run on the Salesforce Platform.

A cloud can be private or public. A **public cloud** is owned and maintained by a cloud service provider, such as Amazon Web Services, and made available to the general public or industry group. Public cloud services are often used for websites with public information and product descriptions, one-time large computing projects, developing and testing new applications, and consumer services such as online storage of data, music, and photos. Google Drive, Dropbox, and Apple iCloud are leading examples of these consumer public cloud services.

A **private cloud** is operated solely for an organization. It may be managed by the organization or a third party and may be hosted either internally or externally. Like public clouds, private clouds are able to allocate storage, computing power, or other resources seamlessly to provide computing resources on an as-needed basis. Companies that want flexible IT resources and a cloud service model while retaining control over their own IT infrastructure are gravitating toward these private clouds.

Because organizations using public clouds do not own the infrastructure, they do not have to make large investments in their own hardware and software. Instead, they purchase their computing services from remote providers and pay only for the amount of computing power they actually use (utility computing) or are billed on a monthly or annual subscription basis. The term **on-demand computing** has also been used to describe such services.

Cloud computing has some drawbacks. Unless users make provisions for storing their data locally, the responsibility for data storage and control is in the hands of the provider. Some companies worry about the security risks related to entrusting their critical data and systems to an outside vendor that also works with other companies. Companies expect their systems to be available 24/7 and do not want to suffer any loss of business capability if cloud infrastructures malfunction. Nevertheless, the trend is for companies to shift more of their computer processing and storage to some form of cloud infrastructure. Startups and small companies with limited IT resources and budgets will find public cloud services especially helpful.

Large firms are most likely to adopt a **hybrid cloud** computing model where they use their own infrastructure for their most essential core activities and adopt public cloud computing for less critical systems or for additional processing capacity during peak business periods. Table 5.2 compares the three cloud computing models. Cloud computing will gradually shift firms from having a fixed infrastructure capacity toward a more flexible infrastructure, some of it owned by the firm and some of it rented from giant computer centers owned by computer hardware vendors. You can find out more about cloud computing in the Learning Tracks for this chapter.

Edge Computing

Having all the laptops, smartphones, tablets, wireless sensor networks, and local on-premise servers used in cloud computing systems interacting with a single central public cloud data center to process all their data can be inefficient

TABLE 5.2   CLOUD COMPUTING MODELS COMPARED

TYPE OF CLOUD	DESCRIPTION	MANAGED BY	USES
Public cloud	Third-party service offering computing, storage, and software services to multiple customers and that is available to the public	Third-party service providers	Companies without major privacy concerns Companies seeking pay-as-you-go IT services Companies lacking IT resources and expertise
Private cloud	Cloud infrastructure operated solely for a single organization and hosted either internally or externally	In-house IT or private third-party host	Companies with stringent privacy and security requirements Companies that must have control over data sovereignty
Hybrid cloud	Combination of private and public cloud services that remain separate entities	In-house IT, private host, third-party providers	Companies requiring some in-house control of IT that are also willing to assign part of their IT infrastructures to a public cloud

and costly. **Edge computing** is a method of optimizing cloud computing systems by performing some data processing on a set of linked servers at the edge of the network, near the source of the data. This reduces the amount of data flowing back and forth between local computers and other devices and the central cloud data center.

Edge computing deployments are useful when sensors or other IoT devices do not need to be constantly connected to a central cloud. For example, an oil rig in the ocean might have thousands of sensors producing large amounts of data, perhaps to confirm that systems are working properly. The data do not necessarily need to be sent over a network as soon as they are produced, so the local edge computing system could compile the data and send daily reports to a central data center or cloud for long-term storage. By only sending important data over the network, the edge computing system reduces the amount of data traversing the network

Edge computing also reduces delays in the transmitting and processing of data because data does not have to travel over a network to a remote data center or cloud for processing. This is ideal for situations where delays of milliseconds can be untenable, such as in financial services or manufacturing.

Green Computing

By curbing hardware proliferation and power consumption, virtualization has become one of the principal technologies for promoting green computing. **Green computing, or green IT**, refers to practices and technologies for designing, manufacturing, using, and disposing of computers, servers, and associated devices such as monitors, printers, storage devices, and networking and communications systems to minimize impact on the environment.

According to Green House Data, the world's data centers use as much energy as the output of 30 nuclear power plants, which amounts to 1.5 percent of all energy use in the world. A corporate data center can easily consume over 100 times more power than a standard office building. All this additional power consumption has a negative impact on the environment and corporate operating costs. Data centers are now being designed with energy efficiency in mind, using state-of-the art air-cooling techniques, energy-efficient equipment, virtualization, and other energy-saving practices. Large companies like Microsoft, Google, Facebook, and Apple are starting to reduce their carbon footprint with clean energy–powered data centers with power-conserving equipment and extensive use of wind and hydropower.

High-Performance and Power-Saving Processors

Another way to reduce power requirements and hardware sprawl is to use more efficient and power-saving processors. Contemporary microprocessors now feature multiple processor cores (which perform the reading and execution of computer instructions) on a single chip. A **multicore processor** is an integrated circuit to which two or more processor cores have been attached for enhanced performance, reduced power consumption, and more efficient simultaneous processing of multiple tasks. This technology enables two or more processing engines with reduced power requirements and heat dissipation to perform tasks faster than a resource-hungry chip with a single processing core. Today you'll find PCs with dual-core, quad-core, six-core, and eight-core processors and servers with 16- and 32-core processors.

Intel and other chip manufacturers are working on microprocessors that minimize power consumption, which is essential for prolonging battery life in small mobile digital devices. Highly power-efficient microprocessors, such as the A9, A10, and A11 processors used in Apple's iPhone and iPad and Intel's Atom processor, are used in lightweight smartphones and tablets, intelligent cars, and healthcare devices.

5-4 What are the current computer software platforms and trends?

There are four major themes in contemporary software platform evolution:

- Linux and open source software
- Java, HTML, and HTML5
- Web services and service-oriented architecture
- Software outsourcing and cloud services

Linux and Open Source Software

Open source software is software produced by a community of several hundred thousand programmers around the world. According to the leading open source professional association, OpenSource.org, open source software is free and can be modified by users. Works derived from the original code must also be free. Open source software is by definition not restricted to any specific operating system or hardware technology.

Popular open source software tools include the Linux operating system, the Apache HTTP web server, the Mozilla Firefox web browser, and the Apache OpenOffice desktop productivity suite. Google's Android mobile operating system and Chrome web browser are based on open source tools. You can find out more about the Open Source Definition from the Open Source Initiative and the history of open source software in the Learning Tracks for this chapter.

Linux

Perhaps the most well-known open source software is Linux, an operating system related to Unix. Linux was created by Finnish programmer Linus Torvalds and first posted on the Internet in August 1991. Linux applications are embedded in cell phones, smartphones, tablet computers, and consumer electronics.

Linux is available in free versions downloadable from the Internet or in low-cost commercial versions that include tools and support from vendors such as Red Hat.

Although Linux is not used in many desktop systems, it is a leading operating system for servers, mainframe computers, and supercomputers. IBM, HP, Intel, Dell, and Oracle have made Linux a central part of their offerings to corporations. Linux has profound implications for corporate software platforms—cost reduction, reliability, and resilience—because Linux can work on all the major hardware platforms.

Software for the Web: Java, HTML, and HTML5

Java is an operating system-independent, processor-independent, object-oriented programming language created by Sun Microsystems that has become the leading interactive programming environment for the web. The Java platform has migrated into mobile phones, tablets, automobiles, music players, game machines, and set-top cable television systems serving interactive content and pay-per-view services. Java software is designed to run on any computer or computing device, regardless of the specific microprocessor or operating system the device uses. For each of the computing environments in which Java is used, a Java Virtual Machine interprets Java programming code for that machine. In this manner, the code is written once and can be used on any machine for which there exists a Java Virtual Machine.

Java developers can create small applet programs that can be embedded in web pages and downloaded to run on a web browser. A **web browser** is an easy-to-use software tool with a graphical user interface for displaying web pages and for accessing the web and other Internet resources. Microsoft's Internet Explorer, Mozilla Firefox, Google Chrome, and Apple Safari browsers are examples. At the enterprise level, Java is being used for more complex e-commerce and e-business applications that require communication with an organization's back-end transaction processing systems.

HTML and HTML5

Hypertext Markup Language (HTML) is a page description language for specifying how text, graphics, video, and sound are placed on a web page and for creating dynamic links to other web pages and objects. Using these links, a user need only point at a highlighted keyword or graphic, click on it, and immediately be transported to another document.

HTML was originally designed to create and link static documents composed largely of text. Today, however, the web is much more social and interactive, and many web pages have multimedia elements—images, audio, and video. Third-party plug-in applications like Flash, Silverlight, and Java have been required to integrate these rich media with web pages. However, these add-ons require additional programming and put strains on computer processing. The next evolution of HTML, called **HTML5**, solves this problem by making it possible to embed images, audio, video, and other elements directly into a document without processor-intensive add-ons. HTML5 makes it easier for web pages to function across different display devices, including mobile devices as well as desktops, and it will support the storage of data offline for apps that run over the web.

Other popular programming tools for web applications include Ruby and Python. Ruby is an object-oriented programming language known for speed and ease of use in building web applications, and Python (praised for its clarity) is being used for building cloud computing applications.

Web Services and Service-Oriented Architecture

Web services refer to a set of loosely coupled software components that exchange information with each other using universal web communication standards and languages. They can exchange information between two different systems regardless of the operating systems or programming languages on which the systems are based. They can be used to build open standard web-based applications linking systems of two different organizations, and they can also be used to create applications that link disparate systems within a single company. Different applications can use web services to communicate with each other in a standard way without time-consuming custom coding.

The foundation technology for web services is **XML**, which stands for Extensible Markup Language. This language was developed in 1996 by the World Wide Web Consortium (W3C, the international body that oversees the development of the web) as a more powerful and flexible markup language than hypertext markup language (HTML) for web pages. Whereas HTML is limited to describing how data should be presented in the form of web pages, XML can perform presentation, communication, and storage of data. In XML, a number is not simply a number; the XML tag specifies whether the number represents a price, a date, or a ZIP code. Table 5.3 illustrates some sample XML statements.

By tagging selected elements of the content of documents for their meanings, XML makes it possible for computers to manipulate and interpret their data automatically and perform operations on the data without human intervention. Web browsers and computer programs, such as order processing or enterprise resource planning (ERP) software, can follow programmed rules for applying and displaying the data. XML provides a standard format for data exchange, enabling web services to pass data from one process to another.

Web services communicate through XML messages over standard web protocols. Companies discover and locate web services through a directory. Using web protocols, a software application can connect freely to other applications without custom programming for each different application with which it wants to communicate. Everyone shares the same standards.

The collection of web services that are used to build a firm's software systems constitutes what is known as a service-oriented architecture. A **service-oriented architecture (SOA)** is set of self-contained services that communicate with each other to create a working software application. Business tasks are accomplished by executing a series of these services. Software developers reuse these services in other combinations to assemble other applications as needed.

Virtually all major software vendors provide tools and entire platforms for building and integrating software applications using web services. Microsoft has incorporated web services tools in its Microsoft .NET platform.

TABLE 5.3 EXAMPLES OF XML

PLAIN ENGLISH	XML
Subcompact	<AUTOMOBILETYPE="Subcompact">
4 passenger	<PASSENGERUNIT="PASS">4</PASSENGER>
$16,800	<PRICE CURRENCY="USD">$16,800</PRICE>

Dollar Rent A Car's systems use web services for its online booking system with Southwest Airline's website. Although both companies' systems are based on different technology platforms, a person booking a flight on Southwest.com can reserve a car from Dollar without leaving the airline's website. Instead of struggling to get Dollar's reservation system to share data with Southwest's information systems, Dollar used Microsoft .NET web services technology as an intermediary. Reservations from Southwest are translated into web services protocols, which are then translated into formats that can be understood by Dollar's computers.

Other car rental companies have linked their information systems to airline companies' websites before. But without web services, these connections had to be built one at a time. Web services provide a standard way for Dollar's computers to "talk" to other companies' information systems without having to build special links to each one. Dollar is now expanding its use of web services to link directly to the systems of a small tour operator and a large travel reservation system as well as a wireless website for cell phones and smartphones. It does not have to write new software code for each new partner's information systems or each new wireless device (see Figure 5.11).

Software Outsourcing and Cloud Services

Today, many business firms continue to operate legacy systems that continue to meet a business need and that would be extremely costly to replace. But they will purchase or rent most of their new software applications from external sources. Figure 5.12 illustrates the rapid growth in external sources of software for U.S. firms.

FIGURE 5.11   HOW DOLLAR RENT A CAR USES WEB SERVICES

Dollar Rent A Car uses web services to provide a standard intermediate layer of software to "talk" to other companies' information systems. Dollar Rent A Car can use this set of web services to link to other companies' information systems without having to build a separate link to each firm's systems.

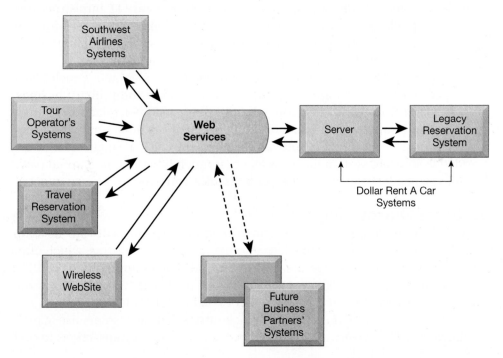

FIGURE 5.12 CHANGING SOURCES OF FIRM SOFTWARE

In 2017, U.S. firms spent an estimated $380 billion on software. About 47 percent ($179 billion) of that originated outside the firm, provided by a variety of vendors. About 13 percent ($49 billion) was provided by SaaS vendors as an online cloud-based service.

Sources: BEA National Income and Product Accounts, 2018.

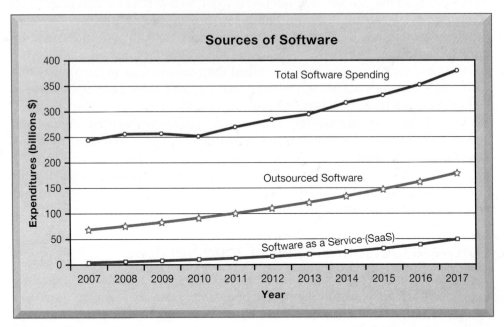

There are three external sources for software: software packages from a commercial software vendor (most ERP systems), outsourcing custom application development to an external vendor (which may or may not be offshore), and cloud-based software services and tools (SaaS/PaaS).

Software Packages and Enterprise Software

We have already described software packages for enterprise applications as one of the major types of software components in contemporary IT infrastructures. A **software package** is a prewritten commercially available set of software programs that eliminates the need for a firm to write its own software programs for certain functions, such as payroll processing or order handling.

Enterprise application software vendors such as SAP and Oracle have developed powerful software packages that can support the primary business processes of a firm worldwide from warehousing, customer relationship management, and supply chain management to finance and human resources. These large-scale enterprise software systems provide a single, integrated, worldwide software system for firms at a cost much less than they would pay if they developed it themselves. Chapter 9 discusses enterprise systems in detail.

Software Outsourcing

Software **outsourcing** enables a firm to contract custom software development or maintenance of existing legacy programs to outside firms, which often operate offshore in low-wage areas of the world. For example, in 2013, IKEA announced a six-year offshore IT outsourcing deal with German infrastructure solutions firm Wincor Nixdorf. Wincor Nixdorf set up 12,000 point-of- sale (POS) systems in 300 IKEA stores in 25 countries. These systems use Wincor Nixdorf's POS TP.net software to control furniture checkout transactions in each store and consolidate all data across the retail group. Wincor Nixdorf provides IKEA with services that include operation and customization of the systems, as well as updating the software and applications running on them. Having a single software provider offshore helped IKEA reduce the work to run the stores (Existek, 2017). Offshore software outsourcing firms have primarily provided lower-level maintenance, data entry, and call center operations, although more sophisticated and experienced offshore firms, particularly in India, have been hired for new-program development. However, as wages offshore rise and the costs of managing offshore projects are factored in (see Chapter 13), some work that would have been sent offshore is returning to domestic companies.

Cloud-Based Software Services and Tools

In the past, software such as Microsoft Word or Adobe Illustrator came in a box and was designed to operate on a single machine. Today, you're more likely to download the software from the vendor's website or to use the software as a cloud service delivered over the Internet and pay a subscription fee.

Cloud-based software and the data it uses are hosted on powerful servers in data centers and can be accessed with an Internet connection and standard web browser. In addition to free or low-cost tools for individuals and small businesses provided by Google or Yahoo, enterprise software and other complex business functions are available as services from the major commercial software vendors. Instead of buying and installing software programs, subscribing companies rent the same functions from these services, with users paying either on a subscription or per-transaction basis. A leading example of software as a service (SaaS) is Salesforce.com, described earlier in this chapter, which provides on-demand software services for customer relationship management.

In order to manage their relationship with an outsourcer or technology service provider, firms need a contract that includes a **service level agreement (SLA)**. The SLA is a formal contract between customers and their service providers that defines the specific responsibilities of the service provider and the level of service expected by the customer. SLAs typically specify the nature and level of services provided, criteria for performance measurement, support options, provisions for security and disaster recovery, hardware and software ownership and upgrades, customer support, billing, and conditions for terminating the agreement. We provide a Learning Track on this topic.

Mashups and Apps

The software you use for both personal and business tasks today may be composed of interchangeable components that integrate freely with other applications on the Internet. Individual users and entire companies mix and match these software components to create their own customized applications and to share information with others. The resulting software applications are called **mashups**. The idea is to take different sources and produce a new work that is greater than the sum of its parts. You have performed a mashup if you've ever personalized your Facebook profile or your blog with a capability to display videos or slide shows.

Web mashups combine the capabilities of two or more online applications to create a kind of hybrid that provides more customer value than the original sources alone. For instance, ZipRealty uses Google Maps and data provided by an online real estate database. **Apps** are small, specialized software programs that run on the Internet, on your computer, or on your mobile phone or tablet and are generally delivered over the Internet. Google refers to its online services as apps. But when we talk about apps today, most of the attention goes to the apps that have been developed for the mobile digital platform. It is these apps that turn smartphones and tablets into general-purpose computing tools. There are now millions of apps for the IOS and Android operating systems.

Some downloaded apps do not access the web, but many do, providing faster access to web content than traditional web browsers. Apps provide a streamlined non-browser pathway for users to perform a number of tasks, ranging from reading the newspaper to shopping, searching, personal health monitoring, playing games, and buying. They increasingly are used by managers as gateways to their firm's enterprise systems. Because so many people are now accessing the Internet from their mobile devices, some say that apps are "the new browsers." Apps are also starting to influence the design and function of traditional websites as consumers are attracted to the look and feel of apps and their speed of operation.

Many apps are free or purchased for a small charge, much less than conventional software, which further adds to their appeal. The success of these mobile platforms depends in large part on the quantity and the quality of the apps they provide. Apps tie the customer to a specific hardware platform: As the user adds more and more apps to his or her mobile phone, the cost of switching to a competing mobile platform rises.

At the moment, the most commonly downloaded apps are games, news and weather, maps/navigation, social networking, music, and video/movies. But there are also serious apps for business users that make it possible to create and edit documents, connect to corporate systems, schedule and participate in meetings, track shipments, and dictate voice messages (see the Chapter 1 Interactive Session on Management). Most large online retailers have apps for consumers for researching and buying goods and services online.

5-5 What are the challenges of managing IT infrastructure and management solutions?

Creating and managing a coherent IT infrastructure raises multiple challenges: dealing with platform and technology change (including cloud and mobile computing), management and governance, and making wise infrastructure investments.

Dealing with Platform and Infrastructure Change

As firms grow, they often quickly outgrow their infrastructure. As firms shrink, they can get stuck with excessive infrastructure purchased in better times. How can a firm remain flexible if investments in IT infrastructure are fixed-cost purchases and licenses? How well does the infrastructure scale? **Scalability** refers to the ability of a computer, product, or system to expand to serve a large number of users without breaking down. New applications, mergers and acquisitions, and changes in business volume all affect computer workload and must be considered when planning hardware capacity.

Firms using mobile computing and cloud computing platforms will require new policies, procedures, and tools for managing these platforms. They will need to inventory all of their mobile devices in business use and develop policies and tools for tracking, updating, and securing them, and for controlling the data and applications that run on them. Firms often turn to **mobile device management (MDM)** software, which monitors, manages, and secures mobile devices that are deployed across multiple mobile service providers and across multiple mobile operating systems being used in the organization. MDM tools enable the IT department to monitor mobile usage, install or update mobile software, back up and restore mobile devices, and remove software and data from devices that are stolen or lost.

Firms using cloud computing and SaaS will need to fashion new contractual arrangements with remote vendors to make sure that the hardware and software for critical applications are always available when needed and that they meet corporate standards for information security. It is up to business management to determine acceptable levels of computer response time and availability for the firm's mission-critical systems to maintain the level of business performance that is expected.

Management and Governance

A long-standing issue among information system managers and CEOs has been the question of who will control and manage the firm's IT infrastructure. Chapter 2 introduced the concept of IT governance and described some issues it addresses. Other important questions about IT governance are: Should departments and divisions have the responsibility of making their own information technology decisions, or should IT infrastructure be centrally controlled and managed? What is the relationship between central information systems management and business unit information systems management? How will infrastructure costs be allocated among business units? Each organization will need to arrive at answers based on its own needs.

Making Wise Infrastructure Investments

IT infrastructure is a major investment for the firm. If too much is spent on infrastructure, it lies idle and constitutes a drag on the firm's financial performance. If too little is spent, important business services cannot be delivered and the firm's competitors (who spent the right amount) will outperform the under-investing firm. How much should the firm spend on infrastructure? This question is not easy to answer.

A related question is whether a firm should purchase and maintain its own IT infrastructure components or rent them from external suppliers, including those offering cloud services. The decision either to purchase your own IT assets or to rent them from external providers is typically called the *rent-versus-buy* decision.

Cloud computing is a low-cost way to increase scalability and flexibility, but firms should evaluate this option carefully in light of security requirements and impact on business processes and workflows. In some instances, the cost of renting software adds up to more than purchasing and maintaining an application in-house, or firms can overspend on cloud services (Loten, 2018). Yet there are many benefits to using cloud services including significant reductions in hardware, software, human resources, and maintenance costs. Moving to cloud computing allows firms to focus on their core businesses rather than technology issues.

Total Cost of Ownership of Technology Assets
The actual cost of owning technology resources includes the original cost of acquiring and installing hardware and software as well as ongoing administration costs for hardware and software upgrades, maintenance, technical support, training, and even utility and real estate costs for running and housing

TABLE 5.4 TOTAL COST OF OWNERSHIP (TCO) COST COMPONENTS	
INFRASTRUCTURE COMPONENT	COST COMPONENTS
Hardware acquisition	Purchase price of computer hardware equipment, including computers, terminals, storage, and printers
Software acquisition	Purchase or license of software for each user
Installation	Cost to install computers and software
Training	Cost to provide training for information systems specialists and end users
Support	Cost to provide ongoing technical support, help desks, and so forth
Maintenance	Cost to upgrade the hardware and software
Infrastructure	Cost to acquire, maintain, and support related infrastructure, such as networks and specialized equipment (including storage backup units)
Downtime	Cost of lost productivity if hardware or software failures cause the system to be unavailable for processing and user tasks
Space and energy	Real estate and utility costs for housing and providing power for the technology

the technology. The **total cost of ownership (TCO)** model can be used to analyze these direct and indirect costs to help firms determine the actual cost of specific technology implementations. Table 5.4 describes the most important components to consider in a TCO analysis.

When all these cost components are considered, the TCO for a PC might run up to three times the original purchase price of the equipment. Gains in productivity and efficiency from equipping employees with mobile computing devices must be balanced against increased costs from integrating these devices into the firm's IT infrastructure and from providing technical support. Other cost components include fees for wireless airtime, end-user training, help desk support, and software for special applications. Costs are higher if the mobile devices run many different applications or need to be integrated into back-end systems such as enterprise applications.

Hardware and software acquisition costs account for only about 20 percent of TCO, so managers must pay close attention to administration costs to understand the full cost of the firm's hardware and software. It is possible to reduce some of these administration costs through better management. Many large firms are saddled with redundant, incompatible hardware and software because their departments and divisions have been allowed to make their own technology purchases.

In addition to switching to cloud services, these firms could reduce their TCO through greater centralization and standardization of their hardware and software resources. Companies could reduce the size of the information systems staff required to support their infrastructure if the firm minimizes the number of different computer models and pieces of software that employees are allowed to use. In a centralized infrastructure, systems can be administered from a central location and troubleshooting can be performed from that location.

Competitive Forces Model for IT Infrastructure Investment

Figure 5.13 illustrates a competitive forces model you can use to address the question of how much your firm should spend on IT infrastructure.

FIGURE 5.13   COMPETITIVE FORCES MODEL FOR IT INFRASTRUCTURE

There are six factors you can use to answer the question "How much should our firm spend on IT infrastructure?"

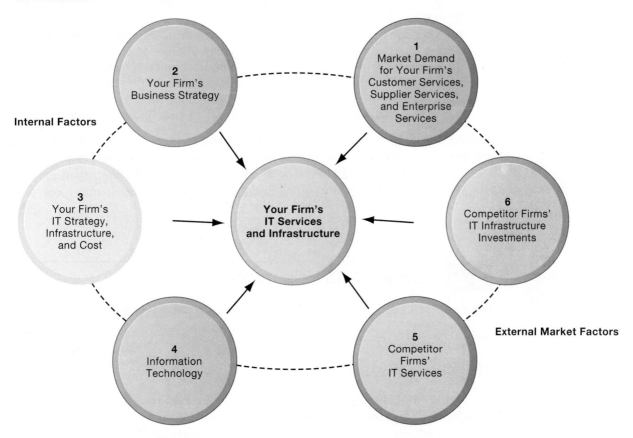

Market demand for your firm's services. Make an inventory of the services you currently provide to customers, suppliers, and employees. Survey each group, or hold focus groups to find out if the services you currently offer are meeting the needs of each group. For example, are customers complaining of slow responses to their queries about price and availability? Are employees complaining about the difficulty of finding the right information for their jobs? Are suppliers complaining about the difficulties of discovering your production requirements?

Your firm's business strategy. Analyze your firm's five-year business strategy and try to assess what new services and capabilities will be required to achieve strategic goals.

Your firm's IT strategy, infrastructure, and cost. Examine your firm's information technology plans for the next five years and assess its alignment with the firm's business plans. Determine the total IT infrastructure costs. You will want to perform a TCO analysis. If your firm has no IT strategy, you will need to devise one that takes into account the firm's five-year strategic plan.

Information technology assessment. Is your firm behind the technology curve or at the bleeding edge of information technology? Both situations are to be avoided. It is usually not desirable to spend resources on advanced technologies that are still experimental, often expensive, and sometimes unreliable. You want to spend on technologies for which standards have been established; IT vendors are competing on cost, not design; and where there are multiple suppliers. However, you do not want to put off investment in new technologies or allow competitors to develop new business models and capabilities based on the new technologies.

Competitor firm services. Try to assess what technology services competitors offer to customers, suppliers, and employees. Establish quantitative and qualitative measures to compare them to those of your firm. If your firm's service levels fall short, your company is at a competitive disadvantage. Look for ways your firm can excel at service levels.

Competitor firm IT infrastructure investments. Benchmark your expenditures for IT infrastructure against your competitors. Many companies are quite public about their innovative expenditures on IT. If competing firms try to keep IT expenditures secret, you may be able to find IT investment information in public companies' SEC Form 10-K annual reports to the federal government when those expenditures affect a firm's financial results.

Your firm does not necessarily need to spend as much as or more than your competitors. Perhaps it has discovered much less expensive ways of providing services, and this can lead to a cost advantage. Alternatively, your firm may be spending far less than competitors, and experiencing commensurate poor performance and losing market share.

5-6 How will MIS help my career?

Here is how Chapter 5 and this book can help you find a job as an entry-level IT consultant.

The Company

A1 Tech IT Consulting, a national technology consulting firm headquartered in Atlanta, is looking for an entry-level IT consultant. The company partners with technology vendors to create and sell leading-edge technology solutions based on cloud, network, and managed IT services to small, medium-sized, and enterprise-sized companies. The company has 65 employees and is noted for outstanding customer service.

Position Description

The entry-level IT consultant will work with the firm's account managers to maintain good relationships with existing clients and help its technology consultants create solutions and proposals for prospective customers. The company will provide on-the-job training about the technology industry and its technology consulting process. Job responsibilities include:

- Providing research on potential and existing clients and the competitive landscape.
- Managing digital marketing campaigns.
- Assisting in identifying potential business opportunities.
- Preparing periodic reports on screening, tracking, and monitoring clients and prospects.

Job Requirements

- Bachelor's degree or equivalent
- Ability to communicate well with clients by phone, by email, and face-to-face
- Strong organizational, presentation, and writing skills

- Ability to work in a fast-paced environment and collaborate effectively as a team member
- Proficiency in Microsoft Office (Word, Excel, and PowerPoint)
- Strong organizational, presentation, and writing skills and willingness to learn

Interview Questions

1. What do you know about cloud computing and managed IT services? Are you familiar with common operating systems, security, and data management platforms? Have you ever used these services on the job? What did you do with them?
2. Have you had much face-to-face contact with customers? Can you describe what work you did with customers? Have you ever helped customers with a technology problem?
3. Do you have any digital marketing experience?
4. Can you give us an example of a sales-related problem or other business problem that you helped solve? Do you do any writing and analysis? Can you provide examples?
5. What is your level of proficiency with Microsoft Office? What work have you done with Excel spreadsheets?

Author Tips

1. Review this chapter and also Chapters 6 and 8 of this text, paying special attention to cloud computing, networking technology, and managed technology services.
2. Use the web to research the company and how it works with other technology companies to provide its IT services. Learn what you can about these partner companies as well and the tools and services they offer.
3. Inquire exactly how you would be using Microsoft Office, and if possible provide examples of how you used these tools to solve problems in the classroom or for a job assignment. Bring examples of your writing (including some from your Digital Portfolio described in MyLab MIS) demonstrating your analytical skills and project experience.
4. Indicate that you are very interested in learning more about the technology industry and technologies and services used by the company.
5. Review the company's LinkedIn page, Facebook, and Twitter to learn about strategic trends and important issues for this company.

REVIEW SUMMARY

5-1 What is IT infrastructure, and what are the stages and drivers of IT infrastructure evolution?

IT infrastructure is the shared technology resources that provide the platform for the firm's specific information system applications. IT infrastructure includes hardware, software, and services that are shared across the entire firm.

The five stages of IT infrastructure evolution are the mainframe era, the personal computer era, the client/server era, the enterprise computing era, and the cloud and mobile computing era. Moore's Law deals with the exponential increase in processing power and decline in the cost of computer technology, stating that every 18 months the power of microprocessors doubles and the price of computing falls in half. The Law of Mass Digital Storage deals with the exponential decrease in the cost of storing data, stating that the number of kilobytes of data that can be stored on magnetic media for $1 roughly doubles every 15 months. Metcalfe's Law states that a network's value to participants grows exponentially as the network takes on more members. The rapid decline in costs of communication and growing agreement in the technology industry to use computing and communications standards are also driving an explosion of computer use.

5-2 What are the components of IT infrastructure?

Major IT infrastructure components include computer hardware platforms, operating system platforms, enterprise software platforms, networking and telecommunications platforms, database management software, Internet platforms, and consulting services and systems integrators.

5-3 What are the current trends in computer hardware platforms?

Increasingly, computing is taking place on a mobile digital platform. Quantum computing is an emerging technology that could dramatically boost processing power through the ability to be in more than one state at the same time. Consumerization of IT is the business use of information technology that originated in the consumer market. Virtualization organizes computing resources so that their use is not restricted by physical configuration or geographic location. In cloud computing, firms and individuals obtain computing power and software as services over a network, including the Internet, rather than purchasing and installing the hardware and software on their own computers. Edge computing helps optimize cloud computing by performing some data processing on a set of linked servers at the edge of the network, near the source of the data. A multicore processor is a microprocessor to which two or more processing cores have been attached for enhanced performance. Green computing includes practices and technologies for producing, using, and disposing of information technology hardware to minimize negative impact on the environment.

5-4 What are the current computer software platforms and trends?

Open source software is produced and maintained by a global community of programmers and is often downloadable for free. Linux is a powerful, resilient open source operating system that can run on multiple hardware platforms and is used widely to run web servers. Java is an operating system– and hardware-independent programming language that is the leading interactive programming environment for the web. HTML5 makes it possible to embed images, audio, and video directly into a web document without add-on programs. Web services are loosely coupled software components based on open web standards that work with any application software and operating system. They can be used as components of web-based applications linking the systems of two different organizations or to link disparate systems of a single company. Companies are purchasing their new software applications from outside sources, including software packages, by outsourcing custom application development to an external vendor (that may be offshore), or by renting online software services (SaaS). Mashups combine two different software services to create new software applications and services. Apps are software applications that run on mobile devices and are delivered over the Internet.

5-5 What are the challenges of managing IT infrastructure and management solutions?

Major challenges include dealing with platform and infrastructure change, infrastructure management and governance, and making wise infrastructure investments. Solution guidelines include using a competitive forces model to determine how much to spend on IT infrastructure and where to make strategic infrastructure investments, and establishing the total cost of ownership (TCO) of information technology assets. The total cost of owning technology resources includes not only the original cost of computer hardware and software but also costs for hardware and software upgrades, maintenance, technical support, and training. Many firms are turning to cloud computing in an effort to reduce their IT platform costs. Firms use tools for mobile device management (MDM) to monitor, manage, and secure mobile devices that are deployed across the enterprise.

Key Terms

Android, 178

Application server, 169

Apps, 195

BYOD, 182

Chrome OS, 178

Clients, 169

Client/server computing, 169

Cloud computing, 170

MyLab MIS

To complete the problems with MyLab MIS, go to EOC Discussion Questions in MyLab MIS.

Review Questions

5-1 What is IT infrastructure, and what are the stages and drivers of IT infrastructure evolution?

- Define IT infrastructure from both a technology and a services perspective.

- List each of the eras in IT infrastructure evolution and describe its distinguishing characteristics.

- Define and describe the following: web server, application server, multitiered client/server architecture.

- Describe Moore's Law and the Law of Mass Digital Storage.

- Describe how network economics, declining communications costs, and technology standards affect IT infrastructure.

5-2 What are the components of IT infrastructure?

- List and describe the components of IT infrastructure that firms need to manage.

5-3 What are the current trends in computer hardware platforms?

- Describe the evolving mobile platform, consumerization of IT, and cloud computing.

- Explain how businesses can benefit from virtualization, green computing, and multicore processors.

5-4 What are the current computer software platforms and trends?

- Define and describe open source software and Linux and explain their business benefits.

- Define Java and HTML5 and explain why they are important.

- Define and describe web services and the role played by XML.

- Name and describe the three external sources for software.

- Define and describe software mashups and apps.

5-5 What are the challenges of managing IT infrastructure and management solutions?

- Name and describe the management challenges posed by IT infrastructure.

- Explain how using a competitive forces model and calculating the TCO of technology assets help firms make good infrastructure investments.

Discussion Questions

5-6
MyLab MIS
Why is selecting computer hardware and software for the organization an important management decision? What management, organization, and technology issues should be considered when selecting computer hardware and software?

5-7
MyLab MIS
Should organizations use software service providers for all their software needs?

Why or why not? What management, organization, and technology factors should be considered when making this decision?

5-8
MyLab MIS
What are the advantages and disadvantages of cloud computing?

Hands-On MIS Projects

The projects in this section give you hands-on experience in developing solutions for managing IT infrastructures and IT outsourcing, using spreadsheet software to evaluate alternative desktop systems, and using web research to budget for a sales conference. Visit MyLab MIS to access this chapter's Hands-On MIS Projects.

Management Decision Problems

5-9 The University of Pittsburgh Medical Center (UPMC) relies on information systems to operate 19 hospitals, a network of other care sites, and international and commercial ventures. Demand for additional servers and storage technology was growing by 20 percent each year. UPMC was setting up a separate server for every application, and its servers and other computers were running a number of different operating systems, including several versions of Unix and Windows. UPMC had to manage technologies from many different vendors, including Hewlett-Packard (HP), Sun Microsystems, Microsoft, and IBM. Assess the impact of this situation on business performance. What factors and management decisions must be considered when developing a solution to this problem?

5-10 Qantas Airways, Australia's leading airline, faces cost pressures from high fuel prices and lower levels of global airline traffic. To remain competitive, the airline must find ways to keep costs low while providing a high level of customer service. Qantas had a 30-year-old data center. Management had to decide whether to replace its IT infrastructure with newer technology or outsource it. What factors should be considered by Qantas management when deciding whether to outsource? If Qantas decides to outsource, list and describe points that should be addressed in a service level agreement.

Improving Decision Making: Using a Spreadsheet to Evaluate Hardware and Software Options

Software skills: Spreadsheet formulas
Business skills: Technology pricing

5-11 In this exercise, you will use spreadsheet software to calculate the cost of desktop systems, printers, and software.

Use the Internet to obtain pricing information on hardware and software for an office of 30 people. You will need to price 30 PC desktop systems (monitors, computers, and keyboards) manufactured by Lenovo, Dell, and HP. (For the purposes of this exercise, ignore the fact that desktop systems usually come with preloaded software packages.) Also obtain pricing on 15 desktop printers manufactured by HP, Canon, and Brother. Each desktop system must satisfy the minimum specifications shown in tables that you can find in MyLab MIS.

Also obtain pricing on 30 licenses or copies of the most recent versions of Microsoft Office 365 Business and Apache Open Office (formerly Oracle Open Office) and on 30 copies of Microsoft Windows 10 Pro. Each desktop productivity solution should contain software for word processing, spreadsheets, database, and presentations. Prepare a spreadsheet showing your research results for the desktop system, printer, and software combination offering the best performance and pricing per worker over a two-year period. Because every two workers share one printer (15 printers/30 systems), your calculations should assume only half a printer cost per worker.

Improving Decision Making: Using Web Research to Budget for a Sales Conference

Software skills: Internet-based software
Business skills: Researching transportation and lodging costs

5-12 The Foremost Composite Materials Company is planning a two-day sales conference for October 19–20, starting with a reception on the evening of October 18. The conference consists of all-day meetings that the entire sales force, numbering 120 sales representatives and their 16 managers, must attend. Each sales representative requires his or her own room, and the company needs two common meeting rooms, one large enough to hold the entire sales force plus a few visitors (200) and the other able to hold half the force. Management has set a budget of $195,000 for the representatives' room rentals. The company would like to hold the conference in either Miami or Marco Island, Florida, at a Hilton- or Marriott-owned hotel.

Use the Hilton and Marriott websites to select a hotel in whichever of these cities would enable the company to hold its sales conference within its budget and meet its sales conference requirements. Then locate flights arriving the afternoon prior to the conference. Your attendees will be coming from Los Angeles (51), San Francisco (30), Seattle (22), Chicago (19), and Pittsburgh (14). Determine costs of each airline ticket from these cities. When you are finished, create a budget for the conference. The budget will include the cost of each airline ticket, the room cost, and $70 per attendee per day for food.

Collaboration and Teamwork Project

Evaluating Server and Mobile Operating Systems

5-13 Form a group with three or four of your classmates. Choose server or mobile operating systems to evaluate. You might research and compare the capabilities and costs of Linux versus Unix or the most recent version of the Windows operating system for servers. Alternatively, you could compare the capabilities of the Android mobile operating system with iOS for the iPhone. If possible, use Google Docs and Google Drive or Google Sites to brainstorm, organize, and develop a presentation of your findings for the class.

Is BYOD Good for Business?
CASE STUDY

Just about everyone who has a smartphone wants to be able to bring it to work and use it on the job, and many employers would like workers to do so. A survey of BYOD trends by MarketsandMarkets found that adoption rates among North American companies approached 50 percent by the start of 2018. Research from Sapho workplace productivity experts found the average worker saves 81 minutes per week in productivity by using a personal device at work.

Will BYOD become the new normal? Not necessarily. Half of all enterprises believe that BYOD represents a growing problem for their organizations, according to a number of studies. Although BYOD can improve employee job satisfaction and productivity, it also can cause a number of problems if not managed properly. Support for personally owned devices is more difficult than it is for company-supplied devices, the cost of managing mobile devices can increase, and protecting corporate data and networks becomes more difficult.

When every employee brings his or her own device to work, IT departments lose almost all control over the hardware. They can't control what apps or programs are installed, how the devices are secured, or what files are downloaded. In the past, the firm was able to control who had what technology in order to prevent privacy breaches, hacking, and unauthorized access to corporate information. Inability to control the hardware means more vulnerabilities. That is the big tradeoff with BYOD: offering employees greater flexibility while potentially exposing the company to danger.

BYOD advocates have argued that it increases employee productivity, but that is not always the case. When employees bring their own devices to work, they may be tempted to use them on the job for entertainment or catching up with friends. It's incredibly easy for employees to get sucked into an endless black hole of text messaging, YouTube videos, and checking Facebook updates. Productivity will suffer (see the Chapter 7 Interactive Session on Management).

BYOD requires a significant portion of corporate IT resources dedicated to managing and maintaining a large number of devices within the organization.

In the past, companies tried to limit business smartphone use to a single platform. This made it easier to keep track of each mobile device and to roll out software upgrades or fixes because all employees were using the same devices or, at the very least, the same operating system. Today, the mobile digital landscape is much more complicated, with a variety of devices and operating systems on the market that do not have well-developed tools for administration and security. Android has over 80 percent of the worldwide smartphone market, but it is more difficult to use for corporate work than Apple mobile devices using the iOS operating system. iOS is considered a closed system and runs only on a limited number of different Apple mobile devices. In contrast, Android's fragmentation makes it more difficult and costly for corporate IT to manage. There are about 25,000 different models of Android-based devices available around the world, according to a report by OpenSignal, which researches wireless networks and devices. Android's huge consumer market share attracts many hackers. Android is also vulnerable because it has an open source architecture and comes in multiple versions.

If employees are allowed to work with more than one type of mobile device and operating system, companies need an effective way to keep track of all the devices employees are using. To access company information, the company's networks must be configured to receive connections from that device. When employees make changes to their personal phone, such as switching cellular carriers, changing their phone number, or buying a new mobile device altogether, companies will need to quickly and flexibly ensure that their employees are still able to remain productive. Firms need a system that keeps track of which devices employees are using, where the device is located, whether it is being used, and what software it is equipped with. For unprepared companies, keeping track of who gets access to what data could be a nightmare.

With the large variety of mobile devices and operating systems available, providing adequate technical support for every employee could be difficult. When employees are not able to access critical data or encounter other problems with their mobile devices, they will need assistance from the information systems department. Companies that rely on desktop computers tend to have many of the same computers with the same specs and operating systems, making tech support that much easier. Mobility introduces a new layer of variety and complexity to tech support that companies need to be prepared to handle.

There are significant concerns with securing company information accessed with mobile devices. If a device is stolen or compromised, companies need ways to ensure that sensitive or confidential information isn't freely available to anyone. Mobility puts assets and data at greater risk than if they were only located within company walls and on company machines. Marble Security Labs analyzed 1.2 million Android and iOS apps and found that the consumer apps on mobile devices did not adequately protect business information. Companies often use technologies that allow them to wipe data from devices remotely or encrypt data so that if the device is stolen, it cannot be used. You'll find a detailed discussion of mobile security issues in Chapter 8.

Intel was a pioneer in the BYOD movement and has successfully implemented an enterprise-wide policy covering more than 30,000 employee mobile devices. Another major issue surrounding a corporate BYOD policy is the potential lack of trust between workers and management when management has access to personal data on employee devices. To deal with this issue, Intel has established clear-cut guidelines informing employees about exactly what information can and can't be seen when administrators manage personal devices. Intel will quickly respond to any questions employees might have regarding BYOD. The company also allows employees to choose among different levels of mobile access to corporate systems, with each tier accompanied by different levels of security.

SAP, a leading global vendor of enterprise software, is another tech company that has implemented BYOD successfully. The company developed a specialized mobile platform for various work-related applications, enabling employees to work from anywhere with their mobile devices. SAP has also created a security system for decommissioning a mobile device within a minute whenever a smartphone or tablet is lost or stolen. All SAP divisions across the globe have reported some form of success with BYOD. SAP Australia/New Zealand reports that the policy is key in attracting younger workers who are attached to their mobile devices and constantly use the apps.

The global reinsurance giant Swiss Re believes every employee should be able to work in the way they choose and has more and more staff using their own smartphones and tablets to access its intranet and personal information management (PIM) apps. Swiss Re successfully implemented BYOD by choosing a secure, highly scalable Enterprise Mobility Management (EMM) system that could support multiple operating systems, and a local partner to manage all of its technical and organizational aspects.

Over the past six years, 4,500 employee-owned iPhones and iPads have been added to the system alongside existing company devices. About one-third of the smartphones and tablets are company-owned and the other two-thirds are owned by employees of Swiss Re. Swiss Re manages these devices using MobileIron's EMM system, which enables global enterprises to secure and manage modern operating systems in a world of mixed-use mobile devices and desktops. It incorporates identity, context, and privacy enforcement to set the appropriate level of access to enterprise data and services.

The multi-OS EMM solution was rolled out with the help of local partner Nomasis AG. Likewise, Android is a possibility in the future. If it meets the company's security requirements, staff wishing to use Android devices will probably be allowed to do so as part of Swiss Re's BYOD strategy, obviously within the framework of MobileIron.

Supporting nearly all current mobile operating systems is a big technical and organizational challenge for Swiss Re, but management feels it has been worthwhile. Mobile devices have helped the company experience a significant rise in user productivity, because staff can access documents more quickly, whether they're in the office or traveling on business.

Blackstone, a global investment and advisory firm, has implemented a BYOD policy, but it has placed limitations on the types of devices employees can use. Blackstone's BYOD policy only allows employees to use their own Apple products such as iPads. For that company, Apple devices were the easiest to support and required little maintenance compared to other mobile tools. Any other devices would add to the workload of Blackstone's IT department, thus eliminating the cost savings that often come with BYOD. Due to Apple's popularity, few employees have objected.

At Venafi, a cybersecurity company, employees have the option of bringing their own smartphones, tablets, and IT notebooks to work with them or using company-issued devices. The company has a well-developed BYOD policy. Venafi's IT department does not support employees' hardware devices because it would be too difficult to handle all the different mobile devices and software available to consumers. That means employees are responsible for troubleshooting and repairs of their personal equipment. However, Venafi does ensure that each device is securely connected to the corporate network.

According to Tammy Moskites, Venafi CISO and CIO, the biggest challenge in defining a BYOD policy that leaves everyone satisfied has been balancing risk with flexibility. Although Venafi has given employees the choice of using their own mobile devices, it has also written contracts with language describing the terms and conditions for bringing one's own device into work, including the ability to remove company data from the device if needed.

Many corporate BYOD policies restrict access to time-wasting sites like Facebook, YouTube, or Twitter. But Venafi management believes that instead of resorting to measures like blocking YouTube or Facebook and forbidding the use of mobile phones, companies should focus more on performance. As long as the employees are motivated and performing well, they shouldn't be subjected to unnecessary restrictions. Employees typically don't understand the implications of BYOD and the dangers of lax security. Venafi's IT department tries to educate employees about realities of BYOD and gives them the power to use their devices responsibly.

Iftekhar Khan, IT director at Toronto's Chelsea Hotel, remains less sanguine. He believes BYOD might work for his company down the road but not in the immediate future. Khan notes that the hospitality industry and many others still want employees to use corporate-owned devices for any laptop, tablet, or smartphone requiring access to the corporate network. His business has sensitive information and needs that level of control. Although the hotel might possibly save money with BYOD, it's ultimately all about productivity.

Sources: "Swiss Re Chooses MobileIron 'Bring Your Own Device' Technology," www.mobileiron.com, accessed March 9, 2018; "5 BYOD Management Case Studies," Sunviewsoftware.com, accessed March 9, 2018; Stasmayer Incorporated, "The 'Bring Your Own Device' Trend: Is It Worth It?" www.stasmayer.com, accessed March 10, 2018; Lisa Phifer, "The Challenges of a Bring Your Own Device (BYOD) Policy," *Simple MDM*, January 5, 2017; Jonathan Crowl, "The Latest BYOD Trends and Predictions, from Mobile Focus to Endpoint Management." *Mobile Business Insights*, August 14, 2017; Ryan Patrick, "Is a BYOD Strategy Best for Business?" *IT World Canada*, March 22, 2016; Linda Gimmeson, "3 Companies Showing Success With BYOD," Toolbox.com, July 9, 2015; Alan F., "Open Signal: 24,093 Unique and Different Android-Powered Devices Are Available," Phonearena.com, August 5, 2015.

CASE STUDY QUESTIONS

5-14 What are the advantages and disadvantages of allowing employees to use their personal mobile devices for work?

5-15 What management, organization, and technology factors should be addressed when deciding whether to allow employees to use their personal mobile devices for work?

5-16 Evaluate how the companies described in this case study dealt with the challenges of BYOD.

5-17 Allowing employees to use their own smartphones for work will save the company money. Do you agree? Why or why not?

MyLab MIS

Go to the Assignments section of MyLab MIS to complete these writing exercises.

5-18 What are the distinguishing characteristics of cloud computing, and what are the three types of cloud services?

5-19 What is the total cost of ownership of technology assets, and what are its cost components?

Chapter 5 References

Amazon Web Services. "Overview of Amazon Web Services." (April 2017).

Benitez, Jose, Gautam Ray, and Jörg Henseler. "Impact of Information Technology Infrastructure Flexibility on Mergers and Acquisitions." *MIS Quarterly* 42 No. 1 (March 2018).

Butler, Brandon. "Battle of the Clouds: Amazon Web Services vs. Microsoft Azure vs. Google Cloud Platform." *Network World* (February 22, 2017).

Carr, Nicholas. *The Big Switch.* New York: Norton (2008).

Choi, Jae, Derek L. Nazareth, and Hemant K. Jain. "Implementing Service-Oriented Architecture in Organizations." *Journal of Management Information Systems* 26, No. 4 (Spring 2010).

Cisco Systems. "Cisco Global Cloud Index: Forecast and Methodology, 2016–2021 White Paper." (February 1, 2018).

David, Julie Smith, David Schuff, and Robert St. Louis. "Managing Your IT Total Cost of Ownership." *Communications of the ACM* 45, No. 1 (January 2002).

Elumalai, Arul, Kara Sprague, Sid Tandon, and Lareina Yee. "Ten Trends Redefining Enterprise IT Infrastructure." McKinsey & Company (November 2017).

Existek. "Offshore Outsourcing: 3 Examples of Successful IT Outsourcing." (June 22, 2017).

Flamm, Kenneth. "Measuring Moore's Law: Evidence from Price, Cost, and Quality Indexes." University of Texas at Austin Preliminary Draft (2017).

Flinders, Karl. "Ofcom Outsources IT Management to Indian Services Supplier NIIT." *Computer Weekly* (January 12, 2016).

Follow, Jaewon Kang. "IBM Bets on Next-Gen Technologies as it Tries to Stave Off Rivals." TheStreet.com (May 5, 2016).

Gartner, Inc. "Gartner Forecasts Worldwide Public Cloud Services Revenue to Reach $260 Billion in 2017." (October 12, 2017).

_____. "Gartner Says Global IT Spending to Reach $3.7 Trillion in 2018." (January 18, 2018).

Guo, Zhiling, and Dan Ma. "A Model of Competition Between Perpetual Software and Software as a Service." *MIS Quarterly* 42 No. 1 (March 2018).

International Data Corporation. "Worldwide Public Cloud Services Spending Forecast to Double by 2019, According to IDC." (January 21, 2016).

Internet World Stats. "World Internet Usage and Population Statistics." Internetworldstats.com, accessed March 15, 2018.

Kauffman, Robert J., and Julianna Tsai. "The Unified Procurement Strategy for Enterprise Software: A Test of the 'Move to the Middle' Hypothesis." *Journal of Management Information Systems* 26, No. 2 (Fall 2009).

Letschin, Michael. "Six Trends That Will Change How You Think About Data Storage." *Information Management* (February 8, 2016).

Li, Shengli, Hsing Kenneth Cheng, Yang Duan, and Yu-Chen Yang. "A Study of Enterprise Software Licensing Models." *Journal of Management Information Systems* 34 No. 1 (2017).

Loten, Angus. "Rush to the Cloud Creates Risk of Overspending." *Wall Street Journal* (July 25, 2018).

Lyman, Peter, and Hal R. Varian. "How Much Information 2003?" University of California at Berkeley School of Information Management and Systems (2003).

Markoff, John. "Moore's Law Running Out of Room, Tech Looks for a Successor." *New York Times* (May 4, 2016).

Mearian, Lucas. "Data Storage Goes from $1M to 2 Cents Per Gigabyte." *Computerworld* (March 23, 2017).

Mell, Peter, and Tim Grance. "The NIST Definition of Cloud Computing." Version 15. *NIST* (October 17, 2009).

Metz, Cade. "Chips off the Old Block: Computers Are Taking Design Cues from Human Brains." *New York Times* (September 16, 2017).

Moore, Gordon. "Cramming More Components Onto Integrated Circuits," *Electronics* 38, No. 8 (April 19, 1965).

Netmarketshare. "Desktop Operating System Market Share." www.netmarketshare.com, accessed March 10, 2018.

Retana, German F., Chris Forman, Sridhar Narasimhan, Marius Florin Niculescu, and D. J. Wu. "Technology Support and Post-Adoption IT Service Use: Evidence from the Cloud." *MIS Quarterly* 42, No. 3 (September 2018).

Schuff, David, and Robert St. Louis. "Centralization vs. Decentralization of Application Software." *Communications of the ACM* 44, No. 6 (June 2001).

Song, Peijian, Ling Xue, Arun Rai, and Cheng Zha. "The Ecosystem of Software Platform: A Study of Asymmetric Cross-Side Network Effects and Platform Governance." *MIS Quarterly* 42 No. 1 (March 2018).

Stango, Victor. "The Economics of Standards Wars." *Review of Network Economics* 3, Issue 1 (March 2004).

Susarla, Anjana, Anitesh Barua, and Andrew B. Whinston. "A Transaction Cost Perspective of the 'Software as a Service' Business Model." *Journal of Management Information Systems* 26, No. 2 (Fall 2009).

Taft, Darryl K. "Application Development: Java Death Debunked: 10 Reasons Why It's Still Hot." *eWeek* (February 22, 2012).

Uotila, Juha, Thomas Keil, and Markku Maula. "Supply-Side Network Effects and the Development of Information Technology Standards." *MIS Quarterly* 41 No. 4 (December 2017).

Weitzel, Tim. *Economics of Standards in Information Networks.* Heidelberg, New York: Physica-Verlag (2004).

Foundations of Business Intelligence: Databases and Information Management

LEARNING OBJECTIVES

After reading this chapter, you will be able to answer the following questions:

6-1 What are the problems of managing data resources in a traditional file environment?

6-2 What are the major capabilities of database management systems (DBMS), and why is a relational DBMS so powerful?

6-3 What are the principal tools and technologies for accessing information from databases to improve business performance and decision making?

6-4 Why are information policy, data administration, and data quality assurance essential for managing the firm's data resources?

6-5 How will MIS help my career?

CHAPTER CASES

Data Management Helps the Charlotte Hornets Learn More About Their Fans

Kraft Heinz Finds a New Recipe for Analyzing Its Data

Databases Where the Data Aren't There

How Reliable Is Big Data?

VIDEO CASES

Dubuque Uses Cloud Computing and Sensors to Build a Smarter City

Brooks Brothers Closes In on Omnichannel Retail

Maruti Suzuki Business Intelligence and Enterprise Databases

MyLab MIS

Discussion Questions: 6-5, 6-6, 6-7; **Hands-on MIS Projects** 6-8, 6-9, 6-10, 6-11; **Writing Assignments:** 6-17, 6-18; **eText with Conceptual Animations**

Data Management Helps the Charlotte Hornets Learn More About Their Fans

The NBA's Charlotte Hornets have millions of fans, but until recently they didn't know very much about them. The Charlotte, North Carolina–based basketball team had many millions of records of fan data—online ticket and team gear purchases, food and beverage purchases at games, and comments about the team on social media. Every time a fan performs one of these actions, more data about that fan are created. Three million records of food and beverage purchase transactions are generated during each Hornets game. There was too much unorganized customer data for decision makers to digest.

All of this accumulating data, which came from many different sources, started to overtax the team's Microsoft Dynamics customer relationship management system. There were 12 to 15 different sources of data on Hornets fan behavior and they were maintained in separate data repositories that could not communicate with each other. It became increasingly difficult for the Hornets to understand their fans and how they were interacting with the organization.

Five years ago, Hornets management decided to improve its approach to data management. The team needed technology that could easily maintain data from many different sources and 12 different vendors and it needed to be able to combine and integrate what amounted to 12 different profiles on each fan into a single profile. This would enable the Hornets to understand each fan's behavior in much greater detail and offer them a more personalized experience.

© Oleksii Sidorov/Shutterstock

Under the leadership of Chris Zeppenfeld, the Hornets' senior director of business intelligence, the team implemented a data warehouse that would consolidate all of the Hornets' customer data from its various data sources in a single location where the data could be easily accessed and analyzed by business users. The warehouse was based on a SAP HANA database optimized to process very large quantities of data at ultra-high speed and included Phizzle Fan Tracker™ software to cleanse, streamline, and combine millions of fan records to create a single profile for each Hornets fan. Phizzle Fan Tracker is a fan engagement platform designed to consolidate, analyze, and act on multiple data sources. The platform's data aggregation capabilities, innovative data visualization tools, and social listening solutions provide sports properties and brands the capability to gather and analyze digital, social, and real-world fan engagements. Fan Tracker works with the SAP HANA database to consolidate customer profiles, analyze and act on real-time online behavior, and consolidate all existing data sources to uniquely identify fan records. The solution provides a unified overview and deeper understanding of each fan, allowing clubs to offer their fans a more personalized experience.

By using Fan Tracker and a unified data warehouse, the Hornets have compiled and synthesized 25 million fan and consumer interactions, saving over $1.5 million in consulting expenses. They now have a real-time data profile for every one of their 1.5 million fans, which includes up-to-the minute behavioral data on each fan from third-party applications as well as the Hornets' own sources. Each profile reveals detailed insights into a fan's behavior including sentiment, purchase history, interactions, and fan value across multiple points of contact. Zeppenfeld believes that better fan data management has helped the team rank among the top five NBA franchises for new full season ticket sales each year.

Sources: Jim O'Donnell, "Charlotte Hornets Use Phizzle Built on HANA to Analyze Fan Behavior," SearchSAPtechtarget.com, February 11, 2018; "NBA Team Charlotte Hornets/SAP Case Study," www.phizzle.com, accessed February 12, 2018; and Mark J. Burns, "Why The Charlotte Hornets Are Using Phizzle To Streamline Their Data Warehouse," *Sport Techie*, September 2016.

The experience of the Charlotte Hornets illustrates the importance of data management. Business performance depends on what a firm can or cannot do with its data. The Charlotte Hornets NBA basketball team was a thriving business, but both operational efficiency and management decision making were hampered by fragmented data stored in multiple locations that were difficult to access and analyze. How businesses store, organize, and manage their data has an enormous impact on organizational effectiveness.

The chapter-opening diagram calls attention to important points raised by this case and this chapter. The Charlotte Hornets had accumulated very large quantities of fan data from many different sources. Marketing campaigns and personalized offers to fans were not as effective as they could have been because it was so difficult to assemble and understand the data required to obtain a detailed understanding of each customer. The solution was to combine the Hornets' customer data from all sources in a data warehouse that provided a single source of data for reporting and analysis and use Fan Tracker software to consolidate disparate pieces of customer data into a single profile for each customer. The Hornets had to reorganize their data into a standard company-wide format; establish rules, responsibilities, and procedures for accessing and using the data; and provide tools for making the data accessible to users for querying and reporting.

The data warehouse integrated company data from all of its disparate sources into a single comprehensive database that could be queried directly. The data were reconciled to prevent multiple profiles on the same customer. The solution improved customer marketing, sales, and service while reducing costs. The Hornets increased their ability to quickly analyze very large quantities of data by using SAP HANA high-speed database technology.

The data warehouse boosted operational efficiency and decision making by making more comprehensive and accurate customer data available and by

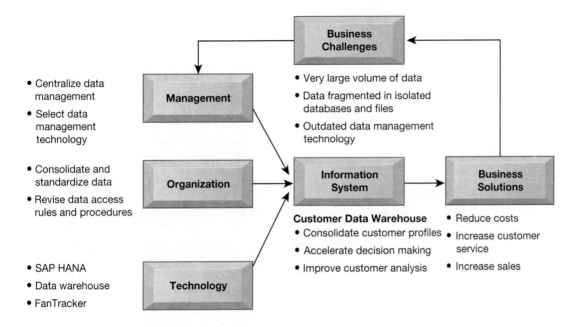

making it easier to access all the business's data on each customer. By helping the Hornets understand their own customers better, the solution increased opportunities for selling to customers as well as the effectiveness of marketing and sales campaigns.

Here are some questions to think about: What was the business impact of the Hornets' data management problems? How did better use of the Hornets' customer data improve operational efficiency and management decision making?

6-1 What are the problems of managing data resources in a traditional file environment?

An effective information system provides users with accurate, timely, and relevant information. Accurate information is free of errors. Information is timely when it is available to decision makers when it is needed. Information is relevant when it is useful and appropriate for the types of work and decisions that require it.

You might be surprised to learn that many businesses don't have timely, accurate, or relevant information because the data in their information systems have been poorly organized and maintained. That's why data management is so essential. To understand the problem, let's look at how information systems arrange data in computer files and traditional methods of file management.

File Organization Terms and Concepts

A computer system organizes data in a hierarchy that starts with bits and bytes and progresses to fields, records, files, and databases (see Figure 6.1). A **bit** represents the smallest unit of data a computer can handle. A group of bits, called a **byte**, represents a single character, which can be a letter, a number, or another symbol. A grouping of characters into a word, a group of words, or a complete number (such as a person's name or age) is called a **field**. A group of related fields, such as the student's name, the course taken, the date, and the grade, comprises a **record**; a group of records of the same type is called a **file**.

FIGURE 6.1 **THE DATA HIERARCHY**

A computer system organizes data in a hierarchy that starts with the bit, which represents either a 0 or a 1. Bits can be grouped to form a byte to represent one character, number, or symbol. Bytes can be grouped to form a field, and related fields can be grouped to form a record. Related records can be collected to form a file, and related files can be organized into a database.

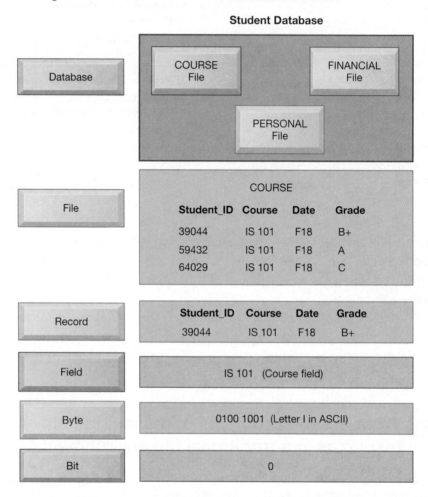

For example, the records in Figure 6.1 could constitute a student course file. A group of related files makes up a database. The student course file illustrated in Figure 6.1 could be grouped with files on students' personal histories and financial backgrounds to create a student database.

A record describes an entity. An **entity** is a person, place, thing, or event on which we store and maintain information. Each characteristic or quality describing a particular entity is called an **attribute**. For example, Student_ID, Course, Date, and Grade are attributes of the entity COURSE. The specific values that these attributes can have are found in the fields of the record describing the entity COURSE.

Problems with the Traditional File Environment

In most organizations, systems tended to grow independently without a companywide plan. Accounting, finance, manufacturing, human resources, and sales and marketing all developed their own systems and data files. Figure 6.2 illustrates the traditional approach to information processing.

FIGURE 6.2 TRADITIONAL FILE PROCESSING

The use of a traditional approach to file processing encourages each functional area in a corporation to develop specialized applications. Each application requires a unique data file that is likely to be a subset of the master file. These subsets of the master file lead to data redundancy and inconsistency, processing inflexibility, and wasted storage resources.

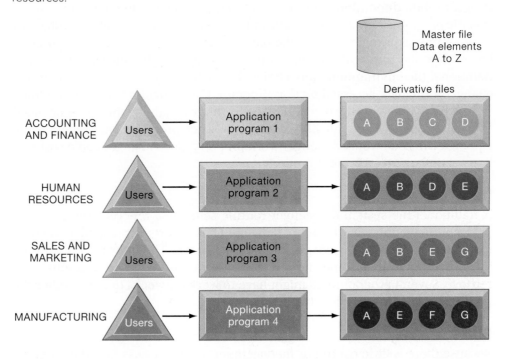

Each application, of course, required its own files and its own computer program to operate. For example, the human resources functional area might have a personnel master file, a payroll file, a medical insurance file, a pension file, a mailing list file, and so forth, until tens, perhaps hundreds, of files and programs existed. In the company as a whole, this process led to multiple master files created, maintained, and operated by separate divisions or departments. As this process goes on for 5 or 10 years, the organization is saddled with hundreds of programs and applications that are very difficult to maintain and manage. The resulting problems are data redundancy and inconsistency, program-data dependence, inflexibility, poor data security, and an inability to share data among applications.

Data Redundancy and Inconsistency

Data redundancy is the presence of duplicate data in multiple data files so that the same data are stored in more than one place or location. Data redundancy occurs when different groups in an organization independently collect the same piece of data and store it independently of each other. Data redundancy wastes storage resources and also leads to **data inconsistency**, where the same attribute may have different values. For example, in instances of the entity COURSE illustrated in Figure 6.1, the Date may be updated in some systems but not in others. The same attribute, Student_ID, might also have different names in different systems throughout the organization. Some systems might use Student_ID and others might use ID, for example.

Additional confusion can result from using different coding systems to represent values for an attribute. For instance, the sales, inventory, and manufacturing systems of a clothing retailer might use different codes to represent clothing size.

One system might represent clothing size as "extra large," whereas another might use the code "XL" for the same purpose. The resulting confusion would make it difficult for companies to create customer relationship management, supply chain management, or enterprise systems that integrate data from different sources.

Program-Data Dependence

Program-data dependence refers to the coupling of data stored in files and the specific programs required to update and maintain those files such that changes in programs require changes to the data. Every traditional computer program has to describe the location and nature of the data with which it works. In a traditional file environment, any change in a software program could require a change in the data accessed by that program. One program might be modified from a five-digit to a nine-digit ZIP code. If the original data file were changed from five-digit to nine-digit ZIP codes, then other programs that required the five-digit ZIP code would no longer work properly. Such changes could cost millions of dollars to implement properly.

Lack of Flexibility

A traditional file system can deliver routine scheduled reports after extensive programming efforts, but it cannot deliver ad hoc reports or respond to unanticipated information requirements in a timely fashion. The information required by ad hoc requests is somewhere in the system but may be too expensive to retrieve. Several programmers might have to work for weeks to put together the required data items in a new file.

Poor Security

Because there is little control or management of data, access to and dissemination of information may be out of control. Management might have no way of knowing who is accessing or even making changes to the organization's data.

Lack of Data Sharing and Availability

Because pieces of information in different files and different parts of the organization cannot be related to one another, it is virtually impossible for information to be shared or accessed in a timely manner. Information cannot flow freely across different functional areas or different parts of the organization. If users find different values for the same piece of information in two different systems, they may not want to use these systems because they cannot trust the accuracy of their data.

6-2 What are the major capabilities of database management systems (DBMS), and why is a relational DBMS so powerful?

Database technology cuts through many of the problems of traditional file organization. A more rigorous definition of a **database** is a collection of data organized to serve many applications efficiently by centralizing the data and controlling redundant data. Rather than storing data in separate files for each application, data appear to users as being stored in only one location. A single database services multiple applications. For example, instead of a corporation storing employee data in separate information systems and separate files for personnel, payroll, and benefits, the corporation could create a single common human resources database (see Figure 6.3).

FIGURE 6.3   HUMAN RESOURCES DATABASE WITH MULTIPLE VIEWS

A single human resources database provides many different views of data, depending on the information requirements of the user. Illustrated here are two possible views, one of interest to a benefits specialist and one of interest to a member of the company's payroll department.

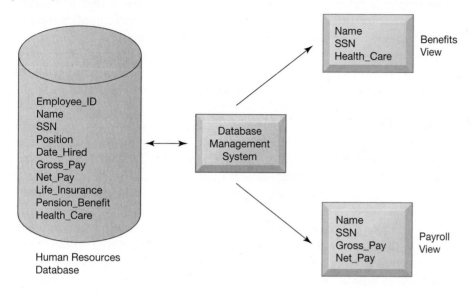

Database Management Systems

A **database management system (DBMS)** is software that enables an organization to centralize data, manage them efficiently, and provide access to the stored data by application programs. The DBMS acts as an interface between application programs and the physical data files. When the application program calls for a data item, such as gross pay, the DBMS finds this item in the database and presents it to the application program. Using traditional data files, the programmer would have to specify the size and format of each data element used in the program and then tell the computer where they were located.

The DBMS relieves the programmer or end user from the task of understanding where and how the data are actually stored by separating the logical and physical views of the data. The *logical view* presents data, as they would be perceived by end users or business specialists, whereas the *physical view* shows how data are actually organized and structured on physical storage media.

The database management software makes the physical database available for different logical views required by users. For example, for the human resources database illustrated in Figure 6.3, a benefits specialist might require a view consisting of the employee's name, social security number, and health insurance coverage. A payroll department member might need data such as the employee's name, social security number, gross pay, and net pay. The data for all these views are stored in a single database, where they can be more easily managed by the organization.

How a DBMS Solves the Problems of the Traditional File Environment

A DBMS reduces data redundancy and inconsistency by minimizing isolated files in which the same data are repeated. The DBMS may not enable the organization to eliminate data redundancy entirely, but it can help control redundancy. Even if the organization maintains some redundant data, using a DBMS eliminates data inconsistency because the DBMS can help the organization ensure that every occurrence of redundant data has the same values. The DBMS uncouples programs and data, enabling data to stand on their own. The description of the data used by the program does not have to be specified in detail each time a different program is written. Access and availability of information will be increased and program development and maintenance costs reduced because users and programmers can perform ad hoc queries of the database for many simple applications without having to write complicated programs. The DBMS enables the organization to centrally manage data, their use, and security. Data sharing throughout the organization is easier because the data are presented to users as being in a single location rather than fragmented in many different systems and files.

Relational DBMS

Contemporary DBMS use different database models to keep track of entities, attributes, and relationships. The most popular type of DBMS today for PCs as well as for larger computers and mainframes is the **relational DBMS**. Relational databases represent data as two-dimensional tables (called relations). Tables may be referred to as files. Each table contains data on an entity and its attributes. Microsoft Access is a relational DBMS for desktop systems, whereas DB2, Oracle Database, and Microsoft SQL Server are relational DBMS for large mainframes and midrange computers. MySQL is a popular open source DBMS.

Let's look at how a relational database organizes data about suppliers and parts (see Figure 6.4). The database has a separate table for the entity SUPPLIER and a table for the entity PART. Each table consists of a grid of columns and rows of data. Each individual element of data for each entity is stored as a separate field, and each field represents an attribute for that entity. Fields in a relational database are also called columns. For the entity SUPPLIER, the supplier identification number, name, street, city, state, and ZIP code are stored as separate fields within the SUPPLIER table and each field represents an attribute for the entity SUPPLIER.

The actual information about a single supplier that resides in a table is called a row. Rows are commonly referred to as records, or in very technical terms, as **tuples**. Data for the entity PART have their own separate table.

The field for Supplier_Number in the SUPPLIER table uniquely identifies each record so that the record can be retrieved, updated, or sorted. It is called a **key field**. Each table in a relational database has one field that is designated as its **primary key**. This key field is the unique identifier for all the information in any row of the table and this primary key cannot be duplicated. Supplier_Number is the primary key for the SUPPLIER table and Part_Number is the primary key for the PART table. Note that Supplier_Number appears in both the SUPPLIER and PART tables. In the SUPPLIER table, Supplier_Number is the primary key. When the field Supplier_Number appears in the PART table, it is called a **foreign key** and is essentially a lookup field to look up data about the supplier of a specific part.

Operations of a Relational DBMS

Relational database tables can be combined easily to deliver data required by users, provided that any two tables share a common data element. Suppose we wanted to find in this database the names of suppliers who could provide us with part number 137 or part number 150. We would need information from two tables: the SUPPLIER table and the PART table. Note that these two files have a shared data element: Supplier_Number.

In a relational database, three basic operations, as shown in Figure 6.5, are used to develop useful sets of data: select, join, and project. The *select*

FIGURE 6.4 RELATIONAL DATABASE TABLES

A relational database organizes data in the form of two-dimensional tables. Illustrated here are tables for the entities SUPPLIER and PART showing how they represent each entity and its attributes. Supplier_Number is a primary key for the SUPPLIER table and a foreign key for the PART table.

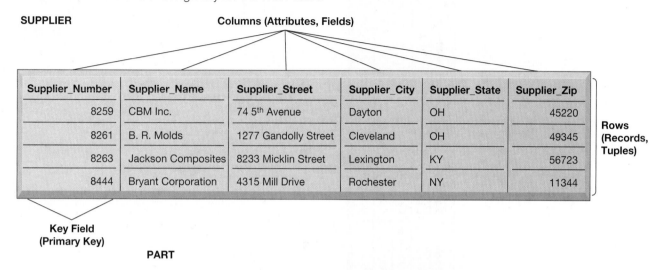

operation creates a subset consisting of all records in the file that meet stated criteria. Select creates, in other words, a subset of rows that meet certain criteria. In our example, we want to select records (rows) from the PART table where the Part_Number equals 137 or 150. The *join* operation combines relational tables to provide the user with more information than is available in individual tables. In our example, we want to join the now-shortened PART table (only parts 137 or 150 will be presented) and the SUPPLIER table into a single new table.

The *project* operation creates a subset consisting of columns in a table, permitting the user to create new tables that contain only the information required. In our example, we want to extract from the new table only the following columns: Part_Number, Part_Name, Supplier_Number, and Supplier_Name.

Capabilities of Database Management Systems

A DBMS includes capabilities and tools for organizing, managing, and accessing the data in the database. The most important are its data definition language, data dictionary, and data manipulation language.

FIGURE 6.5 THE THREE BASIC OPERATIONS OF A RELATIONAL DBMS

The select, join, and project operations enable data from two different tables to be combined and only selected attributes to be displayed.

SUPPLIER

Supplier_Number	Supplier_Name	Supplier_Street	Supplier_City	Supplier_State	Supplier_Zip
8259	CBM Inc.	74 5th Avenue	Dayton	OH	45220
8261	B. R. Molds	1277 Gandolly Street	Cleveland	OH	49345
8263	Jackson Components	8233 Micklin Street	Lexington	KY	56723
8444	Bryant Corporation	4315 Mill Drive	Rochester	NY	11344

Join by Supplier_Number

PART

Part_Number	Part_Name	Unit_Price	Supplier_Number
137	Door latch	22.00	8259
145	Side mirror	12.00	8444
150	Door molding	6.00	8263
152	Door lock	31.00	8259
155	Compressor	54.00	8261
178	Door handle	10.00	8259

Select Part_Number = 137 or 150

Part_Number	Part_Name	Supplier_Number	Supplier_Name
137	Door latch	8259	CBM Inc.
150	Door molding	8263	Jackson Components

Project selected columns

FIGURE 6.6 ACCESS DATA DICTIONARY FEATURES

Microsoft Access has a rudimentary data dictionary capability that displays information about the size, format, and other characteristics of each field in a database. Displayed here is the information maintained in the SUPPLIER table. The small key icon to the left of Supplier_Number indicates that it is a key field.

Courtesy of Microsoft Corporation

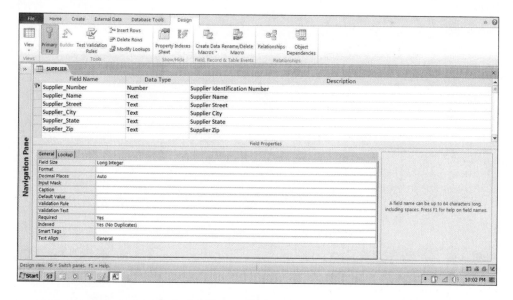

DBMS have a **data definition** capability to specify the structure of the content of the database. It would be used to create database tables and to define the characteristics of the fields in each table. This information about the database would be documented in a data dictionary. A **data dictionary** is an automated or manual file that stores definitions of data elements and their characteristics.

Microsoft Access has a rudimentary data dictionary capability that displays information about the name, description, size, type, format, and other properties of each field in a table (see Figure 6.6). Data dictionaries for large corporate databases may capture additional information, such as usage, ownership (who in the organization is responsible for maintaining the data), authorization, security, and the individuals, business functions, programs, and reports that use each data element.

Querying and Reporting

DBMS includes tools for accessing and manipulating information in databases. Most DBMS have a specialized language called a **data manipulation language** that is used to add, change, delete, and retrieve the data in the database. This language contains commands that permit end users and programming specialists to extract data from the database to satisfy information requests and develop applications. The most prominent data manipulation language today is **Structured Query Language**, or **SQL**. Figure 6.7 illustrates the SQL query

FIGURE 6.7 EXAMPLE OF AN SQL QUERY

Illustrated here are the SQL statements for a query to select suppliers for parts 137 or 150. They produce a list with the same results as Figure 6.5.

```
SELECT PART.Part_Number, PART.Part_Name, SUPPLIER.Supplier_Number,
SUPPLIER.Supplier_Name
FROM PART, SUPPLIER
WHERE PART.Supplier_Number = SUPPLIER.Supplier_Number AND
Part_Number = 137 OR Part_Number = 150;
```

FIGURE 6.8 AN ACCESS QUERY

Illustrated here is how the query in Figure 6.7 would be constructed using Microsoft Access query-building tools. It shows the tables, fields, and selection criteria used for the query.

Courtesy of Microsoft Corporation

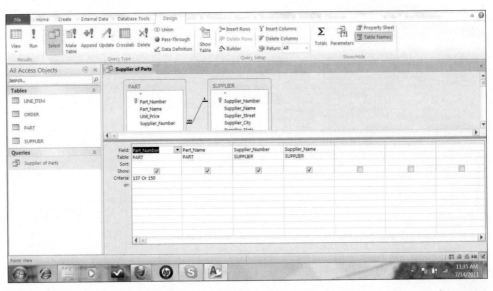

that would produce the new resultant table in Figure 6.5. You can find out more about how to perform SQL queries in our Learning Tracks for this chapter.

Users of DBMS for large and midrange computers, such as DB2, Oracle, or SQL Server, would employ SQL to retrieve information they needed from the database. Microsoft Access also uses SQL, but it provides its own set of user-friendly tools for querying databases and for organizing data from databases into more polished reports.

In Microsoft Access, you will find features that enable users to create queries by identifying the tables and fields they want and the results and then selecting the rows from the database that meet particular criteria. These actions in turn are translated into SQL commands. Figure 6.8 illustrates how the same query as the SQL query to select parts and suppliers would be constructed using the Microsoft Access query-building tools.

Microsoft Access and other DBMS include capabilities for report generation so that the data of interest can be displayed in a more structured and polished format than would be possible just by querying. Crystal Reports is a popular report generator for large corporate DBMS, although it can also be used with Access. Access also has capabilities for developing desktop system applications. These include tools for creating data entry screens, reports, and developing the logic for processing transactions.

Designing Databases

To create a database, you must understand the relationships among the data, the type of data that will be maintained in the database, how the data will be used, and how the organization will need to change to manage data from a companywide perspective. The database requires both a conceptual design and a physical design. The conceptual, or logical, design of a database is an abstract model of the database from a business perspective, whereas the physical design shows how the database is actually arranged on direct-access storage devices.

FIGURE 6.9 AN UNNORMALIZED RELATION FOR ORDER

An unnormalized relation contains repeating groups. For example, there can be many parts and suppliers for each order. There is only a one-to-one correspondence between Order_Number and Order_Date.

ORDER (Before Normalization)

| Order_ Number | Order_ Date | Part_ Number | Part_ Name | Unit_ Price | Part_ Quantity | Supplier_ Number | Supplier_ Name | Supplier_ Street | Supplier_ City | Supplier_ State | Supplier_ Zip |

Normalization and Entity-Relationship Diagrams

The conceptual database design describes how the data elements in the database are to be grouped. The design process identifies relationships among data elements and the most efficient way of grouping data elements together to meet business information requirements. The process also identifies redundant data elements and the groupings of data elements required for specific application programs. Groups of data are organized, refined, and streamlined until an overall logical view of the relationships among all the data in the database emerges.

To use a relational database model effectively, complex groupings of data must be streamlined to minimize redundant data elements and awkward many-to-many relationships. The process of creating small, stable, yet flexible and adaptive data structures from complex groups of data is called **normalization**. Figures 6.9 and 6.10 illustrate this process.

In the particular business modeled here, an order can have more than one part, but each part is provided by only one supplier. If we build a relation called ORDER with all the fields included here, we would have to repeat the name and address of the supplier for every part on the order, even though the order is for parts from a single supplier. This relationship contains what are called repeating data groups because there can be many parts on a single order to a given supplier. A more efficient way to arrange the data is to break down ORDER into smaller relations, each of which describes a single entity. If we go step by step and normalize the relation ORDER, we emerge with the relations illustrated in Figure 6.10. You can find out more about normalization, entity-relationship diagramming, and database design in the Learning Tracks for this chapter.

FIGURE 6.10 NORMALIZED TABLES CREATED FROM ORDER

After normalization, the original relation ORDER has been broken down into four smaller relations. The relation ORDER is left with only two attributes, and the relation LINE_ITEM has a combined, or concatenated, key consisting of Order_Number and Part_Number.

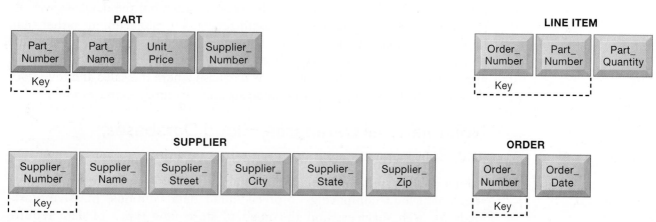

PART

| Part_ Number | Part_ Name | Unit_ Price | Supplier_ Number |

Key

LINE ITEM

| Order_ Number | Part_ Number | Part_ Quantity |

Key

SUPPLIER

| Supplier_ Number | Supplier_ Name | Supplier_ Street | Supplier_ City | Supplier_ State | Supplier_ Zip |

Key

ORDER

| Order_ Number | Order_ Date |

Key

FIGURE 6.11 AN ENTITY-RELATIONSHIP DIAGRAM

This diagram shows the relationships between the entities SUPPLIER, PART, LINE_ITEM, and ORDER that might be used to model the database in Figure 6.10.

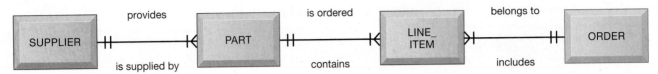

Relational database systems try to enforce **referential integrity** rules to ensure that relationships between coupled tables remain consistent. When one table has a foreign key that points to another table, you may not add a record to the table with the foreign key unless there is a corresponding record in the linked table. In the database we examined earlier in this chapter, the foreign key Supplier_Number links the PART table to the SUPPLIER table. We may not add a new record to the PART table for a part with Supplier_Number 8266 unless there is a corresponding record in the SUPPLIER table for Supplier_Number 8266. We must also delete the corresponding record in the PART table if we delete the record in the SUPPLIER table for Supplier_Number 8266. In other words, we shouldn't have parts from nonexistent suppliers!

Database designers document their data model with an **entity-relationship diagram**, illustrated in Figure 6.11. This diagram illustrates the relationship between the entities SUPPLIER, PART, LINE_ITEM, and ORDER. The boxes represent entities. The lines connecting the boxes represent relationships. A line connecting two entities that ends in two short marks designates a one-to-one relationship. A line connecting two entities that ends with a crow's foot topped by a short mark indicates a one-to-many relationship. Figure 6.11 shows that one ORDER can contain many LINE_ITEMs. (A PART can be ordered many times and appear many times as a line item in a single order.) Each PART can have only one SUPPLIER, but many PARTs can be provided by the same SUPPLIER.

It can't be emphasized enough: If the business doesn't get its data model right, the system won't be able to serve the business well. The company's systems will not be as effective as they could be because they'll have to work with data that may be inaccurate, incomplete, or difficult to retrieve. Understanding the organization's data and how they should be represented in a database is perhaps the most important lesson you can learn from this course.

For example, Famous Footwear, a shoe store chain with more than 800 locations in 49 states, could not achieve its goal of having "the right style of shoe in the right store for sale at the right price" because its database was not properly designed for rapidly adjusting store inventory. The company had an Oracle relational database running on a midrange computer, but the database was designed primarily for producing standard reports for management rather than for reacting to marketplace changes. Management could not obtain precise data on specific items in inventory in each of its stores. The company had to work around this problem by building a new database where the sales and inventory data could be better organized for analysis and inventory management.

Non-relational Databases, Cloud Databases, and Blockchain

For more than 30 years, relational database technology has been the gold standard. Cloud computing, unprecedented data volumes, massive workloads for web services, and the need to store new types of data require database alternatives to the traditional relational model of organizing data in the form of tables, columns, and rows. Companies are turning to "NoSQL" non-relational database technologies for this purpose. **Non-relational database management systems** use a more flexible data model and are designed for managing large data sets across many distributed machines and for easily scaling up or down. They are useful for accelerating simple queries against large volumes of structured and unstructured data, including web, social media, graphics, and other forms of data that are difficult to analyze with traditional SQL-based tools.

There are several different kinds of NoSQL databases, each with its own technical features and behavior. Oracle NoSQL Database is one example, as is Amazon's SimpleDB, one of the Amazon Web Services that run in the cloud. SimpleDB provides a simple web services interface to create and store multiple data sets, query data easily, and return the results. There is no need to predefine a formal database structure or change that definition if new data are added later.

MetLife's MongoDB open source NoSQL database brings together data from more than 70 separate administrative systems, claims systems, and other data sources, including semi-structured and unstructured data, such as images of health records and death certificates. The NoSQL database can handle structured, semi-structured, and unstructured information without requiring tedious, expensive, and time-consuming database mapping to normalize all data to a rigid schema, as required by relational databases.

Cloud Databases and Distributed Databases

Among the services Amazon and other cloud computing vendors provide are relational database engines. Amazon Relational Database Service (Amazon RDS) offers MySQL, Microsoft SQL Server, Oracle Database, PostgreSQL, or Amazon Aurora as database engines. Pricing is based on usage. Oracle has its own Database Cloud Services using its relational Oracle Database, and Microsoft Azure SQL Database is a cloud-based relational database service based on the Microsoft SQL Server DBMS. Cloud-based data management services have special appeal for web-focused startups or small to medium-sized businesses seeking database capabilities at a lower cost than in-house database products.

Google now offers its Spanner distributed database technology as a cloud service. A **distributed database** is one that is stored in multiple physical locations. Parts or copies of the database are physically stored in one location and other parts or copies are maintained in other locations. Spanner makes it possible to store information across millions of machines in hundreds of data centers around the globe, with special time-keeping tools to synchronize the data precisely in all of its locations and ensure the data are always consistent. Google uses Spanner to support its various cloud services, including Google Photos, AdWords (Google's online ad system), and Gmail, and is now making the technology available to other companies that might need such capabilities to run a global business.

Blockchain

Blockchain is a distributed database technology that enables firms and organizations to create and verify transactions on a network nearly instantaneously without a central authority. The system stores transactions as a distributed ledger among a network of computers The information held in the database is continually reconciled by the computers in the network.

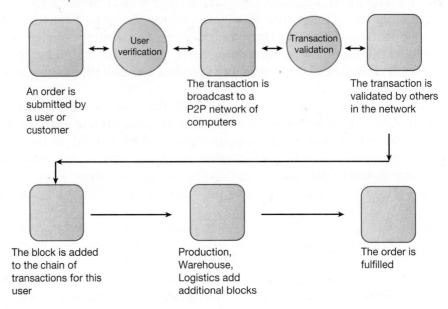

FIGURE 6.12 HOW BLOCKCHAIN WORKS

A blockchain system is a distributed database that records transactions in a peer-to-peer network of computers

The blockchain maintains a continuously growing list of records called blocks. Each block contains a timestamp and link to a previous block. Once a block of data is recorded on the blockchain ledger, it cannot be altered retroactively. When someone wants to add a transaction, participants in the network (all of whom have copies of the existing blockchain) run algorithms to evaluate and verify the proposed transaction. Legitimate changes to the ledger are recorded across the blockchain in a matter of seconds or minutes and records are protected through cryptography. What makes a blockchain system possible and attractive to business firms is encryption and authentication of the actors and participating firms, which ensures that only legitimate actors can enter information, and only validated transactions are accepted. Once recorded, the transaction cannot be changed. Figure 6.12 illustrates how blockchain works for fulfilling an order.

There are many large benefits to firms using blockchain databases. Blockchain networks radically reduce the cost of verifying users, validating transactions, and the risks of storing and processing transaction information across thousands of firms. Instead of thousands of firms building their own private transaction systems, then integrating them with suppliers, shippers, and financial institution systems, blockchain can provide a single, simple, low-cost transaction system for participating firms. Standardization of recording transactions is aided through the use of *smart contracts*. Smart contracts are computer programs that implement the rules governing transactions between firms, e.g., what is the price of products, how will they be shipped, when will the transaction be completed, who will finance the transaction, what are financing terms, and the like.

The simplicity and security that blockchain offers has made it attractive for storing and securing financial transactions, supply chain transactions, medical records, and other types of data. Blockchain is a foundation technology for Bitcoin, Ethereum, and other cryptocurrencies. Chapter 8 provides more detail on securing transactions with blockchain.

6-3 What are the principal tools and technologies for accessing information from databases to improve business performance and decision making?

Businesses use their databases to keep track of basic transactions, such as paying suppliers, processing orders, keeping track of customers, and paying employees. But they also need databases to provide information that will help the company run the business more efficiently and help managers and employees make better decisions. If a company wants to know which product is the most popular or who is its most profitable customer, the answer lies in the data.

The Challenge of Big Data

Most data collected by organizations used to be transaction data that could easily fit into rows and columns of relational database management systems. We are now witnessing an explosion of data from web traffic, email messages, and social media content (tweets, status messages), as well as machine-generated data from sensors (used in smart meters, manufacturing sensors, and electrical meters) or from electronic trading systems. These data may be unstructured or semi-structured and thus not suitable for relational database products that organize data in the form of columns and rows. We now use the term **big data** to describe these data sets with volumes so huge that they are beyond the ability of typical DBMS to capture, store, and analyze.

Big data is often characterized by the "3Vs": the extreme *volume* of data, the wide *variety* of data types and sources, and the *velocity* at which data must be processed. Big data doesn't designate any specific quantity but usually refers to data in the petabyte and exabyte range—in other words, billions to trillions of records, many from different sources. Big data are produced in much larger quantities and much more rapidly than traditional data. For example, a single jet engine is capable of generating 10 terabytes of data in just 30 minutes, and there are more than 25,000 airline flights each day. Twitter generates more than 8 terabytes of data daily. According to the International Data Center (IDC) technology research firm, data are more than doubling every two years, so the amount of data available to organizations is skyrocketing.

Businesses are interested in big data because they can reveal more patterns and interesting relationships than smaller data sets, with the potential to provide new insights into customer behavior, weather patterns, financial market activity, or other phenomena. For example, Shutterstock, the global online image marketplace, stores 24 million images, adding 10,000 more each day. To find ways to optimize the buying experience, Shutterstock analyzes its big data to find out where its website visitors place their cursors and how long they hover over an image before making a purchase. Big data is also finding many uses in the public sector, For example, city governments have been using big data to manage traffic flows and to fight crime.

However, to derive business value from these data, organizations need new technologies and tools capable of managing and analyzing nontraditional data along with their traditional enterprise data. They also need to know what questions to ask of the data and limitations of big data. Capturing, storing, and analyzing big data can be expensive, and information from big data may not necessarily help decision makers. It's important to have a clear understanding of the problem big data will solve for the business. The chapter-ending case explores these issues.

Business Intelligence Infrastructure

Suppose you wanted concise, reliable information about current operations, trends, and changes across the entire company. If you worked in a large company, the data you need might have to be pieced together from separate systems, such as sales, manufacturing, and accounting, and even from external sources, such as demographic or competitor data. Increasingly, you might need to use big data. A contemporary infrastructure for business intelligence has an array of tools for obtaining useful information from all the different types of data used by businesses today, including semi-structured and unstructured big data in vast quantities. These capabilities include data warehouses and data marts, Hadoop, in-memory computing, and analytical platforms. Some of these capabilities are available as cloud services.

Data Warehouses and Data Marts

The traditional tool for analyzing corporate data for the past two decades has been the data warehouse. A **data warehouse** is a database that stores current and historical data of potential interest to decision makers throughout the company. The data originate in many core operational transaction systems, such as systems for sales, customer accounts, and manufacturing, and may include data from website transactions. The data warehouse extracts current and historical data from multiple operational systems inside the organization. These data are combined with data from external sources and transformed by correcting inaccurate and incomplete data and restructuring the data for management reporting and analysis before being loaded into the data warehouse.

The data warehouse makes the data available for anyone to access as needed, but the data cannot be altered. A data warehouse system also provides a range of ad hoc and standardized query tools, analytical tools, and graphical reporting facilities.

Companies often build enterprise-wide data warehouses, where a central data warehouse serves the entire organization, or they create smaller, decentralized warehouses called data marts. A **data mart** is a subset of a data warehouse in which a summarized or highly focused portion of the organization's data is placed in a separate database for a specific population of users. For example, a company might develop marketing and sales data marts to deal with customer information. Bookseller Barnes & Noble used to maintain a series of data marts—one for point-of-sale data in retail stores, another for college bookstore sales, and a third for online sales.

Hadoop

Relational DBMS and data warehouse products are not well suited for organizing and analyzing big data or data that do not easily fit into columns and rows used in their data models. For handling unstructured and semi-structured data in vast quantities, as well as structured data, organizations are using **Hadoop**. Hadoop is an open source software framework managed by the Apache Software Foundation that enables distributed parallel processing of huge amounts of data across inexpensive computers. It breaks a big data problem down into subproblems, distributes them among up to thousands of inexpensive computer processing nodes, and then combines the result into a smaller data set that is easier to analyze. You've probably used Hadoop to find the best airfare on the Internet, get directions to a restaurant, do a search on Google, or connect with a friend on Facebook.

Hadoop consists of several key services, including the Hadoop Distributed File System (HDFS) for data storage and MapReduce for high-performance parallel data processing. HDFS links together the file systems on the numerous nodes in a Hadoop cluster to turn them into one big file system. Hadoop's MapReduce was inspired by Google's MapReduce system for breaking down processing of huge data sets and assigning work to the various nodes in a cluster. HBase, Hadoop's non-relational database, provides rapid access to the data stored on HDFS and a transactional platform for running high-scale real-time applications.

Hadoop can process large quantities of any kind of data, including structured transactional data, loosely structured data such as Facebook and Twitter feeds, complex data such as web server log files, and unstructured audio and video data. Hadoop runs on a cluster of inexpensive servers, and processors can be added or removed as needed. Companies use Hadoop for analyzing very large volumes of data as well as for a staging area for unstructured and semi-structured data before they are loaded into a data warehouse. Yahoo uses Hadoop to track users' behavior so it can modify its home page to fit their interests. Life sciences research firm NextBio uses Hadoop and HBase to process data for pharmaceutical companies conducting genomic research. Top database vendors such as IBM, Hewlett-Packard, Oracle, and Microsoft have their own Hadoop software distributions. Other vendors offer tools for moving data into and out of Hadoop or for analyzing data within Hadoop.

In-Memory Computing

Another way of facilitating big data analysis is to use **in-memory computing**, which relies primarily on a computer's main memory (RAM) for data storage. (Conventional DBMS use disk storage systems.) Users access data stored in system primary memory, thereby eliminating bottlenecks from retrieving and reading data in a traditional, disk-based database and dramatically shortening query response times. In-memory processing makes it possible for very large sets of data, amounting to the size of a data mart or small data warehouse, to reside entirely in memory. Complex business calculations that used to take hours or days are able to be completed within seconds, and this can even be accomplished using handheld devices.

The previous chapter describes some of the advances in contemporary computer hardware technology that make in-memory processing possible, such as powerful high-speed processors, multicore processing, and falling computer memory prices. These technologies help companies optimize the use of memory and accelerate processing performance while lowering costs.

Leading in-memory database products include SAP HANA, Oracle Database In-Memory, and Teradata Intelligent Memory. The chapter-opening case on the Charlotte Hornets and the Interactive Session on the Kraft Company show how organizations are benefiting from in-memory technology.

Analytic Platforms

Commercial database vendors have developed specialized high-speed **analytic platforms** using both relational and non-relational technology that are optimized for analyzing large data sets. Analytic platforms feature preconfigured hardware-software systems that are specifically designed for query processing and analytics. For example, the IBM PureData System for Analytics features tightly integrated database, server, and storage components that handle complex analytic queries 10 to 100 times faster than traditional systems.

Kraft Heinz Finds a New Recipe for Analyzing Its Data

When the Kraft Foods Group and Heinz finalized their merger in July 2015, it was the marriage of two giants. The new Kraft Heinz Company became the fifth-largest consumer-packaged food and beverage organization in the world. The combined company has more than 200 global brands, $26.5 billion in revenue, and over 40,000 employees. Eight of the brands each have annual revenue exceeding $1 billion: Heinz, Maxwell House, Kraft Lunchables, Planters, Velveeta, Philadelphia, and Oscar Mayer. Running these companies required huge amounts of data from all of these brands. This is clearly the world of big data.

To remain profitable, enterprises in the fast-moving consumer goods industry require very lean operations. The uncertain global economy has dampened consumer spending, so companies such as Kraft Heinz must constantly identify opportunities for improving operational efficiencies to protect their profit margins. Kraft Heinz decided to deal with this challenge by focusing on optimizing its supply chain, manufacturing optimal quantities of each of its products, and delivering them to retailers at the best time and least cost to capitalize on consumer demand.

Managing a supply chain as large as that of Kraft Heinz requires timely and accurate data on sales forecasts, manufacturing plans, and logistics, often from multiple sources. To ensure that Kraft Heinz would be able to use all of its enterprise business data effectively, management decided to split the data among two large SAP enterprise resource planning (ERP) systems, one for North American business and the other for all other global business. The combined company also had to rethink its data warehouse.

Before the merger, the North America business had maintained nearly 18 terabytes of data in a SAP Business Warehouse and was using SAP Business Warehouse Accelerator to facilitate operational reporting. SAP Business Warehouse is SAP's data warehouse software for consolidating organizational data and supporting data analytics and reporting. The SAP Business Warehouse (BW) Accelerator is used to speed up database queries. Kraft Heinz management wanted decision makers to obtain more fine-grained views of the data that would reveal new opportunities for improving efficiency, self-service reporting, and real-time analytics.

SAP BW Accelerator was not suitable for these tasks. It could optimize query runtime (the period of time when a query program is running) only for a specific subset of data in the warehouse, and was limited to reporting on selected views of the data. It could not deal with data load and calculation performance and required replication of Business Warehouse data in a separate accelerator. With mushrooming data on the merged company's sales, logistics, and manufacturing, the warehouse was too overtaxed to generate timely reports for decision makers. Moreover, Kraft Heinz's complex data model made building new reports very time-consuming—it could take as much as six months to complete. Kraft Heinz needed a solution that would deliver more detailed reports more quickly without affecting the performance of underlying operational systems.

Kraft Heinz business users had been building some of their own reports using SAP BusinessObjects Analysis edition for Microsoft Office, which integrates with Microsoft Excel and PowerPoint. This tool allows ad hoc multidimensional analysis. What these users needed was to be able to build self-service reports from a single source of data and find an efficient way to collate data from multiple sources to obtain an enterprise-wide view of what was going on.

Kraft Heinz decided to migrate its data warehouse from its legacy database to SAP BW powered by SAP HANA, SAP's in-memory database platform, which dramatically improves the efficiency at which data can be loaded and processed, calculations can be computed, and queries and reports can be run. The new data warehouse would be able to integrate with existing SAP ERP applications driving day-to-day business operations. The company worked with IBM Global Services consultants to cleanse and streamline its existing databases. It archived and purged unwanted or unused data, with the IT department working closely with business professionals to jointly determine what was essential, what was still being used, and what data thought to be unused had been moved to a different functional area of the company.

Cleansing and streamlining data reduced the database size almost 50 percent, to 9 terabytes.

According to Sundar Dittakavi, Kraft Heinz Group Leader of Global Business Intelligence, in addition to providing better insights, the new data warehouse environment has achieved a 98 percent improvement in the production of standard reports. This is due to the 83 percent reduction in load time to execution time to make the data available, and reduction in execution time to complete the analysis. Global key performance indicators for the Kraft side of the business are built into SAP HANA.

Kraft Heinz can now accommodate exploding volumes of data and database queries easily, while maintaining enough processing power to handle unexpected issues. The company is also able to build new reports much faster and the flexibility of SAP HANA makes it much easier to change the company's data model. Now Kraft Heinz can produce new reports for business users in weeks instead of months and give decision makers the insights they need to boost efficiency and lower operating costs.

Sources: Ken Murphy, "The Kraft-Heinz Company Unlocks Recipe for Strategic Business Insight," *SAP Insider Profiles,* January 25, 2017; "The Kraft Heinz Company Migrates SAP Business Warehouse to the Lightning-Fast SAP HANA Database," IBM Corp. and SAP SE 2016; and www.kraftheinzcompany.com, accessed February 15, 2018.

CASE STUDY QUESTIONS

1. Identify the problem in this case study. To what extent was it a technology problem? Were any management and organizational factors involved?

2. How was information technology affecting business performance at Kraft Heinz?

3. How did new technology provide a solution to the problem? How effective was the solution?

4. Identify the management, organizational, and technology factors that had to be addressed in selecting and implementing Kraft-Heinz's new data warehouse solution.

Analytic platforms also include in-memory systems and NoSQL non-relational database management systems and are now available as cloud services.

Figure 6.13 illustrates a contemporary business intelligence technology infrastructure using the technologies we have just described. Current and historical data are extracted from multiple operational systems along with web data, social media data, Internet of Things (IoT) machine-generated data, unstructured audio/visual data, and other data from external sources. Some companies are starting to pour all of these types of data into a data lake. A **data lake** is a repository for raw unstructured data or structured data that for the most part has not yet been analyzed, and the data can be accessed in many ways. The data lake stores these data in their native format until they are needed. The Hadoop Distributed File System (HDFS) is often used to store the data lake contents across a set of clustered computer nodes, and Hadoop clusters may be used to pre-process some of these data for use in the data warehouse, data marts, or an analytic platform, or for direct querying by power users. Outputs include reports and dashboards as well as query results. Chapter 12 discusses the various types of BI users and BI reporting in greater detail.

Analytical Tools: Relationships, Patterns, Trends

Once data have been captured and organized using the business intelligence technologies we have just described, they are available for further analysis using software for database querying and reporting, multidimensional data analysis (OLAP), and data mining. This section will introduce you to these tools, with more detail about business intelligence analytics and applications in Chapter 12.

FIGURE 6.13 CONTEMPORARY BUSINESS INTELLIGENCE INFRASTRUCTURE

A contemporary business intelligence infrastructure features capabilities and tools to manage and analyze large quantities and different types of data from multiple sources. Easy-to-use query and reporting tools for casual business users and more sophisticated analytical toolsets for power users are included.

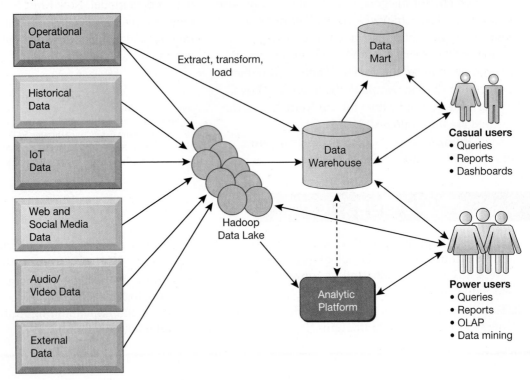

Online Analytical Processing (OLAP)

Suppose your company sells four different products—nuts, bolts, washers, and screws—in the East, West, and Central regions. If you wanted to ask a fairly straightforward question, such as how many washers were sold during the past quarter, you could easily find the answer by querying your sales database. But what if you wanted to know how many washers were sold in each of your sales regions and compare actual results with projected sales?

To obtain the answer, you would need **online analytical processing (OLAP)**. OLAP supports multidimensional data analysis, enabling users to view the same data in different ways using multiple dimensions. Each aspect of information—product, pricing, cost, region, or time period—represents a different dimension. So, a product manager could use a multidimensional data analysis tool to learn how many washers were sold in the East in June, how that compares with the previous month and the previous June, and how it compares with the sales forecast. OLAP enables users to obtain online answers to ad hoc questions such as these in a fairly rapid amount of time, even when the data are stored in very large databases, such as sales figures for multiple years.

Figure 6.14 shows a multidimensional model that could be created to represent products, regions, actual sales, and projected sales. A matrix of actual sales can be stacked on top of a matrix of projected sales to form a cube with six faces. If you rotate the cube 90 degrees one way, the face showing will be product versus actual and projected sales. If you rotate the cube 90 degrees again, you will see region versus actual and projected sales. If you rotate 180 degrees from the original view, you will see projected sales and product versus region.

FIGURE 6.14 MULTIDIMENSIONAL DATA MODEL

This view shows product versus region. If you rotate the cube 90 degrees, the face that will show is product versus actual and projected sales. If you rotate the cube 90 degrees again, you will see region versus actual and projected sales. Other views are possible.

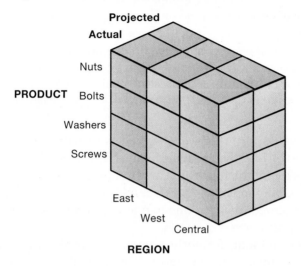

Cubes can be nested within cubes to build complex views of data. A company would use either a specialized multidimensional database or a tool that creates multidimensional views of data in relational databases.

Data Mining

Traditional database queries answer such questions as "How many units of product number 403 were shipped in February 2018?" OLAP, or multidimensional analysis, supports much more complex requests for information, such as "Compare sales of product 403 relative to plan by quarter and sales region for the past two years." With OLAP and query-oriented data analysis, users need to have a good idea about the information for which they are looking.

Data mining is more discovery-driven. Data mining provides insights into corporate data that cannot be obtained with OLAP by finding hidden patterns and relationships in large databases and inferring rules from them to predict future behavior. The patterns and rules are used to guide decision making and forecast the effect of those decisions. The types of information obtainable from data mining include associations, sequences, classifications, clusters, and forecasts.

- *Associations* are occurrences linked to a single event. For instance, a study of supermarket purchasing patterns might reveal that, when corn chips are purchased, a cola drink is purchased 65 percent of the time, but when there is a promotion, cola is purchased 85 percent of the time. This information helps managers make better decisions because they have learned the profitability of a promotion.

- In *sequences*, events are linked over time. We might find, for example, that if a house is purchased, a new refrigerator will be purchased within two weeks 65 percent of the time, and an oven will be bought within one month of the home purchase 45 percent of the time.

- *Classification* recognizes patterns that describe the group to which an item belongs by examining existing items that have been classified and by inferring a set of rules. For example, businesses such as credit card or telephone companies worry about the loss of steady customers. Classification helps discover the characteristics of customers who are likely to leave and can provide a model to help managers predict who those customers are so that the managers can devise special campaigns to retain such customers.

- *Clustering* works in a manner similar to classification when no groups have yet been defined. A data mining tool can discover different groupings within data, such as finding affinity groups for bank cards or partitioning a database into groups of customers based on demographics and types of personal investments.

- Although these applications involve predictions, *forecasting* uses predictions in a different way. It uses a series of existing values to forecast what other values will be. For example, forecasting might find patterns in data to help managers estimate the future value of continuous variables, such as sales figures.

These systems perform high-level analyses of patterns or trends, but they can also drill down to provide more detail when needed. There are data mining applications for all the functional areas of business and for government and scientific work. One popular use for data mining is to provide detailed analyses of patterns in customer data for one-to-one marketing campaigns or for identifying profitable customers.

Caesars Entertainment, formerly known as Harrah's Entertainment, is the largest gaming company in the world. It continually analyzes data about its customers gathered when people play its slot machines or use its casinos and hotels. The corporate marketing department uses this information to build a detailed gambling profile, based on a particular customer's ongoing value to the company. For instance, data mining lets Caesars know the favorite gaming experience of a regular customer at one of its riverboat casinos along with that person's preferences for room accommodations, restaurants, and entertainment. This information guides management decisions about how to cultivate the most profitable customers, encourage those customers to spend more, and attract more customers with high revenue-generating potential. Business intelligence improved Caesars's profits so much that it became the centerpiece of the firm's business strategy.

Text Mining and Web Mining

Unstructured data, most in the form of text files, is believed to account for more than 80 percent of useful organizational information and is one of the major sources of big data that firms want to analyze. Email, memos, call center transcripts, survey responses, legal cases, patent descriptions, and service reports are all valuable for finding patterns and trends that will help employees make better business decisions. **Text mining** tools are now available to help businesses analyze these data. These tools are able to extract key elements from unstructured natural language text, discover patterns and relationships, and summarize the information.

Businesses might turn to text mining to analyze transcripts of calls to customer service centers to identify major service and repair issues or to measure customer sentiment about their company. **Sentiment analysis** software is able to mine text comments in an email message, blog, social media conversation, or survey forms to detect favorable and unfavorable opinions about specific subjects. For example, Kraft Foods uses a Community Intelligence Portal and sentiment analysis to tune into consumer conversations about its products across numerous social networks, blogs, and other websites. Kraft tries to make sense of relevant comments rather than just track brand mentions and can identify customers' emotions and feelings when they talk about how they barbecue and what sauces and spices they use.

The web is another rich source of unstructured big data for revealing patterns, trends, and insights into customer behavior. The discovery and analysis of useful patterns and information from the World Wide Web are called **web mining**. Businesses might turn to web mining to help them understand customer behavior, evaluate the effectiveness of a particular website, or quantify the success of a marketing campaign. For instance, marketers use the Google Trends service, which tracks the popularity of various words and phrases used in Google search queries, to learn what people are interested in and what they are interested in buying.

Web mining looks for patterns in data through content mining, structure mining, and usage mining. Web content mining is the process of extracting knowledge from the content of web pages, which may include text, image, audio, and video data. Web structure mining examines data related to the structure of a particular website. For example, links pointing to a document indicate the popularity of the document, while links coming out of a document indicate the richness or perhaps the variety of topics covered in the document. Web usage mining examines user interaction data recorded by a web server whenever requests for a website's resources are received. The usage data records the user's behavior when the user browses or makes transactions on the website and collects the data in a server log. Analyzing such data can help companies determine the value of particular customers, cross-marketing strategies across products, and the effectiveness of promotional campaigns.

The chapter-ending case describes organizations' experiences as they use the analytical tools and business intelligence technologies we have described to grapple with "big data" challenges.

Databases and the Web

Have you ever tried to use the web to place an order or view a product catalog? If so, you were using a website linked to an internal corporate database. Many companies now use the web to make some of the information in their internal databases available to customers and business partners.

Suppose, for example, a customer with a web browser wants to search an online retailer's database for pricing information. Figure 6.15 illustrates how that customer might access the retailer's internal database over the web. The user accesses the retailer's website over the Internet using a web browser on his or her client PC or mobile device. The user's web browser software requests data from the organization's database, using HTML commands to communicate with the web server. Apps provide even faster access to corporate databases.

Because many back-end databases cannot interpret commands written in HTML, the web server passes these requests for data to software that translates HTML commands into SQL so the commands can be processed by the DBMS

FIGURE 6.15 LINKING INTERNAL DATABASES TO THE WEB

Users access an organization's internal database through the web using their desktop PC browsers or mobile apps.

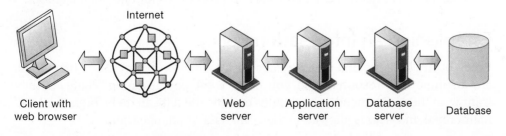

| Client with web browser | Internet | Web server | Application server | Database server | Database |

working with the database. In a client/server environment, the DBMS resides on a dedicated computer called a **database server**. The DBMS receives the SQL requests and provides the required data. Middleware transfers information from the organization's internal database back to the web server for delivery in the form of a web page to the user.

Figure 6.15 shows that the middleware working between the web server and the DBMS is an application server running on its own dedicated computer (see Chapter 5). The application server software handles all application operations, including transaction processing and data access, between browser-based computers and a company's back-end business applications or databases. The application server takes requests from the web server, runs the business logic to process transactions based on those requests, and provides connectivity to the organization's back-end systems or databases. Alternatively, the software for handling these operations could be a custom program or a CGI script. A CGI script is a compact program using the *Common Gateway Interface (CGI)* specification for processing data on a web server.

There are a number of advantages to using the web to access an organization's internal databases. First, web browser software is much easier to use than proprietary query tools. Second, the web interface requires few or no changes to the internal database. It costs much less to add a web interface in front of a legacy system than to redesign and rebuild the system to improve user access.

Accessing corporate databases through the web is creating new efficiencies, opportunities, and business models. ThomasNet.com provides an up-to-date online directory of more than 500,000 suppliers of industrial products, such as chemicals, metals, plastics, rubber, and automotive equipment. Formerly called Thomas Register, the company used to send out huge paper catalogs with this information. Now it provides this information to users online via its website and has become a smaller, leaner company.

Other companies have created entirely new businesses based on access to large databases through the web. One is the social networking service Facebook, which helps users stay connected with each other and meet new people. Facebook features "profiles" with information on over 2.2 billion active users with information about themselves, including interests, friends, photos, and groups with which they are affiliated. Facebook maintains a very large database to house and manage all of this content. There are also many web-enabled databases in the public sector to help consumers and citizens access helpful information.

6-4 Why are information policy, data administration, and data quality assurance essential for managing the firm's data resources?

Setting up a database is only a start. In order to make sure that the data for your business remain accurate, reliable, and readily available to those who need them, your business will need special policies and procedures for data management.

Establishing an Information Policy

Every business, large and small, needs an information policy. Your firm's data are an important resource, and you don't want people doing whatever they want with them. You need to have rules on how the data are to be organized and maintained and who is allowed to view the data or change them.

An **information policy** specifies the organization's rules for sharing, disseminating, acquiring, standardizing, classifying, and inventorying information. Information policy lays out specific procedures and accountabilities, identifying which users and organizational units can share information, where information can be distributed, and who is responsible for updating and maintaining the information. For example, a typical information policy would specify that only selected members of the payroll and human resources department would have the right to change and view sensitive employee data, such as an employee's salary or social security number, and that these departments are responsible for making sure that such employee data are accurate.

If you are in a small business, the information policy would be established and implemented by the owners or managers. In a large organization, managing and planning for information as a corporate resource often require a formal data administration function. **Data administration** is responsible for the specific policies and procedures through which data can be managed as an organizational resource. These responsibilities include developing an information policy, planning for data, overseeing logical database design and data dictionary development, and monitoring how information systems specialists and end-user groups use data.

You may hear the term **data governance** used to describe many of these activities. Promoted by IBM, data governance deals with the policies and processes for managing the availability, usability, integrity, and security of the data employed in an enterprise with special emphasis on promoting privacy, security, data quality, and compliance with government regulations.

A large organization will also have a database design and management group within the corporate information systems division that is responsible for defining and organizing the structure and content of the database and maintaining the database. In close cooperation with users, the design group establishes the physical database, the logical relations among elements, and the access rules and security procedures. The functions it performs are called **database administration**.

Ensuring Data Quality

A well-designed database and information policy will go a long way toward ensuring that the business has the information it needs. However, additional steps must be taken to ensure that the data in organizational databases are accurate and remain reliable.

What would happen if a customer's telephone number or account balance were incorrect? What would be the impact if the database had the wrong price for the product you sold or your sales system and inventory system showed different prices for the same product? Data that are inaccurate, untimely, or inconsistent with other sources of information lead to incorrect decisions, product recalls, and financial losses. Gartner, Inc. reported that more than 25 percent of the critical data in large *Fortune* 1000 companies' databases is inaccurate or incomplete, including bad product codes and product descriptions, faulty inventory descriptions, erroneous financial data, incorrect supplier information, and incorrect employee data. Some of these data quality problems are caused by redundant and inconsistent data produced by multiple systems feeding a data warehouse. For example, the sales ordering system and the inventory management system might both maintain data on the organization's products. However, the sales ordering system might use the term *Item Number* and the inventory system might call the same attribute *Product Number*. The sales, inventory, or manufacturing systems of a clothing retailer might use different codes to represent values for an attribute. One system might represent clothing size as "medium," whereas the other system might use the code "M" for the same purpose. During the design process for the warehouse database, data describing entities, such as a customer, product, or order, should be named and defined consistently for all business areas using the database.

Think of all the times you've received several pieces of the same direct mail advertising on the same day. This is very likely the result of having your name maintained multiple times in a database. Your name may have been misspelled or you used your middle initial on one occasion and not on another or the information was initially entered onto a paper form and not scanned properly into the system. Because of these inconsistencies, the database would treat you as different people! We often receive redundant mail addressed to Laudon, Lavdon, Lauden, or Landon.

If a database is properly designed and enterprise-wide data standards are established, duplicate or inconsistent data elements should be minimal. Most data quality problems, however, such as misspelled names, transposed numbers, or incorrect or missing codes, stem from errors during data input. The incidence of such errors is rising as companies move their businesses to the web and allow customers and suppliers to enter data into their websites that directly update internal systems.

Before a new database is in place, organizations need to identify and correct their faulty data and establish better routines for editing data once their database is in operation. Analysis of data quality often begins with a **data quality audit**, which is a structured survey of the accuracy and level of completeness of the data in an information system. Data quality audits can be performed by surveying entire data files, surveying samples from data files, or surveying end users for their perceptions of data quality.

Data cleansing, also known as *data scrubbing*, consists of activities for detecting and correcting data in a database that are incorrect, incomplete, improperly formatted, or redundant. Data cleansing not only corrects errors but also enforces consistency among different sets of data that originated in separate information systems. Specialized data-cleansing software is available to automatically survey data files, correct errors in the data, and integrate the data in a consistent companywide format.

Data quality problems are not just business problems. They also pose serious problems for individuals, affecting their financial condition and even their jobs. For example, inaccurate or outdated data about consumers' credit histories maintained by credit bureaus can prevent creditworthy individuals from obtaining loans or lower their chances of finding or keeping a job. And as the Interactive Session on Organization describes, incomplete or inaccurate databases also pose problems for criminal justice and public safety.

A small minority of companies allow individual departments to be in charge of maintaining the quality of their own data. However, best data administration practices call for centralizing data governance, standardization of organizational data, data quality maintenance, and accessibility to data assets.

Databases Where the Data Aren't There

On November 5, 2017 Devin Patrick Kelley walked into the First Baptist Church in Sutherland Springs, Texas toting a Ruger AR-556 semi-automatic rifle and fired round after round into the congregation gathered for Sunday morning services. Within a few minutes, he had killed 26 people and injured 20 others. Kelley was later found dead in his SUV with a self-inflicted gunshot wound. The attack was the deadliest mass shooting by an individual in Texas, the fifth-deadliest mass shooting in the United States, as well as the deadliest shooting in an American place of worship in modern history.

This tragedy could have been avoided. Kelley was prohibited by law from purchasing or possessing firearms and ammunition due to a 2012 domestic violence conviction in a court martial while he was serving in the U.S. Air Force. The Air Force failed to record the conviction in the Federal Bureau of Investigation (FBI) National Crime Information Center (NCIC) database, which is used by the National Instant Check System (NICS) to flag prohibited gun purchases. This allowed Kelley to pass background checks and purchase four guns, one in each of the past four years.

Federally licensed firearm dealers are required to check the credentials of every potential buyer against the NICS system containing millions of criminal history records and protection orders. The system is supposed to flag any potential gun buyer who falls in various categories prohibiting a sale including fugitives, convicted felons, or those with dishonorable discharges from the military.

The Air Force acknowledged that it did not inform federal authorities about the domestic violence conviction, which should have prevented Kelley from buying firearms. Ann Stefanek, an Air Force spokesperson, stated that the Air Force would conduct a comprehensive review to ensure records in other cases have been reported correctly. The Defense Department plans to review how all U.S. military services report such cases into the background-check system. Members of the U.S. Senate have called for legislation to improve the completeness of NICS recordkeeping.

Individuals familiar with how NICS works observed that large gaps in information sharing between the military and the Justice Department have created a blind spot in background checks of veterans, allowing those barred from possessing weapons to get clearance. They believed that the failure to flag Kelley more likely reflected a systemic flaw rather than a one-time miss. Robert Belair, a Washington privacy lawyer and expert on the FBI's background-screening system, said the Air Force and other branches of the military seldom submit court-martial records to the FBI's screening database when the offense doesn't lead to a dishonorable discharge because this has never been a priority for the military.

According to a 2016 report by the U.S. Government Accountability Office (GAO), the FBI has struggled to collect domestic abuse records for background checks, in part because incomplete or missing criminal histories make it harder to determine if someone should be banned from obtaining a gun. The GAO focused on reporting by state and local authorities and reported that between 2006 and 2015 about 6,700 firearms were incorrectly transferred to individuals with domestic violence records.

Federal law requires federal departments, including the military branches, to notify the Justice Department at least quarterly about any records they have showing that someone is disqualified from buying a gun. At the state level, however, compliance is voluntary unless specified by state law or federal funding requirements. It isn't known how many court-martial records are submitted to the FBI, which said it couldn't provide the information.

Gaps in databases have also affected other aspects of law enforcement, such as sentencing and parole. The decision to parole O.J. Simpson in October 2017 is an example. Before voting to release O.J. Simpson from prison after nine years, the Nevada parole board discussed in detail the robbery that had put him behind bars and his conduct as an inmate. Members of the Nevada Board of Parole Commissioners stated that before Simpson's 2008 conviction for a Las Vegas hotel robbery, Simpson had no history of a criminal conviction. Although Simpson was acquitted in 1995 of the murders of his former wife Nicole Brown Simpson and Ronald Goldman, in 1989 he had pleaded no contest in Los Angeles to misdemeanor battery of Ms. Simpson, who was then his wife. The Nevada parole board did not have that information. The 1989 conviction was not considered when a four-member panel voted unanimously to release him in October 2017.

When states such as Nevada weigh the risk posed by an inmate, they routinely look through their own records, and also check with the NCIC. Mr. Simpson's 1989 conviction did not appear in the NCIC history when Nevada officials prepared a pre-sentencing report after his 2008 conviction. David M. Smith, hearings examiner for the Nevada parole board, said the parole commissioners relied in part on the information in that 2008 report in assessing whether Mr. Simpson should be released. Smith believed it was impossible to tell whether knowledge of Simpson's misdemeanor conviction would have made a difference in the Nevada parole board's decision.

Omission of Simpson's 1989 conviction in the federal system again highlights the problem of major gaps in federal criminal databases, which rely primarily on accurate and complete reporting by local and state agencies. The Justice Department has reported, for example, that states fail to transmit most of their active arrest warrants from their own databases into the federal system and often neglect to update records to show whether cases resulted in convictions. Some states still rely on paper files, making it likelier that they will not end up in the federal electronic records database, a problem that is more common with older records.

Sources: Kristina Peterson and Jacob Gershman, "Lapses in Gun Buyers' Records Come Under Scrutiny," *Wall Street Journal*, November 7, 2017; Melissa Jeltsen, "Air Force Failed to Enter Church Shooter's Domestic Violence Record In U.S. Database," *Huffington Post*, November 6, 2017; Richard Perez-Pena, "Nevada Parole Board Unaware of O.J. Simpson's Old Conviction," *New York Times*, August 11, 2017; and Eli Rosenberg, Mark Berman, and Wesley Lowery, "Texas Church Gunman Escaped Mental Health Facility in 2012 after Threatening Military Superiors," *Washington Post*, November 7, 2017.

CASE STUDY QUESTIONS

1. Define the problem described in this case. How serious a problem is it?

2. What management, organization, and technology factors contributed to this problem?

3. What is the political and social impact of incomplete recordkeeping in the FBI NCIC and NICS databases?

6-5 How will MIS help my career?

Here is how Chapter 6 and this book can help you find a job as an entry-level data analyst.

The Company

Mega Midwest Power, a large diversified energy company headquartered in Cleveland, Ohio, has an open position for an entry-level data analyst. The company is involved in the distribution, transmission, and generation of electricity as well as energy management and other energy-related services for 5 million customers in the Midwest and mid-Atlantic regions.

Position Description

Job responsibilities include:

- Maintaining the integrity of substation equipment and related data in multiple databases, including SAP.
- Querying databases in multiple systems.
- Modifying systems for proper data management and procedural controls.
- Recommending and implementing process changes based on data problems that are identified.
- Conducting business-specific research, gathering data, and compiling reports and summaries.
- Expanding knowledge of policies, practices, and procedures.

Job Requirements

- BA/BS degree in business, finance, accounting, economics, engineering, or related discipline
- 1–2 years professional work experience desirable
- Knowledge of Microsoft Office tools (Excel, PowerPoint, Access, and Word)
- Strong analytical capabilities, including attention to detail, problem solving, and decision making
- Strong oral and written communication and teamwork skills
- Familiarity with transmission substation equipment desirable

Interview Questions

1. What do you know about substation equipment? Have you ever worked with SAP for Utilities?
2. What do you know about data management and databases? Have you ever worked with data management software? If so, what exactly have you done with it?
3. Tell us what you can do with Access and Excel. What kinds of problems have you used these tools to solve? Did you take courses in Access or Excel?
4. What experience do you have analyzing problems and developing specific solutions? Can you give an example of a problem you helped solve?

Author Tips

1. Do some research on the electric utility industry equipment maintenance and software for electric utility asset management and predictive maintenance. Read blogs from IBM, Deloitte, and Intel about predictive maintenance and watch YouTube videos from GE and IBM on this topic.
2. Review Chapter 6 of this text on data management and databases, along with the Chapter 12 discussion of operational intelligence. Inquire what you would be expected to do with databases in this job position.
3. Do some research on the capabilities of SAP for Utilities and ask exactly how you would be using this software and what skills would be required. Watch SAP's YouTube video on SAP for Utilities.

REVIEW SUMMARY

6-1 What are the problems of managing data resources in a traditional file environment?

Traditional file management techniques make it difficult for organizations to keep track of all of the pieces of data they use in a systematic way and to organize these data so that they can be easily accessed. Different functional areas and groups were allowed to develop their own files independently. Over time, this traditional file management environment creates problems such as data redundancy and inconsistency, program-data dependence, inflexibility, poor security, and lack of data sharing and availability. A database management system (DBMS) solves these problems with software that permits centralization of data and data management so that businesses have a single consistent source for all their data needs. Using a DBMS minimizes redundant and inconsistent files.

6-2 What are the major capabilities of database management systens (DBMS), and why is a relational DBMS so powerful?

The principal capabilities of a DBMS include a data definition capability, a data dictionary capability, and a data manipulation language. The data definition capability specifies the structure and content of the database. The data dictionary is an automated or manual file that stores information about the data in the database, including names, definitions, formats, and descriptions of data elements. The data manipulation language, such as SQL, is a specialized language for accessing and manipulating the data in the database.

The relational database has been the primary method for organizing and maintaining data in information systems because it is so flexible and accessible. It organizes data in two-dimensional tables called relations with rows and columns. Each table contains data about an entity and its attributes. Each row represents a record, and each column represents an attribute or field. Each table also contains a key field to uniquely identify each record for retrieval or manipulation. Relational database tables can be combined easily to deliver data required by users, provided that any two tables share a common data element. Non-relational databases are becoming popular for managing types of data that can't be handled easily by the relational data model. Both relational and non-relational database products are available as cloud computing services. A distributed database is one that is stored in multiple physical locations, including remote cloud computing centers.

Designing a database requires both a logical design and a physical design. The logical design models the database from a business perspective. The organization's data model should reflect its key business processes and decision-making requirements. The process of creating small, stable, flexible, and adaptive data structures from complex groups of data when designing a relational database is termed normalization. A well-designed relational database will not have many-to-many relationships, and all attributes for a specific entity will only apply to that entity. It will try to enforce referential integrity rules to ensure that relationships between coupled tables remain consistent. An entity-relationship diagram graphically depicts the relationship between entities (tables) in a relational database.

6-3   What are the principal tools and technologies for accessing information from databases to improve business performance and decision making?

Contemporary data management technology has an array of tools for obtaining useful information from all the different types of data used by businesses today, including semi-structured and unstructured big data in vast quantities. These capabilities include data warehouses and data marts, Hadoop, in-memory computing, and analytical platforms. OLAP represents relationships among data as a multidimensional structure, which can be visualized as cubes of data and cubes within cubes of data, enabling more sophisticated data analysis. Data mining analyzes large pools of data, including the contents of data warehouses, to find patterns and rules that can be used to predict future behavior and guide decision making. Text mining tools help businesses analyze large unstructured data sets consisting of text. Web mining tools focus on analysis of useful patterns and information from the web, examining the structure of websites and activities of website users, as well as the contents of web pages. Conventional databases can be linked via middleware to the web or a web interface to facilitate user access to an organization's internal data.

6-4   Why are information policy, data administration, and data quality assurance essential for managing the firm's data resources?

Developing a database environment requires policies and procedures for managing organizational data as well as a good data model and database technology. A formal information policy governs the maintenance, distribution, and use of information in the organization. In large corporations, a formal data administration function is responsible for information policy as well as for data planning, data dictionary development, and monitoring data usage in the firm.

Data that are inaccurate, incomplete, or inconsistent create serious operational and financial problems for businesses because they may create inaccuracies in product pricing, customer accounts, and inventory data and lead to inaccurate decisions about the actions that should be taken by the firm. Firms must take special steps to make sure they have a high level of data quality. These include using enterprise-wide data standards, databases designed to minimize inconsistent and redundant data, data quality audits, and data cleansing software.

Key Terms

Analytic platform, 229
Attribute, 214
Big data, 227
Bit, 213

Blockchain, 225
Byte, 213
Data administration, 237
Data cleansing, 238

MyLab MIS

To complete the problems with MyLab MIS, go to the EOC Discussion Questions in MyLab MIS.

Review Questions

6-1 What are the problems of managing data resources in a traditional file environment?

- List and describe each of the components in the data hierarchy.
- Define and explain the significance of entities, attributes, and key fields.
- List and describe the problems of the traditional file environment.

6-2 What are the major capabilities of database management systems (DBMS), and why is a relational DBMS so powerful?

- Define a database and a database management system.
- Name and briefly describe the capabilities of a DBMS.
- Define a relational DBMS and explain how it organizes data.
- List and describe the three operations of a relational DBMS.
- Explain why non-relational databases are useful.
- Define and describe normalization and referential integrity and explain how they contribute to a well-designed relational database.
- Define and describe an entity-relationship diagram and explain its role in database design.

6-3 What are the principal tools and technologies for accessing information from databases to improve business performance and decision making?

- Define big data and describe the technologies for managing and analyzing it.
- List and describe the components of a contemporary business intelligence infrastructure.
- Describe the capabilities of online analytical processing (OLAP).
- Define data mining, describing how it differs from OLAP and the types of information it provides.
- Explain how text mining and web mining differ from conventional data mining.
- Describe how users can access information from a company's internal databases through the web.

6-4 Why are information policy, data administration, and data quality assurance essential for managing the firm's data resources?

- Describe the roles of information policy and data administration in information management.
- Explain why data quality audits and data cleansing are essential.

Discussion Questions

6-5
MyLab MIS
It has been said there is no bad data, just bad management. Discuss the implications of this statement.

6-6
MyLab MIS
To what extent should end users be involved in the selection of a database management system and database design?

6-7
MyLab MIS
What are the consequences of an organization not having an information policy?

Hands-On MIS Projects

The projects in this section give you hands-on experience in analyzing data quality problems, establishing companywide data standards, creating a database for inventory management, and using the web to search online databases for overseas business resources. Visit MyLab MIS to access this chapter's Hands-On MIS Projects.

Management Decision Problems

6-8 Emerson Process Management, a global supplier of measurement, analytical, and monitoring instruments and services based in Austin, Texas, had a new data warehouse designed for analyzing customer activity to improve service and marketing. However, the data warehouse was full of inaccurate and redundant data. The data in the warehouse came from numerous transaction processing systems in Europe, Asia, and other locations around the world. The team that designed the warehouse had assumed that sales groups in all these areas would enter customer names and addresses the same way. In fact, companies in different countries were using multiple ways of entering quote, billing, shipping, and other data. Assess the potential business impact of these data quality problems. What decisions have to be made and steps taken to reach a solution?

6-9 Your industrial supply company wants to create a data warehouse where management can obtain a single corporate-wide view of critical sales information to identify bestselling products, key customers, and sales trends. Your sales and product information are stored in two different systems: a divisional sales system running on a Unix server and a corporate sales system running on an IBM mainframe. You would like to create a single standard format that consolidates these data from both systems. In MyLab MIS, you can review the proposed format along with sample files from the two systems that would supply the data for the data warehouse. Then answer the following questions:

- What business problems are created by not having these data in a single standard format?

- How easy would it be to create a database with a single standard format that could store the data from both systems? Identify the problems that would have to be addressed.

- Should the problems be solved by database specialists or general business managers? Explain.

- Who should have the authority to finalize a single companywide format for this information in the data warehouse?

Achieving Operational Excellence: Building a Relational Database for Inventory Management

Software skills: Database design, querying, and reporting
Business skills: Inventory management

6-10 In this exercise, you will use database software to design a database for managing inventory for a small business. Sylvester's Bike Shop, located in San Francisco, California, sells road, mountain, hybrid, leisure, and children's bicycles. Currently, Sylvester's purchases bikes from three suppliers but plans to add new suppliers in the near future. Using the information found in the tables in MyLab MIS, build a simple relational database to manage information about Sylvester's suppliers and products. Once you have built the database, perform the following activities.

- Prepare a report that identifies the five most expensive bicycles. The report should list the bicycles in descending order from most expensive to least expensive, the quantity on hand for each, and the markup percentage for each.

- Prepare a report that lists each supplier, its products, the quantities on hand, and associated reorder levels. The report should be sorted alphabetically by supplier. For each supplier, the products should be sorted alphabetically.

- Prepare a report listing only the bicycles that are low in stock and need to be reordered. The report should provide supplier information for the items identified.
- Write a brief description of how the database could be enhanced to further improve management of the business. What tables or fields should be added? What additional reports would be useful?

Improving Decision Making: Searching Online Databases for Overseas Business Resources

Software skills: Online databases
Business skills: Researching services for overseas operations

6-11 This project develops skills in searching web-enabled databases with information about products and services in faraway locations.

Your company is located in Greensboro, North Carolina, and manufactures office furniture of various types. You are considering opening a facility to manufacture and sell your products in Australia. You would like to contact organizations that offer many services necessary for you to open your Australian office and manufacturing facility, including lawyers, accountants, import-export experts, and telecommunications equipment and support firms. Access the following online databases to locate companies that you would like to meet with during your upcoming trip: Australian Business Directory Online, AustraliaTrade Now, and the Nationwide Business Directory of Australia. If necessary, use search engines such as Yahoo and Google.

- List the companies you would contact on your trip to determine whether they can help you with these and any other functions you think are vital to establishing your office.
- Rate the databases you used for accuracy of name, completeness, ease of use, and general helpfulness.

Collaboration and Teamwork Project

Identifying Entities and Attributes in an Online Database

6-12 With your team of three or four other students, select an online database to explore, such as AOL Music, iGo.com, or the Internet Movie Database. Explore one of these websites to see what information it provides. Then list the entities and attributes that the company running the website must keep track of in its databases. Diagram the relationship between the entities you have identified. If possible, use Google Docs and Google Drive or Google Sites to brainstorm, organize, and develop a presentation of your findings for the class.

How Reliable Is Big Data?
CASE STUDY

Today's companies are dealing with an avalanche of data from social media, search, and sensors, as well as from traditional sources. According to one estimate, 2.5 quintillion bytes of data per day are generated around the world. Making sense of "big data" to improve decision making and business performance has become one of the primary opportunities for organizations of all shapes and sizes, but it also represents big challenges.

Businesses such as Amazon, YouTube, and Spotify have flourished by analyzing the big data they collect about customer interests and purchases to create millions of personalized recommendations. A number of online services analyze big data to help consumers, including services for finding the lowest price on autos, computers, mobile phone plans, clothing, airfare, hotel rooms, and many other types of goods and services. Big data is also providing benefits in sports (see the chapter-opening case), education, science, health care, and law enforcement.

Analyzing billions of data points collected on patients, healthcare providers, and the effectiveness of prescriptions and treatments has helped the UK National Health Service (NHS) save about 581 million pounds (U.S. $784 million). The data are housed in an Oracle Exadata Database Machine, which can quickly analyze very large volumes of data (review this chapter's discussion of analytic platforms). NHS has used its findings from big data analysis to create dashboards identifying patients taking 10 or more medications at once, and which patients are taking too many antibiotics. Compiling very large amounts of data about drugs and treatments given to cancer patients and correlating that information with patient outcomes has helped NHS identify more effective treatment protocols.

New York City analyzes all the crime-related data it collects to lower the crime rate. Its CompStat crime-mapping program uses a comprehensive citywide database of all reported crimes or complaints, arrests, and summonses in each of the city's 76 precincts to report weekly on crime complaint and arrest activity at the precinct, patrol borough, and citywide levels. CompStat data can be displayed on maps showing crime and arrest locations, crime hot spots, and other relevant information to help precinct commanders quickly identify patterns and trends and deploy police personnel where they are most needed. Big data on criminal activity also powers New York City's Crime Strategies Unit, which targets the worst offenders for aggressive prosecution. Healthcare companies are currently analyzing big data to determine the most effective and economical treatments for chronic illnesses and common diseases and provide personalized care recommendations to patients.

There are limits to using big data. A number of companies have rushed to start big data projects without first establishing a business goal for this new information or key performance metrics to measure success. Swimming in numbers doesn't necessarily mean that the right information is being collected or that people will make smarter decisions. Experts in big data analysis believe too many companies, seduced by the promise of big data, jump into big data projects with nothing to show for their efforts. They start amassing mountains of data with no clear objective or understanding of exactly how analyzing big data will achieve their goal or what questions they are trying to answer. Organizations also won't benefit from big data that has not been properly cleansed, organized, and managed—think data quality.

Just because something can be measured doesn't mean it should be measured. Suppose, for instance, that a large company wants to measure its website traffic in relation to the number of mentions on Twitter. It builds a digital dashboard to display the results continuously. In the past, the company had generated most of its sales leads and eventual sales from trade shows and conferences. Switching to Twitter mentions as the key metric to measure changes the sales department's focus. The department pours its energy and resources into monitoring website clicks and social media traffic, which produce many unqualified leads that never lead to sales.

Although big data is very good at detecting correlations, especially subtle correlations that an analysis of smaller data sets might miss, big data analysis doesn't necessarily show causation or which correlations are meaningful. For example, examining big data might show that from 2006 to 2011 the United States murder rate was highly correlated with the market share of Internet Explorer, since both declined sharply. But that doesn't necessarily mean there is any meaningful connection between the two phenomena. Data analysts need some business knowledge of the problem they are trying to solve with big data.

Big data predictive models don't necessarily give you a better idea of what will happen in the future. Meridian Energy Ltd., an electricity generator and distributor operating in New Zealand and Australia, moved away from using an aging predictive equipment maintenance system. The software was supposed to predict the maintenance needs of all the large equipment the company owns and operates, including generators, wind turbines, transformers, circuit breakers, and industrial batteries. However, the system used outdated modeling techniques and could not actually predict equipment failures. It ran simulations of different scenarios and predicted when assets would fail the simulated tests. The recommendations of the software were useless because they did not accurately predict which pieces of equipment actually failed in the real world. Meridian eventually replaced the old system with IBM's Predictive Maintenance and Quality software, which bases predictions on more real-time data from equipment.

All data sets and data-driven forecasting models reflect the biases of the people selecting the data and performing the analysis. Several years ago, Google developed what it thought was a leading-edge algorithm using data it collected from web searches to determine exactly how many people had influenza and how the disease was spreading. It tried to calculate the number of people with flu in the United States by relating people's location to flu-related search queries on Google. Google consistently overestimated flu rates, when compared to conventional data collected afterward by the U.S. Centers for Disease Control (CDC). Several scientists suggested that Google was "tricked" by widespread media coverage of that year's severe flu season in the United States, which was further amplified by social media coverage. The model developed for forecasting flu trends was based on a flawed assumption—that the incidence of flu-related searches on Googles was a precise indicator of the number of people who actually came down with the flu. Google's algorithm only looked at numbers, not the context of the search results.

In addition to election tampering by hostile nations, insufficient attention to context and flawed assumptions may have played a role in the failure of most political experts to predict Donald Trump's victory over Hillary Clinton in the 2016 presidential election. Trump's victory ran counter to almost every major forecast, which had predicted Clinton's chances of winning to be between 70 to 99 percent.

Tons of data had been analyzed by political experts and the candidates' campaign teams. Clinton ran an overwhelmingly data-driven campaign, and big data had played a large role in Obama's victories in 2008 and 2012. Clinton's team added to the database the Obama campaigns had built, which connected personal data from traditional sources, such as reports from pollsters and field workers, with other data from social media posts and other online behavior as well as data used to predict consumer behavior. The Clinton team assumed that the same voters who supported Obama would turn out for their candidate, and focused on identifying voters in areas with a likelihood of high voter turnout. However, turnout for Clinton among the key groups who had supported Obama—women, minorities, college graduates, and blue-collar workers—fell short of expectations. (Trump had turned to big data as well, but put more emphasis on tailoring campaign messages to targeted voter groups.)

Political experts were misled into thinking Clinton's victory was assured because some predictive models lacked context in explaining potentially wide margins of error. There were shortcomings in polling, analysis, and interpretation, and analysts did not spend enough time examining how the data used in the predictive models were created. Many polls used in election forecasts underestimated the strength of Trump's support. State polls were inaccurate, perhaps failing to capture Republicans who initially refused to vote for Trump and then changed their minds at the last moment. Polls from Wisconsin shortly before the election had put Clinton well ahead of Trump. Polls are important for election predictions, but they are only one of many sources of data that should be consulted. Predictive models were unable to fully determine who would actually turn out to vote as opposed to how people thought they would vote. Analysts overlooked signs that Trump was forging ahead in the battleground states. Britain had a similar surprise when polls mistakenly predicted the nation would vote in June 2016 to stay in the European Union.

And let's not forget that big data poses some challenges to information security and privacy.

As Chapter 4 pointed out, companies are now aggressively collecting and mining massive data sets on people's shopping habits, incomes, hobbies, residences, and (via mobile devices) movements from place to place. They are using such big data to discover new facts about people, to classify them based on subtle patterns, to flag them as "risks" (for example, loan default risks or health risks), to predict their behavior, and to manipulate them for maximum profit.

When you combine someone's personal information with pieces of data from many different sources, you can infer new facts about that person (such as the fact that they are showing early signs of Parkinson's disease, or are unconsciously drawn toward products that are colored blue or green). If asked, most people might not want to disclose such information, but they might not even know such information about them exists. Privacy experts worry that people will be tagged and suffer adverse consequences without due process, the ability to fight back, or even knowledge that they have been discriminated against.

Sources: Linda Currey Post, "Big Data Helps UK National Health Service Lower Costs, Improve Treatments," *Forbes*, February 7, 2018; Michael Jude, "Data Preparation Is the Key to Big Data Success," *InfoWorld*, February 8, 2018; Rajkumar Venkatesan and Christina Black, "Using Big Data: 3 Reasons It Fails and 4 Ways to Make It Work," University of Virginia Darden School of Business Press Release, February 8, 3018; Ed Burns, "When Predictive Models Are Less Than Presidential," *Business Information*, February 2017; Aaron Timms, "Is Donald Trump's Surprise Win a Failure of Big Data? Not Really," *Fortune*, November 14, 2016; Steve Lohr and Natasha Singer, "The Data Said Clinton Would Win. Why You Shouldn't Have Believed It," *New York Times*, November 10, 2016; Nicole Laskowski and Niel Nikolaisen: "Seven Big Data Problems and How to Avoid Them," *TechTarget Inc.*, 2016; Joseph Stromberg, "Why Google Flu Trends Can't Track the Flu (Yet)," smithsonianmag.com, March 13, 2014; and Gary Marcus and Ernest Davis, "Eight (No, Nine!) Problems With Big Data," *New York Times*, April 6, 2014.

CASE STUDY QUESTIONS

6-13 What business benefits did the organizations described in this case achieve by analyzing and using big data?

6-14 Identify two decisions at the organizations described in this case that were improved by using big data and two decisions that big data did not improve.

6-15 List and describe the limitations to using big data.

6-16 Should all organizations try to collect and analyze big data? Why or why not? What management, organization, and technology issues should be addressed before a company decides to work with big data?

MyLab MIS

Go to the Assignments section of MyLab MIS to complete these writing exercises.

6-17 Identify the five problems of a traditional file environment and explain how a database management system solves them.

6-18 Discuss how the following facilitate the management of big data: Hadoop, in-memory computing, analytic platforms.

Chapter 6 References

Aiken, Peter, Mark Gillenson, Xihui Zhang, and David Rafner. "Data Management and Data Administration: Assessing 25 Years of Practice." *Journal of Database Management* (July–September 2011).

Beath, Cynthia, Irma Becerra-Fernandez, Jeanne Ross, and James Short. "Finding Value in the Information Explosion." *MIT Sloan Management Review* 53, No. 4 (Summer 2012).

Bessens, Bart. "Improving Data Quality Using Data Governance." *Big Data Quarterly* (Spring 2018).

Buff, Anne. "Adapting Governance to the Changing Data Landscape." *Big Data Quarterly* 3, No. 4 (Winter 2017).

Bughin, Jacques, John Livingston, and Sam Marwaha. "Seizing the Potential for Big Data." *McKinsey Quarterly* (October 2011).

Caserta, Joe, and Elliott Cordo. "Data Warehousing in the Era of Big Data." *Big Data Quarterly* (January 19, 2016).

Chai, Sen, and Willy Shih. "Why Big Data Isn't Enough." *MIT Sloan Management Review* (Winter 2017).

Clifford, James, Albert Croker, and Alex Tuzhilin. "On Data Representation and Use in a Temporal Relational DBMS." *Information Systems Research* 7, No. 3 (September 1996).

DalleMule, Landro, and Thomas H. Davenport. "What's Your Data Strategy?" *MIT Sloan Management Review* (Winter 2017).

Davenport, Thomas H. *Big Data at Work: Dispelling the Myths, Uncovering the Opportunities*. Boston, MA: Harvard Business School Press (2014).

Devlin, Barry. "The EDW Lives On: The Beating Heart of the Data Lake." *9Sight Consulting* (April 2017).

Eckerson, Wayne W. "Analytics in the Era of Big Data: Exploring a Vast New Ecosystem." *TechTarget* (2012).

Experian Information Solutions. "The 2017 Global Data Management Benchmark Report." (2017).

Henschen, Doug. "MetLife Uses NoSQL for Customer Service Breakthrough." *Information Week* (May 13, 2013).

Hoffer, Jeffrey A., Ramesh Venkataraman, and Heikki Toppi. *Modern Database Management* (12th ed.). Upper Saddle River, NJ: Pearson (2016).

Imhoff, Claudia. "Data Warehouse Appliances and the New World Order of Analytics." *Intelligent Solutions Inc.* (August 2017).

King, Elliot. "Has Data Quality Reached a Turning Point?" *Big Data Quarterly* 3 No. 4 (Winter 2017).

Kroenke, David M., and David Auer. *Database Processing: Fundamentals, Design, and Implementation* (14th ed.). Upper Saddle River, NJ: Pearson (2016).

Lee, Yang W., and Diane M. Strong. "Knowing-Why About Data Processes and Data Quality." *Journal of Management Information Systems* 20, No. 3 (Winter 2004).

Loveman, Gary. "Diamonds in the Datamine." *Harvard Business Review* (May 2003).

Marcus, Gary, and Ernest Davis. "Eight (No, Nine!) Problems with Big Data." *New York Times* (April 6, 2014).

Martens, David, and Foster Provost. "Explaining Data-Driven Document Classifications." *MIS Quarterly* 38, No. 1 (March 2014).

McAfee, Andrew, and Erik Brynjolfsson. "Big Data: The Management Revolution." *Harvard Business Review* (October 2012).

McKendrick, Joe. "Building a Data Lake for the Enterprise." *Big Data Quarterly* (Spring 2018).

McKinsey Global Institute. "Big Data: The Next Frontier for Innovation, Competition, and Productivity." *McKinsey & Company* (2011).

Morrow, Rich. "Apache Hadoop: The Swiss Army Knife of IT." *Global Knowledge* (2013).

Mulani, Narendra. "In-Memory Technology: Keeping Pace with Your Data." *Information Management* (February 27, 2013).

O'Keefe, Kate. "Real Prize in Caesars Fight: Data on Players." *Wall Street Journal* (March 19, 2015).

Redman, Thomas. *Data Driven: Profiting from Your Most Important Business Asset*. Boston: Harvard Business Press (2008).

_____. "Data's Credibility Problem." *Harvard Business Review* (December 2013).

Ross, Jeanne W., Cynthia M. Beath, and Anne Quaadgras. "You May Not Need Big Data After All." *Harvard Business Review* (December 2013).

SAP. "Data Warehousing and the Future." (February 2017).

Shi, Donghui, Jian Guan, Josef Zurada, and Andrew Manikas. "A Data-Mining Approach to Identification of Risk Factors in Safety Management Systems." *Journal of Management Information Systems* 34 No. 4 (2017).

Wallace, David J. "How Caesar's Entertainment Sustains a Data-Driven Culture." *DataInformed* (December 14, 2012).

Zoumpoulis, Spyros, Duncan Simester, and Theos Evgeniou, "Run Field Experiments to Make Sense of Your Big Data." *Harvard Business Review* (November 12, 2015).

7

Telecommunications, the Internet, and Wireless Technology

LEARNING OBJECTIVES

After reading this chapter, you will be able to answer the following questions:

7-1 What are the principal components of telecommunications networks and key networking technologies?

7-2 What are the different types of networks?

7-3 How do the Internet and Internet technology work, and how do they support communication and e-business?

7-4 What are the principal technologies and standards for wireless networking, communication, and Internet access?

7-5 How will MIS help my career?

CHAPTER CASES

Tour de France Wins with Wireless Technology

Net Neutrality: The Battle Rages On

Monitoring Employees on Networks: Unethical or Good Business?

Google, Apple, and Facebook Battle for Your Internet Experience

VIDEO CASES

Telepresence Moves out of the Boardroom and into the Field

Virtual Collaboration with IBM Sametime

MyLab MIS

Discussion Questions: 7-5, 7-6, 7-7; **Hands-on MIS Projects:** 7-8, 7-9, 7-10, 7-11; **Writing Assignments:** 7-17, 7-18; **eText with Conceptual Animations**

Tour de France Wins with Wireless Technology

Every July about two hundred cyclists race across 2,200 miles of the most difficult terrain in France, including steep roads in the Pyrenees and Alps. The Tour de France is considered the world's greatest bicycle race.

The first Tour de France took place 1903, as a way of promoting sales of L'Auto newspapers, initially attracting mostly local competitors and spectators. Thanks to newspapers, radio, and television, coverage and prestige of the event expanded. As with other competitive sports, such as football, baseball, tennis, and soccer, today's Tour de France fans don't just want to just watch a sport; they want to engage with it, and they expect more information and interaction—data-enhanced viewing, live streaming, video on demand, mobile apps, and social media interaction. Digital technology has become essential for attracting fans, athletes, sponsors, and broadcasters.

Up until 2014, Tour de France was a technology laggard. The sport doesn't easily generate real-time statistics. The only source of real-time information was a chalkboard held up by a race executive sitting as a passenger on a motorbike ahead of the cyclists. TV viewers could see timings and the race from numerous camera angles, but little more.

Today, data from Tour de France racing bikes are relayed to TV viewers within two seconds. A small, lightweight tracking sensor is attached to a clip below the saddle of every competing rider's bike. The sensor contains a global positioning system (GPS) chip, a radio frequency (RF) chip, and a rechargeable bat-

© Radu Razvan/Shutterstock

tery. Each sensor transmits data about the bike's GPS position and speed every second, generating over 3 billion data points during the course of the race. These real-time data are combined with feeds from other sources, such as weather services, road gradients, and historical race data from the past few years. Race organizers, broadcasters, teams, TV viewers, and fans using the Tour de France mobile app can now access detailed statistics on the progress of the race and individual riders. Riders wear earpiece radios that relay real-time data to them as they are cycling. The system does not include biometric data to monitor riders' physical performance—the teams keep these data private.

Dimension Data, a global IT services firm headquartered in South Africa, built and operates Tour de France's digital infrastructure. The sensor data from each racing bike are relayed to planes and helicopters flying overhead to cover the race for television. Race data are transmitted to Dimension Data's cloud service, hosted in remote data centers in London and Amsterdam, where powerful algorithms developed by cycling experts analyze the data, including external feeds, to generate real-time information for broadcasters, social media, and the Tour de France race app. Getting the data from bike to viewer only takes two seconds. The system is able to make predictions before and during the race based on current and historic data about riders and the state of the race; for example, the likelihood that the main body of riders might catch up to breakaway riders. The system can also generate rider profiles showing each rider's strengths and weaknesses across different race conditions based on historical race results and performance.

Digital technology has dramatically increased Tour de France fan involvement. Fans are able to see live performance information on their TVs and discuss the results on social media. In 2014, there were only 6 million views of video clips put out by the Tour de France organization. By 2016, that number had soared to 55 million. Seventeen million people access the live-tracking website. The goal is to pull you, the fan, into the race, and it appears Tour de France has succeeded.

Sources: www.letour.fr/en, accessed September 12, 2018; Bryan Glick, "Tour de France Pumps Tech," *Computer Weekly*, August 15–21, 2017; "Tour de France Behind the Scenes: How Dimension Data Rider Live Tracking Works," *DCRainmaker*, July 13, 2017; Dave Michels, "Adding an IoT Dimension to the Tour de France," *Network World*, May 23, 2017; and Scott Gibson, "5 Ways Tour de France Is Winning the Digital Race in 2017," *Dimension Data*, June 29, 2017.

The experience of the Tour de France illustrates some of the powerful capabilities and opportunities provided by contemporary networking technology. The annual Tour de France bicycle race now uses wireless networking and wireless sensor technology to closely track cyclists' speed and position in relation to other variables affecting race outcome, and to deliver race information instantaneously to fans and broadcasters.

The chapter-opening diagram calls attention to important points raised by this case and this chapter. The Tour de France race takes place over a vast and topographically challenging terrain, where it is very difficult to track riders and generate real-time race statistics. This legendary race has many fans, but management realized it could expand its fan base and deepen fan engagement by taking advantage of opportunities presented by wireless networking technology and the Internet of Things (IoT). The Tour de France is thus able to provide real-time race statistics, rider profiles, predictions about race outcomes, and content for TV broadcasts and social media, increasing the popularity of the sport and fans' interest. Tour de France cyclists and teams can use this information to improve their performance.

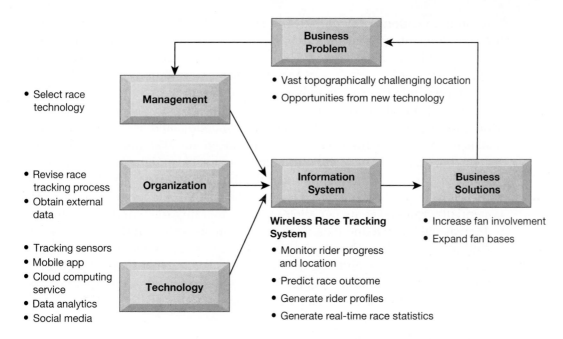

- Select race technology

- Revise race tracking process
- Obtain external data

- Tracking sensors
- Mobile app
- Cloud computing service
- Data analytics
- Social media

Business Problem

- Vast topographically challenging location
- Opportunities from new technology

Management

Organization

Technology

Information System

Wireless Race Tracking System

- Monitor rider progress and location
- Predict race outcome
- Generate rider profiles
- Generate real-time race statistics

Business Solutions

- Increase fan involvement
- Expand fan bases

Here are some questions to think about: Why has wireless technology played such a key role at the Tour de France? Describe how the technology changed the way the Tour de France provided and used data from its races.

7-1 What are the principal components of telecommunications networks and key networking technologies?

If you run or work in a business, you can't do without networks. You need to communicate rapidly with your customers, suppliers, and employees. Until about 1990, businesses used the postal system or telephone system with voice or fax for communication. Today, however, you and your employees use computers, email, text messaging, the Internet, mobile phones, and mobile computers connected to wireless networks for this purpose. Networking and the Internet are now nearly synonymous with doing business.

Networking and Communication Trends

Firms in the past used two fundamentally different types of networks: telephone networks and computer networks. Telephone networks historically handled voice communication, and computer networks handled data traffic. Telephone companies built telephone networks throughout the twentieth century by using voice transmission technologies (hardware and software), and these companies almost always operated as regulated monopolies throughout the world. Computer companies originally built computer networks to transmit data between computers in different locations.

Thanks to continuing telecommunications deregulation and information technology innovation, telephone and computer networks are converging into a single digital network using shared Internet-based standards and technology.

Telecommunications providers today, such as AT&T and Verizon, offer data transmission, Internet access, mobile phone service, and television programming as well as voice service. Cable companies, such as Cablevision and Comcast, offer voice service and Internet access. Computer networks have expanded to include Internet telephone and video services.

Both voice and data communication networks have also become more powerful (faster), more portable (smaller and mobile), and less expensive. For instance, the typical Internet connection speed in 2000 was 56 kilobits per second, but today the majority of U.S. households have high-speed **broadband** connections provided by telephone and cable TV companies running at 3 to 20 megabits (millions of bits per second). The cost for this service has fallen exponentially, from 50 cents per kilobit in 2000 to a tiny fraction of a cent today.

Increasingly, voice and data communication, as well as Internet access, are taking place over broadband wireless platforms such as mobile phones, mobile handheld devices, and PCs in wireless networks. More than 70 percent of Internet users (232 million people) in the United States use smartphones and tablets to access the Internet, as well as desktop PCs.

What Is a Computer Network?

If you had to connect the computers for two or more employees in the same office, you would need a computer network. In its simplest form, a network consists of two or more connected computers. Figure 7.1 illustrates the major hardware, software, and transmission components in a simple network: a client computer and a dedicated server computer, network interfaces, a connection medium, network operating system software, and either a hub or a switch.

FIGURE 7.1 COMPONENTS OF A SIMPLE COMPUTER NETWORK

Illustrated here is a simple computer network consisting of computers, a network operating system (NOS) residing on a dedicated server computer, cable (wiring) connecting the devices, switches, and a router.

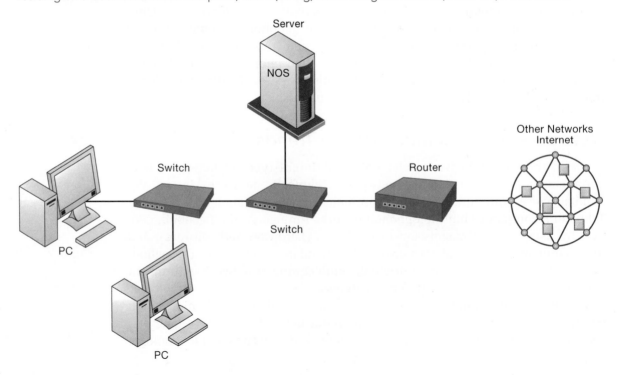

Each computer on the network contains a network interface device to link the computer to the network. The connection medium for linking network components can be a telephone wire, coaxial cable, or radio signal in the case of cell phone and wireless local area networks (Wi-Fi networks).

The **network operating system (NOS)** routes and manages communications on the network and coordinates network resources. It can reside on every computer in the network or primarily on a dedicated server computer for all the applications on the network. A server is a computer on a network that performs important network functions for client computers, such as displaying web pages, storing data, and storing the network operating system (hence controlling the network). Microsoft Windows Server and Linux are the most widely used network operating systems.

Most networks also contain a switch or a hub acting as a connection point between the computers. **Hubs** are simple devices that connect network components, sending a packet of data to all other connected devices. A **switch** has more intelligence than a hub and can filter and forward data to a specified destination on the network.

What if you want to communicate with another network, such as the Internet? You would need a router. A **router** is a communications processor that routes packets of data through different networks, ensuring that the data sent get to the correct address.

Network switches and routers have proprietary software built into their hardware for directing the movement of data on the network. This can create network bottlenecks and makes the process of configuring a network more complicated and time-consuming. **Software-defined networking (SDN)** is a networking approach in which many of these control functions are managed by one central program, which can run on inexpensive commodity servers that are separate from the network devices themselves. This is especially helpful in a cloud computing environment with many pieces of hardware because it allows a network administrator to manage traffic loads in a flexible and more efficient manner.

Networks in Large Companies

The network we've just described might be suitable for a small business, but what about large companies with many locations and thousands of employees? As a firm grows, its small networks can be tied together into a corporate-wide networking infrastructure. The network infrastructure for a large corporation consists of a large number of these small local area networks linked to other local area networks and to firmwide corporate networks. A number of powerful servers support a corporate website, a corporate intranet, and perhaps an extranet. Some of these servers link to other large computers supporting back-end systems.

Figure 7.2 provides an illustration of these more-complex, larger-scale corporate-wide networks. Here the corporate network infrastructure supports a mobile sales force using mobile phones and smartphones, mobile employees linking to the company website, and internal company networks using mobile wireless local area networks (Wi-Fi networks). In addition to these computer networks, the firm's infrastructure may include a separate telephone network that handles most voice data. Many firms are dispensing with their traditional telephone networks and using Internet telephones that run on their existing data networks (described later).

As you can see from this figure, a large corporate network infrastructure uses a wide variety of technologies—everything from ordinary telephone service

FIGURE 7.2 CORPORATE NETWORK INFRASTRUCTURE

Today's corporate network infrastructure is a collection of many networks from the public switched telephone network to the Internet to corporate local area networks linking workgroups, departments, or office floors.

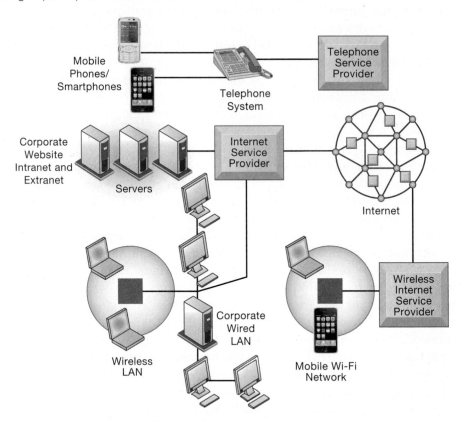

and corporate data networks to Internet service, wireless Internet, and mobile phones. One of the major problems facing corporations today is how to integrate all the different communication networks and channels into a coherent system that enables information to flow from one part of the corporation to another and from one system to another.

Key Digital Networking Technologies

Contemporary digital networks and the Internet are based on three key technologies: client/server computing, the use of packet switching, and the development of widely used communications standards (the most important of which is Transmission Control Protocol/Internet Protocol, or TCP/IP) for linking disparate networks and computers.

Client/Server Computing

Client/server computing, introduced in Chapter 5, is a distributed computing model in which some of the processing power is located within small, inexpensive client computers and resides literally on desktops or laptops or in handheld devices. These powerful clients are linked to one another through a network that is controlled by a network server computer. The server sets the rules of communication for the network and provides every client with an address so others can find it on the network.

Client/server computing has largely replaced centralized mainframe computing in which nearly all the processing takes place on a central large mainframe computer. Client/server computing has extended computing to departments, workgroups, factory floors, and other parts of the business that could not be served by a centralized architecture. It also makes it possible for personal computing devices such as PCs, laptops, and mobile phones to be connected to networks such as the Internet. The Internet is the largest implementation of client/server computing.

Packet Switching

Packet switching is a method of slicing digital messages into parcels called packets, sending the packets along different communication paths as they become available, and then reassembling the packets once they arrive at their destinations (see Figure 7.3). Prior to the development of packet switching, computer networks used leased, dedicated telephone circuits to communicate with other computers in remote locations. In circuit-switched networks, such as the telephone system, a complete point-to-point circuit is assembled, and then communication can proceed. These dedicated circuit-switching techniques were expensive and wasted available communications capacity—the circuit was maintained regardless of whether any data were being sent.

Packet switching is more efficient. Messages are first broken down into small fixed bundles of data called packets. The packets include information for directing the packet to the right address and for checking transmission errors along with the data. The packets are transmitted over various communications channels by using routers, each packet traveling independently. Packets of data originating at one source will be routed through many paths and networks before being reassembled into the original message when they reach their destinations.

TCP/IP and Connectivity

In a typical telecommunications network, diverse hardware and software components need to work together to transmit information. Different components in a network communicate with each other by adhering to a common set of

---

**FIGURE 7.3   PACKET-SWITCHED NETWORKS AND PACKET
COMMUNICATIONS**

Data are grouped into small packets, which are transmitted independently over various communications channels and reassembled at their final destination.

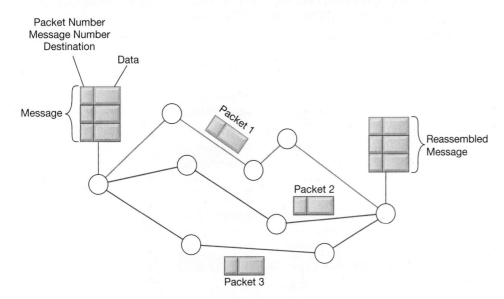

rules called protocols. A **protocol** is a set of rules and procedures governing transmission of information between two points in a network.

In the past, diverse proprietary and incompatible protocols often forced business firms to purchase computing and communications equipment from a single vendor. However, today, corporate networks are increasingly using a single, common, worldwide standard called **Transmission Control Protocol/Internet Protocol (TCP/IP)**. TCP/IP was developed during the early 1970s to support U.S. Department of Defense Advanced Research Projects Agency (DARPA) efforts to help scientists transmit data among different types of computers over long distances.

TCP/IP uses a suite of protocols, the main ones being TCP and IP. TCP refers to the Transmission Control Protocol, which handles the movement of data between computers. TCP establishes a connection between the computers, sequences the transfer of packets, and acknowledges the packets sent. IP refers to the Internet Protocol (IP), which is responsible for the delivery of packets and includes the disassembling and reassembling of packets during transmission. Figure 7.4 illustrates the four-layered Department of Defense reference model for TCP/IP, and the layers are described as follows:

1. Application layer. The Application layer enables client application programs to access the other layers and defines the protocols that applications use to exchange data. One of these application protocols is the Hypertext Transfer Protocol (HTTP), which is used to transfer web page files.

2. Transport layer. The Transport layer is responsible for providing the Application layer with communication and packet services. This layer includes TCP and other protocols.

3. Internet layer. The Internet layer is responsible for addressing, routing, and packaging data packets called IP datagrams. The Internet Protocol is one of the protocols used in this layer.

4. Network Interface layer. At the bottom of the reference model, the Network Interface layer is responsible for placing packets on and receiving them from the network medium, which could be any networking technology.

Two computers using TCP/IP can communicate even if they are based on different hardware and software platforms. Data sent from one computer to the other passes downward through all four layers, starting with the sending

---

FIGURE 7.4 **THE TRANSMISSION CONTROL PROTOCOL/INTERNET PROTOCOL (TCP/IP) REFERENCE MODEL**

This figure illustrates the four layers of the TCP/IP reference model for communications.

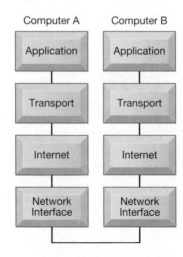

computer's Application layer and passing through the Network Interface layer. After the data reach the recipient host computer, they travel up the layers and are reassembled into a format the receiving computer can use. If the receiving computer finds a damaged packet, it asks the sending computer to retransmit it. This process is reversed when the receiving computer responds.

7-2 What are the different types of networks?

Let's look more closely at alternative networking technologies available to businesses.

Signals: Digital Versus Analog

There are two ways to communicate a message in a network: an analog signal or a digital signal. An *analog signal* is represented by a continuous waveform that passes through a communications medium and has been used for audio communication. The most common analog devices are the telephone handset, the speaker on your computer, or your iPhone earphone, all of which create analog waveforms that your ear can hear.

A *digital signal* is a discrete, binary waveform rather than a continuous waveform. Digital signals communicate information as strings of two discrete states: 1 bits and 0 bits, which are represented as on-off electrical pulses. Computers use digital signals and require a modem to convert these digital signals into analog signals that can be sent over (or received from) telephone lines, cable lines, or wireless media that use analog signals (see Figure 7.5). **Modem** stands for modulator-demodulator. Cable modems connect your computer to the Internet by using a cable network. DSL modems connect your computer to the Internet using a telephone company's landline network. Wireless modems perform the same function as traditional modems, connecting your computer to a wireless network that could be a cell phone network or a Wi-Fi network.

Types of Networks

There are many kinds of networks and ways of classifying them. One way of looking at networks is in terms of their geographic scope (see Table 7.1).

Local Area Networks

If you work in a business that uses networking, you are probably connecting to other employees and groups via a local area network. A **local area network (LAN)** is designed to connect personal computers and other digital devices

FIGURE 7.5 FUNCTIONS OF THE MODEM

A modem is a device that translates digital signals into analog form (and vice versa) so that computers can transmit data over analog networks such as telephone and cable networks.

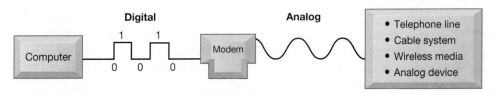

TABLE 7.1 TYPES OF NETWORKS

TYPE	AREA
Local area network (LAN)	Up to 500 meters (half a mile); an office or floor of a building
Campus area network (CAN)	Up to 1,000 meters (a mile); a college campus or corporate facility
Metropolitan area network (MAN)	A city or metropolitan area
Wide area network (WAN)	A regional, transcontinental, or global area

within a half-mile or 500-meter radius. LANs typically connect a few computers in a small office, all the computers in one building, or all the computers in several buildings in close proximity. LANs also are used to link to long-distance wide area networks (WANs, described later in this section) and other networks around the world, using the Internet.

Review Figure 7.1, which could serve as a model for a small LAN that might be used in an office. One computer is a dedicated network server, providing users with access to shared computing resources in the network, including software programs and data files.

The server determines who gets access to what and in which sequence. The router connects the LAN to other networks, which could be the Internet, or another corporate network, so that the LAN can exchange information with networks external to it. The most common LAN operating systems are Windows and Linux.

Ethernet is the dominant LAN standard at the physical network level, specifying the physical medium to carry signals between computers, access control rules, and a standardized set of bits that carry data over the system. Originally, Ethernet supported a data transfer rate of 10 megabits per second (Mbps). Newer versions, such as Gigabit Ethernet, support a data transfer rate of 1 gigabit per second (Gbps).

The LAN illustrated in Figure 7.1 uses a client/server architecture in which the network operating system resides primarily on a single server, and the server provides much of the control and resources for the network. Alternatively, LANs may use a **peer-to-peer** architecture. A peer-to-peer network treats all processors equally and is used primarily in small networks with ten or fewer users. The various computers on the network can exchange data by direct access and can share peripheral devices without going through a separate server.

Larger LANs have many clients and multiple servers, with separate servers for specific services such as storing and managing files and databases (file servers or database servers), managing printers (print servers), storing and managing email (mail servers), or storing and managing web pages (web servers).

Metropolitan and Wide Area Networks

Wide area networks (WANs) span broad geographical distances—regions, states, continents, or the entire globe. The most universal and powerful WAN is the Internet. Computers connect to a WAN through public networks, such as the telephone system or private cable systems, or through leased lines or satellites. A **metropolitan area network (MAN)** is a network that spans a metropolitan area, usually a city and its major suburbs. Its geographic scope falls between a WAN and a LAN.

TABLE 7.2	PHYSICAL TRANSMISSION MEDIA	
TRANSMISSION MEDIUM	DESCRIPTION	SPEED
Twisted pair wire (CAT 5)	Strands of copper wire twisted in pairs for voice and data communications. CAT 5 is the most common 10 Mbps LAN cable. Maximum recommended run of 100 meters.	10–100+ Mbps
Coaxial cable	Thickly insulated copper wire, which is capable of high-speed data transmission and less subject to interference than twisted wire. Currently used for cable TV and for networks with longer runs (more than 100 meters).	Up to 1 Gbps
Fiber-optic cable	Strands of clear glass fiber, transmitting data as pulses of light generated by lasers. Useful for high-speed transmission of large quantities of data. More expensive than other physical transmission media; used for last-mile delivery to customers and the Internet backbone.	15 Mbps to 6+ Tbps
Wireless transmission media	Based on radio signals of various frequencies and includes both terrestrial and satellite microwave systems and cellular networks. Used for long-distance, wireless communication, and Internet access.	Up to 600+ Mbps

Transmission Media and Transmission Speed

Networks use different kinds of physical transmission media, including twisted pair wire, coaxial cable, fiber-optic cable, and media for wireless transmission. Each has advantages and limitations. A wide range of speeds is possible for any given medium, depending on the software and hardware configuration. Table 7.2 compares these media.

Bandwidth: Transmission Speed

The total amount of digital information that can be transmitted through any telecommunications medium is measured in bits per second (bps). One signal change, or cycle, is required to transmit one or several bits; therefore, the transmission capacity of each type of telecommunications medium is a function of its frequency. The number of cycles per second that can be sent through that medium is measured in **hertz**—one hertz is equal to one cycle of the medium.

The range of frequencies that can be accommodated on a particular telecommunications channel is called its **bandwidth**. The bandwidth is the difference between the highest and lowest frequencies that can be accommodated on a single channel. The greater the range of frequencies, the greater the bandwidth and the greater the channel's transmission capacity.

7-3 How do the Internet and Internet technology work, and how do they support communication and e-business?

The Internet has become an indispensable personal and business tool—but what exactly is the Internet? How does it work, and what does Internet technology have to offer for business? Let's look at the most important Internet features.

What Is the Internet?

The Internet is the world's most extensive public communication system. It's also the world's largest implementation of client/server computing and internetworking, linking millions of individual networks all over the world.

This global network of networks began in the early 1970s as a U.S. Department of Defense project to link scientists and university professors around the world.

Most homes and small businesses connect to the Internet by subscribing to an Internet service provider. An **Internet service provider (ISP)** is a commercial organization with a permanent connection to the Internet that sells temporary connections to retail subscribers. EarthLink, NetZero, and AT&T are ISPs. Individuals also connect to the Internet through their business firms, universities, or research centers that have designated Internet domains.

There is a variety of services for ISP Internet connections. Connecting via a traditional telephone line and modem, at a speed of 56.6 kilobits per second (Kbps), used to be the most common form of connection worldwide, but high-speed broadband connections have largely replaced it. Digital subscriber line, cable, satellite Internet connections, and T lines provide these broadband services.

Digital subscriber line (DSL) technologies operate over existing telephone lines to carry voice, data, and video at transmission rates ranging from 385 Kbps all the way up to 3 Mbps, depending on usage patterns and distance. Fios (Verizon's fiber optic cable service) can deliver over 900 Mbps, although most home service delivers 100 Mbps. **Cable Internet connections** provided by cable television vendors use digital cable coaxial lines to deliver high-speed Internet access to homes and businesses. They can provide high-speed access to the Internet of up to 50 Mbps, although most providers offer service ranging from 3 Mbps to 20 Mbps. Where DSL and cable services are unavailable, it is possible to access the Internet via satellite, although some satellite Internet connections have slower upload speeds than other broadband services.

T1 and T3 are international telephone standards for digital communication. They are leased, dedicated lines suitable for businesses or government agencies requiring high-speed guaranteed service levels. **T1 lines** offer guaranteed delivery at 1.54 Mbps, and T3 lines offer delivery at 45 Mbps. The Internet does not provide similar guaranteed service levels but, simply, best effort.

Internet Addressing and Architecture

The Internet is based on the TCP/IP networking protocol suite described earlier in this chapter. Every device connected to the Internet (or another TCP/IP network) is assigned a unique **Internet Protocol (IP) address** consisting of a string of numbers.

When a user sends a message to another user on the Internet or another TCP/IP network, the message is first decomposed into packets. Each packet contains its destination address. The packets are then sent from the client to the network server and from there on to as many other servers as necessary to arrive at a specific computer with a known address. At the destination address, the packets are reassembled into the original message.

The Domain Name System

Because it would be incredibly difficult for Internet users to remember long strings of numbers, an IP address can be represented by a natural language convention called a **domain name**. The **Domain Name System (DNS)** converts domain names to IP addresses. DNS servers maintain a database containing IP addresses mapped to their corresponding domain names. To access a computer on the Internet, users need only specify its domain name, such as Expedia.com,

DNS has a hierarchical structure (see Figure 7.6). At the top of the DNS hierarchy is the root domain. The child domain of the root is called a top-level

FIGURE 7.6   THE DOMAIN NAME SYSTEM

The Domain Name System is a hierarchical system with a root domain, top-level domains, second-level domains, and host computers at the third level.

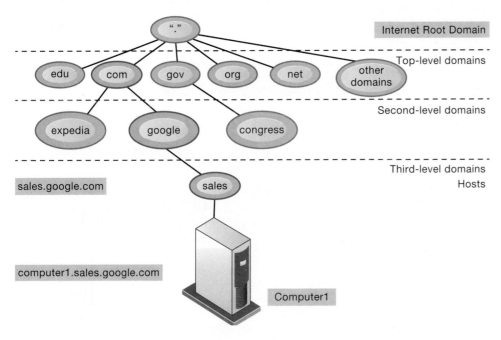

domain, and the child domain of a top-level domain is called a second-level domain. Top-level domains are two- and three-character names you are familiar with from surfing the web; for example, .com, .edu, .gov, and the various country codes such as .ca for Canada or .it for Italy. Second-level domains have two parts, designating a top-level name and a second-level name—such as buy.com, nyu.edu, or amazon.ca. A host name at the bottom of the hierarchy designates a specific computer on either the Internet or a private network.

The following list shows the most common domain extensions currently available and officially approved. Countries also have domain names such as .uk, .au, and .fr (United Kingdom, Australia, and France, respectively), and there is a new class of internationalized top-level domains that use non-English characters. In the future, this list will expand to include many more types of organizations and industries as follows:

.com Commercial organizations/businesses

.edu Educational institutions

.gov U.S. government agencies

.mil U.S. military

.net Network computers

.org Any type of organization

.biz Business firms

.info Information providers

Internet Architecture and Governance

Internet data traffic is carried over transcontinental high-speed backbone networks that generally operate in the range of 155 Mbps to 2.5 Gbps (see Figure 7.7). These trunk lines are typically owned by long-distance telephone

FIGURE 7.7 INTERNET NETWORK ARCHITECTURE

The Internet backbone connects to regional networks, which in turn provide access to Internet service providers, large firms, and government institutions. Network access points (NAPs) and metropolitan area exchanges (MAEs) are hubs where the backbone intersects regional and local networks and where backbone owners connect with one another.

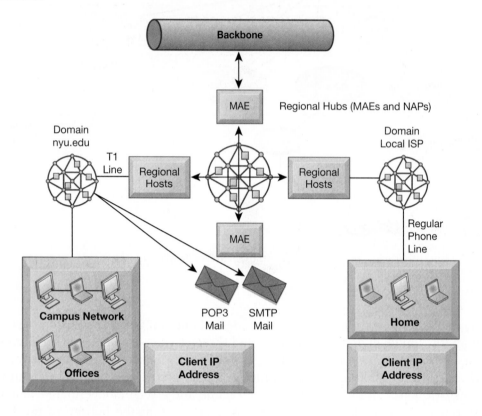

companies (called *network service providers*) or by national governments. Local connection lines are owned by regional telephone and cable television companies in the United States and in other countries that connect retail users in homes and businesses to the Internet. The regional networks lease access to ISPs, private companies, and government institutions.

Each organization pays for its own networks and its own local Internet connection services, a part of which is paid to the long-distance trunk line owners. Individual Internet users pay ISPs for using their service, and they generally pay a flat subscription fee, no matter how much or how little they use the Internet. A debate is now raging on whether this arrangement should continue or whether heavy Internet users who download large video and music files should pay more for the bandwidth they consume. The Interactive Session on Organizations explores this topic by examining the pros and cons of net neutrality.

No one owns the Internet, and it has no formal management. However, worldwide Internet policies are established by a number of professional organizations and government bodies, including the Internet Architecture Board (IAB), which helps define the overall structure of the Internet; the Internet Corporation for Assigned Names and Numbers (ICANN), which manages the domain name system; and the World Wide Web Consortium (W3C), which sets Hypertext Markup Language and other programming standards for the web.

Net Neutrality: The Battle Rages On

What kind of Internet user are you? Do you primarily use the Net to do a little email and online banking? Or are you online all day, watching YouTube videos, downloading music files, or playing online games? Do you use your iPhone to stream TV shows and movies on a regular basis? If you're a power Internet or smartphone user, you are consuming a great deal of bandwidth.

To manage all the data flowing over the Internet, it will be necessary to build new networks. Internet service providers (ISPs) assert that expanding their networks would require passing on burdensome costs to consumers. These companies believe differential pricing methods, which include data caps and metered use—charging based on the amount of bandwidth consumed—are the fairest way to finance necessary investments in their network infrastructures. However, metering Internet use is not universally accepted because of an ongoing debate about net neutrality.

Net neutrality is the idea that Internet service providers must allow customers equal access to content and applications, regardless of the source or nature of the content. Until recently, the Internet has been neutral, with all Internet traffic treated equally on a first-come, first-served basis by Internet backbone owners. However, this arrangement prevents telecommunications and cable companies from charging differentiated prices based on the amount of bandwidth consumed by the content being delivered over the Internet.

Net neutrality advocates include the Electronic Frontier Foundation; data-intensive web businesses such as Netflix, Amazon, and Google; major consumer groups; and a host of bloggers and small businesses. They argue that differentiated pricing would impose heavy costs on heavy bandwidth users such as YouTube, Skype, and other innovative services, preventing high-bandwidth startup companies from gaining traction. Net neutrality supporters also argue that without net neutrality, ISPs that are also cable companies, such as Comcast, might block online streaming video from Netflix or Hulu to force customers to use the cable company's on-demand movie rental services.

It was thought that the issue of net neutrality had been definitively settled by the 2015 ruling of the Federal Communications Commission (FCC) under the Obama administration, which considered broadband Internet services as a utility under Title II of the Communications Act. This ruling gave the FCC broad power over Internet providers. Internet service providers could not discriminate against any lawful content by blocking websites or apps, slow the transmission of data based on the nature of the content as long as it was legal, or create an Internet fast lane for companies and consumers who pay premiums and a slow lane for those who don't.

All that changed under the Trump administration, which opposes net neutrality as part of its push for government-wide deregulation. In December 2017, the FCC voted to repeal its net neutrality rules for Internet providers. Trump's FCC chair, Ajit Pai, has asserted that before net neutrality rules were put into effect in 2015, service providers had not engaged in any of the practices the rules prohibit. Pai believes that ending net neutrality could help lower prices for consumers, because Internet service providers could offset their costs with the use of paid prioritization deals with websites for faster delivery of their content.

Pro-net neutrality groups immediately countered, predicting that repealing net neutrality would lead to a faster, pricier, and more confusing Internet. Deregulation could create a "two-tier" Internet, in which Internet service providers will start charging fees to websites and apps, and slow down or block the sites that don't pay up. As a result, users will have unfettered access to only part of the Internet, with the rest either inaccessible or slow.

Consumer advocates have further argued that if net neutrality rules are eliminated, broadband providers will begin selling Internet services in bundles, similar to how cable television is sold today. For example, if you wanted to access Facebook and Twitter under a bundling system, you might have to pay for a premium social media package. Consumers could suffer from pay-to-play deals. A fast lane could be occupied by big Internet and media companies and affluent households, while everyone else would be relegated to a slow lane.

Some small businesses worry that repealing net neutrality would create an unfair playing field favoring industry giants. Websites and services of e-commerce startups might run slower than those run by the big Internet players such as Netflix or Facebook. Remote workers of all kinds, including freelancers and franchisees could similarly face higher costs to do their jobs from home.

Opponents of net neutrality have countered that the biggest barrier to a company becoming the next Google, Facebook, Netflix, or Amazon isn't the end of net neutrality but Google, Facebook, Netflix, and Amazon themselves. These companies are already spending vast sums of money to push their ever-higher bandwidth content to consumers. Many lawsuits challenging the FCC's new Internet policy have been filed since the new FCC rules took effect. The battle for net neutrality is not over.

Sources: Cecelia Kang, "Flurry of Lawsuits Filed to Fight Repeal of Net Neutrality," *New York Times*, January 16, 2018; Nick Piette, "Net Neutrality: Why It's Vital for Digital Transformation," *Information Week*, February 9, 2018; Aaron Byrd and Natalia V. Osipova, "Why Net Neutrality Was Repealed and How It Affects You," *New York Times*, December 21, 2017; and "Christopher Mims, Get Ready for a Faster, Pricier, and More Confusing Internet," *Wall Street Journal*, December 18, 2017.

CASE STUDY QUESTIONS

1. What is net neutrality? Who's in favor of net neutrality? Who's opposed? Why?

2. What would be the impact on individual users, businesses, and government if Internet providers switched to a tiered service model for transmission over landlines and wireless?

3. It has been said that net neutrality is the most important issue facing the Internet since the advent of the Internet. Discuss the implications of this statement.

4. Are you in favor of enforcing Internet neutrality? Why or why not?

These organizations influence government agencies, network owners, ISPs, and software developers with the goal of keeping the Internet operating as efficiently as possible. The Internet must also conform to the laws of the sovereign nation-states in which it operates as well as to the technical infrastructures that exist within the nation-states. Although in the early years of the Internet and the web there was very little legislative or executive interference, this situation is changing as the Internet plays a growing role in the distribution of information and knowledge, including content that some find objectionable.

The Future Internet: IPv6 and Internet2

The Internet was not originally designed to handle billions of users and the transmission of massive quantities of data. Because of sheer Internet population growth, the world is about to run out of available IP addresses using the old addressing convention. The old system based on 32-bit addresses is being replaced by a new version of IP addressing called **IPv6** (Internet Protocol version 6), which contains 128-bit addresses (2 to the power of 128), or more than a quadrillion possible unique addresses. IPv6 is compatible with most modems and routers sold today, and IPv6 will fall back to the old addressing system if IPv6 is not available on local networks. The transition to IPv6 will take several years as systems replace older equipment.

Internet2 is an advanced networking consortium representing more than 500 U.S. universities, private businesses, and government agencies working with 94,000 institutions across the United States and international networking partners from more than 100 countries. To connect these communities, Internet2 developed a high-capacity, 100 Gbps network that serves as a test bed for leading-edge technologies that may eventually migrate to the public Internet, including large-scale network performance measurement and management tools, secure identity and access management tools, and capabilities such as scheduling high-bandwidth, high-performance circuits.

Internet Services and Communication Tools

The Internet is based on client/server technology. Individuals using the Internet control what they do through client applications on their computers, such as web browser software. The data, including email messages and web pages, are stored on servers. A client uses the Internet to request information from a particular web server on a distant computer, and the server sends the requested information back to the client over the Internet. Client platforms today include not only PCs and other computers but also smartphones and tablets.

Internet Services

A client computer connecting to the Internet has access to a variety of services. These services include email, chatting and instant messaging, electronic discussion groups, **Telnet**, **File Transfer Protocol (FTP)**, and the web. Table 7.3 provides a brief description of these services.

Each Internet service is implemented by one or more software programs. All the services may run on a single server computer, or different services may be allocated to different machines. Figure 7.8 illustrates one way these services can be arranged in a multitiered client/server architecture.

Email enables messages to be exchanged from computer to computer, with capabilities for routing messages to multiple recipients, forwarding messages, and attaching text documents or multimedia files to messages. Most email today is sent through the Internet. The cost of email is far lower than equivalent voice, postal, or overnight delivery costs, and email messages can arrive anywhere in the world in a matter of seconds.

Chatting enables two or more people who are simultaneously connected to the Internet to hold live, interactive conversations. **Chat** systems now support voice and video chat as well as written conversations. Many online retail businesses offer chat services on their websites to attract visitors, to encourage repeat purchases, and to improve customer service.

Instant messaging is a type of chat service that enables participants to create their own private chat channels. The instant messaging system alerts the user whenever someone on his or her private list is online so that the user can initiate a chat session with other individuals. Instant messaging systems for consumers include Yahoo! Messenger, Google Hangouts, AOL Instant Messenger,

TABLE 7.3 MAJOR INTERNET SERVICES

CAPABILITY	FUNCTIONS SUPPORTED
Email	Person-to-person messaging; document sharing
Chatting and instant messaging	Interactive conversations
Newsgroups	Discussion groups on electronic bulletin boards
Telnet	Logging on to one computer system and doing work on another
File Transfer Protocol (FTP)	Transferring files from computer to computer
World Wide Web	Retrieving, formatting, and displaying information (including text, audio, graphics, and video) by using hypertext links

FIGURE 7.8 CLIENT/SERVER COMPUTING ON THE INTERNET

Client computers running web browsers and other software can access an array of services on servers over the Internet. These services may all run on a single server or on multiple specialized servers.

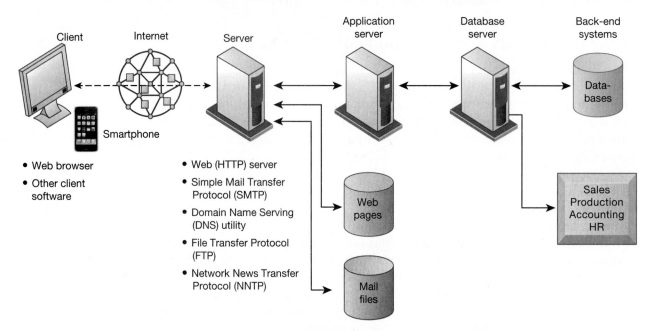

and Facebook Messenger. Companies concerned with security use proprietary communications and messaging systems such as IBM Sametime.

Newsgroups are worldwide discussion groups posted on Internet electronic bulletin boards on which people share information and ideas on a defined topic such as radiology or rock bands. Anyone can post messages on these bulletin boards for others to read.

Employee use of email, instant messaging, and the Internet is supposed to increase worker productivity, but the accompanying Interactive Session on Management shows that this may not always be the case. Many company managers now believe they need to monitor and even regulate their employees' online activity, but is this ethical? Although there are some strong business reasons companies may need to monitor their employees' email and web activities, what does this mean for employee privacy?

Voice over IP

The Internet has also become a popular platform for voice transmission and corporate networking. **Voice over IP (VoIP)** technology delivers voice information in digital form using packet switching, avoiding the tolls charged by local and long-distance telephone networks (see Figure 7.9). Calls that would ordinarily be transmitted over public telephone networks travel over the corporate network based on the Internet protocol, or over the public Internet. Voice calls can be made and received with a computer equipped with a microphone and speakers or with a VoIP-enabled telephone.

Cable firms such as Time Warner and Cablevision provide VoIP service bundled with their high-speed Internet and cable offerings. Skype offers free VoIP worldwide using a peer-to-peer network, and Google has its own free VoIP service.

Although up-front investments are required for an IP phone system, VoIP can reduce communication and network management costs by 20 to 30 percent. For example, VoIP saves Virgin Entertainment Group $700,000 per year in

FIGURE 7.9   HOW VOICE OVER IP WORKS

A VoIP phone call digitizes and breaks up a voice message into data packets that may travel along different routes before being reassembled at the final destination. A processor nearest the call's destination, called a gateway, arranges the packets in the proper order and directs them to the telephone number of the receiver or the IP address of the receiving computer.

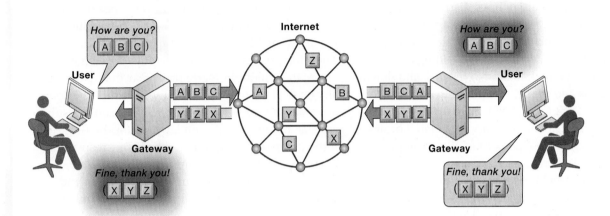

long-distance bills. In addition to lowering long-distance costs and eliminating monthly fees for private lines, an IP network provides a single voice-data infrastructure for both telecommunications and computing services. Companies no longer have to maintain separate networks or provide support services and personnel for each type of network.

Unified Communications

In the past, each of the firm's networks for wired and wireless data, voice communications, and videoconferencing operated independently of each other and had to be managed separately by the information systems department. Now, however, firms can merge disparate communications modes into a single universally accessible service using unified communications technology. **Unified communications** integrates disparate channels for voice communications, data communications, instant messaging, email, and electronic conferencing into a single experience by which users can seamlessly switch back and forth between different communication modes. Presence technology shows whether a person is available to receive a call.

CenterPoint Properties, a major Chicago area industrial real estate company, used unified communications technology to create collaborative websites for each of its real estate deals. Each website provides a single point for accessing structured and unstructured data. Integrated presence technology lets team members email, instant message, call, or videoconference with one click.

Virtual Private Networks

What if you had a marketing group charged with developing new products and services for your firm with members spread across the United States? You would want them to be able to email each other and communicate with the home office without any chance that outsiders could intercept the communications. Large private networking firms offer secure, private, dedicated networks to customers, but this is expensive. A lower-cost solution is to create a virtual private network within the public Internet.

INTERACTIVE SESSION   MANAGEMENT

Monitoring Employees on Networks: Unethical or Good Business?

The Internet has become an extremely valuable business tool, but it's also a huge distraction for workers on the job. Employees are wasting valuable company time by surfing inappropriate websites (Facebook, shopping, sports, etc.), sending and receiving personal email, texting to friends, and downloading videos and music. According to a survey by International Data Corp (IDC), 30 to 40 percent of Internet access is spent on non-work-related browsing, and a staggering 60 percent of all online purchases are made during working hours.

Many companies have begun monitoring employee use of email and the Internet, sometimes without their knowledge. Many tools are now available for this purpose, including Veriato Investigator, OsMonitor, Work Examiner, Mobistealth, and Spytech. These products enable companies to record online searches, monitor file downloads and uploads, record keystrokes, keep tabs on emails, create transcripts of chats, or take certain screenshots of images displayed on computer screens. Instant messaging, text messaging, and social media monitoring are also increasing. Microsoft offers software called MyAnalytics, which assembles data from emails, calendars, and other sources to show employees how they spend their time, how often they are in touch with key contacts, and whether they multitask too much. It also aggregates the data for managers to see how their teams are doing.

Although U.S. companies have the legal right to monitor employee Internet and email activity while they are at work, is such monitoring unethical, or is it simply good business?

Managers worry about the loss of time and employee productivity when employees are focusing on personal rather than company business. Too much time on personal business translates into lost revenue. Some employees may even be billing time they spend pursuing personal interests online to clients, thus overcharging them.

If personal traffic on company networks is too high, it can also clog the company's network so that legitimate business work cannot be performed. GMI Insurance Services, which serves the U.S. transportation industry, found that employees were downloading a great deal of music and streaming video and storing the files on company servers. GMI's server backup space was being eaten up.

When employees use email or the web (including social networks) at employer facilities or with employer equipment, anything they do, including anything illegal, carries the company's name. Therefore, the employer can be traced and held liable. Management in many firms fear that racist, sexually explicit, or other potentially offensive material accessed or traded by their employees could result in adverse publicity and even lawsuits for the firm. Even if the company is found not to be liable, responding to lawsuits could run up huge legal bills. Companies also fear leakage of confidential information and trade secrets through email or social networks. U.S. companies have the legal right to monitor what employees are doing with company equipment during business hours. The question is whether electronic surveillance is an appropriate tool for maintaining an efficient and positive workplace. Some companies try to ban all personal activities on corporate networks— zero tolerance. Others block employee access to specific websites or social sites, closely monitor email messages, or limit personal time on the web.

IT Authorities, a Tampa, Florida–based infrastructure management and support organization, is using Veriato 360 employee monitoring software to help improve employee productivity. The company implemented the software in 2016 to reduce what it believed to be "inefficient activities." According to CEO Jason Caras, knowing that managers can see whether employees are working and exactly how they are working is a huge deterrent to wasteful activity. For IT Authorities specifically, Veriato 360 tracks and records the websites employees are visiting, what documents they are transmitting (and how), what they are sending (and to whom) in email and instant messaging, and even how long they might have been away from their computers at any given time. With Veriato 360, companies such as IT Authorities are able to identify "normal" patterns of activity for an individual's job, as well as any anomalies, so they can quickly address any potential productivity loss before it costs their company thousands or even millions of dollars in lost work.

A Proofpoint survey found that one in five large U.S. companies had fired an employee for violating email policies. Among managers who fired employees for Internet misuse, the majority did so because the employees' email contained sensitive, confidential, or embarrassing information.

No solution is problem-free, but many consultants believe companies should write corporate policies on employee email, social media, and Internet use. Many workers are unaware that employers have the right to monitor and collect data about them. The policies should include explicit ground rules that state, by position or level, under what circumstances employees can use company facilities for email, blogging, or web surfing. The policies should also inform employees whether these activities are monitored and explain why.

The rules should be tailored to specific business needs and organizational cultures. For example, investment firms will need to allow many of their employees access to other investment sites. A company dependent on widespread information sharing, innovation, and independence could very well find that monitoring creates more problems than it solves.

Sources: "Technology Is Making It Possible for Employers to Monitor More Work Activity than Ever," *Economist*, April 3, 2018; www.privacyrights.org, accessed April 5, 2018; "Electronic Surveillance of Employees," www.thebalance.com, accessed April 5, 2018; "Office Slacker Stats," www.staffmonitoring.com, accessed May 3, 2017; "How Do Employers Monitor Internet Usage at Work?" wisegeek.org, accessed April 15, 2017; and Veriato, "Veriato 360 Helps IT Authorities Quickly Increase Employee Productivity," March 15, 2017.

CASE STUDY QUESTIONS

1. Should managers monitor employee email and Internet usage? Why or why not?

2. Describe an effective email and web use policy for a company.

3. Should managers inform employees that their web behavior is being monitored? Or should managers monitor secretly? Why or why not?

A **virtual private network (VPN)** is a secure, encrypted, private network that has been configured within a public network to take advantage of the economies of scale and management facilities of large networks, such as the Internet (see Figure 7.10). A VPN provides your firm with secure, encrypted communications at a much lower cost than the same capabilities offered by traditional non-Internet providers that use their private networks to secure communications. VPNs also provide a network infrastructure for combining voice and data networks.

Several competing protocols are used to protect data transmitted over the public Internet, including Point-to-Point Tunneling Protocol (PPTP). In a process called *tunneling*, packets of data are encrypted and wrapped inside IP packets. By adding this wrapper around a network message to hide its content, business firms create a private connection that travels through the public Internet.

The Web

The web is the most popular Internet service. It's a system with universally accepted standards for storing, retrieving, formatting, and displaying information by using a client/server architecture. Web pages are formatted using hypertext, embedded links that connect documents to one another and that also link pages to other objects, such as sound, video, or animation files. When you click a graphic and a video clip plays, you have clicked a hyperlink. A typical **website** is a collection of web pages linked to a home page.

Hypertext

Web pages are based on a standard Hypertext Markup Language (HTML), which formats documents and incorporates dynamic links to other documents and other objects stored in the same or remote computers (see Chapter 5). Web

FIGURE 7.10   A VIRTUAL PRIVATE NETWORK USING THE INTERNET

This VPN is a private network of computers linked using a secure tunnel connection over the Internet. It protects data transmitted over the public Internet by encoding the data and wrapping them within the Internet protocol. By adding a wrapper around a network message to hide its content, organizations can create a private connection that travels through the public Internet.

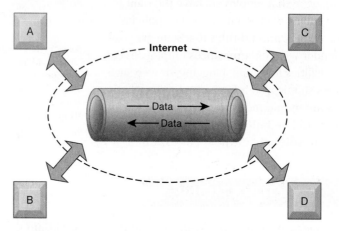

pages are accessible through the Internet because web browser software operating your computer can request web pages stored on an Internet host server by using the **Hypertext Transfer Protocol (HTTP)**. HTTP is the communications standard that transfers pages on the web. For example, when you type a web address in your browser, such as http://www.sec.gov, your browser sends an HTTP request to the sec.gov server requesting the home page of sec.gov.

HTTP is the first set of letters at the start of every web address, followed by the domain name, which specifies the organization's server computer that is storing the web page. Most companies have a domain name that is the same as or closely related to their official corporate name. The directory path and web page name are two more pieces of information within the web address that help the browser track down the requested page. Together, the address is called a **uniform resource locator (URL)**. When typed into a browser, a URL tells the browser software exactly where to look for the information. For example, in the URL http://www.megacorp.com/content/features/082610. html, *http* names the protocol that displays web pages, www.megacorp.com is the domain name, content/features is the directory path that identifies where on the domain web server the page is stored, and 082610.html is the web page name and the name of the format it is in. (It is an HTML page.)

Web Servers

A web server is software for locating and managing stored web pages. It locates the web pages a user requests on the computer where they are stored and delivers the web pages to the user's computer. Server applications usually run on dedicated computers, although they can all reside on a single computer in small organizations.

The leading web servers in use today are Microsoft Internet Information Services (IIS) and Apache HTTP Server. Apache is an open source product that is free of charge and can be downloaded from the web.

Searching for Information on the Web

No one knows for sure how many web pages there really are. The surface web is the part of the web that search engines visit and about which information is recorded. For instance, Google indexed an estimated 35 trillion pages in 2017, and this reflects a large portion of the publicly accessible web page population, estimated to be 60 trillion pages. But there is a deep web that contains an estimated 1 trillion additional pages, many of them proprietary (such as the pages of *Wall Street Journal Online*, which cannot be visited without a subscription or access code), or that are stored in protected corporate databases. Facebook, with web pages of text, photos, and media for more than 2 billion members, is a closed web, and its pages are not completely searchable by Google or other search engines. A small portion of the deep web called the dark web has been intentionally hidden from search engines, uses masked IP addresses, and is accessible only with a special web browser in order to preserve anonymity.

Search Engines   Obviously, with so many web pages, finding specific ones that can help you or your business, nearly instantly, is an important problem. The question is, how can you find the one or two pages you really want and need out of billions of indexed web pages? **Search engines** attempt to solve the problem of finding useful information on the web nearly instantly and, arguably, they are the killer app of the Internet era. Today's search engines can sift through HTML files; files of Microsoft Office applications; PDF files; and audio, video, and image files. There are hundreds of search engines in the world, but the vast majority of search results come from Google, Baidu, Yahoo, and Microsoft's Bing (see Figure 7.11). While we typically think of Amazon as an online store, it is also a powerful product search engine.

Web search engines started out in the early 1990s as relatively simple software programs that roamed the nascent web, visiting pages and gathering information about the content of each page. The first search engines were simple keyword indexes of all the pages they visited, leaving users with lists of pages that may not have been truly relevant to their search.

In 1994, Stanford University computer science students David Filo and Jerry Yang created a hand-selected list of their favorite web pages and called it "Yet Another Hierarchical Officious Oracle," or Yahoo. Yahoo was not initially a search engine but rather an edited selection of websites organized by categories the editors found useful. Currently, Yahoo relies on Microsoft's Bing for search results.

In 1998, Larry Page and Sergey Brin, two other Stanford computer science students, released their first version of Google. This search engine was different. Not only did it index each web page's words but it also ranked search results

---

FIGURE 7.11   TOP DESKTOP/LAPTOP WEB SEARCH ENGINES WORLDWIDE

Google is the world's most popular search engine.

Source: Based on data from Net Market Share, April 2018.

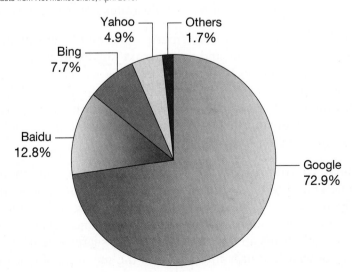

FIGURE 7.12 HOW GOOGLE WORKS

The Google search engine is continuously crawling the web, indexing the content of each page, calculating its popularity, and storing the pages so that it can respond quickly to user requests to see a page. The entire process takes about half a second.

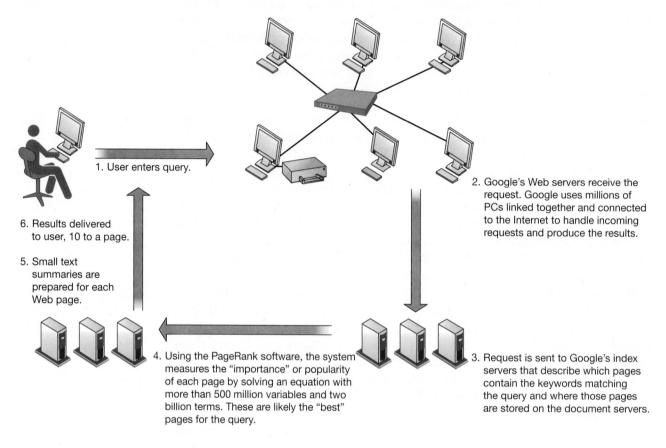

1. User enters query.

2. Google's Web servers receive the request. Google uses millions of PCs linked together and connected to the Internet to handle incoming requests and produce the results.

6. Results delivered to user, 10 to a page.

5. Small text summaries are prepared for each Web page.

4. Using the PageRank software, the system measures the "importance" or popularity of each page by solving an equation with more than 500 million variables and two billion terms. These are likely the "best" pages for the query.

3. Request is sent to Google's index servers that describe which pages contain the keywords matching the query and where those pages are stored on the document servers.

based on the relevance of each page. Page patented the idea of a page ranking system (called *PageRank System*), which essentially measures the popularity of a web page by calculating the number of sites that link to that page as well as the number of pages to which it links. The premise is that popular web pages are more relevant to users. Brin contributed a unique web crawler program that indexed not only keywords on a page but also combinations of words (such as authors and the titles of their articles). These two ideas became the foundation for the Google search engine. Figure 7.12 illustrates how Google works.

Mobile Search Mobile search from smartphones and tablets makes up more than 50 percent of all searches and will expand rapidly in the next few years. Google, Amazon, and Yahoo have developed new search interfaces to make searching and shopping from smartphones more convenient. Google revised its search algorithm to favor sites that look good on smartphone screens. Although smartphones are widely used to shop, actual purchases typically take place on laptops or desktops, followed by tablets.

Semantic Search Another way for search engines to become more discriminating and helpful is to make search engines capable of understanding what we are really looking for. Called **semantic search**, the goal is to build a search engine that can really understand human language and behavior. Google and other search engine firms are attempting to refine search engine algorithms to capture more of what the user intended and the meaning of a search. Rather than evaluate each word separately in a search, Google's Hummingbird search algorithm tries to evaluate an entire sentence, focusing on the meaning behind the words. For instance, if your search is a long sentence like "Google annual report selected financial data 2018," Hummingbird should be able to figure out that you really want Google's parent company Alphabet's SEC Form 10K report filed with the Securities and Exchange Commission in February 2018.

Google searches also take advantage of Knowledge Graph, an effort of the search algorithm to anticipate what you might want to know more about as you search on a topic. Results of the knowledge graph appear on the right of the screen on many search result pages and contain more information about the topic or person you are searching on. For example, if you search "Lake Tahoe," the search engine will return basic facts about Tahoe (altitude, average temperature, and local fish), a map, and hotel accommodations. Google has made **predictive search** part of most search results. This part of the search algorithm guesses what you are looking for and suggests search terms as you type your search words.

Social Search One problem with Google and mechanical search engines is that they are so thorough. Enter a search for "ultra computers" and, in 0.2 seconds, you will receive over 300 million responses! **Social search** is an effort to provide fewer, more relevant, and trustworthy search results based on a person's network of social contacts. In contrast to the top search engines that use a mathematical algorithm to find pages that satisfy your query, social search would highlight content that was created or touched by members of your social network.

Facebook Search is a social network search engine that responds to user search queries with information from the user's social network of friends and connections. Facebook Search relies on the huge amount of data on Facebook that is, or can be, linked to individuals and organizations. You might use Facebook Search to search for Boston restaurants that your friends like or pictures of your friends before 2016.

Visual Search and the Visual Web Although search engines were originally designed to search text documents, the explosion of photos and videos on the Internet created a demand for searching and classifying these visual objects. Facial recognition software can create a digital version of a human face. Facebook has a tag suggest function to assist users in tagging their friends in photos. You can also search for people on Facebook by using their digital image to find and identify them. Facebook is now using artificial intelligence technology to make its facial recognition capabilities more accurate.

Searching photos, images, and video has become increasingly important as the web becomes more visual. The **visual web** refers to websites such as Pinterest, where pictures replace text documents, where users search pictures, and where pictures of products replace display ads for products. Pinterest is a social networking site that provides users (as well as brands) with an online board to which they can pin interesting pictures. Pinterest had 200 million active monthly users worldwide in 2018. Instagram is another example of the visual web. Instagram is a photo and video sharing site that allows users to take pictures, enhance them, and share them with friends on other social sites such as Facebook and Twitter. In 2018, Instagram had 800 million monthly active users.

Intelligent Agent Shopping Bots Chapter 11 describes the capabilities of software agents with built-in intelligence that can gather or filter information and perform other tasks to assist users. **Shopping bots** use intelligent agent software for searching the Internet for shopping information. Shopping bots such as MySimon or PriceGrabber, and travel search tools like Trivago, can help people interested in making a purchase or renting a vacation room filter and retrieve information according to criteria the users have established, and in some cases negotiate with vendors for price and delivery terms.

Search Engine Marketing Search engines have become major advertising platforms and shopping tools by offering what is now called **search engine marketing**. Searching for information is one of the web's most popular activities; it is estimated that 242 million people in the United States will use search engines by 2019 and 215 million will use mobile search by that time. With this huge audience, search engines are the foundation for the most lucrative form of online marketing and advertising: search engine marketing. When users enter a search term on Google, Bing, Yahoo, or any of the other sites serviced by these search engines, they receive two types of listings: sponsored links, for which advertisers have paid to be listed (usually at the top of the search results page), and unsponsored, organic search results. In addition, advertisers can purchase small text boxes on the side of search results pages. The paid, sponsored advertisements are the fastest growing form of Internet advertising and are powerful new marketing tools that precisely match consumer interests with advertising messages at the right moment. Search engine marketing monetizes the value of the search process. In 2018, search engine marketing was expected to generate $42 billion, or 44.2 percent of digital ad spending, nearly half of all online advertising ($93 billion) (eMarketer, 2018). About 90 percent of Google's revenue of $110 billion in 2017 came from online advertising, and 90 percent of that ad revenue came from search engine marketing (Alphabet, 2018).

Because search engine marketing is so effective (it has the highest click-through rate and the highest return on ad investment), companies seek to optimize their websites for search engine recognition. The better optimized the page is, the higher a ranking it will achieve in search engine result listings. **Search engine optimization (SEO)** is the process of improving the quality and volume of web traffic to a website by employing a series of techniques that help a website achieve a higher ranking with the major search engines when certain keywords and phrases are put into the search field. One technique is to make sure that the keywords used in the website description match the keywords likely to be used as search terms by prospective customers. For example, your website is more likely to be among the first ranked by search engines if it uses the keyword *lighting* rather than *lamps* if most prospective customers are searching for *lighting*. It is also advantageous to link your website to as many other websites as possible because search engines evaluate such links to determine the popularity of a web page and how it is linked to other content on the web.

Search engines can be gamed by scammers who create thousands of phony website pages and link them to a single retailer's site in an attempt to fool Google's search engine. Firms can also pay so-called link farms to link to their site. Google changed its search algorithm in 2012 to deal with this problem by examining the quality of links more carefully with the intent of down-ranking sites that have a suspicious pattern of sites linking to them.

In general, search engines have been very helpful to small businesses that cannot afford large marketing campaigns. Because shoppers are looking for a specific product or service when they use search engines, they are what marketers call hot prospects—people who are looking for information and often intending to buy. Moreover, search engines charge only for click-throughs to a site. Merchants do not have to pay for ads that don't work, only for ads that receive a click. Consumers benefit from search engine marketing because ads for merchants appear only when consumers are looking for a specific product. Thus, search engine marketing saves consumers cognitive energy and reduces search costs (including the cost of transportation needed to search for products physically). One study estimated the global value of search to both merchants and consumers to be more than $800 billion, with about 65 percent of the benefit going to consumers in the form of lower search costs and lower prices (McKinsey & Company, 2011).

Sharing Information on the Web

Today's websites don't just contain static content—they enable people to collaborate, share information, and create new services and content online. Today's web can support interactivity, real-time user control, social participation (sharing), and user-generated content. The technologies and services behind these features include cloud computing, software mashups and apps, blogs, RSS, wikis, and social networks. We have already described cloud computing, mashups, and apps in Chapter 5 and introduced social networks in Chapter 2.

A **blog**, the popular term for a weblog, is a personal website that typically contains a series of chronological entries (newest to oldest) by its author and links to related web pages. The blog may include a *blogroll* (a collection of links to other blogs) and *trackbacks* (a list of entries in other blogs that refer to a post on the first blog). Most blogs allow readers to post comments on the blog entries as well. The act of creating a blog is often referred to as blogging. Blogs can be hosted by a third-party service such as Blogger.com or TypePad.com, and blogging features have been incorporated into social networks such as Facebook and collaboration platforms such as IBM Notes. WordPress is a leading open source blogging tool and content management system. **Microblogging**, used in Twitter or other platforms with serious space or size constraints, is a type of blogging that features very small elements of content such as short sentences, individual images, or video links.

Blog pages are usually based on templates provided by the blogging service or software. Therefore, millions of people without HTML skills of any kind can post their own web pages and share content with others. The totality of blog-related websites is often referred to as the **blogosphere**. Although blogs have become popular personal publishing tools, they also have business uses (see Chapters 2 and 10).

If you're an avid blog reader, you might use RSS to keep up with your favorite blogs without constantly checking them for updates. **RSS**, which stands for Really Simple Syndication or Rich Site Summary, pulls specified content from websites and feeds it automatically to users' computers. RSS reader software gathers material from the websites or blogs that you tell it to scan and brings new information from those sites to you. RSS readers are available through websites such as Google and Yahoo, and they have been incorporated into the major web browsers and email programs.

Blogs allow visitors to add comments to the original content, but they do not allow visitors to change the original posted material. **Wikis**, in contrast, are collaborative websites on which visitors can add, delete, or modify content, including the work of previous authors. *Wiki* comes from the Hawaiian word for "quick."

Wiki software typically provides a template that defines layout and elements common to all pages, displays user-editable software program code, and then renders the content into an HTML-based page for display in a web browser. Some wiki software allows only basic text formatting, whereas other tools allow the use of tables, images, or even interactive elements, such as polls or games.

Most wikis provide capabilities for monitoring the work of other users and correcting mistakes.

Because wikis make information sharing so easy, they have many business uses. The U.S. Department of Homeland Security's National Cyber Security Center (NCSC) deployed a wiki to facilitate information sharing with other federal agencies on threats, attacks, and responses and as a repository for technical and standards information. Pixar Wiki is a collaborative community wiki for publicizing the work of Pixar Animation Studios. The wiki format allows anyone to create or edit an article about a Pixar film.

Social networking sites enable users to build communities of friends and professional colleagues. Members typically create a profile—a web page for posting photos, videos, audio files, and text—and then share these profiles with others on the service identified as their friends or contacts. Social networking sites are highly interactive, offer real-time user control, rely on user-generated content, and are broadly based on social participation and sharing of content and opinions. Leading social networking sites include Facebook, Twitter, and LinkedIn (for professional contacts).

Social networking has radically changed how people spend their time online; how people communicate and with whom; how business people stay in touch with customers, suppliers, and employees; how providers of goods and services learn about their customers; and how advertisers reach potential customers. The large social networking sites are also application development platforms where members can create and sell software applications to other members of the community. Facebook alone has more than 7 million apps and websites integrated with it, including applications for gaming, video sharing, and communicating with friends and family. We talk more about business applications of social networking in Chapters 2 and 10, and you can find social networking discussions in many other chapters of this book.

The Future Web

The future Internet is becoming visible. Its key features are more tools for individuals to make sense out of the trillions of pages on the Internet, or the millions of apps available for smartphones and a visual, even three-dimensional (3D) web where you can walk through pages in a 3D environment. (Review the discussion of semantic search and visual search earlier in this chapter.)

Even closer in time is a pervasive web that controls everything from a city's traffic lights and water usage, to the lights in your living room, to your car's rear view mirror, not to mention managing your calendar and appointments. This is referred to as the **Internet of Things (IoT)** and is based on billions of Internet-connected sensors throughout our physical world. Objects, animals, or people are provided with unique identifiers and the ability to transfer data over a network without requiring human-to-human or human-to-computer interaction. Firms such as General Electric, IBM, HP, and Oracle, and hundreds of smaller startups, are exploring how to build smart machines, factories, and cities through extensive use of remote sensors and fast cloud computing. We provide more detail on this topic in the following section.

The App Internet is another element in the future web. The growth of apps within the mobile platform is astounding. More than 80 percent of mobile minutes in the United States are generated through apps, as opposed to browsers. Apps give users direct access to content and are much faster than loading a browser and searching for content.

Other complementary trends leading toward a future web include more widespread use of cloud computing and software as a service (SaaS) business models, ubiquitous connectivity among mobile platforms and Internet access devices, and the transformation of the web from a network of separate siloed applications and content into a more seamless and interoperable whole.

7-4   What are the principal technologies and standards for wireless networking, communication, and Internet access?

Welcome to the wireless revolution! Cell phones, smartphones, tablets, and wireless-enabled personal computers have morphed into portable media and computing platforms that let you perform many of the computing tasks you used to do at your desk, and a whole lot more. We introduced smartphones in our discussions of the mobile digital platform in Chapters 1 and 5. **Smartphones** such as the iPhone, Android phones, and BlackBerry combine the functionality of a cell phone with that of a mobile laptop computer with Wi-Fi capability. This makes it possible to combine music, video, Internet access, and telephone service in one device. A large part of the Internet is becoming a mobile, access-anywhere, broadband service for the delivery of video, music, and web search.

Cellular Systems

Today 81 percent of U.S. adults own mobile phones, and 69 percent own smartphones (eMarketer, 2018). Mobile is now the leading digital platform, with total activity on smartphones and tablets accounting for two-thirds of digital media time spent, and smartphone apps alone capturing more than half of digital media time (Comscore, 2017).

Digital cellular service uses several competing standards. In Europe and much of the rest of the world outside the United Sates, the standard is Global System for Mobile Communications (GSM). GSM's strength is its international roaming capability. There are GSM cell phone systems in the United States, including T-Mobile and AT&T.

A competing standard in the United States is Code Division Multiple Access (CDMA), which is the system Verizon and Sprint use. CDMA was developed by the military during World War II. It transmits over several frequencies, occupies the entire spectrum, and randomly assigns users to a range of frequencies over time, making it more efficient than GSM.

Earlier generations of cellular systems were designed primarily for voice and limited data transmission in the form of short text messages. Today wireless carriers offer 3G and 4G networks. **3G networks**, with transmission speeds ranging from 144 Kbps for mobile users in, say, a car, to more than 2 Mbps for stationary users, offer transmission speeds appropriate for email and web browsing, but are too slow for videos. **4G networks** have much higher speeds, up to 100 Mbps download and 50 Mbps upload, with more than enough capacity for watching high-definition video on your smartphone. Long Term Evolution (LTE) and mobile Worldwide Interoperability for Microwave Access (WiMax—see the following section) are the current 4G standards.

The next generation of wireless technology, called **5G**, is still under development. 5G will support transmission of huge amounts of data in the gigabit range, with fewer transmission delays and the ability to connect many more devices (such as sensors and smart devices) at once than existing cellular systems. 5G technology will be needed for self-driving vehicles, smart cities, and extensive use of the Internet of Things. AT&T, Verizon, and other carriers are starting to launch 5G networks.

Wireless Computer Networks and Internet Access

An array of technologies provides high-speed wireless access to the Internet for PCs and mobile devices. These new high-speed services have extended Internet access to numerous locations that could not be covered by traditional wired Internet services and have made ubiquitous computing, anywhere, anytime, a reality.

Bluetooth

Bluetooth is the popular name for the 802.15 wireless networking standard, which is useful for creating small **personal area networks (PANs)**. It links up to eight devices within a 10-meter area using low-power, radio-based communication and can transmit up to 722 Kbps in the 2.4-GHz band.

Wireless phones, pagers, computers, printers, and computing devices using Bluetooth communicate with each other and even operate each other without direct user intervention (see Figure 7.13). For example, a person could direct a notebook computer to send a document file wirelessly to a printer. Bluetooth connects wireless keyboards and mice to PCs or cell phones to earpieces without wires. Bluetooth has low power requirements, making it appropriate for battery-powered handheld computers or cell phones.

Although Bluetooth lends itself to personal networking, it has uses in large corporations. For example, FedEx drivers use Bluetooth to transmit the delivery data captured by their handheld computers to cellular transmitters, which forward the data to corporate computers. Drivers no longer need to spend time docking their handheld units physically in the transmitters, and Bluetooth has saved FedEx $20 million per year.

FIGURE 7.13   A BLUETOOTH NETWORK (PAN)

Bluetooth enables a variety of devices, including cell phones, smartphones, wireless keyboards and mice, PCs, and printers, to interact wirelessly with each other within a small, 30-foot (10-meter) area. In addition to the links shown, Bluetooth can be used to network similar devices to send data from one PC to another, for example.

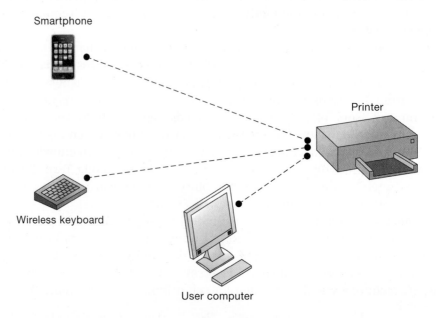

Smartphone

Printer

Wireless keyboard

User computer

Wi-Fi and Wireless Internet Access

The 802.11 set of standards for wireless LANs and wireless Internet access is also known as **Wi-Fi**. The first of these standards to be widely adopted was 802.11b, which can transmit up to 11 Mbps in the unlicensed 2.4-GHz band and has an effective distance of 30 to 50 meters. The 802.11g standard can transmit up to 54 Mbps in the 2.4-GHz range. 802.11n is capable of transmitting over 100 Mbps. Today's PCs and tablets have built-in support for Wi-Fi, as do the iPhone, iPad, and other smartphones.

In most Wi-Fi communication, wireless devices communicate with a wired LAN using access points. An access point is a box consisting of a radio receiver/transmitter and antennas that links to a wired network, router, or hub.

Figure 7.14 illustrates an 802.11 wireless LAN that connects a small number of mobile devices to a larger wired LAN and to the Internet. Most wireless devices are client machines. The servers that the mobile client stations need to use are on the wired LAN. The access point controls the wireless stations and acts as a bridge between the main wired LAN and the wireless LAN. The access point also controls the wireless stations.

The most popular use for Wi-Fi today is for high-speed wireless Internet service. In this instance, the access point plugs into an Internet connection, which could come from a cable service or DSL telephone service. Computers within range of the access point use it to link wirelessly to the Internet.

Hotspots are locations with one or more access points providing wireless Internet access and are often in public places. Some hotspots are free or do not

---

FIGURE 7.14   AN 802.11 WIRELESS LAN

Mobile laptop computers equipped with network interface cards link to the wired LAN by communicating with the access point. The access point uses radio waves to transmit network signals from the wired network to the client adapters, which convert them to data that the mobile device can understand. The client adapter then transmits the data from the mobile device back to the access point, which forwards the data to the wired network.

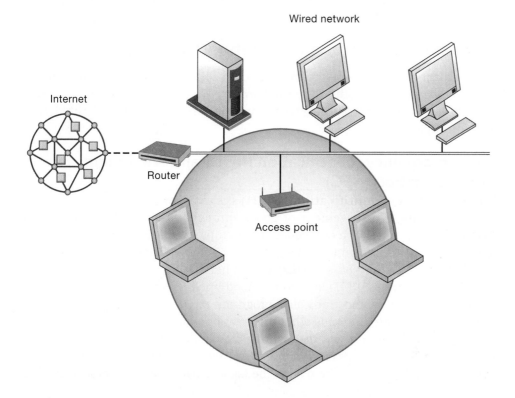

require any additional software to use; others may require activation and the establishment of a user account by providing a credit card number over the web.

Businesses of all sizes are using Wi-Fi networks to provide low-cost wireless LANs and Internet access. Wi-Fi hotspots can be found in hotels, airport lounges, libraries, cafes, and college campuses to provide mobile access to the Internet. Dartmouth College is one of many campuses where students now use Wi-Fi for research, course work, and entertainment.

Wi-Fi technology poses several challenges, however. One is Wi-Fi's security features, which make these wireless networks vulnerable to intruders. We provide more detail about Wi-Fi security issues in Chapter 8.

Another drawback of Wi-Fi networks is susceptibility to interference from nearby systems operating in the same spectrum, such as wireless phones, microwave ovens, or other wireless LANs. However, wireless networks based on the 802.11n standard solve this problem by using multiple wireless antennas in tandem to transmit and receive data and technology called MIMO (multiple input multiple output) to coordinate multiple simultaneous radio signals.

WiMax

A surprisingly large number of areas in the United States and throughout the world do not have access to Wi-Fi or fixed broadband connectivity. The range of Wi-Fi systems is no more than 300 feet from the base station, making it difficult for rural groups that don't have cable or DSL service to find wireless access to the Internet.

The Institute of Electrical and Electronics Engineers (IEEE) developed a family of standards known as WiMax to deal with these problems. **WiMax**, which stands for Worldwide Interoperability for Microwave Access, is the popular term for IEEE Standard 802.16. It has a wireless access range of up to 31 miles and transmission speed of 30–40 Mbps (and up to 1 Gbps for fixed stations).

WiMax antennas are powerful enough to beam high-speed Internet connections to rooftop antennas of homes and businesses that are miles away. Cellular handsets and laptops with WiMax capabilities are appearing in the marketplace. Mobile WiMax is one of the 4G network technologies we discussed earlier in this chapter.

RFID and Wireless Sensor Networks

Mobile technologies are creating new efficiencies and ways of working throughout the enterprise. In addition to the wireless systems we have just described, radio frequency identification systems and wireless sensor networks are having a major impact.

Radio Frequency Identification (RFID) and Near Field Communication (NFC)

Radio frequency identification (RFID) systems provide a powerful technology for tracking the movement of goods throughout the supply chain. RFID systems use tiny tags with embedded microchips containing data about an item and its location to transmit radio signals over a short distance to RFID readers. The RFID readers then pass the data over a network to a computer for processing. Unlike bar codes, RFID tags do not need line-of-sight contact to be read.

The RFID tag is electronically programmed with information that can uniquely identify an item plus other information about the item such as its location, where and when it was made, or its status during production. The reader emits radio waves in ranges anywhere from 1 inch to 100 feet. When an RFID tag comes within the range of the reader, the tag is activated and starts sending data.

FIGURE 7.15   HOW RFID WORKS

RFID uses low-powered radio transmitters to read data stored in a tag at distances ranging from 1 inch to 100 feet. The reader captures the data from the tag and sends them over a network to a host computer for processing.

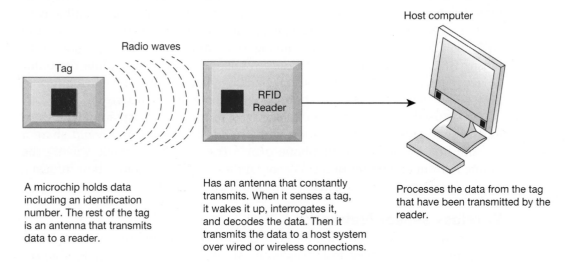

Host computer

Radio waves

Tag

RFID Reader

A microchip holds data including an identification number. The rest of the tag is an antenna that transmits data to a reader.

Has an antenna that constantly transmits. When it senses a tag, it wakes it up, interrogates it, and decodes the data. Then it transmits the data to a host system over wired or wireless connections.

Processes the data from the tag that have been transmitted by the reader.

The reader captures these data, decodes them, and sends them back over a wired or wireless network to a host computer for further processing (see Figure 7.15). Both RFID tags and antennas come in a variety of shapes and sizes.

In inventory control and supply chain management, RFID systems capture and manage more detailed information about items in warehouses or in production than bar coding systems. If a large number of items are shipped together, RFID systems track each pallet, lot, or even unit item in the shipment. This technology may help companies such as Walmart improve receiving and storage operations by improving their ability to see exactly what stock is stored in warehouses or on retail store shelves. Macy's uses RFID technology to track individual items for sale on store shelves.

Walmart has installed RFID readers at store receiving docks to record the arrival of pallets and cases of goods shipped with RFID tags. The RFID reader reads the tags a second time just as the cases are brought onto the sales floor from backroom storage areas. Software combines sales data from Walmart's point-of-sale systems and the RFID data regarding the number of cases brought out to the sales floor. The program determines which items will soon be depleted and automatically generates a list of items to pick in the warehouse to replenish store shelves before they run out. This information helps Walmart reduce out-of-stock items, increase sales, and further shrink its costs.

The cost of RFID tags used to be too high for widespread use, but now it starts at around 7 cents per tag in the United States. As the price decreases, RFID is starting to become cost-effective for many applications.

In addition to installing RFID readers and tagging systems, companies may need to upgrade their hardware and software to process the massive amounts of data produced by RFID systems—transactions that could add up to tens or hundreds of terabytes.

Software is used to filter, aggregate, and prevent RFID data from overloading business networks and system applications. Applications often need to be redesigned to accept large volumes of frequently generated RFID data and to share those data with other applications. Major enterprise software vendors now offer RFID-ready versions of their supply chain management applications.

Tap-and-go services like Apple Pay or Google Wallet use an RFID-related technology called **near field communication (NFC)**. NFC is a short-range wireless connectivity standard that uses electromagnetic radio fields to enable two compatible devices to exchange data when brought within a few centimeters of each other. A smartphone or other NFC-compatible device sends out radio frequency signals that interact with an NFC tag found in compatible card readers or smart posters. The signals create a current that flows through the NFC tag, allowing the device and the tag to communicate with one another. In most cases the tag is passive and only sends out information while the other device (such as a smartphone) is active and can both send and receive information. (There are NFC systems where both components are active.)

NFC is used in wireless payment services, to retrieve information, and even to exchange videos or information with friends on the go. You could share a website link by passing your phone over a friend's phone, while waving the phone in front of a poster or display containing an NFC tag could show information about what you're viewing at a museum or exhibit.

Wireless Sensor Networks

If your company wanted state-of-the art technology to monitor building security or detect hazardous substances in the air, it might deploy a wireless sensor network. **Wireless sensor networks (WSNs)** are networks of interconnected wireless devices that are embedded in the physical environment to provide measurements of many points over large spaces. These devices have built-in processing, storage, and radio frequency sensors and antennas. They are linked into an interconnected network that routes the data they capture to a computer for analysis. These networks range from hundreds to thousands of nodes. Figure 7.16 illustrates one type of wireless sensor network, with data from individual nodes flowing across the network to a server with greater processing power. The server acts as a gateway to a network based on Internet technology.

FIGURE 7.16   A WIRELESS SENSOR NETWORK

The small circles represent lower-level nodes, and the larger circles represent higher-level nodes. Lower-level nodes forward data to each other or to higher-level nodes, which transmit data more rapidly and speed up network performance.

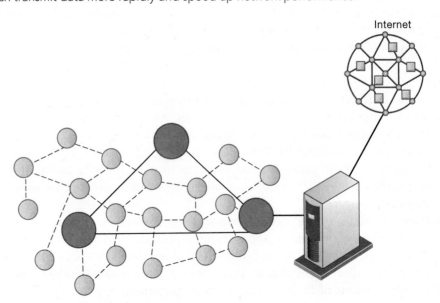

Wireless sensor networks are valuable for uses such as monitoring environmental changes; monitoring traffic or military activity; protecting property; efficiently operating and managing machinery and vehicles; establishing security perimeters; monitoring supply chain management; or detecting chemical, biological, or radiological material.

Output from RFID systems and wireless networks is fueling the Internet of Things (IoT), introduced earlier in this chapter, in which machines such as jet engines, power plant turbines, or agricultural sensors constantly gather data and send the data over the Internet for analysis. The data might signal the need to take action such as replacing a part that's close to wearing out, restocking a product on a store shelf, starting the watering system for a soybean field, or slowing down a turbine. Over time, more and more everyday physical objects will be connected to the Internet and will be able to identify themselves to other devices, creating networks that can sense and respond as data changes. The Tour de France race tracking system, described in the chapter-opening case, is an example of an IoT application. You'll find more examples of the Internet of Things in Chapters 2 and 12.

7-5 How will MIS help my career?

Here is how Chapter 7 and this book can help you find a job as an automotive digital advisor.

The Company

A1 Western Car Dealers, a large and fast-growing southern California automobile dealership, is looking for an automotive digital advisor to run its digital marketing program. The company has more than 500 vehicles for sale, 170 employees, and three locations for selling and servicing new and used vehicles.

Position Description

The automotive digital assistant will be part of a team assisting the dealership group with online marketing, including search engine optimization (SEO) and search engine marketing (SEM), social media and reputation management, and website management. Job responsibilities include coordinating efforts for the dealership owner, dealership managers, and marketing manager in the following areas:

- Online advertising, SEO, and SEM.
- Social media management, including managing the dealership's overall social media and content calendar and developing new content.
- Online reputation management.
- Website management.
- Maintaining the dealership's blog.

Job Requirements

- College graduate in marketing
- Knowledge of digital marketing and social media
- Microsoft Office skills
- Knowledge of automotive sales and content management systems desirable

Interview Questions

1. Have you ever taken any digital marketing courses?
2. Have you any experience running a digital marketing campaign? Did you use SEO and SEM? How did you measure the effectiveness of your social media campaign and audience growth?
3. Do you have any experience with social media management software?
4. Do you have any experience with online reputation management or online inventory management?
5. Have you ever maintained a blog?
6. What is your level of proficiency with Microsoft Office software?

Author Tips

1. Review the discussions of search, search engine marketing, and blogs in this chapter and also the discussions of e-commerce marketing and building an e-commerce presence in Chapter 10.
2. Use the web to learn more about SEO, SEM, social media management, and online reputation management and software tools used for this work. Look into how to generate metrics reports using standardized tools and how to put together analyses and recommendations based on the social media data.
3. Look at how major auto dealers in large metropolitan areas are using social media channels. Are they creating content on YouTube, Instagram, Facebook, and Twitter? Which channels are generating higher levels of audience engagement?
4. Inquire about exactly what you would have to do for website management and required software skills.
5. Inquire about the Microsoft Office skills you would need for this job. Bring examples of the work you have done with this software.

REVIEW **SUMMARY**

7-1 What are the principal components of telecommunications networks and key networking technologies?

A simple network consists of two or more connected computers. Basic network components include computers, network interfaces, a connection medium, network operating system software, and either a hub or a switch. The networking infrastructure for a large company includes the traditional telephone system, mobile cellular communication, wireless local area networks, videoconferencing systems, a corporate website, intranets, extranets, and an array of local and wide area networks, including the Internet.

Contemporary networks have been shaped by the rise of client/server computing, the use of packet switching, and the adoption of Transmission Control Protocol/Internet Protocol (TCP/IP) as a universal communications standard for linking disparate networks and computers, including the Internet. Protocols provide a common set of rules that enable communication among diverse components in a telecommunications network.

7-2 What are the different types of networks?

The principal physical transmission media are twisted copper telephone wire, coaxial copper cable, fiber-optic cable, and wireless transmission.

Local area networks (LANs) connect PCs and other digital devices within a 500-meter radius and are used today for many corporate computing tasks. Wide area networks (WANs) span broad geographical distances, ranging from several miles to entire continents and are often private networks that are independently managed. Metropolitan area networks (MANs) span a single urban area.

Digital subscriber line (DSL) technologies, cable Internet connections, and T1 lines are often used for high-capacity Internet connections.

7-3 How do the Internet and Internet technology work, and how do they support communication and e-business?

The Internet is a worldwide network of networks that uses the client/server model of computing and the TCP/IP network reference model. Every computer on the Internet is assigned a unique numeric IP address. The Domain Name System (DNS) converts IP addresses to more user-friendly domain names. Worldwide Internet policies are established by organizations and government bodies such as the Internet Architecture Board (IAB) and the World Wide Web Consortium (W3C).

Major Internet services include email, newsgroups, chatting, instant messaging, Telnet, FTP, and the web. Web pages are based on Hypertext Markup Language (HTML) and can display text, graphics, video, and audio. Website directories, search engines, and RSS technology help users locate the information they need on the web. RSS, blogs, social networking, and wikis are current information-sharing capabilities of the web. The future web will feature more semantic search, visual search, prevalence of apps, and interconnectedness of many different devices (Internet of Things).

Firms are also starting to realize economies by using VoIP technology for voice transmission and virtual private networks (VPNs) as low-cost alternatives to private WANs.

7-4 What are the principal technologies and standards for wireless networking, communication, and Internet access?

Cellular networks are evolving toward high-speed, high-bandwidth, digital packet-switched transmission. Broadband 3G networks are capable of transmitting data at speeds ranging from 144 Kbps to more than 2 Mbps. 4G networks are capable of transmission speeds of 100 Mbps, and 5G networks capable of transmitting in the gigabit range are starting to be rolled out.

Major cellular standards include Code Division Multiple Access (CDMA), which is used primarily in the United States, and Global System for Mobile Communications (GSM), which is the standard in Europe and much of the rest of the world.

Standards for wireless computer networks include Bluetooth (802.15) for small personal area networks (PANs), Wi-Fi (802.11) for local area networks (LANs), and WiMax (802.16) for metropolitan area networks (MANs).

Radio frequency identification (RFID) systems provide a powerful technology for tracking the movement of goods by using tiny tags with embedded data about an item and its location. RFID readers read the radio signals transmitted by these tags and pass the data over a network to a computer for processing. Wireless sensor networks (WSNs) are networks of interconnected wireless sensing and transmitting devices that are embedded in the physical environment to provide measurements of many points over large spaces.

Key Terms

3G networks, 279

4G networks, 279

5G networks, 279

Bandwidth, 261

Blog, 277

Blogosphere, 277

Bluetooth, 280

Broadband, 254

Cable Internet connections, 262

Chat, 267

Digital subscriber line (DSL), 262

Domain name, 262

Domain Name System (DNS), 262

Email, 267

File Transfer Protocol (FTP), 267

Hertz, 261

Hotspots, 281

Hubs, 255

Hypertext Transfer Protocol (HTTP), 272

Instant messaging, 267

Internet of Things (IoT), 278

Internet Protocol (IP) address, 262

Internet service provider (ISP), 262

Internet2, 266

IPv6, 266

Local area network (LAN), 259

Metropolitan area network (MAN), 260

Microblogging, 277

Modem, 259

Near field communication (NFC), 284

Network operating system (NOS), 255

Packet switching, 257

Peer-to-peer, 260

Personal area networks (PANs), 280

MyLab MIS

To complete the problems with MyLab MIS, go to the EOC Discussion Questions in MyLab MIS.

Review Questions

7-1 What are the principal components of telecommunications networks and key networking technologies?

- Describe the features of a simple network and the network infrastructure for a large company.
- Name and describe the principal technologies and trends that have shaped contemporary telecommunications systems.

7-2 What are the different types of networks?

- Define an analog and a digital signal.
- Distinguish between a LAN, MAN, and WAN.

7-3 How do the Internet and Internet technology work, and how do they support communication and e-business?

- Define the Internet, describe how it works, and explain how it provides business value.
- Explain how the Domain Name System (DNS) and IP addressing system work.

- List and describe the principal Internet services.
- Define and describe VoIP and virtual private networks and explain how they provide value to businesses.
- List and describe alternative ways of locating information on the web.
- Describe how online search technologies are used for marketing.

7-4 What are the principal technologies and standards for wireless networking, communication, and Internet access?

- Define Bluetooth, Wi-Fi, WiMax, and 3G, 4G, and 5G networks.
- Describe the capabilities of each and for which types of applications each is best suited.
- Define RFID, explain how it works, and describe how it provides value to businesses.
- Define WSNs, explain how they work, and describe the kinds of applications that use them.

Discussion Questions

7-5 MyLab MIS It has been said that within the next few years, smartphones will become the single most important digital device we own. Discuss the implications of this statement.

7-6 MyLab MIS Should all major retailing and manufacturing companies switch to RFID? Why or why not?

7-7 MyLab MIS What are some of the issues to consider in determining whether the Internet would provide your business with a competitive advantage?

Hands-On MIS Projects

The projects in this section give you hands-on experience evaluating and selecting communications technology, using spreadsheet software to improve selection of telecommunications services, and using web search engines for business research. Visit MyLab MIS to access this chapter's Hands-On MIS Projects.

Management Decision Problems

7-8   Your company supplies ceramic floor tiles to Home Depot, Lowe's, and other home improvement stores. You have been asked to start using radio frequency identification tags on each case of tiles you ship to help your customers improve the management of your products and those of other suppliers in their warehouses. Use the web to identify the cost of hardware, software, and networking components for an RFID system for your company. What factors should be considered? What are the key decisions that have to be made in determining whether your firm should adopt this technology?

7-9   BestMed Medical Supplies Corporation sells medical and surgical products and equipment from more than 700 manufacturers to hospitals, health clinics, and medical offices. The company employs 500 people at seven locations in western and midwestern states, including account managers, customer service and support representatives, and warehouse staff. Employees communicate by traditional telephone voice services, email, instant messaging, and cell phones. Management is inquiring about whether the company should adopt a system for unified communications. What factors should be considered? What are the key decisions that must be made in determining whether to adopt this technology? Use the web, if necessary, to find out more about unified communications and its costs.

Improving Decision Making: Using Spreadsheet Software to Evaluate Wireless Services

Software skills: Spreadsheet formulas, formatting
Business skills: Analyzing telecommunications services and costs

7-10   In this project, you'll use the web to research alternative wireless services and use spreadsheet software to calculate wireless service costs for a sales force.
You would like to equip your sales force of 35, based in St. Louis, Missouri, with mobile phones that have capabilities for voice transmission, text messaging, Internet access, and taking and sending photos. Use the web to select two wireless providers that offer nationwide voice and data service as well as good service in your home area. Examine the features of the mobile handsets and wireless plans offered by each of these vendors. Assume that each of the 35 salespeople will need to spend three hours per weekday between 8 a.m. and 6 p.m. on mobile voice communication, send 30 text messages per weekday, use 1 gigabyte of data per month, and send five photos per week. Use your spreadsheet software to determine the wireless service and handset that will offer the best pricing per user over a two-year period. For the purposes of this exercise, you do not need to consider corporate discounts.

Achieving Operational Excellence: Using Web Search Engines for Business Research

Software skills: Web search tools
Business skills: Researching new technologies

7-11   This project will help develop your Internet skills in using web search engines for business research.
Use Google and Bing to obtain information about ethanol as an alternative fuel for motor vehicles. If you wish, try some other search engines as well. Compare the volume and quality of information you find with each search tool. Which tool is the easiest to use? Which produced the best results for your research? Why?

Collaboration and Teamwork Project

Evaluating Smartphones

7-12   Form a group with three or four of your classmates. Compare the capabilities of Apple's iPhone with a smartphone from another vendor with similar features. Your analysis should consider the purchase cost of each device, the wireless networks where each device can operate, plan and handset costs, and the services available for each device. You should also consider other capabilities of each device, including available software, security features, and the ability to integrate with existing corporate or PC applications. Which device would you select? On what criteria would you base your selection? If possible, use Google Docs and Google Drive or Google Sites to brainstorm, organize, and develop a presentation of your findings for the class.

Google, Apple, and Facebook Battle for Your Internet Experience
CASE STUDY

Three Internet titans—Google, Apple, and Facebook—are in an epic struggle to dominate your Internet experience, and caught in the crossfire are search, music, video, and other media along with the devices you use for all of these things. Mobile devices with advanced functionality and ubiquitous Internet access are rapidly overtaking traditional desktop machines as the most popular form of computing. Today, people spend more than half their time online using mobile devices that take advantage of a growing cloud of computing capacity. It's no surprise, then, that today's tech titans are aggressively battling for control of this brave new online world.

Apple, which started as a personal computer company, quickly expanded into software and consumer electronics. Since upending the music industry with its iPod MP3 player, and the iTunes digital music service, Apple took mobile computing by storm with the iPhone, iPod Touch, and iPad. Now Apple wants to be the computing platform of choice for the Internet.

Apple's competitive strength is based not on its hardware platform alone but on its superior user interface and mobile software applications, in which it is a leader. Apple's App Store offers more than 2 million apps for mobile and tablet devices. Applications greatly enrich the experience of using a mobile device, and whoever creates the most appealing set of devices and applications will derive a significant competitive advantage over rival companies. Apps are the new equivalent of the traditional browser.

Apple thrives on its legacy of innovation. In 2011, it unveiled Siri (Speech Interpretation and Recognition Interface), a combination search/navigation tool and personal assistant. Siri promises personalized recommendations that improve as it gains user familiarity—all from a verbal command. Google countered by quickly releasing its own AI tool, Google Now. Facebook has developed an intelligent assistant called M.

Apple faces strong competition for its phones and tablets both in the United States and in developing markets like China from inexpensive Chinese smartphones and from Samsung Android phones that have larger screens and lower prices. iPhone sales have started to slow, but Apple is not counting on hardware devices alone for future growth. Services have always played a large part in the Apple ecosystem, and they have emerged as a major revenue source. Apple has more than 1.3 billion active devices in circulation, creating a huge installed base of users willing to purchase services and a source of new revenue streams. Apple's services business, which includes Apple's music (both downloads and subscriptions), video sales and rentals, books, apps (including in-app purchases, subscriptions and advertising), iCloud storage, and payments, has been growing at a double-digit rate.

As Apple rolls out more gadgets, such as the Watch and HomePod, its services revenue will continue to expand and diversify. According to CEO Tim Cook, Apple has become one of the largest service businesses in the world. This service-driven strategy is not without worry because both Google and Facebook offer stiff competition in the services area.

Google continues to be the world's leading search engine, accounting for about 75 percent of web searches from laptop and desktop devices and over 90 percent of the mobile search market. (Google is also the default search engine for the iPhone). About 84 percent of the revenue from Google's parent company Alphabet comes from ads, most of them on Google's search engine. Google dominates online advertising. However, Google is slipping in its position as the gateway to the Internet. New search startups focus on actions and apps instead of the web. Facebook has become an important gateway to the web as well. In 2005, Google had purchased the Android open source mobile operating system to compete in mobile computing. Google provides Android at no cost to smartphone manufacturers, generating revenue indirectly through app purchases and advertising. Many different manufacturers have adopted Android as a standard. In contrast, Apple allows only its own devices to use its proprietary operating system, and all the apps it sells can run only on Apple products. Android is deployed on over 80 percent of smartphones worldwide; is the most common operating system for tablets; and runs on watches, car dashboards, and TVs—more than 4,000 distinct devices. Google wants to extend Android to as many devices as possible.

Google's Android could gain even more market share in the coming years, which could be problematic for Apple as it tries to maintain customer loyalty and keep software developers focused on the iOS platform. Whoever has the dominant smartphone operating system will have control over the apps where smartphone users spend most of their time and built-in channels for serving ads to mobile devices. Although Google search technology can't easily navigate the mobile apps where users are spending most of their time, Google is starting to index the content inside mobile apps and provide links pointing to that content featured in Google's search results on smartphones. Since more than half of global search queries come from mobile devices, the company revised its search algorithms to add "mobile friendliness" to the 200 or so factors it uses to rank websites on its search engine. This favors sites that look good on smartphone screens. The cost-per-click paid for mobile ads has trailed desktop ads, but the gap between computer and mobile ads fees is narrowing. Google instituted a design change to present a cleaner mobile search page.

Seven Google products and services, including Search, YouTube, and Maps, have more than a billion users each. The Android operating system software has over 2 billion monthly active users. Google's ultimate goal is to knit its services and devices together so that Google users will interact with the company seamlessly all day long and everyone will want to use Google. Much of Google's efforts to make its search and related services more powerful and user-friendly in the years ahead are based on the company's investments in artificial intelligence and machine learning (see Chapter 11). These technologies already have been implemented in applications such as voice search, Google Translate, and spam filtering. The goal is to evolve search into more of a smart assistance capability, where computers can understand what people are saying and respond conversationally with the right information at the right moment. Allo is a smart messaging app for iOS and Android that can learn your texting patterns over time to make conversations more expressive and productive. It suggests automatic replies to incoming messages, and you can get suggestions and even book a restaurant reservation without leaving the chat. Google Assistant is meant to provide a continuing, conversational dialogue between users and the search engine.

Facebook is the world's largest social networking service, with over 2 billion monthly active users.

People use Facebook to stay connected with their friends and family and to express what matters most to them. Facebook Platform enables developers to build applications and websites that integrate with Facebook to reach its global network of users and to build personalized and social products. Facebook is so pervasive and appealing that it has become users' primary gateway to the Internet. For a lot of people, Facebook *is* the Internet. Whatever they do on the Internet is through Facebook.

Facebook has persistently worked on ways to convert its popularity and trove of user data into advertising dollars, with the expectation that these dollars will increasingly come from mobile smartphones and tablets. As of early 2018, over 95 percent of active user accounts worldwide accessed the social network via smartphone. Facebook ads allow companies to target its users based on their real identities and expressed interests rather than educated guesses derived from web-browsing habits and other online behavior.

At the end of the first quarter of 2018, 98 percent of Facebook's global revenue came from advertising, and 89 percent of that ad revenue was from mobile advertising. Many of those ads are highly targeted by age, gender, and other demographics. Facebook is now a serious competitor to Google in the mobile ad market and is even trying to compete with emerging mobile platforms. Together, Facebook and Google dominate the digital ad industry and have been responsible for almost all of its growth. Facebook has overhauled its home page to give advertisers more opportunities and more information with which to target markets. The company is expanding advertising in products such as the Instagram feed, Stories, WhatsApp, Facebook Watch, and Messenger, although the majority of ad revenue still comes from its news feed. Facebook has its own personalized search tool to challenge Google's dominance of search. Facebook CEO Mark Zuckerberg is convinced that social networking is the ideal way to use the web and to consume all of the other content people might desire, including news and video. That makes it an ideal marketing platform for companies. But he also knows that Facebook can't achieve long-term growth and prosperity based on social networking alone. During the past few years Facebook has moved into virtual reality, messaging, video, and more.

Facebook is challenging YouTube as the premier destination for personal videos, developing its own TV programming, and making its messages "smarter" by deploying chatbots. Chatbots are stripped-down software agents that understand what you type or say and respond by answering questions or executing tasks, and they run in the background of Facebook's Messenger service (see Chapter 11). Within Facebook Messenger, you can order a ride from Uber, get news updates, check your flight status, or use augmented reality to imagine what a new Nike sneaker looks like by superimposing a 3-D model of that sneaker atop images or video. A new standalone app will allow users to stream videos in their news feed through set-top boxes such as Apple Inc.'s Apple TV and Amazon.com Inc.'s Fire TV, as well as Samsung Internet-connected TVs.

Zuckerberg has said that he intends to help bring the next billion people online by attracting users in developing countries with affordable web connectivity. Facebook has launched several services in emerging markets, such as the Free Basics service designed to get people online so they can explore web applications, including its social network. Facebook wants to beam the Internet to underserved areas through the use of drones and satellites along with other technologies. Zuckerberg thinks that Facebook could eventually be an Internet service provider to underserved areas.

Monetization of personal data drives both Facebook and Google's business models. However, this practice also threatens individual privacy. The consumer surveillance underlying Facebook and Google's free services has come under siege from users, regulators, and legislators on both sides of the Atlantic. Calls for restricting Facebook and Google's collection and use of personal data have gathered steam, especially after recent revelations about Russian agents trying to use Facebook to sway American voters and Facebook's uncontrolled sharing of user data with third-party companies (see the Chapter 4 ending case study). Both companies will have to come to terms with the European Union's new privacy law, called the General Data Protection Regulation (GDPR), that requires companies to obtain consent from users before processing their data, and which may inspire more stringent privacy legislation in the United States. Business models that depend less on ads and more on subscriptions have been proposed, although any effort to curb the use of consumer data would put the business model of the ad-supported Internet—and

possibly Facebook and Google—at risk. Apple emphasizes its privacy protection features and does not share customer data with others.

These tech giants are also being scrutinized for monopolistic behavior. In the United States, Google drives 89 percent of Internet search, 95 percent of young adults on the Internet use a Facebook product, and Google and Apple provide 99 percent of mobile phone operating systems. Critics have called for breaking up these mega-companies or regulating them as Standard Oil and AT&T once were. In July 2018 European regulators fined Google $5 billion for forcing cellphone makers that use the company's Android operating system to install Google search and browser apps. Have these companies become so large that they are squeezing consumers and innovation? How governments answer this question will also affect how Apple, Google, and Facebook will fare and what kind of Internet experience they will be able to provide.

Sources: Associated Press, "EU Fines Google a Record $5 Million over Mobile Practices," July 18, 2018; Christopher Mims, "How Apps, Music and More Can Buoy Apple Beyond the iPhone," *Wall Street Journal*, February 4, 2018; "Search Engine Market Share," www.netmarketshare.com, accessed April 16, 2018; "Facebook's Advertising Revenue Worldwide from 2009 to 2017 (in Million U.S. Dollars)," statista.com, accessed April 17, 2018; David Streitfeld, Natasha Singer, and Steven Erlanger, "How Calls for Privacy May Upend Business for Facebook and Google," *New York Times*, March 24, 2018; Natasha Singer, "Timeline: Facebook and Google Under Regulators' Glare," *New York Times*, March 24, 2018; David Streitfeld, "Google Wants to Be Everywhere with Everyone," *New York Times*, May 17, 2017; Tim Bajarin, "Learning This 1 Thing Helped Me Understand Apple's Strategy," *Time*, April 3, 2017; and Mathew Ingram, "How Google and Facebook Have Taken Over the Digital Ad Industry," *Fortune*, January 4, 2017.

CASE STUDY QUESTIONS

7-13 Compare the business models and core competencies of Google, Apple, and Facebook.

7-14 Why is mobile computing so important to these three firms? Evaluate the mobile strategies of each firm.

7-15 Which company and business model do you think is most likely to dominate the Internet, and why?

7-16 What difference would it make to a business or to an individual consumer if Apple, Google, or Facebook dominated the Internet experience? Explain your answer.

MyLab MIS

Go to the Assignments section of MyLab MIS to complete these writing exercises.

7-17 Compare the capabilities of today's web with those of the future web.

7-18 How do social search, semantic search, and mobile search differ from searching for information on the web using conventional search engines?

Chapter 7 References

Alphabet, Inc. "Form 10K for the Fiscal Year Ending December 31, 2017." Securities and Exchange Commission, filed February 1, 2018.

Chiang, I. Robert, and Jhih-Hua Jhang-Li. "Delivery Consolidation and Service Competition Among Internet Service Providers." *Journal of Management Information Systems* 34, No. 3 (Winter 2014).

Comscore. "The 2017 Mobile App Report." (2017).

Eliason, Andy. "23 Search Engine Facts and Stats You Oughta Know." SEO.com, accessed May 8, 2017.

eMarketer. "US Ad Spending: The eMarketer Forecast for 2018." (2018).

"Facebook Company Statistics." www.statisticbrain.com, accessed April 18, 2018.

IBM Global Technology Services. "Software-Defined Networking in the New Business Frontier." (July 2015).

Iyer, Bala. "To Project the Trajectory of the Internet of Things, Look to the Software Industry." *Harvard Business Review* (February 25, 2016).

Manyika, James, Michael Chui, Peter Bisson, Jonathan Woetzel, Richard Dobbs, Jacques Bughin, and Dan Aharon. "Unlocking the Potential of the Internet of Things." *McKinsey Global Institute* (2015).

McKinsey & Company. "The Impact of Internet Technologies: Search." (July 2011).

Miller, Rich. "5G Wireless: A New Network to Enable the Data Deluge." *Data Center Frontier* (July 13, 2017).

National Telecommunications and Information Agency. "NTIA Announces Intent to Transition Key Internet Domain Name Functions." (March 14, 2014).

Panko, Raymond R., and Julia L. Panko. *Business Data Networks and Security*, 11th ed. (Upper Saddle River, NJ: Prentice-Hall, 2018).

Pew Research Center. "Mobile Fact Sheet." (January 12, 2017).

Segan, Sascha. "What Is 5G?" *PC Magazine* (May 1, 2017).

Varian, Hal. "Executive Assistants for Everyone." *MIT Sloan Management Review* (Fall 2016).

Wang, Weiquan, and Izak Benbasat. "Empirical Assessment of Alternative Designs for Enhancing Different Types of Trusting Beliefs in Online Recommendation Agents." *Journal of Management Information Systems* 33, No. 3 (2016).

8

Securing Information Systems

LEARNING OBJECTIVES

After reading this chapter, you will be able to answer the following questions:

8-1 Why are information systems vulnerable to destruction, error, and abuse?

8-2 What is the business value of security and control?

8-3 What are the components of an organizational framework for security and control?

8-4 What are the most important tools and technologies for safeguarding information resources?

8-5 How will MIS help my career?

CHAPTER CASES

Hackers Target the U.S. Presidential Election: What Happened?

Meltdown and Spectre Haunt the World's Computers

How Secure Is the Cloud?

Is the Equifax Hack the Worst Ever—and Why?

VIDEO CASES

Stuxnet and Cyberwarfare

Cyberespionage: The Chinese Threat

Instructional Videos:

Sony PlayStation Hacked; Data Stolen from 77 Million Users

Meet the Hackers: Anonymous Statement on Hacking Sony

MyLab MIS

Discussion Questions: 8-5, 8-6, 8-7; **Hands-on MIS Projects:** 8-8, 8-9, 8-10, 8-11;
Writing Assignments: 8-17, 8-18; **eText with Conceptual Animations**

Hackers Target the U.S. Presidential Election: What Happened?

In September 2015, Special Agent Adrian Hawkins of the U.S. Federal Bureau of Investigation (FBI) phoned the Democratic National Committee (DNC) with troubling news about its computer network: At least one DNC computer system had been penetrated by hackers linked to the Russian government. Yared Tamene, the DNC tech-support contractor who fielded the calls, conducted a cursory search of the DNC computer system logs to look for signs of hacking. He stated that he did not look too hard, even after Special Agent Hawkins called back and left messages repeatedly over the next several weeks, because he thought the call might be a prank call from an imposter.

The DNC hack was the first sign of a Russian-led cyberwarfare campaign to disrupt the 2016 presidential election. DNC chairwoman Debbie Wasserman Schultz was forced to resign, and a torrent of confidential documents from the DNC and the Clinton campaign were released by WikiLeaks to the press during the campaign. In a stunning upset, Donald Trump won the presidential election, and his victory may have been facilitated by revelations in the leaked documents.

Several Russian hacker groups associated with Russian intelligence were identified as the source of the cyberattacks. The Russian hackers had moved freely through the DNC network for nearly 7 months before top DNC officials were alerted to the attack and hired cybersecurity firm CrowdStrike to beef up their system protection. The DNC computer system was replaced, and all laptops were turned in and their hard drives wiped clean to get rid of infected information.

In the meantime, the hackers gained access to systems of the Clinton campaign. The

© Andriy Popov/123RF

hackers did not have to use any sophisticated tools to gain access and were able to deploy phishing emails to trick legitimate system users into revealing passwords for accessing the system. Clinton campaign aide Charles Delavan clicked on an email sent to the personal account of campaign chairman John Podesta thinking it was legitimate and opened another door for the Russians. Whenever someone clicked on a phishing message, the Russians would enter the network, "exfiltrate" documents of interest, and stockpile them for intelligence purposes. By the summer of 2016, Democrats' private emails and confidential documents were posted on WikiLeaks and other websites day after day and reported by the media.

The DNC thought it was well protected against cyberattacks but only had a fraction of the security budget that a corporation its size would have. It had a standard email spam-filtering service for blocking phishing attacks and malware created to resemble legitimate email, but it did not have the most advanced systems in place to track suspicious traffic.

Hacking during the 2016 presidential election went beyond the DNC and the Clinton campaign. Russian hackers tried to infiltrate at least 21 states' election systems and to delete or alter voter data in Illinois. (Officials don't believe the attackers changed any result.)

On July 13, 2018 a federal grand jury indicted 12 Russian intelligence officers as part of special counsel Robert Mueller's investigation into alleged Russian meddling during the 2016 presidential campaign. The officers were charged with engaging in a sustained effort to hack networks of the Democratic Congressional Campaign Committee, the Democratic National Committee, and Hillary Clinton's campaign. There is mounting evidence that Russian hackers are continuing to target U.S. state election systems, looking for opportunities to influence primaries, the 2018 midterm Congressional elections, and eventually the 2020 presidential campaign. Russian hackers have also been actively trying to influence elections in Europe as well.

Sources: Lucien Bruggeman and Mike Levine, "Mueller indicts 12 Russian Intel Officers for Hacking Democrats," *Good Morning America*, July 13, 2018; Joseph O'Sullivan, "With Russian Hacking Fresh in Mind, Washington State Beefs Up Elections Cybersecurity," *Seattle Times*, July 8, 2018; Erin Kelly, "Russia So Far Not Mounting Robust Hacking Effort Against U.S. Election, Official Says," *USA Today*, July 11, 2018; Harold Stark, "How Russia 'Hacked' Us in 2016 [And What We did Wrong]," *Forbes*, January 24, 2017; Sue Marquette Poremba, "Data Security Lessons from the DNC Hack," *ITBusinessEdge*, March 7, 2017; Mark Moore, "Russian Hackers Infiltrated Voter Databases in Dozens of States," *New York Post*, June 13, 2017; and Eric Lipton, David E. Sanger, and Scott Shane, "The Perfect Weapon: How Russian Cyberpower Invaded the U.S.," *New York Times*, December 13, 2016.

Efforts to disrupt the 2016 U.S presidential election and other recent elections illustrate some of the reasons why organizations need to pay special attention to information systems security. IT security breaches that enabled Russian hackers to penetrate information systems used by the Democratic Party have the potential to change the course of elections—and possibly the fate of nations. Weak IT security has been responsible for many billions of dollars of corporate and consumer financial losses as well.

The chapter-opening diagram calls attention to important points raised by this case and this chapter. The DNC and the Clinton campaign lacked IT security awareness, tools, and expertise to prevent employees from naively responding to hackers' phishing attacks. Also at work were human ignorance, error, and carelessness, evidenced by the DNC's unwillingness to respond quickly to the FBI's hacker attack warning and DNC and Clinton campaign members' inability to identify bogus phishing emails. Although the DNC and the Clinton campaign thought they had sufficient security tools to fend off unwanted intruders, they were not enough to protect them and the presidential campaign from Russian influence. Eventually the Democrats hired outside security experts to beef up system protection.

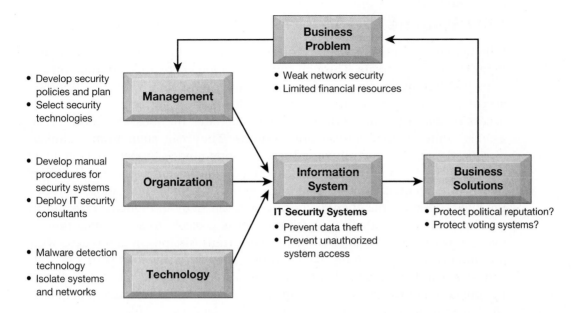

We will probably never really know exactly how much revelations from the emails exposed by the hackers affected the 2016 election outcome. But we do know that what happened was very serious and most likely a preview of future electoral trouble around the world. Equally disturbing, the security vulnerabilities that facilitated the DNC and Clinton campaign hacks are commonplace in businesses and other organizations as well.

Here are some questions to think about: What security vulnerabilities were exploited by the hackers? What management, organizational, and technological factors contributed to these security weaknesses? What was the business impact of these problems? Could the election hacking have been prevented?

8-1 Why are information systems vulnerable to destruction, error, and abuse?

Can you imagine what would happen if you tried to link to the Internet without a firewall or antivirus software? Your computer would be disabled within a few seconds, and it might take you many days to recover. If you used the computer to run your business, you might not be able to sell to your customers or place orders with your suppliers while it was down. And you might find that your computer system had been penetrated by outsiders, who perhaps stole or destroyed valuable data, including confidential payment data from your customers. If too much data was destroyed or divulged, your business might never be able to recover!

In short, if you operate a business today, you need to make security and control a top priority. **Security** refers to the policies, procedures, and technical measures used to prevent unauthorized access, alteration, theft, or physical damage to information systems. **Controls** are methods, policies, and organizational procedures that ensure the safety of the organization's assets, the accuracy and reliability of its records, and operational adherence to management standards.

Why Systems are Vulnerable

When large amounts of data are stored in electronic form, they are vulnerable to many kinds of threats. Through communications networks, information systems in different locations are interconnected. The potential for unauthorized access or damage is not limited to a single location but can occur at many access points in the network. Figure 8.1 illustrates the most common threats against contemporary information systems. They can stem from technical, organizational, and environmental factors compounded by poor management decisions. In the multitier client/server computing environment illustrated here, vulnerabilities exist at each layer and in the communications between the layers. Users at the client layer can cause harm by introducing errors or by accessing systems without authorization. It is possible to access data flowing over networks, steal valuable data during transmission, or alter data without authorization. Radiation may disrupt a network at various points as well. Intruders can launch denial-of-service attacks or malicious software to disrupt the operation of websites. Those capable of penetrating corporate systems can steal, destroy, or alter corporate data stored in databases or files.

Systems malfunction if computer hardware breaks down, is not configured properly, or is damaged by improper use or criminal acts. Errors in programming, improper installation, or unauthorized changes cause computer software to fail. Power failures, floods, fires, or other natural disasters can also disrupt computer systems.

Domestic or offshore partnering with another company contributes to system vulnerability if valuable information resides on networks and computers outside the organization's control. Without strong safeguards, valuable data could be lost, be destroyed, or fall into the wrong hands, revealing important trade secrets or information that violates personal privacy.

Portability makes cell phones, smartphones, and tablet computers easy to lose or steal. Smartphones share the same security weaknesses as other Internet devices and are vulnerable to malicious software and penetration from outsiders. Smartphones that corporate employees use often contain sensitive data such as

FIGURE 8.1 **CONTEMPORARY SECURITY CHALLENGES AND VULNERABILITIES**

The architecture of a web-based application typically includes a web client, a server, and corporate information systems linked to databases. Each of these components presents security challenges and vulnerabilities. Floods, fires, power failures, and other electrical problems can cause disruptions at any point in the network.

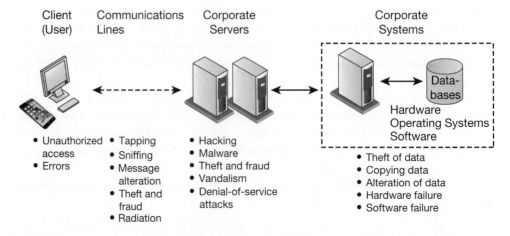

Client (User)	Communications Lines	Corporate Servers	Corporate Systems
• Unauthorized access • Errors	• Tapping • Sniffing • Message alteration • Theft and fraud • Radiation	• Hacking • Malware • Theft and fraud • Vandalism • Denial-of-service attacks	Hardware Operating Systems Software • Theft of data • Copying data • Alteration of data • Hardware failure • Software failure

sales figures, customer names, phone numbers, and email addresses. Intruders may also be able to access internal corporate systems through these devices.

Internet Vulnerabilities

Large public networks, such as the Internet, are more vulnerable than internal networks because they are virtually open to anyone. The Internet is so huge that when abuses do occur, they can have an enormously widespread impact. When the Internet links to the corporate network, the organization's information systems are even more vulnerable to actions from outsiders.

Vulnerability has also increased from widespread use of email, instant messaging (IM), and peer-to-peer (P2P) file-sharing programs. Email may contain attachments that serve as springboards for malicious software or unauthorized access to internal corporate systems. Employees may use email messages to transmit valuable trade secrets, financial data, or confidential customer information to unauthorized recipients. Instant messaging activity over the Internet can in some cases be used as a back door to an otherwise secure network. Sharing files over P2P networks, such as those for illegal music sharing, can also transmit malicious software or expose information on either individual or corporate computers to outsiders.

Wireless Security Challenges

Both Bluetooth and Wi-Fi networks are susceptible to hacking by eavesdroppers. Local area networks (LANs) using the 802.11 standard can be easily penetrated by outsiders armed with laptops, wireless cards, external antennae, and hacking software. Hackers use these tools to detect unprotected networks, monitor network traffic, and, in some cases, gain access to the Internet or to corporate networks.

Wi-Fi transmission technology was designed to make it easy for stations to find and hear one another. The service set identifiers (SSIDs) that identify the access points in a Wi-Fi network are broadcast multiple times and can be picked up fairly easily by intruders' sniffer programs (see Figure 8.2). Wireless networks in many locations do not have basic protections against **war driving**, in which eavesdroppers drive by buildings or park outside and try to intercept wireless network traffic.

An intruder who has associated with an access point by using the correct SSID is capable of accessing other resources on the network. For example, the intruder could use the Windows operating system to determine which other users are connected to the network, access their computer hard drives, and open or copy their files.

Intruders also use the information they have gleaned to set up rogue access points on a different radio channel in physical locations close to users to force a user's radio network interface controller (NIC) to associate with the rogue access point. Once this association occurs, hackers using the rogue access point can capture the names and passwords of unsuspecting users.

Malicious Software: Viruses, Worms, Trojan Horses, and Spyware

Malicious software programs are referred to as **malware** and include a variety of threats such as computer viruses, worms, and Trojan horses. (See Table 8.1.) A **computer virus** is a rogue software program that attaches itself to other software programs or data files to be executed, usually without user knowledge or permission. Most computer viruses deliver a payload. The payload may be

FIGURE 8.2 WI-FI SECURITY CHALLENGES

Many Wi-Fi networks can be penetrated easily by intruders using sniffer programs to obtain an address to access the resources of a network without authorization.

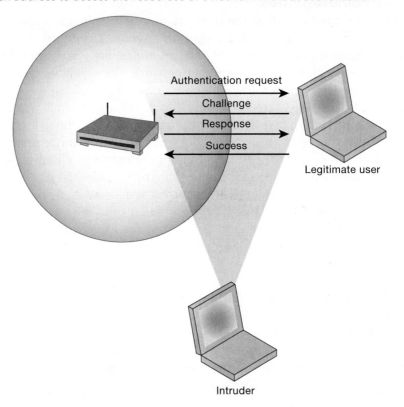

relatively benign, such as instructions to display a message or image, or it may be highly destructive—destroying programs or data, clogging computer memory, reformatting a computer's hard drive, or causing programs to run improperly. Viruses typically spread from computer to computer when humans take an action, such as sending an email attachment or copying an infected file.

Worms are independent computer programs that copy themselves from one computer to other computers over a network. Unlike viruses, worms can operate on their own without attaching to other computer program files and rely

TABLE 8.1 EXAMPLES OF MALICIOUS CODE

NAME	TYPE	DESCRIPTION
Cryptolocker	Ransomware/Trojan	Hijacks users' photos, videos, and text documents; encrypts them with virtually unbreakable asymmetric encryption; and demands ransom payment for them.
Conficker	Worm	First detected in November 2008 and still a problem. Uses flaws in Windows software to take over machines and link them into a virtual computer that can be commanded remotely. Had more than 5 million computers worldwide under its control. Difficult to eradicate.
Sasser.ftp	Worm	First appeared in May 2004. Spread over the Internet by attacking random IP addresses. Causes computers to continually crash and reboot and infected computers to search for more victims. Affected millions of computers worldwide and caused an estimated $14.8 billion to $18.6 billion in damages.
ILOVEYOU	Virus	First detected on May 3, 2000. Script virus written in Visual Basic script and transmitted as an attachment to email with the subject line ILOVEYOU. Overwrites music, image, and other files with a copy of itself and did an estimated $10 billion to $15 billion in damage.

less on human behavior to spread rapidly from computer to computer. Worms destroy data and programs as well as disrupt or even halt the operation of computer networks.

Worms and viruses are often spread over the Internet from files of downloaded software; from files attached to email transmissions; or from compromised email messages, online ads, or instant messaging. Viruses have also invaded computerized information systems from infected external storage devices or infected machines. Especially prevalent today are **drive-by downloads**, consisting of malware that comes with a downloaded file that a user intentionally or unintentionally requests.

Hackers can do to a smartphone just about anything they can do to any Internet-connected device: request malicious files without user intervention, delete files, transmit files, install programs running in the background to monitor user actions, and potentially convert the smartphone to a robot in a botnet to send email and text messages to anyone. According to IT security experts, mobile devices now pose the greatest security risks, outpacing those from larger computers. Kaspersky Lab reported that it had detected 5.7 million mobile malicious installation packages in 2017 (Kaspersky Lab, 2018).

Android, which is the world's leading mobile operating system, is the mobile platform targeted by most hackers. Mobile device viruses pose serious threats to enterprise computing because so many wireless devices are now linked to corporate information systems.

Blogs, wikis, and social networking sites such as Facebook, Twitter, and LinkedIn have emerged as new conduits for malware. Members are more likely to trust messages they receive from friends, even if this communication is not legitimate. For example, a malware strain called FacexWorm appeared inside Facebook Messenger in 2018. Clicking a link via Facebook Messenger takes the victim to a fake YouTube page, which tries to trick the user into installing a YouTube extension for the popular Chrome browser. From there the malware can steal passwords or try to steal cryptocurrency funds such as Bitcoin.

The Internet of Things (IoT) introduces additional security challenges from the Internet-linked devices themselves, their platforms and operating systems, their communications, and even the systems to which they're connected. New security tools will be required to protect IoT devices and platforms from both information attacks and physical tampering, to encrypt their communications, and to address new challenges such as attacks that drain batteries. Many IoT devices such as sensors have simple processors and operating systems that may not support sophisticated security approaches.

Panda Security reported that in 2017 it had identified and neutralized a total of 75 million malware files, about 285,000 new samples a day (Panda Security, 2017).

Many malware infections are Trojan horses. A **Trojan horse** is a software program that appears to be benign but then does something other than expected. The Trojan horse is not itself a virus because it does not replicate, but it is often a way for viruses or other malicious code to be introduced into a computer system. The term *Trojan horse* is based on the huge wooden horse the Greeks used to trick the Trojans into opening the gates to their fortified city during the Trojan War.

An example of a modern-day Trojan horse is the ZeuS (Zbot) Trojan, which infected more than 3.6 million computers in 2009 and still poses a threat. It has been used to steal login credentials for banking by surreptitiously capturing people's keystrokes as they use their computers. Zeus is spread mainly through drive-by downloads and phishing, and recent variants have been difficult to eradicate.

SQL injection attacks exploit vulnerabilities in poorly coded web application software to introduce malicious program code into a company's systems and networks. These vulnerabilities occur when a web application fails to validate properly or filter data a user enters on a web page, which might occur when ordering something online. An attacker uses this input validation error to send a rogue SQL query to the underlying database to access the database, plant malicious code, or access other systems on the network. Malware known as **ransomware** is proliferating on both desktop and mobile devices. Ransomware tries to extort money from users by taking control of their computers, blocking access to files, or displaying annoying pop-up messages. For example, the ransomware called WannaCry that attacked computers in more than 150 countries in May 2017 encrypts an infected computer's files, forcing users to pay hundreds of dollars to regain access. You can get ransomware from downloading an infected attachment, clicking a link inside an email, or visiting the wrong website.

Some types of **spyware** also act as malicious software. These small programs install themselves surreptitiously on computers to monitor user web-surfing activity and serve up advertising. Thousands of forms of spyware have been documented. Many users find such spyware annoying and an infringement on their privacy. Some forms of spyware are especially nefarious. **Keyloggers** record every keystroke made on a computer to steal serial numbers for software, to launch Internet attacks, to gain access to email accounts, to obtain passwords to protected computer systems, or to pick up personal information such as credit card or bank account numbers. The Zeus Trojan described earlier uses keylogging. Other spyware programs reset web browser home pages, redirect search requests, or slow performance by taking up too much computer resources.

Hackers and Computer Crime

A **hacker** is an individual who intends to gain unauthorized access to a computer system. Within the hacking community, the term *cracker* is typically used to denote a hacker with criminal intent, although in the public press, the terms *hacker* and *cracker* are used interchangeably. Hackers gain unauthorized access by finding weaknesses in the security protections websites and computer systems employ. Hacker activities have broadened beyond mere system intrusion to include theft of goods and information as well as system damage and **cybervandalism**, the intentional disruption, defacement, or even destruction of a website or corporate information system.

Spoofing and Sniffing

Hackers attempting to hide their true identities often spoof, or misrepresent, themselves by using fake email addresses or masquerading as someone else. **Spoofing** may also involve redirecting a web link to an address different from the intended one, with the site masquerading as the intended destination. For example, if hackers redirect customers to a fake website that looks almost exactly like the true site, they can then collect and process orders, effectively stealing business as well as sensitive customer information from the true site. We will provide more detail about other forms of spoofing in our discussion of computer crime.

A **sniffer** is a type of eavesdropping program that monitors information traveling over a network. When used legitimately, sniffers help identify potential network trouble spots or criminal activity on networks, but when used for criminal purposes, they can be damaging and very difficult to detect. Sniffers enable hackers to steal proprietary information from anywhere on a network, including email messages, company files, and confidential reports.

Denial-of-Service Attacks

In a **denial-of-service (DoS) attack**, hackers flood a network server or web server with many thousands of false communications or requests for services to crash the network. The network receives so many queries that it cannot keep up with them and is thus unavailable to service legitimate requests. A **distributed denial-of-service (DDoS)** attack uses numerous computers to inundate and overwhelm the network from numerous launch points.

Although DoS attacks do not destroy information or access restricted areas of a company's information systems, they often cause a website to shut down, making it impossible for legitimate users to access the site. For busy e-commerce sites, these attacks are costly; while the site is shut down, customers cannot make purchases. Especially vulnerable are small and midsize businesses whose networks tend to be less protected than those of large corporations.

Perpetrators of DDoS attacks often use thousands of zombie PCs infected with malicious software without their owners' knowledge and organized into a **botnet**. Hackers create these botnets by infecting other people's computers with bot malware that opens a back door through which an attacker can give instructions. The infected computer then becomes a slave, or zombie, serving a master computer belonging to someone else. When hackers infect enough computers, they can use the amassed resources of the botnet to launch DDoS attacks, phishing campaigns, or unsolicited spam email.

Ninety percent of the world's spam and 80 percent of the world's malware are delivered by botnets. A recent example is the Mirai botnet, which infected numerous IoT devices (such as Internet-connected surveillance cameras) in October 2016 and then used them to launch a DDoS attack against Dyn, whose servers monitor and reroute Internet traffic. The Mirai botnet overwhelmed the Dyn servers, taking down Etsy, GitHub, Netflix, Shopify, SoundCloud, Spotify, Twitter, and a number of other major websites. A Mirai botnet variant attacked financial firms in January 2018.

Computer Crime

Most hacker activities are criminal offenses, and the vulnerabilities of systems we have just described make them targets for other types of **computer crime** as well. Computer crime is defined by the U.S. Department of Justice as "any violations of criminal law that involve a knowledge of computer technology for their perpetration, investigation, or prosecution." Table 8.2 provides examples of the computer as both a target and an instrument of crime.

No one knows the magnitude of computer crime—how many systems are invaded, how many people engage in the practice, or the total economic damage. According to the Ponemon Institute's 2017 Annual Cost of Cyber Crime Study, the average annualized cost of cybercrime security for benchmarked companies in seven different countries was $11.7 million (Ponemon Institute, 2017a). Many companies are reluctant to report computer crimes because the crimes may involve employees or that publicizing vulnerability will hurt their reputations. The most economically damaging kinds of computer crime are DoS attacks, activities of malicious insiders, and web-based attacks.

Identity Theft

With the growth of the Internet and electronic commerce, identity theft has become especially troubling. **Identity theft** is a crime in which an imposter obtains key pieces of personal information, such as social security numbers, driver's license numbers, or credit card numbers, to impersonate someone else. The information may be used to obtain credit, merchandise, or services in the name

TABLE 8.2 EXAMPLES OF COMPUTER CRIME

COMPUTERS AS TARGETS OF CRIME

Breaching the confidentiality of protected computerized data

Accessing a computer system without authority

Knowingly accessing a protected computer to commit fraud

Intentionally accessing a protected computer and causing damage negligently or deliberately

Knowingly transmitting a program, program code, or command that intentionally causes damage to a protected computer

Threatening to cause damage to a protected computer

COMPUTERS AS INSTRUMENTS OF CRIME

Theft of trade secrets

Unauthorized copying of software or copyrighted intellectual property, such as articles, books, music, and video

Schemes to defraud

Using email or messaging for threats or harassment

Intentionally attempting to intercept electronic communication

Illegally accessing stored electronic communications, including email and voice mail

Transmitting or possessing child pornography by using a computer

of the victim or to provide the thief with false credentials. Identity theft has flourished on the Internet, with credit card files a major target of website hackers (see the chapter-ending case study). According to the 2018 Identity Fraud Study by Javelin Strategy & Research, identity fraud affected 16.7 million U.S. consumers in 2017, and they lost nearly $17 billion to identity fraud that year (Javelin, 2018).

One increasingly popular tactic is a form of spoofing called **phishing**. Phishing involves setting up fake websites or sending email messages that look like those of legitimate businesses to ask users for confidential personal data. The email message instructs recipients to update or confirm records by providing social security numbers, bank and credit card information, and other confidential data, either by responding to the email message, by entering the information at a bogus website, or by calling a telephone number. eBay, PayPal, Amazon.com, Walmart, and a variety of banks have been among the top spoofed companies. In a more targeted form of phishing called *spear phishing*, messages appear to come from a trusted source, such as an individual within the recipient's own company or a friend.

Phishing techniques called evil twins and pharming are harder to detect. **Evil twins** are wireless networks that pretend to offer trustworthy Wi-Fi connections to the Internet, such as those in airport lounges, hotels, or coffee shops. The bogus network looks identical to a legitimate public network. Fraudsters try to capture passwords or credit card numbers of unwitting users who log on to the network.

Pharming redirects users to a bogus web page, even when the individual types the correct web page address into his or her browser. This is possible if pharming perpetrators gain access to the Internet address information Internet service providers (ISPs) store to speed up web browsing and flawed software on ISP servers allows the fraudsters to hack in and change those addresses.

According to the Ponemon Institute's 2017 Cost of a Data Breach Study, the average cost of a data breach among the 419 companies it surveyed globally was $3.62 million (Ponemon, 2017b). Moreover, brand damage can be significant although hard to quantify. In addition to the data breaches described in case studies for this chapter, Table 8.3 describes other major data breaches.

The U.S. Congress addressed the threat of computer crime in 1986 with the Computer Fraud and Abuse Act, which makes it illegal to access a computer

TABLE 8.3	MAJOR DATA BREACHES
DATA BREACH	DESCRIPTION
Yahoo	In September and December 2016, Yahoo disclosed that it had been the target of two of the biggest data breaches ever, with sensitive information stolen from more than 1 billion user accounts in 2013 and 500 million in 2014. State-sponsored hackers found a way to forge credentials to log into some users' accounts without a password. These data breaches forced Yahoo to lower its selling price by $300 million when it was acquired by Verizon in June 2017. In October 2017, Verizon reported that every single Yahoo account had actually been hacked—3 billion accounts, including email, Tumblr, Flickr, and Fantasy.
Anthem Health Insurance	In February 2015, hackers stole the personal information on more than 80 million customers of the giant health insurer, including names, birthdays, medical IDs, social security numbers, and income data. No medical or credit information was stolen. This was the largest healthcare breach ever recorded.
Sony	In November 2014, hackers stole more than 100 terabytes of corporate data, including trade secrets, email, personnel records, and copies of films for future release. Malware erased data from Sony's corporate systems, leading to hundreds of millions of dollars in losses as well as a tarnished brand image. Sony was hacked earlier in April 2011 when intruders obtained personal information, including credit, debit, and bank account numbers, from more than 100 million PlayStation Network users and Sony Online Entertainment users.
Home Depot	Hacked in 2014 with a malicious software program that plundered store registers while disguising itself as antivirus software. Fifty-six million credit card accounts were compromised, and 53 million customer email addresses were stolen.
eBay	Cyberattack on eBay servers during February and March 2014 compromised a database containing customer names, encrypted passwords, email addresses, physical addresses, phone numbers, and birthdates; 145 million people were affected.

system without authorization. Most states have similar laws, and nations in Europe have comparable legislation. Congress passed the National Information Infrastructure Protection Act in 1996 to make malware distribution and hacker attacks to disable websites federal crimes.

U.S. legislation, such as the Wiretap Act, Wire Fraud Act, Economic Espionage Act, Electronic Communications Privacy Act, CAN-SPAM Act, and Protect Act of 2003, covers computer crimes involving intercepting electronic communication, using electronic communication to defraud, stealing trade secrets, illegally accessing stored electronic communications, using email for threats or harassment, and transmitting or possessing child pornography. A proposed federal Data Security and Breach Notification Act would mandate organizations that possess personal information to put in place "reasonable" security procedures to keep the data secure and notify anyone affected by a data breach, but it has not been enacted.

Click Fraud

When you click an ad displayed by a search engine, the advertiser typically pays a fee for each click, which is supposed to direct potential buyers to its products. **Click fraud** occurs when an individual or computer program fraudulently clicks an online ad without any intention of learning more about the advertiser or making a purchase. Click fraud has become a serious problem at Google and other websites that feature pay-per-click online advertising.

Some companies hire third parties (typically from low-wage countries) to click a competitor's ads fraudulently to weaken them by driving up their marketing costs. Click fraud can also be perpetrated with software programs doing the clicking, and botnets are often used for this purpose. Search engines such as Google attempt to monitor click fraud and have made some changes to curb it.

Global Threats: Cyberterrorism and Cyberwarfare

The cyber criminal activities we have described—launching malware, DoS attacks, and phishing probes—are borderless. Attack servers for malware are now hosted in more than 200 countries and territories. The leading sources of malware attacks include the United States, China, Brazil, India, Germany, and Russia. The global nature of the Internet makes it possible for cybercriminals to operate—and to do harm—anywhere in the world.

Internet vulnerabilities have also turned individuals and even entire nation-states into easy targets for politically motivated hacking to conduct sabotage and espionage. **Cyberwarfare** is a state-sponsored activity designed to cripple and defeat another state or nation by penetrating its computers or networks to cause damage and disruption. One example is the efforts of Russian hackers to disrupt the U.S. elections described in the chapter-opening case. The infamous 2014 hack on Sony has been attributed to state actors from North Korea. In 2017, the WannaCry and Petya cyber attacks, masquerading as ransomware, caused large-scale disruptions in Ukraine as well as to the UK's National Health Service, pharmaceutical giant Merck, and other organizations around the world. Russians were suspected of conducting a cyberattack on Ukraine during a period of political turmoil in 2014. Cyberwarfare also includes defending against these types of attacks.

Cyberwarfare is more complex than conventional warfare. Although many potential targets are military, a country's power grids, dams, financial systems, communications networks, and even voting systems can also be crippled. Non-state actors such as terrorists or criminal groups can mount attacks, and it is often difficult to tell who is responsible. Nations must constantly be on the alert for new malware and other technologies that could be used against them, and some of these technologies developed by skilled hacker groups are openly for sale to interested governments.

Cyberwarfare attacks have become much more widespread, sophisticated, and potentially devastating. Between 2011 and 2015, foreign hackers stole source code and blueprints to the oil and water pipelines and power grid of the United States and infiltrated the Department of Energy's networks 150 times. Over the years, hackers have stolen plans for missile tracking systems, satellite navigation devices, surveillance drones, and leading-edge jet fighters.

According to U.S. intelligence, more than 30 countries are developing offensive cyberattack capabilities, including Russia, China, Iran, and North Korea. Their cyberarsenals include collections of malware for penetrating industrial, military, and critical civilian infrastructure controllers; email lists and text for phishing attacks on important targets; and algorithms for DoS attacks. U.S. cyberwarfare efforts are concentrated in the United States Cyber Command, which coordinates and directs the operations and defense of Department of Defense information networks and prepares for military cyberspace operations. Cyberwarfare poses a serious threat to the infrastructure of modern societies, since their major financial, health, government, and industrial institutions rely on the Internet for daily operations.

Internal Threats: Employees

We tend to think the security threats to a business originate outside the organization. In fact, company insiders pose serious security problems. Studies have found that user lack of knowledge is the single greatest cause of network security breaches. Many employees forget their passwords to access computer systems or allow coworkers to use them, which compromises the system.

Malicious intruders seeking system access sometimes trick employees into revealing their passwords by pretending to be legitimate members of the company in need of information. This practice is called **social engineering**, and the chapter-opening case shows how it was used to gain access to the Clinton campaign system.

Software Vulnerability

Software errors pose a constant threat to information systems, causing untold losses in productivity and sometimes endangering people who use or depend on systems. Growing complexity and size of software programs, coupled with demands for rapid delivery to markets, have contributed to an increase in software flaws or vulnerabilities. For example, in February 2017 Cloudflare, a service provider that helps optimize website performance and security, reported that it had just fixed a software defect that had leaked sensitive data for months. The data included user passwords, cookies, and other authentication data. Although the amount of data leaked appeared to be small, the bug could have affected any of Cloudflare's 5.5 million customers (McMillan, 2017).

A major problem with software is the presence of hidden **bugs** or program code defects. Studies have shown that it is virtually impossible to eliminate all bugs from large programs. The main source of bugs is the complexity of decision-making code. A relatively small program of several hundred lines will contain tens of decisions leading to hundreds or even thousands of paths. Important programs within most corporations are usually much larger, containing tens of thousands or even millions of lines of code, each with many times the choices and paths of the smaller programs.

Zero defects cannot be achieved in larger programs. Complete testing simply is not possible. Fully testing programs that contain thousands of choices and millions of paths would require thousands of years. Even with rigorous testing, you would not know for sure that a piece of software was dependable until the product proved itself after much operational use.

Flaws in commercial software not only impede performance but also create security vulnerabilities that open networks to intruders. Each year security firms identify thousands of software vulnerabilities in Internet and PC software. An example is the Heartbleed bug, which is a flaw in OpenSSL, an open-source encryption technology that an estimated two-thirds of web servers use. Hackers could exploit the bug to access visitors' personal data as well as a site's encryption keys, which can be used to collect even more protected data.

Especially troublesome are **zero-day vulnerabilities**, which are holes in the software unknown to its creator. Hackers then exploit this security hole before the vendor becomes aware of the problem and hurries to fix it. This type of vulnerability is called *zero-day* because the author of the software has zero days after learning about it to patch the code before it can be exploited in an attack. Sometimes security researchers spot the software holes, but more often, they remain undetected until an attack has occurred.

To correct software flaws once they are identified, the software vendor creates small pieces of software called **patches** to repair the flaws without disturbing the proper operation of the software. It is up to users of the software to track these vulnerabilities, test, and apply all patches. This process is called *patch management*.

Because a company's IT infrastructure is typically laden with multiple business applications, operating system installations, and other system services, maintaining patches on all devices and services a company uses is often time-consuming and costly. Malware is being created so rapidly that companies have very little time to respond between the time a vulnerability and a patch are announced and the time malicious software appears to exploit the vulnerability.

Newly Discovered Vulnerabilities in Microprocessor Design

The Interactive Session on Technology describes newly discovered vulnerabilities stemming from flaws in the design of computer microprocessor chips, which enable hackers using malicious software programs to gain access to data that were thought to be completely protected. These vulnerabilities affect nearly every computer chip manufactured in the last 20 years.

8-2 What is the business value of security and control?

Companies have very valuable information assets to protect. Systems often house confidential information about individuals' taxes, financial assets, medical records, and job performance reviews. They also can contain information on corporate operations, including trade secrets, new product development plans, and marketing strategies. Government systems may store information on weapons systems, intelligence operations, and military targets. These information assets have tremendous value, and the repercussions can be devastating if they are lost, destroyed, or placed in the wrong hands. Systems that are unable to function because of security breaches, disasters, or malfunctioning technology can have permanent impacts on a company's financial health. Some experts believe that 40 percent of all businesses will not recover from application or data losses that are not repaired within three days.

Inadequate security and control may result in serious legal liability. Businesses must protect not only their own information assets but also those of customers, employees, and business partners. Failure to do so may open the firm to costly litigation for data exposure or theft. An organization can be held liable for needless risk and harm created if the organization fails to take appropriate protective action to prevent loss of confidential information, data corruption, or breach of privacy. For example, Target had to pay $39 million to several U.S. banks servicing Mastercard that were forced to reimburse Target customers millions of dollars when those customers lost money due to a massive 2013 hack of Target's payment systems affecting 40 million people. Target also paid $67 million to Visa for the data hack and $10 million to settle a class-action lawsuit brought by Target customers. Developing a sound security and control framework that protects business information assets is of critical importance to the entire enterprise, including senior management. It can no longer be limited to the IT department (Rothrock et al., 2018).

Legal and Regulatory Requirements for Electronic Records Management

U.S. government regulations are forcing companies to take security and control more seriously by mandating the protection of data from abuse, exposure, and unauthorized access. Firms face new legal obligations for the retention and storage of electronic records as well as for privacy protection.

Meltdown and Spectre Haunt the World's Computers

In early January 2018, computer users all over the world were shocked to learn that nearly every computer chip manufactured in the last 20 years contained fundamental security flaws that make it possible for attackers to obtain access to data that were thought to be completely protected. Security researchers had discovered the flaws in late 2017. The flaws arise from features built into the chips that help them run faster. The vulnerability enables a malicious program to gain access to data it should never be able to see.

There are two specific variations of these flaws, called Meltdown and Spectre. Meltdown was so named because it "melts" security boundaries normally enforced by hardware. By exploiting Meltdown, an attacker can use a program running on a computer to gain access to data from all over that machine that the program shouldn't normally be able to see, including data belonging to other programs and data to which only administrators should have access. (A system administrator is responsible for the upkeep, configuration, and reliable operation of computer systems.) Meltdown only affects specific kinds of Intel chips produced since 1995.

Spectre is not manufacturer-specific and affects nearly all modern processors. It requires more intimate knowledge of the victim program's inner workings. Spectre's name comes from speculative execution, in which a chip is able to start work on predicted future operations in order to work faster. In this case, the system is tricked into incorrectly anticipating application behavior. The name also suggests that Spectre will be much more difficult to neutralize. Other attacks in the same family will no doubt be discovered, and Spectre will be haunting us for some time.

With both Meltdown and Spectre, an attacker can make a program reveal some of its own data that should have been kept secret. For example, Spectre could harness JavaScript code on a website to trick a web browser into revealing user and password information. Meltdown could be exploited to view data owned by other users and also virtual servers hosted on the same hardware, which is especially dangerous for cloud computing host computers. The most worrisome aspect of Meltdown and Spectre is that security vulnerabilities are not from flawed software but from the fundamental design of hardware platforms beneath the software.

There is no evidence that Spectre and Meltdown have been exploited, but this would be difficult to detect. Moreover, the security flaws are so fundamental and widespread that they could become catastrophic, especially for cloud computing services where many users share machines. According to researchers at global security software firm McAfee, these vulnerabilities are especially attractive to malicious actors because the attack surface is so unprecedented and the impacts of leaking highly sensitive data are so harmful. According to Forester, performance of laptops, desktops, tablets, and smartphones will be less affected. The fundamental vulnerability behind Meltdown and Spectre is at the hardware level, and thus cannot be patched directly. Technology software vendors are only able to release software fixes that work around the problems. Such fixes mitigate vulnerabilities by altering or disabling the way software code makes use of speculative execution and caching features built into the underlying hardware. (Caching is a technique to speed computer memory access by locating a small amount of memory storage on the CPU chip rather than from a separate RAM chip for memory.) Since these features were designed to improve system performance, working around them can slow systems down. Experts initially predicted system performance could be degraded as much as 30 percent, but a slowdown of 5 to 10 percent seems more typical.

Major software vendors have rolled out workaround patches. Cloud vendors have taken measures to patch their underlying infrastructures, with their customers expected to install the patches for their operating systems and applications. Microsoft released operating system patches for Windows 7 and all later versions, which also apply to Microsoft's Internet Explorer and Edge browsers. Apple released patched versions of its Safari browser and iOS, macOS, and tvOS operating systems. Google provided a list of which Chromebook models will or won't need patches and released a patch for its Chrome browser. Older operating systems such as Windows XP and millions of third-party low-cost Android phones that don't get security updates from Google will most likely never be patched. Organizations should apply updates and patches to browser software as soon as they are available. And since these vulnerabilities could enable attackers to steal passwords from user device memory when running JavaScript from a web page, it is recommended that users be instructed to always close their web browsers when not in use. Forrester also recommends that enterprises should use other techniques to protect data from users and organizations that have not applied the fixes.

However, the only way to truly fix Meltdown and Spectre is to replace affected processors. Redesigning

and producing new processors and architectures may take five to ten years to hit the market. If anything good can be said about Spectre and Meltdown, it is that they have focused more global attention on software and hardware security and the need to develop more robust system architectures for secure computing.

Sources: Josh Fruhlinger, "Spectre and Meltdown Explained: What They Are, How They Work, What's at Risk," *CSO*, January 15, 2018; Warwick Ashford, "Meltdown and Spectre a Big Deal for Enterprises," *Computer Weekly*, January 9, 2018; Laura Hautala, "Spectre and Meltdown: Details You Need on Those Big Chip Flaws," CNET, January 8, 2018.

CASE STUDY QUESTIONS

1. How dangerous are Spectre and Meltdown? Explain your answer.
2. Compare the threats of Spectre and Meltdown to cloud computing centers, corporate data centers, and individual computer and smartphone users.
3. How would you protect against Spectre and Meltdown if you were running a public cloud computing center, if you ran a corporate data center, and if you were an individual computer user?

If you work in the healthcare industry, your firm will need to comply with the Health Insurance Portability and Accountability Act (HIPAA) of 1996. **HIPAA** outlines medical security and privacy rules and procedures for simplifying the administration of healthcare billing and automating the transfer of healthcare data between healthcare providers, payers, and plans. It requires members of the healthcare industry to retain patient information for six years and ensure the confidentiality of those records. It specifies privacy, security, and electronic transaction standards for healthcare providers handling patient information, providing penalties for breaches of medical privacy, disclosure of patient records by email, or unauthorized network access.

If you work in a firm providing financial services, your firm will need to comply with the Financial Services Modernization Act of 1999, better known as the **Gramm-Leach-Bliley Act** after its congressional sponsors. This act requires financial institutions to ensure the security and confidentiality of customer data. Data must be stored on a secure medium, and special security measures must be enforced to protect such data on storage media and during transmittal.

If you work in a publicly traded company, your company will need to comply with the Public Company Accounting Reform and Investor Protection Act of 2002, better known as the **Sarbanes-Oxley Act** after its sponsors Senator Paul Sarbanes of Maryland and Representative Michael Oxley of Ohio. This act was designed to protect investors after the financial scandals at Enron, WorldCom, and other public companies. It imposes responsibility on companies and their management to safeguard the accuracy and integrity of financial information that is used internally and released externally. One of the Learning Tracks for this chapter discusses Sarbanes-Oxley in detail.

Sarbanes-Oxley is fundamentally about ensuring that internal controls are in place to govern the creation and documentation of information in financial statements. Because information systems are used to generate, store, and transport such data, the legislation requires firms to consider information systems security and other controls required to ensure the integrity, confidentiality, and accuracy of their data. Each system application that deals with critical financial reporting data requires controls to make sure the data are accurate. Controls to secure the corporate network, prevent unauthorized access to systems and data, and ensure data integrity and availability in the event of disaster or other disruption of service are essential as well.

Electronic Evidence and Computer Forensics

Security, control, and electronic records management have become essential for responding to legal actions. Much of the evidence today for stock fraud, embezzlement, theft of company trade secrets, computer crime, and many civil cases is in digital form. In addition to information from printed or typewritten pages, legal cases today increasingly rely on evidence represented as digital data stored on portable storage devices, CDs, and computer hard disk drives as well as in email, instant messages, and e-commerce transactions over the Internet.

In a legal action, a firm is obligated to respond to a discovery request for access to information that may be used as evidence, and the company is required by law to produce those data. The cost of responding to a discovery request can be enormous if the company has trouble assembling the required data or the data have been corrupted or destroyed. Courts now impose severe financial and even criminal penalties for improper destruction of electronic documents.

An effective electronic document retention policy ensures that electronic documents, email, and other records are well organized, accessible, and neither retained too long nor discarded too soon. It also reflects an awareness of how to preserve potential evidence for computer forensics. **Computer forensics** is the scientific collection, examination, authentication, preservation, and analysis of data held on or retrieved from computer storage media in such a way that the information can be used as evidence in a court of law. It deals with the following problems:

- Recovering data from computers while preserving evidential integrity
- Securely storing and handling recovered electronic data
- Finding significant information in a large volume of electronic data
- Presenting the information to a court of law

Electronic evidence may reside on computer storage media in the form of computer files and as *ambient data*, which are not visible to the average user. An example might be a file that has been deleted on a PC hard drive. Data that a computer user may have deleted on computer storage media can often be recovered through various techniques. Computer forensics experts try to recover such hidden data for presentation as evidence.

An awareness of computer forensics should be incorporated into a firm's contingency planning process. The CIO, security specialists, information systems staff, and corporate legal counsel should all work together to have a plan in place that can be executed if a legal need arises. You can find out more about computer forensics in the Learning Tracks for this chapter.

8-3 What are the components of an organizational framework for security and control?

Even with the best security tools, your information systems won't be reliable and secure unless you know how and where to deploy them. You'll need to know where your company is at risk and what controls you must have in place to protect your information systems. You'll also need to develop a security policy and plans for keeping your business running if your information systems aren't operational.

Information Systems Controls

Information systems controls are both manual and automated and consist of general and application controls. **General controls** govern the design, security, and use of computer programs and the security of data files in general throughout the organization's information technology infrastructure. On the whole, general controls apply to all computerized applications and consist of a combination of hardware, software, and manual procedures that create an overall control environment.

General controls include software controls, physical hardware controls, computer operations controls, data security controls, controls over the systems development process, and administrative controls. Table 8.4 describes the functions of each of these controls.

Application controls are specific controls unique to each computerized application, such as payroll or order processing. They include both automated and manual procedures that ensure that only authorized data are completely and accurately processed by that application. Application controls can be classified as (1) input controls, (2) processing controls, and (3) output controls.

Input controls check data for accuracy and completeness when they enter the system. There are specific input controls for input authorization, data conversion, data editing, and error handling. *Processing controls* establish that data are complete and accurate during updating. *Output controls ensure* that the results of

TABLE 8.4 GENERAL CONTROLS

TYPE OF GENERAL CONTROL	DESCRIPTION
Software controls	Monitor the use of system software and prevent unauthorized access and use of software programs, system software, and computer programs.
Hardware controls	Ensure that computer hardware is physically secure and check for equipment malfunction. Organizations that are critically dependent on their computers also must make provisions for backup or continued operation to maintain constant service.
Computer operations controls	Oversee the work of the computer department to ensure that programmed procedures are consistently and correctly applied to the storage and processing of data. They include controls over the setup of computer processing jobs and backup and recovery procedures for processing that ends abnormally.
Data security controls	Ensure that valuable business data files maintained internally or by an external hosting service are not subject to unauthorized access, change, or destruction while they are in use or in storage.
Implementation controls	Audit the systems development process at various points to ensure that the process is properly controlled and managed.
Administrative controls	Formalize standards, rules, procedures, and control disciplines to ensure that the organization's general and application controls are properly executed and enforced.

computer processing are accurate, complete, and properly distributed. You can find more detail about application and general controls in our Learning Tracks.

Information systems controls should not be an afterthought. They need to be incorporated into the design of a system and should consider not only how the system will perform under all possible conditions but also the behavior of organizations and people using the system.

Risk Assessment

Before your company commits resources to security and information systems controls, it must know which assets require protection and the extent to which these assets are vulnerable. A risk assessment helps answer these questions and determine the most cost-effective set of controls for protecting assets.

A **risk assessment** determines the level of risk to the firm if a specific activity or process is not properly controlled. Not all risks can be anticipated and measured, but most businesses will be able to acquire some understanding of the risks they face. Business managers working with information systems specialists should try to determine the value of information assets, points of vulnerability, the likely frequency of a problem, and the potential for damage. For example, if an event is likely to occur no more than once a year, with a maximum of a $1000 loss to the organization, it is not wise to spend $20,000 on the design and maintenance of a control to protect against that event. However, if that same event could occur at least once a day, with a potential loss of more than $300,000 a year, $100,000 spent on a control might be entirely appropriate.

Table 8.5 illustrates sample results of a risk assessment for an online order processing system that processes 30,000 orders per day. The likelihood of each exposure occurring over a one-year period is expressed as a percentage. The next column shows the highest and lowest possible loss that could be expected each time the exposure occurred and an average loss calculated by adding the highest and lowest figures and dividing by two. The expected annual loss for each exposure can be determined by multiplying the average loss by its probability of occurrence.

This risk assessment shows that the probability of a power failure occurring in a one-year period is 30 percent. Loss of order transactions while power is down could range from $5000 to $200,000 (averaging $102,500) for each occurrence, depending on how long processing is halted. The probability of embezzlement occurring over a yearly period is about 5 percent, with potential losses ranging from $1000 to $50,000 (and averaging $25,500) for each occurrence. User errors have a 98 percent chance of occurring over a yearly period, with losses ranging from $200 to $40,000 (and averaging $20,100) for each occurrence.

After the risks have been assessed, system builders will concentrate on the control points with the greatest vulnerability and potential for loss. In this case, controls should focus on ways to minimize the risk of power failures and user errors because anticipated annual losses are highest for these areas.

TABLE 8.5 ONLINE ORDER PROCESSING RISK ASSESSMENT

EXPOSURE	PROBABILITY OF OCCURRENCE (%)	LOSS RANGE/AVERAGE ($)	EXPECTED ANNUAL LOSS ($)
Power failure	30%	$5000–$200,000 ($102,500)	$30,750
Embezzlement	5%	$1000–$50,000 ($25,500)	$1275
User error	98%	$200–$40,000 ($20,100)	$19,698

Security Policy

After you've identified the main risks to your systems, your company will need to develop a security policy for protecting the company's assets. A **security policy** consists of statements ranking information risks, identifying acceptable security goals, and identifying the mechanisms for achieving these goals. What are the firm's most important information assets? Who generates and controls this information in the firm? What existing security policies are in place to protect the information? What level of risk is management willing to accept for each of these assets? Is it willing, for instance, to lose customer credit data once every 10 years? Or will it build a security system for credit card data that can withstand the once-in-a-hundred-years disaster? Management must estimate how much it will cost to achieve this level of acceptable risk.

The security policy drives other policies determining acceptable use of the firm's information resources and which members of the company have access to its information assets. An **acceptable use policy (AUP)** defines acceptable uses of the firm's information resources and computing equipment, including desktop and laptop computers, mobile devices, telephones, and the Internet. A good AUP defines unacceptable and acceptable actions for every user and specifies consequences for noncompliance.

Figure 8.3 is one example of how an organization might specify the access rules for different levels of users in the human resources function. It specifies what portions of a human resource database each user is permitted to access, based on the information required to perform that person's job. The database contains sensitive personal information such as employees' salaries, benefits, and medical histories.

FIGURE 8.3 ACCESS RULES FOR A PERSONNEL SYSTEM

These two examples represent two security profiles or data security patterns that might be found in a personnel system. Depending on the security profile, a user would have certain restrictions on access to various systems, locations, or data in an organization.

SECURITY PROFILE 1	
User: Personnel Dept. Clerk	
Location: Division 1	
Employee Identification Codes with This Profile:	00753, 27834, 37665, 44116
Data Field Restrictions	Type of Access
All employee data for Division 1 only	Read and Update
• Medical history data	None
• Salary	None
• Pensionable earnings	None

SECURITY PROFILE 2	
User: Divisional Personnel Manager	
Location: Division 1	
Employee Identification Codes with This Profile: 27321	
Data Field Restrictions	Type of Access
All employee data for Division 1 only	Read Only

The access rules illustrated here are for two sets of users. One set of users consists of all employees who perform clerical functions, such as inputting employee data into the system. All individuals with this type of profile can update the system but can neither read nor update sensitive fields, such as salary, medical history, or earnings data. Another profile applies to a divisional manager, who cannot update the system but who can read all employee data fields for his or her division, including medical history and salary. We provide more detail about the technologies for user authentication later on in this chapter.

Disaster Recovery Planning and Business Continuity Planning

If you run a business, you need to plan for events, such as power outages, floods, earthquakes, or terrorist attacks, that will prevent your information systems and your business from operating. **Disaster recovery planning** devises plans for the restoration of disrupted computing and communications services. Disaster recovery plans focus primarily on the technical issues involved in keeping systems up and running, such as which files to back up and the maintenance of backup computer systems or disaster recovery services.

For example, MasterCard maintains a duplicate computer center in Kansas City, Missouri, to serve as an emergency backup to its primary computer center in St. Louis. Rather than build their own backup facilities, many firms contract with cloud-based disaster recovery services or firms such as SunGard Availability Services that provide sites with spare computers around the country where subscribing firms can run their critical applications in an emergency.

Business continuity planning focuses on how the company can restore business operations after a disaster strikes. The business continuity plan identifies critical business processes and determines action plans for handling mission-critical functions if systems go down. For example, Healthways, a well-being improvement company headquartered in Franklin, Tennessee, implemented a business continuity plan that identified the business processes of nearly 70 departments across the enterprise and the impact of system downtime on those processes. Healthways pinpointed its most critical processes and worked with each department to devise an action plan.

Business managers and information technology specialists need to work together on both types of plans to determine which systems and business processes are most critical to the company. They must conduct a business impact analysis to identify the firm's most critical systems and the impact a systems outage would have on the business. Management must determine the maximum amount of time the business can survive with its systems down and which parts of the business must be restored first.

The Role of Auditing

How does management know that information systems security and controls are effective? To answer this question, organizations must conduct comprehensive and systematic audits. An **information systems audit** examines the firm's overall security environment as well as controls governing individual information systems. The auditor should trace the flow of sample transactions through the system and perform tests, using, if appropriate, automated audit software. The information systems audit may also examine data quality.

FIGURE 8.4 SAMPLE AUDITOR'S LIST OF CONTROL WEAKNESSES

This chart is a sample page from a list of control weaknesses that an auditor might find in a loan system in a local commercial bank. This form helps auditors record and evaluate control weaknesses and shows the results of discussing those weaknesses with management as well as any corrective actions management takes.

Function: Loans Location: Peoria, IL		Prepared by: J. Ericson Date: June 16, 2018		Received by: T. Benson Review date: June 28, 2018	
Nature of Weakness and Impact	**Chance for Error/Abuse**		**Notification to Management**		
	Yes/ No	Justification	Report date	Management response	
User accounts with missing passwords	Yes	Leaves system open to unauthorized outsiders or attackers	5/10/18	Eliminate accounts without passwords	
Network configured to allow some sharing of system files	Yes	Exposes critical system files to hostile parties connected to the network	5/10/18	Ensure only required directories are shared and that they are protected with strong passwords	
Software patches can update production programs without final approval from Standards and Controls group	No	All production programs require management approval; Standards and Controls group assigns such cases to a temporary production status			

Security audits review technologies, procedures, documentation, training, and personnel. A thorough audit will even simulate an attack or disaster to test the response of the technology, information systems staff, and business employees.

The audit lists and ranks all control weaknesses and estimates the probability of their occurrence. It then assesses the financial and organizational impact of each threat. Figure 8.4 is a sample auditor's listing of control weaknesses for a loan system. It includes a section for notifying management of such weaknesses and for management's response. Management is expected to devise a plan for countering significant weaknesses in controls.

8-4 What are the most important tools and technologies for safeguarding information resources?

Businesses have an array of technologies for protecting their information resources. They include tools for managing user identities, preventing unauthorized access to systems and data, ensuring system availability, and ensuring software quality.

Identity Management and Authentication

Midsize and large companies have complex IT infrastructures and many systems, each with its own set of users. **Identity management** software automates the process of keeping track of all these users and their system privileges, assigning each user a unique digital identity for accessing each system. It also includes tools for authenticating users, protecting user identities, and controlling access to system resources.

To gain access to a system, a user must be authorized and authenticated. **Authentication** refers to the ability to know that a person is who he or she claims to be. Authentication is often established by using **passwords** known only to authorized users. An end user uses a password to log on to a computer system and may also use passwords for accessing specific systems and files. However, users often forget passwords, share them, or choose poor passwords that are easy to guess, which compromises security. Password systems that are too rigorous hinder employee productivity. When employees must change complex passwords frequently, they often take shortcuts, such as choosing passwords that are easy to guess or keeping their passwords at their workstations in plain view. Passwords can also be sniffed if transmitted over a network or stolen through social engineering.

New authentication technologies, such as tokens, smart cards, and biometric authentication, overcome some of these problems. A **token** is a physical device, similar to an identification card, that is designed to prove the identity of a single user. Tokens are small gadgets that typically fit on key rings and display passcodes that change frequently. A **smart card** is a device about the size of a credit card that contains a chip formatted with access permission and other data. (Smart cards are also used in electronic payment systems.) A reader device interprets the data on the smart card and allows or denies access.

Biometric authentication uses systems that read and interpret individual human traits, such as fingerprints, irises, and voices to grant or deny access. Biometric authentication is based on the measurement of a physical or behavioral trait that makes each individual unique. It compares a person's unique characteristics, such as the fingerprints, face, voice, or retinal image, against a stored profile of these characteristics to determine any differences between these characteristics and the stored profile. If the two profiles match, access is granted. Fingerprint and facial recognition technologies are just beginning

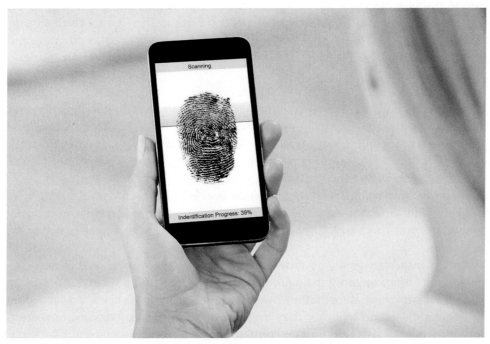

This smartphone has a biometric fingerprint reader for fast yet secure access to files and networks. New models of PCs and smartphones are starting to use biometric identification to authenticate users.

to be used for security applications, with many PC laptops (and some smartphones) equipped with fingerprint identification devices and some models with built-in webcams and face recognition software. Financial service firms such as Vanguard and Fidelity have implemented voice authentication systems for their clients.

The steady stream of incidents in which hackers have been able to access traditional passwords highlights the need for more secure means of authentication. **Two-factor authentication** increases security by validating users through a multistep process. To be authenticated, a user must provide two means of identification, one of which is typically a physical token, such as a smartcard or chip-enabled bank card, and the other of which is typically data, such as a password or personal identification number (PIN). Biometric data, such as fingerprints, iris prints, or voice prints, can also be used as one of the authenticating mechanisms. A common example of two-factor authentication is a bank card; the card itself is the physical item, and the PIN is the other piece of data that goes with it.

Firewalls, Intrusion Detection Systems, and Anti-malware Software

Without protection against malware and intruders, connecting to the Internet would be very dangerous. Firewalls, intrusion detection systems, and anti-malware software have become essential business tools.

Firewalls

Firewalls prevent unauthorized users from accessing private networks. A firewall is a combination of hardware and software that controls the flow of incoming and outgoing network traffic. It is generally placed between the organization's private internal networks and distrusted external networks, such as the Internet, although firewalls can also be used to protect one part of a company's network from the rest of the network (see Figure 8.5).

The firewall acts like a gatekeeper that examines each user's credentials before it grants access to a network. The firewall identifies names, IP addresses, applications, and other characteristics of incoming traffic. It checks this information against the access rules that the network administrator has programmed into the system. The firewall prevents unauthorized communication into and out of the network.

In large organizations, the firewall often resides on a specially designated computer separate from the rest of the network, so no incoming request directly accesses private network resources. There are a number of firewall screening technologies, including static packet filtering, stateful inspection, Network Address Translation, and application proxy filtering. They are frequently used in combination to provide firewall protection.

Packet filtering examines selected fields in the headers of data packets flowing back and forth between the trusted network and the Internet, examining individual packets in isolation. This filtering technology can miss many types of attacks.

Stateful inspection provides additional security by determining whether packets are part of an ongoing dialogue between a sender and a receiver. It sets up state tables to track information over multiple packets. Packets are accepted or rejected based on whether they are part of an approved conversation or attempting to establish a legitimate connection.

FIGURE 8.5 A CORPORATE FIREWALL

The firewall is placed between the firm's private network and the public Internet or another distrusted network to protect against unauthorized traffic.

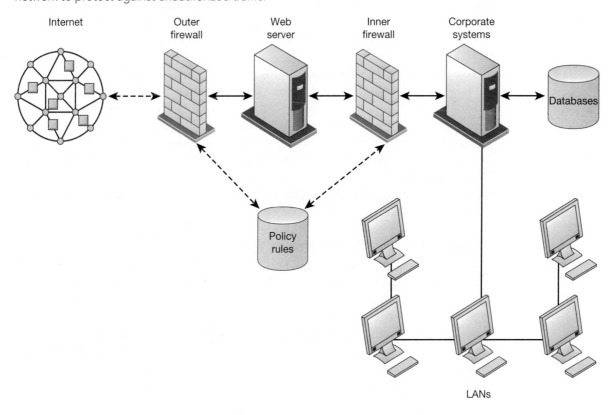

Network Address Translation (NAT) can provide another layer of protection when static packet filtering and stateful inspection are employed. NAT conceals the IP addresses of the organization's internal host computer(s) to prevent sniffer programs outside the firewall from ascertaining them and using that information to penetrate internal systems.

Application proxy filtering examines the application content of packets. A proxy server stops data packets originating outside the organization, inspects them, and passes a proxy to the other side of the firewall. If a user outside the company wants to communicate with a user inside the organization, the outside user first communicates with the proxy application, and the proxy application communicates with the firm's internal computer. Likewise, a computer user inside the organization goes through the proxy to talk with computers on the outside.

To create a good firewall, an administrator must maintain detailed internal rules identifying the people, applications, or addresses that are allowed or rejected. Firewalls can deter, but not completely prevent, network penetration by outsiders and should be viewed as one element in an overall security plan.

Intrusion Detection Systems

In addition to firewalls, commercial security vendors now provide intrusion detection tools and services to protect against suspicious network traffic and attempts to access files and databases. **Intrusion detection systems** feature full-time monitoring tools placed at the most vulnerable points or hot spots of corporate networks to detect and deter intruders continually. The system generates an alarm if it finds a suspicious or anomalous event. Scanning software looks for patterns indicative of known methods of computer attacks such as bad passwords, checks to see whether important files have been removed or modified, and sends warnings of vandalism or system administration errors. The intrusion detection tool can also be customized to shut down a particularly sensitive part of a network if it receives unauthorized traffic.

Anti-malware Software

Defensive technology plans for both individuals and businesses must include anti-malware protection for every computer. **Anti-malware software** prevents, detects, and removes malware, including computer viruses, computer worms, Trojan horses, spyware, and adware. However, most anti-malware software is effective only against malware already known when the software was written. To remain effective, the software must be continually updated. Even then it is not always effective because some malware can evade detection. Organizations need to use additional malware detection tools for better protection.

Unified Threat Management Systems

To help businesses reduce costs and improve manageability, security vendors have combined into a single appliance various security tools, including firewalls, virtual private networks, intrusion detection systems, and web content filtering and anti-spam software. These comprehensive security management products are called **unified threat management (UTM)** systems. UTM products are available for all sizes of networks. Leading UTM vendors include Fortinet, Sophos, and Check Point, and networking vendors such as Cisco Systems and Juniper Networks provide some UTM capabilities in their products.

Securing Wireless Networks

The initial security standard developed for Wi-Fi, called Wired Equivalent Privacy (WEP), is not very effective because its encryption keys are relatively easy to crack. WEP provides some margin of security, however, if users remember to enable it. Corporations can further improve Wi-Fi security by using it in conjunction with virtual private network (VPN) technology when accessing internal corporate data.

In June 2004, the Wi-Fi Alliance industry trade group finalized the 802.11i specification (also referred to as Wi-Fi Protected Access 2 or WPA2) that replaces WEP with stronger security standards. Instead of the static encryption keys used in WEP, the new standard uses much longer keys that continually change, making them harder to crack. The most recent specification is WPA3, introduced in 2018.

Encryption and Public Key Infrastructure

Many businesses use encryption to protect digital information that they store, physically transfer, or send over the Internet. **Encryption** is the process of transforming plain text or data into cipher text that cannot be read by anyone other than the sender and the intended receiver. Data are encrypted by using a secret numerical code, called an encryption key, that transforms plain data into cipher text. The message must be decrypted by the receiver.

Two methods for encrypting network traffic on the web are SSL and S-HTTP. **Secure Sockets Layer (SSL)** and its successor, Transport Layer Security (TLS), enable client and server computers to manage encryption and decryption activities as they communicate with each other during a secure web session. **Secure Hypertext Transfer Protocol (S-HTTP)** is another protocol used for encrypting data flowing over the Internet, but it is limited to individual messages, whereas SSL and TLS are designed to establish a secure connection between two computers.

The capability to generate secure sessions is built into Internet client browser software and servers. The client and the server negotiate what key and what level of security to use. Once a secure session is established between the client and the server, all messages in that session are encrypted.

Two methods of encryption are symmetric key encryption and public key encryption. In symmetric key encryption, the sender and receiver establish a secure Internet session by creating a single encryption key and sending it to the receiver so both the sender and receiver share the same key. The strength of the encryption key is measured by its bit length. Today, a typical key will be 56 to 256 bits long (a string of from 56 to 256 binary digits) depending on the level of security desired. The longer the key, the more difficult it is to break the key. The downside is that the longer the key, the more computing power it takes for legitimate users to process the information.

The problem with all symmetric encryption schemes is that the key itself must be shared somehow among the senders and receivers, which exposes the key to outsiders who might just be able to intercept and decrypt the key. A more secure form of encryption called **public key encryption** uses two keys: one shared (or public) and one totally private as shown in Figure 8.6. The keys are mathematically related so that data encrypted with one key can be decrypted using only the other key. To send and receive messages, communicators first create separate pairs of private and public keys. The public key is kept in a directory, and the private key must be kept secret. The sender encrypts a message with the recipient's public key. On receiving the message, the recipient uses his or her private key to decrypt it.

Digital certificates are data files used to establish the identity of users and electronic assets for protection of online transactions (see Figure 8.7). A digital certificate system uses a trusted third party, known as a certificate authority (CA), to validate a user's identity. There are many CAs in the United States and around the world, including Symantec, GoDaddy, and Comodo.

The CA verifies a digital certificate user's identity offline. This information is put into a CA server, which generates an encrypted digital certificate containing owner identification information and a copy of the owner's public key. The certificate authenticates that the public key belongs to the designated owner.

FIGURE 8.6 PUBLIC KEY ENCRYPTION

A public key encryption system can be viewed as a series of public and private keys that lock data when they are transmitted and unlock data when they are received. The sender locates the recipient's public key in a directory and uses it to encrypt a message. The message is sent in encrypted form over the Internet or a private network. When the encrypted message arrives, the recipient uses his or her private key to decrypt the data and read the message.

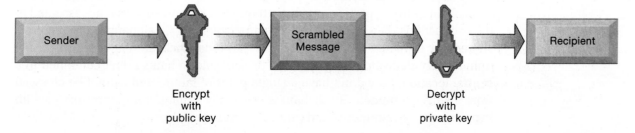

FIGURE 8.7 DIGITAL CERTIFICATES

Digital certificates help establish the identity of people or electronic assets. They protect online transactions by providing secure, encrypted, online communication.

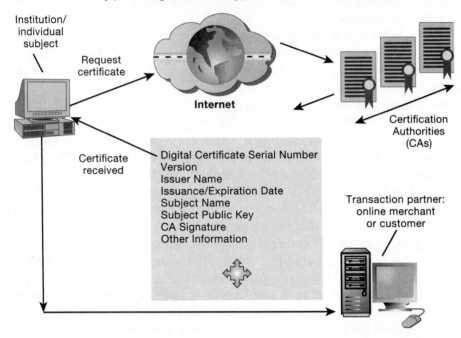

The CA makes its own public key available either in print or perhaps on the Internet. The recipient of an encrypted message uses the CA's public key to decode the digital certificate attached to the message, verifies it was issued by the CA, and then obtains the sender's public key and identification information contained in the certificate. By using this information, the recipient can send an encrypted reply. The digital certificate system would enable, for example, a credit card user and a merchant to validate that their digital certificates were issued by an authorized and trusted third party before they exchange data. **Public key infrastructure (PKI)**, the use of public key cryptography working with a CA, is now widely used in e-commerce.

Securing Transactions with Blockchain

Blockchain, which we introduced in Chapter 6, is gaining attention as an alternative approach for securing transactions and establishing trust among multiple parties. A blockchain is a chain of digital "blocks" that contain records of transactions. Each block is connected to all the blocks before and after it, and the blockchains are continually updated and kept in sync This makes it difficult to tamper with a single record because one would have to change the block containing that record as well as those linked to it to avoid detection.

Once recorded, a blockchain transaction cannot be changed. The records in a blockchain are secured through cryptography, and all transactions are encrypted. Blockchain network participants have their own private keys that are assigned to the transactions they create and act as a personal digital signature. If a record is altered, the signature will become invalid, and the blockchain network will know immediately that something is amiss. Because blockchains aren't contained in a central location, they don't have a single point of failure and cannot be changed from a single computer. Blockchain is especially suitable for environments with high security requirements and mutually unknown actors.

Ensuring System Availability

As companies increasingly rely on digital networks for revenue and operations, they need to take additional steps to ensure that their systems and applications are always available. Firms such as those in the airline and financial services industries with critical applications requiring online transaction processing have traditionally used fault-tolerant computer systems for many years to ensure 100 percent availability. In **online transaction processing**, transactions entered online are immediately processed by the computer. Multitudinous changes to databases, reporting, and requests for information occur each instant.

Fault-tolerant computer systems contain redundant hardware, software, and power supply components that create an environment that provides continuous, uninterrupted service. Fault-tolerant computers use special software routines or self-checking logic built into their circuitry to detect hardware failures and automatically switch to a backup device. Parts from these computers can be removed and repaired without disruption to the computer or downtime. **Downtime** refers to periods of time in which a system is not operational.

Controlling Network Traffic: Deep Packet Inspection

Have you ever tried to use your campus network and found that it was very slow? It may be because your fellow students are using the network to download music or watch YouTube. Bandwidth-consuming applications such as file-sharing programs, Internet phone service, and online video can clog and slow down corporate networks, degrading performance. A technology called **deep packet inspection (DPI)** helps solve this problem. DPI examines data files and sorts out low-priority online material while assigning higher priority to business-critical files. Based on the priorities established by a network's operators, it decides whether a specific data packet can continue to its destination or should be blocked or delayed while more important traffic proceeds.

Security Outsourcing

Many companies, especially small businesses, lack the resources or expertise to provide a secure high-availability computing environment on their own. They can outsource many security functions to **managed security service providers (MSSPs)** that monitor network activity and perform vulnerability testing and intrusion detection. SecureWorks, AT&T, Verizon, IBM, Perimeter eSecurity, and Symantec are leading providers of MSSP services.

Security Issues for Cloud Computing and the Mobile Digital Platform

Although cloud computing and the emerging mobile digital platform have the potential to deliver powerful benefits, they pose new challenges to system security and reliability. We now describe some of these challenges and how they should be addressed.

Security in the Cloud

When processing takes place in the cloud, accountability and responsibility for protection of sensitive data still reside with the company owning that data. Understanding how the cloud computing provider organizes its services and manages the data is critical (see the Interactive Session on Management).

INTERACTIVE SESSION MANAGEMENT

How Secure Is the Cloud?

Over the last several years, many companies have altered their IT strategies to shift an increasing share of their applications and data to public-cloud infrastructure and platforms. However, using the public cloud disrupts traditional cybersecurity models that many companies have built up over years. As a result, as companies make use of the public cloud, they need to revise their cybersecurity practices in order to consume public-cloud services in a way that enables them both to protect critical data and to fully exploit the speed and agility that these services provide.

Managing security and privacy for cloud services is similar to managing traditional IT infrastructures. However, the risks may be different because some, but not all, responsibilities shift to the cloud service provider. The category of cloud service (IaaS, PaaS, or SaaS) affects exactly how these responsibilities are shared. For IaaS, the provider typically supplies and is responsible for securing basic IT resources such as machines, storage systems, and networks. The cloud services customer is typically responsible for its operating system, applications, and corporate data placed into the cloud computing environment. This means that most of the responsibility for securing the applications and the corporate data falls on the customer.

Cloud service customers should carefully review their cloud services agreement with their cloud provider to make sure their applications and data hosted in cloud services are secured in accordance with their security and compliance policies. But that's not all. Although many organizations know how to manage security for their own data center—they're unsure of exactly what they need to do when they shift computing work to the cloud. They need new tool sets and skill sets to manage cloud security from their end to configure and launch cloud instances, manage identity and access controls, update security controls to match configuration changes, and protect workloads and data. There's a misconception among many IT departments that whatever happens in the cloud is not their responsibility. It is essential to update security requirements developed for enterprise data centers to produce requirements suitable for the use of cloud services. Organizations using cloud services often need to apply additional controls at the user, application, and data level.

Cloud service providers have made great strides in tightening security for their areas of responsibility. Amazon's security for its cloud service leaves little to chance. The company keeps careful constraints around its staff, watches what they do every day, and instructs service teams to restrict access to data through tooling and automation. Amazon also rotates security credentials for authentication and verification of identity and changes them frequently—sometimes in a matter of hours.

The biggest threats to cloud data for most companies involve lack of software patching or misconfiguration. Many organizations have been breached because they neglected to apply software patches to newly identified security vulnerabilities when they became available or waited too long to do so. (See the discussion of patch management earlier in this chapter.) Companies have also experienced security breaches because they did not configure aspects of cloud security that were their responsibility. Some users forget to set up AWS bucket password protection. (A bucket is a logical unit of storage in Amazon Web Services [AWS] Simple Storage Solution S3 storage service. Buckets are used to store objects, which consist of data and metadata that describes the data.) Others don't understand basic security features in Amazon such as resource-based access policies (access control lists) or bucket permissions checks, unwittingly exposing data to the public Internet.

Financial publisher Dow Jones & Co. confirmed reports in July 2017 that it may have publicly exposed personal and financial information of 2.2 million customers, including subscribers to *The Wall Street Journal* and *Barron's*. The leak was traced back to a configuration error in a repository in AWS S3 security. Dow Jones had intended to provide semi-public access to select customers over the Internet. However, it wound up granting access to download the data via a URL to "authenticated users," which included anyone who registered (for free) for an AWS account. Accenture, Verizon, Viacom, Tesla, and Uber Technologies are other high-profile names in the steady stream of companies that have exposed sensitive information via AWS S3 security misconfigurations. Such misconfigurations were often performed by employees who lacked security experience when security configurations should have been handled by skilled IT professionals. Stopping AWS bucket misconfigurations may also require enacting policies that limit the damage caused by careless or untrained employees.

Although customers have their choice of security configurations for the cloud, Amazon has been taking its own steps to prevent misconfigurations. In November 2017, the company updated its AWS dashboard, encasing *public* in bright orange on the AWS S3 console so that cloud customers could easily see the status of access permissions to buckets and their objects. This helps everyone see more

easily when an Amazon S3 bucket is open to the public. Amazon also added default encryption to all objects when they are stored in an AWS bucket and access control lists for cross-region replication. Another new tool called Zelkova examines AWS S3 security policies to help users identify which one is more permissive than the others. Amazon Macie is a managed service that uses machine learning to detect personally identifiable information and intellectual property, and has been available for S3 since August 2017.

Sources: Kathleen Richards, "New Cloud Threats as Attackers Embrace the Power of the Cloud," SearchCloudSecurity.com, April 3, 2018; "AWS S3 Security Falls Short at High-profile Companies," SearchCloudSecurity.com, April 2018; "Making a Secure Transition to the Public Cloud," *McKinsey & Company,* January 2018; and "Security for Cloud Computing: Ten Steps to Ensure Success," Cloud Standards Customer Council, December 2017.

CASE STUDY QUESTIONS

1. What kinds of security problems does cloud computing pose? How serious are they? Explain your answer.

2. What management, organization, and technology factors are responsible for cloud security problems? To what extent is cloud security a management issue?

3. What steps can organizations take to make their cloud-based systems more secure?

4. Should companies use the public cloud to run their mission-critical systems? Why or why not?

Cloud computing is highly distributed. Cloud applications reside in large remote data centers and server farms that supply business services and data management for multiple corporate clients. To save money and keep costs low, cloud computing providers often distribute work to data centers around the globe where work can be accomplished most efficiently. When you use the cloud, you may not know precisely where your data are being hosted.

Virtually all cloud providers use encryption to secure the data they handle while the data are being transmitted. However, if the data are stored on devices that also store other companies' data, it's important to ensure that these stored data are encrypted as well. DDoS attacks are especially harmful because they render cloud services unavailable to legitimate customers.

Companies expect their systems to be running 24/7. Cloud providers still experience occasional outages, but their reliability has increased to the point where a number of large companies are using cloud services for part of their IT infrastructures. Most keep their critical systems in-house or in private clouds.

Cloud users need to confirm that regardless of where their data are stored, they are protected at a level that meets their corporate requirements. They should stipulate that the cloud provider store and process data in specific jurisdictions according to the privacy rules of those jurisdictions. Cloud clients should find how the cloud provider segregates their corporate data from those of other companies and ask for proof that encryption mechanisms are sound. It's also important to know how the cloud provider will respond if a disaster strikes, whether the provider will be able to restore your data completely, and how long this should take. Cloud users should also ask whether cloud providers will submit to external audits and security certifications. These kinds of controls can be written into the service level agreement (SLA) before signing with a cloud provider. The Cloud Security Alliance (CSA) has created industrywide standards for cloud security, specifying best practices to secure cloud computing.

Securing Mobile Platforms

If mobile devices are performing many of the functions of computers, they need to be secured like desktops and laptops against malware, theft, accidental loss, unauthorized access, and hacking attempts. Mobile devices accessing corporate systems and data require special protection. Companies should make sure that their corporate security policy includes mobile devices, with additional details on how mobile devices should be supported, protected, and used. They will need mobile device management tools to authorize all devices in use; to maintain accurate inventory records on all mobile devices, users, and applications; to control updates to applications; and to lock down or erase lost or stolen devices so they can't be compromised. Data loss prevention technology can identify where critical data are saved, who is accessing the data, how data are leaving the company, and where the data are going. Firms should develop guidelines stipulating approved mobile platforms and software applications as well as the required software and procedures for remote access of corporate systems. The organization's mobile security policy should forbid employees from using unsecured, consumer-based applications for transferring and storing corporate documents and files or sending such documents and files to oneself by email without encryption. Companies should encrypt communication whenever possible. All mobile device users should be required to use the password feature found in every smartphone.

Ensuring Software Quality

In addition to implementing effective security and controls, organizations can improve system quality and reliability by employing software metrics and rigorous software testing. Software metrics are objective assessments of the system in the form of quantified measurements. Ongoing use of metrics allows the information systems department and end users to measure the performance of the system jointly and identify problems as they occur. Examples of software metrics include the number of transactions that can be processed in a specified unit of time, online response time, the number of payroll checks printed per hour, and the number of known bugs per hundred lines of program code. For metrics to be successful, they must be carefully designed, formal, objective, and used consistently.

Early, regular, and thorough testing will contribute significantly to system quality. Many view testing as a way to prove the correctness of work they have done. In fact, we know that all sizable software is riddled with errors, and we must test to uncover these errors.

Good testing begins before a software program is even written, by using a *walkthrough*—a review of a specification or design document by a small group of people carefully selected based on the skills needed for the particular objectives being tested. When developers start writing software programs, coding walkthroughs can also be used to review program code. However, code must be tested by computer runs. When errors are discovered, the source is found and eliminated through a process called *debugging*. You can find out more about the various stages of testing required to put an information system into operation in Chapter 12. Our Learning Tracks also contain descriptions of methodologies for developing software programs that contribute to software quality.

8-5 How will MIS help my career?

Here is how Chapter 8 and this book can help you find an entry-level job as an identity access and management support specialist.

The Company

No. 1 Value Supermarkets, a major supermarket grocery store chain headquartered in Plano, Texas, is looking to fill an entry-level position for an identity access and management support specialist. The company has 59 retail locations in 23 Texas cities, more than 8,000 workers, and nearly a million weekly shoppers.

Position Description

The identity access and management support specialist will be responsible for monitoring the company's identity management system to ensure that the company is meeting its audit and compliance controls. This position reports to the company's security operations manager. Job responsibilities include:

- Performing data integrity testing of identity management system integrations with business applications.
- Integrating Windows Active Directory files with the identity management system.
- Maintaining information on system user roles and privileges.

Job Requirements

- Bachelor's degree
- Proficiency with computers
- Ability to multitask and work independently
- Attention to detail
- Strong time management skills
- Ability to communicate with both technical and non-technical staff

Interview Questions

1. What do you know about authentication and identity management? Have you ever worked with identity management or other IT security systems? What did you do with this software?

2. Have you ever worked with Windows Active Directory? What exactly did you do with this software?

3. What knowledge and experience do you have with ensuring data integrity?

4. Can you give an example of a situation where you had to multitask and manage your time and how you handled it?

5. Can you tell us about the computer experience you've had? What software tools have you worked with?

Author Tips

1. Review the last two sections of this chapter, especially the discussions of identity management and authentication. Also review the Chapter 6 discussions of data integrity and data quality.

2. Use the web to find out more about identity management, data integrity testing, leading identity management software tools, and Windows Active Directory.

3. Use the web to find out more about the company, the kinds of systems it uses, and who might be using those systems.

REVIEW **SUMMARY**

8-1 Why are information systems vulnerable to destruction, error, and abuse?

Digital data are vulnerable to destruction, misuse, error, fraud, and hardware or software failures. The Internet is designed to be an open system and makes internal corporate systems more vulnerable to actions from outsiders. Hackers can unleash denial-of-service (DoS) attacks or penetrate corporate networks, causing serious system disruptions. Wi-Fi networks can easily be penetrated by intruders using sniffer programs to obtain an address to access the resources of the network. Malware can disable systems and websites, with mobile devices a major target. The dispersed nature of cloud computing makes it difficult to track unauthorized activity or to apply controls from afar. Software presents problems because software bugs may be impossible to eliminate and because software vulnerabilities can be exploited by hackers and malicious software. End users often introduce errors.

8-2 What is the business value of security and control?

Lack of sound security and control can cause firms relying on computer systems for their core business functions to lose sales and productivity. Information assets, such as confidential employee records, trade secrets, or business plans, lose much of their value if they are revealed to outsiders or if they expose the firm to legal liability. Laws, such as HIPAA, the Sarbanes-Oxley Act, and the Gramm-Leach-Bliley Act, require companies to practice stringent electronic records management and adhere to strict standards for security, privacy, and control. Legal actions requiring electronic evidence and computer forensics also require firms to pay more attention to security and electronic records management.

8-3 What are the components of an organizational framework for security and control?

Firms need to establish a good set of both general and application controls for their information systems. A risk assessment evaluates information assets, identifies control points and control weaknesses, and determines the most cost-effective set of controls. Firms must also develop a coherent corporate security policy and plans for continuing business operations in the event of disaster or disruption.

The security policy includes policies for acceptable use and identity management. Comprehensive and systematic information systems auditing helps organizations determine the effectiveness of security and controls for their information systems.

8-4 What are the most important tools and technologies for safeguarding information resources?

Firewalls prevent unauthorized users from accessing a private network when it is linked to the Internet. Intrusion detection systems monitor private networks for suspicious network traffic and attempts to access corporate systems. Passwords, tokens, smart cards, and biometric authentication are used to authenticate system users. Anti-malware software checks computer systems for infections by viruses and worms and often eliminates the malicious software. Encryption, the coding and scrambling of messages, is a widely used technology for securing electronic transmissions over unprotected networks. Blockchain technology enables companies to create and verify tamper-proof transactions on a network without a central authority. Digital certificates combined with public key encryption provide further protection of electronic transactions by authenticating a user's identity. Companies can use fault-tolerant computer systems to make sure that their information systems are always available. Use of software metrics and rigorous software testing help improve software quality and reliability.

Key Terms

Acceptable use policy (AUP), 314
Anti-malware software, 320
Application controls, 312
Authentication, 317
Biometric authentication, 317
Botnet, 303
Bugs, 307
Business continuity planning, 315
Click fraud, 305
Computer crime, 303
Computer forensics, 311
Computer virus, 299
Controls, 297
Cybervandalism, 302
Cyberwarfare, 306
Deep packet inspection (DPI), 323
Denial-of-service (DoS) attack, 303
Digital certificates, 321
Disaster recovery planning, 315
Distributed denial-of-service (DDoS) attack, 303
Downtime, 323
Drive-by download, 301
Encryption, 320
Evil twin, 304
Fault-tolerant computer systems, 323
Firewall, 318
General controls, 312
Gramm-Leach-Bliley Act, 310
Hacker, 302
HIPAA, 310
Identity management, 316
Identity theft, 303

Information systems audit, 315
Intrusion detection systems, 319
Keyloggers, 302
Malware, 299
Managed security service providers (MSSPs), 323
Online transaction processing, 323
Password, 317
Patches, 307
Pharming, 304
Phishing, 304
Public key encryption, 321
Public key infrastructure (PKI), 322
Ransomware, 302
Risk assessment, 313
Sarbanes-Oxley Act, 310
Secure Hypertext Transfer Protocol (S-HTTP), 321
Secure Sockets Layer (SSL), 320
Security, 297
Security policy, 314
Smart card, 317
Sniffer, 302
Social engineering, 307
Spoofing, 302
Spyware, 302
SQL injection attack, 302
Token, 317
Trojan horse, 301
Two-factor authentication, 318
Unified threat management (UTM), 320
War driving, 299
Worm, 300
Zero-day vulnerabilities, 307

MyLab MIS

To complete the problems with MyLab MIS, go to the EOC Discussion Questions in MyLab MIS.

Review Questions

8-1 Why are information systems vulnerable to destruction, error, and abuse?

- List and describe the most common threats against contemporary information systems.
- Define malware and distinguish among a virus, a worm, and a Trojan horse.
- Define a hacker and explain how hackers create security problems and damage systems.
- Define computer crime. Provide two examples of crime in which computers are targets and two examples in which computers are used as instruments of crime.
- Define identity theft and phishing and explain why identity theft is such a big problem today.
- Describe the security and system reliability problems employees create.
- Explain how software defects affect system reliability and security.

8-2 What is the business value of security and control?

- Explain how security and control provide value for businesses.
- Describe the relationship between security and control and recent U.S. government regulatory requirements and computer forensics.

8-3 What are the components of an organizational framework for security and control?

- Define general controls and describe each type of general control.

- Define application controls and describe each type of application control.
- Describe the function of risk assessment and explain how it is conducted for information systems.
- Define and describe the following: security policy, acceptable use policy, and identity management.
- Explain how information systems auditing promotes security and control.

8-4 What are the most important tools and technologies for safeguarding information resources?

- Name and describe three authentication methods.
- Describe the roles of firewalls, intrusion detection systems, and anti-malware software in promoting security.
- Explain how encryption protects information.
- Describe the role of encryption and digital certificates in a public key infrastructure.
- Distinguish between disaster recovery planning and business continuity planning.
- Identify and describe the security problems cloud computing poses.
- Describe measures for improving software quality and reliability.

Discussion Questions

8-5
MyLab MIS
Security isn't simply a technology issue, it's a business issue. Discuss.

8-6
MyLab MIS
If you were developing a business continuity plan for your company, where would you start? What aspects of the business would the plan address?

8-7
MyLab MIS
Suppose your business had an e-commerce website where it sold goods and accepted credit card payments. Discuss the major security threats to this website and their potential impact. What can be done to minimize these threats?

Hands-On MIS Projects

The projects in this section give you hands-on experience analyzing security vulnerabilities, using spreadsheet software for risk analysis, and using web tools to research security outsourcing services. Visit MyLab MIS to access this chapter's Hands-On MIS Projects.

Management Decision Problems

8-8 Zynga is a leading online gaming company, offering web and mobile versions of games such as Farmville, Zynga Poker, Hit it Rich!, and CSR Racing. Zynga's games are available on a number of global platforms, including Apple iOS, Google Android, Facebook, and Zynga.com, and have been played by over 1 billion people. Prepare a security analysis for this Internet-based business. What kinds of threats should it anticipate? What would be their impact on the business? What steps can it take to prevent damage to its websites and continuing operations?'

8-9 A survey of your firm's IT infrastructure has identified a number of security vulnerabilities. Review the data about these vulnerabilities, which can be found in a table in MyLab MIS. Use the table to answer the following questions:

- Calculate the total number of vulnerabilities for each platform. What is the potential impact on the organization of the security problems for each computing platform?

- If you only have one information systems specialist in charge of security, which platforms should you address first in trying to eliminate these vulnerabilities? Second? Third? Last? Why?

- Identify the types of control problems these vulnerabilities illustrate and explain the measures that should be taken to solve them.

- What does your firm risk by ignoring the security vulnerabilities identified?

Improving Decision Making: Using Spreadsheet Software to Perform a Security Risk Assessment

Software skills: Spreadsheet formulas and charts
Business skills: Risk assessment

8-10 This project uses spreadsheet software to calculate anticipated annual losses from various security threats identified for a small company.

Mercer Paints is a paint manufacturing company located in Alabama that uses a network to link its business operations. A security risk assessment that management requested identified a number of potential exposures. These exposures, their associated probabilities, and average losses are summarized in a table, which can be found in MyLab MIS. Use the table to answer the following questions:

- In addition to the potential exposures listed, identify at least three other potential threats to Mercer Paints, assign probabilities, and estimate a loss range.

- Use spreadsheet software and the risk assessment data to calculate the expected annual loss for each exposure.

- Present your findings in the form of a chart. Which control points have the greatest vulnerability? What recommendations would you make to Mercer Paints? Prepare a written report that summarizes your findings and recommendations.

Improving Decision Making: Evaluating Security Outsourcing Services

Software skills: Web browser and presentation software
Business skills: Evaluating business outsourcing services

8-11 This project will help develop your Internet skills in using the web to research and evaluate security outsourcing services.

You have been asked to help your company's management decide whether to outsource security or keep the security function within the firm. Search the web to find information to help you decide whether to outsource security and to locate security outsourcing services.

- Present a brief summary of the arguments for and against outsourcing computer security for your company.

- Select two firms that offer computer security outsourcing services and compare them and their services.

- Prepare an electronic presentation for management, summarizing your findings. Your presentation should make the case of whether your company should outsource computer security. If you believe your company should outsource, the presentation should identify which security outsourcing service you selected and justify your decision.

Collaboration and Teamwork Project

Evaluating Security Software Tools

8-12 With a group of three or four students, use the web to research and evaluate security products from two competing vendors, such as for anti-malware software, firewalls, or antispyware software. For each product, describe its capabilities, for what types of businesses it is best suited, and its cost to purchase and install. Which is the best product? Why? If possible, use Google Docs and Google Drive or Google Sites to brainstorm, organize, and develop a presentation of your findings for the class.

Is the Equifax Hack the Worst Ever—and Why?

CASE STUDY

Equifax (along with TransUnion and Experian) is one of the three main U.S. credit bureaus, which maintain vast repositories of personal and financial data used by lenders to determine credit-worthiness when consumers apply for a credit card, mortgage, or other loans. The company handles data on more than 820 million consumers and more than 91 million businesses worldwide and manages a database with employee information from more than 7,100 employers, according to its website. These data are provided by banks and other companies directly to Equifax and the other credit bureaus. Consumers have little choice over how credit bureaus collect and store their personal and financial data.

Equifax has more data on you than just about anyone else. If any company needs airtight security for its information systems, it should be credit reporting bureaus such as Equifax. Unfortunately this has not been the case.

On September 7, 2017 Equifax reported that from mid-May through July 2017 hackers had gained access to some of its systems and potentially the personal information of about 143 million U.S. consumers, including Social Security numbers and driver's license numbers. Credit card numbers for 209,000 consumers and personal information used in disputes for 182,000 people were also compromised. Equifax reported the breach to law enforcement and also hired a cybersecurity firm to investigate. The size of the breach, importance, and quantity of personal information compromised by this breach are considered unprecedented.

Immediately after Equifax discovered the breach, three top executives, including Chief Financial Officer John Gamble, sold shares worth a combined $1.8 million, according to Securities and Exchange Commission filings. A company spokesman claimed the three executives had no knowledge that an intrusion had occurred at the time they sold their shares on August 1 and August 2. Bloomberg reported that the share sales were not planned in advance. On October 4, 2017 Equifax CEO Richard Smith testified before Congress and apologized for the breach.

The size of the Equifax data breach was second only to the Yahoo breach of 2013, which affected data of all of Yahoo's 3 billion customers. The Equifax breach was especially damaging because of the amount of sensitive personal and financial data stored by Equifax that was stolen, and the role such data play in securing consumers' bank accounts, medical histories, and access to financing. In one swoop the hackers gained access to several essential pieces of personal information that could help attackers commit fraud. According to Avivah Litan, a fraud analyst at Gartner Inc., on a scale of risk to consumers of 1 to 10, this is a 10.

After taking Equifax public in 2005, CEO Smith transformed the company from a slow-growing credit-reporting company (1–2 percent organic growth per year) into a global data powerhouse. Equifax bought companies with databases housing information about consumers' employment histories, savings, and salaries, and expanded internationally. The company bought and sold pieces of data that enabled lenders, landlords, and insurance companies to make decisions about granting credit, hiring job seekers, and renting an apartment. Equifax was transformed into a lucrative business housing $12 trillion of consumer wealth data. In 2016, the company generated $3.1 billion in revenue.

Competitors privately observed that Equifax did not upgrade its technological capabilities to keep pace with its aggressive growth. Equifax appeared to be more focused on growing data it could commercialize.

Hackers gained access to Equifax systems containing customer names, Social Security numbers, birth dates, and addresses. These four pieces of data are generally required for individuals to apply for various types of consumer credit, including credit cards and personal loans. Criminals who have access to such data could use it to obtain approval for credit using other people's names. Credit specialist and former Equifax manager John Ulzheimer calls this is a "nightmare scenario" because all four critical pieces of information for identity theft are in one place.

The hack involved a known vulnerability in Apache Struts, a type of open-source software Equifax and other companies use to build websites. This software vulnerability had been publicly identified in March 2017, and a patch to fix it was released at that time. That means Equifax had the information to eliminate this vulnerability two months before the breach occurred. It did nothing.

Weaknesses in Equifax security systems were evident well before the big hack. A hacker was able to access credit-report data between April 2013 and January 2014. The company discovered that it mistakenly exposed consumer data as a result of a "technical error" that occurred during a 2015 software change. Breaches in 2016 and 2017 compromised information on consumers' W-2 forms that were stored by Equifax units. Additionally, Equifax disclosed in February 2017 that a "technical issue" compromised credit information of some consumers who used identity-theft protection services from LifeLock.

Analyses earlier in 2017 performed by four companies that rank the security status of companies based on publicly available information showed that Equifax was behind on basic maintenance of websites that could have been involved in transmitting sensitive consumer information. Cyberrisk analysis firm Cyence rated the danger of a data breach at Equifax during the next 12 months at 50 percent. It also found the company performed poorly when compared with other financial-services companies. The other analyses gave Equifax a higher overall ranking, but the company fared poorly in overall web-services security, application security, and software patching.

A security analysis by Fair Isaac Corporation (FICO), a data analytics company focusing on credit scoring services, found that by July 14 public-facing websites run by Equifax had expired certificates, errors in the chain of certificates, or other web-security issues. Certificates are used to validate that a user's connection with a website is legitimate and secure.

The findings of the outside security analyses appear to conflict with public declarations by Equifax executives that cybersecurity was a top priority. Senior executives had previously said cybersecurity was one of the fastest-growing areas of expense for the company. Equifax executives touted Equifax's focus on security in an investor presentation that took place weeks after the company had discovered the attack.

Equifax has not revealed specifics about the attack, but either its databases were not encrypted or hackers were able to exploit an application vulnerability that provided access to data in an unencrypted state. Experts think—and hope—that the hackers were unable to access all of Equifax's encrypted

databases to match up information such as driver license or Social Security numbers needed to create a complete data profile for identity theft.

Equifax management stated that although the hack potentially accessed data on approximately 143 million U.S. consumers, it had found no evidence of unauthorized activity in the company's core credit reporting databases. The hack triggered an uproar among consumers, financial organizations, privacy advocates, and the press. Equifax lost one-third of its stock market value. Equifax CEO Smith resigned, with the CSO (chief security officer) and CIO departing the company as well. Banks will have to replace approximately 209,000 credit cards that were stolen in the breach, a major expense. Lawsuits are in the works.

Unfortunately the worst impact will be on consumers themselves, because the theft of uniquely identifying personal information such as Social Security numbers, address history, debt history, and birth dates could have a permanent effect. These pieces of critical personal data could be floating around the Dark Web for exploitation and identity theft for many years. Such information would help hackers answer the series of security questions that are often required to access financial accounts. According to Pamela Dixon, executive director of the World Privacy Forum, "This is about as bad as it gets." If you have a credit report, there's at least a 50 percent chance or more that your data were stolen in this breach.

The data breach exposed Equifax to legal and financial challenges, although the regulatory environment is likely to become more lenient under the current presidential administration. It already is too lenient. Credit reporting bureaus such as Equifax are very lightly regulated. Given the scale of the data compromised, the punishment for breaches is close to nonexistent. There is no federally sanctioned insurance or audit system for data storage, the way the Federal Deposit Insurance Corporation provides insurance for banks after losses. For many types of data, there are few licensing requirements for housing personally identifiable information. In many cases, terms-of-service documents indemnify companies against legal consequences for breaches.

Experts said it was highly unlikely that any regulatory body would shut Equifax down over this breach. The company is considered too critical to the American financial system. The two regulators that do have jurisdiction over Equifax, the Federal Trade

Commission and the Consumer Financial Protection Bureau, declined to comment on any potential punishments over the credit agency's breach.

Even after one of the most serious data breaches in history, no one is really in a position to stop Equifax from continuing to do business as usual. And the scope of the problem is much wider. Public policy has no good way to heavily punish companies that fail to safeguard our data. The United States and other countries have allowed the emergence of huge phenomenally detailed databases full of personal information available to financial companies, technology companies, medical organizations, advertisers, insurers, retailers, and the government.

Equifax has offered very weak remedies for consumers. People can go to the Equifax website to see if their information has been compromised. The site asks customers to provide their last name and the last six digits of their Social Security number. However, even if they do that, they do not necessarily learn whether they were affected. Instead, the site provides an enrollment date for its protection service. Equifax offered a free year of credit protection service to consumers enrolling before November 2017. Obviously, all of these measures won't help much because stolen personal data will be available to hackers on the Dark Web for years to come. Governments involved in state-sponsored cyberwarfare are able to use the data to populate databases of detailed personal and medical information that can be used for blackmail or future attacks. Ironically, the credit-protection service that Equifax is offering requires subscribers to waive their legal rights to seek compensation from Equifax for their losses in order to use the service, while Equifax goes unpunished. On March 1, 2018, Equifax announced that the breach had compromised an additional 2.4 million more Americans' names and driver's license numbers.

Harmful data breaches keep happening. In almost all cases, even when the data concerns tens or hundreds of millions of people, companies such as Equifax and Yahoo that were hacked continue to operate. There will be hacks—and afterward, there will be more. Companies need to be even more diligent about incorporating security into every aspect of their IT infrastructure and systems development activities. According to Litan, to prevent data breaches such as Equifax's, organizations need many layers of security controls. They need to assume that prevention methods are going to fail.

Sources: Selena Larson, "Equifax Says Hackers Stole More than Previously Reported," CNN, March 1, 2018; AnnaMaria Andriotis and Michael Rapoport, "Equifax Upends CEO's Drive to Be a Data Powerhouse," *Wall Street Journal*, September 22, 2017; AnnaMaria Andriotis and Robert McMillan, "Equifax Security Showed Signs of Trouble Months Before Hack," *Wall Street Journal*, September 26, 2017; AnnaMaria Andriotis and Ezequiel Minaya, "Equifax Reports Data Breach Possibly Affecting 143 Million Consumers," *Wall Street Journal*, September 7, 2017; Tara Siegel Bernard and Stacy Cowley, "Equifax Hack Exposes Regulatory Gaps, Leaving Customers Vulnerable," *New York Times*, September 8, 2017; Farhad Manjoo, "Seriously, Equifax? This Is a Breach No One Should Get Away With," *New York Times*, September 8, 2017; Eileen Chang, "Why Equifax Breach of 143 Million Consumers Should Freak You Out," thestreet.com, September 8, 2017; Tara Siegel Bernard, Tiffany Hsu, Nicole Perlroth, and Ron Lieber, "Equifax Says Cyberattack May Have Affected 143 Million Customers," *New York Times*, September 7, 2017; and Nicole Perlroth and Cade Metz, "What We Know and Don't Know About the Equifax Hack," *New York Times*, September 14, 2017.

CASE STUDY QUESTIONS

8-13 Identify and describe the security and control weaknesses discussed in this case.

8-14 What management, organization, and technology factors contributed to these problems?

8-15 Discuss the impact of the Equifax hack.

8-16 How can future data breaches like this one be prevented? Explain your answer.

MyLab MIS

Go to the Assignments section of MyLab MIS to complete these writing exercises.

8-17 Describe three spoofing tactics employed in identity theft by using information systems.

8-18 Describe four reasons mobile devices used in business are difficult to secure.

Chapter 8 References

Anderson, Chad, Richard L. Baskerville, and Mala Kaul. "Information Security Control Theory: Achieving a Sustainable Reconciliation Between Sharing and Protecting the Privacy of Information." *Journal of Management Information Systems* 34 No. 4 (2017).

Bauer, Harald, Ondrej Burkacky, and Christian Knochenhauer. "Security in the Internet of Things." *McKinsey and Company* (May 2017).

Carson, Brant, Giulio Romanelli, Patricia Walsh, and Askhat Zhumaev. "Blockchain Beyond the Hype: What Is the Strategic Business Value?" *McKinsey and Company* (June 2018).

Cloud Standards Customer Council. "Security for Cloud Computing: Ten Steps to Ensure Success, Version 3.0" (December 2017).

Esteves, Jose, Elisabete Ramalho, and Guillermo de Haro. "To Improve Cybersecurity, Think Like a Hacker." *MIT Sloan Management Review* (Spring 2017).

Goode, Sigi, Hartmut Hoehle, Viswanath Venkatesh, and Susan A. Brown. "User Compensation as a Data Breach Recovery Action: An Investigation of the Sony PlayStation Network Breach." *MIS Quarterly* 41 No. 3 (September 2017).

Gwebu, Kholekile L., Jing Wang, and Li Wang. "The Role of Corporate Reputation and Crisis Response Strategies in Data Breach Management." *Journal of Management Information Systems* 35 No. 2 (2018).

Hui, Kai-Lung, Seung Hyun Kim, and Qiu-Hong Wang. "Cybercrime Deterrence and International Legislation: Evidence from Distributed Denial of Service Attacks." *MIS Quarterly* 41, No. 2 (June 2017).

Iansiti, Marco, and Karim R. Lakhani. "The Truth About Blockchain." *Harvard Business Review* (January–February 2017).

Javelin Strategy & Research. "2018 Identity Fraud Study." (February 6, 2018).

Kaminski, Piotr, Chris Rezek, Wolf Richter, and Marc Sorel. "Protecting Your Digital Assets." McKinsey & Company (January 2017).

Kaspersky Lab. "Mobile Malware Evolution 2017." (2018).

McMillan, Robert. "Software Bug at Internet Service Provider Sparks Privacy Concerns." *Wall Street Journal* (February 24, 2017).

Menard, Philip, Gregory J. Bott, and Robert E. Crossler. "User Motivations in Protecting Information Security: Protection Motivation Theory Versus Self-Determination Theory." *Journal of Management Information Systems* 34 No. 4 (2017).

Moody, Gregory D., Mikko Siponen, and Seppo Pahnila. "Toward a Unified Model of Information Security Policy Compliance." *MIS Quarterly* 42 No. 1 (March 2018).

Panda Security. "Cybersecurity Predictions 2018." (2017).

Panko, Raymond R., and Julie L. Panko. *Business Data Networks and Security,* 11th ed. (Upper Saddle River, NJ: Pearson, 2019).

Ponemon Institute. "2017 Cost of Cybercrime Study and the Risk of Business Innovation." (2017a).

_____. "2017 Cost of Data Breach Study: Global Analysis." (2017b).

Rothrock, Ray A., James Kaplan, and Friso Van der Oord. "The Board's Role in Managing Cybersecurity Risks." *MIT Sloan Management Review* (Winter 2018).

Samtani, Sagar, Ryan Chinn, Hsinchun Chen, and Jay F. Nunamaker. "Exploring Emerging Hacker Assets and Key Hackers for Proactive Cyber Threat Intelligence." *Journal of Management Information Systems* 34 No. 4 (2017).

Symantec Corporation. "Internet Security Threat Report." (2018).

Tapscott, Don, and Alex Tapscott. "How Blockchain Will Change Organizations." *MIT Sloan Management Review* (Winter 2017).

Verizon. "2018 Data Breach Investigations Report." (2018).

Wang, Jingguo, Manish Gupta, and H. Raghav Rao. "Insider Threats in a Financial Institution: Analysis of Attack-Proneness of Information Systems Applications." *MIS Quarterly* 39, No. 1 (March 2015).

Young, Carl S. "The Enemies of Data Security: Convenience and Collaboration." *Harvard Business Review* (February 11, 2015).

Key System Applications for the Digital Age

PART THREE examines the core information system applications businesses are using today to improve operational excellence and decision making. These applications include enterprise systems; systems for supply chain management, customer relationship management, artificial intelligence, and knowledge management; e-commerce applications; and business intelligence systems. This part answers questions such as: How can enterprise applications improve business performance? How do firms use e-commerce to extend the reach of their businesses? How can systems improve decision making and help companies benefit from artificial intelligence and knowledge management?

9

Achieving Operational Excellence and Customer Intimacy: Enterprise Applications

LEARNING OBJECTIVES

After reading this chapter, you will be able to answer the following questions:

9-1 How do enterprise systems help businesses achieve operational excellence?

9-2 How do supply chain management systems coordinate planning, production, and logistics with suppliers?

9-3 How do customer relationship management systems help firms achieve customer intimacy?

9-4 What are the challenges that enterprise applications pose, and how are enterprise applications taking advantage of new technologies?

9-5 How will MIS help my career?

CHAPTER CASES

Avon Beautifies Its Supply Chain

Soma Bay Prospers with ERP in the Cloud

Kenya Airways Flies High with Customer Relationship Management

Clemens Food Group Delivers with New Enterprise Applications

VIDEO CASES

Life Time Fitness Gets in Shape with Salesforce CRM

Instructional Video:
GSMS Protects Patients by Serializing Every Bottle of Drugs

MyLab MIS

Discussion Questions: 9-5, 9-6, 9-7; **Hands-on MIS Projects:** 9-8, 9-9, 9-10, 9-11;
Writing Assignments: 9-17, 9-18; **eText with Conceptual Animations**

Avon Beautifies Its Supply Chain

Avon Products Inc. is the oldest beauty company in the United States, and has been in business for over 130 years. It manufactures and sells cosmetics, fragrances, toiletries, accessories, apparel, and various decorative home furnishings. Avon is also the world's leading direct seller of beauty and related products, with 6 million independent door-to-door sales representatives in 143 countries and over $8 billion in annual revenue. Avon also sells through other channels, including the Internet, catalog, and physical outlets.

To survive in a highly competitive, fast-changing industry, motivate representatives, and stimulate sales, Avon launches marketing campaigns with fresh products and promotions every few weeks. To be successful, Avon must be able to anticipate and react quickly to market trends and customer preferences. Avon processes 50,000 orders each day and there is little margin for error. Avon's warehouses must stock the items customers want and deliver them quickly, often to remote locations around the globe.

Until recently, Avon's global supply chain was not up to the task. Avon had recently expanded operations in Europe, the Middle East, and Africa, but there was no central planning function responsible for demand, inventory, and supply planning across the enterprise. Production planning at Avon's three factories in Germany, the United Kingdom, and Poland was highly manual, inflexible, and incapable of supporting Avon's growth in new markets.

© Casimiro PT/Shutterstock

To improve how the company dealt with product availability and inventory, Avon implemented JDA Software's Manufacturing and Intelligent Fulfillment solutions to centralize planning for demand, inventory, and supply across its entire global enterprise. The software helps Avon achieve consistent forecast accuracy in an environment that includes challenges of shorter product lifecycles, seasonality, multiple sales channels, frequent promotions, and continuously changing localized shopper preferences. JDA Intelligent Fulfillment helps companies make intelligent and profitable distribution decisions. The software helps reduce inventory levels and costs, improve customer service, and support more agile, profitable, and responsive operations, meeting the needs of many different types of Avon markets in a single implementation.

The JDA software collects supply chain data about inventory, future sales demands, transport schedules, and sales history from Avon's many markets. The system uses these data along with JDA advanced planning parameters to create a strategic distribution and manufacturing plan. The system also provides Avon with a list of inventory imbalances, service risks, and shipping requirements. Avon can now streamline order processing across borders and respond more quickly to changes in customer demand.

JDA's capabilities for advanced planning and distribution, coupled with its flexibility, made it possible for Avon to meet the needs of many different types of Avon markets with a single system. Avon implemented the JDA software across 29 markets in Europe, Middle East, and Africa (EMEA) within four months, delivering training across the EMEA region in eight languages. Since Avon implemented the JDA supply chain solution, its cost of servicing customers has been reduced, while its customer service rating has increased to 99.5 percent. Inventory levels have dropped by 17 percent in just six months, providing immediate savings of $20 million. Avon now has complete visibility into all aspects of its supply chain and will be able to enter new countries and markets much more easily.

Sources: https://jda.com, accessed January 21, 2018; https://about.avon.com, accessed January 20, 2018; and "Avon Supply Chain Makeover," JDA Software Group, 2016.

Avon's problems with planning, inventory, and supply in a global multichannel marketplace illustrate the critical role of supply chain management systems in business. Avon's business performance was impeded because it could not balance supply and constantly changing demand for its products in many different markets around the world. Avon's existing systems were highly manual and lacked the flexibility to support Avon's growth in new markets. Products were not always available when customers ordered them. Sometimes this left the company holding too much inventory it couldn't sell or not enough at the right time or place to fulfill customer orders.

The chapter-opening diagram calls attention to important points raised by this case and this chapter. Avon competes in the global beauty industry where customer tastes change rapidly, demand is very volatile, and the company is expected to come up quickly with enticing new products. The company's supply chain is far-reaching and complex, servicing customers ordering items in many different locations around the globe. Avon's legacy systems were unable to coordinate demand, inventory, and supply planning across its entire global enterprise. Implementing JDA software tools for supply chain planning and fulfillment has made it much easier for Avon's management to access and analyze demand data for forecasting, inventory planning, and fulfillment, greatly improving both decision making and operational efficiency across the global enterprise.

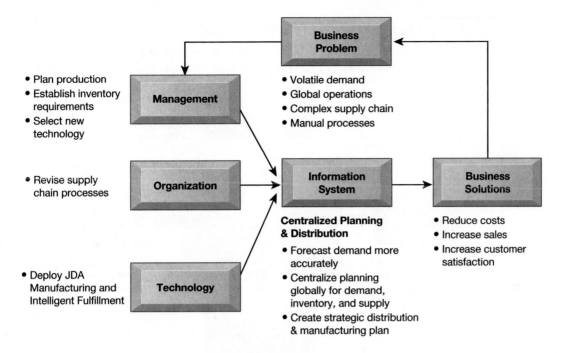

- Plan production
- Establish inventory requirements
- Select new technology

Management

- Revise supply chain processes

Organization

- Deploy JDA Manufacturing and Intelligent Fulfillment

Technology

Business Problem

- Volatile demand
- Global operations
- Complex supply chain
- Manual processes

Information System

Centralized Planning & Distribution

- Forecast demand more accurately
- Centralize planning globally for demand, inventory, and supply
- Create strategic distribution & manufacturing plan

Business Solutions

- Reduce costs
- Increase sales
- Increase customer satisfaction

Here are some questions to think about: How is Avon's business model affected by having an inefficient supply chain? How did JDA software tools improve the way Avon ran its business?

9-1 How do enterprise systems help businesses achieve operational excellence?

Around the globe, companies are increasingly becoming more connected, both internally and with other companies. If you run a business, you'll want to be able to react instantaneously when a customer places a large order or when a shipment from a supplier is delayed. You may also want to know the impact of these events on every part of the business and how the business is performing at any point in time, especially if you're running a large company. Enterprise systems provide the integration to make this possible. Let's look at how they work and what they can do for the firm.

What are Enterprise Systems?

Imagine that you had to run a business based on information from tens or even hundreds of databases and systems, none of which could speak to one another. Imagine your company had 10 major product lines, each produced in separate factories, and each with separate and incompatible sets of systems controlling production, warehousing, and distribution.

At the very least, your decision making would often be based on manual hard-copy reports, often out of date, and it would be difficult to understand what is happening in the business as a whole. Sales personnel might not be able to tell at the time they place an order whether the ordered items are in inventory, and manufacturing could not easily use sales data to plan for new production. You now have a good idea of why firms need a special enterprise system to integrate information.

FIGURE 9.1 HOW ENTERPRISE SYSTEMS WORK

Enterprise systems feature a set of integrated software modules and a central database by which business processes and functional areas throughout the enterprise can share data.

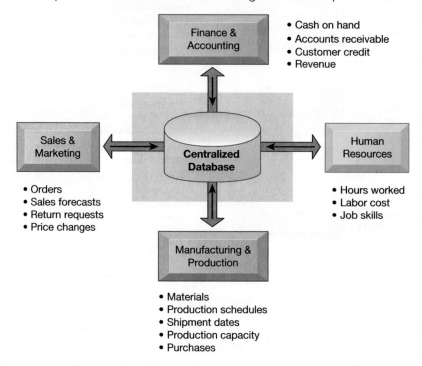

Chapter 2 introduced enterprise systems, also known as enterprise resource planning (ERP) systems, which are based on a suite of integrated software modules and a common central database. The database collects data from many divisions and departments in a firm and from a large number of key business processes in manufacturing and production, finance and accounting, sales and marketing, and human resources, making the data available for applications that support nearly all an organization's internal business activities. When new information is entered by one process, the information is made immediately available to other business processes (see Figure 9.1).

If a sales representative places an order for tire rims, for example, the system verifies the customer's credit limit, schedules the shipment, identifies the best shipping route, and reserves the necessary items from inventory. If inventory stock is insufficient to fill the order, the system schedules the manufacture of more rims, ordering the needed materials and components from suppliers. Sales and production forecasts are immediately updated. General ledger and corporate cash levels are automatically updated with the revenue and cost information from the order. Users can tap into the system and find out where that particular order is at any minute. Management can obtain information at any point in time about how the business is operating. The system can also generate enterprise-wide data for management analyses of product cost and profitability.

Enterprise Software

Enterprise software is built around thousands of predefined business processes that reflect best practices. Table 9.1 describes some of the major business processes that enterprise software supports.

Companies implementing this software first have to select the functions of the system they wish to use and then map their business processes to the predefined

TABLE 9.1 BUSINESS PROCESSES SUPPORTED BY ENTERPRISE SYSTEMS
Financial and accounting processes, including general ledger, accounts payable, accounts receivable, fixed assets, cash management and forecasting, product-cost accounting, cost-center accounting, asset accounting, tax accounting, credit management, and financial reporting
Human resources processes, including personnel administration, time accounting, payroll, personnel planning and development, benefits accounting, applicant tracking, time management, compensation, workforce planning, performance management, and travel expense reporting
Manufacturing and production processes, including procurement, inventory management, purchasing, shipping, production planning, production scheduling, material requirements planning, quality control, distribution, transportation execution, and plant and equipment maintenance
Sales and marketing processes, including order processing, quotes, contracts, product configuration, pricing, billing, credit checking, incentive and commission management, and sales planning

business processes in the software. (One of our Learning Tracks shows how SAP enterprise software handles the procurement process for a new piece of equipment.) Configuration tables provided by the software manufacturer enable the firm to tailor a particular aspect of the system to the way it does business. For example, the firm could use these tables to select whether it wants to track revenue by product line, geographical unit, or distribution channel.

If the enterprise software does not support the way the organization does business, companies can rewrite some of the software to support the way their business processes work. However, enterprise software is unusually complex, and extensive customization may degrade system performance, compromising the information and process integration that are the main benefits of the system. If companies want to reap the maximum benefits from enterprise software, they must change the way they work to conform to the business processes defined by the software.

To implement a new enterprise system, Tasty Baking Company identified its existing business processes and then translated them into the business processes built into the SAP ERP software it had selected. To ensure that it obtained the maximum benefits from the enterprise software, Tasty Baking Company deliberately planned for customizing less than 5 percent of the system and made very few changes to the SAP software itself. It used as many tools and features that were already built into the SAP software as it could. SAP has more than 3,000 configuration tables for its enterprise software.

Leading enterprise software vendors include SAP, Oracle, IBM, Infor Global Solutions, and Microsoft. Versions of enterprise software packages are designed for small and medium-sized businesses and on-demand software services running in the cloud (see the chapter-opening case and Section 9-4).

Business Value of Enterprise Systems

Enterprise systems provide value by both increasing operational efficiency and providing firmwide information to help managers make better decisions. Large companies with many operating units in different locations have used enterprise systems to enforce standard practices and data so that everyone does business the same way worldwide.

Coca-Cola, for instance, implemented a SAP enterprise system to standardize and coordinate important business processes in 200 countries. Lack of standard, companywide business processes had prevented the company from using its worldwide buying power to obtain lower prices for raw materials and from reacting rapidly to market changes.

Enterprise systems help firms respond rapidly to customer requests for information or products. Because the system integrates order, manufacturing, and delivery data, manufacturing is better informed about producing only what customers have ordered, procuring exactly the right number of components or raw materials to fill actual orders, staging production, and minimizing the time that components or finished products are in inventory.

Alcoa, the world's leading producer of aluminum and aluminum products with operations spanning 31 countries and more than 200 locations, had initially been organized around lines of business, each of which had its own set of information systems. Many of these systems were redundant and inefficient. Alcoa's costs for executing requisition-to-pay and financial processes were much higher, and its cycle times were longer than those of other companies in its industry. (Cycle time refers to the total elapsed time from the beginning to the end of a process.) The company could not operate as a single worldwide entity.

After implementing enterprise software from Oracle, Alcoa eliminated many redundant processes and systems. The enterprise system helped Alcoa reduce requisition-to-pay cycle time by verifying receipt of goods and automatically generating receipts for payment. Alcoa's accounts payable transaction processing dropped 89 percent. Alcoa was able to centralize financial and procurement activities, which helped the company reduce nearly 20 percent of its worldwide costs.

Enterprise systems provide much valuable information for improving management decision making. Corporate headquarters has access to up-to-the-minute data on sales, inventory, and production and uses this information to create more accurate sales and production forecasts. Enterprise software includes analytical tools to use data the system captures to evaluate overall organizational performance. Enterprise system data have common standardized definitions and formats that are accepted by the entire organization. Performance figures mean the same thing across the company. Enterprise systems allow senior management to find out easily at any moment how a particular organizational unit is performing, determine which products are most or least profitable, and calculate costs for the company as a whole. For example, Alcoa's enterprise system includes functionality for global human resources management that shows correlations between investment in employee training and quality, measures the companywide costs of delivering services to employees, and measures the effectiveness of employee recruitment, compensation, and training. The Interactive Session on Management describes more of these benefits in detail.

9-2 How do supply chain management systems coordinate planning, production, and logistics with suppliers?

If you manage a small firm that makes a few products or sells a few services, chances are you will have a small number of suppliers. You could coordinate your supplier orders and deliveries by using just a telephone and fax machine. But if you manage a firm that produces more complex products and services, you will have hundreds of suppliers, and each of your suppliers will have its own set of suppliers. Suddenly, you will need to coordinate the activities of hundreds or even thousands of other firms to produce your products and services. Supply chain management (SCM) systems, which we introduced in Chapter 2, are an answer to the problems of supply chain complexity and scale.

Soma Bay Prospers with ERP in the Cloud

Soma Bay is a 10-million-square-mile resort community on the Egyptian shore of the Red Sea. It has many attractions that make it a first-class vacation paradise, including five hotels, a championship golf course, water sport facilities, a world-class spa, and luxury vacation homes. Soma Bay Development Company is headquartered in Hurghada, Egypt and has more than 2,000 employees.

Unfortunately, political upheavals and economic conditions have taken a toll on occupancy rates and profitability. When President Hosni Mubarak was overthrown during the Egyptian revolution of 2011, there was a sharp devaluation of Egyptian currency. In the years that followed, political conditions stabilized and the Egyptian economy recovered, but the tourism industry lost U.S. $1.3 billion after the downing of a commercial airliner over the Sinai Desert in late 2015. Soma Bay Development Company's hotel occupancy rates plummeted from more than 50 percent in 2015 to 25 percent in the first quarter of 2016.

Foreign exchange fluctuations and political upheavals are forces beyond Soma Bay's control, but what the company's management can do during downturns is react intelligently by closely monitoring operations and costs. This is possible thanks to the company's use of a JD Edwards Enterprise One ERP system from Oracle with applications and data residing in Oracle's Cloud Infrastructure as a Service (Oracle Cloud IaaS).

In the past, Soma Bay Development Company had tried to run much of the company using unwieldy Excel-based systems. Managers had to manually manipulate spreadsheets to understand the basic drivers of profitability, and it often took too long to obtain the information needed for sound decision making. These systems made it difficult for Soma Bay to manage its aggressive growth plans, which included construction of 1000 new homes over a five-year period.

Mohammed Serry, Soma Bay Company's CFO, and his team selected JD Edwards Enterprise One for a solution because it could create standardized business processes across functional areas and provide timely reports that explain the profitability of each business unit using a standard chart of accounts. The software can identify the profitability drivers and growth drivers of a business. Enterprise One

seamlessly combines data from the general ledger and other financial systems with data from operational systems.

Soma Bay's Enterprise One cloud platform makes it easy to create cash flow reports, project management reports, accounts receivable aging reports, facility management reports, and key performance indicator reports throughout Soma Bay's distributed organization. Company management also appreciates Oracle Cloud IaaS disaster recovery capabilities. Several years ago, water from an upper floor flooded Soma Bay's Cairo data center. The company was able to restore data and resume operations quickly because it had backups stored in Oracle Cloud.

JD Edwards Enterprise One contains more than 80 separate application modules designed to support a wide range of business processes. The software suite also features mobile applications that support both iOS and Android and can be used on smartphones and tablets. Soma Bay uses the JD Edwards Enterprise One modules for Financials, Procurement, Inventory Management, Job Cost, Real Estate Management, Homebuilder Management, Capital Asset Maintenance, Service Management, and Time and Labor. JD Edwards Enterprise One Homebuilder Management helps Soma Bay coordinate activities and analyze profitability throughout its home-building cycle down to the lot level. JD Edwards Enterprise One Real Estate Management streamlines financial, operational, and facilities management processes for finished properties, coordinating tasks among teams and providing a comprehensive management view of each unit. The Job Cost module shows ongoing costs for the real estate business, which helps management allocate expenses for materials, labor, and other needs and also track expenses against the budgets and forecasts established at the outset of each facilities management project. Managers can identify projects with codes and merge them with financial account numbers to determine budget expenses versus actual expenses. They can thereby verify if complex projects are on track and share expense data among divisions.

The Enterprise One software creates currency-neutral financial reports. This helps reconcile revenue from Soma Bay's tourism division (which caters to Germany and other parts of Europe) with its home sales division (which is aimed primarily at Egyptians) to neutralize the effect of different currencies on financial results. Home building accounts for about 25 percent of corporate revenue.

Having a dual revenue stream mitigates risks. If the tourism business is slow, Soma Bay still has revenue from the real estate business, and vice versa. The ERP system provides the data required to closely track costs. For example, in 2017 Soma Bay spent 100 million Egyptian pounds (equivalent to approximately U.S. $5.7 million) on new construction. The Enterprise One system provided the information about cash management and cash flow for sustaining this level of expansion. Soma Bay can carefully monitor cash flow and payments to contractors.

During the 2016 downturn, Soma Bay used the Enterprise One cost management and profitability capabilities to provide detailed financial data that helped managers carefully control fixed operating expenses, helping to minimize losses. Enterprise One provided a solid understanding of costs and profitability, even though revenue came from different currencies and markets. It was able to show the impact of falling occupancy rates on the business, excluding foreign exchange effect, to help management measure overall performance by legal entity. This knowledge helped Soma Bay weather the downturn and implement an aggressive turnaround plan.

Today, 95 percent of Soma Bay staff members use the Enterprise One software in some capacity. The company has a more stable operating model. Occupancy rates at its five hotels are rising. Soma Bay Development Company is building 500 vacation homes in six seaside communities. According to Cherif Samir, Financial Controller for Soma Bay, being able to track every penny the company spends on a project has revolutionized the business.

Sources: www.searchoracle.com, accessed January 30, 2018; David Baum, "Destination: Cloud," *Profit Magazine*, Fall 2017; and www.somabay.com, accessed January 31, 2018.

CASE STUDY QUESTIONS

1. Identify and describe the problem discussed in this case. What management, organization, and technology factors contributed to the problem?

2. Why was an ERP system required for a solution? How did having a cloud-based ERP system contribute to the solution?

3. What were the business benefits of Soma Bay's new enterprise system? How did it change decision making and the way the company operated?

The Supply Chain

A firm's **supply chain** is a network of organizations and business processes for procuring raw materials, transforming these materials into intermediate and finished products, and distributing the finished products to customers. It links suppliers, manufacturing plants, distribution centers, retail outlets, and customers to supply goods and services from source through consumption. Materials, information, and payments flow through the supply chain in both directions.

Goods start out as raw materials and, as they move through the supply chain, are transformed into intermediate products (also referred to as components or parts) and, finally, into finished products. The finished products are shipped to distribution centers and from there to retailers and customers. Returned items flow in the reverse direction from the buyer back to the seller.

Let's look at the supply chain for Nike sneakers as an example. Nike designs, markets, and sells sneakers, socks, athletic clothing, and accessories throughout the world. Its primary suppliers are contract manufacturers with factories in China, Thailand, Indonesia, Brazil, and other countries. These companies fashion Nike's finished products.

FIGURE 9.2 NIKE'S SUPPLY CHAIN

This figure illustrates the major entities in Nike's supply chain and the flow of information upstream and downstream to coordinate the activities involved in buying, making, and moving a product. Shown here is a simplified supply chain, with the upstream portion focusing only on the suppliers for sneakers and sneaker soles.

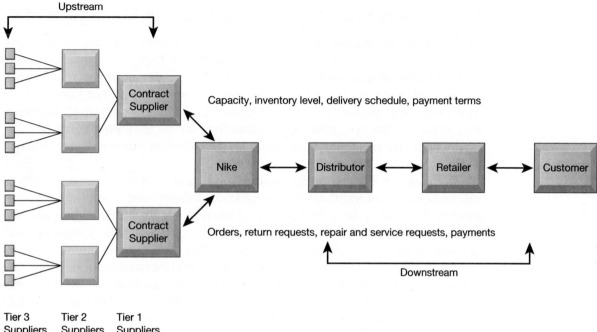

Nike's contract suppliers do not manufacture sneakers from scratch. They obtain components for the sneakers—the laces, eyelets, uppers, and soles—from other suppliers and then assemble them into finished sneakers. These suppliers in turn have their own suppliers. For example, the suppliers of soles have suppliers for synthetic rubber, suppliers for chemicals used to melt the rubber for molding, and suppliers for the molds into which to pour the rubber. Suppliers of laces have suppliers for their thread, for dyes, and for the plastic lace tips.

Figure 9.2 provides a simplified illustration of Nike's supply chain for sneakers; it shows the flow of information and materials among suppliers, Nike, Nike's distributors, retailers, and customers. Nike's contract manufacturers are its primary suppliers. The suppliers of soles, eyelets, uppers, and laces are the secondary (Tier 2) suppliers. Suppliers to these suppliers are the tertiary (Tier 3) suppliers.

The *upstream* portion of the supply chain includes the company's suppliers, the suppliers' suppliers, and the processes for managing relationships with them. The *downstream* portion consists of the organizations and processes for distributing and delivering products to the final customers. Companies that manufacture, such as Nike's contract suppliers of sneakers, also manage their own *internal supply chain processes* for transforming materials, components, and services their suppliers furnish into finished products or intermediate products (components or parts) for their customers and for managing materials and inventory.

The supply chain illustrated in Figure 9.2 has been simplified. It only shows two contract manufacturers for sneakers and only the upstream supply chain for sneaker soles. Nike has hundreds of contract manufacturers turning out finished sneakers, socks, and athletic clothing, each with its own set of suppliers.

The upstream portion of Nike's supply chain actually comprises thousands of entities. Nike also has numerous distributors and many thousands of retail stores where its shoes are sold, so the downstream portion of its supply chain is also large and complex.

Information Systems and Supply Chain Management

Inefficiencies in the supply chain, such as parts shortages, underused plant capacity, excessive finished goods inventory, or high transportation costs, are caused by inaccurate or untimely information. For example, manufacturers may keep too many parts in inventory because they do not know exactly when they will receive their next shipments from their suppliers. Suppliers may order too few raw materials because they do not have precise information on demand. These supply chain inefficiencies waste as much as 25 percent of a company's operating costs.

If a manufacturer had perfect information about exactly how many units of product customers wanted, when they wanted them, and when they could be produced, it would be possible to implement a highly efficient **just-in-time strategy**. Components would arrive exactly at the moment they were needed, and finished goods would be shipped as they left the assembly line.

In a supply chain, however, uncertainties arise because many events cannot be foreseen—uncertain product demand, late shipments from suppliers, defective parts or raw materials, or production process breakdowns. To satisfy customers, manufacturers often deal with such uncertainties and unforeseen events by keeping more material or products in inventory than they think they may actually need. The *safety stock* acts as a buffer for the lack of flexibility in the supply chain. Although excess inventory is expensive, low fill rates are also costly because business may be lost from canceled orders.

One recurring problem in supply chain management is the **bullwhip effect**, in which information about the demand for a product gets distorted as it passes from one entity to the next across the supply chain. A slight rise in demand for an item might cause different members in the supply chain—distributors, manufacturers, suppliers, secondary suppliers (suppliers' suppliers), and tertiary suppliers (suppliers' suppliers' suppliers)—to stockpile inventory so each has enough just in case. These changes ripple throughout the supply chain, magnifying what started out as a small change from planned orders and creating excess inventory, production, warehousing, and shipping costs (see Figure 9.3).

For example, Procter & Gamble (P&G) found it had excessively high inventories of its Pampers disposable diapers at various points along its supply chain because of such distorted information. Although customer purchases in stores were fairly stable, orders from distributors spiked when P&G offered aggressive price promotions. Pampers and Pampers' components accumulated in warehouses along the supply chain to meet demand that did not actually exist. To eliminate this problem, P&G revised its marketing, sales, and supply chain processes and used more accurate demand forecasting.

The bullwhip effect is tamed by reducing uncertainties about demand and supply when all members of the supply chain have accurate and up-to-date information. If all supply chain members share dynamic information about inventory levels, schedules, forecasts, and shipments, they have more precise knowledge about how to adjust their sourcing, manufacturing, and distribution plans. Supply chain management systems provide the kind of information that helps members of the supply chain make better purchasing and scheduling decisions.

FIGURE 9.3 THE BULLWHIP EFFECT

Inaccurate information can cause minor fluctuations in demand for a product to be amplified as one moves further back in the supply chain. Minor fluctuations in retail sales for a product can create excess inventory for distributors, manufacturers, and suppliers.

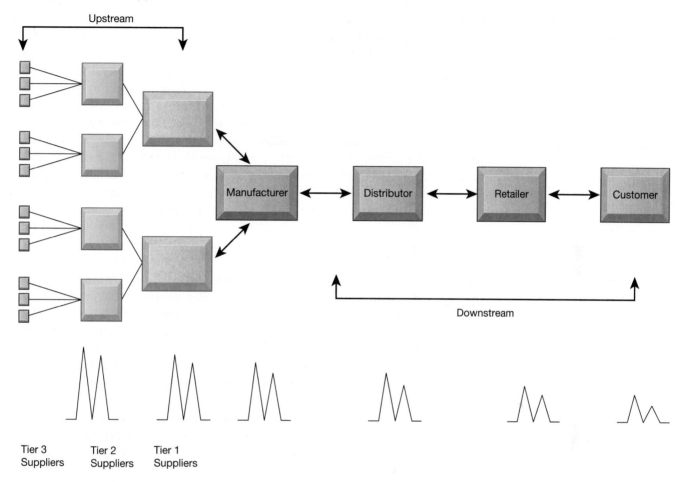

Supply Chain Management Software

Supply chain software is classified as either software to help businesses plan their supply chains (supply chain planning) or software to help them execute the supply chain steps (supply chain execution). **Supply chain planning systems** enable the firm to model its existing supply chain, generate demand forecasts for products, and develop optimal sourcing and manufacturing plans. Such systems help companies make better decisions, such as determining how much of a specific product to manufacture in a given time period; establishing inventory levels for raw materials, intermediate products, and finished goods; determining where to store finished goods; and identifying the transportation mode to use for product delivery.

For example, if a large customer places a larger order than usual or changes that order on short notice, it can have a widespread impact throughout the supply chain. Additional raw materials or a different mix of raw materials may need to be ordered from suppliers. Manufacturing may have to change job scheduling. A transportation carrier may have to reschedule deliveries. Supply chain planning software makes the necessary adjustments to production and distribution plans. Information about changes is shared among the relevant supply chain members so that their work can be coordinated. One of the most important—and complex—supply chain planning functions is **demand planning**, which determines how much product a business needs to make to satisfy all its customers' demands. JDA Software, SAP, and Oracle all offer supply chain management solutions.

Supply chain execution systems manage the flow of products through distribution centers and warehouses to ensure that products are delivered to the right locations in the most efficient manner. They track the physical status of goods, the management of materials, warehouse and transportation operations, and financial information involving all parties. An example is the Warehouse Management System (WMS) that Haworth Incorporated uses. Haworth is a world-leading manufacturer and designer of office furniture, with distribution centers in four states. The WMS tracks and controls the flow of finished goods from Haworth's distribution centers to its customers. Acting on shipping plans for customer orders, the WMS directs the movement of goods based on immediate conditions for space, equipment, inventory, and personnel.

Global Supply Chains and the Internet

Before the Internet, supply chain coordination was hampered by the difficulties of making information flow smoothly among disparate internal supply chain systems for purchasing, materials management, manufacturing, and distribution. It was also difficult to share information with external supply chain partners because the systems of suppliers, distributors, or logistics providers were based on incompatible technology platforms and standards. Enterprise and supply chain management systems enhanced with Internet technology supply some of this integration.

A manager uses a web interface to tap into suppliers' systems to determine whether inventory and production capabilities match demand for the firm's products. Business partners use web-based supply chain management tools to collaborate online on forecasts. Sales representatives access suppliers' production schedules and logistics information to monitor customers' order status.

Global Supply Chain Issues

More and more companies are entering international markets, outsourcing manufacturing operations, and obtaining supplies from other countries as well as selling abroad. Their supply chains extend across multiple countries and regions. There are additional complexities and challenges to managing a global supply chain.

Global supply chains typically span greater geographic distances and time differences than domestic supply chains and have participants from a number of countries. Performance standards may vary from region to region or from nation to nation. Supply chain management may need to reflect foreign government regulations and cultural differences.

The Internet helps companies manage many aspects of their global supply chains, including sourcing, transportation, communications, and international finance. Today's apparel industry, for example, relies heavily on outsourcing to contract manufacturers in China and other low-wage countries. Apparel companies are starting to use the web to manage their global supply chain and production issues. (Review the discussion of Li & Fung in Chapter 3.)

In addition to contract manufacturing, globalization has encouraged outsourcing warehouse management, transportation management, and related operations to third-party logistics providers, such as UPS Supply Chain Solutions and Schneider National. These logistics services offer web-based software to give their customers a better view of their global supply chains. Customers can check a secure website to monitor inventory and shipments, helping them run their global supply chains more efficiently.

Demand-Driven Supply Chains: From Push to Pull Manufacturing and Efficient Customer Response

In addition to reducing costs, supply chain management systems facilitate efficient customer response, enabling the workings of the business to be driven more by customer demand. (We introduced efficient customer response systems in Chapter 3.)

Earlier supply chain management systems were driven by a push-based model (also known as build-to-stock). In a **push-based model**, production master schedules are based on forecasts or best guesses of demand for products, and products are pushed to customers. With new flows of information made possible by web-based tools, supply chain management more easily follows a pull-based model. In a **pull-based model**, also known as a demand-driven or build-to-order model, actual customer orders or purchases trigger events in the supply chain. Transactions to produce and deliver only what customers have ordered move up the supply chain from retailers to distributors to manufacturers and eventually to suppliers. Only products to fulfill these orders move back down the supply chain to the retailer. Manufacturers use only actual order demand information to drive their production schedules and the procurement of components or raw materials, as illustrated in Figure 9.4. Walmart's continuous replenishment system described in Chapter 3 is an example of the pull-based model.

The Internet and Internet technology make it possible to move from sequential supply chains, where information and materials flow sequentially from company to company, to concurrent supply chains, where information flows in many directions simultaneously among members of a supply chain network. Complex supply networks of manufacturers, logistics suppliers, outsourced manufacturers, retailers, and distributors can adjust immediately to changes in schedules or orders. Ultimately, the Internet will enable a digital logistics nervous system for supply chains (see Figure 9.5).

FIGURE 9.4 PUSH- VERSUS PULL-BASED SUPPLY CHAIN MODELS

The difference between push- and pull-based models is summarized by the slogan "Make what we sell, not sell what we make."

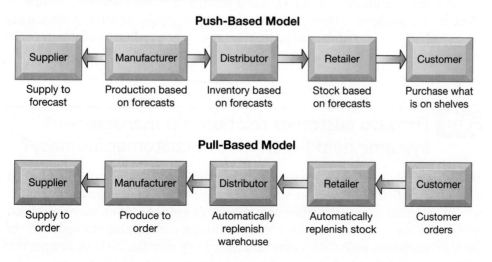

Push-Based Model

Supplier	Manufacturer	Distributor	Retailer	Customer
Supply to forecast	Production based on forecasts	Inventory based on forecasts	Stock based on forecasts	Purchase what is on shelves

Pull-Based Model

Supplier	Manufacturer	Distributor	Retailer	Customer
Supply to order	Produce to order	Automatically replenish warehouse	Automatically replenish stock	Customer orders

| FIGURE 9.5 | THE EMERGING INTERNET-DRIVEN SUPPLY CHAIN |

The emerging Internet-driven supply chain operates like a digital logistics nervous system. It provides multidirectional communication among firms, networks of firms, and e-marketplaces so that entire networks of supply chain partners can immediately adjust inventories, orders, and capacities.

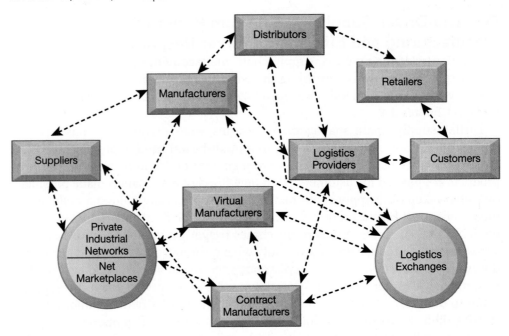

Business Value of Supply Chain Management Systems

You have just seen how supply chain management systems enable firms to streamline both their internal and external supply chain processes and provide management with more accurate information about what to produce, store, and move. By implementing a networked and integrated supply chain management system, companies match supply to demand, reduce inventory levels, improve delivery service, speed product time to market, and use assets more effectively.

Total supply chain costs represent the majority of operating expenses for many businesses and in some industries approach 75 percent of the total operating budget. Reducing supply chain costs has a major impact on firm profitability.

In addition to reducing costs, supply chain management systems help increase sales. If a product is not available when a customer wants it, customers often try to purchase it from someone else. More precise control of the supply chain enhances the firm's ability to have the right product available for customer purchases at the right time.

9-3 How do customer relationship management systems help firms achieve customer intimacy?

You've probably heard phrases such as "the customer is always right" or "the customer comes first." Today these words ring truer than ever. Because competitive advantage based on an innovative new product or service is often very short lived, companies are realizing that their most enduring competitive strength may be their relationships with their customers. Some say that the basis of competition has switched from who sells the most products and services to who "owns" the customer and that customer relationships represent a firm's most valuable asset.

What Is Customer Relationship Management?

What kinds of information would you need to build and nurture strong, long-lasting relationships with customers? You'd want to know exactly who your customers are, how to contact them, whether they are costly to service and sell to, what kinds of products and services they are interested in, and how much money they spend on your company. If you could, you'd want to make sure you knew each of your customers well, as if you were running a small-town store. And you'd want to make your good customers feel special.

In a small business operating in a neighborhood, it is possible for business owners and managers to know their customers well on a personal, face-to-face basis, but in a large business operating on a metropolitan, regional, national, or even global basis, it is impossible to know your customer in this intimate way. In these kinds of businesses, there are too many customers and too many ways that customers interact with the firm (over the web, the phone, email, blogs, and in person). It becomes especially difficult to integrate information from all these sources and deal with the large number of customers.

A large business's processes for sales, service, and marketing tend to be highly compartmentalized, and these departments do not share much essential customer information. Some information on a specific customer might be stored and organized in terms of that person's account with the company. Other pieces of information about the same customer might be organized by products that were purchased. In this traditional business environment, there is no convenient way to consolidate all this information to provide a unified view of a customer across the company.

This is where customer relationship management systems help. Customer relationship management (CRM) systems, which we introduced in Chapter 2, capture and integrate customer data from all over the organization, consolidate the data, analyze the data, and then distribute the results to various systems and customer touch points across the enterprise. A **touch point** (also known as a contact point) is a method of interaction with the customer, such as telephone, email, customer service desk, conventional mail, Facebook, Twitter, website, wireless device, or retail store. Well-designed CRM systems provide a single enterprise view of customers that is useful for improving both sales and customer service (see Figure 9.6.)

Good CRM systems provide data and analytical tools for answering questions such as these: What is the value of a particular customer to the firm over his or her lifetime? Who are our most loyal customers? Who are our most profitable customers? What do these profitable customers want to buy? Firms use the answers to these questions to acquire new customers, provide better service and support to existing customers, customize their offerings more precisely to customer preferences, and provide ongoing value to retain profitable customers.

Customer Relationship Management Software

Commercial CRM software packages range from niche tools that perform limited functions, such as personalizing websites for specific customers, to large-scale enterprise applications that capture myriad interactions with customers, analyze them with sophisticated reporting tools, and link to other major enterprise applications, such as supply chain management and enterprise systems. The more comprehensive CRM packages contain modules for **partner relationship management (PRM)** and **employee relationship management (ERM)**.

FIGURE 9.6 CUSTOMER RELATIONSHIP MANAGEMENT (CRM)

CRM systems examine customers from a multifaceted perspective. These systems use a set of integrated applications to address all aspects of the customer relationship, including customer service, sales, and marketing.

PRM uses many of the same data, tools, and systems as customer relationship management to enhance collaboration between a company and its selling partners. If a company does not sell directly to customers but rather works through distributors or retailers, PRM helps these channels sell to customers directly. It provides a company and its selling partners with the ability to trade information and distribute leads and data about customers, integrating lead generation, pricing, promotions, order configurations, and availability. It also provides a firm with tools to assess its partners' performances so it can make sure its best partners receive the support they need to close more business.

ERM software deals with employee issues that are closely related to CRM, such as setting objectives, employee performance management, performance-based compensation, and employee training. Major CRM application software vendors include Oracle, SAP, Salesforce.com, and Microsoft Dynamics CRM.

Customer relationship management systems typically provide software and online tools for sales, customer service, and marketing. We briefly describe some of these capabilities.

Sales Force Automation

Sales force automation (SFA) modules in CRM systems help sales staff increase productivity by focusing sales efforts on the most profitable customers, those who are good candidates for sales and services. SFA modules provide sales prospect and contact information, product information, product configuration capabilities, and sales quote generation capabilities. Such software can assemble information about a particular customer's past purchases to help the salesperson make personalized recommendations. SFA modules enable sales, marketing, and shipping departments to share customer and prospect information easily. SFA increases each salesperson's efficiency by reducing the cost per sale as well as the cost of acquiring new customers and retaining old ones. SFA modules also provide capabilities for sales forecasting, territory management, and team selling.

Customer Service

Customer service modules in CRM systems provide information and tools to increase the efficiency of call centers, help desks, and customer support staff. They have capabilities for assigning and managing customer service requests.

One such capability is an appointment or advice telephone line. When a customer calls a standard phone number, the system routes the call to the correct service person, who inputs information about that customer into the system only once. When the customer's data are in the system, any service representative can handle the customer relationship. Improved access to consistent and accurate customer information helps call centers handle more calls per day and decrease the duration of each call. Thus, call centers and customer service groups achieve greater productivity, reduced transaction time, and higher quality of service at lower cost. The customer is happier because he or she spends less time on the phone restating his or her problem to customer service representatives.

CRM systems may also include web-based self-service capabilities: The company website can be set up to provide inquiring customers personalized support information as well as the option to contact customer service staff by phone for additional assistance.

Marketing

CRM systems support direct-marketing campaigns by providing capabilities for capturing prospect and customer data, for providing product and service information, for qualifying leads for targeted marketing, and for scheduling and tracking direct-marketing mailings or email (see Figure 9.7). Marketing modules also include tools for analyzing marketing and customer data, identifying profitable and unprofitable customers, designing products and services to satisfy specific customer needs and interests, and identifying opportunities for cross-selling.

Cross-selling is the marketing of complementary products to customers. (For example, in financial services, a customer with a checking account might be sold a money market account or a home improvement loan.) CRM tools also

---

FIGURE 9.7 HOW CRM SYSTEMS SUPPORT MARKETING

Customer relationship management software provides a single point for users to manage and evaluate marketing campaigns across multiple channels, including email, direct mail, telephone, the web, and social media.

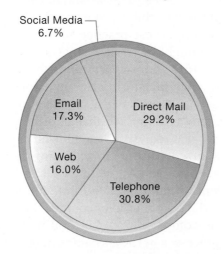

Responses by Channel for January 2019
Promotional Campaign

Social Media 6.7%
Email 17.3%
Direct Mail 29.2%
Web 16.0%
Telephone 30.8%

FIGURE 9.8 **CRM SOFTWARE CAPABILITIES**

The major CRM software products support business processes in sales, service, and marketing, integrating customer information from many sources. Included is support for both the operational and analytical aspects of CRM.

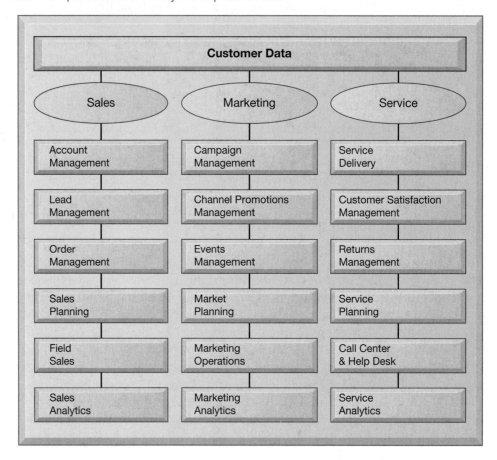

help firms manage and execute marketing campaigns at all stages, from planning to determining the rate of success for each campaign.

Figure 9.8 illustrates the most important capabilities for sales, service, and marketing processes found in major CRM software products. Like enterprise software, this software is business-process driven, incorporating hundreds of business processes thought to represent best practices in each of these areas. To achieve maximum benefit, companies need to revise and model their business processes to conform to the best-practice business processes in the CRM software.

Figure 9.9 illustrates how a best practice for increasing customer loyalty through customer service might be modeled by CRM software. Directly servicing customers provides firms with opportunities to increase customer retention by singling out profitable long-term customers for preferential treatment. CRM software can assign each customer a score based on that person's value and loyalty to the company and provide that information to help call centers route each customer's service request to agents who can best handle that customer's needs. The system would automatically provide the service agent with a detailed profile of that customer that includes his or her score for value and loyalty. The service agent would use this information to present special offers or additional services to the customer to encourage the customer to keep transacting business with the company. You will find more information on other best-practice business processes in CRM systems in our Learning Tracks.

FIGURE 9.9   CUSTOMER LOYALTY MANAGEMENT PROCESS MAP

This process map shows how a best practice for promoting customer loyalty through customer service would be modeled by customer relationship management software. The CRM software helps firms identify high-value customers for preferential treatment.

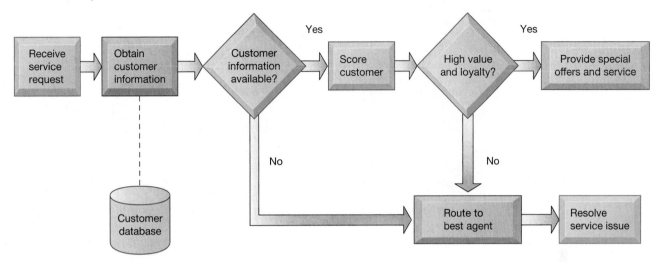

Operational and Analytical CRM

All of the applications we have just described support either the operational or analytical aspects of customer relationship management. **Operational CRM** includes customer-facing applications, such as tools for sales force automation, call center and customer service support, and marketing automation. **Analytical CRM** includes applications that analyze customer data generated by operational CRM applications to provide information for improving business performance.

Analytical CRM applications are based on data from operational CRM systems, customer touch points, and other sources that have been organized in data warehouses or analytic platforms for use in online analytical processing (OLAP), data mining, and other data analysis techniques (see Chapter 6). Customer data collected by the organization might be combined with data from other sources, such as customer lists for direct-marketing campaigns purchased from other companies or demographic data. Such data are analyzed to identify buying patterns, to create segments for targeted marketing, and to pinpoint profitable and unprofitable customers (see Figure 9.10).

Another important output of analytical CRM is the customer's lifetime value to the firm. **Customer lifetime value (CLTV)** is based on the relationship between the revenue produced by a specific customer, the expenses incurred in acquiring and servicing that customer, and the expected life of the relationship between the customer and the company.

Business Value of Customer Relationship Management Systems

Companies with effective customer relationship management systems realize many benefits, including increased customer satisfaction, reduced direct-marketing costs, more effective marketing, and lower costs for customer acquisition and retention. Information from CRM systems increases sales revenue

FIGURE 9.10 ANALYTICAL CRM

Analytical CRM uses a customer data warehouse or analytic platform and tools to analyze customer data collected from the firm's customer touch points and from other sources.

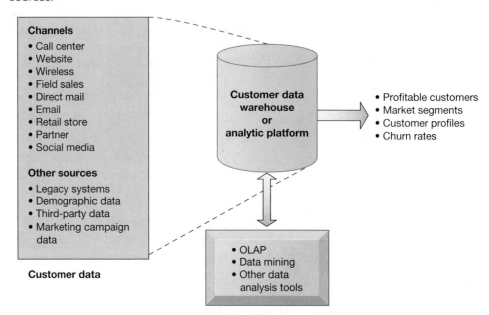

by identifying the most profitable customers and segments for focused marketing and cross-selling (see the Interactive Session on Organizations).

Customer churn is reduced as sales, service, and marketing respond better to customer needs. The **churn rate** measures the number of customers who stop using or purchasing products or services from a company. It is an important indicator of the growth or decline of a firm's customer base.

9-4 What are the challenges that enterprise applications pose, and how are enterprise applications taking advantage of new technologies?

Many firms have implemented enterprise systems and systems for supply chain and customer relationship management because they are such powerful instruments for achieving operational excellence and enhancing decision making. But precisely because they are so powerful in changing the way the organization works, they are challenging to implement. Let's briefly examine some of these challenges as well as new ways of obtaining value from these systems.

Enterprise Application Challenges

Promises of dramatic reductions in inventory costs, order-to-delivery time, more efficient customer response, and higher product and customer profitability make enterprise systems and systems for SCM and CRM very alluring. But to obtain this value, you must clearly understand how your business has to change to use these systems effectively.

Enterprise applications involve complex pieces of software that are very expensive to purchase and implement. It might take a large *Fortune* 500 company several years to complete a large-scale implementation of an enterprise system

Kenya Airways Flies High with Customer Relationship Management

Kenya Airways is the flag carrier of Kenya and ranks among the top ten African airlines in terms of seat capacity, with a fleet of 33 aircraft covering 53 destinations domestically and abroad. It is the only African airline in the SkyTeam alliance, whose 20 members include Delta Airlines, Air France, Alitalia, Aeromexico, China Airlines, and Korean Air, and is expected to live up to a very high global standard.

One area of the business that needed improvement was the airline's relationship to its customers. Africa's current population of 1 billion is expected to reach 1.5 billion within a decade, with a rapidly growing middle class in many countries. Until recently, Kenya Airways was unable to fully capitalize on this market opportunity because it didn't know enough about its customers. Although the airline had added more planes, passenger numbers had been decreasing, partly due to the fear of Ebola virus outbreaks, regional terrorism, and increased competition from Persian Gulf carriers. Profitability suffered.

The airline didn't know who clicked on its email campaigns. It was advertising mostly on billboards, in newspapers, and on flyers, with no way to measure the effectiveness of those campaigns. Management could not tell what its sales representatives in different offices were doing. Data on customers were located in many different repositories, such as spreadsheets and files in company and partner travel agent offices, reservation systems, and airport check-ins, and the data were not integrated. Without a single repository for customer data, Kenya Airways was unable to identify the preferences, special needs, or other personal characteristics of its "guests," who included commercial traders, business executives, government officials, students, missionaries, and medical tourists. Marketing, sales, and customer service activities were operating in the dark. For example, each May the airline would send every customer in its scattered data repositories a Mother's Day greeting, although many of the recipients were not mothers.

In 2014 Kenya Airways initiated a multiyear program to automate and integrate all of its customer data so that it could engage in effective customer relationship management using Oracle's Marketing, Sales, Data, and Service Clouds. Oracle Marketing Cloud provides a cloud-based platform to connect firms' marketing data, centrally orchestrate cross-channel customer interactions, engage the right audience, and analyze performance. It includes tools for managing marketing automation campaigns, providing cross-channel customer experiences, creating and managing engaging content, "listening" to customer conversations about a product, brand or service, and engaging with messaging (social marketing).

A few weeks after implementing Oracle Marketing Cloud, the airline ran its first automated marketing campaign, which directed emails, SMS texts, and social media posts about special holiday season fares to Kenyan emigrants in Dubai. Kenya Airways then created campaigns to promote new and expanded routes to Hanoi and Zanzibar. As time went on, the airline's marketing team became more skillful at tracking revenue flows generated by those campaigns and identifying new sources of data to target the campaigns more effectively. Kenya Airways Marketing Automation Lead, Harriet Luyai, reported in early 2015 that "reachable contacts" rose from 40 percent to 89 percent, open rates on marketing emails rose from 40 percent to 65 percent, and the airline's "acquisition rate"—the percentage of respondents who opt in to its campaigns—was up to 20 percent. The airline can measure the impact of marketing campaigns on ticket sales. Campaigns that previously took three days to execute using an agency now take 30 minutes and are much less expensive.

After implementing Oracle Marketing Cloud, Kenya Airways started using Oracle Sales Cloud to automate its sales activities and Oracle RightNow Cloud Service for its customer service activities, linking all three clouds in one central data repository. Marketing, sales, and service could now integrate their customer data and coordinate business processes. The airline pulled together information on age, income, education level, job function, job level, revenue generated for the airline, geography, status, preferences, interest areas, service calls, email activity, form submissions, and purchase history to help it create very detailed customer profiles for personalizing offerings.

To help the Kenya Airways marketing team drive additional revenue by converting leads to ticket sales, increasing website traffic, and increasing social followers, the airline implemented Oracle Social Cloud.

This tool helps the Kenya Airways customer service team follow social media posts and discussions about the airline's services and respond to questions and problems within 30 minutes. It also helps agents prioritize their follow-up posts and manage workflows for the appropriate approvals and for troubleshooting.

Although Kenya Airways had a customer loyalty program, it had previously been unable to identify high-value customers. Now Kenya Airways can track all its high-value customers and show how much revenue each customer generates. It can also segment customers across the customer life cycle, making it possible to distinguish a new customer from a longtime high-value customer. Kenya Airways now has a 360-degree view of each of its customers.

It took much more time to implement the Oracle Cloud suite than Kenya Airways had

originally estimated—more than a year instead of six months. The required data, which resided in many different applications, needed to be cleansed to make sure they were all in the right format before they could be transferred to the new data repository. Much of this work was manual. Airline staff had to be trained in new ways of working with digital CRM tools because so much of its work had previously been manual. Kenya Airways management feels the airline has been richly rewarded for this effort.

Sources: "Company View of Kenya Airways PLC," www.bloomberg.com, accessed January 31, 2018; Rob Preston, "First-Class Flight," *Profit Magazine*, August 2016; www.kenya-airways.com, accessed January 31, 2018; "Kenya Airways Turns to McKinsey for Turnaround Strategy," Consultancy.uk, February 8, 2016; and Tilde Herrera, "Kenya Airways Fuels with Data to Lift Marketing," October 29, 2015.

CASE STUDY QUESTIONS

1. What was the problem at Kenya Airways described in this case? What management, organization, and technology factors contributed to this problem?

2. What was the relationship of customer relationship management to Kenya Airways' business performance and business strategy?

3. Describe Kenya Airway's solution to its problem. What management, organization, and technology issues had to be addressed by the solution?

4. How effective was this solution? How did it affect the way Kenya Airways ran its business and its business performance?

or a system for SCM or CRM. According to a 2018 survey of 237 ERP users conducted by Panorama Consulting Solutions, ERP projects took an average of 17.4 months to complete, and 44 percent of the projects delivered 50 percent or less of the expected benefits. Approximately 64 percent of these projects experienced cost overruns, and 79 percent exceeded their initial timelines (Panorama Consulting Solutions, 2018). Changes in project scope and additional customization work add to implementation delays and costs.

Enterprise applications require not only deep-seated technological changes but also fundamental changes in the way the business operates. Companies must make sweeping changes to their business processes to work with the software. Employees must accept new job functions and responsibilities. They must learn how to perform a new set of work activities and understand how the information they enter into the system can affect other parts of the company. This requires new organizational learning and should also be factored into ERP implementation costs.

SCM systems require multiple organizations to share information and business processes. Each participant in the system may have to change some of its processes and the way it uses information to create a system that best serves the supply chain as a whole.

Some firms experienced enormous operating problems and losses when they first implemented enterprise applications because they didn't understand how much organizational change was required. For example, Kmart had trouble getting products to store shelves when it first implemented i2 Technologies (now JDA Software) SCM software. The i2 software did not work well with Kmart's promotion-driven business model, which created sharp spikes in demand for products. Supermarket giant Woolworth's Australia encountered data-related problems when it transitioned from an antiquated home-grown ERP system to SAP. Weekly profit-and-loss reports tailored for individual stores couldn't be generated for nearly 18 months. The company had to change its data collection procedures, but failed to understand its own processes or properly document these business processes.

Enterprise applications also introduce switching costs. When you adopt an enterprise application from a single vendor, such as SAP, Oracle, or others, it is very costly to switch vendors, and your firm becomes dependent on the vendor to upgrade its product and maintain your installation.

Enterprise applications are based on organization-wide definitions of data. You'll need to understand exactly how your business uses its data and how the data would be organized in a CRM, SCM, or ERP system. CRM systems typically require some data cleansing work.

Enterprise software vendors are addressing these problems by offering pared-down versions of their software and fast-start programs for small and medium-sized businesses and best-practice guidelines for larger companies. Companies are also achieving more flexibility by using cloud applications for functions not addressed by the basic enterprise software so that they are not constrained by a single do-it-all type of system.

Companies adopting enterprise applications can also save time and money by keeping customizations to a minimum. For example, Kennametal, a $2 billion metal-cutting tools company in Pennsylvania, had spent $10 million over 13 years maintaining an ERP system with more than 6,400 customizations. The company replaced it with a plain-vanilla, uncustomized version of SAP enterprise software and changed its business processes to conform to the software. Office Depot avoided customization when it moved from in-house systems to the Oracle ERP Cloud. The retailer is using best practices embedded in Oracle's Supply Chain Management Cloud and in its cloud-based Human Capital Management (HCM) and Enterprise Performance Management (EPM) systems. By not customizing its Oracle ERP applications, Office Depot simplified its information systems and reduced the cost of maintaining and managing them (Thibodeau, 2018).

Next-Generation Enterprise Applications

Today, enterprise application vendors are delivering more value by becoming more flexible, user-friendly, web-enabled, mobile, and capable of integration with other systems. Stand-alone enterprise systems, customer relationship management systems, and SCM systems are becoming a thing of the past. The major enterprise software vendors have created what they call *enterprise solutions, enterprise suites,* or e-business suites to make their CRM, SCM, and ERP systems work closely with each other and link to systems of customers and suppliers.

Next-generation enterprise applications also include cloud solutions as well as more functionality available on mobile platforms. Large enterprise software vendors such as SAP, Oracle, Microsoft, and Epicor now feature cloud versions of their flagship ERP systems and also cloud-based products for small and medium-sized businesses (as described earlier in the Interactive Session on Management). SAP, for example, offers SAP S/4HANA Cloud for large companies, and SAP Business ByDesign and SAP Business One enterprise software for medium-sized and small businesses. Microsoft offers the Dynamics 365 cloud version of its ERP and CRM software. Cloud-based enterprise systems are also offered by smaller vendors such as NetSuite.

The undisputed global market leader in cloud-based CRM systems is Salesforce.com, which we described in Chapter 5. Salesforce.com delivers its service through Internet-connected computers or mobile devices, and it is widely used by small, medium-sized, and large enterprises. As cloud-based products mature, more companies, including very large *Fortune* 500 firms, are choosing to run all or part of their enterprise applications in the cloud.

Social CRM

CRM software vendors are enhancing their products to take advantage of social networking technologies. These social enhancements help firms identify new ideas more rapidly, improve team productivity, and deepen interactions with customers (see Chapter 10). Using **social CRM** tools, businesses can better engage with their customers by, for example, analyzing their sentiments about their products and services.

Social CRM tools enable a business to connect customer conversations and relationships from social networking sites to CRM processes. The leading CRM vendors now offer such tools to link data from social networks to their CRM software. SAP, Salesforce.com, and Oracle CRM products now feature technology to monitor, track, and analyze social media activity on Facebook, LinkedIn, Twitter, YouTube, and other sites. Business intelligence and analytics software vendors such as SAS also have capabilities for social media analytics (with several measures of customer engagement across a variety of social networks) along with campaign management tools for testing and optimizing both social and traditional web-based campaigns.

Salesforce.com connected its system for tracking leads in the sales process with social-listening and social-media marketing tools, enabling users to tailor their social-marketing dollars to core customers and observe the resulting comments. If an ad agency wants to run a targeted Facebook or Twitter ad, these capabilities make it possible to aim the ad specifically at people in the client's lead pipeline who are already being tracked in the CRM system. Users will be able to view tweets as they take place in real time and perhaps uncover new leads. They can also manage multiple campaigns and compare them all to figure out which ones generate the highest click-through rates and cost per click.

Business Intelligence in Enterprise Applications

Enterprise application vendors have added business intelligence features to help managers obtain more meaningful information from the massive amounts of data these systems generate, including data from the Internet of Things (IoT). SAP now makes it possible for its enterprise applications to use HANA in-memory computing technology so that they are capable of much more rapid and complex data analysis. Included are tools for flexible reporting; ad hoc analysis; interactive dashboards; what-if scenario analysis; data visualization; and machine learning to analyze very large bodies of data, make connections, make predictions, and provide recommendations for operations optimization. For example, SAP created a machine learning and neural network application (see Chapter 11) that recognizes patterns associated with machine performance in the oil and gas industry. The software automatically generates notifications of potential machine failures and sends them to SAP Plant Maintenance, which planners use to schedule machine repair and replacement (Franken, 2018).

The major enterprise application vendors offer portions of their products that work on mobile handhelds. You can find out more about this topic in our Learning Track on Wireless Applications for Customer Relationship Management, Supply Chain Management, and Healthcare.

9-5 How will MIS help my career?

Here is how Chapter 9 and this book can help you find a job as a manufacturing management trainee.

The Company

XYZ Global Industrial Components is a large Michigan-headquartered company with 40 global manufacturing facilities and more than 4,000 employees worldwide, and it has an open position for a new college graduate in its Manufacturing Management Program. The company produces fastener, engineered, and linkage and suspension components for automotive, heavy-duty trucks, aerospace, electric utility, telecommunications, and other industries worldwide.

Position Description

The Manufacturing Management Program is a rotational, two-year program designed to nurture and train future managers by enabling recent college graduates to acquire critical skills and industry experience in plant, technical, and corporate environments. Job responsibilities include:

- Working with business units and project teams on systems implementation, including implementation of ERP and JDA manufacturing systems.
- Understanding business processes and data requirements for each business unit.
- Proficiency in supporting and conducting business requirement analysis sessions.
- Tracking and documenting changes to functional and business specifications.
- Writing user documentation, instructions, and procedures.
- Monitoring and documenting post-implementation problems and revision requests.

Job Requirements

- Bachelor's degree in IT, MIS, engineering, or related field or equivalent, with a GPA higher than 3.0
- Demonstrated skills in Microsoft Office Suite
- Strong written and verbal communication skills
- Proven track record of accomplishments both inside and outside the educational setting
- Experience in a leadership role in a team

Interview Questions

- Describe the projects you have worked on in a team. Did you play a leadership role? Exactly what did you do to help your team achieve its goal? Were any of these projects IT projects?
- What do you know about ERP or JDA manufacturing systems? Have you ever worked with them? What exactly did you do with these systems?
- Tell us what you can do with Microsoft Office software. Which tools have you used? Do you have any Access and Excel skills? What kinds of problems have you used these tools to solve? Did you take courses in Access or Excel?

Author Tips

1. Do some research on the company, its industry, and the kinds of challenges it faces. Look through the company's LinkedIn page and read their posts over the past twelve months. Are there any key trends in the LinkedIn posts for this company?

2. Review this text's Chapter 9 on enterprise applications, Chapter 13 on developing systems, and Chapter 14 on IT project management and implementation.

3. View YouTube videos created by major IT consulting firms that discuss the latest trends in manufacturing technology and enterprise systems.

4. Inquire how you would be using Microsoft Office tools for the job and what Excel and Access skills you would be expected to demonstrate. Bring examples of the work you have done with this software. Show that you would be eager to learn what you don't know about these tools to fulfill your job assignments.

5. Bring examples of your writing (including some from your Digital Portfolio described in MyLab MIS) demonstrating your analytical skills and project experience.

REVIEW **SUMMARY**

9-1 How do enterprise systems help businesses achieve operational excellence?

Enterprise software is based on a suite of integrated software modules and a common central database. The database collects data from and feeds the data into numerous applications that can support nearly all of an organization's internal business activities. When one process enters new information, the information is made available immediately to other business processes.

Enterprise systems support organizational centralization by enforcing uniform data standards and business processes throughout the company and a single unified technology platform. The firmwide data that enterprise systems generate help managers evaluate organizational performance.

9-2 How do supply chain management systems coordinate planning, production, and logistics with suppliers?

Supply chain management (SCM) systems automate the flow of information among members of the supply chain so they can use it to make better decisions about when and how much to purchase, produce, or ship. More accurate information from supply chain management systems reduces uncertainty and the impact of the bullwhip effect.

Supply chain management software includes software for supply chain planning and for supply chain execution. Internet technology facilitates the management of global supply chains by providing the connectivity for organizations in different countries to share supply chain information. Improved communication among supply chain members also facilitates efficient customer response and movement toward a demand-driven model.

9-3 How do customer relationship management systems help firms achieve customer intimacy?

Customer relationship management (CRM) systems integrate and automate customer-facing processes in sales, marketing, and customer service, providing an enterprise-wide view of customers. Companies can use this customer knowledge when they interact with customers to provide them with better service or sell new products and services. These systems also identify profitable or unprofitable customers or opportunities to reduce the churn rate.

The major customer relationship management software packages provide capabilities for both operational CRM and analytical CRM. They often include modules for managing relationships with selling partners (partner relationship management) and for employee relationship management.

9-4   What are the challenges that enterprise applications pose, and how are enterprise applications taking advantage of new technologies?

Enterprise applications are difficult to implement. They require extensive organizational change, large new software investments, and careful assessment of how these systems will enhance organizational performance. Enterprise applications cannot provide value if they are implemented atop flawed processes or if firms do not know how to use these systems to measure performance improvements. Employees require training to prepare for new procedures and roles. Attention to data management is essential.

Enterprise applications are now more flexible, web-enabled, and capable of integration with other systems, using web services and service-oriented architecture (SOA). They also can run in cloud infrastructures or on mobile platforms. CRM software has added social networking capabilities to enhance internal collaboration, deepen interactions with customers, and use data from social networking sites. Enterprise applications are incorporating business intelligence capabilities for analyzing the large quantities of data they generate.

Key Terms

Analytical CRM, 357
Bullwhip effect, 348
Churn rate, 358
Cross-selling, 355
Customer lifetime value (CLTV), 357
Demand planning, 350
Employee relationship management (ERM), 353
Enterprise software, 342
Just-in-time strategy, 348
Operational CRM, 357

Partner relationship management (PRM), 353
Pull-based model, 351
Push-based model, 351
Sales force automation (SFA), 354
Social CRM, 362
Supply chain, 346
Supply chain execution systems, 350
Supply chain planning systems, 349
Touch point, 353

MyLab MIS

To complete the problems with MyLab MIS, go to the EOC Discussion Questions in MyLab MIS.

Review Questions

9-1   How do enterprise systems help businesses achieve operational excellence?

- Define an enterprise system and explain how enterprise software works.
- Describe how enterprise systems provide value for a business.

9-2   How do supply chain management systems coordinate planning, production, and logistics with suppliers?

- Define a supply chain and identify each of its components.
- Explain how supply chain management systems help reduce the bullwhip effect and how they provide value for a business.
- Define and compare supply chain planning systems and supply chain execution systems.
- Describe the challenges of global supply chains and how Internet technology can help companies manage them better.

- Distinguish between a push-based and a pull-based model of supply chain management and explain how contemporary supply chain management systems facilitate a pull-based model.

9-3   How do customer relationship management systems help firms achieve customer intimacy?

- Define customer relationship management and explain why customer relationships are so important today.
- Describe how partner relationship management (PRM) and employee relationship management (ERM) are related to customer relationship management (CRM).
- Describe the tools and capabilities of customer relationship management software for sales, marketing, and customer service.
- Distinguish between operational and analytical CRM.

9-4 What are the challenges that enterprise applications pose, and how are enterprise applications taking advantage of new technologies?

- List and describe the challenges enterprise applications pose.
- Explain how these challenges can be addressed.

- Describe how enterprise applications are taking advantage of cloud computing and business intelligence.
- Define social CRM and explain how customer relationship management systems are using social networking.

Discussion Questions

9-5
MyLab MIS
Supply chain management is less about managing the physical movement of goods and more about managing information. Discuss the implications of this statement.

9-6
MyLab MIS
If a company wants to implement an enterprise application, it had better do its homework. Discuss the implications of this statement.

9-7
MyLab MIS
Which enterprise application should a business install first: ERP, SCM, or CRM? Explain your answer.

Hands-On MIS Projects

The projects in this section give you hands-on experience analyzing business process integration, suggesting supply chain management and customer relationship management applications, using database software to manage customer service requests, and evaluating supply chain management business services. Visit MyLab MIS to access this chapter's Hands-On MIS Projects,

Management Decision Problems

9-8 Toronto-based Mercedes-Benz Canada, with a network of 55 dealers, did not know enough about its customers. Dealers provided customer data to the company on an ad hoc basis. Mercedes did not force dealers to report this information. There was no real incentive for dealers to share information with the company. How could CRM and PRM systems help solve this problem?

9-9 Office Depot sells a wide range of office supply products and services in the United States and internationally. The company tries to offer a wider range of office supplies at lower cost than other retailers by using just-in-time replenishment and tight inventory control systems. It uses information from a demand forecasting system and point-of-sale data to replenish its inventory in its 1,600 retail stores. Explain how these systems help Office Depot minimize costs and any other benefits they provide. Identify and describe other supply chain management applications that would be especially helpful to Office Depot.

Improving Decision Making: Using Database Software to Manage Customer Service Requests

Software skills: Database design; querying and reporting
Business skills: Customer service analysis

9-10 In this exercise, you'll use database software to develop an application that tracks customer service requests and analyzes customer data to identify customers meriting priority treatment.

Prime Service is a large service company that provides maintenance and repair services for close to 1,200 commercial businesses in New York, New Jersey, and Connecticut. Its customers include businesses of all sizes. Customers with service needs call into its customer service department with requests for repairing heating ducts, broken windows, leaky roofs, broken water pipes, and other problems. The company assigns each request a number and writes down the service request number, the identification number of the customer account, the date of the request, the type of equipment requiring repair, and a brief description of the problem. The service requests are handled on a first-come-first-served basis. After the service work has been completed, Prime calculates the cost of the work, enters the price on the service request form, and bills the client. This arrangement treats the most important and profitable clients—those with accounts of more than $70,000—no differently from its clients with small accounts. Management would like to find a way to provide its best customers with better service. It would also like to know which types of service problems occur most frequently so that it can make sure it has adequate resources to address them.

Prime Service has a small database with client account information, which can be found in MyLab MIS. Use database software to design a solution that would enable Prime's customer service representatives to identify the most important customers so that they could receive priority service. Your solution will require more than one table. Populate your database with at least 10 service requests. Create several reports that would be of interest to management, such as a list of the highest—and lowest—priority accounts and a report showing the most frequently occurring service problems. Create a report listing service calls that customer service representatives should respond to first on a specific date.

Achieving Operational Excellence: Evaluating Supply Chain Management Services

Software skills: Web browser and presentation software
Business skills: Evaluating supply chain management services

9-11 In addition to carrying goods from one place to another, some trucking companies provide supply chain management services and help their customers manage their information. In this project, you'll use the web to research and evaluate two of these business services. Investigate the websites of two companies, UPS and Schneider National, to see how these companies' services can be used for supply chain management. Then respond to the following questions:

- What supply chain processes can each of these companies support for its clients?
- How can customers use the websites of each company to help them with supply chain management?
- Compare the supply chain management services these companies provide. Which company would you select to help your firm manage its supply chain? Why?

Collaboration and Teamwork Project

Analyzing Enterprise Application Vendors

9-12 With a group of three or four other students, use the web to research and evaluate the products of two vendors of enterprise application software. You could compare, for example, the SAP and Oracle enterprise systems, the supply chain management systems from JDA Software and SAP, or the customer relationship management systems of Oracle and Salesforce.com. Use what you have learned from these companies' websites to compare the software products you have selected in terms of business functions supported, technology platforms, cost, and ease of use. Which vendor would you select? Why? Would you select the same vendor for a small business (50–300 employees) as well as for a large one? If possible, use Google Docs and Google Drive or Google Sites to brainstorm, organize, and develop a presentation of your findings for the class.

Clemens Food Group Delivers with New Enterprise Applications

CASE STUDY

Clemens Food Group is known for helping its customers bring home the bacon, and other products as well. Based in Hatfield, Pennsylvania, Clemens Food is a vertically coordinated company that includes antibiotic-free hog farming, food production, logistical services, and transportation. Using a responsive pork production system, the company focuses on supplying the highest-quality products to its partners as well as advanced solutions that simplify partners' operations.

The Clemens Food Group family of services and brands include pork product producers Hatfield Quality Meats and Nick's Sausage Company, as well as logistics and transportation firms (PV Transport), and CFC Logistics Country View Family Farms, a hog procurement and production company managing over 100 family farms raising hogs under contract. Clemens Food Group products are sold by grocers and food service operators in the northeastern and mid-Atlantic regions of the United States. The Clemens Food Group raises and processes about five million hogs per year, managing procurement, production, and logistics services from birth to finished food products. Clemens has 3,350 employees.

For a company in the perishable goods industry such as Clemens Food to be profitable, it must have a firm grasp on the timeliness and accuracy of orders and very precise information about the status of its products and warehouse activities throughout its network of farms and production facilities. Accuracy in determining yields, costs, and prices in a wildly fluctuating market can make a difference of millions of dollars. Unfortunately, Clemens Food's legacy systems were no longer able to keep up with production and support future growth. Management realized the company needed a new platform to provide better visibility into production, more efficient planning, and tighter control of available-to-promise processes. (Available-to-promise [ATP] provides a response to customer order inquiries, generating available quantities of the requested product and delivery due dates.) Clemens Food also wanted real-time information about plant profitability, including daily profitability margins on an order-by-order basis.

In 2010, Clemens Food created a five-year plan to modernize its IT infrastructure with an integrated platform for systems to optimize its supply network and improve scheduling, optimization, and margin visibility in its multi-business operations. The plan gained steam in 2014 when Clemens Food announced it would develop a third pork processing plant comprising 550,000 square feet in Coldwater Township, Michigan. The addition of this facility could significantly increase volume and double revenue if it was backed by a more modern IT platform. Clemens Food's existing ERP system needed to be replaced by one that could handle increased volume and multi-plant complexities.

Joshua Rennells, Senior Vice President at Clemens Food Group, and his team extensively researched new technologies. A key requirement was to use proven best technology for what works in the perishable food industry. Where there is market volatility and inherent risks in selling a perishable product, precise information on yields and costs is especially important. Clemens Food believed SAP software was the best solution for helping the company achieve growth targets and share data across organizational boundaries with a fully integrated state-of-the-art system, and Rennells believed that the SAP S/4HANA platform would not require another significant upgrade for 15 years.

SAP S/4HANA is a business suite that is based on the SAP HANA in-memory computing platform. It features enterprise resource planning software meant to cover all day-to-day processes of an enterprise and also integrates portions of SAP Business Suite products for customer relationship management, supplier relationship management, and supply chain management. SAP S/4HANA is available in on-premises, cloud, and hybrid computing platforms.

Rather than implement the new system incrementally, Clemens Food chose to implement SAP S/4HANA Finance, along with functionality for materials management and production planning in a sweeping "big-bang" approach across the enterprise. The new system needed to be operational in time for the opening of the Coldwater plant. According to Rennells, Clemens Food had used a phased approach for its previous ERP implementation 15 years earlier. That prior rollout ended up taking several years and resulted in heavy customization. By the time Clemens Food migrated to SAP S/4HANA, its legacy ERP system was linked to more than 70 applications.

Taking a big-bang approach was the only way to be up and running before the Coldwater plant went live.

Being in the perishables industry made it imperative for Clemens Food to have master data in place when the new system went live to avoid disruptions to production or shipping capabilities. (Master data play a key role in the core operation of a business, such as data about customers, employees, inventory, or suppliers, and are typically shared by multiple users and groups across an organization.) The master data in Clemens Food's legacy system had quite a few flaws that showed up in testing. Clemens Food needed a rigorous master data cleansing effort.

Clemens Food selected itelligence Group implementation consultants to help with its master data and other migration issues. itelligence Group is a global SAP Platinum Partner with over 25 years of experience. It offers a full range of services from implementation consulting to managed services for its clients. Clemens Food Group identified itelligence as a partner with deep SAP food-specific knowledge and experience, including fresh and processed meat. itelligence Group had a proprietary Hog Procurement solution available for Clemens that helped deliver an on-time and on-budget project with minimal disruption to the business.

itelligence Group had experience guiding other meat-processing companies through similar large-scale implementations. Rennells wanted itelligence to act as business process experts to help Clemens Food re-examine the way it did things. Clemens Food followed itelligence's suggestions about modifications, budget management, the overall testing cycle, and the philosophy of implementation.

One especially valuable piece of project guidance from itelligence was to encourage project members to see the implementation as being led by the business rather than just an IT project. Clemens Foods started out with the project being IT-led, but after five months assigned internal leaders of the business to be the project leads. That switch forced the project team to be more objective through all the different testing phases. After each testing cycle, they had objective scoring from the dedicated team leads who viewed the project as a business process improvement. That helped the project team move closer to a finished product, rather than waiting until going live to find out it missed the mark. Including the business as equal partners when updates were instituted helped ensure that customizations were avoided.

Two Clemens Food production plants went live on SAP S/4HANA in May 2017, three months before the Coldwater facility began operations. There were no business disruptions. To avoid disruption of production or shipping capabilities, the company had built in some planned downtime for production to address any issues with shipping or procurement, which are tied to the Coldwater plant's main distribution system. The planned downtime also ensured that any master data flaws potentially discovered through testing would be cleaned up and master data would be in place before the system actually went live. Management had anticipated it would take about six months to stabilize the new system, and that turned out to be accurate.

Sales forecasting in the meat-processing industry has unique challenges because of the many variables from dealing with perishable products, raw material by-products, and seasonality considerations. Every Thursday, Clemens Food had run a sales report on its old legacy system that showed the previous week's sales. Information about actual profitability was delayed. Now, the company can measure profitability on an invoice-by-invoice basis, and it knows the profitability of each order right away. Prices change daily in the perishable food business, so the importance of having real-time information about profitability can't be overstated.

Deeper insights and visibility from the new system have improved customer service. With available-to-promise processes running on SAP S/4HANA and with SAP S/4HANA integrated with the company's warehouse management system, Clemens Food can assure customers placing a phone order whether there is inventory available. In the pork industry, this can be an extremely complicated task, since a single hog can be broken down into hundreds of by-products. Before implementing SAP S/4HANA, Clemens Food was able to provide the same assurance only when an order was ready for shipment.

Once the new system is fully stabilized, Clemens Food plans a reporting upgrade, using SAP HANA Live views with its existing SAP BusinessObjects Business Intelligence suite. The company now has a single "source of truth," and data are integrated, whereas in the past it had to deal with similar data spread over multiple systems. With a single source of truth and the ability to put information at people's fingertips, Clemens Foods can create dashboards and focus on making reporting far simpler than it's ever been.

Sources: Ken Murphy, "Clemens Food Group Corrals the Power of the Digital Core," *SAP Insider*, January 24, 2018; www. itelligencegroup.com, accessed March 27, 2018; "Clemens Food Group LLC," www.vault.com, accessed March 27, 2018; and www. clemensfoodgroup.com, accessed March 27, 2018.

CASE STUDY QUESTIONS

9-13 Why would supply chain management be so important for Clemens Food Group?

9-14 What problem was the company facing? What management, organization, and technology factors contributed to the problem?

9-15 Was SAP S/4HANA a good solution for Clemens Food Group? Explain your answer.

9-16 What management, organization, and technology issues had to be addressed to implement SAP S/4HANA at Clemens Food Group?

MyLab MIS

Go to the Assignments section of MyLab MIS to complete these writing exercises.

9-17 What are three reasons a company would want to implement an enterprise resource planning (ERP) system and two reasons it might not want to do so?

9-18 What are the sources of data for analytical CRM systems? Provide three examples of outputs from analytical CRM systems.

Chapter 9 References

Bowers, Melissa R., Adam G. Petrie, and Mary C. Holcomb." Unleashing the Potential of Supply Chain Analytics." MIT Sloan Management Review (Fall 2017).

Bozarth, Cecil, and Robert B. Handfield. *Introduction to Operations and Supply Chain Management*, 5th ed. (Upper Saddle River, NJ: Prentice-Hall, 2019).

D'Avanzo, Robert, Hans von Lewinski, and Luk N. van Wassenhove. "The Link Between Supply Chain and Financial Performance." *Supply Chain Management Review* (November 1, 2003).

Davenport, Thomas H. *Mission Critical: Realizing the Promise of Enterprise Systems.* (Boston: Harvard Business School Press, 2000).

Franken, Govert. "SAP AI: Machine Learning in Oil and Gas." blogs.sap.com, accessed April 11, 2018.

Fruhlinger, Josh, and Thomas Wailgum. "15 Famous ERP Disasters, Dustups and Disappointments." *CIO* (July 10, 2017).

Hitt, Lorin, D. J. Wu, and Xiaoge Zhou. "Investment in Enterprise Resource Planning: Business Impact and Productivity Measures." *Journal of Management Information Systems* 19, No. 1 (Summer 2002).

Hu, Michael, and Sean T. Monahan. "Sharing Supply Chain Data in the Digital Era." *MIT Sloan Management Review* (Fall 2015).

Kitchens, Brent, David, Dobolyi, Jingjing Li, and Ahmed Abbasi. "Advanced Customer Analytics: Strategic Value Through Integration of Relationship-Oriented Big Data." *Journal of Management Information Systems* 35, No. 2 (2018).

Klein, Richard, and Arun Rai. "Interfirm Strategic Information Flows in Logistics Supply Chain Relationships." *MIS Quarterly* 33, No. 4 (December 2009).

Laudon, Kenneth C. "The Promise and Potential of Enterprise Systems and Industrial Networks." Working paper, The Concours Group. Copyright Kenneth C. Laudon (1999).

Lee, Hau L., V. Padmanabhan, and Seugin Whang. "The Bullwhip Effect in Supply Chains." *Sloan Management Review* (Spring 1997).

Liang, Huigang, Zeyu Peng, Yajiong Xue, Xitong Guo, and Nengmin Wang. "Employees' Exploration of Complex Systems: An Integrative View." *Journal of Management Information Systems* 32, No. 1 (2015).

Maklan, Stan, Simon Knox, and Joe Peppard. "When CRM Fails." *MIT Sloan Management Review* 52, No. 4 (Summer 2011).

Malik, Yogesh, Alex Niemeyer, and Brian Ruwadi. "Building the Supply Chain of the Future." *McKinsey Quarterly* (January 2011).

Nadeau, Michael. "ERP Heads for the Cloud." *CIO* (September 20 2016).

_____. "Hybrid ERP Matures as Companies Develop Better Strategies." *CIO* (February 22, 2017).

Oracle Corporation. "Alcoa Implements Oracle Solution 20% Below Projected Cost, Eliminates 43 Legacy Systems." www.oracle.com, accessed August 21, 2005.

Panorama Consulting Solutions. "2018 ERP Report" (2018).

Rai, Arun, Paul A. Pavlou, Ghiyoung Im, and Steve Du. "Interfirm IT Capability Profiles and Communications for Cocreating Relational Value: Evidence from the Logistics Industry." *MIS Quarterly* 36, No. 1 (March 2012).

Ranganathan, C., and Carol V. Brown. "ERP Investments and the Market Value of Firms: Toward an Understanding of Influential ERP Project Variables." *Information Systems Research* 17, No. 2 (June 2006).

Sarker, Supreteek, Saonee Sarker, Arvin Sahaym, and Bjørn-Andersen. "Exploring Value Cocreation in Relationships Between an ERP Vendor and Its Partners: A Revelatory Case Study." *MIS Quarterly* 36, No. 1 (March 2012).

Seldon, Peter B., Cheryl Calvert, and Song Yang. "A Multi-Project Model of Key Factors Affecting Organizational Benefits from Enterprise Systems." *MIS Quarterly* 34, No. 2 (June 2010).

Sodhi, ManMohan S., and Christopher S. Tang. "Supply Chains Built for Speed and Customization." *MIT Sloan Management Review* (Summer 2017).

Strong, Diane M., and Olga Volkoff. "Understanding Organization-Enterprise System Fit: A Path to Theorizing the Information Technology Artifact." *MIS Quarterly* 34, No. 4 (December 2010).

Sykes, Tracy Ann, Viswanath Venkatesh, and Jonathan L. Johnson. "Enterprise System Implementation and Employee Job

Performance: Understanding the Role of Advice Networks." *MIS Quarterly* 38, No. 1 (March 2014).

Tate, Wendy L., Diane Mollenkopf, Theodore Stank, and Andrea Lago da Silva. "Integrating Supply and Demand." *MIT Sloan Management Review* (Summer 2015).

Thibodeau, Patrick. "Office Depot Says 'No' to Oracle ERP Cloud Customizations." *TechTarget* (February 1, 2018).

Tian, Feng, and Sean Xin Xu. "How Do Enterprise Resource Planning Systems Affect Firm Risk? Post-Implementation Impact." *MIS Quarterly* 39, No. 1 (March 2015).

"Top 5 Reasons ERP Implementations Fail and What You Can Do About It." Ziff Davis (2013).

Van Caeneghem, Alexander, and Jean-Marie Becquevort. "Turning on ERP Systems Can Turn Off People." *CFO* (February 5, 2016).

Wailgum, Thomas. "What Is ERP? A Guide to Enterprise Resource Planning Systems." *CIO* (July 27, 2017).

Wong, Christina W. Y., Kee-Hung Lai, and T. C. E. Cheng. "Value of Information Integration to Supply Chain Management: Roles of Internal and External Contingencies." *Journal of Management Information Systems* 28, No. 3 (Winter 2012).

Zhang, Jonathan Z., George F. Watson IV, and Robert W. Palmatier. "Customer Relationships Evolve—So Must Your CRM Strategy." *MIT Sloan Management Review* (May 1, 2018).

10

E-commerce: Digital Markets, Digital Goods

LEARNING OBJECTIVES

After reading this chapter, you will be able to answer the following questions:

10-1 What are the unique features of e-commerce, digital markets, and digital goods?

10-2 What are the principal e-commerce business and revenue models?

10-3 How has e-commerce transformed marketing?

10-4 How has e-commerce affected business-to-business transactions?

10-5 What is the role of m-commerce in business, and what are the most important m-commerce applications?

10-6 What issues must be addressed when building an e-commerce presence?

10-7 How will MIS help my career?

CHAPTER CASES

YouTube Transforms the Media Landscape
Uber: Digital Disruptor
"Socializing" with Customers
A Nasty Ending for Nasty Gal

VIDEO CASES

Walmart Takes On Amazon: A Battle of IT and Management Systems
Groupon: Deals Galore
Etsy: A Marketplace and Community

Instructional Videos:
Walmart's E-commerce Fulfillment Center Network
Behind the Scenes of an Amazon Warehouse

MyLab MIS

Discussion Questions: 10-7, 10-8, 10-9; **Hands-on MIS Projects:** 10-10, 10-11, 10-12, 10-13; **Writing Assignments:** 10-18, 10-19; **eText with Conceptual Animations**

Youtube Transforms the Media Landscape

The first video posted on YouTube was a 19-second clip from 2005 of one of the company's founders standing in front of the San Diego Zoo elephant cage. Who would have thought that the online video-sharing service would mushroom into the world's second most popular website, with more than 1.8 billion monthly users? YouTube viewers worldwide now watch more than 5 billion YouTube videos per day. Three hundred hours of video are uploaded to YouTube every minute.

YouTube allows users to view, rate, share, add to favorites, report, and comment on videos and subscribe to other users' video channels. Although hundreds of millions of people love to post YouTube videos of their growing children, dogs, and cats, YouTube offers much more: clips from major motion pictures and TV shows, music videos, sports videos, videos from companies promoting their brands, and numerous "how-to" videos about home repair, gardening, and computer troubleshooting. Most YouTube content has been uploaded by individuals, but media corporations such as CBS, the BBC, Vevo, and Hulu offer some of their material via YouTube as part of a partnership program.

© Bloomicon/Shutterstock

YouTube maintains very large databases for video content and tracking the behavior of its users. It carefully mines data to give each user personalized video recommendations that will entice that person to watch longer. There are so many eyeballs affixed to YouTube—it's a gold mine for marketers, and YouTube content gets richer by the minute. More than half of YouTube views come from mobile devices.

YouTube was purchased by Google in 2006 and benefits from Google's enormous reach, since Google handles about 80 percent of global Internet searches. YouTube revenue comes from ads accompanying videos that are targeted to site content and audiences. YouTube also offers subscription-based premium channels, film rentals, and a subscription service called YouTube Red that provides ad-free access to the website and some exclusive content. It is unclear if YouTube is actually profitable at this point. Experts believe that annual costs for running and maintaining YouTube exceed $6 billion.

Once known as a magnet for pirated video, YouTube has been embraced by Hollywood and the entertainment world. Almost every movie trailer or music video is released onto YouTube; all major sports leagues upload highlights there; and networks supplement traditional programming with videos that can be shared, like the talk show host James Corden's "Carpool Karaoke" series. YouTube has become a major destination entertainment site, and it is about to alter the media landscape even further.

YouTube has joined services targeting consumers who want to give up cable or satellite TV without losing access to live television. In early 2017, YouTube announced a subscription service called YouTube TV. For $40 per month, the service offers more than 60 channels, including the major networks, FX, ESPN, and the Disney Channel, as well as the ability to store an unlimited number of programs on a cloud-based digital video recorder for up to six accounts. YouTube TV subscribers will be able to watch content on any platform, including PCs, tablets, smartphones, and big-screen TVs.

After the cost of acquiring all this television content is considered, Google may not make much on YouTube TV subscription revenue. That's fine right now, because Google is using YouTube TV to break into the television advertising market, selling targeted advertising in ad slots that typically went to cable operators. In the long term, that could be significant: Roughly $70 billion is spent annually in the United States on TV ads.

Sources: David Pierce, "Why You Should Cut Cable—and What You'll Miss," *Wall Street Journal*, February 14, 2018; Douglas MacMillan, "Investors Want More Transparency about YouTube's Sales, Profit," *Wall Street Journal*, April 10, 2018; "37 Mind Blowing YouTube Facts, Figures and Statistics—2018," *MerchDope*, August 4, 2018; www.tv.youtube.com, accessed July 30, 2018; Jack Nicas, "YouTube Tops 1 Billion Hours of Video a Day, on Pace to Eclipse TV," *Wall Street Journal*, February 27, 2017; Jack Nicas and Shalini Ramachandran, "Google's YouTube to Launch $35-a-Month Web-TV Service," *Wall Street Journal*, February 28, 2017; and Peter Kafka and Rani Molla, "2017 Was the Year Digital Ad Spending Finally Beat TV," *Recode*, December 4, 2017.

YouTube exemplifies some of the major trends in e-commerce today. It does not sell a product, it sells an innovative service, as e-commerce businesses are increasingly trying to do. YouTube's service delivers streaming video content either for free (supported by advertising) or by subscription, and also enables users to upload and store their own videos. YouTube makes use of advanced data mining and search technology to generate revenue from advertising. YouTube is "social," linking people to each other through their shared interests and fascination with video. And it is mobile: YouTube can be viewed on smartphones and tablets as well as conventional computers and TV screens, and more than half of YouTube views are on mobile devices.

The chapter-opening diagram calls attention to important points raised by this case and this chapter. YouTube's primary business challenge is how to take advantage of opportunities presented by the Internet and new developments in search and data mining technology to wring profits from the billions of videos it streams to viewers. Obviously YouTube had to make major investments in technology to support video uploads and downloads, gigantic databases of videos and users, tagging images, and social networking tools. YouTube generates revenue from ads targeted to video viewers and from subscriptions to its streaming content services, including its new lineup of major TV channels. It is unclear

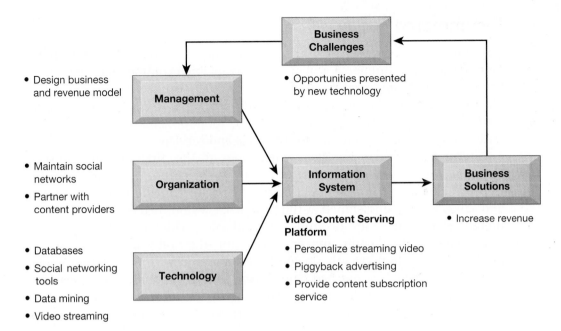

whether YouTube has achieved long-term profitability, but it is very valuable to Google as another outlet for its advertising.

Here are some questions to think about: How does YouTube provide value? Why is YouTube an expensive business to operate? Is it a viable business model? Why or why not?

10-1 What are the unique features of e-commerce, digital markets, and digital goods?

In 2019, purchasing goods and services online by using smartphones, tablets, and desktop computers is ubiquitous. In 2019, an estimated 224 million Americans (about 92 percent of the Internet population) will shop online, and 195 million will purchase something online, as did millions of others worldwide. Although most purchases still take place through traditional channels, e-commerce continues to grow rapidly and to transform the way many companies do business (eMarketer, 2018h). E-commerce is composed of three major segments: retail goods, travel and services, and online content. In 2019, e-commerce consumer sales of goods ($598 billion), travel and services ($213 billion), and online content ($23 billion) will total about $830 billion. Sales of retail goods alone will be about 11 percent of total U.S. retail sales of $5.9 trillion, and are growing at 12 percent annually (compared with 3.3 percent for traditional retailers) (eMarketer, 2018e; 2018c). E-commerce is still a small part of the much larger retail goods market that takes place in physical stores. E-commerce has expanded from the desktop and home computer to mobile devices, from an isolated activity to a new social commerce, and from a *Fortune* 1000 commerce with a national audience to local merchants and consumers whose location is known to mobile devices. At the top 100 e-commerce retail sites, more than half of online shoppers arrive from their smartphones, and 48 percent of e-commerce sales are now mobile, while 52 percent of purchases occur on the desktop. The key words for understanding this new e-commerce in 2019 are "social, mobile, local" (eMarketer, 2018d).

E-commerce Today

E-commerce refers to the use of the Internet and the web to transact business. More formally, e-commerce is about digitally enabled commercial transactions between and among organizations and individuals. For the most part, this refers to transactions that occur over the Internet and the web. Commercial transactions involve the exchange of value (e.g., money) across organizational or individual boundaries in return for products and services.

E-commerce began in 1995 when one of the first Internet portals, Netscape.com, accepted the first ads from major corporations and popularized the idea that the web could be used as a new medium for advertising and sales. No one envisioned at the time what would turn out to be an exponential growth curve for e-commerce retail sales, which doubled and tripled in the early years. E-commerce grew at double-digit rates until the recession of 2008–2009, when growth slowed to a crawl and revenues flattened (see Figure 10.1), which is not bad considering that traditional retail sales were shrinking by 5 percent annually. Since then, offline retail sales have increased only a few percentage points a year, whereas online e-commerce has been a stellar success.

The very rapid growth in e-commerce in the early years created a market bubble in e-commerce stocks, which burst in March 2001. A large number of e-commerce companies failed during this process. Yet for many others, such as Amazon, eBay, Expedia, and Google, the results have been more positive: soaring revenues, fine-tuned business models that produce profits, and rising stock prices. By 2006, e-commerce revenues returned to solid growth and have continued to be the fastest-growing form of retail trade in the United States, Europe, and Asia.

- Online consumer sales (including travel and digital content) will grow to an estimated $830 billion in 2019, an increase of more than 12 percent over 2018 with 195 million people purchasing online and an additional 224 million shopping and gathering information but not purchasing (eMarketer, 2017b).

FIGURE 10.1 THE GROWTH OF E-COMMERCE

Retail e-commerce revenues grew 15–25 percent per year until the recession of 2008–2009, when they slowed measurably. In 2018, e-commerce revenues grew at an estimated 12 percent annually.

Sources: Based on data from eMarketer, "US Retail Ecommerce Sales, 2018–2022," 2018c; eMarketer, "US Digital Travel Sales, 2018–2022," 2018a; and eMarketer chart, "US Mobile Downloads and In-App Revenues, 2013–2017," 2017a.

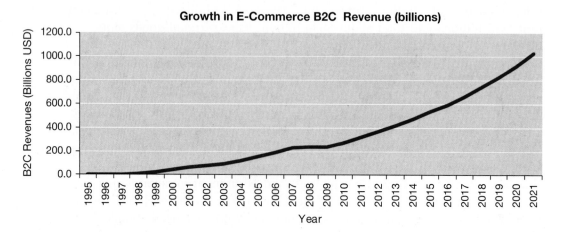

The Internet influences more than $2 trillion in retail commerce that takes place in physical stores, about 40 percent of all retail sales.

- The number of individuals of all ages online in the United States is expected to grow to 279 million in 2018, up from 147 million in 2004. In the world, more than 3.7 billion people are now connected to the Internet. Growth in the overall Internet population has spurred growth in e-commerce (Internet World Stats, 2018).

- Approximately 106 million U.S. households will have broadband access to the Internet in 2018, representing about 82 percent of all households.

- About 232 million Americans will access the Internet by using a smartphone in 2019. Mobile e-commerce has begun a rapid growth based on apps, ringtones, downloaded entertainment, and location-based services. Mobile e-commerce will account for about $267 billion in 2019, 44 percent of all e-commerce. Mobile phones and tablets are becoming the most common Internet access device. Currently, more than 80 percent of all mobile phone users access the Internet using their phones, although they also use their desktops (eMarketer, 2018b).

- B2B e-commerce (use of the Internet for business-to-business commerce and collaboration among business partners) expanded to more than $7.7 trillion. Table 10.1 highlights these new e-commerce developments.

The New E-commerce: Social, Mobile, Local

One of the biggest changes is the extent to which e-commerce has become more social, mobile, and local. Online marketing once consisted largely of creating a corporate website, buying display ads on Yahoo, purchasing search-related ads on Google, and sending email messages. The workhorse of online marketing was the display ad. It still is, but it's increasingly being replaced by video ads, which are far more effective. Display ads from the very beginning of the Internet were based on television ads, where brand messages were flashed before millions of users who were not expected to respond immediately, ask questions, or make observations. If the ads did not work, the solution was often to repeat the ad. The primary measure of success was how many eyeballs (unique visitors) a website produced and how many impressions a marketing campaign generated. (An impression was one ad shown to one person.) Both of these measures were carryovers from the world of television, which measures marketing in terms of audience size and ad views.

From Eyeballs to Conversations: Conversational Commerce

After 2007, all this changed with the rapid growth of Facebook and other social sites, the explosive growth of smartphones beginning with the Apple iPhone, and the growing interest in local marketing. What's different about the new world of social-mobile-local e-commerce is the dual and related concepts of conversations and engagement. In the popular literature, this is often referred to as conversational commerce. Marketing in this new period is based on firms engaging in multiple online conversations with their customers, potential customers, and even critics. Your brand is being talked about on the web and social media (that's the conversation part), and marketing your firm, building, and restoring your brands require you to locate, identify, and participate in these conversations. Social marketing means all things social: listening, discussing, interacting, empathizing, and engaging. The emphasis in online marketing has shifted from a focus on eyeballs to a focus on participating in customer-oriented conversations. In this sense, social marketing is not simply a new ad channel

TABLE 10.1 THE GROWTH OF E-COMMERCE

BUSINESS TRANSFORMATION

E-commerce remains the fastest-growing form of commerce when compared to physical retail stores, services, and entertainment. Social, mobile, and local commerce have become the fastest-growing forms of e-commerce.

The breadth of e-commerce offerings grows, especially in the services economy of social networking, travel, entertainment, retail apparel, jewelry, appliances, and home furnishings.

The online demographics of shoppers broaden to match that of ordinary shoppers.

Pure e-commerce business models are refined further to achieve higher levels of profitability, and traditional retail firms, such as Walmart, JCPenney, L.L.Bean, and Macy's, are developing omnichannel business models to strengthen their dominant physical retail assets. Walmart, the world's largest retailer, has decided to take on Amazon with a more than $1 billion investment in its e-commerce efforts.

Small businesses and entrepreneurs continue to flood the e-commerce marketplace, often riding on the infrastructures created by industry giants, such as Amazon, Apple, and Google, and increasingly taking advantage of cloud-based computing resources.

Mobile e-commerce has taken off in the United States with location-based services and entertainment downloads, including e-books, movies, music, and television shows. Mobile e-commerce will generate more than $267 billion in 2019.

TECHNOLOGY FOUNDATIONS

Wireless Internet connections (Wi-Fi, WiMax, and 4G smartphones) continue to expand.

Powerful smartphones and tablet computers provide access to music, web surfing, and entertainment as well as voice communication. Podcasting and streaming take off as platforms for distribution of video, radio, and user-generated content.

Mobile devices expand to include wearable computers such as Apple Watch and Fitbit trackers.

The Internet broadband foundation becomes stronger in households and businesses as communication prices fall.

Social networking apps and sites such as Facebook, Twitter, LinkedIn, Instagram, and others seek to become a major new platform for e-commerce, marketing, and advertising. Facebook has 2.2 billion users worldwide and 214 million in the United States (Facebook, 2018).

Internet-based models of computing, such as smartphone apps, cloud computing, software as a service (SaaS), and database software greatly reduce the cost of e-commerce websites.

NEW BUSINESS MODELS EMERGE

More than 70 percent of the Internet population has joined an online social network, created blogs, and shared photos and music. Together, these sites create an online audience as large as that of television that is attractive to marketers. In 2018, social networking will account for an estimated 15 percent of online time. Social sites have become the primary gateway to the Internet in news, music, and, increasingly, products and services. (eMarketer, 2018f)

The traditional advertising industry is disrupted as online advertising grows twice as fast as TV and print advertising; Google, Yahoo, and Facebook display more than 1 trillion ads a year.

On-demand service e-commerce sites such as Uber, Lyft, and Airbnb extend the market creator business model (on-demand model) to new areas of the economy.

Newspapers and other traditional media adopt online, interactive models but are losing advertising revenues to the online players despite gaining online readers. The *New York Times* succeeds in capturing more than 2.8 million subscribers, growing at 25 percent annually and adding 400,000 new digital subscribers in 2018. Book publishing continues to grow slowly at 5 percent because of the growth in e-books and the continuing appeal of traditional books.

Online entertainment business models offering television, movies, music, and games grow with cooperation among the major copyright owners in Hollywood and New York and with Internet distributors such as Apple, Amazon, Google, YouTube, and Facebook. Increasingly, the online distributors are moving into movie and TV production. Cable television is in modest decline, as some viewers cut or reduce their cable subscriptions and rely on Internet-based alternatives such as Roku or YouTube TV.

but a collection of technology-based tools for communicating with shoppers. The leading social commerce platforms are Facebook, Instagram, Twitter, and Pinterest.

In the past, firms could tightly control their brand messaging and lead consumers down a funnel of cues that ended in a purchase. That is not true of social marketing. Consumer purchase decisions are increasingly driven by the conversations, choices, tastes, and opinions of their social network. Social marketing is all about firms participating in and shaping this social process.

From the Desktop to the Smartphone

Traditional online marketing (browser-based, search, display ads, video ads, email, and games) still constitutes the majority (58 percent) of all online marketing ($107 billion), but it's growing much more slowly than social-mobile-local marketing. Mobile marketing now constitutes 70 percent of all online marketing. The marketing dollars are following customers and shoppers from the PC to mobile devices (eMarketer, 2018g)

Social, mobile, and local e-commerce are connected. As mobile devices become more powerful, they are more useful for accessing Facebook and other social sites. As mobile devices become more widely adopted, customers can use them to find local merchants, and merchants can use them to alert customers in their neighborhood of special offers.

Why E-commerce Is Different

Why has e-commerce grown so rapidly? The answer lies in the unique nature of the Internet and the web. Simply put, the Internet and e-commerce technologies are much richer and more powerful than previous technology revolutions such as radio, television, and the telephone. Table 10.2 describes the unique features of the Internet and web as a commercial medium. Let's explore each of these unique features in more detail.

Ubiquity

In traditional commerce, a marketplace is a physical place, such as a retail store, that you visit to transact business. E-commerce is ubiquitous, meaning

TABLE 10.2 EIGHT UNIQUE FEATURES OF E-COMMERCE TECHNOLOGY

E-COMMERCE TECHNOLOGY DIMENSION	BUSINESS SIGNIFICANCE
Ubiquity. Internet/web technology is available everywhere: at work, at home, and elsewhere by desktop and mobile devices. Mobile devices extend service to local areas and merchants.	The marketplace is extended beyond traditional boundaries and is removed from a temporal and geographic location. Marketspace is created; shopping can take place anytime, anywhere. Customer convenience is enhanced, and shopping costs are reduced.
Global Reach. The technology reaches across national boundaries, around the earth.	Commerce is enabled across cultural and national boundaries seamlessly and without modification. The marketspace includes, potentially, billions of consumers and millions of businesses worldwide.
Universal Standards. There is one set of technology standards, namely Internet standards.	With one set of technical standards across the globe, disparate computer systems can easily communicate with each other.
Richness. Video, audio, and text messages are possible.	Video, audio, and text marketing messages are integrated into a single marketing message and consumer experience.
Interactivity. The technology works through interaction with the user.	Consumers are engaged in a dialogue that dynamically adjusts the experience to the individual and makes the consumer a participant in the process of delivering goods to the market.
Information Density. The technology reduces information costs and raises quality.	Information processing, storage, and communication costs drop dramatically, whereas currency, accuracy, and timeliness improve greatly. Information becomes plentiful, cheap, and more accurate.
Personalization/Customization. The technology allows personalized messages to be delivered to individuals as well as to groups.	Personalization of marketing messages and customization of products and services are based on individual characteristics.
Social Technology. The technology supports content generation and social networking.	New Internet social and business models enable user content creation and distribution and support social networks.

that it is available just about everywhere all the time. It makes it possible to shop from your desktop, at home, at work, or even from your car, using smartphones. The result is called a **marketspace**—a marketplace extended beyond traditional boundaries and removed from a temporal and geographic location.

From a consumer point of view, ubiquity reduces **transaction costs**—the costs of participating in a market. To transact business, it is no longer necessary to spend time or money traveling to a market, and much less mental effort is required to make a purchase.

Global Reach

E-commerce technology permits commercial transactions to cross cultural and national boundaries far more conveniently and cost effectively than is true in traditional commerce. As a result, the potential market size for e-commerce merchants is roughly equal to the size of the world's online population (estimated to be more than 3 billion).

In contrast, most traditional commerce is local or regional—it involves local merchants or national merchants with local outlets. Television, radio stations, and newspapers, for instance, are primarily local and regional institutions with limited, but powerful, national networks that can attract a national audience but not easily cross national boundaries to a global audience.

Universal Standards

One strikingly unusual feature of e-commerce technologies is that the technical standards of the Internet and, therefore, the technical standards for conducting e-commerce are universal standards. All nations around the world share them and enable any computer to link with any other computer regardless of the technology platform each is using. In contrast, most traditional commerce technologies differ from one nation to the next. For instance, television and radio standards differ around the world, as does cellular telephone technology.

The universal technical standards of the Internet and e-commerce greatly lower **market entry costs**—the cost merchants must pay simply to bring their goods to market. At the same time, for consumers, universal standards reduce **search costs**—the effort required to find suitable products.

Richness

Information **richness** refers to the complexity and content of a message. Traditional markets, national sales forces, and small retail stores have great richness; they can provide personal, face-to-face service, using aural and visual cues when making a sale. The richness of traditional markets makes them powerful selling or commercial environments. Prior to the development of the web, there was a trade-off between richness and reach; the larger the audience reached, the less rich the message. The web makes it possible to deliver rich messages with text, audio, and video simultaneously to large numbers of people.

Interactivity

Unlike any of the commercial technologies of the twentieth century, with the possible exception of the telephone, e-commerce technologies are interactive, meaning they allow for two-way communication between merchant and consumer and peer-to-peer communication among friends. Television, for instance, cannot ask viewers any questions or enter conversations with them, and it cannot request customer information to be entered on a form. In contrast, all these activities are possible on an e-commerce website or mobile app. Interactivity allows an online merchant to engage a consumer in ways similar to a face-to-face experience but on a massive, global scale.

Information Density

The Internet and the web vastly increase **information density**—the total amount and quality of information available to all market participants, consumers, and merchants alike. E-commerce technologies reduce information collection, storage, processing, and communication costs while greatly increasing the currency, accuracy, and timeliness of information.

Information density in e-commerce markets make prices and costs more transparent. **Price transparency** refers to the ease with which consumers can find out the variety of prices in a market; **cost transparency** refers to the ability of consumers to discover the actual costs merchants pay for products.

There are advantages for merchants as well. Online merchants can discover much more about consumers than in the past. This allows merchants to segment the market into groups that are willing to pay different prices and permits the merchants to engage in **price discrimination**—selling the same goods, or nearly the same goods, to different targeted groups at different prices. For instance, an online merchant can discover a consumer's avid interest in expensive, exotic vacations and then pitch high-end vacation plans to that consumer at a premium price, knowing this person is willing to pay extra for such a vacation. At the same time, the online merchant can pitch the same vacation plan at a lower price to a more price-sensitive consumer. Information density also helps merchants differentiate their products in terms of cost, brand, and quality.

Personalization/Customization

E-commerce technologies permit **personalization**. Merchants can target their marketing messages to specific individuals by adjusting the message to a person's clickstream behavior, name, interests, and past purchases. The technology also permits **customization**—changing the delivered product or service based on a user's preferences or prior behavior. Given the interactive nature of e-commerce technology, much information about the consumer can be gathered in the marketplace at the moment of purchase. With the increase in information density, a great deal of information about the consumer's past purchases and behavior can be stored and used by online merchants.

The result is a level of personalization and customization unthinkable with traditional commerce technologies. For instance, you may be able to shape what you see on television by selecting a channel, but you cannot change the content of the channel you have chosen. In contrast, online news outlets such as the *Wall Street Journal Online* allow you to select the type of news stories you want to see first and give you the opportunity to be alerted when certain events happen.

Social Technology: User Content Generation and Social Networking

In contrast to previous technologies, the Internet and e-commerce technologies have evolved to be much more social by allowing users to create and share with their friends (and a larger worldwide community) content in the form of text, videos, music, or photos. By using these forms of communication, users can create new social networks and strengthen existing ones.

All previous mass media, including the printing press, use a broadcast model (one-to-many) in which content is created in a central location by experts (professional writers, editors, directors, and producers), with audiences concentrated in huge numbers to consume a standardized product. The new Internet and e-commerce empower users to create and distribute content on a large scale and permit users to program their own content consumption. The Internet provides a unique many-to-many model of mass communications.

Key Concepts in E-commerce: Digital Markets and Digital Goods in a Global Marketplace

The location, timing, and revenue models of business are based in some part on the cost and distribution of information. The Internet has created a digital marketplace where millions of people all over the world can exchange massive amounts of information directly, instantly, and free. As a result, the Internet has changed the way companies conduct business and increased their global reach.

The Internet reduces information asymmetry. An **information asymmetry** exists when one party in a transaction has more information that is important for the transaction than the other party. That information helps determine their relative bargaining power. In digital markets, consumers and suppliers can see the prices being charged for goods, and in that sense, digital markets are said to be more transparent than traditional markets.

For example, before automobile retailing sites appeared on the web, there was significant information asymmetry between auto dealers and customers. Only the auto dealers knew the manufacturers' prices, and it was difficult for consumers to shop around for the best price. Auto dealers' profit margins depended on this asymmetry of information. Today's consumers have access to a legion of websites providing competitive pricing information, and three-fourths of U.S. auto buyers use the Internet to shop around for the best deal. Thus, the web has reduced the information asymmetry surrounding an auto purchase. The Internet has also helped businesses seeking to purchase from other businesses reduce information asymmetries and locate better prices and terms.

Digital markets are very flexible and efficient because they operate with reduced search and transaction costs, lower **menu costs** (merchants' costs of changing prices), greater price discrimination, and the ability to change prices dynamically based on market conditions. In **dynamic pricing**, the price of a product varies depending on the demand characteristics of the customer or the supply situation of the seller. For instance, online retailers from Amazon to Walmart change prices on thousands of products based on time of day, demand for the product, and users' prior visits to their sites. Using big data analytics, some online firms can adjust prices at the individual level based on behavioral targeting parameters such as whether the consumer is a price haggler (who will receive a lower price offer) versus a person who accepts offered prices and does not search for lower prices. Prices can also vary by zip code. Uber, along with other ride services, uses surge pricing to adjust prices of a ride based on demand (which always rises during storms and major conventions).

These new digital markets can either reduce or increase switching costs, depending on the nature of the product or service being sold, and they might cause some extra delay in gratification due to shipping times. Unlike a physical market, you can't immediately consume a product such as clothing purchased over the web (although immediate consumption is possible with digital music downloads and other digital products).

FIGURE 10.2 THE BENEFITS OF DISINTERMEDIATION TO THE CONSUMER

The typical distribution channel has several intermediary layers, each of which adds to the final cost of a product, such as a sweater. Removing layers lowers the final cost to the customer.

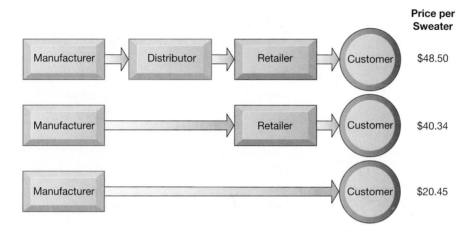

Price per Sweater

Manufacturer → Distributor → Retailer → Customer	$48.50
Manufacturer → Retailer → Customer	$40.34
Manufacturer → Customer	$20.45

Digital markets provide many opportunities to sell directly to the consumer, bypassing intermediaries such as distributors or retail outlets. Eliminating intermediaries in the distribution channel can significantly lower purchase transaction costs. To pay for all the steps in a traditional distribution channel, a product may have to be priced as high as 135 percent of its original cost to manufacture.

Figure 10.2 illustrates how much savings result from eliminating each of these layers in the distribution process. By selling directly to consumers or reducing the number of intermediaries, companies can raise profits while charging lower prices. The removal of organizations or business process layers responsible for intermediary steps in a value chain is called **disintermediation**. E-commerce has also given rise to a completely new set of new intermediaries such as Amazon, eBay, PayPal, and Blue Nile. Therefore, disintermediation differs from one industry to another.

Disintermediation is affecting the market for services. Airlines and hotels operating their own reservation sites online earn more per ticket because they have eliminated travel agents as intermediaries. Table 10.3 summarizes the differences between digital markets and traditional markets.

Digital Goods

The Internet digital marketplace has greatly expanded sales of **digital goods**—goods that can be delivered over a digital network. Music tracks, video, Hollywood movies, software, newspapers, magazines, and books can all be expressed, stored, delivered, and sold as purely digital products. For the most part, digital goods are intellectual property, which is defined as "works of the mind." Intellectual property is protected from misappropriation by copyright, patent, trademark, and trade secret laws (see Chapter 4). Today, all these products are delivered as digital streams or downloads while their physical counterparts decline in sales.

In general, for digital goods, the marginal cost of producing another unit is about zero (it costs nothing to make a copy of a music file). However, the cost of producing the original first unit is relatively high—in fact, it is nearly the total cost of the product because there are few other costs of inventory and distribution. Costs of delivery over the Internet are very low, marketing costs often

TABLE 10.3 DIGITAL MARKETS COMPARED WITH TRADITIONAL MARKETS

	DIGITAL MARKETS	TRADITIONAL MARKETS
Information asymmetry	Asymmetry reduced	Asymmetry high
Search costs	Low	High
Transaction costs	Low (sometimes virtually nothing)	High (time, travel)
Delayed gratification	High (or lower in the case of a digital good)	Lower: purchase now
Menu costs	Low	High
Dynamic pricing	Low cost, instant	High cost, delayed
Price discrimination	Low cost, instant	High cost, delayed
Market segmentation	Low cost, moderate precision	High cost, less precision
Switching costs	Higher/lower (depending on product characteristics)	High
Network effects	Strong	Weaker
Disintermediation	More possible/likely	Less possible/unlikely

remain the same, and pricing can be highly variable. On the Internet, the merchant can change prices as often as desired because of low menu costs.

The impact of the Internet on the market for these kinds of digital goods is nothing short of revolutionary, and we see the results around us every day. Businesses dependent on physical products for sales—such as bookstores, music stores, book publishers, music labels, and film studios—face the possibility of declining sales and even destruction of their businesses. Newspaper and magazine subscriptions to hard copies are declining, while online readership and subscriptions are expanding.

Total record label industry revenues fell nearly 50 percent from $14 billion in 1999 to about $7.7 billion in 2016, due almost entirely to the rapid decline in CD album sales and the growth of digital music services (both legal and illegal music piracy). But revenues increased in 2017 by 16 percent to $8.7 billion primarily through the growth of paid subscriptions (RIAA.com, 2018). The Apple iTunes Store has sold more than 50 billion songs for 99 cents each since opening in 2003, providing a digital distribution model that has restored some of the revenues lost to digital music channels. Yet the download business is rapidly fading at Apple, down more than 25 percent in recent years, as streaming becomes the dominant consumer path to music. Since iTunes, illegal downloading has been cut in half, and legitimate online music sales (both downloads and streaming) amounted to $5.7 billion in 2017. As cloud streaming services expand, illegal downloading will decline further. Digital music sales, both digital download and streaming, account for more than 80 percent of all music revenues. The music labels make only about 32 cents from a single track download and only 0.5 cents for a streamed track. Although the record labels make revenue from ownership of the song (both words and music), the artists who perform the music make virtually nothing from streamed music. Artists' earnings on a streamed song on an ad-supported platform like Spotify are pennies per million streams.

Hollywood has been less severely disrupted than the music industry by illegal digital distribution platforms, because it is more difficult to download high-quality, pirated copies of full-length movies and because of the availability of low-cost, high-quality legal movies. Hollywood has struck lucrative distribution deals with Netflix, Google, Hulu, Amazon, and Apple, making it convenient to download and pay for high-quality movies and television series.

TABLE 10.4 HOW THE INTERNET CHANGES THE MARKETS FOR DIGITAL GOODS

	DIGITAL GOODS	TRADITIONAL GOODS
Marginal cost/unit	Zero	Greater than zero, high
Cost of production	High (most of the cost)	Variable
Copying cost	Approximately zero	Greater than zero, high
Distributed delivery cost	Low	High
Inventory cost	Low	High
Marketing cost	Variable	Variable
Pricing	More variable (bundling, random pricing games)	Fixed, based on unit costs

These arrangements are not enough to compensate entirely for the loss in DVD sales, which fell 60 percent from 2006 to 2017. Digital format streaming and downloads grew by 20 percent in 2017 and, for the first time, consumers viewed more downloaded movies than DVDs or related physical products. As with television series, the demand for feature-length Hollywood movies appears to be expanding, in part because of the growth of smartphones, tablets, and smart TVs, making it easier to watch movies in more locations.

In 2019, about 258 million Internet users are expected to view movies, about 82 percent of the adult Internet population. There is little doubt that the Internet is becoming a major movie distribution and television channel that rivals cable television, and someday may replace cable television entirely (see the chapter-opening case).

Table 10.4 describes digital goods and how they differ from traditional physical goods (eMarketer, 2018i)

10-2 What are the principal e-commerce business and revenue models?

E-commerce is a fascinating combination of business models and new information technologies. Let's start with a basic understanding of the types of e-commerce and then describe e-commerce business and revenue models.

Types of E-commerce

There are many ways to classify electronic commerce transactions—one is by looking at the nature of the participants. The three major electronic commerce categories are business-to-consumer (B2C) e-commerce, business-to-business (B2B) e-commerce, and consumer-to-consumer (C2C) e-commerce.

- **Business-to-consumer (B2C)** electronic commerce involves retailing products and services to individual shoppers. Amazon, Walmart, and iTunes are examples of B2C commerce. BarnesandNoble.com, which sells books, software, and music to individual consumers, is an example of B2C e-commerce.

- **Business-to-business (B2B)** electronic commerce involves sales of goods and services among businesses. Elemica's website for buying and selling chemicals and energy is an example of B2B e-commerce.

- **Consumer-to-consumer (C2C)** electronic commerce involves consumers selling directly to consumers. For example, eBay, the giant web auction site, enables people to sell their goods to other consumers by auctioning their merchandise off to the highest bidder or for a fixed price. eBay acts as a middleman by creating a digital platform for peer-to-peer commerce. Craigslist is the platform most consumers use to buy from and sell directly to others.

Another way of classifying electronic commerce transactions is in terms of the platforms participants use in a transaction. Until recently, most e-commerce transactions took place using a desktop PC connected to the Internet over a wired network. Several wireless mobile alternatives have emerged, such as smartphones and tablet computers. The use of handheld wireless devices for purchasing goods and services from any location is termed **mobile commerce or m-commerce**. All three types of e-commerce transactions can take place using m-commerce technology, which we discuss in detail in Section 10.3.

E-commerce Business Models

Changes in the economics of information described earlier have created the conditions for entirely new business models to appear while destroying older business models. Table 10.5 describes some of the most important Internet business models that have emerged. All, in one way or another, use the Internet (including apps on mobile devices) to add extra value to existing products and services or to provide the foundation for new products and services.

Portal

Portals are gateways to the web and are often defined as those sites that users set as their home page. Some definitions of a portal include search engines such as

TABLE 10.5 INTERNET BUSINESS MODELS

CATEGORY	DESCRIPTION	EXAMPLES
E-tailer	Sells physical products directly to consumers or to individual businesses.	Amazon Blue Nile
Transaction broker	Saves users money and time by processing online sales transactions and generating a fee each time a transaction occurs.	ETrade.com Expedia
Market creator	Provides a digital environment where buyers and sellers can meet, search for products, display products, and establish prices for those products; can serve consumers or B2B e-commerce, generating revenue from transaction fees.	eBay Priceline.com Exostar Elemica
Content provider	Creates revenue by providing digital content, such as news, music, photos, or video, over the web. The customer may pay to access the content, or revenue may be generated by selling advertising space.	WSJ.com GettyImages.com iTunes.com MSN Games
Community provider	Provides an online meeting place where people with similar interests can communicate and find useful information.	Facebook Twitter
Portal	Provides initial point of entry to the web along with specialized content and other services.	Yahoo MSN AOL
Service provider	Provides applications such as photo sharing, video sharing, and user-generated content as services; provides other services such as online data storage and backup.	Google Docs Photobucket.com Dropbox

Google and Bing even if few make these sites their home page. Portals such as Yahoo, Facebook, MSN, and AOL offer web search tools as well as an integrated package of content and services such as news, email, instant messaging, maps, calendars, shopping, music downloads, video streaming, and more all in one place. The portal business model now provides a destination site where users start their web searching and linger to read news, find entertainment, meet other people, and, of course, be exposed to advertising. Facebook is a very different kind of portal based on social networking, and in 2018 Americans will spend more than half their online time at Facebook, about two hours per day! Portals generate revenue primarily by attracting very large audiences, charging advertisers for display ad placement (similar to traditional newspapers), collecting referral fees for steering customers to other sites, and charging for premium services. In 2019, portals (not including Google, Facebook, or Bing) will generate an estimated $10 billion in display ad revenues. Although there are hundreds of portal/search engine sites, the top portals (Yahoo, MSN, and AOL) gather more than 80 percent of the Internet portal traffic because of their superior brand recognition.

E-tailer

Online retail stores, often called **e-tailers**, come in all sizes, from giant Amazon with 2017 retail sales revenues of more than $178 billion to tiny local stores that have websites. An e-tailer is similar to the typical brick-and-mortar storefront, except that customers only need to connect to the Internet to check their inventory and place an order. Altogether, online retail (the sale of physical goods online) will generate about $598 billion in revenues in 2019. The value proposition of e-tailers is to provide convenient, low-cost shopping 24/7; large selections; and consumer choice. Some e-tailers, such as Walmart.com or Staples.com, referred to as bricks-and-clicks, are subsidiaries or divisions of existing physical stores and carry the same products. Others, however, operate only in the virtual world, without any ties to physical locations. Ashford.com and eVitamins.com are examples of this type of e-tailer. Several other variations of e-tailers—such as online versions of direct-mail catalogs, online malls, and manufacturer-direct online sales—also exist.

Content Provider

E-commerce has increasingly become a global content channel. *Content* is defined broadly to include all forms of intellectual property. **Intellectual property** refers to tangible and intangible products of the mind for which the creator claims a property right. Content providers distribute information content—such as digital video, music, photos, text, and artwork—over the web. The value proposition of online content providers is that consumers can conveniently find a wide range of content online and purchase this content inexpensively to be played or viewed on multiple computer devices or smartphones.

Providers do not have to be the creators of the content (although sometimes they are, like Disney.com) and are more likely to be Internet-based distributors of content produced and created by others. For example, Apple sells music tracks at its iTunes Store, but it does not create or commission new music.

The phenomenal popularity of Internet-connected mobile devices such as the iPhone, iPod, and iPad has enabled new forms of digital content delivery from podcasting to mobile streaming. **Podcasting** is a method of publishing audio or video broadcasts through the Internet, allowing subscribing users to download audio or video files onto their personal computers, smartphones, tablets, or portable music players. **Streaming** is a publishing method for music and video files that flows a continuous stream of content to a user's device without being stored locally on the device.

Estimates vary, but total online content will generate about $23 billion in 2019, one of the fastest-growing e-commerce segments, growing at an estimated 18 percent annual rate.

Transaction Broker

Sites that process transactions for consumers normally handled in person, by phone, or by mail are transaction brokers. The largest industries using this model are financial services and travel services. The online transaction broker's primary value propositions are savings of money and time and providing an extraordinary inventory of financial products or travel packages in a single location. Online stockbrokers and travel booking services charge fees that are considerably less than traditional versions of these services. Fidelity Financial Services and Expedia are the largest online financial and travel service firms based on a transaction broker model.

Market Creator

Market creators build a digital environment in which buyers and sellers can meet, display products, search for products, and establish prices. The value proposition of online market creators is that they provide a platform where sellers can easily display their wares and purchasers can buy directly from sellers. Online auction markets such as eBay and Priceline are good examples of the market creator business model. Another example is Amazon's Merchants platform (and similar programs at eBay), where merchants are allowed to set up stores on Amazon's website and sell goods at fixed prices to consumers. The so-called on-demand economy (mistakenly often referred to as the sharing economy), exemplified by Uber (described in the Interactive Session on Organizations) and Airbnb, is based on the idea of a market creator building a digital platform where supply meets demand; for instance, spare auto or room rental capacity finds individuals who want transportation or lodging. Crowdsource funding markets such as Kickstarter.com bring together private equity investors and entrepreneurs in a funding marketplace.

Service Provider

Whereas e-tailers sell products online, service providers offer services online. Photo sharing and online sites for data backup and storage all use a service provider business model. Software is no longer a physical product with a CD in a box but, increasingly, software as a service (SaaS) that you subscribe to online rather than purchase from a retailer, such as Office 365. Google has led the way in developing online software service applications such as G Suite, Google Sites, Gmail, and online data storage services. Salesforce.com is a major provider of cloud-based software for customer management (see Chapter 5).

Community Provider (Social Networks)

Community providers are sites that create a digital online environment where people with similar interests can transact (buy and sell goods); share interests, photos, and videos; communicate with like-minded people; receive interest-related information; and even play out fantasies by adopting online personalities called *avatars*. Social networking sites Facebook, Tumblr, Instagram, LinkedIn, and Twitter and hundreds of other smaller, niche sites all offer users community-building tools and services. Social networking sites have been the fastest-growing websites in recent years, often doubling their audience size in a year.

INTERACTIVE SESSION ORGANIZATIONS

Uber: Digital Disruptor

You're in New York, Paris, Chicago, or another major city and need a ride. Instead of trying to hail a cab, you pull out your smartphone and tap the Uber app. A Google map pops up displaying your nearby surroundings. You select a spot on the screen designating an available driver, and the app secures the ride, showing how long it will take for the ride to arrive and how much it will cost. Once you reach your destination, the fare is automatically charged to your credit card. No fumbling for money.

Rates take into account the typical factors of time and distance but also demand. Uber's software predicts areas where rides are likely to be in high demand at different times of the day. This information appears on a driver's smartphone so that the driver knows where to linger and, ideally, pick up customers within minutes of a request for a ride. Uber also offers a higher-priced town car service for business executives and a ride-sharing service. Under certain conditions, if demand is high, Uber can be more expensive than taxis, but it still appeals to riders by offering a reliable, fast, convenient alternative to traditional taxi services.

Uber runs much leaner than a traditional taxi company does. Uber does not own taxis and has no maintenance and financing costs. It does not have employees, so it claims, but instead calls the drivers independent contractors, who receive a cut of each fare. Uber is not encumbered with employee costs such as workers' compensation, minimum wage requirements, background checks on drivers, driver training, health insurance, or commercial licensing costs. Uber has shifted the costs of running a taxi service entirely to the drivers and to the customers using their cell phones. Drivers pay for their own cars, fuel, and insurance. What Uber does is provide a smartphone-based platform that enables people who want a service—like a taxi—to find a provider who can meet that need.

Uber relies on user reviews of drivers and the ride experience to identify problematic drivers and driver reviews of customers to identify problematic passengers. It also sets standards for cleanliness. It uses the reviews to discipline drivers. Uber does not publicly report how many poorly rated drivers or passengers there are in its system. Uber also uses software that monitors sensors in drivers' smartphones to monitor their driving behavior.

Uber is headquartered in San Francisco and was founded in 2009 by Travis Kalanick and Garrett Camp. In 2018, it had more than 3 million drivers working in 600 cities worldwide, generating revenue of 2.6 billion in the first quarter of 2018. After paying for drivers, marketing, and other operating expenses, Uber still operated at a loss. More than 75 million people use Uber. However, Uber's over-the-top success has created its own set of challenges.

By digitally disrupting a traditional and highly regulated industry, Uber has ignited a firestorm of opposition from existing taxi services in the United States and around the world. Who can compete with an upstart firm offering a 40 percent price reduction when demand for taxis is low? (When demand is high, Uber prices surge.) What city or state wants to give up regulatory control over passenger safety, protection from criminals, driver training, and a healthy revenue stream generated by charging taxi firms for a taxi license?

If Uber is the poster child for the new on-demand economy, it's also an iconic example of the social costs and conflict associated with this new kind of business model. Uber has been accused of denying its drivers the benefits of employee status by classifying them as contractors, violating public transportation laws and regulations throughout the United States and the world, abusing the personal information it has collected on ordinary people, increasing traffic congestion, undermining public transportation, and failing to protect public safety by refusing to perform sufficient criminal, medical, and financial background checks on its drivers. Uber's brand image has been further tarnished by negative publicity about its aggressive, unrestrained workplace culture and the behavior of CEO Kalanick.

Uber has taken some remediating steps. It enhanced its app to make it easier for drivers to take breaks while they are on the job. Drivers can now also be paid instantly for each ride they complete rather than weekly and see on the app's dashboard how much they have earned. Uber added an option to its app for passengers to tip its U.S. drivers, and

Kalanick resigned as head of Uber in June 2017. (He was replaced by Dara Khosrowshahi.)

Critics fear that Uber and other on-demand firms have the potential for creating a society of part-time, low-paid, temp work, displacing traditionally full-time, secure jobs—the so-called Uberization of work. According to one study, half of Uber drivers earn less than the minimum wage in their state. Uber responds by saying it is lowering the cost of transportation, expanding the demand for ride services, and expanding opportunities for car drivers, whose pay is about the same as other taxi drivers.

Does Uber have a sustainable business model? The company is still not profitable, and continues to subsidize the cost of many of its rides. Uber has competitors, including Lyft in the United States and local firms in Asia and Europe. New, smaller, competing firms offering app-based cab-hailing services are cropping up, such as Sidecar and Via. Established taxi firms in New York and other cities are launching their own hailing apps and trumpeting their fixed-rate prices.

Uber is pressing on, with new services for same-day deliveries, business travel accounts, and heavy investments in self-driving cars, which management believes will be key to lowering labor costs and ensuring long-term profitability. After a self-driving Uber car struck and killed a woman in Tempe, Arizona in March 2018, Arizona suspended autonomous vehicle testing in the state, and Uber stopped testing autonomous cars in California, Pittsburgh, and Toronto. Even before the accident, Uber's self-driving cars were having trouble driving through construction zones and next to tall vehicles like big truck rigs. Test drivers had to take over the car almost every mile. It is still too early to tell whether Uber and other on-demand businesses will succeed.

Sources: Steven Hill, "New Leadership Has Not Changed Uber," *New York Times*, March 26, 2018; Bloomberg, "Uber Revenue Spiked 70% Last Quarter, But It Still Lost Tons of Money," May 24, 2018; Daisuke Wakabashai, "Uber's Self-Driving Cars Were Struggling Before Arizona Crash," *New York Times*, March 23, 2018; Craig Smith, "100 Amazing Uber Statistics, Demographics and Facts (July 2018)," *DMR*, July 29, 2018; "Rob Berger, "Uber Settlement Takes Customers for a Ride," *Forbes*, April 22, 2016; and Mike Isaac and Noam Scheiber, "Uber Settles Cases with Concessions, But Drivers Stay Freelancers," *New York Times,* April 21, 2016.

CASE STUDY QUESTIONS

1. Analyze Uber using the competitive forces and value chain models. What is its competitive advantage?

2. What is the relationship between information technology and Uber's business model? Explain your answer.

3. How disruptive is Uber?

4. Is Uber a viable business? Explain your answer.

E-commerce Revenue Models

A firm's **revenue model** describes how the firm will earn revenue, generate profits, and produce a superior return on investment. Although many e-commerce revenue models have been developed, most companies rely on one, or some combination, of the following six revenue models: advertising, sales, subscription, free/freemium, transaction fee, and affiliate.

Advertising Revenue Model

In the **advertising revenue model**, a website generates revenue by attracting a large audience of visitors who can then be exposed to advertisements. The advertising model is the most widely used revenue model in e-commerce, and arguably, without advertising revenues, the web would be a vastly different experience from what it is now because people would be asked to pay for access to content. Content on the web—everything from news to videos and opinions—is free to visitors because advertisers pay the production and distribution costs in return for the right to expose visitors to ads. Companies will spend an estimated $125 billion on online advertising in 2019 (in the form of a paid message on a website, paid search listing, video, app, game, or other online medium, such as instant messaging). About $90 billion of this will be for mobile ads. Mobile ads will account for 72 percent of all digital advertising. In the past five years, advertisers have increased online spending and cut outlays on traditional channels such as radio and newspapers. In 2019, online advertising will grow at 18 percent and constitute about 53 percent of all advertising in the United States (eMarketer, 2018g).

Websites with the largest viewership or that attract a highly specialized, differentiated viewership and are able to retain user attention (stickiness) can charge higher advertising rates. Yahoo, for instance, derives nearly all its revenue from display ads (banner ads), video ads, and, to a lesser extent, search engine text ads. Google and Facebook derive well over 90 percent of their revenue from advertising, including selling keywords (AdWords), selling ad spaces (AdSense), and selling display ad spaces to advertisers. Facebook alone displays one-third of the trillion display ads shown on all sites in 2019.

Sales Revenue Model

In the **sales revenue model**, companies derive revenue by selling goods, information, or services to customers. Companies such as Amazon (which sells books, music, and other products), LLBean.com, and Gap.com all have sales revenue models. Content providers make money by charging for downloads of entire files such as music tracks (iTunes Store) or books or for downloading music and/or video streams (Hulu.com TV shows). Apple has pioneered and strengthened the acceptance of micropayments. **Micropayment systems** provide content providers with a cost-effective method for processing high volumes of very small monetary transactions (anywhere from 25 cents to $5.00 per transaction). The largest micropayment system on the web is Apple's iTunes Store, which has more than 1 billion customers worldwide who purchase individual music tracks for 99 cents and feature-length movies for various prices.

Subscription Revenue Model

In the **subscription revenue model**, a website offering content or services charges a subscription fee for access to some or all of its offerings on an ongoing basis. Content providers often use this revenue model. For instance, the online version of *Consumer Reports* provides access to premium content, such as detailed ratings, reviews, and recommendations, only to subscribers for a $35.00 annual fee. Netflix is one of the most successful subscriber sites with over 100 million customers worldwide in 2018. To be successful, the subscription model requires the content to be perceived as differentiated, having high added value, and not readily available elsewhere or easily replicated. Other companies offering content or services online on a subscription basis include Match.com (dating services), Ancestry.com (genealogy research), and Microsoft Xbox Live.

Free/Freemium Revenue Model

In the **free/freemium revenue model**, firms offer basic services or content for free and charge a premium for advanced or special features. For example, Google offers free applications but charges for premium services. Pandora, the subscription radio service, offers a free service with limited play time and advertising and a premium service with unlimited play. The idea is to attract very large audiences with free services and then convert some of this audience to pay a subscription for premium services. One problem with this model is converting people from being freeloaders into paying customers. "Free" can be a powerful model for losing money. None of the freemium music streaming sites have earned a profit to date. Nevertheless, they are finding that free service with ad revenue is more profitable than the paid subscriber part of their business.

Transaction Fee Revenue Model

In the **transaction fee revenue model**, a company receives a fee for enabling or executing a transaction. For example, eBay provides an online auction marketplace and receives a small transaction fee from a seller if the seller is successful in selling an item. E*Trade, an online stockbroker, receives transaction fees each time it executes a stock transaction on behalf of a customer. The transaction revenue model enjoys wide acceptance in part because the true cost of using the platform is not immediately apparent to the user.

Online financial services, from banking to payment systems, rely on a transaction fee model. While online banking and services are dominated by large banks with millions of customers, start-up financial technology firms, also known as **FinTech** firms, have grown rapidly to compete with banks for peer-to-peer (P2P), bill payment, money transfer, lending, crowdsourcing, financial advice, and account aggregation services. The largest growth in FinTech has involved P2P payment services, such as Venmo and Square, two among hundreds of FinTech firms competing in this space with banks and online payment giants such as PayPal (PayPal purchased Venmo in 2013). FinTech firms are typically not profitable and are often bought out by larger financial service firms for their technology and customer base.

Affiliate Revenue Model

In the **affiliate revenue model**, websites (called *affiliate websites*) send visitors to other websites in return for a referral fee or percentage of the revenue from any resulting sales. Referral fees are also referred to as lead generation fees. For example, MyPoints makes money by connecting companies to potential customers by offering special deals to its members. When members take advantage of an offer and make a purchase, they earn points they can redeem for free products and services, and MyPoints receives a referral fee. Community feedback sites such as Epinions and Yelp receive much of their revenue from steering potential customers to websites where they make a purchase. Amazon uses affiliates that steer business to the Amazon website by placing the Amazon logo on their blogs. Personal blogs often contain display ads as part of affiliate programs. Some bloggers are paid directly by manufacturers, or receive free products, for speaking highly of products and providing links to sales channels.

10-3 How has e-commerce transformed marketing?

Although e-commerce and the Internet have changed entire industries and enabled new business models, no industry has been more affected than marketing and marketing communications.

The Internet provides marketers with new ways of identifying and communicating with millions of potential customers at costs far lower than traditional

TABLE 10.6 ONLINE AD SPENDING BY FORMATS (BILLIONS)

MARKETING FORMAT	2018 REVENUE	DESCRIPTION
Search engine	$53.3	Text ads targeted at precisely what the customer is looking for at the moment of shopping and purchasing. Sales oriented.
Display ads	$67.1	Banner ads (pop-ups and leave-behinds) with interactive features; increasingly behaviorally targeted to individual web activity. Brand development and sales. Includes social media and blog display ads.
Video	$21.2	Fastest-growing format, engaging and entertaining; behaviorally targeted, interactive. Branding and sales.
Classified	$2.1	Job, real estate, and services ads; interactive, rich media, and personalized to user searches. Sales and branding.
Rich media	$18.3	Animations, games, and puzzles. Interactive, targeted, and entertaining. Branding orientation.
Lead generation	$2.3	Marketing firms that gather sales and marketing leads online and then sell them to online marketers for a variety of campaign types. Sales or branding orientation.
Sponsorships	$2.1	Online games, puzzles, contests, and coupon sites sponsored by firms to promote products. Sales orientation.
Email	$0.47	Effective, targeted marketing tool with interactive and rich media potential. Sales oriented.

Source: Based on eMarketer, "Digital Ad Spending by Format,, 2018" eMarketer, March 2018.

media, including search engine marketing, data mining, recommender systems, and targeted email. The Internet enables **long tail marketing**. Before the Internet, reaching a large audience was very expensive, and marketers had to focus on attracting the largest number of consumers with popular hit products, whether music, Hollywood movies, books, or cars. In contrast, the Internet allows marketers to find potential customers inexpensively for products where demand is very low. For instance, the Internet makes it possible to sell independent music profitably to very small audiences. There's always some demand for almost any product. Put a string of such long tail sales together and you have a profitable business.

The Internet also provides new ways—often instantaneous and spontaneous—to gather information from customers, adjust product offerings, and increase customer value. Table 10.6 describes the leading marketing and advertising formats used in e-commerce.

Behavioral Targeting

Many e-commerce marketing firms use **behavioral targeting** techniques to increase the effectiveness of banners, rich media, and video ads. Behavioral targeting refers to tracking the clickstreams (history of clicking behavior) of individuals on thousands of websites to understand their interests and intentions and expose them to advertisements that are uniquely suited to their online behavior. Marketers and most researchers believe this more precise understanding of the customer leads to more efficient marketing (the firm pays for ads only to those shoppers who are most interested in their products) and larger sales and revenues. Unfortunately, behavioral targeting of millions of web users also leads to the invasion of personal privacy without user consent. When consumers lose trust in their web experience, they tend not to purchase anything. Backlash is growing against the aggressive uses of personal information as consumers seek out safer havens for purchasing and messaging. Snapchat offers

FIGURE 10.3 WEBSITE VISITOR TRACKING

E-commerce websites and advertising platforms like Google's DoubleClick have tools to track a shopper's every step through an online store and then across the web as shoppers move from site to site. Close examination of customer behavior at a website selling women's clothing shows what the store might learn at each step and what actions it could take to increase sales.

Courtesy of Google Inc.

The shopper clicks on the home page. The store can tell that the shopper arrived from the Yahoo portal at 2:30 PM (which might help determine staffing for customer service centers) and how long she lingered on the home page (which might indicate trouble navigating the site). Tracking beacons load cookies on the shopper's browser to follow her across the Web.

The shopper clicks on blouses, then clicks to view a woman's pink blouse. The shopper clicks to select this item in a size 10 in pink and clicks to place it in her shopping cart. This information can help the store determine which sizes and colors are most popular. If the visitor moves to a different site, ads for pink blouses will appear from the same or a different vendor.

From the shopping cart page, the shopper clicks to close the browser to leave the website without purchasing the blouse. This action could indicate the shopper changed her mind or that she had a problem with the website's checkout and payment process. Such behavior might signal that the website was not well designed.

disappearing messages, and even Facebook has retreated by making its default for new posts "for friends only."

Behavioral targeting takes place at two levels: at individual websites or from within apps and on various advertising networks that track users across thousands of websites. All websites collect data on visitor browser activity and store it in a database. They have tools to record the site that users visited prior to coming to the website, where these users go when they leave that site, the type of operating system they use, browser information, and even some location data. They also record the specific pages visited on the particular site, the time spent on each page of the site, the types of pages visited, and what the visitors purchased (see Figure 10.3). Firms analyze this information about customer interests and behavior to develop precise profiles of existing and potential customers. In addition, most major websites have hundreds of tracking programs on their home pages, which track your clickstream behavior across the web by following you from site to site and re-target ads to you by showing you the same ads on different sites. The leading online advertising network is Google's DoubleClick.

This information enables firms to understand how well their website is working, create unique personalized web pages that display content or ads for products or services of special interest to each user, improve the customer's experience, and create additional value through a better understanding of the shopper (see Figure 10.4). By using personalization technology to modify the web pages presented to each customer, marketers achieve some of the benefits of using individual salespeople at dramatically lower costs. For instance, General Motors will show a Chevrolet banner ad to women emphasizing safety and utility, whereas men will receive ads emphasizing power and ruggedness.

FIGURE 10.4 WEBSITE PERSONALIZATION

Firms can create unique personalized web pages that display content or ads for products or services of special interest to individual users, improving the customer experience and creating additional value.

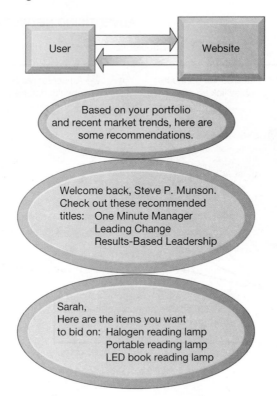

It's a short step from ad networks to programmatic ad buying. Ad networks create real-time bidding platforms (RTB) where marketers bid in an automated environment for highly targeted slots available from web publishers. Here, ad platforms can predict how many targeted individuals will view the ads, and ad buyers can estimate how much this exposure is worth to them.

What if you are a large national advertising company or global manufacturer trying to reach millions of consumers? With millions of websites, working with each one would be impractical. Advertising networks solve this problem by creating a network of several thousand of the most popular websites millions of people visit, tracking the behavior of these users across the entire network, building profiles of each user, and then selling these profiles to advertisers in a real-time bidding environment. Popular websites download dozens of web-tracking cookies, bugs, and beacons, which report user online behavior to remote servers without the users' knowledge. Looking for young, single consumers with college degrees, living in the Northeast, in the 18–34 age range who are interested in purchasing a European car? Advertising networks can identify and deliver thousands of people who fit this profile and expose them to ads for European cars as they move from one website to another. Estimates vary, but behaviorally targeted ads are generally 10 times more likely to produce a consumer response than a randomly chosen banner or video ad (see Figure 10.5). So-called advertising exchanges use this same technology to auction access to people with very specific profiles to advertisers in a few milliseconds. In 2016, about 50 percent of online display ads were

FIGURE 10.5 HOW AN ADVERTISING NETWORK SUCH AS DOUBLECLICK WORKS

Advertising networks and their use of tracking programs have become controversial among privacy advocates because of their ability to track individual consumers across the Internet.

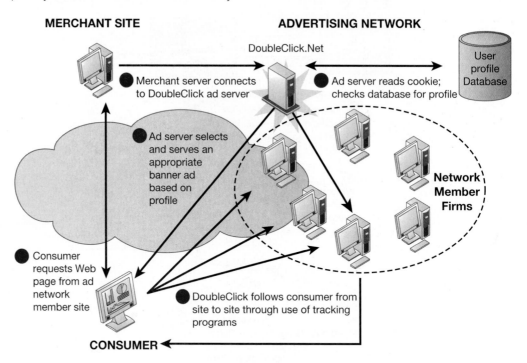

targeted ads developed by programmatic ad buys, and the rest depended on the context of the pages shoppers visited—the estimated demographics of visitors, or so-called blast-and-scatter advertising—which is placed randomly on any available page with minimal targeting, such as time of day or season.

It's another short step to **native advertising**. Native advertising involves placing ads in social network newsfeeds or within traditional editorial content, such as a newspaper article. This is also referred to as organic advertising, where content and advertising are in very close proximity or integrated together.

Two-thirds (68 percent) of Internet users disapprove of search engines and websites tracking their online behavior to aim targeted ads at them. Twenty-eight percent of those surveyed approve of behavioral targeting because they believe it produces more relevant ads and information. A majority of Americans want a Do Not Track option in browsers that will stop websites from collecting information about their online behavior. More than 50 percent are very concerned about the wealth of personal data online; 86 percent have taken steps to mask their online behavior; 25 percent of web users use ad-blocking software (Rainie, 2016).

Social E-commerce and Social Network Marketing

In 2019, one of the fastest-growing media for branding and marketing is social media. Companies will spend an estimated $30 billion in 2019 using social networks such as Facebook, Instagram, Twitter, and LinkedIn to reach millions of consumers who spend hours a day on social sites. Expenditures for social media marketing are much smaller than for television, magazines, and even newspapers, but this will change in the future. Social networks in the offline world are collections of people who voluntarily communicate with one another over an extended period of time. Online social networks, such as Facebook, Instagram, Pinterest, LinkedIn, Twitter, and Tumblr, along with other sites with social components, are websites that enable users to communicate with one another, form group and individual relationships, and share interests, values, and ideas.

Social e-commerce is commerce based on the idea of the digital **social graph**, a mapping of all significant online social relationships. The social graph is synonymous with the idea of a social network used to describe offline relationships. You can map your own social graph (network) by drawing lines from yourself to the 10 closest people you know. If they know one another, draw lines between these people. If you are ambitious, ask these 10 friends to list and draw in the names of the 10 people closest to them. What emerges from this exercise is a preliminary map of your social network. Now imagine if everyone on the Internet did the same and posted the results to a very large database with a website. Ultimately, you would end up with Facebook or a site like it.

According to small world theory, you are only six links away from any other person on earth. If you entered your personal address book, which has, say, 100 names in it, in a list and sent it to your friends, and they in turn entered 50 new names of their friends, and so on, five times, the social network created would encompass 31 billion people! The social graph is therefore a collection of millions of personal social graphs (and all the people in them).

If you understand the interconnectedness of people, you will see just how important this concept is to e-commerce: The products and services you buy will influence the decisions of your friends, and their decisions will in turn influence you. If you are a marketer trying to build and strengthen a brand, you can take advantage of the fact that people are enmeshed in social networks, share interests and values, and communicate and influence one another. As a marketer, your target audience is not a million isolated people watching a TV show but the social network of people who watch the show and the viewers' personal networks. Moreover, online social networks are where the largest Internet audiences are located. Table 10.7 describes the features of social commerce that are driving its growth.

Facebook, with 74 percent of all social marketing in the United States and 208 million U.S. monthly visitors in 2018, receives most of the public attention given to social networking. The other top four social sites are also growing, though at far slower rates than in the past. LinkedIn had 93 million visitors a month in 2018. Twitter grew to reach 146 million active users in 2018, with stronger offshore growth than in the United States. Pinterest hit the top 50 websites with 110 million users, a 25 percent increase from 2017. According to analysts, 25 percent of the total time spent online in the United States was spent on social network sites (about 56 minutes a day), and social networking is the most common online activity. The fastest-growing smartphone applications are social network apps; nearly half of smartphone users visit social sites daily. More than 70 percent of all visits to Facebook in 2018 came from smartphones.

At **social shopping** sites such as Pinterest you can swap shopping ideas with friends. Facebook offers the "like" button to let your friends know you admire a product, service, or content and, in some cases, purchase something online. Facebook processes around 5 billion likes a day worldwide. Online communities are also ideal venues to employ viral marketing techniques. Online viral marketing is like traditional word-of-mouth marketing except that the word can

TABLE 10.7 FEATURES OF SOCIAL COMMERCE

SOCIAL COMMERCE FEATURE	DESCRIPTION
Newsfeed	A stream of notifications from friends and advertisers that social users find on their home pages.
Timelines	A stream of photos and events in the past that create a personal history for users, one that can be shared with friends.
Social sign-on	Websites allow users to sign into their sites through their social network pages on Facebook or another social site. This allows websites to receive valuable social profile information from Facebook and use it in their own marketing efforts.
Collaborative shopping	An environment where consumers can share their shopping experiences with one another by viewing products, chatting, or texting. Friends can chat online about brands, products, and services.
Network notification	An environment where consumers can share their approval (or disapproval) of products, services, or content or share their geolocation, perhaps a restaurant or club, with friends. Facebook's ubiquitous "like" button is an example, as are Twitter's tweets and followers.
Social search (recommendations)	An environment where consumers can ask their friends for advice on purchases of products, services, and content. Although Google can help you find things, social search can help you evaluate the quality of things by listening to the evaluations of your friends or their friends. For instance, Amazon's social recommender system can use your Facebook social profile to recommend products.

spread across an online community at the speed of light and go much further geographically than a small network of friends.

The Wisdom of Crowds

Creating sites where thousands, even millions, of people can interact offers business firms new ways to market and advertise and to discover who likes (or hates) their products. In a phenomenon called the **wisdom of crowds**, some argue that large numbers of people can make better decisions about a wide range of topics or products than a single person or even a small committee of experts.

Obviously, this is not always the case, but it can happen in interesting ways. In marketing, the wisdom of crowds concept suggests that firms should consult with thousands of their customers first as a way of establishing a relationship with them and, second, to understand better how their products and services are used and appreciated (or rejected). Actively soliciting the comments of your customers builds trust and sends the message to your customers that you care what they are thinking and that you need their advice.

Beyond merely soliciting advice, firms can be actively helped in solving some business problems by using **crowdsourcing**. For instance, BMW launched a crowdsourcing project to enlist the aid of customers in designing an urban vehicle for 2025. Kickstarter.com is arguably one of the most famous e-commerce crowdfunding sites where visitors invest in start-up companies. Other examples include Caterpillar working with customers to design better machinery, IKEA for designing furniture, and Pepsico using Super Bowl viewers to build an online video.

Marketing through social media is still in its early stages, and companies are experimenting in hopes of finding a winning formula. Social interactions and customer sentiment are not always easy to manage, presenting new challenges for companies eager to protect their brands. The Interactive Session on Management provides specific examples of companies' social marketing efforts using Facebook and Twitter.

INTERACTIVE SESSION MANAGEMENT

"Socializing" with Customers

More than 3 billion people worldwide use social media, making it an obvious platform for companies seeking to engage consumers, amplify product messages, discover trends and influencers, build brand awareness, and take action on customer requests and recommendations. More than 80 million businesses have Facebook brand pages, enabling users to interact with the brand through blogs, comment pages, contests, and offerings on the brand page. The "like" button gives users a chance to share with their social network their feelings about content they are viewing and websites they are visiting. With like buttons on many millions of websites, Facebook can track user behavior on other sites and then sell this information to marketers. Facebook also sells display ads to firms that appear on users' home pages and most other pages in the Facebook interface such as photos and apps. Twitter features such as "promoted tweets" and "promoted trends" enable advertisers to have their tweets displayed more prominently when Twitter users search for certain keywords.

Mack Trucks, a leading U.S. truck manufacturer, used a social marketing campaign to attract customers, drivers, and dealers when it launched its new Anthem model. Mack had traditionally used print ads in trucking publications, brochures, and industry trade shows as its primary marketing channels when rolling out a new product. However, these channels did not enable Mack to tailor and deliver different messages for different customers. For example, a manager of a large fleet might be most interested in fuel efficiency, while an owner-operator might be more attracted to design style. Mack's marketing team continued to use traditional channels for broad awareness and relied on social marketing to focus on segmentation and metrics.

Starting in July 2017 Mack launched a series of biweekly YouTube videos to build excitement for the Anthem model, followed by a live stream of the Anthem unveiling on YouTube and Facebook in September of that year. Mack netted 7,000 email addresses from the teaser campaign, with 3,700 people viewing the live stream of the launch event. These are considered significant numbers for a product costing over U.S. $100,000. Mack's marketing team also launched a comprehensive social media campaign directing the company's 174,000 Facebook followers, 24,000 Twitter followers, 15,000 LinkedIn followers, 15,000 YouTube subscribers, and other social communities to photos, videos, text summaries, and other content describing every aspect of the new Anthem line. These activities were credited with attracting more than 40,000 new social followers to the Mack brand.

Mack uses Oracle Eloqua Marketing Cloud Service and Oracle Social Cloud to link social activity to 175,000 profiles in its Oracle Eloqua database of customers and prospects. The digital marketing team thus knows if a person in the database clicked on a Facebook post to view an Anthem-related video or looked for other information on the company's website. Compelling personalized content helps engage prospects and move them further along the sales process until they ask to talk to a Mack dealer. At that point, the prospect is considered a qualified lead. Oracle Social Cloud alerts team members when the Mack Anthem is mentioned on various social sites, and they can respond where appropriate.

Mack also enlisted celebrity influencers for the Anthem campaign. Country music artist Steve Moakler recorded a road song called *Born Ready* for the Anthem launch and dedicated it to drivers. More than 55,000 people viewed Moakler's performance on YouTube. The marketing team also produced a YouTube video with the Oakland Raiders' Khalil Mack called *What Makes a Mack,* and it attracted over 75,000 viewers. Mack is developing a broad-based influence program identifying customers and drivers who will be among the first to view new products and serve as active advocates on social media.

More than 9,300 people opted into some aspect of the Mack Anthem campaign, generating about 1,700 qualified leads. The Anthem landing page has attracted over 146,000 visitors, who can watch the Moakler video and obtain information on every aspect of the new truck line. Mack's senior management is very pleased with the results and the detail and precision of digital marketing information. Vice President of Marketing John Walsh can see what happens with every dollar Mack spends.

An estimated 90 percent of customers are influenced by online reviews, and nearly half of U.S. social media users actively seek customer service through social media. As a result, marketing is now placing much more emphasis on customer satisfaction and service. Social media monitoring helps marketers and business owners understand more about buyers' likes, dislikes, and complaints concerning products, additional products or product modifications customers want, and how people are talking about a brand (positive or negative sentiment).

Prompted by customer social media comments about meats other than roast beef, fast-food sandwich restaurant chain Arby's launched a "Meat Mountain" campaign poster showing various meats other than roast beef. Arby's customers mistakenly thought the poster displayed a new sandwich and, through social media, indicated they were anxious to try it. Arby's then responded with a new $10 Meat Mountain sandwich.

Social media campaigns can be tricky to orchestrate, and the results are not always predictable. When social followers of Donald Trump called for boycotting Nordstrom for dropping Ivanka Trump's clothing line from its stores, Nordstrom's stock price rose, and the company outperformed many of its retail industry rivals in the months that followed. Nordstrom customers remained loyal to the brand. Previous Trump tweets calling out other brands such as Lockheed Martin had hurt stock share prices. In September 2016, San Antonio–based Miracle Mattress provoked angry social media backlash when it posted a Facebook video advertising a "Twin Towers Sale." The video encouraged customers to "remember 9/11" and "get any size mattress for a twin price." Miracle Mattress removed the video from its Facebook timeline, and owner Mike Bonanno posted an apology letter.

Sources: Rob Preston, "Open Road," *Profit Magazine*, Spring 2018; Melody Hahm, "26-Year-Old Launches Instagram-Fueled Fast Fashion Brand," *Yahoo Finance*, July 25, 2018; Craig Smith, "844 Amazing Facebook Statistics (July 2018) by the Numbers," *Dmr*, July 30, 2018; www.Macktrucks.com, accessed July 29, 2018; Janet Morrissey, "Brands Heed Social Media. They're Advised Not to Forget Word of Mouth," *New York Times*, November 26, 2017; Farhad Manjoo "How Battling Brands Online Has Gained Urgency, and Impact," *New York Times*, June 21, 2017; and Lindsay Friedman, "The 12 Worst Social-Media Fails of 2016," www.entrepreneur.com, September 22, 2016.

CASE STUDY QUESTIONS

1. Assess the management, organization, and technology issues for using social media technology to engage with customers.

2. What are the advantages and disadvantages of using social media for advertising, brand building, market research, and customer service?

3. Give an example of a business decision in this case study that was facilitated by using social media to interact with customers.

4. Should all companies use social media technology for customer service and marketing? Why or why not? What kinds of companies are best suited to use these platforms?

10-4 How has e-commerce affected business-to-business transactions?

Trade between business firms (business-to-business commerce, or B2B) represents a huge marketplace. The total amount of B2B trade in the United States in 2019 is estimated to be about $13.5 trillion, with B2B e-commerce (online B2B) contributing about $6.2 trillion of that amount (U.S. Bureau of the Census, 2018; authors' estimates). By 2020, B2B e-commerce is expected to grow to about $6.9 trillion in the United States.

The process of conducting trade among business firms is complex and requires considerable human intervention; therefore, it consumes significant resources. Some firms estimate that each corporate purchase order for support products costs them, on average, at least $100 in administrative overhead, including processing paper, approving purchase decisions, using the telephone and fax machines to search for products and arrange for purchases, arranging for shipping, and receiving the goods. Across the economy, this adds up to trillions of dollars annually spent for procurement processes that could be automated. If even just a portion of inter-firm trade were automated and parts of the entire procurement process were assisted by the Internet, literally trillions of dollars might be released for more productive uses, consumer prices potentially would fall, productivity would increase, and the economic wealth of the nation would expand. This is the promise of B2B e-commerce. The challenge of B2B e-commerce is changing existing patterns and systems of procurement and designing and implementing new Internet and cloud-based B2B solutions.

Electronic Data Interchange (EDI)

B2B e-commerce refers to the commercial transactions that occur among business firms. Increasingly, these transactions are flowing through a variety of Internet-enabled mechanisms. About 80 percent of online B2B e-commerce is still based on proprietary systems for **Electronic Data Interchange (EDI)**. EDI enables the computer-to-computer exchange between two organizations of standard transactions such as invoices, bills of lading, shipment schedules, or purchase orders. Transactions are automatically transmitted from one information system to another through a network, eliminating the printing and handling of paper at one end and the inputting of data at the other. Each major industry in the United States and much of the rest of the world has EDI standards that define the structure and information fields of electronic transactions for that industry.

EDI originally automated the exchange of documents such as purchase orders, invoices, and shipping notices. Although many companies still use EDI for document automation, firms engaged in just-in-time inventory replenishment and continuous production use EDI as a system for continuous replenishment. Suppliers have online access to selected parts of the purchasing firm's production and delivery schedules and automatically ship materials and goods to meet prespecified targets without intervention by firm purchasing agents (see Figure 10.6).

Although many organizations still use private networks for EDI, they are increasingly web-enabled because Internet technology provides a much more flexible and low-cost platform for linking to other firms. Businesses can extend digital technology to a wider range of activities and broaden their circle of trading partners.

FIGURE 10.6   ELECTRONIC DATA INTERCHANGE (EDI)

Companies use EDI to automate transactions for B2B e-commerce and continuous inventory replenishment. Suppliers can automatically send data about shipments to purchasing firms. The purchasing firms can use EDI to provide production and inventory requirements and payment data to suppliers.

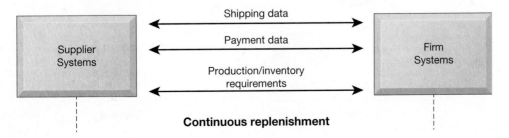

Procurement, for example, involves not only purchasing goods and materials but also sourcing, negotiating with suppliers, paying for goods, and making delivery arrangements. Businesses can now use the Internet to locate the lowest-cost supplier, search online catalogs of supplier products, negotiate with suppliers, place orders, make payments, and arrange transportation. They are not limited to partners linked by traditional EDI networks.

New Ways of B2B Buying and Selling

The Internet and web technology enable businesses to create electronic storefronts for selling to other businesses using the same techniques as used for B2C commerce. Alternatively, businesses can use Internet technology to create extranets or electronic marketplaces for linking to other businesses for purchase and sale transactions.

Private industrial networks typically consist of a large firm using a secure website to link to its suppliers and other key business partners (see Figure 10.7). The buyer owns the network, and it permits the firm and designated suppliers, distributors, and other business partners to share product design and development, marketing, production scheduling, inventory management, and unstructured communication, including graphics and email. Another term for a private industrial network is a **private exchange**.

An example is VW Group Supply, which links the Volkswagen Group and its suppliers. VW Group Supply handles 90 percent of all global purchasing for Volkswagen, including all automotive and parts components.

Net marketplaces, which are sometimes called e-hubs, provide a single, digital marketplace based on Internet technology for many buyers and sellers (see Figure 10.8). They are industry-owned or operate as independent intermediaries between buyers and sellers. Net marketplaces generate revenue

FIGURE 10.7 A PRIVATE INDUSTRIAL NETWORK

A private industrial network, also known as a private exchange, links a firm to its suppliers, distributors, and other key business partners for efficient supply chain management and other collaborative commerce activities.

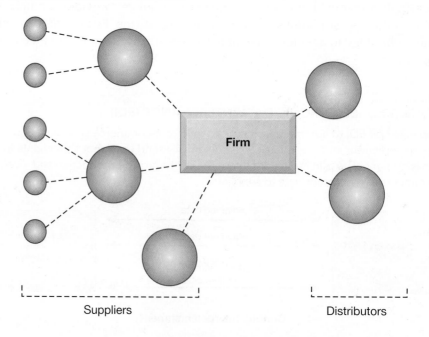

Suppliers   Distributors

FIGURE 10.8   A NET MARKETPLACE

Net marketplaces are online marketplaces where multiple buyers can purchase from multiple sellers.

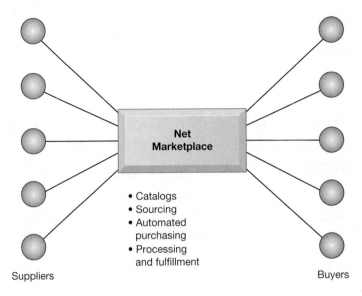

- Catalogs
- Sourcing
- Automated purchasing
- Processing and fulfillment

Suppliers   Buyers

from purchase and sale transactions and other services provided to clients. Participants in Net marketplaces can establish prices through online negotiations, auctions, or requests for quotations, or they can use fixed prices.

There are many types of Net marketplaces and ways of classifying them. Some sell direct goods and some sell indirect goods. **Direct goods** are goods used in a production process, such as sheet steel for auto body production. **Indirect goods** are all other goods not directly involved in the production process, such as office supplies or products for maintenance and repair. Some Net marketplaces support contractual purchasing based on long-term relationships with designated suppliers, and others support short-term spot purchasing, where goods are purchased based on immediate needs, often from many suppliers.

Some Net marketplaces serve vertical markets for specific industries, such as automobiles, telecommunications, or machine tools, whereas others serve horizontal markets for goods and services that can be found in many industries, such as office equipment or transportation.

Exostar is an example of an industry-owned Net marketplace, focusing on long-term contract purchasing relationships and on providing common networks and computing platforms for reducing supply chain inefficiencies. This aerospace and defense industry-sponsored Net marketplace was founded jointly by BAE Systems, Boeing, Lockheed Martin, Raytheon, and Rolls-Royce plc to connect these companies to their suppliers and facilitate collaboration. More than 125,000 trading partners in the commercial, military, and government sectors use Exostar's sourcing, e-procurement, and collaboration tools for both direct and indirect goods.

Exchanges are independently owned third-party Net marketplaces that connect thousands of suppliers and buyers for spot purchasing. Many exchanges provide vertical markets for a single industry, such as food, electronics, or industrial equipment, and they primarily deal with direct inputs. For example, Go2Paper enables a spot market for paper, board, and craft among buyers and sellers in the paper industries from more than 75 countries.

Exchanges proliferated during the early years of e-commerce, but many have failed. Suppliers were reluctant to participate because the exchanges encouraged competitive bidding that drove prices down and did not offer any long-term relationships with buyers or services to make lowering prices worthwhile. Many essential direct purchases are not conducted on a spot basis because they require contracts and consideration of issues such as delivery timing, customization, and quality of products.

10-5 What is the role of m-commerce in business, and what are the most important m-commerce applications?

Walk down the street in any major metropolitan area and count how many people are pecking away at their iPhones, Samsungs, or BlackBerrys. Ride the trains or fly the planes, and you'll see fellow travelers reading an online newspaper, watching a video on their phone, or reading a novel on their Kindle. As the mobile audience has expanded in leaps and bounds, mobile advertising and m-commerce have taken off.

In 2019, retail m-commerce will account for about 48 percent of all e-commerce, with about $270 billion in annual revenues generated by retail goods and services, apps, advertising, music, videos, ring tones, movies, television, and location-based services such as local restaurant locators and traffic updates. M-commerce is the fastest-growing form of e-commerce, expanding at a rate of 30 percent or more per year, and is estimated to grow to $500 billion by 2022 (see Figure 10.9) (eMarketer, 2018d).

FIGURE 10.9 MOBILE RETAIL COMMERCE REVENUES

Mobile e-commerce is the fastest-growing type of B2C e-commerce and represented about 34 percent of all e-commerce in 2018.

Sources: Data from eMarketer chart "Retail Mcommerce Sales, US, (billions) 2018–2022," eMarketer, 2018d

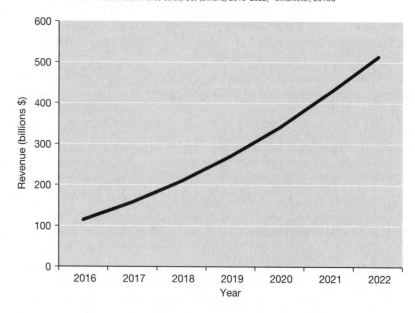

The main areas of growth in mobile e-commerce are mass market retailing such as Amazon; sales of digital content such as music, TV shows, movies, and e-books; and in-app sales to mobile devices. On-demand firms such as Uber (described earlier in this chapter) and Airbnb are location-based services, and examples of mobile commerce as well. Larger mobile screens and more-convenient payment procedures also play a role in the expansion of m-commerce.

Location-Based Services and Applications

Location-based services include geosocial, geoadvertising, and geoinformation services. Seventy-four percent of smartphone owners use location-based services. What ties these activities together and is the foundation for mobile commerce is the global positioning system (GPS)–enabled map services available on smartphones. A **geosocial service** can tell you where your friends are meeting. **Geoadvertising services** can tell you where to find the nearest Italian restaurant, and **geoinformation services** can tell you the price of a house you are looking at or about special exhibits at a museum you are passing. In 2019, the fastest-growing and most popular location-based services are on-demand economy firms such as Uber, Lyft, Airbnb, and hundreds more that provide services to users in local areas and are based on the user's location (or, in the case of Airbnb, the user's intended travel location).

Waze is an example of a popular, social geoinformation service. Waze is a GPS-based map and navigational app for smartphones, now owned by Google. Waze locates the user's car on a digital map using GPS and, like other navigation programs, collects information on the user's speed and direction continuously. What makes Waze different is that it collects traffic information from users who submit accident reports, speed traps, landmarks, street fairs, protests, and even addresses. Waze uses this information to come up with suggested alternative routes, travel times, and warnings and can even make recommendations for gas stations along the way. The Waze app is used extensively by Uber and Lyft drivers and more than 50 million other drivers in the United States.

Foursquare and new offerings by Facebook and Google are examples of geosocial services. Geosocial services help you find friends, or your friends to find you, by checking in to the service, announcing your presence in a restaurant or other place. Your friends are instantly notified. About 20 percent of smartphone owners use geosocial services.

Foursquare provides a location-based social networking service to over 60 million registered individual users, who can connect with friends, update their location, and provide reviews and tips for enjoying a location. Points are awarded for checking in at designated venues. Users choose to post their check-ins on their accounts on Twitter, Facebook, or both. Users also earn badges by checking in at locations with certain tags, for check-in frequency, or for the time of check-in.

Connecting people to local merchants in the form of geoadvertising is the economic foundation for mobile commerce. Geoadvertising sends ads to users based on their GPS locations. Smartphones report their locations back to Google and Apple. Merchants buy access to these consumers when they come within range of a merchant. For instance, Kiehl Stores, a cosmetics retailer, sent special offers and announcements to customers who came within 100 yards of their store.

Other Mobile Commerce Services

Banks and credit card companies have developed services that let customers manage their accounts from their mobile devices. JPMorgan Chase and Bank of America customers can use their cell phones to check account balances, transfer funds, and pay bills. Apple Pay for the iPhone and Apple Watch, along with other Android and Windows smartphone models, allow users to charge items to their credit card accounts with a swipe of their phone. (See our Learning Track on mobile payment systems.)

The mobile advertising market is the fastest-growing online ad platform, racking up a forecast $90 billion in ad revenue in 2019 and growing at 20 percent annually. Ads eventually move to where the eyeballs are, and increasingly that means mobile phones and, to a lesser extent, tablets. Google is the largest mobile advertising market, posting about $23 billion in mobile ads or 60 percent of its total ad revenue, with Facebook number two with $19.4 billion (90 percent of its total digital ad business). Google is displaying ads linked to cell phone searches by users of the mobile version of its search engine; ads are embedded in games, videos, and other mobile applications.

Shopkick is a mobile application that enables retailers such as Best Buy, Sports Authority, and Macy's to offer coupons to people when they walk into their stores. The Shopkick app automatically recognizes when the user has entered a partner retail store and offers a new virtual currency called kickbucks, which can be redeemed for store gift cards.

Fifty-five percent of online retailers now have m-commerce websites—simplified versions of their websites that enable shoppers to use cell phones to shop and place orders. Virtually all large traditional and online retailers such as Sephora, Home Depot, Amazon, and Walmart have apps for m-commerce sales. In 2019, more than 66 percent of m-commerce sales will occur within apps rather than mobile web browsers. Browser commerce has, at least for mobile users, become app commerce.

10-6 What issues must be addressed when building an e-commerce presence?

Building a successful e-commerce presence requires a keen understanding of business, technology, and social issues as well as a systematic approach. Today, an e-commerce presence is not just a corporate website but also includes a social network site on Facebook, a Twitter feed, and smartphone apps where customers can access your services. Developing and coordinating all these customer venues can be difficult. A complete treatment of the topic is beyond the scope of this text, and students should consult books devoted to just this topic (Laudon and Traver, 2019). The two most important management challenges in building a successful e-commerce presence are (1) developing a clear understanding of your business objectives and (2) knowing how to choose the right technology to achieve those objectives.

Develop an E-commerce Presence Map

E-commerce has moved from being a PC-centric activity on the web to a mobile and tablet-based activity. Currently, a majority of Internet users in the United States use smartphones and tablets to shop for goods and services,

FIGURE 10.10 **E-COMMERCE PRESENCE MAP**

An e-commerce presence requires firms to consider the four types of presence, with specific platforms and activities associated with each.

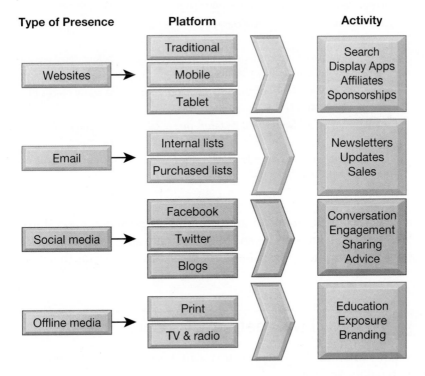

look up prices, enjoy entertainment, and access social sites, less so to make purchases. Your potential customers use these various devices at different times during the day and involve themselves in different conversations, depending what they are doing—touching base with friends, tweeting, or reading a blog. Each of these is a touch point where you can meet the customer, and you have to think about how you develop a presence in these different virtual places. Figure 10.10 provides a roadmap to the platforms and related activities you will need to think about when developing your e-commerce presence.

Figure 10.10 illustrates four kinds of e-commerce presence: websites, email, social media, and offline media. You must address different platforms for each of these types. For instance, in the case of website presence, there are three platforms: traditional desktop, tablets, and smartphones, each with different capabilities. Moreover, for each type of e-commerce presence, there are related activities you will need to consider. For instance, in the case of websites, you will want to engage in search engine marketing, display ads, affiliate programs, and sponsorships. Offline media, the fourth type of e-commerce presence, is included here because many firms use multiplatform or integrated marketing by which print ads refer customers to websites.

Develop a Timeline: Milestones

Where would you like to be a year from now? It's very helpful for you to have a rough idea of the time frame for developing your e-commerce presence when you begin. You should break your project down into a small number of phases that could be completed within a specified time. Table 10.8 illustrates a one-year

TABLE 10.8 E-COMMERCE PRESENCE TIMELINE		
PHASE	ACTIVITY	MILESTONE
Phase 1: Planning	Envision web presence; determine personnel.	Web mission statement
Phase 2: Website development	Acquire content; develop a site design; arrange for hosting the site.	Website plan
Phase 3: Web implementation	Develop keywords and metatags; focus on search engine optimization; identify potential sponsors.	A functional website
Phase 4: Social media plan	Identify appropriate social platforms and content for your products and services.	A social media plan
Phase 5: Social media implementation	Develop Facebook, Twitter, and Pinterest presence.	Functioning social media presence
Phase 6: Mobile plan	Develop a mobile plan; consider options for porting your website to smartphones.	A mobile media plan

timeline for the development of an e-commerce presence for a start-up company devoted to fashions for teenagers. You can also find more detail about developing an e-commerce website in the Learning Tracks for this chapter.

10.7 How will MIS help my career?

Here is how Chapter 10 and this text can help you find a job as a junior e-commerce data analyst.

The Company

SportsFantasy Empire, a technology company that creates digital sports competitions, is looking for a recent college graduate to fill a junior e-commerce data analyst position. SportsFantasy Empire offers players the opportunity to compete through web and mobile devices in fantasy sports contests for cash prizes. The company was founded in 2012 and is headquartered in Los Angeles, with additional offices in San Francisco and New York.

Job Description

The junior e-commerce data analyst will work with SportsFantasy Empire's analytics team to analyze large volumes of data to derive business insights about the company's games and customers that will increase revenue. Job responsibilities include:

- Setting up contest sizing that defines the user experience and business efficiency.
- Optimizing acquisition spending and marketing strategies to drive growth.
- Identifying ways to improve customer gameplay through on-site changes.
- Measuring how new features or site changes are driving changes in customer behavior.
- Developing standard reporting for key business results, including reports on contest performance, player activity, segment performance, and key player performance.

Job Requirements

- Bachelor's degree in engineering, mathematics, business, or a related field
- E-commerce data analytics experience desirable
- Knowledge of statistics
- Demonstrated history of independently developing new insights from data
- Experience with model building, SQL, SAS, or other programming language desirable
- Strong communication and organizational skills
- Avid fantasy sports player a plus

Interview Questions

1. Do you play fantasy sports? How often? Have you ever worked with data about fantasy sports? Why do you think you would be a good fit for this job?
2. What is your background in statistics? What courses did you take? Have you any job experience where you had to use statistics?
3. Have you ever analyzed data about website performance or online customer behavior?
4. What do you know about the cost of acquiring a customer through social media channels (i.e., measuring the average customer acquisition cost on social networks; acquisition vs. retention costs)?
5. How would you propose working with our non-technical teams in telling a story about customer data insights so that they are able to drive customer engagement and loyalty and execute more effectively?
6. What is your proficiency level with SQL or SAS and site analytics tools? Have you ever used these tools on the job? What did you do with them?
7. Can you give an example of a problem you solved using data analytics? Did you do any writing and analysis? Can you provide examples?

Author Tips

1. Review this chapter and also the discussion of search and search engine marketing in Chapter 7. To qualify for this job, you should also have taken course work in statistics. Course work or on-the-job training in SQL and SAS would also be helpful.
2. Use the web to do more research on the company. Try to find out more about its strategy, competitors, and business challenges. Additionally, review the company's social media channels from the past 12 months. Are there any trends you can identify or certain themes the social media channels seem to focus on?
3. Be prepared to talk about SportsFantasy Empire's games as well as the games offered by competitors to show you are familiar with the industry. Inquire about some of the ways the company fine-tunes its online presence. Be prepared to give an example of how you think a fantasy game could improve its online presence.
4. Use the web to find examples of data analytics used by fantasy sports companies.

10-1 What are the unique features of e-commerce, digital markets, and digital goods?

E-commerce involves digitally enabled commercial transactions between and among organizations and individuals. Unique features of e-commerce technology include ubiquity, global reach, universal technology standards, richness, interactivity, information density, capabilities for personalization and customization, and social technology. E-commerce is becoming increasingly social, mobile, and local.

Digital markets are said to be more transparent than traditional markets, with reduced information asymmetry, search costs, transaction costs, and menu costs along with the ability to change prices dynamically based on market conditions. Digital goods, such as music, video, software, and books, can be delivered over a digital network. Once a digital product has been produced, the cost of delivering that product digitally is extremely low.

10-2 What are the principal e-commerce business and revenue models?

E-commerce business models are e-tailers, transaction brokers, market creators, content providers, community providers, service providers, and portals. The principal e-commerce revenue models are advertising, sales, subscription, free/freemium, transaction fee, and affiliate.

10-3 How has e-commerce transformed marketing?

The Internet provides marketers with new ways of identifying and communicating with millions of potential customers at costs far lower than traditional media. Crowdsourcing using the wisdom of crowds helps companies learn from customers to improve product offerings and increase customer value. Behavioral targeting techniques increase the effectiveness of banner, rich media, and video ads. Social commerce uses social networks and social network sites to improve targeting of products and services.

10-4 How has e-commerce affected business-to-business transactions?

B2B e-commerce generates efficiencies by enabling companies to locate suppliers, solicit bids, place orders, and track shipments in transit electronically. Net marketplaces provide a single, digital marketplace for many buyers and sellers. Private industrial networks link a firm with its suppliers and other strategic business partners to develop highly efficient and responsive supply chains.

10-5 What is the role of m-commerce in business, and what are the most important m-commerce applications?

M-commerce is especially well suited for location-based applications such as finding local hotels and restaurants, monitoring local traffic and weather, and providing personalized location-based marketing. Mobile phones and handhelds are being used for mobile bill payment, banking, securities trading, transportation schedule updates, and downloads of digital content such as music, games, and video clips. M-commerce requires wireless portals and special digital payment systems that can handle micropayments. The GPS capabilities of smartphones make geoadvertising, geosocial, and geoinformation services possible.

10-6 What issues must be addressed when building an e-commerce presence?

Building a successful e-commerce presence requires a clear understanding of the business objectives to be achieved and selection of the right platforms, activities, and timeline to achieve those objectives. An e-commerce presence includes not only a corporate website but also a presence on Facebook, Twitter, and other social networking sites and smartphone apps.

Key Terms

Advertising revenue model, 390

Affiliate revenue model, 392

Behavioral targeting, 393

Business-to-business (B2B), 385

Business-to-consumer (B2C), 385

Community providers, 388

Consumer-to-consumer (C2C), 385

Cost transparency, 381

MyLab MIS

To complete the problems with MyLab MIS, go to the EOC Discussion Questions in MyLab MIS.

Review Questions

10-1 What are the unique features of e-commerce, digital markets, and digital goods?

- Name and describe four business trends and three technology trends shaping e-commerce today.
- List and describe the eight unique features of e-commerce.
- Define a digital market and digital goods and describe their distinguishing features.

10-2 What are the principal e-commerce business and revenue models?

- Name and describe the principal e-commerce business models.
- Name and describe the e-commerce revenue models.

10-3 How has e-commerce transformed marketing?

- Explain how social networking and the wisdom of crowds help companies improve their marketing.
- Define behavioral targeting and explain how it works at individual websites and on advertising networks.

- Define the social graph and explain how it is used in e-commerce marketing.

10-4 How has e-commerce affected business-to-business transactions?

- Explain how Internet technology supports business-to-business electronic commerce.
- Define and describe Net marketplaces and explain how they differ from private industrial networks (private exchanges).

10-5 What is the role of m-commerce in business, and what are the most important m-commerce applications?

- List and describe important types of m-commerce services and applications.

10-6 What issues must be addressed when building an e-commerce presence?

- List and describe the four types of e-commerce presence.

Discussion Questions

10-7
MyLab MIS How does the Internet change consumer and supplier relationships?

10-8
MyLab MIS The Internet may not make corporations obsolete, but the corporations will have to change their business models. Do you agree? Why or why not?

10-9
MyLab MIS How have social technologies changed e-commerce?

Hands-On MIS Projects

The projects in this section give you hands-on experience developing e-commerce strategies for businesses, using spreadsheet software to research the profitability of an e-commerce company, and using web tools to research and evaluate e-commerce hosting services. Visit MyLab MIS to access this chapter's Hands-On MIS Projects.

Management Decision Problems

10-10 Columbiana is a small, independent island in the Caribbean that has many historical buildings, forts, and other sites along with rain forests and striking mountains. A few first-class hotels and several dozen less-expensive accommodations lie along its beautiful white-sand beaches. The major airlines have regular flights to Columbiana, as do several small airlines. Columbiana's government wants to increase tourism and develop new markets for the country's tropical agricultural products. How can an e-commerce presence help? What Internet business model would be appropriate? What functions should the e-commerce presence perform?

10-11 Explore the websites of the following companies: Swatch, Lowe's, and Priceline. Determine which of these websites would benefit most from adding a company-sponsored blog to the website. List the business benefits of the blog. Specify the intended audience for the blog. Decide who in the company should author the blog and select some topics for the blog.

Improving Decision Making: Using Spreadsheet Software to Analyze a Dot-com Business

Software skills: Spreadsheet downloading, formatting, and formulas
Business skills: Financial statement analysis

10-12 Pick one e-commerce company on the Internet—for example, Ashford, Yahoo, or Priceline. Study the web pages that describe the company and explain its purpose and structure. Use the web to find articles that comment on the company. Then visit the Securities and Exchange Commission's website at www.sec.gov to access the company's 10-K (annual report) form showing income statements and balance sheets. Select only the sections of the 10-K form containing the desired portions of financial statements that you need to examine and download them into your spreadsheet. (MyLab MIS provides more detailed instructions on how to download this 10-K data into a spreadsheet.) Create simplified spreadsheets of the company's balance sheets and income statements for the past three years.

- Is the company a dot-com success, borderline business, or failure? What information provides the basis of your decision? Why? When answering these questions, pay special attention to the company's three-year trends in revenues, costs of sales, gross margins, operating expenses, and net margins.

- Prepare an overhead presentation (with a minimum of five slides), including appropriate spreadsheets or charts, and present your work to your professor and classmates.

Achieving Operational Excellence: Evaluating E-commerce Hosting Services

Software skills: Web browser software
Business skills: Evaluating e-commerce hosting services

10-13 This project will help develop your Internet skills in evaluating commercial services for hosting an e-commerce site for a small start-up company.

You would like to set up a website to sell towels, linens, pottery, and tableware from Portugal and are examining services for hosting small business Internet storefronts. Your website should be able to take secure credit card payments and calculate shipping costs and taxes. Initially, you would like to display photos and descriptions of 40 products. Visit Wix, GoDaddy, and iPage and compare the range of e-commerce hosting services they offer to small businesses, their capabilities, and their costs. Examine the tools they provide for creating an e-commerce site. Compare these services and decide which you would use if you were actually establishing a web store. Write a brief report indicating your choice and explaining the strengths and weaknesses of each service.

Collaboration and Teamwork Project

Performing a Competitive Analysis of E-commerce Sites

10-14 Form a group with three or four of your classmates. Select two businesses that are competitors in the same industry and that use their websites for electronic commerce. Visit these websites. You might compare, for example, the websites for Pandora and Spotify, Amazon and BarnesandNoble.com, or E*Trade and TD Ameritrade. Prepare an evaluation of each business's website in terms of its functions, user friendliness, and ability to support the company's business strategy. Which website does a better job? Why? Can you make some recommendations to improve these websites? If possible, use Google Docs and Google Drive or Google Sites to brainstorm, organize, and develop a presentation of your findings for the class.

A Nasty Ending for Nasty Gal
CASE STUDY

In 2006, Sophia Amoruso was a 22-year-old hitch-hiking, dumpster-diving community college drop-out with a lot of time on her hands. After reading a book called *Starting an eBay Business for Dummies*, she launched an eBay store called Nasty Gal Vintage, named after a song and 1975 album by the jazz singer Betty Davis, second wife of the legendary Miles Davis.

Nasty Gal's styling was edgy and fresh—a little bit rock and roll, a little bit disco, modern, but never hyper-trendy. Eight years after its founding, Nasty Gal had sold more than $100 million in new and vintage clothing and accessories, employed more than 350 people, had more than a million fans on Facebook and Instagram, and was a global brand. It looked like a genuine e-commerce success story. Or was it?

When Amoruso began her business, she did everything herself out of her tiny San Francisco apartment—merchandising, photographing, copywriting, and shipping. She got up at the crack of dawn to make 6 a.m. estate sales, haggled with thrift stores, spent hours photoshopping the images she styled and shot photos herself using models she recruited herself, and ensured that packaging was high quality.

She would inspect items to make sure they were in good enough shape to sell. She zipped zippers, buttoned buttons, connected hooks, folded each garment, and slid it into a clear plastic bag that was sealed with a sticker. Then she boxed the item and affixed a shipping label on it. She had to assume that her customers were as particular and as concerned with aesthetics as she was.

Amoruso had taken photography classes at a community college, where she learned to understand the importance of silhouette and composition. She bought vintage pieces with dramatic silhouettes—a coat with a big funnel collar, a '50s dress with a flared skirt, or a Victorian jacket with puffy sleeves. Exaggerating everything about the silhouette through the angle from which it was photographed helped Amoruso produce tiny thumbnails for eBay that attracted serious bidders. She was able to take an object, distill what was best about it, and then exaggerate those qualities so they were visible even in its tiniest representation. When the thumbnail was enlarged, it looked amazing.

Amoruso has been a heavy user of social tools to promote her business. When she first started out, she used MySpace, where she attracted a cult following of more than 60,000 fans. The company gained traction on social media with Nasty Gal's aesthetic that could be both high and low, edgy and glossy.

Amoruso took customer feedback very seriously and believed customers were at the center of everything Nasty Gal did. When she sold on eBay, she learned to respond to every customer comment to help her understand precisely who was buying her goods and what they wanted. Amoruso said that the content Nasty Gal customers created has always been a huge part of the Nasty Gal brand. It was very important to see how customers wore Nasty Gal's pieces and the types of photographs they took. They were inspiring.

Social media is built on sharing, and Nasty Gal gave its followers compelling images, words, and content to share and talk about each day. They could be a crazy vintage piece, a quote, or a behind-the-scenes photo. At most companies the person manning the Twitter and Facebook accounts is far removed from senior management. Amoruso did not always author every Nasty Gal tweet, but she still read every comment. If the customers were unhappy about something, she wanted to hear about it right away. At other businesses, it might take months for customer feedback to filter up to the CEO. When Nasty Gal first joined Snapchat, Amoruso tested the water with a few Snaps, and Nasty Gal followers responded in force.

In June 2008, Amoruso moved Nasty Gal Vintage off eBay and onto its own destination website, www.nastygal.com. In 2012, Nasty Gal began selling clothes under its own brand label and also invested $18 million in a 527,000-square-foot national distribution center in Shepherdsville, Kentucky, to handle its own shipping and logistics. Venture capitalists Index Ventures provided at least $40 million in funding. Nasty Gal opened a brick-and-mortar store in Los Angeles in 2014 and another in Santa Monica in 2015.

With growing direct-to-consumer demand and higher inventory replenishment requirements driven by new store openings, Nasty Gal invested in a new warehouse management system. The warehouse management system investment was designed to increase warehouse productivity and shorten order cycle times so that Nasty Gal's supply chain could better service its mushrooming sales. (Order cycle time refers to the time period between placing of one order and the next order.) The company selected HighJump's Warehouse Management System (WMS) with the goal of increasing visibility and overall productivity while keeping fill rates above 99 percent. (The fill rate is the percentage of orders satisfied from stock at hand.)

Key considerations were scalability and capabilities for handling retail replenishment in addition to direct-to-consumer orders. HighJump's implementation team customized the WMS software to optimize the business processes that worked best for an e-commerce retailer that ships most of its items straight to the customer, with a small subset going to retail stores. The WMS software was also configured to support processes that would scale with future growth. Picking efficiency and fill rates shot up, with fill rates above 99 percent, even though order volume climbed.

Nasty Gal experienced tremendous growth in its early years, being named *INC Magazine's* fastest-growing retailer in 2012 and earning a number one ranking in *Internet Retailer's* Top 500 Guide in 2016. By 2011, annual sales hit $24 million and then nearly $100 million in 2012. However, sales started dropping to $85 million in 2014 and then $77 million in 2015. Nasty Gal's rapid expansion had been fueled by heavy spending in advertising and marketing. This is a strategy used by many start-ups, but it only pays off in the long run if one-time buyers become loyal shoppers. Otherwise, too much money is spent on online marketing like banner ads and paying for influencers. If a company pays $70 on marketing to acquire a customer and that customer only buys once from it, the company won't make money. A company that spends $200 million to make $100 million in revenue is not a sustainable business. Nasty Gal had a "leaky bucket" situation: Once it burned through its fundraising capital and cut down on marketing, sales continued to drop.

Nasty Gal couldn't hold onto customers. Some were dissatisfied with product quality, but many were more attracted to fast-fashion retailers such as Zara and H&M, which both deliver a wider array of trendy clothes through online and bricks-and-mortar stores at lower prices and are constantly changing their merchandise. The actual market for the Nasty Gal brand was quickly saturated. There was a limit to the number of women Nasty Gal appealed to: Nasty Gal had a California cool, young girl look, and it was unclear how attractive it was in other parts of the United States and around the world.

Nasty Gal also wasted money on things that didn't warrant large expenditures. The company quintupled the size of its headquarters by moving into a 50,300-square-foot location in downtown Los Angeles in 2013—far more space than the company needed, according to industry experts. The company had also opened a 500,000-square-foot fulfillment center in Kentucky to handle its own distribution and logistics as well as two bricks-and-mortar stores in Los Angeles and Santa Monica. Even in the hyper-trendy fashion business, companies have to closely monitor production, distribution, and expenses for operations to move products at a scale big enough to make a profit. Nasty Gal's mostly young staff focused too much on the creative side of the business.

While it was growing, Nasty Gal built its management team, hiring sizzling junior talent from retail outlets such as Urban Outfitters. But their traditional retail backgrounds clashed with the start-up mentality. As Nasty Gal expanded, Amoruso's own fame also grew, and she was sidetracked by other projects. She wrote two books. The first, titled *#Girlboss*, described the founding of Nasty Gal and Amoruso's business philosophy and was adapted by Netflix into a show with Amoruso as executive producer. (The series was cancelled in June 2017 after just one season.) Employees complained about Amoruso's management style and lack of focus.

Amoruso resigned as chief executive in 2015 but remained on Nasty Gal's board of directors until the company filed for Chapter 11 bankruptcy on November 9, 2016. Between 2015 and 2016, Nasty Gal had raised an additional $24 million in equity and debt financing from venture-focused Stamos Capital Partners LP and Hercules Technology Growth Capital Inc. Even though the funding helped Nasty Gal stay afloat, the company still had trouble paying for new inventory, rent, and other operating expenses.

Within weeks of filing for Chapter 11 protection, Nasty Gal sold its brand name and other intellectual property on February 28, 2017, for $20 million to a rival online fashion site, the United Kingdom's Boohoo.com. Boohoo is operating Nasty Gal as a standalone website, but Nasty Gal's stores are closing. Boohoo believes Nasty Gal's arresting style and loyal customer base will complement Boohoo and expand global opportunities for growth. Many customers have complained about the quality of fabric and customer service.

Amoruso subsequently turned to developing Girlboss—a media company that hosts a website, a podcast, and two annual conferences, called the Girlboss Rally. She also launched the Girlboss Foundation, which has given out $130,000 to women-owned small businesses.

Sources: Cady Drell, "Sophia Amoruso on the Strange and Difficult Upside of Making Big Mistakes." *Elle*, July 24, 2018; Aundrea Cline-Thomas, "How Girlboss's Sophia Amoruso Continues to Chart Her Career Course," www.nbcnews.com, July 26, 2018; Sarah Chaney, "How Nasty Gal Went from an $85 Million Company to Bankruptcy," *Wall Street Journal*,

February 24, 2017; Shan Li, "Nasty Gal, Once a Fashion World Darling, Went Bankrupt: What Went Wrong?," *Los Angeles Times*, February 24, 2017; "Case Study Nasty Gal," *HighJump*, 2016; and Yelena Shuster, "NastyGal Founder Sophia Amoruso on How to Become a #GirlBoss," *Elle*, May 15, 2014.

CASE STUDY QUESTIONS

10-15 How was social media related to Nasty Gal's business model? To what extent was Nasty Gal a "social" business?

10-16 What management, organization, and technology problems were responsible for Nasty Gal's failure as a business?

10-17 Could Nasty Gal have avoided bankruptcy? Explain your answer.

MyLab MIS

Go to the Assignments section of MyLab MIS to complete these writing exercises.

10-18 Describe the six features of social commerce. Provide an example for each feature, describing how a business could use that feature for selling to consumers online.

10-19 List and describe the main activities involved in building an e-commerce presence.

Chapter 10 References

Almquist, Eric, Jamie Cleghorn, and Lori Sherer. "The B2B Elements of Value." Harvard Business Review (March–April 2018).

Bapna, Ravi, Jui Ramaprasad, and Akmed Umyarov. "Monetizing Freemium Comunities: Does Paying for Premium Increase Social Engagement?"*MIS Quarterly* 42, No. 3 (September 2018).

Bell, David R., Santiago Gallino, and Antonio Moreno. "The Store Is Dead - Long Live the Store." *MIT Sloan Management Review* (Spring 2018).

Brynjolfsson, Erik, Tomer Geva, and Shachar Reichman. "Crowd-Squared: Amplifying the Predictive Power of Search Trend Data." *MIS Quarterly* 40, No. 4 (December 2016).

"Do Search Ads Really Work?" *Harvard Business Review* (March–April 2017).

eMarketer. "US Mobile Downloads and In-App Revenue." (November, 2017a).

_____. "US Time Spent with Media." eMarketer Chart (April 2017b).

_____. "Digital Travel Sales 2018–2022." eMarketer (June 2018a.)

_____. "Internet Users by Device, 2016–2022." eMarketer (February 2018b).

_____. "Retail Ecommerce Sales 2018–2022." eMarketer (May 2018c.)

_____. "Retail Mcommerce Sales 2018–2022." eMarketer (July 2018d.)

_____. "Retail Sales North America 2018–2022." eMarketer (May 2018e).

_____. "Social Network Share of Average Time Spent Per Day with Digital Media by Platform." 2015–2020, eMarketer (April 2018f.)

_____. "US Ad Spending." eMarketer (April 2018g.)

_____. "US Digital Users Estimates for 2018." eMarketer (March 2018h).

_____. "US Digital Video Viewers and Penetration, 2016–2022." eMarketer (February 2018i).

Facebook. "Stats." https://newsroom.fb.com, accessed July 20, 2018.

Fang, Xiao, and Paul Jen-Hwa Hu. "Top Persuader Prediction for Social Networks." *MIS Quarterly* 42 No. 1 (March 2018).

Gomber, Peter, Robert J. Kauffman, Chris Parker, and Bruce W. Weber. "On the Fintech Revolution: Interpreting the Forces of Innovation, Disruption, and Transformation in Financial Services." *Journal of Management Information Systems* 35 No. 1 (2018).

Gosline, Renee Richardson, Jeffrey Lee, and Glen Urban. "The Power of Customer Stories in Digital Marketing." *MIT Sloan Management Review* (Summer 2017).

Gunarathne, Priyanga, Huaxia Rui, and Abraham Seidmann. "When Social Media Delivers Customer Service: Differential Customer Treatment in the Airline Industry." *MIS Quarterly* 42 No. 2 (June 2018).

Hoang, Ai-Phuong, and Robert J. Kauffman. "Content Sampling, Household Informedness, and the Consumption of Digital Information Goods." *Journal of Management Information Systems* 35 No. 2 (2018).

Hong, Yili, Paul A. Pavlou, Nan Shi, and Kanliang Wang. "On the Role of Fairness and Social Distance in Designing Effective Social Referral Systems." *MIS Quarterly* 41 No. 3 (September 2017).

Hu, Nan, Paul A. Pavlou, and Jie Zhang. "On Self-Selection Biases in Online Product Reviews." *MIS Quarterly* 41, No. 2 (June 2017).

Huang, Ni, Yili Hong, and Gordon Burtch. "Social Network Integration and User Content Generation: Evidence from Natural Experiments." *MIS Quarterly* 41 No. 4 (December 2017).

Internet World Stats. "Internet Users in the World." Internetworldstats.com (2018).

John, Leslie K., Daniel Mochon, Oliver Emrich, and Janet Schwartz. "What's the Value of a 'Like'?" *Harvard Business Review* (March–April 2017).

Kwark, Young, Jianqing Chen, and Srinivasan Raghunathan. "Platform or Wholesale? A Strategic Tool for Online Retailers to Benefit from Third-Party Information." *MIS Quarterly* 41 No. 3 (September 2017).

Laudon, Kenneth C., and Carol Guercio Traver. *E-commerce: Business, Technology, Society*, 15th ed. (Upper Saddle River, NJ: Prentice-Hall, 2019).

Lin Zhije, Khim-Yong Goh, and Cheng-Suang Heng. "The Demand Effects of Product Recommendation Networks: An Empirical Analysis of Network Diversity and Stability." *MIS Quarterly* 41, No. 2 (June 2017).

Liu, Qianqian Ben, and Elena Karahanna. "The Dark Side of Reviews: The Swaying Effects of Online Product Reviews on Attribute Preference Construction." *MIS Quarterly* 41, No. 2 (June 2017).

Luo, Xueming, Bin Gu, Jie Zhang, and Chee Wei Phang. "Expert Blogs and Consumer Perceptions of Competing Brands." *MIS Quarterly* 41, No. 2 (June 2017).

Mo, Jiahui, Sumit Sarkar, and Syam Menon. "Know When to Run: Recommendations in Crowdsourcing Contests." *MIS Quarterly* 42, No. 3 (September 2018).

Oh, Hyelim, Animesh Animesh, and Alain Pinsonneault. "Free Versus For-a-Fee: The Impact of a Paywall on the Pattern and Effectiveness of Word-of-Mouth via Social Media." *MIS Quarterly* 40, No. 1 (March 2016).

Orlikowski, Wanda, and Susan V. Scott. "The Algorithm and the Crowd: Considering the Materiality of Service Innovation." *MIS Quarterly* 39, No. 1 (March 2015).

Rainie, Lee. "Americans' Complicated Feelings about Social Media in an Era of Privacy Concerns." Pew Research Center (May 2018).

_____. "The State of Privacy in Post-Snowden America." Pew Research Center (September 21, 2016).

RIAA.com, accessed July 30, 2018.

Schlager, Tobias, Christian Hildebrand, Gerald Häubl, Nikolaus Franke, and Andreas Herrmann. "Social Product-Customization Systems: Peer Input, Conformity, and Consumers' Evaluation of Customized Products." *Journal of Management Information Systems* 35 No.1 (2018).

Shuk, Ying Ho, and Kai H. Lim. "Nudging Moods to Induce Unplanned Purchases in Imperfect Mobile Personalization Conexts." MIS Quarterly 42, No. 3 (September 2018).

U.S. Bureau of the Census. "E-Stats." www.census.gov, accessed July 8, 2018.

Ye, Shun, Siva Viswanathan, and Il-Horn Hann. "The Value of Reciprocity in Online Barter Markets: An Empirical Investigation." *MIS Quarterly* 42 No. 2 (June 2018).

11

Managing Knowledge and Artificial Intelligence

LEARNING OBJECTIVES

After reading this chapter, you will be able to answer the following questions:

11-1 What is the role of knowledge management systems in business?

11-2 What are artificial intelligence (AI) and machine learning? How do businesses use AI?

11-3 What types of systems are used for enterprise-wide knowledge management, and how do they provide value for businesses?

11-4 What are the major types of knowledge work systems, and how do they provide value for firms?

11-5 How will MIS help my career?

CHAPTER CASES

Machine Learning Helps Akershus University Hospital Make Better Treatment Decisions

Sargent & Lundy Learns to Manage Employee Knowledge

The Reality of Virtual Reality

Can Cars Drive Themselves—And Should They?

VIDEO CASES

How IBM's Watson Became a Jeopardy Champion

Alfresco: Open Source Document Management and Collaboration

MyLab MIS

Discussion Questions: 11-5, 11-6, 11-7; **Hands-on MIS Projects:** 11-8, 11-9, 11-10, 11-11; **Writing Assignments:** 11-17, 11-18; **eText with Conceptual Animations**

Machine Learning Helps Akershus University Hospital Make Better Treatment Decisions

The healthcare industry is deluged with big data, including patient histories, clinical records, charts, and test results. Medical information is now doubling every 3 years and will be doubling every 73 days by 2020. How can healthcare professionals keep up with the knowledge in their field, and how can they use this knowledge to make more informed decisions about treatment options and managing healthcare costs when there is way too much data for humans to easily analyze and absorb?

One of the many health care organizations struggling with this problem is Akershus University Hospital (Ahus), a Norwegian public university hospital serving approximately 500,000 inhabitants around Oslo, Norway, and employing 9,500 people. Ahus had amassed huge volumes of data on patients and treatments, but much of this information was in unstructured, textual reports that made it extremely difficult and time-consuming to extract meaningful information. Combing through thousands of complex clinical documents was impossible to complete manually.

© Panchenko Vladimir/Shutterstock

Working with Capgemini consultants, Ahus is trying to solve this problem by using artificial intelligence technology in IBM Watson Explorer. IBM Watson Explorer is a *cognitive computing* platform that can analyze structured and unstructured data to uncover trends and patterns that would be difficult, if not impossible, for humans to discern. It uses natural language processing to search data expressed in everyday language like ordinary speech and machine learning algorithms to improve search results. Natural language processing technology makes it possible for a machine to understand, analyze, and derive meaning from human language. Machine learning software can identify patterns in very large databases without explicit programming, although with significant human training. IBM Watson Explorer is able to rapidly mine large volumes of data, interpret speech and text, pick up on nuances of meaning and context, answer questions, draw conclusions, and learn from its experience. It can make inferences and correlations about the content it ingests and rank potential responses for a user to select.

The hospital's image diagnostic department wanted to improve the use of CT examinations in emergencies. Ahus used IBM Watson Explorer to analyze when its CT scans performed on pediatric patients in emergency situations fell within recommended guidelines. CT scans can be life-saving in critical circumstances, but the radiation can also be potentially harmful, so CT scans should not be overused. A large amount of Ahus's CT scan data was in text format. Ahus used Watson Explorer to gather unstructured data from more than 5,000 anonymous CT examination reports and apply machine learning and natural language processing techniques to learn how often CT scans were undertaken and the findings of those scans.

Ahus and Capgemini implemented the project over a period of seven weeks during the summer of 2016. Watson had to learn the language used in medicine and understand the context of how that language is used. Capgemini adapted the technology to the Norwegian language, and Ahus trained Watson to understand medical words and phrases. The project also created a classification schema, teaching Watson to distinguish files that reported positive scan results and those that reported negative results, and categorize the data accordingly.

After several tests, Watson Explorer attained an accuracy level of 99 percent for content classification. The final analysis confirmed that frequency of CT scanning at Ahus was at an acceptable level, and that the hospital was striking the right balance between the probability of positive gains in relation to the potential harmful effects. It would have taken a team of people months and perhaps years to analyze the same amount of data that Watson could process in minutes.

Sources: IBM Corporation. "Akershus University Hospital," and "IBM Watson Explorer," www.ibm.com, accessed May 17, 2018; and "Akershus University Hospital Optimizes the Use of CT Examinations," www.capgemini.com, accessed May 18, 2018.

Akershus University Hospital's use of artificial intelligence techniques such as machine learning and natural language processing to determine whether its CT scans fell within recommended guidelines shows how organizational performance can benefit by using technology to facilitate the acquisition and application of knowledge. Facilitating access to knowledge, using knowledge tools to create and utilize new knowledge, and using that knowledge to improve business processes are vital to success and survival for both private business firms and public organizations.

The chapter-opening diagram calls attention to important points raised by this case and this chapter. Like other medical facilities, Akershus University Hospital was what is termed "data rich but knowledge poor." It had vast quantities of patient and treatment data, but they were largely unstructured and very difficult to analyze for information and insights. AI techniques such as machine learning and natural language processing helped Ahus obtain new insights and knowledge from thousands of CT scan records so that it could optimize treatments and ensure doctors and staff were following best practices.

Here are some questions to think about: How did using IBM Watson Explorer help Akershus University Hospital improve its knowledge? What was the impact on the hospital's business processes?

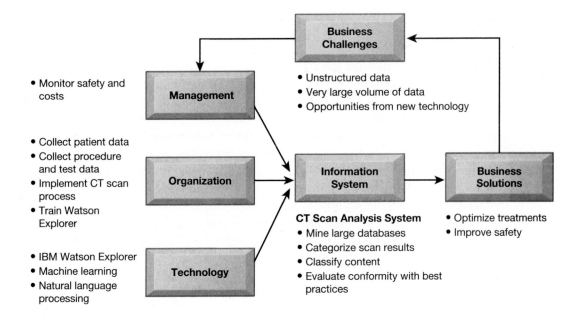

- Monitor safety and costs

Management

Business Challenges
- Unstructured data
- Very large volume of data
- Opportunities from new technology

- Collect patient data
- Collect procedure and test data
- Implement CT scan process
- Train Watson Explorer

Organization

Information System

Business Solutions

- IBM Watson Explorer
- Machine learning
- Natural language processing

Technology

CT Scan Analysis System
- Mine large databases
- Categorize scan results
- Classify content
- Evaluate conformity with best practices

- Optimize treatments
- Improve safety

11-1 What is the role of knowledge management systems in business?

Knowledge management and collaboration systems are among the fastest-growing areas of corporate and government software investment. The past decade has shown an explosive growth in research on knowledge and knowledge management in the economics, management, and information systems fields.

Knowledge management and collaboration are closely related. Knowledge that cannot be communicated and shared with others is nearly useless. Knowledge becomes useful and actionable when shared throughout the firm. We have already described the major tools for collaboration and social business in Chapter 2. In this chapter, we will focus on knowledge management systems and be mindful that communicating and sharing knowledge are becoming increasingly important.

We live in an information economy in which the major source of wealth and prosperity is the production and distribution of information and knowledge. At least 20 percent of the total economic output of the United States, $4 trillion, derives from the output of the information and knowledge sectors of the economy, which employs an estimated minimum of 30 million people (U.S. Department of Labor, 2017; Bureau of Economic Analysis, 2018).

Knowledge management has become an important theme at many large business firms as managers realize that much of their firm's value depends on the firm's ability to create and manage knowledge. Studies have found that a substantial part of a firm's stock market value is related to its intangible assets, of which knowledge is one important component, along with brands, reputations, and unique business processes. Well-executed knowledge-based projects have been known to produce extraordinary returns on investment, although the impacts of knowledge-based investments are difficult to measure (Gu and Lev, 2001).

Important Dimensions of Knowledge

There is an important distinction between data, information, knowledge, and wisdom. Chapter 1 defines **data** as flows of events or transactions captured by an organization's systems that are useful for transacting but little else. To turn data into useful *information*, a firm must expend resources to organize data into categories of understanding, such as monthly, daily, regional, or store-based reports of total sales. To transform information into **knowledge**, a firm must expend additional resources to discover patterns, rules, and contexts where the knowledge works. Finally, **wisdom** is thought to be the collective and individual experience of applying knowledge to the solution of problems. Wisdom involves where, when, and how to apply knowledge.

Knowledge is both an individual attribute and a collective attribute of the firm. Knowledge is a cognitive, even a physiological, event that takes place inside people's heads. It is also stored in libraries and records, shared in lectures, and stored by firms in the form of business processes and employee know-how. Knowledge residing in the minds of employees that has not been documented is called **tacit knowledge**, whereas knowledge that has been documented is called **explicit knowledge**. Knowledge can reside in email, voice mail, graphics, and unstructured documents as well as structured documents. Knowledge is generally believed to have a location, either in the minds of humans or in specific business processes. Knowledge is "sticky" and not universally applicable or easily moved. Finally, knowledge is thought to be situational and contextual. For example, you must know when to perform a procedure as well as how to perform it. Table 11.1 reviews these dimensions of knowledge.

We can see that knowledge is a different kind of firm asset from, say, buildings and financial assets; that knowledge is a complex phenomenon; and that there are many aspects to the process of managing knowledge. We can also

TABLE 11.1 IMPORTANT DIMENSIONS OF KNOWLEDGE

KNOWLEDGE IS A FIRM ASSET

Knowledge is an intangible asset.

The transformation of data into useful information and knowledge requires organizational resources.

Knowledge is not subject to the law of diminishing returns as are physical assets but instead experiences network effects because its value increases as more people share it.

KNOWLEDGE HAS DIFFERENT FORMS

Knowledge can be either tacit or explicit (codified).

Knowledge involves know-how, craft, and skill.

Knowledge involves knowing how to follow procedures.

Knowledge involves knowing why, not simply when, things happen (causality).

KNOWLEDGE HAS A LOCATION

Knowledge is a cognitive event involving mental models and maps of individuals.

There is both a social and an individual basis of knowledge.

Knowledge is "sticky" (hard to move), situated (enmeshed in a firm's culture), and contextual (works only in certain situations).

KNOWLEDGE IS SITUATIONAL

Knowledge is conditional; knowing when to apply a procedure is just as important as knowing the procedure (conditional).

Knowledge is related to context; you must know how to use a certain tool and under what circumstances.

recognize that knowledge-based core competencies of firms—the two or three things that an organization does best—are key organizational assets. Knowing how to do things effectively and efficiently in ways that other organizations cannot duplicate is a primary source of profit and competitive advantage that cannot be purchased easily by competitors in the marketplace.

For instance, having a unique build-to-order production system constitutes a form of knowledge and perhaps a unique asset that other firms cannot copy easily. With knowledge, firms become more efficient and effective in their use of scarce resources. Without knowledge, firms become less efficient and less effective in their use of resources and ultimately fail.

Organizational Learning and Knowledge Management

Like humans, organizations create and gather knowledge using a variety of organizational learning mechanisms. Through collection of data, careful measurement of planned activities, trial and error (experimentation), and feedback from customers and the environment in general, organizations gain experience. Organizations that learn adjust their behavior to reflect that learning by creating new business processes and by changing patterns of management decision making. This process of change is called **organizational learning**. Arguably, organizations that can sense and respond to their environments rapidly will survive longer than organizations that have poor learning mechanisms.

The Knowledge Management Value Chain

Knowledge management refers to the set of business processes developed in an organization to create, store, transfer, and apply knowledge. Knowledge management increases the ability of the organization to learn from its environment and to incorporate knowledge into its business processes. Figure 11.1 illustrates the value-adding steps in the knowledge management value chain. Each stage in the value chain adds value to raw data and information as they are transformed into usable knowledge.

In Figure 11.1, information systems activities are separated from related management and organizational activities, with information systems activities on the top of the graphic and organizational and management activities below. One apt slogan of the knowledge management field is "Effective knowledge management is 80 percent managerial and organizational and 20 percent technological."

In Chapter 1, we define *organizational and management capital* as the set of business processes, culture, and behavior required to obtain value from investments in information systems. In the case of knowledge management, as with other information systems investments, supportive values, structures, and behavior patterns must be built to maximize the return on investment in knowledge management projects. In Figure 11.1, the management and organizational activities in the lower half of the diagram represent the investment in organizational capital required to obtain substantial returns on the information technology (IT) investments and systems shown in the top half of the diagram.

Knowledge Acquisition

Organizations acquire knowledge in a number of ways, depending on the type of knowledge they seek. The first knowledge management systems sought to build corporate repositories of documents, reports, presentations, and best practices. These efforts have been extended to include unstructured documents (such as email). In other cases, organizations acquire knowledge by developing

FIGURE 11.1 THE KNOWLEDGE MANAGEMENT VALUE CHAIN

Knowledge management today involves both information systems activities and a host of enabling management and organizational activities.

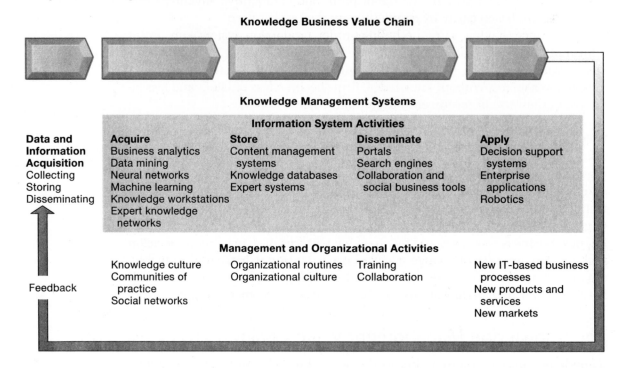

online expert networks so that employees can "find the expert" in the company who is personally knowledgeable.

In still other cases, firms must acquire new knowledge by discovering patterns in corporate data via machine learning (including neural networks, genetic algorithms, natural language processing, and other AI techniques), or by using knowledge workstations where engineers can discover new knowledge. These various efforts are described throughout this chapter. A coherent and organized knowledge system also requires business analytics using data from the firm's transaction processing systems that track sales, payments, inventory, customers, and other vital areas as well as data from external sources such as news feeds, industry reports, legal opinions, scientific research, and government statistics.

Knowledge Storage

Once they are discovered, documents, patterns, and expert rules must be stored so they can be retrieved and used by employees. Knowledge storage generally involves the creation of a database. Document management systems that digitize, index, and tag documents according to a coherent framework are large databases adept at storing collections of documents. Expert systems also help corporations preserve the knowledge that is acquired by incorporating that knowledge into organizational processes and culture. Each of these is discussed later in this chapter and in the following chapter.

Management must support the development of planned knowledge storage systems, encourage the development of corporate-wide schemas for indexing documents, and reward employees for taking the time to update and store documents properly. For instance, it would reward the sales force for submitting names of prospects to a shared corporate database of prospects where all sales personnel can identify each prospect and review the stored knowledge.

Knowledge Dissemination

Portals, email, instant messaging, wikis, social business tools, and search engine technology have added to an existing array of collaboration tools for sharing calendars, documents, data, and graphics (see Chapter 2). Contemporary technology has created a deluge of information and knowledge. How can managers and employees discover, in a sea of information and knowledge, that which is really important for their decisions and their work? Here, training programs, informal networks, and shared management experience communicated through a supportive culture help managers focus their attention on what is important.

Knowledge Application

Regardless of what type of knowledge management system is involved, knowledge that is not shared and applied to the practical problems facing firms and managers does not add business value. To provide a return on investment, organizational knowledge must become a systematic part of management decision making and become situated in systems for decision support (described in Chapter 12). Ultimately, new knowledge must be built into a firm's business processes and key application systems, including enterprise applications for managing crucial internal business processes and relationships with customers and suppliers. Management supports this process by creating—based on new knowledge—new business practices, new products and services, and new markets for the firm.

Building Organizational and Management Capital: Collaboration, Communities of Practice, and Office Environments

In addition to the activities we have just described, managers can help by developing new organizational roles and responsibilities for the acquisition of knowledge, including the creation of chief knowledge officer executive positions, dedicated staff positions (knowledge managers), and communities of practice. **Communities of practice (COPs)** are informal social networks of professionals and employees within and outside the firm who have similar work-related activities and interests. The activities of these communities include self-education and group education, conferences, online newsletters, and day-to-day sharing of experiences and techniques to solve specific work problems. Many organizations, such as IBM, the U.S. Federal Highway Administration, and the World Bank, have encouraged the development of thousands of online communities of practice. These communities of practice depend greatly on software environments that enable collaboration and communication.

COPs can make it easier for people to reuse knowledge by pointing community members to useful documents, creating document repositories, and filtering information for newcomers. COPs' members act as facilitators, encouraging contributions and discussion. COPs can also reduce the learning curve for new employees by providing contacts with subject matter experts and access to a community's established methods and tools. Finally, COPs can act as a spawning ground for new ideas, techniques, and decision-making behavior.

FIGURE 11.2 **MAJOR TYPES OF KNOWLEDGE MANAGEMENT SYSTEMS**

There are three major categories of knowledge management systems, and each can be broken down further into more specialized types of knowledge management systems.

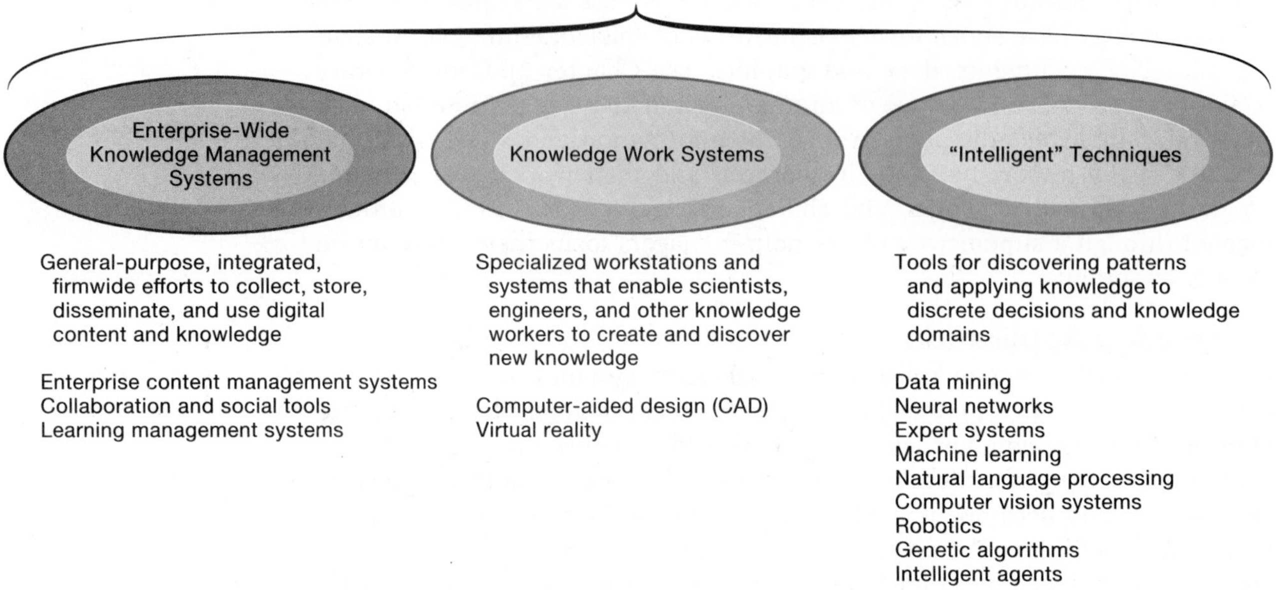

Enterprise-Wide Knowledge Management Systems	Knowledge Work Systems	"Intelligent" Techniques
General-purpose, integrated, firmwide efforts to collect, store, disseminate, and use digital content and knowledge	Specialized workstations and systems that enable scientists, engineers, and other knowledge workers to create and discover new knowledge	Tools for discovering patterns and applying knowledge to discrete decisions and knowledge domains
Enterprise content management systems Collaboration and social tools Learning management systems	Computer-aided design (CAD) Virtual reality	Data mining Neural networks Expert systems Machine learning Natural language processing Computer vision systems Robotics Genetic algorithms Intelligent agents

Types of Knowledge Management Systems

There are essentially three major types of knowledge management systems: enterprise-wide knowledge management systems, knowledge work systems, and "intelligent" techniques. Figure 11.2 shows the knowledge management systems applications for each of these major categories.

Enterprise-wide knowledge management systems are general-purpose firmwide efforts to collect, store, distribute, and apply digital content and knowledge. These systems include capabilities for searching for information, storing both structured and unstructured data, and locating employee expertise within the firm. They also include supporting technologies such as portals, search engines, collaboration and social business tools, and learning management systems.

The development of powerful networked workstations and software for assisting engineers and scientists in the discovery of new knowledge has led to the creation of knowledge work systems such as computer-aided design (CAD), visualization, simulation, and virtual reality systems. **Knowledge work systems (KWS)** are specialized systems built for engineers, scientists, and other knowledge workers charged with discovering and creating new knowledge for a company. We discuss knowledge work applications in detail in Section 11-4.

Knowledge management also includes a diverse group of **"intelligent" techniques**, such as data mining, expert systems, machine learning, neural networks, natural language processing, computer vision systems, robotics, genetic algorithms, and intelligent agents. These techniques have different objectives, from a focus on discovering knowledge (data mining and neural networks) to distilling knowledge in the form of rules for a computer program (expert systems) to discovering optimal solutions for problems (genetic algorithms). Section 11-2 provides more detail about these "intelligent" techniques.

11-2 What are artificial intelligence (AI) and machine learning? How do businesses use AI?

"Intelligent" techniques are often described as **artificial intelligence (AI)**. There are many definitions of artificial intelligence. In the most ambitious vision, AI involves the attempt to build computer systems that think and act like humans. Humans see, hear, and communicate with natural languages, make decisions, plan for the future, achieve goals, perceive patterns in their environments, and learn, among many other capabilities. Humans also love, hate, and choose what objectives they want to pursue. These are the foundations of what is called "human intelligence" and what is called "common sense" or generalized intelligence.

So far the "Grand Vision" of AI remains a distant dream: there are no computer programs that have demonstrated generalized human intelligence or common sense. Human intelligence is vastly more complex than the most sophisticated computer programs and covers a broader range of activities than is currently possible with "intelligent" computer systems and devices.

A narrow definition of artificial intelligence is far more realistic and useful. Stripped of all the hyperbole, artificial intelligence programs are like all computer programs: They take data input from the environment, process that data, and produce outputs. AI programs differ from traditional software programs in the techniques and technologies they use to input and process data. AI systems today can perform many tasks that would be impossible for humans to accomplish, and can equal or come close to humans in tasks such as interpreting CT scans, recognizing faces and voices, playing games like chess or Go, or besting human experts in certain well-defined tasks. In many industries they are transforming how business is done, where people are employed, and how they do their jobs.

Evolution of AI

In the last decade, significant progress has been made within this limited vision of AI. The major forces driving the rapid evolution of AI are the development of Big Data databases generated by the Internet, e-commerce, the Internet of Things, and social media. Secondary drivers include the drastic reduction in the cost of computer processing and the growth in the power of processors. And finally, the growth of AI has relied on the refinement of algorithms by tens of thousands of AI software engineers and university AI research centers, along with significant investment from business and governments. There have been few fundamental conceptual breakthroughs in AI in this period, or in understanding how humans think. Many of the algorithms and statistical techniques were developed decades earlier but could not be implemented and refined on such a large scale as is currently possible.

Progress has been significant: Image recognition programs have gone from 25 percent error rates down to less than 3 percent in 2018; natural language speech recognition errors have dropped from 15 percent to 6 percent; and in translation among common languages, Google's Translate program achieves about 85 percent accuracy compared to humans (Technology Quarterly, 2017; Hirschberg and Manning, 2016). These advances have made possible personal assistants like Siri (Apple), Alexa (Amazon), Cortana (Microsoft), and Now (Google), as well as speech-activated systems in automobiles.

In a famous 1950 paper, computer scientist Alan Turing defined an artificially intelligent computer program as one that a human could have a conversation with and not be able to tell it was a computer (Turing, 1950). We still cannot have a genuine conversation with a computer AI system because it has no genuine understanding of the world, no common sense, and does not truly understand humans. Nevertheless, AI systems can be enormously helpful to humans and business firms.

Major Types of AI

Artificial intelligence is a family of programming techniques and technologies, each of which has advantages in select applications. Table 11.2 describes the major types of AI: expert systems, machine learning, neural networks, deep learning, genetic algorithms, natural language processing, computer vision systems, robotics, and intelligent agents. Let's take a look at each type of AI and understand how it is used by businesses and other organizations.

Expert Systems

Expert systems were developed in the 1970s and were the first large-scale applications of AI in business and other organizations. They account for an estimated 20 percent of all AI systems today. Expert systems capture the knowledge of individual experts in an organization through in-depth interviews, and represent that knowledge as sets of rules. These rules are then converted into computer code in the form of IF-THEN rules. Such programs are often used to develop apps that walk users through a process of decision making.

Expert systems provide benefits such as improved decisions, reduced errors, reduced costs, reduced training time, and better quality and service. They have been used in applications for making decisions about granting credit and for diagnosing equipment problems, as well as in medical diagnostics, legal research, civil engineering, building maintenance, drawing up building plans, and educational technology (personalized learning and responsive testing)

TABLE 11.2 MAJOR TYPES OF AI TECHNIQUES

Expert systems	Represent the knowledge of experts as a set of rules that can be programmed so that a computer can assist human decision makers.
Machine learning	Software that can identify patterns in very large databases without explicit programming although with significant human training.
Neural networks and deep learning	Loosely based on human neurons, algorithms that can be trained to classify objects into known categories based on data inputs. Deep learning uses multiple layers of neural networks to reveal the underlying patterns in data, and in some limited cases identify patterns without human training.
Genetic algorithms	Algorithms based loosely on evolutionary natural selection and mutation, commonly used to generate high-quality solutions to optimization and search problems.
Natural language processing	Algorithms that make it possible for a computer to understand and analyze natural human language.
Computer vision systems	Systems that can view and extract information from real-world images.
Robotics	Use of machines that can substitute for human movements as well as computer systems for their control and information processing.
Intelligent agents	Software agents that use built-in or learned knowledge to perform specific tasks or services for an individual.

FIGURE 11.3 RULES IN AN EXPERT SYSTEM

An expert system contains a number of rules to be followed. The rules are interconnected, the number of outcomes is known in advance and is limited, there are multiple paths to the same outcome, and the system can consider multiple rules at a single time. The rules illustrated are for simple credit-granting expert systems.

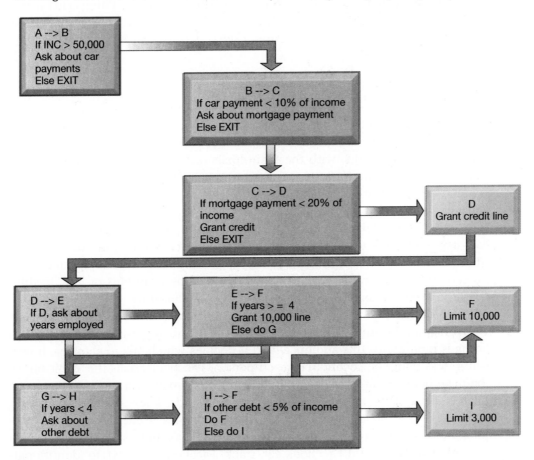

(Maor, 2003; Mishra, 2016). For instance, if you were the project manager of a 14-story office building and were given the task of configuring the building's air conditioning system, which has hundreds of parts and subassemblies, an expert system could walk you through the process by asking a series of questions, producing an order to suppliers, and providing an overall cost estimate for the project, all in a matter of hours rather than weeks. See Figure 11.3 for an expert system for credit granting.

How Expert Systems Work

Expert systems model human knowledge as a set of rules that collectively are called the **knowledge base**. Expert systems can have from a handful to many thousands of rules, depending on the complexity of the decision-making problem. The strategy used to search through the collection of rules and formulate conclusions is called the **inference engine**. The inference engine works by searching through the rules and firing those rules that are triggered by facts the user gathers and enters.

Expert systems have a number of limitations, the most important of which is that even experts can't explain how they make decisions: they know more than they can say. People drive cars, for instance, but are challenged to say how they do it. The knowledge base can become chaotic as the number of rules can reach into the thousands. In rapidly changing environments, say medical diagnosis, the rules change and need to be continually updated. Expert systems are not useful for dealing with unstructured problems that managers and employees typically encounter, and do not use real-time data to guide their decisions. Expert systems do not scale well to the kinds of very large data sets produced by the Internet and the Internet of Things (IoT), and they are expensive to build. For these reasons, expert system development has slowed in the last decade to small domains of expert knowledge such as automobile diagnosis.

Machine Learning

More than 75 percent of AI development today involves some kind of **machine learning (ML)** accomplished by neural networks, genetic algorithms, and deep learning networks, with the main focus on finding patterns in data, and classifying data inputs into known (and unknown) outputs. Machine learning is based on an entirely different AI paradigm than expert systems. In machine learning there are no experts, and there is no effort to write computer code for rules reflecting an expert's understanding. Instead, ML begins with very large data sets with tens to hundreds of millions of data points and automatically finds patterns and relationships by analyzing a large set of examples and making a statistical inference. Table 11.3 provides some examples of how leading business firms are using various types of machine learning.

Facebook has over 200 million monthly users in the United States who spend an average of 35 minutes on site daily. The firm displays an estimated 1 billion ads monthly to this audience, and it decides which ads to show each person in less than one second. For each person, Facebook bases this decision on the prior behavior of its users, including information shared (posts, comments, Likes), the activity of their social network friends, background information supplied to Facebook (age, gender, location, devices used), information supplied by advertisers (email address, prior purchases), and user activity on apps and other websites that Facebook can track. Facebook uses ML to identify patterns in the dataset, and to estimate the probability that any specific user will click on a particular ad based on the patterns of behavior they have identified.

TABLE 11.3 EXAMPLES OF MACHINE LEARNING

WellsFargo	Aiera system reads and analyzes a half-million documents daily for 1,600 stocks, and produces buy and sell calls for 550 stocks followed by their wealth management unit.
Allstate Insurance	Amelia system uses deep learning and natural language processing to assist call center employees in handling customer queries. Trained on 40 insurance topics, it understands context, and learns from experience.
Netflix	Recommender system based on video similarity algorithm uses statistical and machine learning to develop a personalized selection of videos for each of its 125 million subscribers worldwide.
Amazon	Alexa uses machine learning and speech recognition for its intelligent voice-controlled personal assistant.
Schindler Group	Monitors over one million elevators and walkways using GE's Predix operating system and machine learning to make predictions about needed maintenance.
PayPal	Uses machine learning algorithms to identify patterns of fraud for 170 million customers who generate four billion transactions annually.

Analysts estimate that Facebook uses at least 100,000 servers located in several very large-scale "hyper datacenters" to perform this task. At the end of this process is a simple show ad/no show ad result.

The current response rate (click rate) to Facebook ads is about 0.1 percent, roughly four times that of an untargeted display ad although not as good as targeted email campaigns (about 3 percent), or Google Search ads (about 2 percent). All of the very large Internet consumer firms, including Amazon, Alphabet's Google, Microsoft, Alibaba, Tencent, Netflix, and Baidu, use similar ML algorithms. Obviously, no human or group of humans could achieve these results given the enormous database size, the speed of transactions, or the complexity of working in real time. The benefits of ML illustrated by this brief example come down to an extraordinary ability to recognize patterns at the scale of millions of people in a matter of seconds, and classify objects into discrete categories.

Supervised and Unsupervised Learning

Nearly all machine learning today involves **supervised learning**, in which the system is "trained" by providing specific examples of desired inputs and outputs identified by humans in advance. A very large database is developed, say ten million photos posted on the Internet, and then split into two sections, one a development database and the other a test database. Humans select a target, let's say to identify all photos that contain a car image. Humans feed a large collection of verified pictures that contain a car image into a neural network (described below) that proceeds iteratively through the development database in millions of cycles, until eventually the system can identify photos with a car. The machine learning system is then tested using the test database to ensure the algorithms can achieve the same results with different photos. In many cases, but not all, machine learning can come close to or equal human efforts, but on a very much larger scale. Over time, with tweaking by programmers, and by making the database even bigger, using ever larger computing systems, the system will improve its performance, and in that sense, can learn. Supervised learning is one technique used to develop autonomous vehicles that need to be able to recognize objects around them, such as people, other cars, buildings, and lines on the pavement to guide them (see the chapter-ending case study).

In **unsupervised learning**, the same procedures are followed, but humans do not feed the system examples. Instead, the system is asked to process the development database and report whatever patterns it finds. For instance, in a seminal research effort often referred to "The Cat Paper," researchers collected 10 million YouTube photos from videos and built an ML system that could detect human faces without labeling or "teaching" the machine with verified human face photos (Le et al., 2011). Researchers developed a brute force neural network computer system composed of 1,000 machines with 16,000 core processors loaned by Google. The systems processors had a total of 1 billion connections to one another, creating a very large network that imitated on a small scale the neurons and synapses (connections) of a human brain. The result was a system that could detect human faces in photos, as well as cat faces and human bodies. The system was then tested on 22,000 object images on ImageNet (a large online visual database), and achieved a 16 percent accuracy rate. In principle then, it is possible to create machine learning systems that can "teach themselves" about the world without human intervention. But there's a long way to go: we wouldn't want to use autonomous cars that were guided by systems with a 16 percent accuracy rate! Nevertheless, this research was a 75 percent improvement over previous efforts.

To put this in perspective, a one-year-old human baby can recognize faces, cats, tables, doors, windows, and hundreds of other objects it has been exposed to, and continuously catalogs new experiences that it seeks out by itself for recognition in the future. But babies have a huge computational advantage over our biggest ML research systems. The human adult brain has an estimated 84 billion neurons, each with over 10,000 connections to other neurons (synapses), and over one trillion total connections in its network (brain). Modern *homo sapiens* have been programed (by nature) for an estimated 300,000 years, and their predecessors for 2.5 million years. For these reasons, machine learning is applicable today in a very limited number of situations where there are very large databases and computing facilities, most desired outcomes are already defined by humans, the output is binary (0,1), and where there is a very talented and large group of software and system engineers working the problem.

Neural Networks

A neural network is composed of interconnected units called neurons. Each neuron can take data from other neurons, and transfer data to other neurons in the system. The artificial neurons are not biological physical entities as in the human brain, but instead are software programs and mathematical models that perform the input and output function of neurons. The strength of the connections (weight) can be controlled by researchers using a Learning Rule, an algorithm that systematically alters the strength of the connections among the neurons to produce the final desired output that could be identifying a picture of a cancer tumor, fraudulent credit card transactions, or suspicious telephone calling patterns.

Neural networks find patterns and relationships in very large amounts of data that would be too complicated and difficult for a human being to analyze by using machine learning algorithms and computational models that are loosely based on how the biological human brain is thought to operate. Neural networks are **pattern detection programs**. Neural networks learn patterns from large quantities of data by sifting through the data, and ultimately finding pathways through the network of thousands of neurons. Some pathways are more successful than others in their ability to identify objects like cars, animals, faces, and voices. There may be millions of pathways through the data. An algorithm (the Learning Rule mentioned above) identifies these successful paths, and strengthens the connection among neurons in these pathways. This process is repeated thousands or millions of times until only the most successful pathways are identified. The Learning Rule identifies the best or optimal pathways through the data. At some point, after millions of pathways are analyzed, the process stops when an acceptable level of pattern recognition is reached, for instance, successfully identifying cancer tumors about as well as humans, or even better than humans.

Figure 11.4 represents one type of neural network comprising an input layer, a processing layer, and an output layer. Humans train the network by feeding it a set of outcomes they want the machine to learn. For instance, if the objective is to build a system that can identify patterns in fraudulent credit card purchases, the system is trained using actual examples of fraudulent transactions. The data set may be composed of a million examples of fraudulent transactions. The data set is divided into two segments: a training data set, and a test data set. The training data set is used to train the system. After millions of test runs, the program hopefully will identify the best path through the data. To verify the accuracy of the system, it is then used on the test data set, which the

FIGURE 11.4 HOW A NEURAL NETWORK WORKS

A neural network uses rules it "learns" from patterns in data to construct a hidden layer of logic. The hidden layer then processes inputs, classifying them based on the experience of the model. In this example, the neural network has been trained to distinguish between valid and fraudulent credit card purchases.

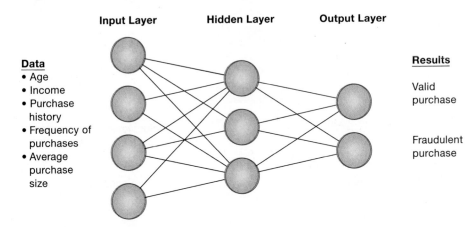

system has not analyzed before. If successful, the system will be tested on new data sets. The neural network in Figure 11.4 has learned how to identify a likely fraudulent credit card purchase.

Neural network applications in medicine, science, and business address problems in pattern classification, prediction, and control and optimization. In medicine, neural network applications are used for screening patients for coronary artery disease, for diagnosing epilepsy and Alzheimer's disease, and for performing pattern recognition of pathology images, including certain cancers. The financial industry uses neural networks to discern patterns in vast pools of data that might help investment firms predict the performance of equities, corporate bond ratings, or corporate bankruptcies. Visa International uses a neural network to help detect credit card fraud by monitoring all Visa transactions for sudden changes in the buying patterns of cardholders. Table 11.4 provides examples of neural networks.

TABLE 11.4 EXAMPLES OF NEURAL NETWORKS

FUNCTIONALITY	INPUTS	PROCESS	OUTPUTS/APPLICATION
Computer vision	Millions of digital images, videos, or sensors	Recognize patterns in images, and objects	Photo tagging; facial recognition; autonomous vehicles
Speech recognition	Digital soundtracks, voices	Recognize patterns and meaning in soundtracks and speech	Digital assistants, chatbots, help centers
Machine controls, diagnostics	Internet of Things: thousands of sensors	Identify operational status, patterns of failure	Preventive maintenance; quality control
Language translation	Millions of sentences in various languages	Identify patterns in multiple languages	Translate sentences from one language to another
Transaction analysis	Millions of loan applications, stock trades, phone calls	Identify patterns in financial and other transactions	Fraud control; theft of services; stock market predictions
Targeted online ads	Millions of browser histories	Identify clusters of consumers; preferences	Programmatic advertising

FIGURE 11.5 A DEEP LEARNING NETWORK

Deep learning networks consist of many layers of neural networks working in a hierarchical fashion to detect patterns. Shown here is an expanded look at layer 1. Other layers have the same structure.

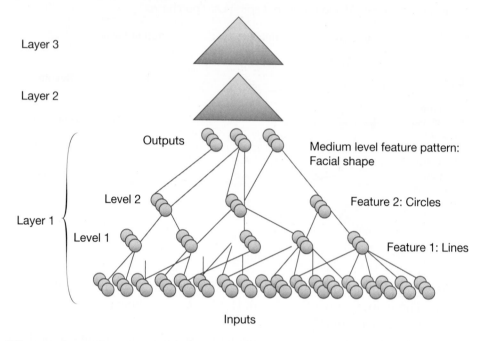

"Deep Learning" Neural Networks

"Deep learning" neural networks are more complex, with many layers of transformation of the input data to produce a target output. Collections of neurons are called nodes or layers. Deep learning networks are in their infancy, and are used almost exclusively for pattern detection on unlabeled data where the system is not told what to look for specifically but to simply discover patterns in the data. The system is expected to be self-taught. See Figure 11.5.

For instance, in our earlier example of unsupervised learning involving a machine learning system that could identify cats (The Cat Paper) and other objects without training, the system used was a deep learning network. It consisted of three layers of neural networks (layers 1, 2, and 3). Each of these layers has two levels of pattern detection (levels 1 and 2). Each level was developed to identify a low-level feature of the photos: layer 1 identified lines in the photos, and layer 2 identified circles. The result of the first layer may be blobs and fuzzy edges. Second and third layers refine the images emerging from the first layer, until at the end of the process the system can distinguish cats, dogs, and humans, although in this case not very well, with a 16 percent accuracy rate.

Many pundits believe deep learning networks come closer to the "Grand Vision" of AI where ML systems would be capable of learning like a human being. Others who work in ML and deep learning are more critical (Marcus, 2018; Pearl 2016).

Limitations of Neural Networks and Machine Learning

Neural networks have a number of limitations currently. They require very large data sets to identify patterns. There are often many patterns in large data sets that are nonsensical, and it takes humans to choose which patterns "make sense." Many patterns in large data sets are ephemeral: there may be a pattern in the stock market, or the performance of professional sports teams, but they do not last long. In many important decision situations there are no large data sets. Should you apply to College A or College B? Should we merge with another company?

Neural networks, machine learning systems, and the people who work with them cannot explain how the system arrived at a particular solution. For instance, in the case of the IBM Watson computer playing Jeopardy, researchers could not say exactly why Watson chose the answers it did, only that they were either right or wrong. Most real-world ML applications in business involve classifying digital objects into simple binary categories (yes or no; 0 or 1). But many of the significant problems facing managers, firms, and organizations do not have binary solutions. Neural networks may not perform well if their training covers too little or too much data. AI systems have no sense of ethics: they may recommend actions that are illegal or immoral. In most current applications, AI systems are best used as tools for relatively low-level decisions, aiding, but not substituting for managers.

Genetic Algorithms

Genetic algorithms are another form of machine learning. Genetic algorithms are useful for finding the optimal solution for a specific problem by examining a very large number of alternative solutions for that problem. Their method of solving problems is based on ideas inspired by evolutionary biology such as inheritance, mutation, selection, and crossover (recombination).

A genetic algorithm works by searching a population of randomly generated strings of binary digits to identify the right string representing the best possible solution for the problem. As solutions alter and combine, the worst ones are discarded and the better ones survive to go on to produce even better solutions.

In Figure 11.6, each string corresponds to one of the variables in the problem. One applies a test for fitness, ranking the strings in the population according to their level of desirability as possible solutions. After the initial population is evaluated for fitness, the algorithm then produces the next generation of

FIGURE 11.6 THE COMPONENTS OF A GENETIC ALGORITHM

This example illustrates an initial population of "chromosomes," each representing a different solution. The genetic algorithm uses an iterative process to refine the initial solutions so that the better ones, those with the higher fitness, are more likely to emerge as the best solution.

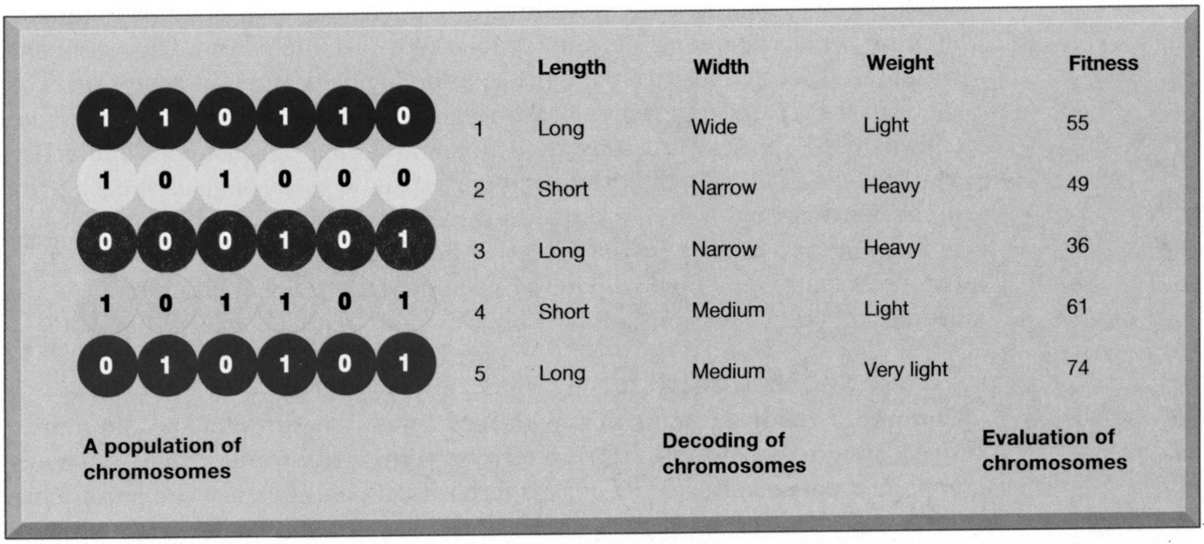

		Length	Width	Weight	Fitness
1 1 0 1 1 0	1	Long	Wide	Light	55
1 0 1 0 0 0	2	Short	Narrow	Heavy	49
0 0 0 1 0 1	3	Long	Narrow	Heavy	36
1 0 1 1 0 1	4	Short	Medium	Light	61
0 1 0 1 0 1	5	Long	Medium	Very light	74
A population of chromosomes			Decoding of chromosomes	Evaluation of chromosomes	

strings, consisting of strings that survived the fitness test plus offspring strings produced from mating pairs of strings, and tests their fitness. The process continues until a solution is reached.

Genetic algorithms are used to solve problems that are very dynamic and complex, involving hundreds or thousands of variables or formulas. The problem must be one whose range of possible solutions can be represented genetically and for which criteria can be established for evaluating fitness. Genetic algorithms expedite the solution because they can evaluate many solution alternatives quickly to find the best one. For example, General Electric engineers used genetic algorithms to help optimize the design for jet turbine aircraft engines, in which each design change required changes in up to 100 variables. The supply chain management software from JDA software uses genetic algorithms to optimize production-scheduling models, incorporating hundreds of thousands of details about customer orders, material and resource availability, manufacturing and distribution capability, and delivery dates.

Natural Language Processing, Computer Vision Systems, and Robotics

Other important AI techniques include natural language processing, computer vision systems, and robotics.

Natural Language Processing

Human language is not always precise. It is often ambiguous, and meanings of words can depend on complex variables such as slang, regional dialects, and social context. **Natural language processing (NLP)** makes it possible for a computer to understand and analyze natural language—language that human beings instinctively use, not language specially formatted to be understood by computers. NLP algorithms are typically based on machine learning, including deep learning, which can learn how to identify a speaker's intent from many examples. Akershus University Hospital, described in the chapter-opening case, used NLP and IBM Watson Explorer to sift through thousands of medical records with unstructured textual data expressed in everyday language like natural speech. The algorithms could read text on a medical record and interpret its meaning. You can also see natural language processing at work in leading search engines such as Google, spam filtering systems, and text mining sentiment analysis (discussed in Chapter 6).

Tokyo-based Mizuho Bank employs advanced speech recognition technology, IBM® Watson™ content analytics software, and a cloud services infrastructure to improve contact center agents' interactions with customers. After converting the customer's speech to textual data, the solution applies natural language processing algorithms based on machine learning analysis of interactions with thousands of customers. The system learns more and more from each customer interaction so that it can eventually infer the customer's specific needs or goals at each point of the conversation. It then formulates the optimal response, which is delivered in real time as a prompt on the agent's screen. By helping contact center agents more efficiently sense and respond to customer needs, this solution reduced the average duration of customer interactions by more than 6 percent (IBM, 2018).

Computer Vision Systems

Computer vision systems deal with how computers can emulate the human visual system to view and extract information from real-world images. Such systems incorporate image processing, pattern recognition, and image understanding.

An example is Facebook's facial recognition tool called DeepFace, which is nearly as accurate as the human brain in recognizing a face. DeepFace will help Facebook improve the accuracy of Facebook's existing facial recognition capabilities to ensure that every photo of a Facebook user is connected to that person's Facebook account. Computer vision systems are also used in autonomous vehicles such as drones and self-driving cars (see the chapter-ending case), industrial machine vision systems (e.g., inspecting bottles), military applications, and robotic tools.

In 2017, the National Basketball Association (NBA) decided to allow sponsors to place small logo patches representing their brands on player uniforms. This advertising investment turned out to be worth its multi-million-dollar cost. According to GumGum, an AI company focusing on computer vision technology, the image placed by The Goodyear Tire & Rubber Co. on the uniforms of the Cleveland Cavaliers generated $3.4 million in value from social media exposure alone during the first half of the baseball season. GumGum develops algorithms that enable computers to identify what's happening in imagery. GumGum used computer vision technology to thoroughly analyze broadcast and social media content for placement, exposure, and duration involving Goodyear images that appeared in online or in TV-generated NBA content. Instead of humans trying to monitor the number of times a logo appeared on a screen, GumGum's *vision technology* tracks and reports the data (Albertson, 2018).

Robotics

Robotics deals with the design, construction, operation, and use of movable machines that can substitute for humans along with computer systems for their control, sensory feedback, and information processing. Robots cannot substitute entirely for people but are programmed to perform a specific series of actions automatically. They are often are used in dangerous environments (such as bomb detection and deactivation), manufacturing processes, military operations (drones), and medical procedures (surgical robots). Many employees now worry whether robots will replace people entirely and take away their jobs (see the Chapter 4 Interactive Session on Organizations).

The most widespread use of robotic technology has been in manufacturing. For example, automobile assembly lines employ robots to do heavy lifting, welding, applying glue, and painting. People still do most of the final assembly of cars, especially when installing small parts or wiring that needs to be guided into place. A Renault SA plant in Cleon, France, now uses robots from Universal Robots AS of Denmark to drive screws into engines, especially those that go into places people find hard to access. The robots verify that parts are properly fastened and check to make sure the correct part is being used. The Renault robots are also capable of working in proximity to people and slowing down or stopping to avoid hurting them.

Intelligent Agents

Intelligent agents are software programs that work in the background without direct human intervention to carry out specific tasks for an individual user, business process, or software application. The agent uses a limited built-in or learned knowledge base to accomplish tasks or make decisions on the user's behalf, such as deleting junk email, scheduling appointments, or finding the cheapest airfare to California.

There are many intelligent agent applications today in operating systems, application software, email systems, mobile computing software, and network tools. Of special interest to business are intelligent agent bots that search for information on the Internet. Chapter 7 describes how shopping bots help consumers find products they want and assist them in comparing prices and other features.

Although some software agents are programmed to follow a simple set of rules, others are capable of learning from experience and adjusting their behavior using machine learning and natural language processing. Siri, a virtual assistant application on Apple's iPhone and iPad, is an example. Siri uses natural language processing to answer questions, make recommendations, and perform actions. The software adapts to the user's individual preferences over time and personalizes results, performing tasks such as getting directions, scheduling appointments, and sending messages. Similar products include Google Now, Microsoft's Cortana, and Amazon's Alexa.

Chatbots (chatterbots) are software agents designed to simulate a conversation with one or more human users via textual or auditory methods. They try to understand what you type or say and respond by answering questions or executing tasks. They provide automated conversations that allow users to do things like check the weather, manage personal finances, shop online, and receive help when they have questions for customer service. Vodafone, a multinational telecommunications company, uses a chatbot to answer 80,000 questions per month, reducing contact center calls for 75 percent of the customers it chats with. Vodafone staff use the chatbot to access accurate, up-to-date information on Vodafone products and services. Facebook has integrated chatbots into its Messenger messaging app so that an outside company with a Facebook brand page can interact with Facebook users through the chat program. Today's chatbots perform very basic functions but will become more technologically advanced in the future.

Procter & Gamble (P&G) used intelligent agent technology to make its supply chain more efficient (see Figure 11.7). It modeled a complex supply chain as a group of semiautonomous agents representing individual supply chain components such as trucks, production facilities, distributors, and retail stores. The behavior of each agent is programmed to follow rules that mimic actual behavior, such as "order an item when it is out of stock." Simulations using the agents enable the company to perform what-if analyses on inventory levels, in-store stockouts, and transportation costs.

Using intelligent agent models, P&G discovered that trucks should often be dispatched before being fully loaded. Although transportation costs would be higher using partially loaded trucks, the simulation showed that retail store stockouts would occur less often, thus reducing the number of lost sales, which would more than make up for the higher distribution costs. Agent-based modeling has saved P&G $300 million annually on an investment of less than 1 percent of that amount.

11-3 What types of systems are used for enterprise-wide knowledge management, and how do they provide value for businesses?

Firms must deal with at least three kinds of knowledge. Some knowledge exists within the firm in the form of structured text documents (reports and presentations). Decision makers also need knowledge that is semistructured, such as email, voice mail, chat room exchanges, videos, digital pictures,

FIGURE 11.7 INTELLIGENT AGENTS IN P&G'S SUPPLY CHAIN NETWORK

Intelligent agents are helping Procter & Gamble shorten the replenishment cycles for products such as a box of Tide.

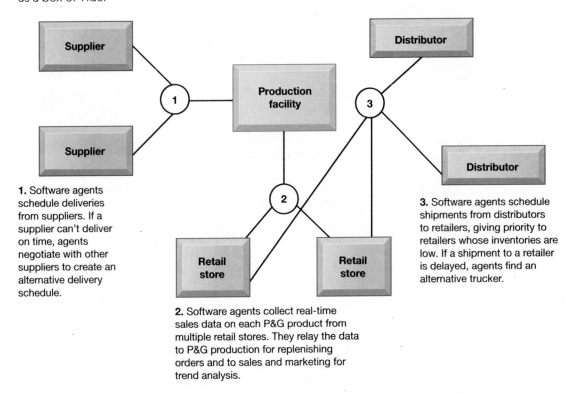

1. Software agents schedule deliveries from suppliers. If a supplier can't deliver on time, agents negotiate with other suppliers to create an alternative delivery schedule.

2. Software agents collect real-time sales data on each P&G product from multiple retail stores. They relay the data to P&G production for replenishing orders and to sales and marketing for trend analysis.

3. Software agents schedule shipments from distributors to retailers, giving priority to retailers whose inventories are low. If a shipment to a retailer is delayed, agents find an alternative trucker.

brochures, or bulletin board postings. In still other cases, there is no formal or digital information of any kind, and the knowledge resides in the heads of employees. Much of this knowledge is tacit knowledge that is rarely written down. Enterprise-wide knowledge management systems deal with all three types of knowledge.

Enterprise Content Management Systems

Businesses today need to organize and manage both structured and semistructured knowledge assets. **Structured knowledge** is explicit knowledge that exists in formal documents as well as in formal rules that organizations derive by observing experts and their decision-making behaviors. But according to experts, at least 80 percent of an organization's business content is semistructured or unstructured—information in folders, messages, memos, proposals, emails, graphics, electronic slide presentations, and even videos created in different formats and stored in many locations.

Enterprise content management (ECM) systems help organizations manage both types of information. They have capabilities for knowledge capture, storage, retrieval, distribution, and preservation to help firms improve their business processes and decisions. Such systems include corporate repositories of documents, reports, presentations, and best practices, as well as capabilities for collecting and organizing semistructured knowledge such as email (see Figure 11.8). Major enterprise content management systems also enable users to access external sources of information, such as news feeds and research, and to communicate via email, chat/instant messaging,

---

FIGURE 11.8 **AN ENTERPRISE CONTENT MANAGEMENT SYSTEM**

An enterprise content management system has capabilities for classifying, organizing, and managing structured and semistructured knowledge and making it available throughout the enterprise.

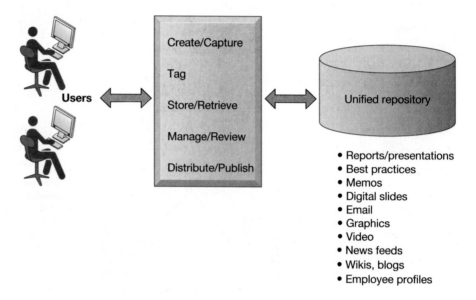

discussion groups, and videoconferencing. They are starting to incorporate blogs, wikis, and other enterprise social networking tools. Open Text Corporation, IBM, and Oracle are leading vendors of enterprise content management software.

A key problem in managing knowledge is the creation of an appropriate classification scheme, or **taxonomy**, to organize information into meaningful categories so that it can be easily accessed. Once the categories for classifying knowledge have been created, each knowledge object needs to be "tagged," or classified, so that it can be easily retrieved. Enterprise content management systems have capabilities for tagging, interfacing with corporate databases and content repositories, and creating enterprise knowledge portals that provide a single point of access to information resources.

Firms in publishing, advertising, broadcasting, and entertainment have special needs for storing and managing unstructured digital data such as photographs, graphic images, video, and audio content. For example, Coca-Cola must keep track of all the images of the Coca-Cola brand that have been created in the past at all of the company's worldwide offices to prevent both redundant work and variation from a standard brand image. **Digital asset management systems** help companies classify, store, and distribute these digital objects.

Locating and Sharing Expertise

Some of the knowledge businesses need is not in the form of a digital document but instead resides in the memory of individual experts in the firm. Contemporary enterprise content management systems, along with the systems for collaboration and social business introduced in Chapter 2, have capabilities for locating experts and tapping their knowledge. These include online directories of corporate experts and their profiles with details about their job experience, projects, publications, and educational degrees, and repositories of expert-generated content. Specialized search tools make it easier for employees to find the appropriate expert in a company. For knowledge resources outside the firm, social networking and social business tools enable users to bookmark web pages of interest, tag these bookmarks with keywords, and share the tags and web page links with other people.

Learning Management Systems

Companies need ways to keep track of and manage employee learning and to integrate it more fully into their knowledge management and other corporate systems. A **learning management system (LMS)** provides tools for the management, delivery, tracking, and assessment of various types of employee learning and training.

Contemporary LMS support multiple modes of learning, including CD-ROM, downloadable videos, web-based classes, live instruction in classes or online, and group learning in online forums and chat sessions. The LMS consolidates mixed-media training, automates the selection and administration of courses, assembles and delivers learning content, and measures learning effectiveness. The Interactive Session on Management shows how Sargent & Lundy used learning management and enterprise collaboration systems to increase sharing of employee expertise and employee learning.

Businesses run their own learning management systems, but they are also turning to publicly available **massive open online courses (MOOCs)** to educate their employees. A MOOC is an online course made available via the web to very large numbers of participants. Companies view MOOCs as a new way to design and deliver online learning where learners can collaborate with each other, watch short videos, and participate in threaded discussion groups. Firms such as Microsoft, AT&T, and Tenaris have developed their own MOOCs, while others such as Bank of America and Qualcomm are adapting publicly available MOOCs aligned with their core competencies.

11-4 What are the major types of knowledge work systems, and how do they provide value for firms?

The enterprise-wide knowledge systems we have just described provide a wide range of capabilities that can be used by many if not all the workers and groups in an organization. Firms also have specialized systems for knowledge workers to help them create new knowledge and to ensure that this knowledge is properly integrated into the business.

Knowledge Workers and Knowledge Work

Knowledge workers, which we introduced in Chapter 1, include researchers, designers, architects, scientists, and engineers who primarily create knowledge and information for the organization. Knowledge workers usually have high levels of education and memberships in professional organizations and are often asked to exercise independent judgment as a routine aspect of their work. For example, knowledge workers create new products or find ways of improving existing ones. Knowledge workers perform three key roles that

INTERACTIVE SESSION MANAGEMENT

Sargent & Lundy Learns to Manage Employee Knowledge

Sargent & Lundy is a 125-year-old firm providing comprehensive engineering, project management, and consulting services for complex power generation and power transmission projects. During its 125-year history, the company has designed 958 power plants all over the world. The headquarters are in Chicago, with global offices in Canada and the United Arab Emirates. Sargent & Lundy is noted for its industry knowledge, engineering expertise, and high-quality work. Approximately 87 percent of its 2,500 employees are engineers and designers.

The company takes pride in the depth of knowledge of its employee experts and their loyalty to the firm. On average, employees stay with the company for 15 years—often much longer. Sargent & Lundy tries to cross-utilize its staff in various types of work because it believes they are the best people for the job. Deanna Myers, Sargent & Lundy's Senior Manager of Learning and Development, works to ensure that employees have the skills, tools, and resources they need to achieve excellence throughout their careers.

In December 2010, Sargent & Lundy's management learned that around half of the company's most experienced employees, including engineers, designers, and power experts, would be eligible to retire by 2015. When they left the company, they would be taking critical business knowledge with them. Although engineers had access to a knowledge database of the firm's documented processes and procedures, experts' tacit knowledge was more difficult to capture.

The company hired a large group of new recruits very quickly to replace the retirees. However, with a worldwide footprint and ambitious expansion plans, the company needed to find better ways of transferring seasoned employees' expertise—including their tacit knowledge—to the new recruits wherever they were located. Corporate training hand learning facilities needed to be centralized and overhauled to make it easier for experts to share industry experience and skills as well as tacit knowledge.

In the past, Sargent & Lundy had used an untracked schedule of instructor-led courses, which often overlapped with existing training. The moment an instructor-led course had finished, the company might have just hired another two or three people who needed that course. This meant that a portion of the employees who really needed the instruction were not getting it. There was no in-house computer-based training available for new employees.

The company decided to transform its learning model and implemented a new talent management platform based on SAP SuccessFactors Learning Management System. SAP SuccessFactors is a cloud-based human capital management (HCM) software suite. It integrates software for orienting and training a new employee, social business and collaboration tools, a learning management system (LMS), performance management, recruiting software, applicant tracking software, succession planning, talent management, and HR analytics to enable companies to manage their employees more strategically and maximize their performance. SAP SuccessFactors provides detailed capabilities for reporting and tracking individual employee development.

Working with company experts, Sargent & Lundy's technical training team used SuccessFactors to develop a wide range of training programs and learning plans for specific technologies. Videos and online courses were added to the company's training arsenal, along with personalized learning plans for people working with specific disciplines and technologies. For example, an electrical engineer working on a transmission project would follow a learning plan with courses and objectives that differed from those of another electrical engineer working on a nuclear plant.

Sargent & Lundy's new recruits wanted more discussion and feedback on how well they were performing on a day-to-day basis, so the company also implemented SAP Jam, SAP's cloud-based social collaboration program. Using SAP Jam made it even easier for employees to share knowledge, often in real time.

Face-to-face meetings are still the primary way for staff to share knowledge about industry trends, best practices, and innovative solutions. But Sargent & Lundy's employees were too geographically scattered to always meet in person. The company's knowledge-sharing model had to change to provide more knowledge sharing and employee conversations online.

Sargent & Lundy's new social platform features online discussion forums covering everything from seismic analysis to specific types of valves.

New employees with questions are able to connect to experts via SAP Jam with just a few mouse clicks. The in-house experts respond to the questions and share their experiences. Before implementing SAP Jam, only a small percentage of regional staff participated in discussions for communities of practice. Sargent & Lundy's Communities of Practice (CoP) program makes it possible for employee experts to collaborate with novice staff around specific topics (see the discussion of CoPs earlier in this chapter).

The main focus of SAP Jam is on discussion groups. When users log in, they are presented with a home feed showing events in the discussion groups to which they subscribe. They can drill down to a specific feed or browse all the CoP groups for topics of interest. There are no restrictions on who can post a question, discussion topic, or article. A designer in the transmission group might look at how designers in other groups solved similar problems by reviewing what these groups discussed in their last CoP

meeting, references and visuals, and which experts or solutions might be helpful.

SAP Jam was launched in late 2015, and in the year that followed there was a 125 percent increase in participation. Many CoP groups are now using SAP Jam, including groups for specific technical topics such as thermo hydraulics and non-technical groups such as one for women in leadership. Employees of all levels can use Jam to discuss topics of interest, find answers to questions, and check facts. Besides improving employee learning, the tool has increased employee engagement. Conversations in SAP Jam have identified areas for process improvement and problems that need immediate technical staff attention.

Sources: www.sargentlundy.com, accessed May 28, 2018; Lauren Bonneau, "Creating a Culture of Collaboration at Sargent & Lundy," *SAP Insider Profiles*, March 24, 2017; and SAP SE, "Sargent & Lundy: Powering the Next Generation on Blended Learning with SAP SuccessFactors Solutions," 2016.

CASE STUDY QUESTIONS

1. How is knowledge management related to Sargent & Lundy's business model?

2. Identify the knowledge management problem faced by Sargent & Lundy. What management, organization, and technology factors contributed to this problem?

3. Describe the solution selected for this problem. Was it effective? Why or why not? How much

did it change the firm's operations and decision making?

4. What management, organization, and technology issues had to be addressed in selecting and implementing the solution?

are critical to the organization and to the managers who work within the organization:

- Keeping the organization current in knowledge as it develops in the external world—in technology, science, social thought, and the arts
- Serving as internal consultants regarding the areas of their knowledge, the changes taking place, and opportunities
- Acting as change agents, evaluating, initiating, and promoting change projects

Requirements of Knowledge Work Systems

Most knowledge workers rely on systems such as word processors, email, videoconferencing, collaboration, and scheduling systems, which are designed to increase worker productivity in the office. However, knowledge workers also require highly specialized knowledge work systems with powerful

| FIGURE 11.9 REQUIREMENTS OF KNOWLEDGE WORK SYSTEMS

Knowledge work systems require strong links to external knowledge bases in addition to specialized hardware and software.

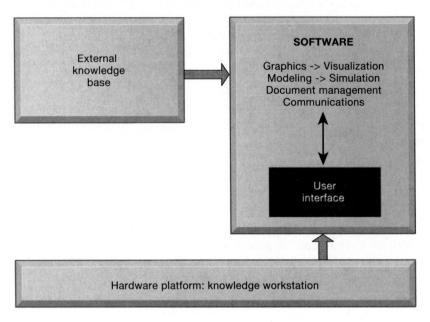

graphics, analytical tools, and communications and document management capabilities.

These systems require sufficient computing power to handle the sophisticated graphics or complex calculations necessary for such knowledge workers as scientific researchers, engineers, and product designers. Because knowledge workers need knowledge from the external world, these systems also must give the worker quick and easy access to external databases. They typically feature user-friendly interfaces that enable users to perform needed tasks without having to spend a great deal of time learning how to use the system. Knowledge workers are highly paid—wasting a knowledge worker's time is simply too expensive. Figure 11.9 summarizes the requirements of knowledge work systems.

Examples of Knowledge Work Systems

Major knowledge work applications include CAD systems and virtual reality systems for simulation and modeling. **Computer-aided design (CAD)** automates the creation and revision of designs, using computers and sophisticated graphics software. Using a more traditional physical design methodology, each design modification requires a mold to be made and a prototype to be tested physically. That process must be repeated many times, which is very expensive and time-consuming. Using a CAD workstation, the designer need only make a physical prototype toward the end of the design process because the design can be easily tested and changed on the computer. The ability of CAD software to provide design specifications for the tooling and manufacturing processes also saves a great deal of time and money while producing a manufacturing process with far fewer problems.

For example, Ford Motor Company used a computer simulation to create an engine cylinder to come up with the most efficient design possible.

Engineers altered that design to account for manufacturing constraints and tested the revised design virtually in models that used decades of data on material properties and engine performance. Ford then created the mold to make a real part that could be bolted onto an engine for further testing. The entire process took days instead of months and cost thousands of dollars instead of millions.

CAD systems can supply data for **3-D printing**, also known as additive manufacturing, which uses machines to make solid objects, layer by layer, from specifications in a digital file. Unlike traditional techniques, by which objects are cut or drilled from molds, resulting in wasted materials, 3-D printing lets workers model an object on a computer and print it out with plastic, metal, or composite materials. 3-D printing is currently used for prototyping, custom manufacturing, and fashioning items with small production runs. Today's 3-D printers can handle materials including plastic, titanium, and human cartilage and produce fully functional components including batteries, transistors, prosthetic devices, LEDs, and other complex mechanisms, and there are now 3-D printing services that run over the cloud, such as that offered by Staples.

Virtual reality (VR) systems have visualization, rendering, and simulation capabilities that go far beyond those of conventional CAD systems. They use interactive graphics software to create computer-generated simulations that are so close to reality that users almost believe they are participating in a real-world situation. In many virtual reality systems, the user dons special clothing, headgear, and equipment, depending on the application. The clothing contains sensors that record the user's movements and immediately transmit that information back to the computer. For instance, to walk through a virtual reality simulation of a house, you would need garb that monitors the movement of your feet, hands, and head. You also would need goggles containing video screens and sometimes audio attachments and feeling gloves so that you can be immersed in the computer feedback.

At NYU Langone Medical Center in New York City, students wearing 3-D glasses are able to "dissect" a virtual cadaver projected on a screen. With the help of a computer, they can move through the virtual body, scrutinizing layers of muscles or watching a close-up of a pumping heart along with bright red arteries and deep blue veins. The 3-D virtual cadaver is a valuable complementary teaching tool. The Interactive Session on Technology describes some of the issues raised by applications of VR technology.

Augmented reality (AR) is a related technology for enhancing visualization by overlaying digital data and images onto a physical real-world environment. The digital technology provides additional information to enhance the perception of reality, making the surrounding real world of the user more interactive and meaningful. The yellow first-down markers shown on televised football games are examples of augmented reality as are medical procedures like image-guided surgery, where data acquired from computerized tomography (CT) and magnetic resonance imaging (MRI) scans or from ultrasound imaging are superimposed on the patient in the operating room. Other industries where AR has caught on include military training, engineering design, robotics, and consumer design. For example, Newport News Shipbuilding, which designs and builds U.S. Navy aircraft carriers, uses AR to inspect a ship near the end of the manufacturing process. By seeing the final design superimposed on the ship, engineers have reduced inspection time by 96 percent—from 36 hours to only 90 minutes (Porter and Heppelmann, 2017).

INTERACTIVE SESSION TECHNOLOGY

The Reality of Virtual Reality

In the past, your best chance of experiencing virtual reality (VR) was to view Hollywood films. Today, this technology has become more sophisticated and immersive, and it is finding more business uses.

Besides entertainment, the most popular virtual reality applications are currently in retail and manufacturing, where an immersive experience can help customers visualize products or teach factory workers how to use complex equipment. Audi has used virtual reality technology in its "dealership in a briefcase" program. By donning an Oculus Rift virtual reality headset, prospective buyers can feel as if they are sitting behind the wheel of a car or opening up the trunk. The VR headset displays in 3-D exactly what you'd see if you were looking over a real-life Audi. Bang & Olufsen headphones simulate the sounds of doors slamming shut and music from the stereo system of the cars being browsed. This VR experience is available for the entire Audi model range and customization options.

Volkswagen Group is experimenting with virtual reality to speed up vehicle design and development and to identify potentially costly design problems earlier in the development cycle. Volkswagen has been able to cut out costly physical prototypes and replace them with immersive, 360-degree views of digitally constructed interior and exterior components of a vehicle using virtual reality HTC Vive headsets. Virtual components of a car, including interior and exterior parts such as buttons, lights, or consoles, can be switched out and replaced easily with a few lines of software code during the design process.

A major drawback of virtual reality is how it isolates people from others and from real-world surroundings because they are immersed in a virtual world encased in a headset. Facebook wants to change that by using virtual reality to create a new type of shared social experience. Facebook envisions a virtual world with an imaginary social space where avatars that look like real people "hang out" with other avatars representing friends and family. CEO Mark Zuckerberg believes virtual reality provides a new and powerful way for his company

to grow, and expects one billion people to use this medium.

In March 2014 Facebook purchased Oculus VR for $2 billion to start working with virtual reality. Oculus produces the Rift high-end VR headset and also Oculus Go, a standalone headset costing only $199 that is supposed to be easier to use than the Rift. A beta version of Spaces, Facebook's virtual reality app for the Oculus Rift, was launched in April 2018. Spaces is intended as a virtual hangout where you can interact with up to four friends, each represented by self-created digital avatars. Inside Spaces you can also video chat with friends via Facebook Messenger, do a Facebook Live broadcast, or take "selfies" in VR to share with Facebook friends.

In Oculus Rooms for the Oculus Go, people can spend time together in a virtual world, chatting, watching a movie, or playing cards. Oculus Go has a virtual reality TV viewing app called Oculus TV where users can "sit" in a 3-D environment with a massive screen and watch video with a friend. Content from Netflix, Hulu Showtime, Redbull, Pluto TV, Facebook video, and ESPN is available. Oculus Venues makes it possible to watch sports or live concerts with friends or other people in virtual reality.

Facebook is trying to create photorealistic avatars, with technology to help users personalize their avatars with more lifelike features and gestures so that they more closely resemble the people they represent. Facebook's avatars are still very cartoon-like. Creating the virtual reality experience Facebook wants carries a hefty price tag—an investment of around $3 billion during the next decade. It is too early to tell whether Facebook can make a virtual reality breakthrough for widespread use.

Not all organizations will benefit from VR. Greg Meyers, CIO at Motorola Solutions, a data communications and telecommunications equipment provider, doesn't see any obvious applications where virtual reality can help drive growth for his company. Virtual reality may be useful for staging more effective meetings, but Meyers feels the company would derive more benefit from using

AI technology to help it make better and faster decisions.

There is a gap between the hype and the reality of what VR can actually do for business. Management needs to ensure that the company will receive concrete returns on investment. Virtual reality shouldn't be viewed as the next platform everyone's going to use, because it's unclear that will be the case, according to Forrester Research analyst J. P. Gownder. A business needs to be able to demonstrate that VR will solve a very specific business problem, and must determine exactly how VR technology can improve its operations, engage customers for highly configurable goods, or deliver new consumer experiences.

Many enterprise applications of immersive technology are still in the piloting and troubleshooting phases. Today's virtual reality technology also lacks strong security and management features appropriate for deployment in the enterprise, where VR applications might need to be linked to the organization's databases and major corporate systems.

According to research analyst Ian Hughes, for most workplace applications, shutting people off from other people and the real world to engage in a virtual experience does not fit well with the way people behave. Rather than a fully simulated work environment, for most tasks, Hughes recommends blending real and virtual worlds. It's better for technology to be extending the real world rather than replacing it.

Sources: Kurt Wagner, "Oculus Go, the Virtual Reality Headset Facebook Hopes Will Bring VR to the Mainstream, Is Finally Here," *Recode,* May 1, 2018; Sara Castellanos, "Volkswagen Brings Sense of Touch to Virtual Reality," *Wall Street Journal,* April 25, 2018; Chuong Nguyen, "Facebook Wants to Make Your Virtual Self Appear as Real as Possible in VR," *Digital Trends,* May 3, 2018; "Virtual and Augmented Reality—Reshaping Business Futures," ETCIO.com, March 12, 2018; Matt Kapko, "Making Waves with Immersive Technologies," *CIO,* May–June 2017; and Lisa Eadiccio, "Inside Facebook's Plan to Take Virtual Reality Mainstream," *Time,* August 2, 2017.

CASE STUDY QUESTIONS

1. If your company wanted to implement a virtual reality application, what management, organization, and technology factors should it consider?

2. Should all businesses use virtual reality? Why or why not? What kinds of organizations will benefit most from this technology?

3. Do you think Facebook's virtual reality strategy will be successful? Explain your answer.

11-5 How will MIS help my career?

Here is how Chapter 11 and this book will help you find an entry-level job as a sales assistant for an AI company.

The Company

RazzleDazzle Technology, an artificial intelligence company based in San Jose, California, is looking for an entry-level sales assistant. RazzleDazzle specializes in computer vision technology, seeking to unlock the value of visual content produced daily across diverse data sets to solve problems for a variety of industries, including advertising and professional sports.

Position Description

The sales assistant will work closely with the sales team on planning and staging events, database management, administrative tasks, and account research to support sales and marketing objectives. Job responsibilities include:

- Using Salesforce.com for lead generation collection, data entry, and maintenance
- Using Excel to update sales team resources
- Scheduling meetings and taking meeting notes
- Assisting with research on sales accounts and new event ideas and locations
- Assisting sales with client meeting preparation
- Assembling promotional materials

Job Requirements

- Recent college graduate.
- Bachelor's degree in marketing, MIS, finance, or liberal arts.
- Strong interest in learning the business and industry.
- Knowledge of Microsoft Office essential.
- Attention to detail, effective communication skills, enthusiastic attitude, and the ability to thrive in a fast-paced environment.

Interview Questions

1. What do you know about our company and about computer vision systems? Have you ever done any work with AI technology?
2. Have you ever worked with Salesforce.com? How have you used the software?
3. What is your proficiency level with Microsoft Office tools? What work have you done with Excel spreadsheets?
4. Can you provide samples of your writing to demonstrate your communication skills and sense of detail?

Author Tips

1. Review the section of this chapter on AI and use the web to find out more about computer vision systems.
2. Use the web and LinkedIn to find out more about this company, its products, services, and competitors and the way it operates. Think about what it needs to support its sales team and how you could specifically contribute.
3. Learn what you can about Salesforce.com, with attention to how it handles lead generation, data entry, and maintenance.
4. Inquire exactly how you would be using Excel in this job. Describe some of the Excel work you have done and perhaps bring samples with you to the interview.

11-1   What is the role of knowledge management systems in business?

Knowledge management is a set of processes to create, store, transfer, and apply knowledge in the organization. Much of a firm's value depends on its ability to create and manage knowledge. Knowledge management promotes organizational learning by increasing the ability of the organization to learn from its environment and to incorporate knowledge into its business processes. There are three major types of knowledge management systems: enterprise-wide knowledge management systems, knowledge work systems, and "intelligent" techniques.

11-2   What are artificial intelligence (AI) and machine learning? How do businesses use AI?

AI involves the attempt to build computer systems that try to think and act like humans. At present, artificial intelligence lacks the flexibility, breadth, and generality of human intelligence, but it can be used to capture, codify, and extend organizational knowledge.

Expert systems capture tacit knowledge from a limited domain of human expertise and express that knowledge in the form of rules. Machine learning software can learn from previous data and examples. It can identify patterns in very large databases without explicit programming, although with significant human training

Neural networks consist of hardware and software that attempt to mimic the thought processes of the human brain. Neural networks are notable for their ability to learn on their own with some training, and to recognize patterns that cannot be easily identified by humans. Deep learning neural networks use multiple layers of neural networks to reveal the underlying patterns in data, and in some limited cases identify patterns without human training

Genetic algorithms develop solutions to particular problems using genetically based processes such as fitness, crossover, and mutation. Genetic algorithms are useful for solving problems involving optimization where many alternatives or variables must be evaluated to generate an optimal solution.

Intelligent agents are software programs with built-in or learned knowledge bases that carry out specific tasks for an individual user, business process, or software application. Intelligent agents can be programmed to navigate through large amounts of data to locate useful information and in some cases act on that information on behalf of the user. Chatbots are software agents designed to simulate a conversation with one or more human users via textual or auditory methods.

Natural language processing technology makes it possible for a machine to understand human language and to process that information. Computer vision systems deal with how computers can emulate the human visual system to view and extract information from real-world images. Robotics deals with the design, construction, operation, and use of movable machines that can substitute for some human actions.

11-3   What types of systems are used for enterprise-wide knowledge management, and how do they provide value for businesses?

Enterprise-wide knowledge management systems are firmwide efforts to collect, store, distribute, and apply digital content and knowledge. Enterprise content management systems provide databases and tools for organizing and storing structured documents and tools for organizing and storing semistructured knowledge, such as email or rich media. Often these systems include group collaboration tools, portals to simplify information access, search tools, tools for locating experts, and tools for classifying information based on a taxonomy that is appropriate for the organization. Learning management systems provide tools for the management, delivery, tracking, and assessment of various types of employee learning and training.

11-4   What are the major types of knowledge work systems, and how do they provide value for firms?

Knowledge work systems (KWS) support the creation of new knowledge and its integration into the organization. KWS require easy access to an external knowledge base; powerful computer hardware that can support software with intensive graphics, analysis, document management, and communications capabilities; and a user-friendly interface. KWS include computer-aided design (CAD) systems, augmented reality applications, and virtual reality systems, which create interactive simulations that behave like the real world, with intensive graphics and powerful modeling capabilities.

Key Terms

3-D printing, 445
Artificial intelligence (AI), 427
Augmented reality (AR), 445
Chatbot, 438
Communities of practice (COPs), 425
Computer-aided design (CAD), 444
Computer vision systems, 436
Data, 422
"Deep learning," 434
Digital asset management systems, 440
Enterprise content management (ECM), 439
Enterprise-wide knowledge management systems, 426
Expert systems, 428
Explicit knowledge, 422
Genetic algorithms, 435
Inference engine, 429
Intelligent agents, 437
"Intelligent" techniques, 426

Knowledge, 422
Knowledge base, 429
Knowledge management, 423
Knowledge work systems (KWS), 426
Learning management system (LMS), 441
Machine learning, 430
Massive open online course (MOOC), 441
Natural language processing (NLP), 436
Neural networks, 432
Organizational learning, 423
Pattern detection program, 432
Robotics, 437
Structured knowledge, 439
Supervised learning, 431
Tacit knowledge, 422
Taxonomy, 440
Unsupervised learning, 431
Virtual reality (VR) systems, 445
Wisdom, 422

MyLab MIS

To complete the problems with the MyLab MIS, go to the EOC Discussion Questions in MyLab MIS.

Review Questions

11-1   What is the role of knowledge management systems in business?

- Define knowledge management and explain its value to businesses.
- Describe the important dimensions of knowledge.
- Distinguish between data, knowledge, and wisdom and between tacit knowledge and explicit knowledge.
- Describe the stages in the knowledge management value chain.

11-2   What are artificial intelligence (AI) and machine learning? How do businesses use AI?

- Define artificial intelligence (AI) and the major AI techniques.
- Define an expert system, describe how it works, and explain its value to business.
- Define machine learning, explain how it works, and give some examples of the kinds of problems it can solve.
- Define neural networks and deep learning neural networks, describing how they work and how they benefit organizations.
- Define and describe genetic algorithms, and intelligent agents. Explain how each works and the kinds of problems for which each is suited.

- Define and describe computer vision systems, natural language processing systems, and robotics and give examples of their applications in organizations.

11-3   What types of systems are used for enterprise-wide knowledge management, and how do they provide value for businesses?

- Define and describe the various types of enterprise-wide knowledge management systems and explain how they provide value for businesses.
- Describe the role of the following in facilitating knowledge management: taxonomies, MOOCs, and learning management systems.

11-4   What are the major types of knowledge work systems, and how do they provide value for firms?

- Define knowledge work systems and describe the generic requirements of knowledge work systems.
- Describe how the following systems support knowledge work: CAD, virtual reality, and augmented reality.

Discussion Questions

11-5
MyLab MIS
Knowledge management is a business process, not a technology. Discuss.

11-6
MyLab MIS
Describe various ways that knowledge management systems could help firms with sales and marketing or with manufacturing and production.

11-7
MyLab MIS
Compare artificial intelligence to human intelligence. How "intelligent" is artificial intelligence today?

Hands-On MIS Projects

The projects in this section give you hands-on experience designing a knowledge portal, identifying opportunities for knowledge management, creating a simple expert system, and using intelligent agents to research products for sale on the web. Visit MyLab MIS to access this chapter's Hands-On MIS Projects.

Management Decision Problems

11-8 U.S. Pharma Corporation is headquartered in New Jersey but has research sites in Germany, France, the United Kingdom, Switzerland, and Australia. Research and development of new pharmaceuticals is key to ongoing profits, and U.S. Pharma researches and tests thousands of possible drugs. The company's researchers need to share information with others within and outside the company, including the U.S. Food and Drug Administration, the World Health Organization, and the International Federation of Pharmaceutical Manufacturers & Associations. Also critical is access to health information sites, such as the U.S. National Library of Medicine, and to industry conferences and professional journals. Design a knowledge portal for U.S. Pharma's researchers. Include in your design specifications relevant internal systems and databases, external sources of information, and internal and external communication and collaboration tools. Design a home page for your portal.

11-9 Canadian Tire is one of Canada's largest companies, with 50,000 employees and 1,100 stores and gas bars (gas stations) across Canada selling sports, leisure, home products, apparel, and financial services as well as automotive and petroleum products. The retail outlets are independently owned and operated. Canadian Tire has been using daily mailings and thick product catalogs to inform its dealers about new products, merchandise setups, best practices, product ordering, and problem resolution, and it is looking for a better way to provide employees with human resources and administrative documents. Describe the problems created by this way of doing business and how knowledge management systems might help.

Improving Decision Making: Building a Simple Expert System for Retirement Planning

Software skills: Spreadsheet formulas and IF function or expert system tool
Business skills: Benefits eligibility determination

11-10 Expert systems typically use a large number of rules. This project has been simplified to reduce the number of rules, but it will give you experience working with a series of rules to develop an application.

When employees at your company retire, they are given cash bonuses. These cash bonuses are based on the length of employment and the retiree's age. To receive a bonus, an employee must be at least 50 years of age and have worked for the company for more than five years. The following table summarizes the criteria for determining bonuses.

LENGTH OF EMPLOYMENT	BONUS
<5 years	No bonus
5–10 years	20 percent of current annual salary
11–15 years	30 percent of current annual salary
16–20 years	40 percent of current annual salary
21–25 years	50 percent of current annual salary
26 or more years	100 percent of current annual salary

Using the information provided, build a simple expert system. Find a demonstration copy of an expert system software tool on the web that you can download. Alternatively, use your spreadsheet software to build the expert system. (If you are using spreadsheet software, we suggest using the IF function so you can see how rules are created.)

Improving Decision Making: Using Intelligent Agents for Comparison Shopping

Software skills: Web browser and shopping bot software
Business skills: Product evaluation and selection

11-11 This project will give you experience using shopping bots to search online for products, find product information, and find the best prices and vendors. Select a digital camera you might want to purchase, such as the Canon PowerShot SX540 or the Olympus Tough TG-5. Visit MySimon (www.mysimon.com), BizRate.com (www.bizrate.com), and Google Shopping to do price comparisons for you. Evaluate these shopping sites in terms of their ease of use, number of offerings, speed in obtaining information, thoroughness of information offered about the product and seller, and price selection. Which site or sites would you use, and why? Which camera would you select, and why? How helpful were these sites for making your decision?

Collaboration and Teamwork Project

Rating Enterprise Content Management Systems

11-12 With a group of classmates, select two enterprise content management (ECM) products, such as those from Oracle, OpenText, and IBM. Compare their features and capabilities. To prepare your analysis, use articles from computer magazines and the websites of the ECM software vendors. If possible, use Google Docs and Google Drive or Google Sites to brainstorm, organize, and develop a presentation of your findings for the class.

Can Cars Drive Themselves—And Should They?

CASE STUDY

Will cars really be able to drive themselves without human operators? Should they? And are they good business investments? Everyone is searching for answers.

Autonomous vehicle technology has reached a point where no automaker can ignore it. Every major auto maker is racing to develop and perfect autonomous vehicles, believing that the market for them could one day reach trillions of dollars. Companies such as Ford, General Motors, Nissan, Mercedes, Tesla, and others have invested billions in autonomous technology research and development. Ford invested $1 billion in AI firm Argo AI, and GM bought a self-driving car startup called Cruise. Ford has set a goal of producing a self-driving car with no pedals by 2021. Ride-hailing companies like Uber and Lyft believe driverless cars that eliminate labor costs are key to their long-term profitability. Cars that drive themselves have been on the road in select locations in California, Arizona, Michigan, Paris, London, Singapore, and Beijing. Waymo, the company that emerged from Google's self-driving car project, predicts that by 2020 its fleet of self-driving Jaguars will make as many as one million trips per day.

A car that is supposed to take over driving from a human requires a very powerful computer system that must process and analyze large amounts of data generated by myriad sensors, cameras, and other devices to control and adjust steering, accelerating, and braking in response to real-time conditions. Key technologies include:

Sensors: Self-driving cars are loaded with sensors of many different types. Sensors on car wheels measure car velocity as it drives and moves through traffic. Ultrasonic sensors measure and track positions of line curbs, sidewalks, and objects very close to the car.

Cameras: Cameras are needed for spotting things like lane lines on the highway, speed signs, and traffic lights. Windshield-mounted cameras create a 3-D image of the road ahead. Cameras behind the rear-view mirror focus on lane markings. Infrared cameras pick up infrared beams emitted from headlamps to extend vision for night driving.

Lidars: Lidars are light detection and ranging devices which sit on top of most self-driving cars.

A lidar fires out millions of laser beams every second, measuring how long they take to bounce back. The lidar takes in a 360-degree view of a car's surroundings, identifying nearby objects with an accuracy up to 2 centimeters. Lidars are very expensive and not yet robust enough for a life of potholes, extreme temperatures, rain, or snow.

GPS: A global positioning system (GPS) pinpoints the car's macro location, and is accurate to within 1.9 meters. Combined with reading from tachometers, gyroscopes, and altimeters, it provides initial positioning.

Radar: Radar bounces radio waves off of objects to help see a car's surroundings, including blind spots, and is especially helpful for spotting big metallic objects, such as other vehicles.

Computer: All the data generated by these technologies needs to be combined, analyzed, and turned into a robot-friendly picture of the world, with instructions on how to move through it, requiring almost supercomputer-like processing power. Its software features obstacle avoidance algorithms, predictive modeling, and "smart" object discrimination (for example, knowing the difference between a bicycle and a motorcycle) to help the vehicle follow traffic rules and navigate obstacles.

Machine Learning, Deep Learning, and Computer Vision Technology: The car's computer system has to be "trained" using machine intelligence and deep learning to do things like detect lane lines and identify cyclists, by showing it millions of examples of the subject at hand. Because the world is too complex to write a rule for every possible scenario, cars must be able to "learn" from experience and figure out how to navigate on their own.

Maps: Before an autonomous car takes to the streets, its developers use cameras and lidars to map its territory in extreme detail. That information helps the car verify its sensor readings, and it is key for any vehicle to know its own location.

Self-driving car companies are notorious for overhyping their progress. Should we believe them? At this point, the outlook for them is clouded.

In March 2018, a self-driving Uber Volvo XC90 operating in autonomous mode struck and killed a woman in Tempe, Arizona. Since the crash, Arizona has suspended autonomous vehicle testing in the state, and Uber is not renewing its permit to test self-driving cars in California. The company has also stopped testing autonomous cars in Pittsburgh and Toronto and it's unclear when it will be revived. Even before the accident, Uber's self-driving cars were having trouble driving through construction zones and next to tall vehicles like big truck rigs. Uber's drivers had to intervene far more frequently than drivers in other autonomous car projects.

The Uber accident raised questions about whether autonomous vehicles were even ready to be tested on public roads and how regulators should deal with this. Autonomous vehicle technology's defenders pointed out that nearly 40,000 people die on U.S. roads every year, and human error causes more than 90 percent of crashes. But no matter how quickly self-driving proliferates, it will be a very long time before the robots can put a serious dent in those numbers and convince everyday folks that they're better off letting the cars do the driving.

While proponents of self-driving cars like Tesla's Elon Musk envision a self-driving world where almost all traffic accidents would be eliminated, and the elderly and disabled could travel freely, most Americans think otherwise. A Pew Research Center survey found that most people did not want to ride in self-driving cars and were unsure if they would make roads more dangerous or safer. Eighty-seven percent wanted a person always behind the wheel, ready to take over if something went wrong.

There's still plenty that needs to be improved before self-driving vehicles could safely take to the road. Autonomous vehicles are not yet able to operate safely in all weather conditions. Heavy rain or snow can confuse current car radar and lidar systems—autonomous vehicles can't operate on their own in such weather conditions. These vehicles also have trouble when tree branches hang too low or bridges and roads have faint lane markings. On some roads, self-driving vehicles will have to make guidance decisions without the benefit of white lines or clear demarcations at the edge of the road, including Botts' Dots (small plastic markers that define lanes). Botts' Dots are not believed to be effective lane-marking for autonomous vehicles.

Computer vision systems are able to reliably recognize objects. What remains challenging is "scene understanding"—for example, the ability to determine whether a bag on the road is empty or is hiding bricks or heavy objects inside. Although autonomous vehicle vision systems are now capable of picking out traffic lights reliably, they are not always able to make correct decisions if traffic lights are not working. This requires experience, intuition, and knowing how to cooperate among multiple vehicles. Autonomous vehicles must also be able to recognize a person moving alongside a road, determine whether that person is riding a bicycle, and how that person is likely to respond and behave. All of that is still difficult for an autonomous vehicle to do right now. Chaotic environments such as congested streets teeming with cars, pedestrians, and cyclists are especially difficult for self-driving cars to navigate.

Driving a car to merge into rapidly flowing lanes of traffic is an intricate task that often requires eye contact with oncoming drivers. How can autonomous vehicles communicate with humans and other machines to let them know what they want to do? Researchers are investigating whether electronic signs and car-to-car communication systems would solve this problem. There's also what's called the "trolley problem": In a situation where a crash is unavoidable, how does a robot car decide whom or what to hit? Should it hit the car coming up on its left or a tree on the side of the road?

A less advanced version of autonomous vehicle technology is already on the market. Cadillac Super Cruise, Nissan ProPilot Assist, and Tesla Autopilot are capable of keeping a car in its lane and a safe distance from other cars, allowing the "driver" behind the wheel to take hands off the wheel, provided that person keeps paying attention and is ready to take control if needed. These less-advanced systems can't see things like stopped fire trucks or traffic lights. But humans haven't made good driving backups because their attention tends to wander. At least two Tesla drivers in the U.S. have died using the system. (One hit a truck in 2016, another hit a highway barrier in 2018.) There is what is called a "handoff problem." A semi-autonomous car needs to be able to determine what its human "driver" is doing and how to get that person to take the wheel when needed.

And let's not forget security. A self-driving car is essentially a collection of networked computers and sensors linked wirelessly to the outside world, and it is no more secure than other networked systems. Keeping systems safe from intruders who want to crash or weaponize cars may prove to be the greatest challenge confronting autonomous vehicles in the future.

Self-driving cars require new ecosystems to support them, much as today's cars are dependent on garages, gasoline stations, and highway systems. New roads, highways, and automotive supply chains will have to be rebuilt for self-driving cars. The big auto makers that build millions of cars a year rely on complex, precise interaction among hundreds of companies, including automotive component suppliers and the services to keep cars running. They need dealers to sell the cars, gas pumps or charging stations to fuel them, body shops to fix them, and parking lots to store them. Manufacturers of autonomous vehicles need to rethink interactions and processes built up over a century. The highway infrastructure will need to change over time to support autonomous vehicles. Waymo has partnered with Avis to take care of its fleet of driverless minivans in Arizona, and it's working with a startup called Trov to insure their passengers. GM is retooling one of its plants to produce Chevrolet Bolts without steering wheels or pedals.

A computer-driven car that can handle any situation as well as a human under all conditions is decades away at best. Many analysts expect the first deployment of self-driving technology will be robot taxi services operating in limited conditions and areas, so their operators can avoid particularly tricky intersections and make sure everything is mapped in fine detail. The Boston Consulting Group predicts that 25 percent of all miles driven in the U.S. by 2030 may be by shared self-driving vehicles. To take a ride, you'd probably have to use predetermined pickup and drop-off points, so your car can always pull over safely and legally. The makers of self-driving cars will be figuring out how much to charge so they can recoup their research and development costs, but not so much as to dissuade potential riders. They'll struggle with regulators and insurance companies over what to do in the inevitable event of a crash.

Some pundits predict that in the next few decades, driverless technology will add $7 trillion to the global economy and save hundreds of thousands of lives. At the same time, it could devastate the auto industry along with gas stations, taxi drivers, and truckers. People might stop buying cars because services like Uber using self-driving cars would be cheaper. This could cause mass unemployment of taxi drivers and large reductions in auto sales. It would also cut down the need for many parking garages and parking spaces, freeing up valuable real estate for other purposes. More people might decide to live further from their workplaces because autonomous vehicles linked to traffic systems would make traffic flow more smoothly and free riders to work, nap, or watch video

while commuting. Some people will prosper. Most will probably benefit, but many will be left behind. Driverless technology is estimated to change one in every nine U.S. jobs, although it will also create new jobs. Another consideration is that the tremendous investment in autonomous vehicles, estimated to be around $32 billion annually, might be better spent on improving public transportation systems like trains and subways. Does America need more cars in sprawling urban areas where highways are already jammed?

The accidents self-driving cars have experienced so far point to the need to create a dependable standard for measuring reliability and safety. In 2018, twenty-nine states have enacted legislation regulating autonomous vehicles, with a few states requiring a safety driver always be in the car ready to take control. U.S. federal regulators have delayed formulating an overarching set of self-driving car standards, leaving a gap for the states to fill. The federal government is only now poised to create its first law for autonomous vehicles. This law is similar to Arizona's and would allow hundreds of thousands of driverless cars to be deployed within a few years and would restrict states from putting up hurdles for the industry.

Sources: Christopher Mims, "Driverless Hype Collides with Merciless Reality," *Wall Street Journal*, September 13, 2018; National Conference of State Legislatures, "Autonomous Vehicles—Self Driving Vehicles Enacted Legislation," June 25, 2018; Jack Karsten and Darrell West, "The State of Self-Driving Car Laws Across the U.S.," Brookings Institute, May 1, 2018; Alex Davies, "The WIRED Guide to Self-Driving Cars," *WIRED*, May 17, 2018; Daisuke Wakabashai, "Uber's Self-Driving Cars Were Struggling Before Arizona Crash," *New York Times*, March 23, 2018; Kevin Roose, "The Self-Driving Car Industry's Biggest Turning Point Yet," *New York Times*, March 29, 2018; Tim Higgins, "VW, Hyundai Turn to Driverless-Car Startup in Silicon Valley," *Wall Street Journal*, January 4, 2018; John Markoff, "A Guide to Challenges Facing Self-Driving Car Technologists," *New York Times*, June 7, 2017; and The Editorial Board, "Would You Buy a Self-Driving Future from These Guys?" *New York Times*, October 14, 2017.

CASE STUDY QUESTIONS

11-13 What are the management, organizational, and technology challenges posed by self-driving car technology?

11-14 Are self-driving cars good business investments? Explain your answer.

11-15 What ethical and social issues are raised by self-driving car technology?

11-16 Will cars really be able to drive themselves without human operators? Should they?

MyLab MIS

Go to the Assignments section of MyLab MIS to complete these writing exercises.

11-17 How do each of the following types of systems acquire and model knowledge: expert system, genetic algorithms, neural network?

11-18 How do enterprise content management systems help organizations manage structured and semistructured knowledge? What are two examples of each type of knowledge handled by these systems?

Chapter 11 References

Agrawal, Ajay, Joshua S. Gans, and Avi Goldfarb. "What to Expect from Artificial Intelligence." *MIT Sloan Management Review* (February 7, 2017).

Albertson, Mark. "NBA Advertisers Chew on Data from GumGum's Computer Vision Tool." *Silicon Angle* (March 22, 2018).

Althuizen, Niek, and Astrid Reichel. "The Effects of IT-Enabled Cognitive Stimulation Tools on Creative Problem Solving: A Dual Pathway to Creativity." *Journal of Management Information Systems* 33, No. 1 (2016).

Bureau of Economic Analysis. "Gross Output by Industry." (April 19, 2018).

Burtka, Michael. "Generic Algorithms." *The Stern Information Systems Review* 1, No. 1 (Spring 1993).

Chui, Michael, James Manyika, and Mehdi Miremadi. "What AI Can and Can't Do (Yet) for Your Business." *McKinsey Quarterly* (January 2018).

D'Aveni, Richard A. "The 3-D Printing Playbook." *Harvard Business Review* (July–August 2018).

Davenport, Thomas H., and Vikram Mahidhar. "What's Your Cognitive Strategy?" *MIT Sloan Management Review* 59, No. 4 (Summer 2018).

Davenport, Thomas H., and Julia Kirby. "Just How Smart Are Smart Machines?" *MIT Sloan Management Review* 57, No. 3 (Spring 2016).

Davenport, Thomas H., and Lawrence Prusak. *Working Knowledge: How Organizations Manage What They Know*. Boston, MA: Harvard Business School Press (1997).

Davenport, Thomas H., Laurence Prusak, and Bruce Strong. "Putting Ideas to Work." *Wall Street Journal* (March 10, 2008).

Davenport, Thomas H., and Rajeev Ronaki. "Artificial Intelligence for the Real World." *Harvard Business Review* (January–February 2018).

Dawar, Niraj. "Marketing in the Age of Alexa." *Harvard Business Review* (May–June 2018).

Dhar, Vasant, and Roger Stein. *Intelligent Decision Support Methods: The Science of Knowledge Work*. Upper Saddle River, NJ: Prentice Hall (1997).

eMarketer. "Artificial Intelligence: What's Now, What's New, and What's Next." (May 2017).

Gelernter, David. "Machines That Will Think and Feel." *Wall Street Journal* (March 18, 2016).

Gu, Feng, and Baruch Lev. "Intangible Assets: Measurements, Drivers, Usefulness." (2001). http://pages.stern.nyu.edu/~blev/.

Hamori, Monoika. "Can MOOCs Solve Your Training Problem?" *Harvard Business Review* (January–February 2018).

Havakhor, Taha, and Rajiv Sabherwal. "Team Processes in Virtual Knowledge Teams: The Effects of Reputation Signals and Network Density." *Journal of Management Information Systems* 35, No. 1 (2018).

Hirschberg, Julia, and Christopher D. Manning. "Advances in Natural Language Processing." *Science* (May 12, 2016).

Holland, John H. "Genetic Algorithms." *Scientific American* (July 1992).

Huang, Peng, Ali Tafti, and Sunil Mithas. "Platform Sponsor Investments and User Contributions in Knowledge Communities: The Role of Knowledge Seeding." *MIS Quarterly* 42, No. 1 (March 2018).

IBM Corporation. "Mizuho Bank." www.ibm.com, accessed May 17, 2018.

Kim, Seung Hyun, Tridas Mukhopadhyay, and Robert E. Kraut. "When Does Repository KMS Use Lift Performance? The Role of Alternative Knowledge Sources and Task Environments." *MIS Quarterly* 40, No. 1 (March 2016).

Kuang, Cliff. "Can AI Be Taught to Explain Itself?" *New York Times* (November 21, 2017).

Kyriakou, Harris, Jeffrey V. Nickerson, and Gaurav Sabnis. "Knowledge Reuse for Customization: Metamodels in an Open Design Community for 3D Printing." *MIS Quarterly* 41, No. 1 (2017).

Le, Quoc V., et al. "Building High-level Features Using Large Scale Unsupervised Learning." arXiv.org:1112.6209, Machine Learning, Cornell University Library (November 2011).

Lev, Baruch. "Sharpening the Intangibles Edge." *Harvard Business Review* (June 1, 2004).

Lohr, Steve. "Is There a Smarter Path to Artificial Intelligence? Some Experts Hope So." *New York Times* (June 20, 2018).

Malone, Thomas W. "How Human-Computer 'Superminds' Are Redefining the Future of Work." *MIT Sloan Management Review* 59, No. 4 (Summer 2018).

Maor, Itzakh., and T. A. Reddy. "Literature Review of Artificial Intelligence and Knowledge-based Expert Systems in Buildings and HVAC&R System Design," in M. Geshwiler, E. Howard, and C. Helms (Eds.), *ASHRAE Transactions* (2003).

Marcus, Gary. "Deep Learning: A Critical Appraisal." (January 2, 2018).

Markoff, John. "How Many Computers to Identify a Cat? 16,000." *New York Times* (June 26, 2012).

McCarthy, John. "Generality in Artificial Intelligence." *Communications of the ACM* (December 1987).

Mims, Christopher. "Without Humans, Artificial Intelligence Is Still Pretty Stupid." *Wall Street Journal* (November 12, 2017).

Mishra, Divya, et. al. "Rule Based Expert System for Medical Diagnosis—A Review." *International Journal of Engineering Technology, Management and Applied Sciences* (December 2016).

Nurmohamed, Zafred, Nabeel Gillani, and Michael Lenox. "New Use for MOOCs: Real-World Problem-Solving." *Harvard Business Review* (July 2013).

Pearl, Judea. "Theoretical Impediments to Machine Learning." (November 2016).

Porter, Michael E., and James Heppelmann. "Why Every Organization Needs an Augmented Reality Strategy." *Harvard Business Review* (November–December 2017).

Pyle, Dorian, and Cristina San Jose. "An Executive's Guide to Machine Learning." *McKinsey Quarterly* (June 2015).

Ross, Jeanne. "The Fundamental Flaw in AI Implementation." *MIT Sloan Management Review* 59, No. 2 (Winter 2018).

Rouse, Margaret. "Natural Language Processing." Searchbusinessanalytics.com (September 27, 2017).

Samuelson, Douglas A., and Charles M. Macal. "Agent-Based Simulation." *OR/MS Today* (August 2006).

Technology Quarterly. "Language: Finding a Voice." *The Economist* (May 1, 2017).

Trantopoulos, Konstantinos, Georg von Krogh, Martin W. Wallin, and Martin Woerter. "External Knowledge and Information Technology: Implications for Process Innovation Performance." *MIS Quarterly* 41, No. 1 (March 2017).

Turing, A. M. "Computing Machinery and Intelligence." *Mind* 49 (1950).

U.S. Department of Labor. "Table 2.1. Employment by Major Industry Sector, 2006, 2016, and Projected 2026." Bureau of Labor Statistics (2017).

Wakabayashi, Daisuke, and Nick Wingfield. "Alexa, We're Still Trying to Figure Out What to Do with You." *New York Times* (January 15, 2018).

Wilson, H. James, and Paul R. Daugherty. "Collaborative Intelligence: Humans and AI Are Joining Forces." *Harvard Business Review* (July–August 2018).

Zhang, Xiaojun, and Viswanath Venkatesh. "A Nomological Network of Knowledge Management System Use: Antecedents and Consequences." *MIS Quarterly* 41, No. 4 (December 2017).

12

Enhancing Decision Making

LEARNING OBJECTIVES

After reading this chapter, you will be able to answer the following questions:

12-1 What are the different types of decisions, and how does the decision-making process work?

12-2 How do information systems support the activities of managers and management decision making?

12-3 How do business intelligence and business analytics support decision making?

12-4 How do different decision-making constituencies in an organization use business intelligence, and what is the role of information systems in helping people working in a group make decisions more efficiently?

12-5 How will MIS help my career?

CHAPTER CASES

Big Data and the Internet of Things Drive Precision Agriculture

Siemens Makes Business Processes More Visible

Anthem Benefits from More Business Intelligence

Is Predix GE's Future?

VIDEO CASES

PSEG Leverages Big Data and Business Analytics Using GE's Predix Platform

FreshDirect Uses Business Intelligence to Manage Its Online Grocery

Business Intelligence Helps the Cincinnati Zoo Work Smarter

MyLab MIS

Discussion Questions: 12-5, 12-6, 12-7; **Hands-on MIS Projects:** 12-8, 12-9, 12-10, 12-11; **Writing Assignments:** 12-17, 12-18; **eText with Conceptual Animations**

Big Data and the Internet of Things Drive Precision Agriculture

By 2050, the world will be populated with an estimated 9 million people, and in order to feed all of them, agricultural output will need to double. Information technology, in the form of the Internet of Things (IoT), wireless and mobile technologies, and automated data collection and analysis is likely to provide part of the solution to this problem.

Purdue University's College of Agriculture is one of the organizations leading the way toward more data-driven farming. The College has developed an agriculture-oriented network with advanced IoT sensors and devices that will allow researchers to study and improve plant growth and food production processes. According to Pat Smoker, director of Purdue Agriculture IT, in West Lafayette, Indiana, every process from farm to table has potential for improvement through better use of information technology.

Purdue College of Agriculture partnered with Hewlett Packard Enterprise (HPE) on a digital agriculture initiative. In fall 2016, the university began installing an Internet of Things (IoT) network on its 1,408-acre research farm, the Agronomy Center for Research and Education (ACRE). The system captures terabytes of data daily from sensors, cameras, and human inputs. To collect, aggregate, process, and transmit

© Ekkasit keatsirikul/123RF

such large volumes of data back to Purdue's HPE supercomputer, the university is deploying a combination of wireless and edge computing technologies (see Chapters 5 and 7). They include solar-powered mobile Wi-Fi hotspots, an adaptive weather tower providing high-speed connectivity across the entire ACRE facility, and the PhenoRover, a semi-automated mobile vehicle that roams throughout ACRE research plots capturing real-time data from plant-based sensors. Purdue is also experimenting with drones for plant-growth data collection. ACRE researchers can enter data into a mobile device on-site and transmit them via the wireless network to an HPE data center for analysis.

Previously, Purdue's faculty had to figure out how to transmit data from the sensors back to the lab, and assign someone to write the software for analyzing the data. The new system is faster and responsive. For example, researchers using mobile devices in the field can transmit data about seed growth back to ACRE labs to analyze the impact of water levels, fertilizer quantities, and soil types. The labs can then communicate the results of their analysis back to the field to allow quick adjustments. Computerized instructions control how planting and spraying machines apply seed and nutrients to a field.

The Purdue project is an example of "precision agriculture," in which data collected and analyzed with digital tools drive decisions about fertilizer levels, planting depth, and irrigation requirements for small sections of fields or individual plants, and automated equipment can apply the ideal treatment for specific weeds.

Large agricultural companies like Monsanto and DuPont are big precision agriculture players, providing computerized data analysis and planting recommendations to farmers who use their seeds, fertilizers, and herbicides. The farmer provides data on his or her farm's field boundaries, historic crop yields, and soil conditions to these companies or another agricultural data analysis company, which analyzes the data along with other data it has collected about seed performance weather conditions, and soil types in different areas. The company doing the data analysis then sends a computer file with recommendations back to the farmer, who uploads the data into computerized planting equipment and follows the recommendations as it plants fields. For example, the recommendations might tell an Iowa corn farmer to lower the number of seeds planted per acre or to plant more seeds per acre in specified portions of the field capable of growing more corn. The farmer might also receive advice on the exact type of seed to plant in different areas and how much fertilizer to apply. In addition to producing higher crop yields, farmers using fertilizer, water, and energy to run equipment more precisely are less wasteful, and this also promotes the health of the planet.

Sources: "Envision: The Big Idea," https://ag.purdue.edu, accessed April 26, 2018; "Precision Agriculture," www.farms.com, accessed April 26, 2018; www.monsanto.com, accessed May 1, 2018; and Eileen McCooey, "Purdue Uses IoT to Reinvent Farming, Boost Output," *Baseline*, December 6, 2017.

Precision agriculture is a powerful illustration of how information systems can dramatically improve decision making. In the past, deciding what to plant, how, where, and when was based on farmers' historical experience with their land and best guesses. Wireless networks, myriad sensors in the field, mobile devices, powerful computers, and big data analytics tools have created systems that can make many of these decisions much more rapidly and accurately.

The chapter-opening diagram calls attention to important points raised by this case and this chapter. There is a worldwide need to increase food production, both to feed a rapidly growing global population and to make farms more profitable. Wireless technology and big data analytics create new opportunities for managing crops almost on a plant-by-plant basis. Managing fields with this level of computerized precision means farmers need to use less fertilizer and less seed per unit of land, potentially saving an individual farmer tens of thousands of dollars while increasing crop yields. Precision agriculture may also help solve the world food crisis.

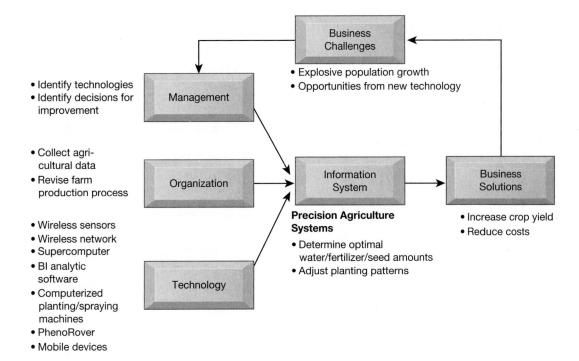

- Identify technologies
- Identify decisions for improvement

- Collect agricultural data
- Revise farm production process

- Wireless sensors
- Wireless network
- Supercomputer
- BI analytic software
- Computerized planting/spraying machines
- PhenoRover
- Mobile devices

Business Challenges

- Explosive population growth
- Opportunities from new technology

Management

Organization

Technology

Information System

Precision Agriculture Systems

- Determine optimal water/fertilizer/seed amounts
- Adjust planting patterns

Business Solutions

- Increase crop yield
- Reduce costs

Here are some questions to think about: How is information technology changing the way farmers run their business? How is precision agriculture changing decision making? Give examples of two decisions that can be improved by using precision agriculture.

12-1 What are the different types of decisions, and how does the decision-making process work?

Decision making in businesses used to be limited to management. Today, lower-level employees are responsible for some of these decisions, as information systems make information available to lower levels of the business. But what do we mean by better decision making? How does decision making take place in businesses and other organizations? Let's take a closer look.

Business Value of Improved Decision Making

What does it mean to the business to make better decisions? What is the monetary value of improved decision making? Table 12.1 attempts to measure the monetary value of improved decision making for a small U.S. manufacturing firm with $280 million in annual revenue and 140 employees. The firm has identified a number of key decisions where new system investments might improve the quality of decision making. The table provides selected estimates of annual value (in the form of cost savings or increased revenue) from improved decision making in selected areas of the business.

We can see from Table 12.1 that decisions are made at all levels of the firm and that some of these decisions are common, routine, and numerous. Although the value of improving any single decision may be small, improving hundreds of thousands of "small" decisions adds up to a large annual value for the business.

TABLE 12.1 BUSINESS VALUE OF ENHANCED DECISION MAKING

EXAMPLE DECISION	DECISION MAKER	NUMBER OF ANNUAL DECISIONS	ESTIMATED VALUE TO FIRM OF A SINGLE IMPROVED DECISION	ANNUAL VALUE
Allocate support to most valuable customers	Accounts manager	12	$100,000	$1,200,000
Predict call center daily demand	Call center management	4	$150,000	$600,000
Decide parts inventory levels daily	Inventory manager	365	$5,000	$1,825,000
Identify competitive bids from major suppliers	Senior management	1	$2,000,000	$2,000,000
Schedule production to fill orders	Manufacturing manager	150	$10,000	$1,500,000
Allocate labor to complete a job	Production floor manager	100	$4,000	$400,000

Types of Decisions

Chapters 1 and 2 showed that there are different levels in an organization. Each of these levels has different information requirements for decision support and responsibility for different types of decisions (see Figure 12.1). Decisions are classified as structured, semi-structured, and unstructured.

Unstructured decisions are those in which the decision maker must provide judgment, evaluation, and insight to solve the problem. Each of these decisions is novel, important, and nonroutine, and there is no well-understood or agreed-on procedure for making them.

Structured decisions, by contrast, are repetitive and routine, and they involve a definite procedure for handling them so that they do not have to be treated each time as if they were new. Many decisions have elements of both

FIGURE 12.1 INFORMATION REQUIREMENTS OF KEY DECISION-MAKING GROUPS IN A FIRM

Senior managers, middle managers, operational managers, and employees have different types of decisions and information requirements.

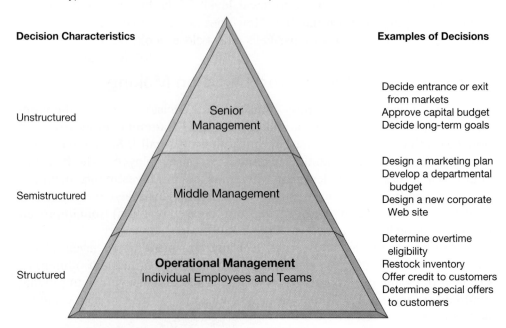

types of decisions and are **semi-structured**, where only part of the problem has a clear-cut answer provided by an accepted procedure. In general, structured decisions are more prevalent at lower organizational levels, whereas unstructured problems are more common at higher levels of the firm.

Senior executives face many unstructured decision situations, such as establishing the firm's 5- or 10-year goals or deciding new markets to enter. Answering the question "Should we enter a new market?" would require access to news, government reports, and industry views as well as high-level summaries of firm performance. However, the answer would also require senior managers to use their own best judgment and poll other managers for their opinions.

Middle managers face more structured decision scenarios, but their decisions may include unstructured components. A typical middle-level management decision might be "Why is the reported order fulfillment report showing a decline over the past six months at a distribution center in Minneapolis?" This middle manager will obtain a report from the firm's enterprise system or distribution management system on order activity and operational efficiency at the Minneapolis distribution center. This is the structured part of the decision. But before arriving at an answer, this middle manager will have to interview employees and gather more unstructured information from external sources about local economic conditions or sales trends.

Operational management and rank-and-file employees tend to make more structured decisions. For example, a supervisor on an assembly line has to decide whether an hourly paid worker is entitled to overtime pay. If the employee worked more than eight hours on a particular day, the supervisor would routinely grant overtime pay for any time beyond eight hours that was clocked on that day.

A sales account representative often has to make decisions about extending credit to customers by consulting the firm's customer database that contains credit information. If the customer met the firm's pre-specified criteria for granting credit, the account representative would grant that customer credit to make a purchase. In both instances, the decisions are highly structured and are routinely made thousands of times each day in most large firms. The answer has been preprogrammed into the firm's payroll and accounts receivable systems.

The Decision-Making Process

Making a decision is a multistep process. Simon (1960) described four different stages in decision making: intelligence, design, choice, and implementation (see Figure 12.2).

Intelligence consists of discovering, identifying, and understanding the problems occurring in the organization—why a problem exists, where, and what effects it is having on the firm.

Design involves identifying and exploring various solutions to the problem.

Choice consists of choosing among solution alternatives.

Implementation involves making the chosen alternative work and continuing to monitor how well the solution is working.

What happens if the solution you have chosen doesn't work? Figure 12.2 shows that you can return to an earlier stage in the decision-making process and repeat it if necessary. For instance, in the face of declining sales, a sales management team may decide to pay the sales force a higher commission for making more sales to spur on the sales effort. If this does not produce sales increases, managers would need to investigate whether the problem stems from

FIGURE 12.2 STAGES IN DECISION MAKING

The decision-making process is broken down into four stages.

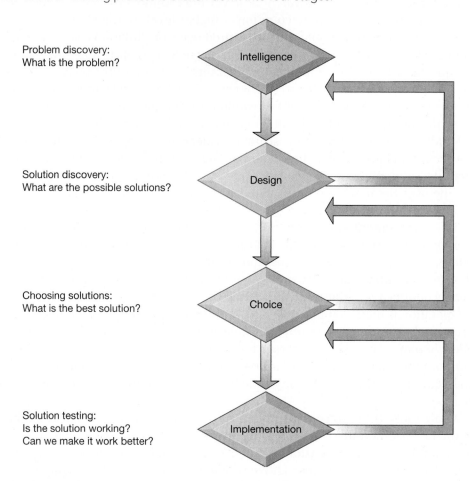

Problem discovery:
What is the problem?

Solution discovery:
What are the possible solutions?

Choosing solutions:
What is the best solution?

Solution testing:
Is the solution working?
Can we make it work better?

poor product design, inadequate customer support, or a host of other causes that call for a different solution.

12-2 How do information systems support the activities of managers and management decision making?

The premise of this book and this chapter is that systems to support decision making produce better decision making by managers and employees, above-average returns on investment for the firm, and ultimately higher profitability. However, information systems cannot improve every decision taking place in an organization. Let's examine the role of managers and decision making in organizations to see why this is so.

Managerial Roles

Managers play key roles in organizations. Their responsibilities range from making decisions, to writing reports, to attending meetings, to arranging birthday parties. We are able to better understand managerial functions and roles by examining classical and contemporary models of managerial behavior.

The **classical model of management**, which describes what managers do, was largely unquestioned for more than 70 years after the 1920s. Henri Fayol and other early writers first described the five classical functions of managers as planning, organizing, coordinating, deciding, and controlling. This description of management activities dominated management thought for a long time, and it is still popular today.

The classical model describes formal managerial functions but does not address exactly what managers do when they plan, decide things, and control the work of others. For this, we must turn to the work of contemporary behavioral scientists who have studied managers in daily action. **Behavioral models** argue that the actual behavior of managers appears to be less systematic, more informal, less reflective, more reactive, and less well organized than the classical model would have us believe.

Observers find that managerial behavior actually has five attributes that differ greatly from the classical description. First, managers perform a great deal of work at an unrelenting pace — studies have found that managers engage in more than 600 different activities each day, with no break in their pace. There is never enough time to do everything for which a CEO is responsible (Porter and Nohria, 2018). Second, managerial activities are fragmented; most activities last for less than nine minutes, and only 10 percent of the activities exceed one hour in duration. Third, managers prefer current, specific, and ad hoc information (printed information often will be too old). Fourth, they prefer oral forms of communication to written forms because oral media provide greater flexibility, require less effort, and bring a faster response. Fifth, managers give high priority to maintaining a diverse and complex web of contacts that acts as an informal information system and helps them execute their personal agendas and short- and long-term goals.

Analyzing managers' day-to-day behavior, Henry Mintzberg found that it could be classified into 10 managerial roles (Mintzberg, 1971). **Managerial roles** are expectations of the activities that managers should perform in an organization. Mintzberg found that these managerial roles fell into three categories: interpersonal, informational, and decisional.

Interpersonal Roles

Managers act as figureheads for the organization when they represent their companies to the outside world and perform symbolic duties, such as giving out employee awards, in their **interpersonal role**. Managers act as leaders, attempting to motivate, counsel, and support subordinates. Managers also act as liaisons between various organizational levels; within each of these levels, they serve as liaisons among the members of the management team. Managers provide time and favors, which they expect to be returned.

Informational Roles

In their **informational role**, managers act as the nerve centers of their organizations, receiving the most concrete, up-to-date information and redistributing it to those who need to be aware of it. Managers are therefore information disseminators and spokespersons for their organizations.

Decisional Roles

Managers make decisions. In their **decisional role**, they act as entrepreneurs by initiating new kinds of activities, they handle disturbances arising in the organization, they allocate resources to staff members who need them, and they negotiate conflicts and mediate between conflicting groups.

TABLE 12.2 MANAGERIAL ROLES AND SUPPORTING INFORMATION SYSTEMS

ROLE	BEHAVIOR	SUPPORT SYSTEMS
INTERPERSONAL ROLES		
Figurehead		Telepresence systems
Leader	Interpersonal	Telepresence, social networks, Twitter
Liaison		Smartphones, social networks
INFORMATIONAL ROLES		
Nerve center		Management information systems, executive support system
Disseminator	Information	Texting, email, social networks
Spokesperson	processing	Webinars, telepresence
DECISIONAL ROLES		
Entrepreneur	Decision	None exist
Disturbance handler	making	None exist
Resource allocator		Business intelligence, decision-support system
Negotiator		None exist

Sources: Authors and Mintzberg, Henry. "Managerial Work: Analysis from Observation." Management Science 18 (October 1971).

Table 12.2, based on Mintzberg's role classifications, is one look at where systems can and cannot help managers. The table shows that information systems are now capable of supporting most, but not all, areas of managerial life.

Real-World Decision Making

We now see that information systems are not helpful for all managerial roles. And in those managerial roles where information systems might improve decisions, investments in information technology do not always produce positive results. There are three main reasons: information quality, management filters, and organizational culture (see Chapter 3).

Information Quality

High-quality decisions require high-quality information. Table 12.3 describes information quality dimensions that affect the quality of decisions.

If the output of information systems does not meet these quality criteria, decision making will suffer. Chapter 6 describes how corporate databases and files have varying levels of inaccuracy and incompleteness, which in turn will degrade the quality of decision making.

TABLE 12.3 INFORMATION QUALITY DIMENSIONS

QUALITY DIMENSION	DESCRIPTION
Accuracy	Do the data represent reality?
Integrity	Are the structure of data and relationships among the entities and attributes consistent?
Consistency	Are data elements consistently defined?
Completeness	Are all the necessary data present?
Validity	Do data values fall within defined ranges?
Timeliness	Are data available when needed?
Accessibility	Are the data accessible, comprehensible, and usable?

Management Filters

Even with timely, accurate information, managers often make bad decisions. Managers (like all human beings) absorb information through a series of filters to make sense of the world around them. Cognitive scientists, behavioral economists, and recently neuro-economists have found that managers, like other humans, are poor at assessing risk, and are risk averse; perceive patterns where none exist; and make decisions based on intuition, feelings, and the framing of the problem as opposed to empirical data (Kahneman, 2011; Tversky and Kahneman, 1986).

For instance, Wall Street firms such as Bear Stearns and Lehman Brothers imploded in 2008 because they underestimated the risk of their investments in complex mortgage securities, many of which were based on subprime loans that were more likely to default. The computer models they and other financial institutions used to manage risk were based on overly optimistic assumptions and overly simplistic data about what might go wrong. Management wanted to make sure that their firms' capital was not all tied up as a cushion against defaults from risky investments, preventing them from investing it to generate profits. So the designers of these risk management systems were encouraged to measure risks in a way that minimized their risk.

Organizational Inertia and Politics

Organizations are bureaucracies with limited capabilities and competencies for acting decisively. When environments change and businesses need to adopt new business models to survive, strong forces within organizations resist making decisions calling for major change. Decisions taken by a firm often represent a balancing of the firm's various interest groups rather than the best solution to the problem.

Studies of business restructuring find that firms tend to ignore poor performance until threatened by outside takeovers, and they systematically blame poor performance on external forces beyond their control—such as economic conditions (the economy), foreign competition, and rising prices—rather than blaming senior or middle management for poor business judgment. When the external business environment is positive and firm performance improves, managers typically credit themselves for the improved performance rather than the positive environment.

High-Velocity Automated Decision Making

Today, many decisions made by organizations are not made by managers—or any humans. For instance, when you enter a query into Google's search engine, Google has to decide which URLs to display in about half a second on average (500 milliseconds). High-frequency traders at electronic stock exchanges execute their trades in under 30 milliseconds.

In high-velocity decision environments, the intelligence, design, choice, and implementation parts of the decision-making process are captured by the software's algorithms. The humans who wrote the software have already identified the problem, designed a method for finding a solution, defined a range of acceptable solutions, and implemented a solution. Obviously, with humans out of the loop, great care needs to be taken to ensure the proper operation of these systems to prevent significant harm.

Organizations in these areas are making decisions faster than what managers can monitor or control. The past few years have seen a series of breakdowns in computerized trading systems, including one on August 1, 2012, when a software error caused Knight Capital to enter millions of faulty trades in less than an hour. The trading glitch created wild surges and plunges in nearly 150 stocks and left Knight with $440 million in losses.

12-3 How do business intelligence and business analytics support decision making?

Chapter 2 introduced you to the different types of systems used for supporting management decision making. At the foundation of all of these decision support systems are a business intelligence and business analytics infrastructure that supplies the data and the analytic tools for supporting decision making.

What Is Business Intelligence?

Business intelligence (BI) is a term used by hardware and software vendors and information technology consultants to describe the infrastructure for warehousing, integrating, reporting, and analyzing data that come from the business environment, including big data. The foundation infrastructure collects, stores, cleans, and makes relevant information available to managers. Think databases, data warehouses, data marts, Hadoop, and analytic platforms, which we described in Chapter 6. *Business analytics (BA)* is also a vendor-defined term that focuses more on tools and techniques for analyzing and understanding data. Think online analytical processing (OLAP), statistics, models, and data mining, which we also introduced in Chapter 6.

Business intelligence and analytics are essentially about integrating all the information streams produced by a firm into a single, coherent, enterprise-wide set of data and then using modeling, statistical analysis tools, and data mining tools to make sense out of all these data so managers can make better decisions and plans. Purdue College of Agriculture, described in the chapter-opening case, is using business intelligence and analytics to help farmers make some very fine-grained decisions about fertilizer levels, planting depth, and irrigation requirements for small sections of fields or individual plants.

It is important to remember that business intelligence and analytics are products defined by technology vendors and consulting firms. Leading providers of these products include Oracle, SAP, IBM, Microsoft, and SAS. A number of BI and BA products now have cloud and mobile versions.

The Business Intelligence Environment

Figure 12.3 gives an overview of a business intelligence environment, highlighting the kinds of hardware, software, and management capabilities that the major vendors offer and that firms develop over time. There are six elements in this business intelligence environment:

- **Data from the business environment:** Businesses must deal with both structured and unstructured data from many different sources, including big data. The data need to be integrated and organized so that they can be analyzed and used by human decision makers.

- **Business intelligence infrastructure:** The underlying foundation of business intelligence is a powerful database system that captures all the relevant data to operate the business. The data may be stored in transactional

> **FIGURE 12.3**　**BUSINESS INTELLIGENCE AND ANALYTICS FOR DECISION SUPPORT**

Business intelligence and analytics require a strong database foundation, a set of analytic tools, and an involved management team that can ask intelligent questions and analyze data.

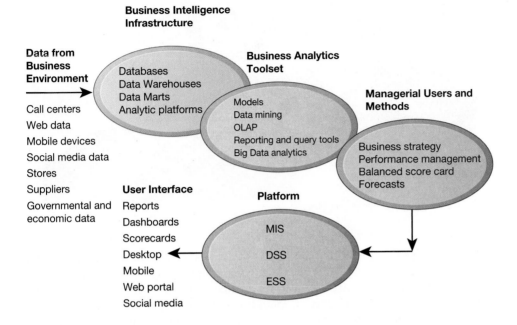

databases or combined and integrated into an enterprise data warehouse or series of interrelated data marts.

- **Business analytics toolset:** A set of software tools are used to analyze data and produce reports, respond to questions posed by managers, and track the progress of the business using key indicators of performance.

- **Managerial users and methods:** Business intelligence hardware and software are only as intelligent as the human beings who use them. Managers impose order on the analysis of data using a variety of managerial methods that define strategic business goals and specify how progress will be measured. These include business performance management and balanced scorecard approaches focusing on key performance indicators and industry strategic analyses focusing on changes in the general business environment, with special attention to competitors. Without strong senior management oversight, business analytics can produce a great deal of information, reports, and online screens that focus on the wrong matters and divert attention from the real issues.

- **Delivery platform—MIS, DSS, ESS:** The results from business intelligence and analytics are delivered to managers and employees in a variety of ways, depending on what they need to know to perform their jobs. MIS, DSS, and ESS, which we introduced in Chapter 2, deliver information and knowledge to different people and levels in the firm—operational employees, middle managers, and senior executives. In the past, these systems could not share data and operated as independent systems. Today, one suite of hardware and software tools in the form of a business intelligence and analytics package is able to integrate all this information and bring it to managers' desktops or mobile platforms.

- **User interface:** Business people often learn quicker from a visual representation of data than from a dry report with columns and rows of information. Today's business analytics software suites feature **data visualization** tools, such as rich graphs, charts, dashboards, and maps. They also are able to

Data visualization tools facilitate creation of graphs, charts, dashboards, and maps to make it easier for users to obtain insights from data.

© NicoElNino/Shutterstock

deliver reports on mobile phones and tablets as well as on the firm's web portal. For example, Tableau Software enables non-technical users to easily create and share customized interactive dashboards to provide business insights from a broad spectrum of data, including data from spreadsheets, corporate databases, and the web. Another example is the process mining software used by Siemens AG to visualize and analyze its business processes (see the Interactive Session on Technology). BA software is adding capabilities to post information on Twitter, Facebook, or internal social media to support decision making in an online group setting rather than in a face-to-face meeting.

Business Intelligence and Analytics Capabilities

Business intelligence and analytics promise to deliver correct, nearly real-time information to decision makers, and the analytic tools help them quickly understand the information and take action. There are six analytic functionalities that BI systems deliver to achieve these ends:

- **Production reports:** These are predefined reports based on industry-specific requirements (see Table 12.4).
- **Parameterized reports:** Users enter several parameters as in a pivot table to filter data and isolate impacts of parameters. For instance, you might want to

TABLE 12.4   EXAMPLES OF BUSINESS INTELLIGENCE PREDEFINED PRODUCTION REPORTS

BUSINESS FUNCTIONAL AREA	PRODUCTION REPORTS
Sales	Forecast sales; sales team performance; cross-selling; sales cycle times
Service/call center	Customer satisfaction; service cost; resolution rates; churn rates
Marketing	Campaign effectiveness; loyalty and attrition; market basket analysis
Procurement and support	Direct and indirect spending; off-contract purchases; supplier performance
Supply chain	Backlog; fulfillment status; order cycle time; bill of materials analysis
Financials	General ledger; accounts receivable and payable; cash flow; profitability
Human resources	Employee productivity; compensation; workforce demographics; retention

INTERACTIVE SESSION TECHNOLOGY

Siemens Makes Business Processes More Visible

Siemens AG is a German manufacturing conglomerate that produces systems and components for industrial automation, healthcare, energy, building, and transportation markets. The company is headquartered in Munich and Berlin, with 372,000 employees worldwide, and global revenue of €83 billion (approximately U.S. $99 billion) in fiscal 2017. Siemens is the largest industrial manufacturing company in Europe, with branch offices abroad. This is clearly a company that prizes innovation and continuous improvement of the efficiency and quality of its business processes.

Siemens has thousands of business processes, some of which are very complex. Management was seeking better ways of making the business more efficient and turned to business process mining technology. In 2014 the company established a unit called Process DAsh (which stands for Data Analytics, smart handling) to actively support global process optimization in all Siemens divisions. It started collecting and analyzing ERP data to identify bottlenecks in its production, delivery, and payment processes using Celonis Process Mining analysis and visualization software for this purpose. Celonis partners with SAP, and its software runs on the SAP HANA in-memory database platform.

Process mining software analyzes data in enterprise application event logs to determine how business processes are actually working in order to identify bottlenecks and other areas of inefficiency so that they can be improved. The technology can analyze millions of transaction records and spot deviations from normal workflows. A push of a button produces a snapshot of an entire business process. Process DAsh used the Celonis software to take all the individual data in a large number of information systems and use them to construct logical models of existing business processes and automatically visualize them. The software documents actual processes in real time, as the sequence of events is taking place.

When process mining software is used to analyze the transaction logs of an ERP or CRM system, data visualization capabilities in the software can show users what processes are running at any given time. An organization might use process mining software to find the cause of unexpected delays in invoice processing by examining the logs of the accounts payable module in its ERP system. Users can see at a glance where inefficiencies occur through bottlenecks, unnecessary detours, and manual interventions, or where compliance issues might arise. Some process mining software, including Celonis, enables users to drill down to view the individual documents associated with a process.

Celonis has capabilities for comparing users' target operating models to the as-is process, providing an automated fit-gap analysis. Celonis analyzes root causes for deviations and performance loss, highlighting the issues which have the greatest impact on process performance. At the touch of a button, the user can see a comparison between the target and actual process and also visualize the main cause of delays and additional expenditure.

If a process model doesn't already exist, the software will try to create one automatically, sometimes using artificial intelligence techniques such as machine learning (see Chapter 11). If a process model is available, the process mining software will compare it to the event log to identify discrepancies and their possible causes. For process modeling, Siemens uses a Celonis tool called Pi Conformance and Machine Learning. The software predicts which customer orders are likely to arrive late using algorithms that continuously learn from Siemens' performance.

Siemens started using Celonis analysis and visualization tools to learn how quickly it pays its suppliers. Some suppliers offer discounts for early payment. Siemens was often unable to take advantage of these discounts because it was unable to pay quickly enough. The company used process mining to analyze data from its ERP, accounting, and payment approval systems to understand why this was happening. Siemens also used process mining to study inefficiencies in the way it takes orders from and is paid by its customers (order-to-cash processes).

Before implementing the Celonis software, Siemens had to manage its business processes manually. Individual supervisors were responsible for specific processes. When things did not go as planned, such as when a machine broke down or a parts shipment arrived late, there was no easy way to determine exactly how these occurrences impacted overall operations.

There was some resistance to process mining among some long-term Siemens managers who thought they already knew how to handle processes efficiently. Lars Reinkemeyer, head of Siemens global process mining services, was able to promote analytics adoption by identifying individuals who were receptive to process mining and enlisting them to promote the new technology. Since Siemens AG implemented process mining, it has been able to identify slowdowns in parts procurement, late

product deliveries, and billing inefficiencies that were costing the company millions of dollars. Siemens AG now has over 2,500 users of Process DAsh worldwide.

Sources: Lindsay Clark, "Siemens Success Sets the Scene for Growth in Process Mining," *Computer Weekly*, April 12, 2018; Julian Baumann, "Siemens Is the World's Biggest User of Process Mining," www.celonis.com, accessed April 22, 2018; "Success Story Siemens," www.celonis.com, accessed April 22, 2018; Margaret Rouse, "Process Mining Software," searchERP.com, Jun 30, 2017; and Ed Burns, "Siemens Uses Process Mining Software to Improve Manufacturing Visibility," SearchBusinessAnalytics.com, December 15, 2016.

CASE STUDY QUESTIONS

1. Identify the problem in this case study. What management, organization, and technology factors contributed to the problem?

2. Describe the capabilities of process mining software. Was this an effective solution? Explain your answer.

3. How did process mining change decision making at Siemens?

4. What management, organization, and technology issues need to be addressed when implementing process mining systems?

enter region and time of day to understand how sales of a product vary by region and time. If you were Starbucks, you might find that customers in the East buy most of their coffee in the morning, whereas in the Northwest customers buy coffee throughout the day. This finding might lead to different marketing and ad campaigns in each region. (See the discussion of pivot tables in Section 12.4.)

- **Dashboards/scorecards:** These are visual tools for presenting performance data defined by users.
- **Ad hoc query/search/report creation:** These allow users to create their own reports based on queries and searches.
- **Drill down:** This is the ability to move from a high-level summary to a more detailed view.
- **Forecasts, scenarios, models:** These include the ability to perform linear forecasting and what-if scenario analysis and analyze data using standard statistical tools.

Predictive Analytics

An important capability of business intelligence analytics is the ability to model future events and behaviors, such as the probability that a customer will respond to an offer to purchase a product. **Predictive analytics** use statistical analysis, data mining techniques, historical data, and assumptions about future conditions to predict future trends and behavior patterns. Variables that can be measured to predict future behavior are identified. For example, an insurance company might use variables such as age, gender, and driving record as predictors of driving safety when issuing auto insurance policies. A collection of such predictors is combined into a predictive model for forecasting future probabilities with an acceptable level of reliability.

FedEx has been using predictive analytics to develop models that predict how customers will respond to price changes and new services, which customers are most at risk of switching to competitors, and how much revenue will be generated by new storefront or drop-box locations. The accuracy rate of FedEx's predictive analytics system ranges from 65 to 90 percent.

Predictive analytics are being incorporated into numerous business intelligence applications for sales, marketing, finance, fraud detection, and healthcare. One of the most well-known applications is credit scoring, which is used throughout the financial services industry. When you apply for a new credit card, scoring models process your credit history, loan application, and purchase data to determine your likelihood of making future credit payments on time. Healthcare insurers have been analyzing data for years to identify which patients are most likely to generate high costs.

Many companies employ predictive analytics to predict response to direct marketing campaigns. They are able to lower their marketing and sales costs by focusing their resources on customers who have been identified as more promising. For instance, Slack Technologies, which provides cloud-based team collaboration tools and services for 6.8 million active users, uses predictive analytics to identify customers who are most likely to use its products very frequently and upgrade to its paid services (McDonough, 2017).

Big Data Analytics

Predictive analytics are starting to use big data from both private and public sectors, including data from social media, customer transactions, and output from sensors and machines. In e-commerce, many online retailers have capabilities for making personalized online product recommendations to their website visitors to help stimulate purchases and guide their decisions about what merchandise to stock. However, most of these product recommendations have been based on the behaviors of similar groups of customers, such as those with incomes under $50,000 or whose ages are between 18 and 25 years. Now some retailers are starting to analyze the tremendous quantities of online and in-store customer data they collect along with social media data to make these recommendations more individualized. These efforts are translating into higher customer spending and customer retention rates. Table 12.5 provides examples of companies using big data analytics.

TABLE 12.5 WHAT BIG DATA ANALYTICS CAN DO

Bank of America	Able to analyze all of its 50 million customers at once to understand each customer across all channels and interactions and present consistent, finely customized offers. Can determine which of its customers has a credit card or a mortgage loan that could benefit from refinancing at a competitor. When the customer visits BofA online, calls a call center, or visits a branch, that information is available for the online app or sales associate to present BofA's competing offer.
Vestas Wind Systems	Improves wind turbine placement for optimal energy output using IBM BigInsights software and an IBM supercomputer to analyze 2.8 petabytes of structured and unstructured data such as weather reports, tidal phases, geospatial and sensor data, satellite images, deforestation maps, and weather modeling research. The analysis, which used to take weeks, can now be completed in less than one hour.
Hunch.com	Analyzes massive database with data from customer purchases, social networks, and signals from around the web to produce a "taste graph" that maps users with their predicted affinity to products, services, and websites. The taste graph includes predictions about 500 million people, 200 million objects (videos, gadgets, books), and 30 billion connections between people and objects. Helps eBay develop more finely customized recommendations on items to offer.
German World Cup Soccer Team	Analyzed very large amounts of video and numeric data about individual player and team performance on itself and competing teams and then used what it had learned to improve how it played and to capitalize on competitors' strengths and weaknesses. Superior use of big data analytics helped the team win the 2014 World Cup.

In the public sector, big data analytics have been driving the movement toward "smart cities," which make intensive use of digital technology to make better decisions about running cities and serving their residents. Public record-keeping has produced warehouses full of property transfers, tax records, corporate filings, environmental compliance audits, restaurant inspections, building maintenance reports, mass transit appraisals, crime data, health department stats, public education records, utility reviews, and more. Municipalities are adding more data captured through sensors, location data from mobile phones, and targeted smartphone apps. Predictive modeling programs now inform public policy decisions on utility management, transportation operation, healthcare delivery, and public safety. What's more, the ability to evaluate how changes in one service affect the operation and delivery of other services enables holistic problem solving that could only be dreamed of a generation ago.

Operational Intelligence and Analytics

Many decisions deal with how to run the business of these cities on a day-to-day basis. These are largely operational decisions, and this type of business activity monitoring is called **operational intelligence**. The Internet of Things is creating huge streams of data from web activities, smartphones, sensors, gauges, and monitoring devices that can be used for operational intelligence about activities inside and outside the organization. Software for operational intelligence and analytics enables organizations to analyze these streams of big data as they are generated in real time. The data-driven farming systems described in the chapter-opening case are one example of operational intelligence. Another is the use of data generated by sensors on trucks, trailers, and intermodal containers owned by Schneider National, one of North America's largest truckload, logistics, and intermodal services providers. The sensors monitor location, driving behaviors, fuel levels, and whether a trailer or container is loaded or empty. Data from fuel tank sensors help Schneider identify the optimal location at which a driver should stop for fuel based on how much is left in the tank, the truck's destination, and fuel prices en route. The chapter-ending case describes how General Electric (GE) is using operational intelligence to monitor and analyze the performance of generators, jet engines, locomotives, and oil-refining gear and to connect these devices to the cloud.

Location Analytics and Geographic Information Systems

Decisions are also based on location data. BI analytics include **location analytics**, the ability to gain business insight from the location (geographic) component of data, including location data from mobile phones, output from sensors or scanning devices, and data from maps. For example, location analytics might help a marketer determine which people to target with mobile ads about nearby restaurants and stores or quantify the impact of mobile ads on in-store visits. Location analytics would help a utility company view and measure outages and their associated costs as related to customer location to help prioritize marketing, system upgrades, and customer service efforts. UPS's package tracking and delivery-routing systems described in Chapter 1 use location analytics, as does an application used by Starbucks to determine where to open new stores. The Starbucks system analyzes very large amounts of location-based data and demographic data to determine the best places to open more stores without harming sales at other Starbucks locations. A user can see on a map local trade areas, retail clusters, demographics, traffic and transportation nodes, and locations with new offices that might be important sources of customers.

Courtesy of U.S. National Oceanic and Atmospheric Administration (NOAA) Office for Coastal Management

The U.S. National Oceanic and Atmospheric Administration (NOAA) Office for Coastal Management provides a web mapping tool to visualize community-level impacts from coastal flooding or sea level rise up to 6 feet above average high tides. Photo simulations of how future flooding might impact local landmarks are also provided, as well as data related to water depth, connectivity, flood frequency, socio-economic vulnerability, and wetland loss and migration.

The Starbucks application is an example of a **geographic information system (GIS)**. GIS provide tools to help decision makers visualize problems that benefit from mapping. GIS software ties location data about the distribution of people or other resources to points, lines, and areas on a map. Some GIS have modeling capabilities for changing the data and automatically revising business scenarios.

GIS might be used to help state and local governments calculate response times to natural disasters and other emergencies, to help banks identify the best location for new branches or ATM terminals, or to help police forces pinpoint locations with the highest incidence of crime.

12-4 How do different decision-making constituencies in an organization use business intelligence, and what is the role of information systems in helping people working in a group make decisions more efficiently?

Earlier in this text and in this chapter, we described the different information constituencies in business firms—from senior managers to middle managers, analysts, and operational employees. This also holds true for BI and BA systems (see Figure 12.4). More than 80 percent of the audience for BI consists of casual users who rely largely on production reports. Senior executives tend to use BI to monitor firm activities using visual interfaces like dashboards and scorecards. Middle managers and analysts are much more likely to be immersed in the data and software, entering queries and slicing and dicing the data along different dimensions. Operational employees will, along with customers and suppliers, be looking mostly at prepackaged reports.

Decision Support for Operational and Middle Management

Operational and middle management are generally charged with monitoring the performance of key aspects of the business, ranging from the downtime of machines on a factory floor to the daily or even hourly sales at franchise food

FIGURE 12.4 BUSINESS INTELLIGENCE USERS

Casual users are consumers of BI output, while intense power users are the producers of reports, new analyses, models, and forecasts.

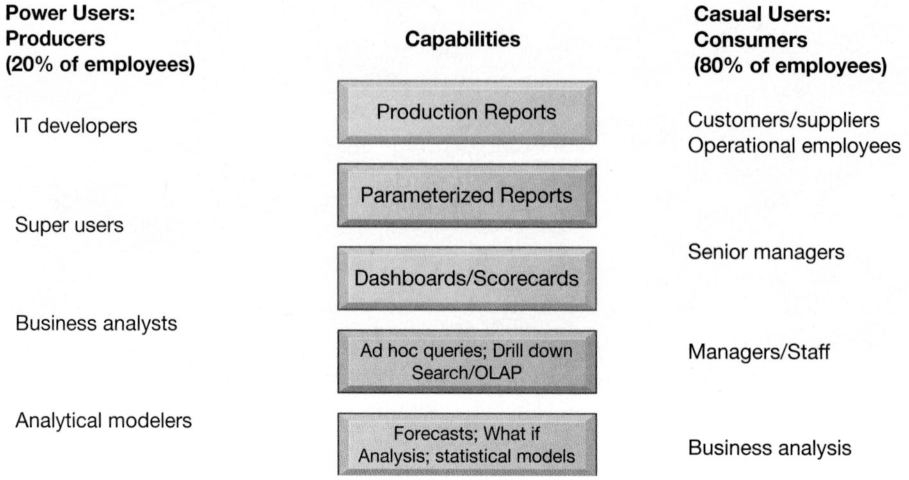

Power Users: Producers (20% of employees)	Capabilities	Casual Users: Consumers (80% of employees)
IT developers	Production Reports	Customers/suppliers Operational employees
Super users	Parameterized Reports	
	Dashboards/Scorecards	Senior managers
Business analysts	Ad hoc queries; Drill down Search/OLAP	Managers/Staff
Analytical modelers	Forecasts; What if Analysis; statistical models	Business analysis

stores to the daily traffic at a company's website. Most of the decisions these managers make are fairly structured. Management information systems (MIS), which we introduced in Chapter 2, are typically used by middle managers to support this type of decision making. Increasingly, middle managers receive these reports online and are able to interactively query the data to find out why events are happening. Managers at this level often turn to exception reports, which highlight only exceptional conditions, such as when the sales quotas for a specific territory fall below an anticipated level or employees have exceeded their spending limits in a dental care plan. Table 12.6 provides some examples of MIS for business intelligence.

Support for Semi-structured Decisions

Some managers are "super users" and keen business analysts who want to create their own reports and use more sophisticated analytics and models to find patterns in data, to model alternative business scenarios, or to test specific hypotheses. Decision-support systems (DSS) are the BI delivery platform for this category of users, with the ability to support semi-structured decision making.

DSS rely more heavily on modeling than MIS, using mathematical or analytical models to perform what-if or other kinds of analysis. "What-if" analysis, working forward from known or assumed conditions, allows the user to vary certain values in test results to predict outcomes if changes occur in those

TABLE 12.6 EXAMPLES OF MIS APPLICATIONS

COMPANY	MIS APPLICATION
California Pizza Kitchen	Inventory Express application "remembers" each restaurant's ordering patterns and compares the amount of ingredients used per menu item to predefined portion measurements established by management. The system identifies restaurants with out-of-line portions and notifies their managers so that corrective actions will be taken.
Black & Veatch	Intranet MIS tracks construction costs for various projects across the United States.
Taco Bell	Total Automation of Company Operations (TACO) system provides information on food, labor, and period-to-date costs for each restaurant.

FIGURE 12.5   SENSITIVITY ANALYSIS

This figure displays the results of a sensitivity analysis of the effect of changing the sales price of a necktie and the cost per unit on the product's break-even point. It answers the question: What happens to the break-even point if the sales price and the cost to make each unit increase or decrease?

Total fixed costs	19000					
Variable cost per unit	3					
Average sales price	17					
Contribution margin	14					
Break-even point	1357					
			Variable Cost per Unit			
Sales	1357	**2**	**3**	**4**	**5**	**6**
Price	14	1583	1727	1900	2111	2375
	15	1462	1583	1727	1900	2111
	16	1357	1462	1583	1727	1900
	17	1267	1357	1462	1583	1727
	18	1188	1267	1357	1462	1583

values. What happens if we raise product prices by 5 percent or increase the advertising budget by $1 million? **Sensitivity analysis** models ask what-if questions repeatedly to predict a range of outcomes when one or more variables are changed multiple times (see Figure 12.5). Backward sensitivity analysis helps decision makers with goal seeking: If I want to sell 1 million product units next year, how much must I reduce the price of the product?

Chapter 6 described multidimensional data analysis and OLAP as key business intelligence technologies. Spreadsheets have a similar feature for multidimensional analysis called a **pivot table**, which manager "super users" and analysts employ to identify and understand patterns in business information that may be useful for semi-structured decision making.

Figure 12.6 illustrates a Microsoft Excel pivot table that examines a large list of order transactions for a company selling online management training videos

FIGURE 12.6   A PIVOT TABLE THAT EXAMINES CUSTOMER REGIONAL DISTRIBUTION AND ADVERTISING SOURCE

In this pivot table, we are able to examine where an online training company's customers come from in terms of region and advertising source.

Courtesy of Microsoft Corporation

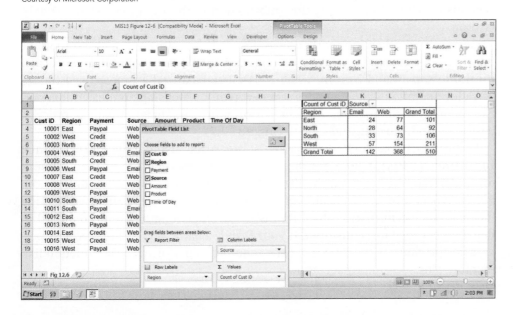

and books. It shows the relationship between two dimensions: the sales region and the source of contact (web banner ad or e-mail) for each customer order. It answers the question: Does the source of the customer make a difference in addition to region? The pivot table in this figure shows that most customers come from the West and that banner advertising produces most of the customers in all the regions.

One of the Hands-On MIS projects for this chapter asks you to use a pivot table to find answers to a number of other questions using the same list of transactions for the online training company as we used in this discussion. The complete Excel file for these transactions is available in MyLab MIS. We also provide a Learning Track on creating pivot tables using Excel.

In the past, much of this modeling was done with spreadsheets and small stand-alone databases. Today these capabilities are incorporated into large enterprise BI systems where they are able to analyze data from large corporate databases. BI analytics include tools for intensive modeling, some of which we described earlier. Such capabilities help Progressive Insurance identify the best customers for its products. Using widely available insurance industry data, Progressive defines small groups of customers, or "cells," such as motorcycle riders age 30 or above with college educations, credit scores over a certain level, and no accidents. For each "cell," Progressive performs a regression analysis to identify factors most closely correlated with the insurance losses that are typical for this group. It then sets prices for each cell and uses simulation software to test whether this pricing arrangement will enable the company to make a profit. These analytic techniques make it possible for Progressive to profitably insure customers in traditionally high-risk categories that other insurers would have rejected.

Decision Support for Senior Management: Balanced Scorecard and Enterprise Performance Management Methods

The purpose of executive support systems (ESS), introduced in Chapter 2, is to help C-level executive managers focus on the really important performance information that affects the overall profitability and success of the firm. There are two parts to developing ESS. First, you will need a methodology for understanding exactly what is "the really important performance information" for a specific firm that executives need, and second, you will need to develop systems capable of delivering this information to the right people in a timely fashion.

Currently, the leading methodology for understanding the really important information needed by a firm's executives is called the **balanced scorecard method** (Kaplan and Norton, 1992, 2004). The balanced scorecard is a framework for operationalizing a firm's strategic plan by focusing on measurable outcomes on four dimensions of firm performance: financial, business process, customer, and learning and growth (Figure 12.7).

Performance on each dimension is measured using **key performance indicators (KPIs)**, which are the measures proposed by senior management for understanding how well the firm is performing along any given dimension. For instance, one key indicator of how well an online retail firm is meeting its customer performance objectives is the average length of time required to deliver a package to a consumer. If your firm is a bank, one KPI of business process performance is the length of time required to perform a basic function like creating a new customer account.

FIGURE 12.7   THE BALANCED SCORECARD FRAMEWORK

In the balanced scorecard framework, the firm's strategic objectives are operationalized along four dimensions: financial, business process, customer, and learning and growth. Each dimension is measured using several KPIs.

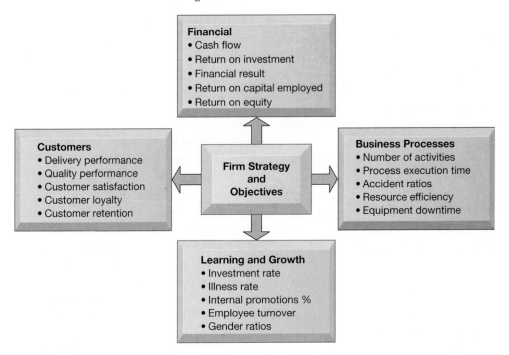

The balanced scorecard framework is thought to be "balanced" because it causes managers to focus on more than just financial performance. In this view, financial performance is past history—the result of past actions—and managers should focus on the things they are able to influence today, such as business process efficiency, customer satisfaction, and employee training. Once a scorecard is developed by consultants and senior executives, the next step is automating a flow of information to executives and other managers for each of the key performance indicators (see the Interactive Session on Management). Once these systems are implemented, they are often referred to as ESS.

Another closely related popular management methodology is **business performance management (BPM)**. Originally defined by an industry group in 2004 (led by the same companies that sell enterprise and database systems like Oracle, SAP, and IBM), BPM attempts to systematically translate a firm's strategies (e.g., differentiation, low-cost producer, market share growth, and scope of operation) into operational targets. Once the strategies and targets are identified, a set of KPIs are developed that measure progress toward the targets. The firm's performance is then measured with information drawn from the firm's enterprise database systems. BPM uses the same ideas as the balanced scorecard but with a stronger strategy flavor.

Corporate data for contemporary ESS are supplied by the firm's existing enterprise applications (enterprise resource planning, supply chain management, and customer relationship management). ESS also provide access to news services, financial market databases, economic information, and whatever other external data senior executives require. ESS also have significant **drill-down** capabilities if managers need more detailed views of data.

INTERACTIVE SESSION   MANAGEMENT

Anthem Benefits from More Business Intelligence

Anthem Inc. is one of the largest health benefit companies in the United States. One in eight Americans receives coverage for their medical care through Anthem's affiliated plans. Anthem also offers a broad range of medical and specialty products, such as life and disability insurance benefits; dental, vision, and behavioral health services; and long-term care insurance and flexible spending accounts. Anthem is headquartered in Indianapolis, Indiana and earned over $90 billion in revenue in 2017.

Anthem has been an industry leader in analyzing data to reduce fraud and waste, cultivate customers, fine-tune its products, and keep healthcare costs low. For example, the company analyzes the data it collects on benefit claims, clinical data, electronic health records, lab results, and call centers to determine each person's risk for an emergency room visit or a stroke. This information helps the company identify opportunities for improvement and individuals who might benefit from additional services or wellness coaching.

Now Anthem is applying its analytical skills internally to sharpen decisions about how to deploy and develop its employees as a strategic resource. Anthem has 56,000 employees and would like better answers to these questions: What is our employee turnover rate for call center staff in Colorado Springs or across the United States? What is the cost of that turnover? Are we differentiating rewards for our top performers? How many of our nurses might retire within the next couple of years? What is the relationship between our time-to-hire metrics and national unemployment rates?

Anthem created a cloud-based People Data Central (PDC) portal, whose interactive "workforce intelligence" dashboard lets HR and other Anthem users access and ask questions such as these using internal and third-party data. The portal serves 56,000 employees and presents data in dashboards, graphs, reports, and other highly visual formats that are easy to comprehend and manipulate.

A high-level "executive scorecard" feature explores the relationship between Human Resources metrics and business outcomes to use in short- and long-term planning. One scorecard report showed the relationship between customer growth, Anthem's net hire

ratio, and total costs associated with internal and external labor. PDC provides a total of seven dashboards on "hire-to-retire" HR operations, 50 summary views from which users can drill down into detailed reports, and links to other relevant data and training sources.

The company also formed a Talent Insights team, whose members include MBAs, PhDs, and CPAs, to develop more sophisticated data analysis and help users work with the data. For example, the Talent Insights team worked with Anthem's Wellness team to examine data on employees who utilize company wellness credits to determine whether this could be correlated with reduced absenteeism and employee turnover. Every month, the team looks at a different slice of data using various indicators such as company performance, employee participation in wellness programs, or reductions in absenteeism. For example, one month the team broke down Anthem's workforce by generational age bands and examined the potential ramifications for company performance, highlighting its analysis in the portal's "insight spotlight" section.

The PDC uses Oracle Human Capital Management (HCM) Cloud and Oracle Business Intelligence Cloud Service. Oracle HCM Cloud is the cloud-based version of Oracle tools for Human Capital Management (human resources management), including tools for talent management and workforce management. Oracle Business Intelligence Cloud Service provides powerful data analytics tools as a cloud service that is available to anyone in the enterprise. The service includes tools for ad hoc query and analysis, interactive dashboards, and reports. Anthem's Oracle-based cloud platform took less than six months to deploy.

Anthem's human resources and talent data used to be scattered among many different systems and spreadsheets, so they were difficult to aggregate and compare. Basic questions such as "What is our turnover rate?" or "How many open positions do we have right now?" produced different answers, depending on who was asked, even within the same location or work group. To improve the HR department's recruiting, hiring, promotion, and employee development programs, Anthem needed better analytic tools and a single standardized enterprise-wide view of its data.

The PDC is able to perform sentiment analysis (see Chapter 6). The portal includes a channel where employees can voice their opinions about their work experiences confidentially, using emojis and limited text entries. The system analyzes these ongoing sentiments to create "team vitals" reports to help management identify and address potential productivity risks. The company often finds information on which it can immediately take action, such as ideas for improving processes or re-prioritizing resources.

The Anthem Talent Insights team is also helping other business groups outside of Human Resources make better use of data. These employees from other functional business areas typically have access only to the data for their business units. Talent

Insights helps them combine these data with HR data so they can answer questions such as how their high-potential employees whose careers are advancing compare with those in other parts of the company. The team developed a model that accurately predicts first-year attrition and identifies the causes of employee turnover. Anthem management is using this information to increase employee retention and create better profiles for future hires.

Sources: Rob Preston, "People Data Central," *Profit Magazine,* Winter 2018; Michael Singer, "Anthem Prescribes Oracle Analytics for Talent Lifecycle," blogs.oracle.com, February 26, 2018; www.antheminc.com, accessed April 24, 2018; and Jennifer Bresnick, "Borrowed from Retail, Anthem's Big Data Analytics Boost Member Engagement," *HealthIT Analytics,* August 4, 2017.

CASE STUDY QUESTIONS

1. Why did Anthem need better data and analytics tools for Human Resources? What management, organization, and technology factors contributed to Anthem's need for better HR data and analytics?

2. Describe the business intelligence capabilities of the PDC portal.

3. What groups in the company benefited from Anthem's new analytics tools? Explain your answer.

4. How did Anthem's new data analytics capabilities change the Human Resources function at the company?

Well-designed ESS help senior executives monitor organizational performance, track activities of competitors, recognize changing market conditions, and identify problems and opportunities. Employees lower down in the corporate hierarchy also use these systems to monitor and measure business performance in their areas of responsibility. For these and other business intelligence systems to be truly useful, the information must be "actionable"—it must be readily available and also easy to use when making decisions. If users have difficulty identifying critical metrics within the reports they receive, employee productivity and business performance will suffer.

Group Decision-Support Systems (GDSS)

The systems we have just described focus primarily on helping you make a decision acting alone. However, what if you are part of a team and need to make a decision as a group? **Group decision-support systems (GDSS)** are available for this purpose. The collaboration environments described in Chapter 2 can be used to help a set of decision makers working together as a group, in the same location or different locations, to solve unstructured problems. Originally, GDSS required dedicated conference rooms with special hardware and software tools to facilitate group decision making. But today GDSS capabilities have evolved along with the power of desktop PCs, the explosion of mobile computing, and the rapid expansion of bandwidth on Wi-Fi and cellular networks. Dedicated rooms for collaboration can be replaced with much less expensive and flexible virtual collaboration rooms that can connect mobile employees with colleagues in the office sitting at desktops in a high-quality video and audio environment.

For example, Cisco's Collaboration Meeting Rooms Hybrid (CMR) allows groups of employees to meet using any device via WebEx video software, which does not require any special network connections, special displays, or complex software. The software to run CMR can be hosted on company servers or in the cloud. The meetings can be scheduled by employees whenever needed. CMR can handle up to 500 participants in a meeting, but that is quite rare. Skype began deploying a similar cloud-based collaboration environment integrated with Microsoft Office called Skype for Business to support online meetings and sharing of documents, audio, and video.

12-5 How will MIS help my career?

Here is how Chapter 12 and this text can help you find a job as an entry-level data analyst.

The Company

Western Well Health, a major provider of healthcare services for the Denver, Colorado metropolitan area, is looking for an entry-level data analyst to perform data analysis and reporting for operational/clinical departments. The company's healthcare network includes 18 hospitals, six senior living communities, urgent care clinics, partner hospitals, and home care and hospice services in Colorado and Western Kansas.

Position Description

The data analyst will be responsible for coordinating a variety of quality and performance measurement initiatives, including satisfaction survey programs, benchmarking and tracking quality of care, clinical outcome performance, and asset utilization. Job responsibilities include:

- Performing data analysis based on SAS data sets, MS Access databases, external websites, and business intelligence platforms to produce reports for key stakeholder groups and decision makers.
- Eliciting data and reporting requirements using interviews, document analysis, requirements workshops, site visits, use cases, data analysis, and workflow analysis.
- Working with staff on the design, maintenance, and distribution of reports and incorporation of reports into the balanced scorecard.
- Analyzing, testing, and modifying databases and reports as needed to meet end user specifications and quality assurance procedures.
- Assisting in enhancing business intelligence reporting tools, dashboards, and mobile BI to improve usability, increase user adoption, and streamline support.

Job Requirements

- Bachelor's degree in Information Systems or Statistics
- Knowledge of Microsoft Access, SQL, and business intelligence tools such as Business Objects, SAS BI, or Tableau

- Data management, analytics, and information system experience preferred
- Some knowledge of the healthcare business and medical record systems desirable
- Project management skills and/or experience desirable

Interview Questions

1. Have you worked with any business intelligence software? Which tools? What is your level of proficiency? Can you give examples of the kinds of data analysis work and reports you used these tools for?

2. In your experience with data analysis and business intelligence, did you ever work with tools that were not as user-friendly as they could have been? What would you have recommended to improve the tool(s) for users?

3. Have you ever developed an analytics report for users from scratch? What BI tools, or tools and data sets, did you use? Can you talk more about how you worked with users to elicit the information requirements for the report?

4. What do you know about the healthcare industry and electronic medical records? Have you ever worked with medical record systems and software? What work did you do with them?

5. Have you ever worked on a project team? What were your responsibilities? Did you play a leadership role?

Author Tips

1. Review the first two sections of this chapter on decision making and also Chapter 6 on data management and Chapter 13 on building systems and information requirements.

2. Use the web to do more research on the company. Try to find out more about its strategy, competitors, and business challenges. Additionally, look at the company's social media channels over the past 12 months. Are there any trends you can identify or certain themes the social media channels seem to focus on?

3. If you don't have experience with the BI software tools required for the job, use the web to learn more about these tools and how other healthcare companies are using them. Go to websites of major consulting companies such as McKinsey & Co., Boston Consulting Group, Bain & Co., and Accenture to read their research articles on how technology is changing the healthcare service industry.

4. Be prepared to bring samples of the querying/reporting work you have done in your course work and your Microsoft Access proficiency.

REVIEW **SUMMARY**

12-1 What are the different types of decisions, and how does the decision-making process work?

The different levels in an organization (strategic, management, operational) have different decision-making requirements. Decisions can be structured, semi-structured, or unstructured, with structured decisions clustering at the operational level of the organization and unstructured decisions at the strategic level. Decision making can be performed by individuals or groups and includes employees as well as operational, middle, and senior managers. There are four stages in decision making: intelligence, design, choice, and implementation.

o information systems support the activities of managers and management decision
|?

y classical models of managerial activities stress the functions of planning, organizing, coordi-
deciding, and controlling. Contemporary research looking at the actual behavior of managers
und that managers' real activities are highly fragmented, variegated, and brief in duration and
managers shy away from making grand, sweeping policy decisions.

Information technology provides new tools for managers to carry out both their traditional and
newer roles, enabling them to monitor, plan, and forecast with more precision and speed than ever
before and to respond more rapidly to the changing business environment. Information systems
have been most helpful to managers by providing support for their roles in disseminating information, providing liaisons between organizational levels, and allocating resources. However, information systems are less successful at supporting unstructured decisions. Where information systems
are useful, information quality, management filters, and organizational culture can degrade decision
making.

12-3 How do business intelligence and business analytics support decision making?

Business intelligence and analytics promise to deliver correct, nearly real-time information to
decision makers, and analytic tools help them quickly understand the information and take action.
A business intelligence environment consists of data from the business environment, the BI infrastructure, a BA toolset, managerial users and methods, a BI delivery platform (MIS, DSS, or ESS), and
the user interface. There are six analytic functionalities that BI systems deliver to achieve these ends:
predefined production reports, parameterized reports, dashboards and scorecards, ad hoc queries and
searches, the ability to drill down to detailed views of data, and the ability to model scenarios and create forecasts. BI analytics are starting to handle big data. Predictive analytics, location analytics, and
operational intelligence are important analytic capabilities.

12-4 How do different decision-making constituencies in an organization use business intelligence, and what is the role of information systems in helping people working in a group make decisions more efficiently?

Operational and middle management are generally charged with monitoring the performance of
their firm. Most of the decisions they make are fairly structured. Management information systems
(MIS) producing routine production reports are typically used to support this type of decision making. For making unstructured decisions, middle managers and analysts will use decision-support
systems (DSS) with powerful analytics and modeling tools, including spreadsheets and pivot tables.
Senior executives making unstructured decisions use dashboards and visual interfaces displaying key
performance information affecting the overall profitability, success, and strategy of the firm. The
balanced scorecard and business performance management are two methodologies used in designing executive support systems (ESS). Group decision-support systems (GDSS) help people working
together in a group arrive at decisions more efficiently.

Key Terms

Balanced scorecard method, 478
Behavioral models, 465
Business performance management (BPM), 479
Choice, 463
Classical model of management, 465
Data visualization, 469
Decisional role, 465
Design, 463
Drill down, 479
Geographic information systems (GIS), 475
Group decision-support systems (GDSS), 481
Implementation, 463
Informational role, 465

Intelligence, 463
Interpersonal role, 465
Key performance indicators (KPIs), 478
Location analytics, 474
Managerial roles, 465
Operational intelligence, 474
Pivot table, 477
Predictive analytics, 472
Semi-structured decisions, 463
Sensitivity analysis, 477
Structured decisions, 462
Unstructured decisions, 462

Review Questions

12-1 What are the different types of decisions, and how does the decision-making process work?

- List and describe the different levels of decision making and decision-making constituencies in organizations. Explain how their decision-making requirements differ.

- Distinguish between unstructured, semi-structured, and structured decisions.

- List and describe the stages in decision making.

12-2 How do information systems support the activities of managers and management decision making?

- Compare the descriptions of managerial behavior in the classical and behavioral models.

- Identify the specific managerial roles that can be supported by information systems.

12-3 How do business intelligence and business analytics support decision making?

- Define and describe business intelligence and business analytics.

- List and describe the elements of a business intelligence environment.

- List and describe the analytic functionalities provided by BI systems.

- Define predictive analytics, location analytics, and operational intelligence and give an example of each.

12-4 How do different decision-making constituencies in an organization use business intelligence, and what is the role of information systems in helping people working in a group make decisions more efficiently?

- List each of the major decision-making constituencies in an organization and describe the types of decisions each makes.

- Describe how MIS, DSS, or ESS provide decision support for each of these groups.

- Define and describe the balanced scorecard method and business performance management.

- Define a group decision-support system (GDSS) and explain how it differs from a DSS.

Discussion Questions

12-5
As a manager or user of information systems, what would you need to know to participate in the design and use of a DSS or an ESS? Why?

12-6
If businesses used DSS, GDSS, and ESS more widely, would managers and employees make better decisions? Why or why not?

12-7
How much can business intelligence and business analytics help companies refine their business strategy? Explain your answer.

Hands-On MIS Projects

The projects in this section give you hands-on experience identifying opportunities for DSS, using a spreadsheet pivot table to analyze sales data, and using online retirement planning tools for financial planning. Visit MyMIS Lab's Multimedia Library to access this chapter's Hands-On MIS Projects.

Management Decision Problems

12-8 Dealerships for Subaru and other automobile manufacturers keep records of the mileage of cars they sell and service. Mileage data are used to remind customers of when they need to schedule service appointments, but they are used for other purposes as well. What kinds of decisions does this piece of data support at the local level and at the corporate level? What would happen if this piece of data were erroneous, for example, showing mileage of 130,000 instead of 30,000? How would it affect decision making? Assess its business impact.

12-9 Applebee's is the largest casual dining chain in the world, with more than 1,900 locations throughout the United States and in 20 other countries. The menu features beef, chicken, and pork items as well as burgers, pasta, and seafood. Applebee's CEO wants to make the restaurant more profitable by developing menus that are tastier and contain more items that customers want and are willing to pay for despite rising costs for gasoline and agricultural products. How might business intelligence help management implement this strategy? What pieces of data would Applebee's need to collect? What kinds of reports would be useful to help management make decisions on how to improve menus and profitability?

Improving Decision Making: Using Pivot Tables to Analyze Sales Data

Software skills: Pivot tables
Business skills: Analyzing sales data

12-10 This project gives you an opportunity to learn how to use Excel's PivotTable feature to analyze a database or data list. Use the data file for Online Management Training Inc. described earlier in the chapter. This is a list of the sales transactions at OMT for one day. You can find this spreadsheet file at MyLab MIS. Use Excel's PivotTable to help you answer the following questions:

- Where are the average purchases higher? The answer might tell managers where to focus marketing and sales resources, or pitch different messages to different regions.
- What form of payment is the most common? The answer could be used to emphasize in advertising the most preferred means of payment.
- Are there any times of day when purchases are most common? Do people buy more products while at work (likely during the day) or at home (likely in the evening)?
- What's the relationship between region, type of product purchased, and average sales price? We provide instructions on how to use Excel PivotTables in our Learning Tracks.

Improving Decision Making: Using a Web-Based DSS for Retirement Planning

Software skills: Internet-based software
Business skills: Financial planning

12-11 This project will help develop your skills in using web-based DSS for financial planning.

The websites for CNN Money and Kiplinger feature web-based DSS for financial planning and decision making. Select either site to plan for retirement. Use your chosen site to determine how much you need to save to have enough income for your retirement. Assume that you are 50 years old and single and plan to retire in 17 years. You have $100,000 in savings. Your current annual income is $85,000. Your goal is to be able to generate an annual retirement income of $60,000, including Social Security payments.

Use the website you have selected to determine how much money you need to save to help you achieve your retirement goal. If you need to calculate your estimated Social Security payments, use the Quick Calculator at the Social Security Administration website.

Critique the site—its ease of use, its clarity, the value of any conclusions reached, and the extent to which the site helps investors understand their financial needs and the financial markets.

Collaboration and Teamwork Project

Investigating Data-Driven Analytics in Sports

12-12 With three or four of your classmates, select a sport, such as football, baseball, basketball, or soccer. Use the web to research how the sport uses data and analytics to improve team performance or increase ticket sales to events. If possible, use Google Docs and Google Drive or Google Sites to brainstorm, organize, and develop a presentation of your findings for the class.

General Electric (GE), one of the world's largest industrial companies with products ranging from turbines to jet engines to medical equipment, has been transitioning to a much more technology-centric business strategy and business model. Jeffrey Immelt, GE's CEO from 2000 to 2017, wanted to turn GE into a top 10 software company by 2020. In 2015 GE set up GE Digital as its own business within the industrial conglomerate for this purpose.

GE has been focusing on electric power generators, jet engines, locomotives, and oil-refining gear, and the software to connect these devices to the cloud. The company is using sensor-generated data from industrial machines to help customers monitor equipment performance, prevent breakdowns, and assess the machines' overall health. This emerging technology opened new opportunities for GE customers to analyze their IoT data while also helping to transform GE from a traditional manufacturer to a modern digital business.

In a number of industries, improving the productivity of existing assets by even a single percentage point can generate significant benefits. This is true of the oil and gas sector, where average recovery rate of an oil well is 35 percent. That means 65 percent of a well's potential is left in the earth because available technology makes it too expensive to extract. If technology can help oil extraction companies raise the recovery rate from 35 to 36 percent, the world's output will increase by 80 billion barrels—the equivalent of three years of global supply.

The oil and gas industry is also deeply affected by unplanned downtime, when equipment cannot operate because of a malfunction. A single unproductive day on a platform can cost a liquefied natural gas (LNG) facility as much as $25 million, and an average midsized LNG facility experiences about five down days a year. That's $125 to $150 million lost. Minimizing downtime is critical, especially considering declining revenues from lower energy prices. GE sees a $1 billion opportunity for its IoT software.

The foundation for all of GE's Industrial Internet (IoT) applications is Predix, a software platform launched in 2015 to collect data from industrial sensors and analyze the information in the cloud. Predix can run on any cloud infrastructure. The platform has open standards and protocols that allow customers to more easily and quickly connect their machines to the Industrial Internet. The platform can accommodate the size and scale of industrial data for every customer at current levels of use, but it also has been designed to scale up as demand grows. Predix can offer apps developed by other companies as well as GE, is available for on-premises or cloud-based deployment, and can be extended by customers with their own data sources, algorithms, and code. Customers may develop their own custom applications for the Predix platform. GE is also building a developer community to create apps that can be hosted on Predix. Predix is not limited to industrial applications. It could be used for analyzing data in healthcare systems, for example. GE now has a Health Cloud running on Predix. Data security is embedded at all platform application layers, and this is essential for companies linking their operations to the Internet.

GE currently uses Predix to monitor and maintain its own industrial products, such as wind turbines, jet engines, and hydroelectric turbine systems. Predix is able to provide GE corporate customers' machine operators and maintenance engineers with real-time information to schedule maintenance checks, improve machine efficiency, and reduce downtime. Helping customers collect and use this operational data proactively would lower costs in GE service agreements. When GE agrees to provide service for a customer's machine, it often comes with a performance guarantee. Proactive identification of potential issues that also takes the cost out of shop visits helps the customer and helps GE.

In early 2013, GE began to use Predix to analyze data across its fleet of machines. By identifying what made one machine more efficient or downtime-prone than another, GE could more tightly manage its operations. For example, by using high-performance analytics, GE learned that some of its jet aircraft engines were beginning to require more frequent unscheduled maintenance. By collecting massive amounts of data and analyzing the data across its entire fleet of machines, GE was able to cluster engine data by operating environment. The company found that the hot and harsh environments in the Middle East and China caused engines to clog, heat up, and lose efficiency, so they required more maintenance. GE found that engines had far fewer of these problems if they were washed more frequently. Fleet analytics helped GE increase engine lifetime and reduce engine maintenance. The company thinks it can save its customers an average of $7 million of jet airplane fuel annually because their engines will be more efficient.

Predix is starting to provide solutions for GE customers. The New York Power Authority, the nation's largest state-owned utility, has been working with GE Digital to build apps that improve the efficiency of its power generation and distribution network. Pilot projects with GE have saved the utility $3 million in costs. The goal is $500 million in savings over the next decade. British oil and gas company BP plc switched from its own software to Predix to monitor conditions in its oil wells. By the end of 2015, BP had equipped 650 of its thousands of oil wells with GE sensors linked to Predix. Each well was outfitted with 20 to 30 sensors to measure pressure and temperature, transmitting 500,000 data points to the Predix cloud every 15 seconds. BP hopes to use the data to predict well flows and the useful life of each well, and ultimately to obtain an enterprise-wide view of its oil fields' performance.

GE identified pipeline risk management as a major challenge for the oil and gas industry. There are 2 million miles of transmission pipe throughout the globe, moving liquid oil or gas from its point of extraction to refining, processing, or market. Pipeline spills are not frequent, but when they occur, they cause serious economic and environmental damage as well as bad publicity for pipeline operators and energy companies. Pipeline operators are always anxious to know where their next rupture will be, but they formerly lacked the data to measure pipeline fitness. Operators had no way of integrating multiple sources of data into one place so they could see and understand the risk in their pipelines.

GE developed a pipeline-management software suite for accessing, managing, and integrating critical data for the safe management of pipelines, including a risk assessment tool to monitor aging infrastructure. GE's risk-assessment solution combines internal and external factors (such as flooding) to provide an accurate, up-to-the minute visual representation of where risk exists in a pipeline. This risk assessment tool enables pipeline operators to see how recent

events affect their risk and make real-time decisions about where field service crews should be deployed along the pipeline. The risk assessment tool visualization and analytics capabilities run on Predix.

GE is also pulling data from weather systems and dig-reporting services to provide a more comprehensive view of a pipeline network. Weather has a sizable impact on risk for pipelines in areas prone to seismic activity, waterways, and washouts. Checking weather patterns along thousands of miles of pipe for rain or flood zones, and integrating those data with other complex pipeline data sets is very difficult to perform manually. But by bringing all relevant data together in one place, GE gives pipeline operators easier access to information to help them address areas with the greatest potential impact.

Besides being able to examine all current risk, pipeline operators would benefit from a "what-if" calculation tool to model hypothetical scenarios, such as assessing the impact of adjusting operating pressures or addressing particular areas of corrosive pipe. GE would give them the tools for a color-coded view of how those actions affect pipeline risk.

Although few businesses have the capital or infrastructure to operate a platform for integrating and analyzing IoT data, GE faces competition from many sources, including giant cloud services suppliers like Amazon, Microsoft, and Google; major business software companies like Oracle, SAP, IBM, and SAS Institute; industrial conglomerates like Siemens, Honeywell, and ABB; and start-ups like C3 IoT, Uptake, and FogHorn Systems. GE's advantage is its longstanding relationships with customers. So far, only 8 percent of GE's industrial customers are using Predix portfolio products.

In November 2017, Jeff Flannery, who had succeeded Immelt as GE's CEO, announced that spending on GE Digital and Predix would be cut by more than 25 percent, or $400 million. Digital initiatives are still critical to the company nevertheless, and Flannery wants Predix to generate $1 billion in annual revenue. However, Flannery wants this accomplished via a "more focused" strategy. In July 2018 the company announced it was seeking a buyer for key parts of its digital unit.

GE had greatly underestimated the challenges of creating all the software needed for analyzing Internet of Things (IoT) data to improve business processes across a wide range of industries. GE's technical expertise lies in designing and manufacturing machines like power jet engines, plant turbines, and medical imaging equipment and in creating the specialized software to control machines in factory operations. It was too much of a stretch for GE Digital to move quickly into cloud-based software to handle all kinds of sensor and machine data and big data analytics for the entire Industrial Internet. GE also faced difficulties adapting its own legacy applications for Predix. GE has many algorithms for monitoring its machines, but they mostly were written in different coding languages and resided on other systems in GE businesses. This made converting the software to run on Predix time consuming and expensive. Predix has been pared back to be primarily a set of software tools to help write applications, as opposed to connecting to layers of code to automate data analysis. GE Digital now focuses on selling products for specific industrial applications tailored to GE's existing industrial customers rather than all-purpose software for the wider industrial world.

Sources: Dana Cimilucca, Dana Mattioli, and Thomas Gryta, "GE Puts Digital Assets on the Block," *Wall Street Journal*, July 30, 2018; Steve Lohr, "GE Makes a Sharp 'Pivot' on Digital," *New York Times*, April 19, 2018; www.ge.com, accessed May 3, 2018; Courtney Biorlin, "GE Predix Platform's Focus Narrows as Flannery Cuts Digital Spending," *Internet of Things Institute*, November 15, 2017; Alwyn Scott, "GE Is Shifting the strategy for Its $12 Billion Digital Business," *Reuters*, August 28, 2017; Laura Winig, "GE's Big Bet on Data and Analytics," *MIT Sloan Management Review,* February 2016; Devin Leonard and Rick Clough, "How GE Exorcised the Ghost of Jack Welch to Become a 124-Year-Old Startup," *Bloomberg Businessweek,* March 21, 2016; and Holly Lugassy, "GE Leverages Pivotal Cloud Foundry to Build Predix, First Cloud for Industry," CloudFoundry.org, May 11, 2016.

CASE STUDY QUESTIONS

12-13 How is GE changing its business strategy and business model? What is the role of information technology in GE's business?

12-14 On what business functions and level of decision making is GE focusing?

12-15 Describe three kinds of decisions that can be supported using Predix. What is the value to the firm of each of those decisions? Explain.

12-16 To what extent is GE becoming a software company? Explain your answer.

MyLab MIS

Go to the Assignments section of MyLab MIS to complete these writing exercises.

12-17 Identify and describe three factors that prevent managers from making good decisions.

12-18 Give three examples of data used in location analytics and explain how each can help businesses.

Chapter 12 References

Breuker, Dominic, Martin Matzner, Patrick Delfmann, and Jörg Becker. "Comprehensible Predictive Models for Business Processes." *MIS Quarterly* 40, No. 4 (September 2016).

Brynjolfsson, Erik, Tomer Geva, and Shachar Reichman. "Crowd-Squared: Amplifying the Predictive Power of Search Trend Data." *MIS Quarterly* 40, No. 4 (December 2016).

Chen, Daniel Q., David S. Preston, and Morgan Swink. "How the Use of Big Data Analytics Affects Value Creation in Supply Chain Management." *Journal of Management Information Systems* 32, No. 4 (2015).

Davenport, Thomas H. "Analytics 3.0." *Harvard Business Review* (December 2013).

Davenport, Thomas H., and Jill Dyche. "Big Data in Big Companies." *International Institute of Analytics* (May 2013).

Davenport, Thomas H., and Jeanne G. Harris. *Competing on Analytics: The New Science of Winning: Updated, with a New Introduction.* Boston: Harvard Business Review Press (2017).

De la Merced, Michael J., and Ben Protess. "A Fast-Paced Stock Exchange Trips over Itself." *New York Times* (March 23, 2012).

Dennis, Alan R., Jay E. Aronson, William G. Henriger, and Edward D. Walker III. "Structuring Time and Task in Electronic Brainstorming." *MIS Quarterly* 23, No. 1 (March 1999).

Dietvorst, Berkeley J. "When People Don't Trust Algorithms." *MIT Sloan Management Review* (July 5, 2017).

Grau, Jeffrey. "How Retailers Are Leveraging 'Big Data' to Personalize Ecommerce." *eMarketer* (2012).

Hardin, Andrew, Clayton A. Looney, and Gregory D. Moody. "Assessing the Credibility of Decisional Guidance Delivered by Information Systems." *Journal of Management Information Systems* 34, No. 4 (2017).

Kahneman, Daniel. *Thinking, Fast and Slow.* New York: Farrar, Straus and Giroux (2011).

Kaplan, Robert S., and David P. Norton. "The Balanced Scorecard: Measures That Drive Performance." *Harvard Business Review* (January–February 1992).

_____. *Strategy Maps: Converting Intangible Assets into Tangible Outcomes.* Boston: Harvard Business School Press (2004).

Leidner, Dorothy E., and Joyce Elam. "The Impact of Executive Information Systems on Organizational Design, Intelligence, and Decision Making." *Organization Science* 6, No. 6 (November–December 1995).

Luca, Michael, Jon Kleinberg, and Sendhil Mullainathan. "Algorithms Need Managers, Too." *Harvard Business Review* (January–February 2016).

Marchand, Donald A., and Joe Peppard. "Why IT Fumbles Analytics." *Harvard Business Review* (January–February 2013).

Martens, David, Foster Provost, Jessica Clark, and Enric Junqué de Fortuny. "Mining Massive Fine-Grained Behavior Data to Improve Predictive Analytics." *MIS Quarterly* 40, No. 4 (December 2016).

McDonough, Brian. "How Slack Uses Big Data to Grow Its Business." *Information Management* (May 3, 2017).

McKinsey Global Institute. "The Age of Analytics: Competing in a Data-Driven World" (December 2016).

Mintzberg, Henry. "Managerial Work: Analysis from Observation." *Management Science* 18 (October 1971).

Porter, Michael E., and Nitin Nohria. "How CEOs Manage Time." *Harvard Business Review* (July–August 2018).

Ransbotham, Sam, David Kiron, and Pamela Kirk Prentice. "Minding the Analytics Gap." *MIT Sloan Management Review* (Spring 2015).

Sharda, Ramesh, Dursan Delen, and Efraim Turban. *Business Intelligence, Analytics, and Data Science: A Managerial Perspective*, 4/e. New York: Pearson (2018).

Shi, Donghui, Jian Guan, Jozef Zurada, and Andrew Manikas. "A Data-Mining Approach to Identification of Risk Factors in Safety Management Systems." *Journal of Management Information Systems* 34, No. 4 (2017).

Simchi-Levi, David. "The New Frontier of Price Optimization." *MIT Sloan Management Review* (Fall 2017).

Simon, H. A. *The New Science of Management Decision*. New York: Harper & Row (1960).

Tversky, Amos, and Daniel Kahneman. "Rational Choice and the Framing of Decisions." *Journal of Business* (1986).

Building and Managing Systems

PART FOUR shows how to use the knowledge acquired in earlier chapters to analyze and design information system solutions to business problems. This part answers questions such as these: How can I develop a solution to an information system problem that provides genuine business benefits? How can the firm adjust to the changes introduced by the new system solution? What alternative approaches are available for building system solutions?

13

Building Information Systems

LEARNING OBJECTIVES

After reading this chapter, you will be able to answer the following questions:

13-1 How does building new systems produce organizational change?

13-2 What are the core activities in the systems development process?

13-3 What are the principal methodologies for modeling and designing systems?

13-4 What are alternative methods for building information systems?

13-5 What are new approaches for system building in the digital firm era?

13-6 How will MIS help my career?

CHAPTER CASES

Cameron International Builds a New System for Financial Reporting

Carter's Redesigns Its Business Processes

Systems Development Is Different for Mobile Apps

Hitachi Consulting Moves Human Resources to the Cloud

VIDEO CASES

IBM: Business Process Management in a SaaS Environment

IBM Helps the City of Madrid with Real-Time BPM Software

Instructional Videos:

BPM Business Process Management Customer Story

Workflow Management Viisualized

MyLab MIS

Discussion Questions: 13-6, 13-7, 13-8; **Hands-on MIS Projects:** 13-9, 13-10, 13-11, 13-12; **Writing Assignments:** 13-19, 13-20; **eText with Conceptual Animations**

Cameron International Builds a New System for Financial Reporting

Cameron International Corporation is a subsidiary of Schlumberger Holdings Corporation and is a global provider of pressure control, processing, flow control, and compression systems as well as project management and aftermarket services for the oil and gas and process industries. Headquartered in Houston, Texas, Cameron has approximately 23,000 employees and maintains a sales and service network that spans five continents.

In 2010 Cameron embarked on an enterprise-wide standardization project to simplify its information technology platform and financial reporting processes. The company consolidated to five profit centers on five business units, with a new reporting structure. Manufacturing plants were to roll up their financial data to profit centers for reporting information such as profit and loss (P&L) statements. This consolidation made it possible for senior managers to use an aggregate view of profit center data to better evaluate the overall financial health of the company. However, Cameron's systems were unable to provide views of data at the manufacturing plant level. Managers seeking plant-level reporting had to input data into one system and then review it in another.

Cameron needed a solution that would include financial data at the plant level in a central, consolidation application. The company evaluated several planning and consolidation software tools and selected SAP Business Planning and Consolidation (SAP BPC) version 7.5. The BPC software delivers planning, budgeting, forecasting, and financial consolidation capabilities in a single application. SAP BPC did provide reporting at the plant level and could be integrated with SAP's ERP system, which Cameron was already using. Each plant would be able to see its P&L statements and any variances as well as data aggregated by profit center.

Cameron implemented the new SAP planning and consolidation system in stages, starting with its U.S. locations, and it ran the system in parallel with its legacy system for a set period. During the parallel rollout, Cameron matched the data from the two systems to ensure the financial data was correct. After running successfully in parallel for two months, the new system went live throughout the company and the legacy system was retired.

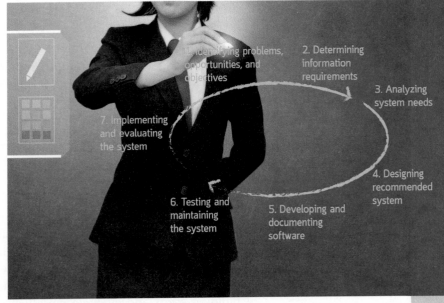

© A. Singkham/123RF

Customization of the SAP software was required. Cameron made software modifications to customize business rules for U.S. eliminations of intercompany transactions. It also used plug-ins to rectify timing differences during data loading. (A plug-in is a software module that can easily be installed to add a specific feature or service to an existing computer program.)

End users, who comprised two-thirds of the project team, actively participated in the development and implementation of the new system. Business users from finance provided systems developers with details about their reporting needs. End users helped review the system's reporting capabilities and outputs to improve the reports prior to putting the system into production. This also helped familiarize users with the new system. Management was pleased because the new system produced financial statements rapidly, exactly the way the business wanted. Implementation of the new system went smoothly, on time and on budget. The new system is more user-friendly, with tools to help finance business users to do more on their own without assistance from IT staff.

With SAP BPC, Cameron has moved from manually pulling data to seamless automation. Users of the new system need only double-click on a profit center to see the data in detail. They can see how many plants there are and the data for each plant. With the legacy system, it took a full day of manual effort to ensure consolidation was done correctly. Business users were spending 90 percent of their time assembling the data and only 10 percent on analyzing information. The level of automation in the new system enables Cameron's business users to now spend 90 percent of their time analyzing reporting results.

Sources: www.sap.com, accessed January 5, 2018; Lauren Bonneau, "Cameron Achieves Complete Plant-Level Visibility with SAP Business Planning and Consolidation," *SAP Insider Profiles*, October 30, 2017; and www.cameron.slb.com, accessed January 5, 2018.

Cameron's experience illustrates some of the steps required to design and build new information systems. Building a new system for financial consolidation entailed analyzing the organization's problems with existing systems, assessing information requirements, selecting appropriate technology, and redesigning business processes and jobs. Management had to oversee the systems-building effort and evaluate benefits and costs. The information requirements were incorporated into the design of the new system, which represented a process of planned organizational change.

The chapter-opening case calls attention to important points raised by this case and this chapter. Cameron had reorganized around five profit centers. Its ability to analyze its financial data by both manufacturing plant and profit center levels was hampered by an outdated legacy consolidation system and inefficient manual processes, which raised costs and slowed down work, and limited the company's ability to quickly and thoroughly analyze its financial data.

The solution was to implement a new business planning and consolidation system that could provide reporting at both manufacturing plant and profit center levels. Cameron's information requirements were incorporated into the system design. The system was more user-friendly. The solution encompassed not just the application of new technology, but changes to corporate culture, business processes, and job functions. Cameron's finance function was able to spend more time on planning and analysis.

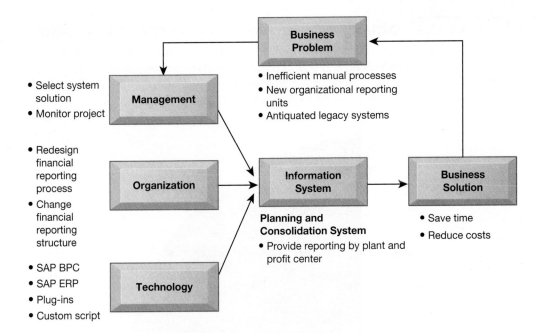

Here are some questions to think about: How did Cameron's new SAP BPC system meet its information requirements? How much did the new system change the way Cameron ran its business?

13-1 How does building new systems produce organizational change?

Building a new information system is one kind of planned organizational change. The introduction of a new information system involves much more than new hardware and software. It also includes changes in jobs, skills, management, and organization. When we design a new information system, we are redesigning the organization. System builders must understand how a system will affect specific business processes and the organization as a whole.

Systems Development and Organizational Change

Information technology can promote various degrees of organizational change, ranging from incremental to far-reaching. Figure 13.1 shows four kinds of structural organizational change that are enabled by information technology: (1) automation, (2) rationalization, (3) business process redesign, and (4) paradigm shifts. Each carries different risks and rewards.

The most common form of IT-enabled organizational change is **automation**. The first applications of information technology involved assisting employees with performing their tasks more efficiently and effectively. Calculating paychecks and payroll registers, giving bank tellers instant access to customer deposit records, and developing a nationwide reservation network for airline ticket agents are all examples of early automation.

A deeper form of organizational change—one that follows quickly from early automation—is **rationalization of procedures**. Automation frequently reveals new bottlenecks in production and makes the existing arrangement of

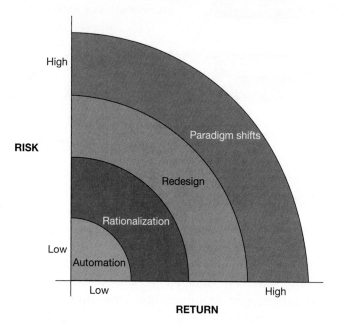

FIGURE 13.1 ORGANIZATIONAL CHANGE CARRIES RISKS AND REWARDS

The most common forms of organizational change are automation and rationalization. These relatively slow-moving and slow-changing strategies present modest returns but little risk. Faster and more comprehensive change—such as redesign and paradigm shifts—carries high rewards but offers substantial chances of failure.

procedures and structures painfully cumbersome. Rationalization of procedures is the streamlining of standard operating procedures. For example, Cameron International's new system for financial reporting is effective not only because it uses computer technology but also because the company simplified its business processes for this function. Fewer manual steps are required.

Rationalization of procedures is often found in programs for making a series of continuous quality improvements in products, services, and operations, such as total quality management (TQM) and Six Sigma. **Total quality management (TQM)** makes achieving quality an end in itself and the responsibility of all people and functions within an organization. TQM derives from concepts developed by American quality experts such as W. Edwards Deming and Joseph Juran, but it was popularized by Japanese organizations. **Six Sigma** is a specific measure of quality, representing 3.4 defects per million opportunities. Most companies cannot achieve this level of quality but use six sigma as a goal for driving ongoing quality improvement programs.

A more powerful type of organizational change is **business process redesign**, in which business processes are analyzed, simplified, and redesigned. Business process redesign reorganizes workflows, combining steps to cut waste and eliminate repetitive, paper-intensive tasks. (Sometimes the new design eliminates jobs as well.) It is much more ambitious than rationalization of procedures, requiring a new vision of how the process is to be organized. The Interactive Session on Organizations presents another example.

Rationalizing procedures and redesigning business processes are limited to specific parts of a business. New information systems can ultimately affect the design of the entire organization by transforming how the organization carries out its business or even the nature of the business. For instance, the long-haul trucking and transportation firm Schneider National used new information systems to change its business model. Schneider created a new business managing

INTERACTIVE SESSION · ORGANIZATIONS

Carter's Redesigns Its Business Processes

Carter's has built a big business dressing little ones and you probably wore some of its products when you were growing up. This company is the largest U.S. branded marketer of apparel exclusively for babies and young children, and includes the OshKosh B'gosh brand. Carter's merchandise is sold online, in over 1,000 company stores in the United States and Canada, and in 18,000 department and specialty stores. The company has annual revenue exceeding $3 billion and is based in Atlanta, Georgia. Carter's financial systems handle hundreds of thousands of transactions each day.

Until recently, the systems Carter's used to process these transactions were heavily manual and paper-based and could no longer keep pace with the company's growth or the increasingly digital business environment. For many years that company had relied on more than 20 legacy financial systems, some of which were homegrown and antiquated. If the systems did not integrate with each other as they should, Carter's used manual processes to keep everything working together. This created bottlenecks that slowed down processing and also increased the chances of human error. For example, managing chargebacks required a great deal of manual data entry and tracking down spreadsheets, emails, folders, and faxes from various systems in order to reconcile a specific chargeback to the appropriate ledger. (A chargeback is the return of funds used to make a purchase to the buyer if the buyer disputes the purchase.)

Carter's management wanted to transform the role of the finance function from preoccupation with transaction processing to focusing more on analyzing financial data and guiding decision making. To accomplish this goal, the company needed process improvements in both the business's finance processes and technology. This meant streamlining and simplifying financial processes so the finance department had more time for analysis and reporting work. In 2015, Carter's launched a "Vision to Value" initiative to achieve this goal.

In addition to replacing outdated systems with more up-to-date technology, including a centralized enterprise resource planning (ERP) system, the project provided an opportunity to modernize financial processes. Carter's selected SAP Business Suite 4 SAP HANA (also known as SAP S/4HANA) software for this purpose and worked with Deloitte Consultants for assistance with systems integration and implementation. SAP S/4HANA is a business software suite based on SAP's proprietary HANA ultra-high-speed data management and computing platform, and is designed to support all day-to-day processes of an enterprise. The new software solution had to interact well with other related systems beyond financials such as order management systems and point of sale systems. SAP S/4HANA offers integration to multiple data sources from many different SAP and non-SAP applications, financial and otherwise.

Business process redesign was as crucial to the success of the project as new technology. Implementing SAP software provided Carter's with the opportunity to transform older and inefficient processes into modern processes reflecting best practices for its line of business and its industry. Carter's had to benchmark its financial processes against these best practices, many of which were incorporated in the SAP software. Thorough benchmarking required questioning the rationale behind every core financial process. For each process based on existing technology, the implementation had to ask whether it could be redesigned on a new technology platform to be more efficient. Carter's also examined whether the process would be better served by remaining on a legacy system rather than migrating to SAP S/4HANA. Carter's decided to keep a process on its existing system unless migrating to SAP S/4HANA provided clear benefits. For the systems that ran core financial processes, SAP S/4HANA was superior.

In July 2016, Carter's went live with SAP S/4HANA Finance with the procure-to-pay, invoice-to-cash, fixed assets, and record-to-report processes supported by the new system. Moving the procure-to-pay process to SAP S/4HANA increased efficiency by eliminating manual data entry and increasing the visibility of a transaction as it flowed through the system. (Procure-to-pay is the process of buying goods and includes the initial decision to make the purchase, the process of selecting the goods, and the transaction to pay for the goods purchased.) Instead of requiring various phone calls, emails, and paper copies of supporting documentation, the software guides the process. The SAP Invoice Management application enables a centralized invoicing process by scanning, reading, and filing invoices via optical character recognition (OCR), which kicks off an invoice workflow through a preset list of coders and approvers all the way to invoice payment. Once invoice information has been entered, it can be accessed automatically anywhere along the process life cycle, and users can view all information related to the invoice transaction on a single screen. For example, when approving an invoice, the system makes it possible for Carter's staff to see the invoice data flowing to accounts payable to start the payment process.

System-generated tracking of chargebacks and an improved capability to monitor chargeback status in the system has created significant time savings and efficiencies in billing and collections. All the information is in the SAP system, so whoever is approving the chargeback can see all the history in one place. In addition to chargeback history, once a chargeback is approved, the system sends a specific chargeback to a specific general ledger. The system has also made processes for fixed assets more efficient by eliminating manual routing and spreadsheet dependence.

Sources: "Transforming a Retail Brand Leader with SAP S/4HANA Finance," events.sap.com, accessed February 24, 2018; Ken Murphy, "A Next-Generation Finance Platform at Carter's," *SAP Insider Profiles*, December 19, 2016; and www.corporate.carters.com, accessed February 26, 2018.

CASE STUDY QUESTIONS

1. How did Carter's previous business processes affect its business performance?

2. What management, organization, and technology factors contributed to Carter's problems with its business processes?

3. Diagram Carter's old and redesigned business process for paying an invoice.

4. Describe the role of technology in Carter's business process changes.

5. How did Carter's redesigned business processes change the way the company worked? What was their business impact? Explain.

logistics for other companies. This more radical form of business change is called a **paradigm shift**. A paradigm shift involves rethinking the nature of the business and the nature of the organization.

Paradigm shifts and business process redesign often fail because extensive organizational change is so difficult to orchestrate (see Chapter 14). Why, then, do so many corporations contemplate such radical change? Because the rewards are equally high (see Figure 13.1). In many instances, firms seeking paradigm shifts and pursuing reengineering strategies achieve stunning, order-of-magnitude increases in their returns on investment (or productivity). Some of these success stories, and some failure stories, are included throughout this book.

Business Process Redesign

Like Cameron International, described in the chapter-opening case, many businesses today are trying to use information technology to improve their business processes. Some of these systems entail incremental process change, but others require more far-reaching redesign of business processes. To deal with these changes, organizations are turning to business process management. **Business process management (BPM)** provides a variety of tools and methodologies to analyze existing processes, design new processes, and optimize those processes. BPM is never concluded because process improvement requires continual change. Companies practicing business process management go through the following steps:

1. **Identify processes for change:** One of the most important strategic decisions that a firm can make is not deciding how to use computers to improve business processes but understanding what business processes need improvement. When systems are used to strengthen the wrong business model or business processes, the business can become more efficient at doing what it should not do. As a result, the firm becomes vulnerable to competitors who may have discovered the right business model. Considerable time and cost may also be spent improving business processes that have little impact on overall firm performance and revenue. Managers need to determine what business processes are the most important and how improving these processes will help business performance.

2. **Analyze existing processes:** Existing business processes should be modeled and documented, noting inputs, outputs, resources, and the sequence of activities. The process design team identifies redundant steps, paper-intensive tasks, bottlenecks, and other inefficiencies.

3. **Design the new process:** Once the existing process is mapped and measured in terms of time and cost, the process design team will try to improve the process by designing a new one. A new streamlined "to-be" process will be documented and modeled for comparison with the old process.

4. **Implement the new process:** Once the new process has been thoroughly modeled and analyzed, it must be translated into a new set of procedures and work rules. New information systems or enhancements to existing systems may have to be implemented to support the redesigned process. The new process and supporting systems are rolled out into the business organization. As the business starts using this process, problems are uncovered and addressed. Employees working with the process may recommend improvements.

5. **Continuous measurement:** Once a process has been implemented and optimized, it needs to be continually measured. Why? Processes may deteriorate over time as employees fall back on old methods, or they may lose their effectiveness if the business experiences other changes.

Figure 13.2 illustrates the "as-is" process for purchasing a book from a physical bookstore. Consider what happens when a customer visits a physical bookstore and searches its shelves for a book. If he or she finds the book, that person takes it to the checkout counter and pays for it via credit card, cash, or check. If the customer is unable to locate the book, he or she must ask a bookstore clerk to search the shelves or check the bookstore's inventory records to see if it is in stock. If the clerk finds the book, the customer purchases it and leaves. If the book is not available locally, the clerk inquires about ordering it for the customer from the bookstore's warehouse or from the book's distributor or publisher. Once the ordered book arrives at the bookstore, a bookstore employee telephones the customer with this information. The customer would have to go to the bookstore again to pick up the book and pay for it. If the bookstore is unable to order the book for the customer, the customer would have to try another bookstore. You can see that this process has many steps and might require the customer to make multiple trips to the bookstore.

Figure 13.3 illustrates how the book-purchasing process can be redesigned by taking advantage of the Internet. The customer accesses an online bookstore over the Internet from his or her computer. He or she searches the bookstore's online catalog for the book he or she wants. If the book is available, the

FIGURE 13.2 AS-IS BUSINESS PROCESS FOR PURCHASING A BOOK FROM A PHYSICAL BOOKSTORE

Purchasing a book from a physical bookstore requires many steps to be performed by both the seller and the customer.

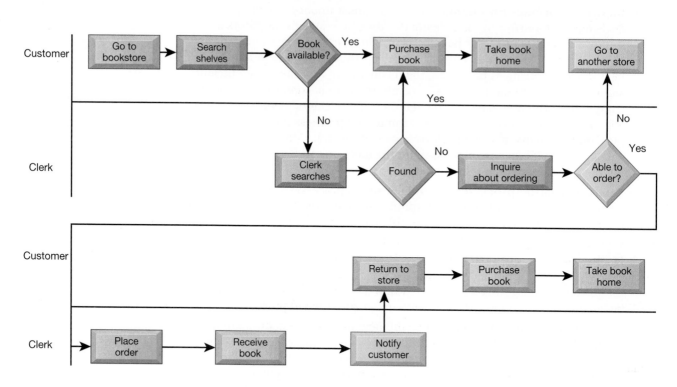

customer orders the book online, supplying credit card and shipping address information, and the book is delivered to the customer's home. If the online bookstore does not carry the book, the customer selects another online bookstore and searches for the book again. This process has far fewer steps than those for purchasing the book in a physical bookstore, requires much less effort on the part of the customer, and requires less sales staff for customer service. The new process is therefore much more efficient and time-saving.

The new process design needs to be justified by showing how much it reduces time and cost or enhances customer service and value. Management first measures the time and cost of the existing process as a baseline. In our example,

FIGURE 13.3 REDESIGNED PROCESS FOR PURCHASING A BOOK ONLINE

Using Internet technology makes it possible to redesign the process for purchasing a book so that it requires fewer steps and consumes fewer resources.

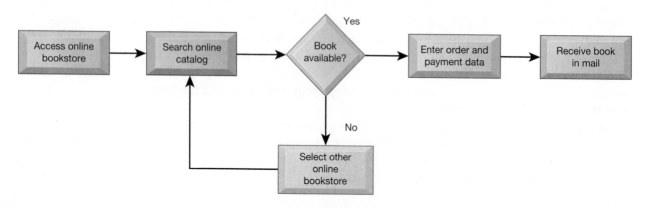

the time required for purchasing a book from a physical bookstore might range from 15 minutes (if the customer immediately finds what he or she wants) to 30 minutes if the book is in stock but has to be located by sales staff. If the book has to be ordered from another source, the process might take one or two weeks and another trip to the bookstore for the customer. If the customer lives far away from the bookstore, the time to travel to the bookstore would have to be factored in. The bookstore will have to pay the costs for maintaining a physical store and keeping the book in stock, for sales staff on site, and for shipment costs if the book has to be obtained from another location.

The new process for purchasing a book online might only take several minutes, although the customer might have to wait several days or a week to have the book delivered and will have to pay a shipping charge. But the customer saves time and money by not having to travel to the bookstore or make additional visits to pick up the book. Booksellers' costs are lower because they do not have to pay for a physical store location or for local inventory.

Although many business process improvements are incremental and ongoing, there are occasions when more radical change must take place. Our example of a physical bookstore redesigning the book-purchasing process so that it can be carried out online is an example of this type of radical, far-reaching change. When properly implemented, business process redesign produces dramatic gains in productivity and efficiency and may even change the way the business is run. In some instances, it drives a "paradigm shift" that transforms the nature of the business itself.

This actually happened in book retailing when Amazon challenged traditional physical bookstores with its online retail model and Kindle e-book reader. By radically rethinking the way a book can be published, purchased, and sold, Amazon and other online bookstores have achieved remarkable efficiencies, cost reductions, and a whole new way of doing business.

BPM poses challenges. Executives report that the largest single barrier to successful business process change is organizational culture. Employees do not like unfamiliar routines and often try to resist change. This is especially true of projects where organizational changes are very ambitious and far-reaching. Managing change is neither simple nor intuitive, and companies committed to extensive process improvement need a good change management strategy (see Chapter 14).

Tools for Business Process Management

Many software firms provide tools for various aspects of BPM, including IBM, Oracle, and TIBCO. These tools help businesses identify and document processes requiring improvement, create models of improved processes, capture and enforce business rules for performing processes, and integrate existing systems to support new or redesigned processes. BPM software tools also provide analytics for verifying that process performance has been improved and for measuring the impact of process changes on key business performance indicators.

For example, American National Insurance Company, which offers life insurance, medical insurance, property casualty insurance, and investment services, used Pegasystems BPM software to streamline customer service processes across four business groups. The software built rules to guide customer service representatives through a single view of a customer's information that was maintained in multiple systems. By eliminating the need to juggle multiple applications simultaneously to handle customer and agent requests, the improved process increased customer service representative workload capacity by 192 percent.

13-2 What are the core activities in the systems development process?

New information systems are an outgrowth of organizational problem solving. A new information system is built as a solution to some type of problem or set of problems the organization perceives it is facing. The problem may be one in which managers and employees realize that the organization is not performing as well as expected or that the organization should take advantage of new opportunities to perform more successfully.

The activities that go into producing an information system solution to an organizational problem or opportunity are called **systems development**. Systems development is a structured kind of problem solved with distinct activities. These activities consist of systems analysis, systems design, programming, testing, conversion, and production and maintenance.

Figure 13.4 illustrates the systems development process. The systems development activities depicted usually take place in sequential order. But some of the activities may need to be repeated or some may take place simultaneously depending on the approach to system building that is being employed (see Section 13-4).

Systems Analysis

Systems analysis is the analysis of a problem that a firm tries to solve with an information system. It consists of defining the problem, identifying its causes, specifying the solution, and identifying the information requirements that must be met by a system solution.

The systems analyst creates a road map of the existing organization and systems, identifying the primary owners and users of data along with existing hardware and software. The systems analyst then details the problems of existing systems. By examining documents, work papers, and procedures, observing system operations, and interviewing key users of the systems, the analyst can identify the problem areas and objectives a solution would achieve. Often, the solution requires building a new information system or improving an existing one.

FIGURE 13.4   THE SYSTEMS DEVELOPMENT PROCESS

Building a system can be broken down into six core activities.

The systems analysis also includes a **feasibility study** to determine whether that solution is feasible, or achievable, from a financial, technical, and organizational standpoint. The feasibility study determines whether the proposed system is expected to be a good investment, whether the technology needed for the system is available and can be handled by the firm's information systems specialists, and whether the organization can handle the changes introduced by the system.

Normally, the systems analysis process identifies several alternative solutions that the organization can pursue and assess the feasibility of each. A written systems proposal report describes the costs and benefits, and the advantages and disadvantages, of each alternative. It is up to management to determine which mix of costs, benefits, technical features, and organizational impacts represents the most desirable alternative.

Establishing Information Requirements

Perhaps the most challenging task of the systems analyst is to define the specific information requirements that must be met by the chosen system solution. At the most basic level, the **information requirements** of a new system involve identifying who needs what information, where, when, and how. Requirements analysis carefully defines the objectives of the new or modified system and develops a detailed description of the functions that the new system must perform. Faulty requirements analysis is a leading cause of systems failure and high systems development costs (see Chapter 14). A system designed around the wrong set of requirements will either have to be discarded because of poor performance or will need to undergo major modifications. Section 13-4 describes alternative approaches to eliciting requirements that help minimize this problem.

Some problems do not require an information system solution but instead need an adjustment in management, additional training, or refinement of existing organizational procedures. If the problem is information-related, systems analysis still may be required to diagnose the problem and arrive at the proper solution.

Systems Design

Systems analysis describes what a system should do to meet information requirements, and **systems design** shows how the system will fulfill this objective. The design of an information system is the overall plan or model for that system. Like the blueprint of a building or house, it consists of all the specifications that give the system its form and structure.

The systems designer details the system specifications that will deliver the functions identified during systems analysis. These specifications should address all of the managerial, organizational, and technological components of the system solution. Table 13.1 lists the types of specifications that would be produced during systems design.

Like houses or buildings, information systems may have many possible designs. Each design represents a unique blend of technical and organizational components. What makes one design superior to others is the ease and efficiency with which it fulfills user requirements within a specific set of technical, organizational, financial, and time constraints.

The Role of End Users

User information requirements drive the entire system-building effort. Users must have sufficient control over the design process to ensure that the system reflects their business priorities and information needs, not the biases of the

TABLE 13.1 SYSTEM DESIGN SPECIFICATIONS

OUTPUT	PROCESSING	DOCUMENTATION
Medium	Computations	Operations documentation
Content	Program modules	Systems documentation
Timing	Required reports	User documentation
INPUT	Timing	CONVERSION
Origins	MANUAL PROCEDURES	Data conversion rules
Flow	What activities	Testing method
Data entry	Who performs them	Conversion strategy
USER INTERFACE	When	TRAINING
Simplicity	How	Training techniques
Efficiency	Where	Training modules
Logic	CONTROLS	ORGANIZATIONAL CHANGES
Feedback	Input controls (characters, limit, reasonableness)	Task redesign
Errors		Job design
DATABASE DESIGN	Processing controls (consistency, record counts)	Process design
Logical data model	Output controls (totals, samples of output)	Organization structure design
Volume and speed requirements		Reporting relationships
Record specifications	Procedural controls (passwords, special forms)	
	SECURITY	
	Access controls	
	Catastrophe plans	
	Audit trails	

technical staff. Working on design increases users' understanding and acceptance of the system. As we describe in Chapter 14, insufficient user involvement in the design effort is a major cause of system failure. However, some systems require more user participation in design than others, and Section 13-4 shows how alternative systems development methods address the user participation issue.

Completing the Systems Development Process

The remaining steps in the systems development process translate the solution specifications established during systems analysis and design into a fully operational information system. These concluding steps consist of programming, testing, conversion, production, and maintenance.

Programming

During the **programming** stage, system specifications that were prepared during the design stage are translated into software program code. Today, many organizations no longer do their own programming for new systems. Instead, they purchase the software that meets the requirements for a new system from external sources such as software packages from a commercial software vendor, software services from a software service provider, or outsourcing firms that develop custom application software for their clients (see Section 13-4).

Testing

Exhaustive and thorough **testing** must be conducted to ascertain whether the system produces the right results. Testing answers the question: Will the system produce the desired results under known conditions? Some companies are starting to use cloud computing services for this work.

The amount of time needed to answer this question has been traditionally underrated in systems project planning (see Chapter 14). Testing is time-consuming: Test data must be carefully prepared, results reviewed, and corrections made in the system. In some instances, parts of the system may have to be redesigned. The risks resulting from glossing over this step are enormous.

Testing an information system can be broken down into three types of activities: unit testing, system testing, and acceptance testing. **Unit testing**, or program testing, consists of testing each program separately in the system. It is widely believed that the purpose of such testing is to guarantee that programs are error-free, but this goal is realistically impossible. Testing should be viewed instead as a means of locating errors in programs, by focusing on finding all the ways to make a program fail. Once they are pinpointed, problems can be corrected.

System testing tests the functioning of the information system as a whole. It tries to determine whether discrete modules will function together as planned and whether discrepancies exist between the way the system actually works and the way it was conceived. Among the areas examined are performance time, capacity for file storage and handling peak loads, recovery and restart capabilities, and manual procedures.

Acceptance testing provides the final certification that the system is ready to be used in a production setting. Systems tests are evaluated by users and reviewed by management. When all parties are satisfied that the new system meets their standards, the system is formally accepted for installation.

The systems development team works with users to devise a systematic test plan. The **test plan** includes all of the preparations for the series of tests we have just described.

Figure 13.5 shows an example of a test plan. The general condition being tested is a record change. The documentation consists of a series of test plan

---

FIGURE 13.5 A SAMPLE TEST PLAN TO TEST A RECORD CHANGE

When developing a test plan, it is imperative to include the various conditions to be tested, the requirements for each condition tested, and the expected results. Test plans require input from both end users and information systems specialists.

Procedure	Address and Maintenance "Record Change Series"		Test Series 2		
	Prepared by:		Date:	Version:	
Test Ref.	Condition Tested	Special Requirements	Expected Results	Output On	Next Screen
2.0	Change records				
2.1	Change existing record	key field	Not allowed		
2.2	Change nonexistent record	Other fields	"Invalid key" message		
2.3	Change deleted record	Deleted record must be available	"Deleted" message		
2.4	Make second record	Change 2.1 above	OK if valid	Transaction file	V45
2.5	Insert record		OK if valid	Transaction file	V45
2.6	Abort during change	Abort 2.5	No change	Transaction file	V45

screens maintained on a database (perhaps a PC database) that is ideally suited to this kind of application.

Conversion

Conversion is the process of changing from the old system to the new system. Four main conversion strategies can be employed: the parallel strategy, the direct cutover strategy, the pilot study strategy, and the phased approach strategy.

In a **parallel strategy**, both the old system and its potential replacement are run together for a time until everyone is assured that the new one functions correctly. This is the safest conversion approach because, in the event of errors or processing disruptions, the old system can still be used as a backup. However, this approach is very expensive, and additional staff or resources may be required to run the extra system.

The **direct cutover strategy** replaces the old system entirely with the new system on an appointed day. It is a very risky approach that can potentially be more costly than running two systems in parallel if serious problems with the new system are found. There is no other system to fall back on. Dislocations, disruptions, and the cost of corrections may be enormous.

The **pilot study strategy** introduces the new system to only a limited area of the organization, such as a single department or operating unit. When this pilot version is complete and working smoothly, it is installed throughout the rest of the organization, either simultaneously or in stages.

The **phased approach strategy** introduces the new system in stages, either by functions or by organizational units. If, for example, the system is introduced by function, a new payroll system might begin with hourly workers who are paid weekly, followed six months later by adding salaried employees (who are paid monthly) to the system. If the system is introduced by organizational unit, corporate headquarters might be converted first, followed by outlying operating units four months later.

Moving from an old system to a new one requires that end users be trained to use the new system. Detailed **documentation** showing how the system works from both a technical and end-user standpoint is finalized during conversion time for use in training and everyday operations. Lack of proper training and documentation contributes to system failure, so this portion of the systems development process is very important.

Production and Maintenance

After the new system is installed and conversion is complete, the system is said to be in **production**. During this stage, the system will be reviewed by both users and technical specialists to determine how well it has met its original objectives and to decide whether any revisions or modifications are in order. In some instances, a formal **post-implementation audit** document is prepared. After the system has been fine-tuned, it must be maintained while it is in production to correct errors, meet requirements, or improve processing efficiency. Changes in hardware, software, documentation, or procedures to a production system to correct errors, meet new requirements, or improve processing efficiency are termed **maintenance**. Routine maintenance consumes a large percentage of many firms' IT budgets, but could be reduced significantly through more up-to-date systems-building practices and technology. Table 13.2 summarizes the systems development activities.

TABLE 13.2 SYSTEMS DEVELOPMENT

CORE ACTIVITY	DESCRIPTION
Systems analysis	Identify problem(s)
	Specify solutions
	Establish information requirements
Systems design	Create design specifications
Programming	Translate design specifications into program code
Testing	Perform unit testing
	Perform systems testing
	Perform acceptance testing
Conversion	Plan conversion
	Prepare documentation
	Train users and technical staff
Production and maintenance	Operate the system
	Evaluate the system
	Modify the system

13-3 What are the principal methodologies for modeling and designing systems?

There are alternative methodologies for modeling and designing systems. Structured methodologies and object-oriented development are the most prominent.

Structured Methodologies

Structured methodologies have been used to document, analyze, and design information systems since the 1970s. **Structured** refers to the fact that the techniques are step by step, with each step building on the previous one. Structured methodologies are top-down, progressing from the highest, most abstract level to the lowest level of detail—from the general to the specific.

Structured development methods are process-oriented, focusing primarily on modeling the processes, or actions that capture, store, manipulate, and distribute data as the data flow through a system. These methods separate data from processes. A separate programming procedure must be written every time someone wants to take an action on a particular piece of data. The procedures act on data that the program passes to them.

The primary tool for representing a system's component processes and the flow of data between them is the **data flow diagram (DFD)**. The data flow diagram offers a logical graphic model of information flow, partitioning a system into modules that show manageable levels of detail. It rigorously specifies the processes or transformations that occur within each module and the interfaces that exist between them.

Figure 13.6 shows a simple data flow diagram for a mail-in university course registration system. The rounded boxes represent processes, which portray the transformation of data. The square box represents an external entity, which is an originator or receiver of information located outside the boundaries of

**FIGURE 13.6   DATA FLOW DIAGRAM FOR MAIL-IN UNIVERSITY
REGISTRATION SYSTEM**

The system has three processes: Verify availability (1.0), Enroll student (2.0), and Confirm
registration (3.0). The name and content of each of the data flows appear adjacent to
each arrow. There is one external entity in this system: the student. There are two data
stores: the student master file and the course file.

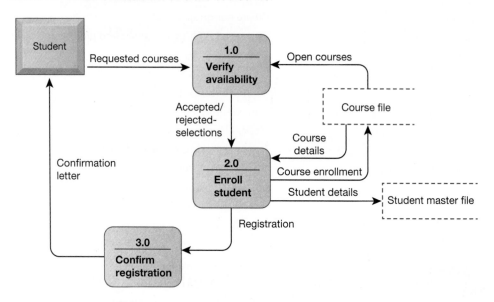

the system being modeled. The open rectangles represent data stores, which
are either manual or automated inventories of data. The arrows represent data
flows, which show the movement between processes, external entities, and
data stores. They contain packets of data with the name or content of each data
flow listed beside the arrow.

This data flow diagram shows that students submit registration forms with
their name, their identification number, and the numbers of the courses they
wish to take. In process 1.0, the system verifies that each course selected is still
open by referencing the university's course file. The file distinguishes courses
that are open from those that have been canceled or filled. Process 1.0 then determines which of the student's selections can be accepted or rejected. Process
2.0 enrolls the student in the courses for which he or she has been accepted.
It updates the university's course file with the student's name and identification number and recalculates the class size. If maximum enrollment has been
reached, the course number is flagged as closed. Process 2.0 also updates the
university's student master file with information about new students or changes
in address. Process 3.0 then sends each student applicant a confirmation of registration letter listing the courses for which he or she is registered and noting
the course selections that could not be fulfilled.

The diagrams can be used to depict higher-level processes as well as lower-
level details. Through leveled data flow diagrams, a complex process can be
broken down into successive levels of detail. An entire system can be divided
into subsystems with a high-level data flow diagram. Each subsystem, in turn,
can be divided into additional subsystems with second-level data flow diagrams,
and the lower-level subsystems can be broken down again until the lowest level
of detail has been reached.

Another tool for structured analysis is a data dictionary, which contains information about individual pieces of data and data groupings within a system

FIGURE 13.7 HIGH-LEVEL STRUCTURE CHART FOR A PAYROLL SYSTEM

This structure chart shows the highest or most abstract level of design for a payroll system, providing an overview of the entire system.

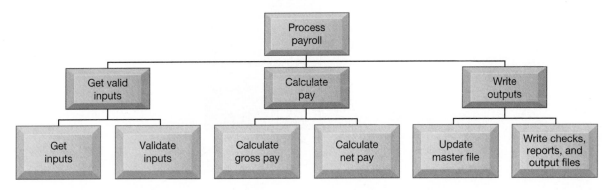

(see Chapter 6). The data dictionary defines the contents of data flows and data stores so that systems builders understand exactly what pieces of data they contain. **Process specifications** describe the transformation occurring within the lowest level of the data flow diagrams. They express the logic for each process.

In structured methodology, software design is modeled using hierarchical structure charts. The **structure chart** is a top-down chart, showing each level of design, its relationship to other levels, and its place in the overall design structure. The design first considers the main function of a program or system, then breaks this function into subfunctions, and decomposes each subfunction until the lowest level of detail has been reached. Figure 13.7 shows a high-level structure chart for a payroll system. If a design has too many levels to fit onto one structure chart, it can be broken down further on more detailed structure charts. A structure chart may document one program, one system (a set of programs), or part of one program.

Object-Oriented Development

Structured methods are useful for modeling processes but do not handle the modeling of data well. They also treat data and processes as logically separate entities, whereas in the real world such separation seems unnatural. Different modeling conventions are used for analysis (the data flow diagram) and for design (the structure chart).

Object-oriented development addresses these issues. Object-oriented development uses the **object** as the basic unit of systems analysis and design. An object combines data and the specific processes that operate on those data. Data encapsulated in an object can be accessed and modified only by the operations, or methods, associated with that object. Instead of passing data to procedures, programs send a message for an object to perform an operation that is already embedded in it. The system is modeled as a collection of objects and the relationships among them. Because processing logic resides within objects rather than in separate software programs, objects must collaborate with each other to make the system work.

Object-oriented modeling is based on the concepts of *class* and *inheritance*. Objects belonging to a certain class, or general category of similar objects, have the features of that class. Classes of objects in turn can inherit all the structure and behaviors of a more general class and then add variables and behaviors unique to each object. New classes of objects are created by choosing an

> **FIGURE 13.8 CLASS AND INHERITANCE**
>
> This figure illustrates how classes inherit the common features of their superclass.

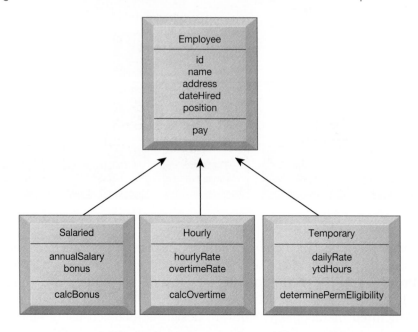

existing class and specifying how the new class differs from the existing class instead of starting from scratch each time.

We can see how class and inheritance work in Figure 13.8, which illustrates the relationships among classes concerning employees and how they are paid. Employee is the common ancestor, or superclass, for the other three classes. Salaried, Hourly, and Temporary are subclasses of Employee. The class name is in the top compartment, the attributes for each class are in the middle portion of each box, and the list of operations is in the bottom portion of each box. The features that are shared by all employees (ID, name, address, date hired, position, and pay) are stored in the Employee superclass, whereas each subclass stores features that are specific to that particular type of employee. Specific to hourly employees, for example, are their hourly rates and overtime rates. A solid line from the subclass to the superclass is a generalization path showing that the subclasses Salaried, Hourly, and Temporary have common features that can be generalized into the superclass Employee.

Object-oriented development is more iterative and incremental than traditional structured development. During analysis, systems builders document the functional requirements of the system, specifying its most important properties and what the proposed system must do. Interactions between the system and its users are analyzed to identify objects, which include both data and processes. The object-oriented design phase describes how the objects will behave and how they will interact with one another. Similar objects are grouped together to form a class, and classes are grouped into hierarchies in which a subclass inherits the attributes and methods from its superclass.

The information system is implemented by translating the design into program code, reusing classes that are already available in a library of reusable software objects, and adding new ones created during the object-oriented design phase. Implementation may also involve the creation of an object-oriented database. The resulting system must be thoroughly tested and evaluated.

Because objects are reusable, object-oriented development could potentially reduce the time and cost of writing software because organizations can reuse software objects that have already been created as building blocks for other applications. New systems can be created by using some existing objects, changing others, and adding a few new objects. Object-oriented frameworks have been developed to provide reusable, semicomplete applications that the organization can further customize into finished applications.

Computer-Aided Software Engineering

Computer-aided software engineering (CASE)—sometimes called *computer-aided systems engineering*—provides software tools to automate the methodologies we have just described to reduce the amount of repetitive work in systems development. CASE tools provide automated graphics facilities for producing charts and diagrams, screen and report generators, data dictionaries, extensive reporting facilities, analysis and checking tools, code generators, and documentation generators. CASE tools also have capabilities for validating design diagrams and specifications. Team members can share their work easily by accessing each other's files to review or modify what has been done. Modest productivity benefits can also be achieved if the tools are used properly, which requires organizational discipline.

13-4 What are alternative methods for building information systems?

Systems differ in terms of their size and technological complexity and in terms of the organizational problems they are meant to solve. A number of systems-building approaches have been developed to deal with these differences. This section describes these alternative methods: the traditional systems life cycle, prototyping, application software packages and cloud software services, end-user development, and outsourcing.

Traditional Systems Life Cycle

The **systems life cycle** is the oldest method for building information systems. The life cycle methodology is a phased approach to building a system, dividing systems development into formal stages, as illustrated in Figure 13.9. Systems development specialists have different opinions on how to partition the systems-building stages, but they roughly correspond to the stages of systems development we have just described.

The systems life cycle methodology maintains a formal division of labor between end users and information systems specialists. Technical specialists, such as systems analysts and programmers, are responsible for much of the systems analysis, design, and implementation work; end users are limited to providing information requirements and reviewing the technical staff's work. The life cycle also emphasizes formal specifications and paperwork, so many documents are generated during the course of a systems project.

The systems life cycle is still used for building large, complex systems that require a rigorous and formal requirements analysis, predefined specifications, and tight controls over the system-building process. However, the systems life cycle approach can be costly, time-consuming, and inflexible. Although systems builders can go back and forth among stages in the life cycle, the systems life cycle is predominantly a "waterfall" approach in which tasks in one stage are completed before work for the next stage begins. Activities can be repeated, but volumes of new

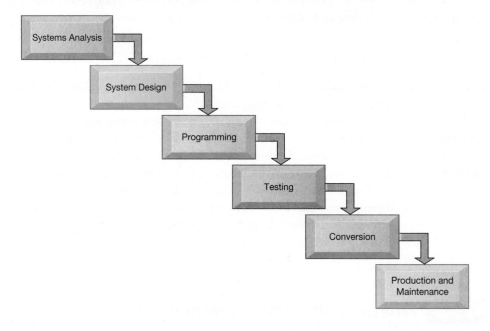

FIGURE 13.9 THE TRADITIONAL SYSTEMS DEVELOPMENT LIFE CYCLE

The systems development life cycle partitions systems development into formal stages, with each stage requiring completion before the next stage can begin.

documents must be generated and steps retraced if requirements and specifications need to be revised. This encourages freezing of specifications relatively early in the development process. The life cycle approach is also not suitable for many small desktop systems, which tend to be less structured and more individualized.

Prototyping

Prototyping consists of building an experimental system rapidly and inexpensively for end users to evaluate. By interacting with the prototype, users can get a better idea of their information requirements. The prototype endorsed by the users can be used as a template to create the final system.

The **prototype** is a working version of an information system or part of the system, but it is meant to be only a preliminary model. Once operational, the prototype will be further refined until it conforms precisely to users' requirements. Once the design has been finalized, the prototype can be converted to a polished production system.

The process of building a preliminary design, trying it out, refining it, and trying again has been called an **iterative** process of systems development because the steps required to build a system can be repeated over and over again. Prototyping is more explicitly iterative than the conventional life cycle, and it actively promotes system design changes. It has been said that prototyping replaces unplanned rework with planned iteration, with each version more accurately reflecting users' requirements.

Steps in Prototyping

Figure 13.10 shows a four-step model of the prototyping process, which consists of the following:

> ***Step 1:*** *Identify the user's basic requirements.* The systems designer (usually an information systems specialist) works with the user only long enough to capture the user's basic information needs.

| FIGURE 13.10   THE PROTOTYPING PROCESS

The process of developing a prototype can be broken down into four steps. Because a prototype can be developed quickly and inexpensively, systems builders can go through several iterations, repeating steps 3 and 4, to refine and enhance the prototype before arriving at the final operational one.

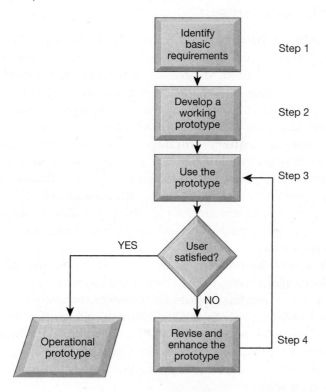

Step 2: *Develop an initial prototype.* The systems designer creates a working prototype quickly, using tools for rapidly generating software.

Step 3: *Use the prototype.* The user is encouraged to work with the system to determine how well the prototype meets his or her needs and to make suggestions for improving the prototype.

Step 4: *Revise and enhance the prototype.* The system builder notes all changes the user requests and refines the prototype accordingly. After the prototype has been revised, the cycle returns to Step 3. Steps 3 and 4 are repeated until the user is satisfied.

When no more iterations are required, the approved prototype then becomes an operational prototype that furnishes the final specifications for the application. Sometimes the prototype is adopted as the production version of the system.

Advantages and Disadvantages of Prototyping

Prototyping is most useful when there is some uncertainty about requirements or design solutions and is often used for designing an information system's **end-user interface** (the part of the system with which end users interact, such as online display and data entry screens, reports, or web pages). Because prototyping encourages intense end-user involvement throughout the systems development life cycle, it is more likely to produce systems that fulfill user requirements.

However, rapid prototyping can gloss over essential steps in systems development. If the completed prototype works reasonably well, management may not see the need for reprogramming, redesign, or full documentation and testing to build a polished production system. Some of these hastily constructed systems may not easily accommodate large quantities of data or a large number of users in a production environment.

End-User Development

End-user development allows end users, with little or no formal assistance from technical specialists, to create simple information systems, reducing the time and steps required to produce a finished application. Using user-friendly query languages and reporting, website development, graphics, and PC software tools, end users can access data, create reports, and develop simple applications on their own with little or no help from professional systems analysts or programmers. A **query language** is a software tool that provides immediate online answers to questions that are not predefined, such as "Who are the highest-performing sales representatives?" Query languages are often tied to data management software (see Chapter 6). For example, CEMEX, an international supplier of products for the construction industry, used Information Builders WebFOCUS to create a self-service reporting portal to visualize financial and operational data.

On the whole, end-user-developed systems can be completed more rapidly than those developed through the conventional systems life cycle. Allowing users to specify their own business needs improves requirements gathering and often leads to a higher level of user involvement and satisfaction with the system. However, end-user software tools still cannot replace conventional tools for some business applications because they cannot easily handle the processing of large numbers of transactions or applications with extensive procedural logic and updating requirements.

End-user computing also poses organizational risks because it occurs outside of traditional mechanisms for information systems management and control. When systems are created rapidly without a formal development methodology, testing and documentation may be inadequate. Control over data can be lost in systems outside the traditional information systems department. To help organizations maximize the benefits of end-user applications development, management should control the development of end-user applications by requiring cost justification of end-user information system projects and by establishing hardware, software, and quality standards for user-developed applications.

Application Software Packages, Software Services, and Outsourcing

Chapter 5 points out that much of today's software is not developed in-house but is purchased from external sources. Firms can rent the software from an online software service provider, they can purchase the software from a commercial vendor as a package to run in-house, or they can have a custom application developed by an outside outsourcing firm.

Application Software Packages and Cloud Software Services

Today many systems are based on commercially available application software packages or cloud software as a service (SaaS). For example, companies can choose to implement Oracle enterprise resource planning, supply chain management, or human capital management software in-house or pay to use this software running on the Oracle Cloud platform. Microsoft Office desktop productivity software comes in both desktop and cloud (Office 365) versions. Many applications are common to all business organizations—for example, payroll, accounts receivable, general ledger, or inventory control. For such universal functions with standard processes that do not change a great deal over time, a more generic system will fulfill the requirements of many organizations.

If a commercial software package or cloud software service can fulfill most of an organization's requirements, the company does not have to write its own software. The company can save time and money by using the prewritten, predesigned, pretested software programs from the software vendor. Package and SaaS vendors supply much of the ongoing maintenance and support for the system, including enhancements to keep the system in line with ongoing technical and business developments. When a package or SaaS solution is pursued, end users will be responsible for supplying the business information requirements for the system, and information systems specialists will provide technical requirements.

If an organization has unique requirements that the package does not meet, these tools include capabilities for customization. **Customization** features allow a commercial software package or cloud-based software to be modified to meet an organization's unique requirements without destroying the integrity of the software. (See the chapter-opening case on Cameron International and the chapter-ending case on Hitachi Consulting for examples.) If a great deal of customization is required, additional programming and customization work may become so expensive and time-consuming that they negate many of the advantages of software packages and services.

When a system is developed using an application software package or a cloud software service, systems analysis will include a formal evaluation of the software package or service in which both end users and information systems specialists will participate. The most important evaluation criteria are the functions provided by the software, flexibility, user-friendliness, hardware requirements, database requirements, installation and maintenance efforts, documentation, vendor quality, and cost. The package or software service evaluation process often is based on a **request for proposal (RFP)**, which is a detailed list of questions submitted to software vendors.

When software from an external source is selected, the organization no longer has total control over the systems design process. Instead of tailoring the systems design specifications directly to user requirements, the design effort will consist of trying to mold user requirements to conform to the features of the package or software service. If the organization's requirements conflict with the way the package or software service works and this software cannot be customized, the organization will have to adapt to the package or software service and change its procedures.

Outsourcing

If a firm does not want to use its internal resources to build or operate information systems, it can outsource the work to an external organization that specializes in providing these services. Cloud computing and software as a service (SaaS) providers, which we described in Chapter 5, are one form of outsourcing. Subscribing companies use the software and computer hardware provided by the service as the technical platform for their systems. In another form of outsourcing, a company could hire an external vendor to design and create the software for its system, but that company would operate the system on its own computers. The outsourcing vendor might be domestic or in another country.

Domestic outsourcing is driven primarily by the fact that outsourcing firms possess skills, resources, and assets that their clients do not have. Installing a new supply chain management system in a very large company might require hiring an additional 30 to 50 people with specific expertise in supply chain management software licensed from a vendor. Rather than hire permanent new employees, most of whom would need extensive training in the new software, and then release them after the new system is built, it makes more sense, and is often less expensive, to outsource this work for a 12-month period.

In the case of **offshore outsourcing**, the decision is much more cost-driven. A skilled programmer in India or Russia earns about $10,000–$30,000 per year compared with about $60,000 or more per year for a comparable programmer in the United States. The Internet and low-cost communications technology have drastically reduced the expense and difficulty of coordinating the work of global teams in offshore locations. In addition to cost savings, many offshore outsourcing firms offer world-class technology assets and skills. Wage inflation outside the United States has recently eroded some of these advantages, and some jobs have moved back to the United States. Firms generally do not outsource the conception, systems analysis, and design of IT systems to offshore firms, but often do outsource programming, testing, maintenance, and daily operation of IT systems.

A firm is most likely to benefit from outsourcing if it takes the time to evaluate all the risks and to make sure outsourcing is appropriate for its particular needs. Any company that outsources its applications must thoroughly understand the project, including its requirements, method of implementation, anticipated benefits, cost components, and metrics for measuring performance.

Many firms underestimate costs for identifying and evaluating vendors of information technology services, for transitioning to a new vendor, for improving internal software development methods to match those of outsourcing vendors, and for monitoring vendors to make sure they are fulfilling their contractual obligations. Companies will need to allocate resources for documenting requirements, sending out RFPs, handling travel expenses, negotiating contracts, and project management. Experts claim it takes from three months to a full year to fully transfer work to an offshore partner and make sure the vendor thoroughly understands your business.

Outsourcing offshore incurs additional costs for coping with cultural differences that drain productivity and dealing with human resources issues, such as terminating or relocating domestic employees. All of these hidden costs undercut some of the anticipated benefits from outsourcing. Firms should be especially cautious when using an outsourcer to develop or to operate applications that give it some type of competitive advantage.

General Motors Corporation (GM) had outsourced 90 percent of its IT services, including its data centers and application development. The company later decided to bring 90 percent of its IT infrastructure in-house, with only 10 percent managed by outsourcers. Lowering costs is important, but GM's primary reason for cutting back outsourcing was to take back control of its information systems, which it believes were preventing the company from responding quickly to competitive opportunities. Bringing information systems in-house will make it easier for GM to standardize and streamline its systems and data centers. Figure 13.11 shows best- and worst-case scenarios for the total cost of an offshore outsourcing project. It shows how much hidden costs affect the total project cost. The best case reflects the lowest estimates for additional costs, and the worst case reflects the highest estimates for these costs. As you can see, hidden costs increase the total cost of an offshore outsourcing project

FIGURE 13.11 TOTAL COST OF OFFSHORE OUTSOURCING

If a firm spends $10 million on offshore outsourcing contracts, that company will actually spend 15.2 percent in extra costs even in the best-case scenario. In the worst-case scenario, where there is a dramatic drop in productivity along with exceptionally high transition and layoff costs, a firm can expect to pay up to 57 percent in extra costs on top of the $10 million outlay for an offshore contract.

TOTAL COST OF OFFSHORE OUTSOURCING				
Cost of outsourcing contract			$10,000,000	
Hidden Costs	Best Case	Additional Cost ($)	Worst Case	Additional Cost ($)
1. Vendor selection	.02%	20,000	2%	200,000
2. Transition costs	2%	200,000	3%	300,000
3. Layoffs & retention	3%	300,000	5%	500,000
4. Lost productivity/cultural issues	3%	300,000	27%	2,700,000
5. Improving development processes	1%	100,000	10%	1,000,000
6. Managing the contract	6%	600,000	10%	1,000,000
Total additional costs		1,520,000		5,700,000
	Outstanding Contract ($)	Additional Cost ($)	Total Cost ($)	Additional Cost
Total cost of outsourcing (TCO) best case	10,000,000	1,520,000	11,520,000	15.2%
Total cost of outsourcing (TCO) worst case	10,000,000	5,700,000	15,700,000	57.0%

by an extra 15 to 57 percent. Even with these extra costs, many firms will benefit from offshore outsourcing if they manage the work well.

13-5 What are new approaches for system building in the digital firm era?

Technologies and business conditions are changing so rapidly that companies are adopting shorter, more informal systems development processes, including those for mobile applications. In addition to using software packages and online software services, businesses are relying more heavily on fast-cycle techniques such as rapid application development, joint application design, agile development, and reusable standardized software components that can be assembled into a complete software system.

Rapid Application Development (RAD), Agile Development, and DevOps

The term **rapid application development (RAD)** refers to the process of creating workable systems in a very short period of time with some flexibility to adapt as a project evolves. RAD includes the use of visual programming and other tools for building graphical user interfaces, iterative prototyping of key system elements, automation of program code generation, and close teamwork among end users and information systems specialists. Simple systems often can be assembled from prebuilt components. The process does not have to be sequential, and key parts of development can occur simultaneously.

Sometimes a technique called **joint application design (JAD)** is used to accelerate the generation of information requirements and to develop the initial systems design. JAD brings end users and information systems specialists together in an interactive session to discuss the system's design. Properly prepared and facilitated, JAD sessions can significantly speed up the design phase and involve users at an intense level.

Agile development focuses on rapid delivery of working software by breaking a large project into a series of small subprojects that are completed in short periods of time using iteration, continuous feedback, and continual user involvement. Each mini-project is worked on by a team as if it were a complete project and regularly released to the client. Improvement or addition of new functionality takes place within the next iteration as developers clarify requirements. Testing occurs early and often throughout the entire development process. Agile methods emphasize face-to-face communication, encouraging people to collaborate and make decisions quickly and effectively.

DevOps builds on agile development principles as an organizational strategy to create a culture and environment that further promote rapid and agile development practices. *DevOps* stands for "development and operations" and emphasizes close collaboration between the software developers who create applications and the IT operational staff who run and maintain the applications. Traditionally, in a large enterprise, an application development team would be in charge of gathering business requirements for an application, designing the application, and writing and testing the software. The operations team would run and maintain the software once it was put into production. Problems arise when the development team is unaware of operational issues that prevent the software from working as expected, requiring additional time and rework to fix the software.

DevOps tries to change this relationship by promoting better and more frequent communication and collaboration between systems development and operations groups and a fast and stable workflow throughout the entire application development life cycle. With this type of organizational change along with agile techniques, standardized processes, and more powerful automated software creation and testing tools, it is possible to build, test, and release applications more rapidly and more frequently. For example, DevOps helps developers at Netflix make hundreds of software changes each day.

Component-Based Development and Web Services

We have already described some of the benefits of object-oriented development for building systems that can respond to rapidly changing business environments, including web applications. To further expedite software creation, groups of objects have been assembled to provide software components for common functions such as a graphical user interface or online ordering capability that can be combined to create large-scale business applications. This approach to software development is called **component-based development**, and it enables a system to be built by assembling and integrating existing software components. Increasingly, these software components are coming from cloud services. Businesses are using component-based development to create their e-commerce applications by combining commercially available components for shopping carts, user authentication, search engines, and catalogs with pieces of software for their own unique business requirements.

Web Services and Service-Oriented Computing

Chapter 5 introduced *web services* as loosely coupled, reusable software components using Extensible Markup Language (XML) and other open protocols and standards that enable one application to communicate with another with no custom programming required to share data and services. In addition to supporting internal and external integration of systems, web services can be used as tools for building new information system applications or enhancing existing systems. Because these software services use a universal set of standards, they promise to be less expensive and less difficult to weave together than proprietary components.

Web services can perform certain functions on their own, and they can also engage other web services to complete more complex transactions, such as checking credit, procurement, or ordering products. By creating software components that can communicate and share data regardless of the operating system, programming language, or client device, web services can provide significant cost savings in systems building while opening up new opportunities for collaboration with other companies.

Mobile Application Development: Designing for a Multiscreen World

Today, employees and customers expect, and even demand, to be able to use a mobile device of their choice to obtain information or perform a transaction anywhere and at any time. To meet these needs, companies will need to develop mobile websites, mobile apps, and native apps as well as traditional information systems.

Once an organization decides to develop mobile apps, it has to make some important choices, including the technology it will use to implement these apps (whether to write a native app or mobile web app) and what to do about a mobile website. A **mobile website** is a version of a regular website that is scaled down in content and navigation for easy access and search on a small mobile screen. (Access Amazon's website from your computer and then from your smartphone to see the difference from a regular website.)

A **mobile web app** is an Internet-enabled app with specific functionality for mobile devices. Users access mobile web apps through their mobile device's web browser. The web app resides primarily on a server, is accessed via the Internet, and doesn't need to be installed on the device. The same application can be used by most devices that can surf the web, regardless of their brand.

A **native app** is a standalone application designed to run on a specific platform and device. The native app is installed directly on a mobile device. Native apps can connect to the Internet to download and upload data, and they can also operate on these data even when not connected to the Internet. For example, an e-book reading app such as Kindle software can download a book from the Internet, disconnect from the Internet, and present the book for reading. Native mobile apps provide fast performance and a high degree of reliability. They are also able to take advantage of a mobile device's particular capabilities, such as its camera or touch features. However, native apps are expensive to develop because multiple versions of an app must be programmed for different mobile operating systems and hardware.

Developing applications for mobile platforms is quite different from development for PCs and their much larger screens. The reduced size of mobile devices makes using fingers and multitouch gestures much easier than typing and using keyboards. Mobile apps need to be optimized for the specific tasks they are to perform, they should not try to carry out too many tasks, and they should be designed for usability. The user experience for mobile interaction is fundamentally different from using a desktop or laptop PC. Saving resources—bandwidth, screen space, memory, processing, data entry, and user gestures—is a top priority.

When a full website created for the desktop shrinks to the size of a smartphone screen, it is difficult for the user to navigate through the site. The user must continually zoom in and out and scroll to find relevant material. Therefore, companies need to design websites specifically for mobile interfaces and create multiple mobile sites to meet the needs of smartphones, tablets, and desktop browsers. This equates to at least three sites with separate content, maintenance, and costs. Currently, websites know what device you are using because your browser will send this information to the server when you log on. Based on this information, the server will deliver the appropriate screen.

One solution to the problem of having multiple websites is to use **responsive web design**. Responsive web design enables websites to change layouts automatically according to the visitor's screen resolution, whether on a desktop, laptop, tablet, or smartphone. Responsive design uses tools such as flexible grid-based layouts, flexible images, and media queries to optimize the design for different viewing contexts. This eliminates the need for separate design and development work for each new device. HTML5, which we introduced in Chapter 5, is also used for mobile application development because it can support cross-platform mobile applications.

The Interactive Session on Technology describes how some companies have addressed the challenges of mobile development we have just identified.

13-6 How will MIS help my career?

Here is how Chapter 13 and this book can help you find a job as an entry-level junior business systems analyst.

The Company

Systems 100 Technology Consultants, a Chicago-based professional technology services firm, provides staffing and information technology consulting services to other U.S. companies and has an open position for an entry-level junior business systems analyst. The company provides business and technology consultants to more than 150 firms in financial services, healthcare, communications, transportation, energy, consumer goods, and technology, helping them implement business and technology initiatives cost-effectively.

Position Description

A junior business systems analyst is expected to work in project teams throughout all phases of the software development life cycle, including defining business requirements, developing detailed design specifications, and working with application developers to build or enhance systems and business processes. Before undertaking assignments, new business systems analysts receive training in the background they will need to succeed in their assignments. The first assignment is to work on a contract basis for a startup data analytics company in Michigan serving mid-sized organizations. The junior business systems analyst would work with a team of data scientists to help clients integrate data sources, cleanse and organize messy data, and improve understanding of patterns and trends.

INTERACTIVE SESSION **TECHNOLOGY**

Systems Development Is Different for Mobile Apps

Just about all businesses today want to deploy mobile apps and they want these apps developed in a very short time frame. That's not so easy.

Developing successful mobile apps poses some unique challenges. The user experience on a mobile device is fundamentally different from that on a PC. There are special features on mobile devices such as location-based services that give firms the potential to interact with customers in meaningful new ways. Firms need to be able to take advantage of those features while delivering an experience that is appropriate to a small screen. There are multiple platforms for mobile software, including iOS, Android, and Windows 10, and a firm may need a different version of an application to run on each of these as well as on devices of different sizes and capabilities. Mobile devices might be tiny and worn on the wrist or they might be large high-definition tablet displays. They might include sensors and audio output and even displays combining real and virtual images. System builders need to understand how, why, and where customers use mobile devices and how these mobile experiences change business interactions and behavior. You can't just port a website or desktop application to a smartphone or tablet. It's a different systems development process. Many enterprises require applications that link to corporate systems and function on the desktop as well as on mobile devices. Take, for example, Great-West Financial, the second largest retirement services company in the United States with approximately $461 billion in assets under its administration. Company employees spend more time serving customers in the field rather than in the office and needed a connection to the company's ERP Financials system from wherever they are working to process accounts payable invoice approvals. Great-West decided to deploy the Dolphin Mobile Approvals app for this purpose.

Great-West selected Dolphin because it could handle all of its SAP workflows in a single app, so that employees did not have to go to one place to approve invoices and another to approve everything else. Great-West configured the app to make its look and feel as similar as possible to the application users accessed on their desktops. The user sees the same data fields on the invoice header and line item

on a mobile device as on a desktop computer screen, and the steps in the invoice approval process are the same. However, given the difficulty of jumping back and forth between different screens on a mobile device, the mobile app incorporates the necessary invoice approval codes into its line-item detail rather than displaying these codes on a PDF attachment. On a desktop, users must sign into the SAP system in order to see an invoice and will receive notification that an invoice is available for approval via email. A pop-up notification on the mobile app eliminates the need for users to log into the app before knowing about an invoice.

Before deploying the mobile app, Great-West had to set up an appropriate mobile infrastructure, considering factors such as security, sign-on, and back-end integration. Since this was the company's first mobile app interfacing to the SAP system, the company had to make sure the mobile app could incorporate the entire workflow from the SAP system and that all the data was encrypted and secure. Great-West purchased 1,000 licenses for the mobile approvals app (which is compatible with both iOS and Android devices) and issued company-owned devices to senior executives and the heaviest invoice users. Remaining users are allowed to use the app on their own devices as long as they conform to the firm's BYOD policy.

For the past few years, United Parcel Service (UPS) has provided customers with a UPS Mobile app to track their shipments and obtain pricing information using smartphones and tablets. UPS developers initially wrote and maintained multiple versions of UPS Mobile, including one for iOS in Objective-C and another for Android in Java. This meant twice the work for UPS mobile developers. The different versions of the app might not be updated at the same time, so customers with different types of devices didn't always have access to the latest features at the same time.

UPS was able to move the UPS Mobile app to a single development platform, but this entailed an enormous amount of work. The company selected Visual Studio Tools for Xamarin for this purpose because it allowed developers to share one C# code base across platforms and deliver fully native apps to customers. Xamarin also had better integration with mobile devices' unique hardware and capabilities. Although UPS had to rebuild more than 130,000 lines of code that had been written over a four-year period, management realized that rewriting UPS Mobile would produce dramatic time and cost savings in the long run. The company went ahead with developing on a single platform. Much of the Xamarin code would need to be developed only once and it could support multiple platforms with great efficiency in the years to come. UPS mobile developers rewrote all versions of UPS Mobile with Visual Studio Tools for Xamarin. UPS can now add a new feature across all mobile devices in weeks and days instead of months.

Sources: Rob Bamforth, "Developers at the Mobile Edge," *Computer Weekly,* January 30–February 5, 2018; Mary K. Pratt, Linda Tucci, "Enterprise Mobile App Development: No Easy Answers," searchCIOtechtarget.com, accessed February 20, 2018; Microsoft, "UPS Paves the Way for Better Service with Faster Development and Artificial Intelligence," September 28, 2017; www.greatwest.com, accessed February 20, 2018; and Ken Murphy, "Great-West Financial Establishes Its Mobile Footprint," *SAP Insider Profiles,* October 31, 2016.

CASE STUDY QUESTIONS

1. What management, organization, and technology challenges need to be addressed when building a mobile application?

2. How does user requirement definition for mobile applications differ from traditional systems analysis?

3. Describe how Great-West's invoice approvals process changed after the mobile application was deployed.

Job Requirements

- Upcoming or recent college graduate, with BA in Management Information Systems, Finance, Psychology, or related field
- 3 to 6-plus months of corporate work or internship experience, including experience working with a project team
- Strong understanding of technology and systems, and business process improvement
- Strong analytical, communication, and problem-solving skills
- Ability to work comfortably in a team environment
- Knowledge and understanding of the software development life cycle and business process improvement
- Knowledge of MS Office applications
- Exposure to SQL desirable but not required

Interview Questions

1. What information systems courses have you taken, including MIS, database, data analytics, and systems development? Can you write SQL queries?

2. Have you worked on any systems development projects? If so, what exactly did you do? What systems development practices did you use?

3. Have you worked on any other kinds of projects, and what role did you play? Do you have samples of the writing or output you produced for these projects?

4. Which Microsoft Office tools have you used? What kinds of problems have you used these tools to solve?

5. Have you any experience with agile software development?

Author Tips

1. Review the discussion of business processes in Chapter 2 and Chapter 13 and the Chapter 14 discussion of IT project management and implementation. Be prepared to talk about any systems development experience you have had, including analyzing or redesigning business processes. Also be prepared to discuss contemporary systems development practices.

2. Inquire about how you would be using SQL and Microsoft Office tools for the job and what skills you would be expected to demonstrate. Bring samples of the work you have done with this software. Express interest in learning what you don't know about these tools to fulfill your job assignments.

3. Bring samples of your writing (including some from your Digital Portfolio described in MyLab MIS) demonstrating your analytical and business application skills and project experience.

REVIEW SUMMARY

13-1 How does building new systems produce organizational change?

Building a new information system is a form of planned organizational change. Four kinds of technology-enabled change are (1) automation, (2) rationalization of procedures, (3) business process redesign, and (4) paradigm shift, with far-reaching changes carrying the greatest risks and rewards. Many organizations are using business process management to redesign workflows and business processes in the hope of achieving dramatic productivity breakthroughs. Business process management is also useful for promoting total quality management (TQM), Six Sigma, and other initiatives for incremental process improvement.

13-2 What are the core activities in the systems development process?

The core activities in systems development are systems analysis, systems design, programming, testing, conversion, production, and maintenance. Systems analysis is the study and analysis of problems of existing systems and the identification of requirements for their solutions. Systems design provides the specifications for an information system solution, showing how its technical and organizational components fit together.

13-3 What are the principal methodologies for modeling and designing systems?

The two principal methodologies for modeling and designing information systems are structured methodologies and object-oriented development. Structured methodologies focus on modeling processes and data separately. The data flow diagram is the principal tool for structured analysis, and the structure chart is the principal tool for representing structured software design. Object-oriented development models a system as a collection of objects that combine processes and data. Object-oriented modeling is based on the concepts of class and inheritance.

13-4 What are alternative methods for building information systems?

The oldest method for building systems is the systems life cycle, which requires that information systems be developed in formal stages. The stages must proceed sequentially and have defined outputs; each requires formal approval before the next stage can commence. The systems life cycle is useful for large projects that need formal specifications and tight management control over each stage of systems building, but it is very rigid and costly.

Prototyping consists of building an experimental system rapidly and inexpensively for end users to interact with and evaluate. Prototyping encourages end-user involvement in systems development and iteration of design until specifications are captured accurately. The rapid creation of prototypes can result in systems that have not been completely tested or documented or that are technically inadequate for a production environment.

Using a software package or online software services (SaaS) reduces the amount of design, programming, testing, installation, and maintenance work required to build a system. Application software packages or SaaS are helpful if a firm does not have the internal information systems staff or financial resources to custom develop a system. To meet an organization's unique requirements, packages may require extensive modifications that can substantially raise development costs.

End-user development is the development of information systems by end users, either alone or with minimal assistance from information systems specialists. End user–developed systems can be created rapidly and informally using user-friendly software tools. However, end-user development may create information systems that do not necessarily meet quality assurance standards and that are not easily controlled by traditional means.

Outsourcing consists of using an external vendor to build (or operate) a firm's information systems instead of the organization's internal information systems staff. Outsourcing can save application development costs or enable firms to develop applications without an internal information systems staff. However, firms risk losing control over their information systems and becoming too dependent on external vendors. Outsourcing also entails hidden costs, especially when the work is sent offshore.

13-5 What are new approaches for system building in the digital firm era?

Companies are turning to rapid application design (RAD), joint application design (JAD), agile development, and reusable software components to accelerate the systems development process. RAD uses object-oriented software, visual programming, prototyping, and tools for very rapid creation of systems. Agile development breaks a large project into a series of small subprojects that are completed in short periods of time using iteration and continuous feedback. Component-based development expedites application development by grouping objects into suites of software components that can be combined to create large-scale business applications. DevOps emphasizes close collaboration between the software developers who create applications and the IT operational staff who run and maintain the applications. Web services provide a common set of standards that enable organizations to link their systems regardless of their technology platform through standard plug-and-play architecture. Mobile application development must pay attention to simplicity, usability, and the need to optimize tasks for tiny screens.

Key Terms

Acceptance testing, 505
Agile development, 518
Automation, 495
Business process management (BPM), 498
Business process redesign, 496
Component-based development, 518
Computer-aided software engineering (CASE), 511
Conversion, 506
Customization, 515
Data flow diagram (DFD), 507
DevOps, 518
Direct cutover strategy, 506
Documentation, 506
End-user development, 514
End-user interface, 513
Feasibility study, 503
Information requirements, 503
Iterative, 512
Joint application design (JAD), 517
Maintenance, 506
Mobile web app, 519
Mobile website, 519
Native app, 519
Object, 509
Object-oriented development, 509
Offshore outsourcing, 516
Paradigm shift, 498

Parallel strategy, 506
Phased approach strategy, 506
Pilot study strategy, 506
Post-implementation audit, 506
Process specifications, 509
Production, 506
Programming, 504
Prototype, 512
Prototyping, 512
Query languages, 514
Rapid application development (RAD), 517
Rationalization of procedures, 495
Request for proposal (RFP), 515
Responsive web design, 520
Six Sigma, 496
Structure chart, 509
Structured, 507
System testing, 505
Systems analysis, 502
Systems design, 503
Systems development, 502
Systems life cycle, 511
Test plan, 505
Testing, 505
Total quality management (TQM), 496
Unit testing, 505

MyLab MIS

To complete the problems with MyLab MIS, go to the EOC Discussion Questions in MyLab MIS.

Review Questions

13-1 How does building new systems produce organizational change?

- Describe each of the four kinds of organizational change that can be promoted with information technology.
- Define business process management and describe the steps required to carry it out.

13-2 What are the core activities in the systems development process?

- Distinguish between systems analysis and systems design. Describe the activities for each.
- Define information requirements and explain why they are difficult to determine correctly.
- Explain why the testing stage of systems development is so important. Name and describe the three stages of testing for an information system.
- Describe the role of programming, conversion, production, and maintenance in systems development.

13-3 What are the principal methodologies for modeling and designing systems?

- Compare object-oriented and traditional structured approaches for modeling and designing systems.

13-4 What are alternative methods for building information systems?

- Define the traditional systems life cycle. Describe its advantages and disadvantages for systems building.

- Define information system prototyping. Describe its benefits and limitations. List and describe the steps in the prototyping process.
- Define an application software package. Explain the advantages and disadvantages of developing information systems based on software packages.
- Define end-user development and describe its advantages and disadvantages. Name some policies and procedures for managing end-user development.
- Describe the advantages and disadvantages of using outsourcing for building information systems.

13-5 What are new approaches for system building in the digital firm era?

- Define rapid application development (RAD), agile development, and DevOps and explain how they can speed up system building.
- Explain how component-based development and web services help firms build and enhance their information systems.
- Explain the features of mobile application development and responsive web design.

Discussion Questions

13-6
MyLab MIS
Why is selecting a systems development approach an important business decision? Who should participate in the selection process?

13-7
MyLab MIS
Some have said that the best way to reduce systems development costs is to use application software packages, SaaS, or user-friendly tools. Do you agree? Why or why not?

13-8
MyLab MIS
Why is it so important to understand how a business process works when trying to develop a new information system?

Hands-On MIS Projects

The projects in this section give you hands-on experience analyzing business processes, designing and building a customer system for auto sales, and analyzing website information requirements.

Management Decision Problems

13-9   For an additional fee, a customer purchasing a Sears Roebuck appliance, such as a washing machine, can purchase a three-year service contract. The contract provides free repair service and parts for the specified appliance using an authorized Sears service provider. When a person with a Sears service contract needs to repair an appliance, such as a washing machine, he or she calls the Sears Repairs & Parts department to schedule an appointment. The department makes the appointment and gives the caller the date and approximate time of the appointment. The repair technician arrives during the designated time frame and diagnoses the problem. If the problem is caused by a faulty part, the technician either replaces the part if he or she is carrying the part or orders the replacement part from Sears. If the part is not in stock at Sears, Sears orders the part and gives the customer an approximate time when the part will arrive. The part is shipped directly to the customer. After the part has arrived, the customer must call Sears to schedule a second appointment for a repair technician to replace the ordered part. This process is very lengthy. It may take two weeks to schedule the first repair visit, another two weeks to order and receive the required part, and another week to schedule a second repair visit after the ordered part has been received.

- Diagram the existing process.
- What is the impact of the existing process on Sears's operational efficiency and customer relationships?
- What changes could be made to make this process more efficient? How could information systems support these changes? Diagram the improved process.

13-10   Management at your agricultural chemicals corporation has been dissatisfied with production planning. Production plans are created using best guesses of demand for each product, which are based on how much of each product has been ordered in the past. If a customer places an unexpected order or requests a change to an existing order after it has been placed, there is no way to adjust production plans. The company may have to tell customers it can't fill their orders, or it may run up extra costs maintaining additional inventory to prevent stock-outs.

At the end of each month, orders are totaled and manually keyed into the company's production planning system. Data from the past month's production and inventory systems are manually entered into the firm's order management system. Analysts from the sales department and from the production department analyze the data from their respective systems to determine what the sales targets and production targets should be for the next month. These estimates are usually different. The analysts then get together at a high-level planning meeting to revise the production and sales targets to take into account senior management's goals for market share, revenues, and profits. The outcome of the meeting is a finalized production master schedule.

The entire production planning process takes 17 business days to complete. Nine of these days are required to enter and validate the data. The remaining days are spent developing and reconciling the production and sales targets and finalizing the production master schedule.

- Draw a diagram of the existing production planning process.
- Analyze the problems this process creates for the company.
- How could an enterprise system solve these problems? In what ways could it lower costs? Diagram what the production planning process might look like if the company implemented enterprise software.

Improving Decision Making: Using Database Software to Design a Customer System for Auto Sales

Software skills: Database design, querying, reporting, and forms
Business skills: Sales lead and customer analysis

13-11   This project requires you to perform a systems analysis and then design a system solution using database software.

Ace Auto Dealers specializes in selling new vehicles from Subaru in Portland, Oregon. The company advertises in local newspapers and is listed as an authorized dealer on the Subaru website and other major websites for auto buyers. The company benefits from a good local word-of-mouth reputation and name recognition.

Ace does not believe it has enough information about its customers. It cannot easily determine which prospects have made auto purchases, nor can it identify which customer touch points have produced the greatest number of sales leads or actual sales so it can focus advertising and marketing more on the channels that generate the most revenue. Are purchasers discovering Ace from newspaper ads, from word of mouth, or from the web?

Prepare a systems analysis report detailing Ace's problem and a system solution that can be implemented using PC database management software. Then use database software to develop a simple system solution. In MyLab MIS, you will find more information about Ace and its information requirements to help you develop the solution.

Achieving Operational Excellence: Analyzing Website Design and Information Requirements

Software skills: Web browser software
Business skills: Information requirements analysis, website design

13-12 Visit the website of your choice and explore it thoroughly. Prepare a report analyzing the various functions provided by that website and its information requirements. Your report should answer these questions: What functions does the website perform? What data does it use? What are its inputs, outputs, and processes? What are some of its other design specifications? Does the website link to any internal systems or systems of other organizations? What value does this website provide the firm?

Collaboration and Teamwork Project

Preparing Website Design Specifications

13-13 With three or four of your classmates, select a system described in this text that uses the web. Review the website for the system you select. Use what you have learned from the website and the description in this book to prepare a report describing some of the design specifications for the system you select. If possible, use Google Docs and Google Drive or Google Sites to brainstorm, organize, and develop a presentation of your findings for the class.

Hitachi Consulting Moves Human Resources to the Cloud

CASE STUDY

Hitachi Consulting Corporation is an international management and technology consulting firm headquartered in Dallas, Texas and a subsidiary of Hitachi Ltd. based in Tokyo, Japan. Hitachi Consulting currently employs approximately 6,500 people in 22 countries, including the United States, Japan, Brazil, China, India, Portugal, Singapore, Spain, the UK, Germany, and Vietnam. Because the company provides consulting services, its employees are its most important resource. To succeed competitively, Hitachi Consulting must ensure that it has the right number of employees with the right skills and expertise wherever and whenever the need for its consulting services arise. The human resources function is especially important in a company of this sort.

Four years ago, Hitachi Consulting decided to grow its business model to include turnkey and custom solutions combining business best practices and leading-edge technologies such as the Internet of Things (IoT) as well as traditional consulting services. Hitachi is doing this across many areas—rail and transportation, energy, water, cities, healthcare, and public safety. A key success factor is to collaborate with partners, clients and other stakeholders across entire industries. These new offerings require people with appropriate talents and skills to deliver Hitachi Consulting's new solution portfolio. The company had to recast its Human Resources department to operate more strategically so that it would have the right human resources in place to do the work.

Hitachi Consulting was saddled with multiple disparate local human resources systems (and in some cases just spreadsheets) that held its valuable employee data. These systems were not integrated with the company's legacy Human Resources system in the United States. There was no way to easily obtain an enterprise-wide view of the company's workforce. When a senior executive requested such company-wide data for decision making, HR staff had to manually assemble and aggregate the necessary data. The process would take days. Dealing with such complex manual processes and siloed data prevented the company from operating under a "single source of truth."

For the company to move forward, its Human Resources function had to be transformed and its legacy HR system needed to be replaced. One top priority was to improve business processes for talent acquisition and development so that Hitachi Consulting could find the right people better, faster, and cheaper. In the past, Hitachi Consulting waited until a new position opened before actively recruiting new talent. Its new HR function sought to cultivate relationships with top candidates, fueled by employee referrals and social networks. Through ongoing dialogues, the HR staff could identify star talent and quickly hire these people when the time was right. Hitachi hoped that the new HR system would reduce recruiting costs, improve candidate experience, engagement, and retention, and expand recognition of Hitachi as an employer of choice.

Another high priority was having a single system of record as the authoritative source of information for all of HCC's regions with a central repository for HR data. With an enterprise-wide cloud application, HR and IT managers could centrally assign authorizations for data access based on roles and responsibilities, while also enforcing global security and regulatory policies. HCC's workforce regularly works at client sites and requires access to enterprise data and applications from tablets and smartphones, so the new solution needed to provide mobile access as well, which was not possible with HCC's legacy systems. Other goals included expanded analytics and reporting capabilities, and a global platform to streamline compensation, benefits, and absence management.

A steering committee composed of HR, business, and IT leadership evaluated various technology options, selecting Oracle HCM Cloud for the solution. Oracle HCM Cloud is a cloud-based system for Human Capital Management (HCM), providing a single global human resources solution to maintain employee records, align common HR processes, attract, develop and retain top talent, improve employee productivity, control labor costs, and address simple and complex employee compensation needs. There are capabilities for recruiting candidates, managing performance, developing careers, providing learning, performing talent reviews, and planning successions.

Hitachi Consulting was growing quickly, and the flexibility of cloud computing was helpful when it had to quickly absorb large numbers of employees from a new acquisition. At one point, Hitachi Consulting had less than two weeks to bring hundreds of new employees into its legacy HR system. With the old system, it was a challenge to ensure the company had sufficient hardware and software resources to accommodate the new employees without overspending for additional infrastructure, or just as risky, keeping a lid on infrastructure expenditures so that the system couldn't handle future growth. With a cloud platform, Hitachi Consulting could simply bring the new employees into the HR application and adjust its contract with Oracle to accommodate the additional head count. Switching computing to a cloud software service provider also would relieve Hitachi Consulting's IT staff from routine data center maintenance tasks, leaving more time for strategic business initiatives, such as creating reports and analyses for decision-makers.

Oracle HCM Cloud met all these requirements, and it also featured a streamlined modern interface that would make the system much easier for employees to use than the antiquated interface of HCC's legacy system. The Oracle cloud platform's flexibility also appealed to the steering committee. With many cloud services, customers must adapt their processes to the services' requirements. Oracle HCM Cloud offers standard processes, but it also lets organizations customize processes when necessary.

The HCC team steering committee also found that Oracle HCM Cloud offered tight security and regulatory controls required to safeguard HR data, some of which is highly sensitive. For years, many companies were reluctant to adopt cloud computing, concerned that outside service providers would not be able to safeguard sensitive data as effectively as systems housed and managed on-site. Over time, cloud computing's reputation for reliability and security has increased. More firms have decided that cloud security is on par with what they could do on premises. The HCC steering committee was convinced that Oracle is addressing the latest security threats and is doing everything as well as or better than the company to protect employee data.

Senior management approved the HR modernization plan in early 2014, with the new system projected to go live in September 2015. The project leaders realized they would need to carefully manage the employee experience so staffers would become comfortable with the changes created by the new system. Both HR and IT staff directly involved with

the HR modernization project also had to perform their usual duties. Project leaders devised a time-sharing plan that pulled individuals into the modernization project when their expertise was most needed, but quickly returned them to their regular jobs to keep HCC's business on track.

Implementation of the Oracle Human Capital Management Cloud to serve Hitachi Consulting's entire global workforce has provided many benefits for Hitachi Consulting. It has reduced the time and cost to hire new employees and improved top talent identification, development, and retention. The employee referral process used to falter because staff members questioned whether their suggestions were actually implemented. With the new system, the referring party is more clearly identified and tagged for eventual rewards if the referral leads to a successful new hire. HCC's referral rate of new talent from current employees has increased from 17 to 35 percent. The company was able to save $1 million in the first year the system was operational by reducing payments to search firms. It has become easier to absorb and integrate employees from acquisitions.

HCC senior executives and regional managers can now access workforce information when making decisions about HCC's new business direction. For example, HCC's senior executives recently asked HCC director of service delivery Matt Revell for the company's employee head count and turnover trends over the last 12 months to evaluate the investments managers were making for people in HCC's sales and solutions organizations. To gather that information in the past, Revell's staff had to request the data from managers in each HCC region and then standardize the information. (This was because some definitions, such as those for full-time employees versus contingent staff, weren't consistent.) Only then could HCC's U.S.-based analytics group aggregate the data and run the final report. Oracle HCM Cloud has centralized all of HCC's HR information and uses a common enterprise-wide set of definitions. Reporting and analytics work can be accomplished much faster and more accurately.

The new centralized system has also made the HR department more efficient by replacing dozens of separate processes that had been running in various regions with standardized practices, and enhancing the ability to strategically analyze employee data. For example, HCC routinely reassigns hundreds of individuals a year to posts outside their home countries for customer engagements that require specialized skills. The new, streamlined global system greatly improved the global transfer process, and it also serves as the system of record that feeds employee data for many mission-critical downstream systems. This has improved data integrity but also greatly improved the global visibility of HCC's workforce, facilitating strategic analysis of global employee data.

HCC transformation experts teach clients that fundamental change is an ongoing process, and that's a lesson the company's HR and IT departments are taking to heart. HCC leaders are now expanding their use of the compensation capabilities available within Oracle HCM Cloud to more closely manage sales force compensation. According to Sona Manzo, vice president of the Oracle HCM Cloud practice at HCC, the company needed time to determine how it would be transforming its sales organization, so it kept sales compensation as a separate initiative,

HCC is continuing to use new capabilities in Oracle HCM Cloud to help its business grow. The new system has been able to handle complex bonus packages tailored for salespeople in each country. For example, "hot skill" bonuses are critical for attracting talent in Asia Pacific locations, but are not used in other regions such as the Americas. HCC will soon be able to track multiple bonus plans in each country and is investigating capabilities that enable managers to request and approve bonus or salary increases via mobile devices.

Sources: April Mazon, "Hitachi Consulting Realizes Significant Value with HCM Cloud Transformation," https://blogs.oracle.com, accessed January 10, 2018; Alan Joch, "Disrupt Yourself," *Profit Magazine,* Summer 2017; and www.hitachiconsulting.com, accessed January 19, 2018.

CASE STUDY QUESTIONS

13-14 Analyze Hitachi Consulting's problems with its legacy human resources system. What management, organization, and technology factors were responsible for these problems? What was the business impact of these problems?

13-15 List and describe the major information requirements for Hitachi's new HR system.

13-16 Was a cloud-based system appropriate for Hitachi Consulting? Why or why not?

13-17 What steps did Hitachi take to make sure its new HR system was successful?

13-18 What were the benefits of the new HR system? How did it change operational activities and decision making at Hitachi Consulting? How successful was this system solution?

MyLab MIS

Go to the Assignments section of MyLab MIS to complete these writing exercises.

13-19 Describe four system conversion strategies.

13-20 Describe the role of end users in developing systems using the traditional systems life cycle, prototyping, application software packages, and end-user development.

Chapter 13 References

AppDynamics. "10 Things Your CIO Should Know about DevOps." www.appdynamics.com, accessed March 3, 2018.

Aron, Ravi, Eric K. Clemons, and Sashi Reddi. "Just Right Outsourcing: Understanding and Managing Risk." *Journal of Management Information Systems* 22, No. 1 (Summer 2005).

Benaroch, Michael, Yossi Lichtenstein, and Lior Fink. "Contract Design Choices and the Balance of Ex Ante and Ex Post Transaction Costs in Software Development Outsourcing." *MIS Quarterly* 40, No. 1 (March 2016).

Bossert, Oliver, Chris Ip, and Irina Starikova. "Beyond Agile: Reorganizing IT for Faster Software Delivery." *McKinsey & Company* (2015).

Chang, Young Bong, Vijay Gurbaxani, and Kiron Ravindran. "Information Technology Outsourcing: Asset Transfer and the Role of Contract." *MIS Quarterly* 41, No. 3 (September 2017).

Comella-Dorda, Santiago, Swati Lohiya, and Gerard Speksnijder. "An Operating Model for Company-Wide Agile Development." *McKinsey & Company* (May 2016).

Edberg, Dana T., Polina Ivanova, and William Kuechler. "Methodology Mashups: An Exploration of Processes Used to Maintain Software." *Journal of Management Information Systems* 28, No. 4 (Spring 2012).

El Sawy, Omar A. *Redesigning Enterprise Processes for E-Business.* McGraw-Hill (2001).

Furneaux, Brent, and Michael Wade. "Impediments to Information Systems Replacement: A Calculus of Discontinuance." *Journal of Management Information Systems* 34, No. 3 (2017).

Gnanasambandam, Chandra, Martin Harrysson, Rahul Mangla, and Shivam Srivastava. "An Executive's Guide to Software Development." *McKinsey & Company* (February 2017).

Goo, Jahyun, Rajiv Kishore, H. R. Rao, and Kichan Nam. "The Role of Service Level Agreements in Relational Management of Information Technology Outsourcing: An Empirical Study." *MIS Quarterly* 33, No. 1 (March 2009).

Hahn, Eugene D., Jonathan P. Doh, and Kraiwinee Bunyaratavej. "The Evolution of Risk in Information Systems Offshoring: The Impact of Home Country Risk, Firm Learning, and Competitive Dynamics." *MIS Quarterly* 33, No. 3 (September 2009).

Hammer, Michael, and James Champy. *Reengineering the Corporation*. New York: HarperCollins (1993).

Hoehle, Hartmut, and Viswanath Venkatesh. "Mobile Application Usability: Conceptualization and Instrument Development." *MIS Quarterly* 39, No. 2 (June 2015).

Hua Ye, Jonathan, and Atreyi Kankanhalli. "User Service Innovation on Mobile Phone Platforms: Investigating Impacts of Lead Userness, Toolkit Support, and Design Autonomy." *MIS Quarterly* 42, No. 1 (March 2018).

Kelleher, Justin. "Debunking the Myths Around Agile Development." *Information Management* (August 21, 2017).

Kendall, Kenneth E., and Julie E. Kendall. *Systems Analysis and Design* (9th ed.). Upper Saddle River, NJ: Prentice Hall (2019).

Kotlarsky, Julia, Harry Scarbrough, and Ilan Oshri. "Coordinating Expertise Across Knowledge Boundaries in Offshore-Outsourcing Projects: The Role of Codification." *MIS Quarterly* 38, No. 2 (June 2014).

Levina, Natalia, and Jeanne W. Ross. "From the Vendor's Perspective: Exploring the Value Proposition in Information Technology Outsourcing." *MIS Quarterly* 27, No. 3 (September 2003).

Mani, Deepa, and Anitesh Barua. "The Impact of Firm Learning on Value Creation in Strategic Outsourcing Relationships." *Journal of Management Information Systems* 32, No. 1 (2015).

McKinsey & Company. "Agile with a Capital 'A': A Guide to the Principles and Pitfalls of Agile Development." (February 2018).

Nelson, H. James, Deborah J. Armstrong, and Kay M. Nelson. "Patterns of Transition: The Shift from Traditional to Object-Oriented Development." *Journal of Management Information Systems* 25, No. 4 (Spring 2009).

Ozer, Muammer, and Doug Vogel. "Contextualized Relationship Between Knowledge Sharing and Performance in Software Development." *Journal of Management Information Systems* 32, No. 2 (2015).

Pollock, Neil, and Sampsa Hyysalo. "The Business of Being a User: The Role of the Reference Actor in Shaping Packaged Enterprise System Acquisition and Development." *MIS Quarterly* 38, No. 2 (June 2014).

Saunders, Adam, and Erik Brynjolfsson. "Valuing Information Technology Related Intangible Assets." *MIS Quarterly* 40, No. 1 (March 2016).

Sircar, Sumit, Sridhar P. Nerur, and Radhakanta Mahapatra. "Revolution or Evolution? A Comparison of Object-Oriented and Structured Systems Development Methods." *MIS Quarterly* 25, No. 4 (December 2001).

Su, Ning, Natalia Levina, and Jeanne W. Ross. "The Long-Tail Strategy for IT Outsourcing." *MIT Sloan Management Review* (Winter 2016).

Valacich, Joseph A., and Joey George. *Modern Systems Analysis and Design*, 8th ed. Upper Saddle River, NJ: Prentice-Hall (2017).

14

Managing Projects

LEARNING OBJECTIVES

After reading this chapter, you will be able to answer the following questions:

14-1 What are the objectives of project management, and why is it so essential in developing information systems?

14-2 What methods can be used for selecting and evaluating information systems projects and aligning them with the firm's business goals?

14-3 How can firms assess the business value of information systems?

14-4 What are the principal risk factors in information systems projects, and how can they be managed?

14-5 How will MIS help my career?

CHAPTER CASES

Sound Project Management Helps Stepan Company Improve Financial Planning and Reporting

ConocoPhillips Implements a New System for Access Control

Arup Moves Project Management to the Cloud

Pennsylvania's Unemployment Compensation Modernization System: Unfinished Business

VIDEO CASES

Blue Cross Blue Shield: Smarter Computing Project

NASA Project Management Challenges

MyLab MIS

Discussion Questions: 14-5, 14-6, 14-7; **Hands-on MIS Projects:** 14-8, 14-9, 14-10, 14-11; **Writing Assignments:** 14-17, 14-18; **eText with Conceptual Animations**

Sound Project Management Helps Stepan Company Improve Financial Planning and Reporting

Stepan Company, headquartered in Northfield, Illinois, is a major global manufacturer of specialty and intermediate chemicals such as surfactants, polymers, and specialty products that are sold to other manufacturers. The company's principal markets include manufacturers of cleaning and washing compounds (including detergents, shampoos, fabric softeners, toothpastes, and household cleaners), paints, cosmetics, food, beverages, nutritional supplements, agricultural products, plastics, furniture, automotive equipment, insulation, and refrigeration. Stepan has 2,000 employees and 18 manufacturing locations worldwide.

For many years, Stepan's corporate financial planning and analysis (FP&A) team managed budgeting and forecasting for global finance using spreadsheets and databases that were not easily consolidated for the enterprise. FP&A was spending a large amount of time maintaining spreadsheets and collecting, aggregating, and extracting data out of its systems. It took hundreds of hours to produce monthly financial statements, and that left little time for analysis and thinking strategically.

During the past decade Stepan expanded quickly and outgrew its legacy reporting and planning processes. In 2014 Stepan embarked on an enterprise-wide business transformation initiative called "DRIVE." One objective was to improve antiquated financial reporting and planning processes globally. The company selected a solution based on SAP Business Planning and Consolidation (BPC), which delivers planning, budgeting, forecasting, and financial consolidation capabilities in a single application and could integrate with Stepan's global SAP ERP system.

© Canbedone/Shutterstock

Stepan's project team for the new system undertook discovery sessions, meetings with improvement and implementation consultants, training courses on applied strategic thinking, and site visits to several peer companies. With assistance from consultants from SAP's analytics group, the team surveyed and personally interviewed employees to determine exactly how much time they spent on management reporting and planning.

The project team built a business case that called for better planning tools. The team presented data to executive management that showed Stepan's finance department lagged behind those of similar-sized chemical companies in working strategically. The team also showed that the number of working days spent on Stepan's budget cycles was roughly double the number spent by other similar-sized companies.

Stepan followed a phased implementation approach. Phase I focused on management reporting and supply chain forecasting. It went live with the functionality for management reporting in January 2017 and functionality for supply chain forecasting and reporting shortly thereafter. Phase II focused on implementing budgeting, forecasting, and profit projection capabilities in the fourth quarter of 2017. Phase III, delivering functionality for full consolidations and external reporting, was scheduled for 2018. Participation of end users with the FP&A project team was critical for data validation. Stepan rolled out functionality to select groups of users before going live for the global finance teams. This approach enabled Stepan to allocate training resources for smaller user groups, even though it would take longer for benefits to materialize.

Project scope and managing user expectations were top priorities. Stepan's FP&A project team clearly defined the scope of the project and made sure to keep the entire company informed about new developments and changes. To counter runaway expectations, the team distributed a list of everything in scope and out of scope for each phase of the project. It produced reference guides with detailed descriptions of the functionality users could expect for every rollout, along with the capabilities of SAP BPC. The project team highlighted each problem the application addressed and tried to educate people throughout the company who might not know much about finance. Stepan's FP&A Senior Manager Andrew Chapmen believed that clearly explaining what was not within the scope of the project was even more important than defining what was within the project's scope.

Stepan is starting to realize benefits from the project, with better tools for slicing and dicing information, less manually intensive processes, and less effort required to analyze costs and see exactly what's driving cost and profitability. The company is becoming a more strategic organization.

Sources: www.stepan.com, accessed January 5, 2018; Ken Murphy, "Planning Tips Scales in Stepan Company's Favor," *SAP Insider Profiles*, August 10, 2017; and www.sap.com, accessed January 5, 2018.

One of the principal challenges posed by information systems is ensuring they deliver genuine business benefits. There is a very high failure rate among information systems projects because organizations have incorrectly assessed their business value or because firms have failed to manage the organizational change surrounding the introduction of new technology. Projects to build or improve information systems require special managerial and organizational techniques to make them effective.

Stepan's management realized this when it undertook its project to implement a new financial planning and consolidation system. The new technology involved changes to important business processes as well as new software. Stepan succeeded with this project because its management clearly understood that strong project management and attention to organizational change were essential to success.

The chapter-opening diagram calls attention to important points raised by this case and this chapter. Stepan's rapid global growth and antiquated budgeting and forecasting processes called for more automated state-of-the art systems that could quickly consolidate financial data for the entire enterprise. Outdated legacy systems made financial operations inefficient, preventing the Financial

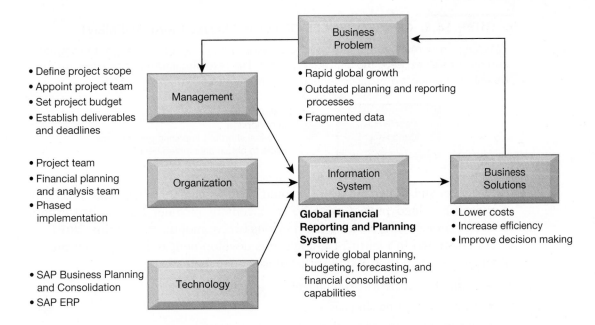

Planning and Analysis group from focusing on improving financial analysis and thinking more strategically. Management wisely assembled a project team, carefully defined the project's scope, and worked closely with SAP specialist consultants and end users with financial business knowledge. The new system was implemented in manageable phases where users could be carefully trained.

Here are some questions to think about: Why was this project successful? Why was it important to pay close attention to project scope?

14-1 What are the objectives of project management, and why is it so essential in developing information systems?

There is a very high failure rate among information systems projects. In nearly every organization, information systems projects take much more time and money to implement than originally anticipated, or the completed system does not work properly. When an information system does not meet expectations or costs too much to develop, companies may not realize any benefit from their information system investment, and the system may not be able to solve the problems for which it was intended. The development of a new system must be carefully managed and orchestrated, and the way a project is executed is likely to be the most important factor influencing its outcome. That's why it's essential to have some knowledge about managing information systems projects and the reasons why they succeed or fail.

Runaway Projects and System Failure

How badly are projects managed? On average, private sector projects are underestimated by half in terms of budget and time required to deliver the complete system promised in the system plan. Many projects are delivered with missing functionality (promised for delivery in later versions). A joint study by McKinsey and Oxford University found that large software projects on average run 66 percent

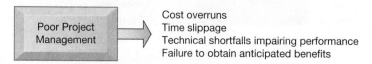

FIGURE 14.1 CONSEQUENCES OF POOR PROJECT MANAGEMENT

Without proper management, a systems development project takes longer to complete and most often exceeds the allocated budget. The resulting information system may not be able to demonstrate any benefits to the organization.

over budget and 33 percent over schedule. Over 50 percent of businesses recently surveyed by cloud project portfolio management provider Innotas had experienced IT project failure within the previous twelve months (Florentine, 2016).

As illustrated in Figure 14.1, a systems development project without proper management will most likely suffer these consequences:

- Costs that vastly exceed budgets
- Unexpected time slippage
- Technical performance that is less than expected
- Failure to obtain anticipated benefits

The systems produced by failed information projects are often not used in the way they were intended or are not used at all. Users often have to develop parallel manual systems to make these systems work.

The actual design of the system may fail to capture essential business requirements or improve organizational performance. Information may not be provided quickly enough to be helpful, it may be in a format that is impossible to digest and use, or it may represent the wrong pieces of data.

The way in which nontechnical business users must interact with the system may be excessively complicated and discouraging. A system may be designed with a poor user interface. The **user interface** is the part of the system with which end users interact. For example, an online input form or data entry screen may be so poorly arranged that no one wants to submit data or request information. System outputs may be displayed in a format that is too difficult to comprehend.

Websites may discourage visitors from exploring further if the web pages are cluttered and poorly arranged, if users cannot easily find the information they are seeking, or if it takes too long to access and display the web page on the user's computer.

Additionally, the data in the system may have a high level of inaccuracy or inconsistency. The information in certain fields may be erroneous or ambiguous, or it may not be organized properly for business purposes. Information required for a specific business function may be inaccessible because the data are incomplete.

Project Management Objectives

A **project** is a planned series of related activities for achieving a specific business objective. Information systems projects include the development of new information systems, enhancement of existing systems, or upgrade or replacement of the firm's information technology (IT) infrastructure.

Project management refers to the application of knowledge, skills, tools, and techniques to achieve specific targets within specified budget and time constraints. Project management activities include planning the work, assessing risk, estimating resources required to accomplish the work, organizing the work, acquiring human and material resources, assigning tasks, directing activities, controlling project execution, reporting progress, and analyzing the results. As in other areas of business, project management for information systems must deal with five major variables: scope, time, cost, quality, and risk.

Scope defines what work is or is not included in a project. For example, the scope of a project for a new order processing system might be to include new modules for inputting orders and transmitting them to production and accounting but not any changes to related accounts receivable, manufacturing, distribution, or inventory control systems. Project management defines all the work required to complete a project successfully and should ensure that the scope of a project does not expand beyond what was originally intended.

Time is the amount of time required to complete the project. Project management typically establishes the amount of time required to complete major components of a project. Each of these components is further broken down into activities and tasks. Project management tries to determine the time required to complete each task and establish a schedule for completing the work.

Cost is based on the time to complete a project multiplied by the cost of human resources required to complete the project. Information systems project costs also include the cost of hardware, software, and work space. Project management develops a budget for the project and monitors ongoing project expenses.

Quality is an indicator of how well the end result of a project satisfies the objectives specified by management. The quality of information systems projects usually boils down to improved organizational performance and decision making. Quality also considers the accuracy and timeliness of information produced by the new system and ease of use.

Risk refers to potential problems that would threaten the success of a project. These potential problems might prevent a project from achieving its objectives by increasing time and cost, lowering the quality of project outputs, or preventing the project from being completed altogether. Section 14.4 describes the most important risk factors for information systems.

14-2 What methods can be used for selecting and evaluating information systems projects and aligning them with the firm's business goals?

Companies typically are presented with many different projects for solving problems and improving performance. There are far more ideas for systems projects than there are resources. Firms will need to select the projects that promise the greatest benefit to the business. Obviously, the firm's overall business strategy should drive project selection. How should managers choose among all the options?

Management Structure for Information Systems Projects

Figure 14.2 shows the elements of a management structure for information systems projects in a large corporation. It helps ensure that the most important projects are given priority.

At the apex of this structure is the corporate strategic planning group and the information systems steering committee. The corporate strategic planning group is responsible for developing the firm's strategic plan, which may require the development of new systems. Often, this group will have developed objective measures of firm performance (called *key performance indicators*, introduced in Chapter 2

FIGURE 14.2 MANAGEMENT CONTROL OF SYSTEMS PROJECTS

Each level of management in the hierarchy is responsible for specific aspects of systems projects, and this structure helps give priority to the most important systems projects for the organization.

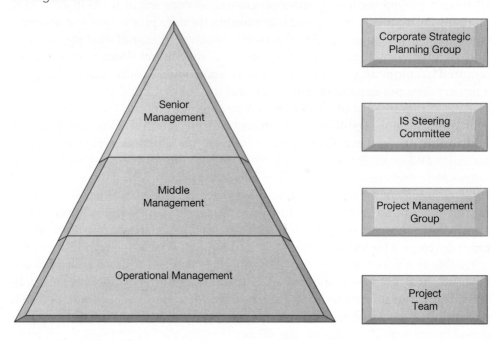

and Chapter 12) and choose to support IT projects that can make a substantial improvement in one or several key performance indicators. These performance indicators are reviewed and discussed by the firm's board of directors.

The information systems steering committee is the senior management group with responsibility for systems development and operation. It is composed of department heads from both end-user and information systems areas. The steering committee reviews and approves plans for systems in all divisions, seeks to coordinate and integrate systems, and occasionally becomes involved in selecting specific information systems projects. This group also has a keen awareness of the key performance indicators decided on by higher-level managers and the board of directors.

The project team is supervised by a project management group composed of information systems managers and end-user managers responsible for overseeing specific information systems projects. The project team is directly responsible for an individual systems project. It consists of systems analysts, specialists from the relevant end-user business areas, application programmers, and perhaps database specialists. The mix of skills and the size of the project team depend on the specific nature of the system solution.

Linking Systems Projects to the Business Plan

In order to identify the information systems projects that will deliver the most business value, organizations need to develop an **information systems plan** that supports their overall business plan and in which strategic systems are incorporated into top-level planning. The plan serves as a road map indicating the direction of systems development (the purpose of the plan), the rationale, the state of current systems, new developments to consider, the management strategy, the implementation plan, and the budget (see Table 14.1).

TABLE 14.1 INFORMATION SYSTEMS PLAN

1. Purpose of the Plan
   Overview of plan contents
   Current business organization and future organization
   Key business processes
   Management strategy

2. Strategic Business Plan Rationale
   Current situation
   Current business organization
   Changing environments
   Major goals of the business plan
   Firm's strategic plan

3. Current Systems
   Major systems supporting business functions and processes
   Current infrastructure capabilities
      Hardware
      Software
      Database
      Networking and Internet
      Cloud services
   Difficulties meeting business requirements
   Anticipated future demands

4. New Developments
   New systems projects
      Project descriptions
      Business rationale
      Applications' role in strategy
   New infrastructure capabilities required
      Hardware
      Software
      Database
      Networking and Internet
      Cloud services

5. Management Strategy
   Acquisition plans
   Milestones and timing
   Organizational realignment
   Management controls
   Major training initiatives
   Human resources strategy

6. Implementation Plan
   Anticipated difficulties in implementation
   Progress reports

7. Budget Requirements
   Requirements
   Potential savings
   Financing
   Acquisition cycle

The plan contains a statement of corporate goals and specifies how information technology will support the attainment of those goals. The report shows how general goals will be achieved by specific systems projects. It identifies specific target dates and milestones that can be used later to evaluate the plan's progress in terms of how many objectives were actually attained in the time frame specified in the plan. The plan indicates the key management decisions, technology, and required organizational change.

In order to plan effectively, firms will need to inventory and document all of their information system applications, IT infrastructure components, and long- and short-term information requirements. For projects in which benefits involve improved decision making, managers should try to identify the decision improvements that would provide the greatest additional value to the firm. They should then develop a set of metrics to quantify the value of more timely and precise information on the outcome of the decision. (See Chapter 12 for more detail on this topic.)

Portfolio Analysis

Once strategic analyses have determined the overall direction of systems development, **portfolio analysis** can be used to evaluate alternative systems projects. Portfolio analysis inventories all of the organization's information systems projects and assets, including infrastructure, outsourcing contracts, and licenses. This portfolio of information systems investments can be described as having a certain profile of risk and benefit to the firm (see Figure 14.3) similar to a financial portfolio.

Each information systems project carries its own set of risks and benefits. (Section 14-4 describes the factors that increase the risks of systems projects.) Firms would try to improve the return on their portfolios of IT assets by balancing the risk and return from their systems investments. Although there is no ideal profile for all firms, information-intensive industries (e.g., finance) should have a few high-risk, high-benefit projects to ensure that they stay current with technology. Firms in non–information-intensive industries should focus on high-benefit, low-risk projects.

Most desirable, of course, are systems with high benefit and low risk. These promise early returns and low risks. Second, high-benefit, high-risk systems should be examined; low-benefit, high-risk systems should be totally avoided; and low-benefit, low-risk systems should be reexamined for the possibility of

---

FIGURE 14.3 A SYSTEM PORTFOLIO

Companies should examine their portfolio of projects in terms of potential benefits and likely risks. Certain kinds of projects should be avoided altogether and others developed rapidly. There is no ideal mix. Companies in different industries have different profiles.

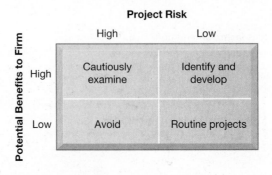

rebuilding and replacing them with more desirable systems having higher benefits. By using portfolio analysis, management can determine the optimal mix of investment risk and reward for their firms, balancing riskier high-reward projects with safer lower-reward ones. Firms where portfolio analysis is aligned with business strategy have been found to have a superior return on their IT assets, better alignment of IT investments with business objectives, and better organization-wide coordination of IT investments (Jeffrey and Leliveld, 2004).

Scoring Models

A **scoring model** is useful for selecting projects where many criteria must be considered. It assigns weights to various features of a system and then calculates the weighted totals. Using Table 14.2, the firm must decide among two alternative enterprise resource planning (ERP) systems. The first column lists the criteria that decision makers will use to evaluate the systems. These criteria are usually the result of lengthy discussions among the decision-making group. Often the most important outcome of a scoring model is not the score but agreement on the criteria used to judge a system.

Table 14.2 shows that this particular company attaches the most importance to capabilities for sales order processing, inventory management, and warehousing. The second column in Table 14.2 lists the weights that decision makers attached to the decision criteria. Columns 3 and 5 show the percentage of requirements for each function that each alternative ERP system can provide. Each vendor's score can be calculated by multiplying the percentage of requirements met for each function by the weight attached to that function. ERP System B has the highest total score.

TABLE 14.2 EXAMPLE OF A SCORING MODEL FOR AN ERP SYSTEM

CRITERIA	WEIGHT	ERP SYSTEM A %	ERP SYSTEM A SCORE	ERP SYSTEM B %	ERP SYSTEM B SCORE
1.0 Order Processing					
1.1 Online order entry	4	67	268	73	292
1.2 Online pricing	4	81	324	87	348
1.3 Inventory check	4	72	288	81	324
1.4 Customer credit check	3	66	198	59	177
1.5 Invoicing	4	73	292	82	328
Total Order Processing			1,370		1,469
2.0 Inventory Management					
2.1 Production forecasting	3	72	216	76	228
2.2 Production planning	4	79	316	81	324
2.3 Inventory control	4	68	272	80	320
2.4 Reports	3	71	213	69	207
Total Inventory Management			1,017		1,079
3.0 Warehousing					
3.1 Receiving	2	71	142	75	150
3.2 Picking/packing	3	77	231	82	246
3.3 Shipping	4	92	368	89	356
Total Warehousing			741		752
Grand Total			3,128		3,300

As with all "objective" techniques, there are many qualitative judgments involved in using the scoring model. This model requires experts who understand the issues and the technology. It is appropriate to cycle through the scoring model several times, changing the criteria and weights, to see how sensitive the outcome is to reasonable changes in criteria. Scoring models are used most commonly to confirm, to rationalize, and to support decisions rather than as the final arbiters of system selection.

14-3 How can firms assess the business value of information systems?

Even if a systems project supports a firm's strategic goals and meets user information requirements, it needs to be a good investment for the firm. The value of systems from a financial perspective essentially revolves around the issue of return on invested capital. Does a particular information system investment produce sufficient returns to justify its costs?

Information System Costs and Benefits

Table 14.3 lists some of the more common costs and benefits of systems. **Tangible benefits** can be quantified and assigned a monetary value. **Intangible benefits**, such as more efficient customer service or enhanced decision making, cannot be immediately quantified but may lead to quantifiable gains in the long run. Transaction and clerical systems that displace labor and save space always produce more measurable, tangible benefits than management information systems, decision-support systems, and computer-supported collaborative work systems (see Chapter 2 and Chapter 12).

Chapter 5 introduced the concept of total cost of ownership (TCO), which is designed to identify and measure the components of information technology expenditures beyond the initial cost of purchasing and installing hardware and software. However, TCO analysis provides only part of the information needed to evaluate an information technology investment because it does not typically deal with benefits, cost categories such as complexity costs, and "soft" and strategic factors discussed later in this section.

Capital Budgeting for Information Systems

To determine the benefits of a particular project, you'll need to calculate all of its costs and all of its benefits. Obviously, a project where costs exceed benefits should be rejected. But even if the benefits outweigh the costs, additional financial analysis is required to determine whether the project represents a good return on the firm's invested capital. **Capital budgeting** models are one of several techniques used to measure the value of investing in long-term capital investment projects.

Capital budgeting methods rely on measures of cash flows into and out of the firm; capital projects generate those cash flows. The investment cost for information systems projects is an immediate cash outflow caused by expenditures for hardware, software, and labor. In subsequent years, the investment may cause additional cash outflows that will be balanced by cash inflows resulting from the investment. Cash inflows take the form of increased sales of more products (for reasons such as new products, higher quality, or increasing market share)

TABLE 14.3 COSTS AND BENEFITS OF INFORMATION SYSTEMS

COSTS

Hardware
Networking
Software
Services
Personnel

TANGIBLE BENEFITS (COST SAVINGS)

Increased productivity
Lower operational costs
Reduced workforce
Lower computer expenses
Lower outside vendor costs
Lower clerical and professional costs
Reduced rate of growth in expenses
Reduced facility costs

INTANGIBLE BENEFITS

Improved asset utilization
Improved resource control
Improved organizational planning
Increased organizational flexibility
More timely information
More information
Increased organizational learning
Legal requirements attained
Enhanced employee goodwill
Increased job satisfaction
Improved decision making
Improved operations
Higher client satisfaction
Better corporate image

or reduced costs in production and operations. The difference between cash outflows and cash inflows is used for calculating the financial worth of an investment. Once the cash flows have been established, several alternative methods are available for comparing different projects and deciding about the investment.

The principal capital budgeting models for evaluating IT projects are the payback method, the accounting rate of return on investment (ROI), net present value, and the internal rate of return (IRR). You can find out more about how these capital budgeting models are used to justify information system investments in the Learning Tracks for this chapter.

Limitations of Financial Models

The traditional focus on the financial and technical aspects of an information system tends to overlook the social and organizational dimensions of information systems that may affect the true costs and benefits of the investment. Many companies' information systems investment decisions do not adequately consider costs from organizational disruptions created by a new system, such as the cost to train end users, the impact that users' learning curves for a new system have on productivity, or the time managers need to spend overseeing new system-related changes. Intangible benefits such as more timely decisions from a new system or enhanced employee learning and expertise may also be overlooked in a traditional financial analysis.

14-4 What are the principal risk factors in information systems projects, and how can they be managed?

We have already introduced the topic of information systems risks and risk assessment in Chapter 8. In this chapter, we describe the specific risks to information systems projects and show what can be done to manage them effectively.

Dimensions of Project Risk

Systems differ dramatically in their size, scope, level of complexity, and organizational and technical components. Some systems development projects are more likely to create the problems we have described earlier or to suffer delays because they carry a much higher level of risk than others. The level of project risk is influenced by project size, project structure, and the level of technical expertise of the information systems staff and project team.

- *Project size.* The larger the project—as indicated by the dollars spent, the size of the implementation staff, the time allocated for implementation, and the number of organizational units affected—the greater the risk. Very large-scale systems projects have a failure rate that is 50 to 75 percent higher than that for other projects because such projects are complex and difficult to control. The organizational complexity of the system—how many units and groups use it and how much it influences business processes—contributes to the complexity of large-scale systems projects just as much as technical characteristics, such as the number of lines of program code, length of project, and budget. In addition, there are few reliable techniques for estimating the time and cost to develop large-scale information systems.

- *Project structure.* Some projects are more highly structured than others. Their requirements are clear and straightforward, so outputs and processes can be easily defined. Users know exactly what they want and what the system should do; there is almost no possibility of the users changing their minds. Such projects run a much lower risk than those with relatively undefined, fluid, and constantly changing requirements; with outputs that cannot be fixed easily because they are subject to users' changing ideas; or with users who cannot agree on what they want.

- *Experience with technology.* The project risk rises if the project team and the information system staff lack the required technical expertise. If the team is unfamiliar with the hardware, system software, application software, or database management system proposed for the project, it is highly likely that the project will experience technical problems or take more time to complete because of the need to master new skills.

Although the difficulty of the technology is one risk factor in information systems projects, the other factors are primarily organizational, dealing with the complexity of information requirements, the scope of the project, and how many parts of the organization will be affected by a new information system.

Change Management and the Concept of Implementation

The introduction or alteration of an information system has a powerful behavioral and organizational impact. Changes in the way that information is defined, accessed, and used to manage the organization's resources often lead to new distributions of authority and power. This internal organizational change breeds resistance and opposition and can lead to the demise of an otherwise good system.

A very large percentage of information systems projects stumble because the process of organizational change surrounding system building was not properly addressed. Successful system building requires careful **change management**.

The Concept of Implementation

To manage the organizational change surrounding the introduction of a new information system effectively, you must examine the process of implementation. **Implementation** refers to all organizational activities working toward the adoption, management, and routinization of an innovation, such as a new information system. In the implementation process, the systems analyst is a **change agent**. The analyst not only develops technical solutions but also redefines the configurations, interactions, job activities, and power relationships of various organizational groups. The analyst is the catalyst for the entire change process and is responsible for ensuring that all parties involved accept the changes created by a new system. The change agent communicates with users, mediates between competing interest groups, and ensures that the organizational adjustment to such changes is complete.

The Role of End Users

System implementation generally benefits from high levels of user involvement and management support. User participation in the design and operation of information systems has several positive results. First, if users are heavily involved in systems design, they have more opportunities to mold the system according to their priorities and business requirements and more opportunities to control the outcome. Second, they are more likely to react positively to the completed system because they have been active participants in the change process. Incorporating user knowledge and expertise leads to better solutions.

The relationship between users and information systems specialists has traditionally been a problem area for information systems implementation efforts. Users and information systems specialists tend to have different backgrounds, interests, and priorities. This is referred to as the **user-designer communications gap**. These differences lead to divergent organizational loyalties, approaches to problem solving, and vocabularies.

Information systems specialists, for example, often have a highly technical, or machine, orientation to problem solving. They look for elegant and sophisticated technical solutions in which hardware and software efficiency is optimized at the expense of ease of use or organizational effectiveness. Users prefer systems that are oriented toward solving business problems or facilitating

TABLE 14.4 THE USER-DESIGNER COMMUNICATIONS GAP

USER CONCERNS	DESIGNER CONCERNS
Will the system deliver the information we need for our work?	What demands will this system put on our servers?
Can we access the data on our smartphones, tablets, and PCs?	What kind of programming demands will this place on our group?
What new procedures do we need to enter data into the system?	Where will the data be stored? What's the most efficient way to store them?
How will the operation of the system change employees' daily routines?	What technologies should we use to secure the data?

organizational tasks. Often the orientations of both groups are so at odds that they appear to speak in different tongues.

These differences are illustrated in Table 14.4, which depicts the typical concerns of end users and technical specialists (information systems designers) regarding the development of a new information system. Communication problems between end users and designers are a major reason why user requirements are not properly incorporated into information systems and why users are driven out of the implementation process.

Systems development projects run a very high risk of failure when there is a pronounced gap between users and technical specialists and when these groups continue to pursue different goals. Under such conditions, users are often driven away from the project. Because they cannot comprehend what the technicians are saying, users conclude that the entire project is best left in the hands of the information specialists alone.

Management Support and Commitment

If an information systems project has the backing and commitment of management at various levels, it is more likely to be perceived positively by both users and the technical information services staff. Both groups will believe that their participation in the development process will receive higher-level attention and priority. They will be recognized and rewarded for the time and effort they devote to implementation. Management backing also ensures that a systems project receives sufficient funding and resources to be successful. Furthermore, to be enforced effectively, all the changes in work habits and procedures and any organizational realignments associated with a new system depend on management backing. If a manager considers a new system a priority, the system will more likely be treated that way by his or her subordinates. According to the Project Management Institute, executive sponsors who are actively engaged is the leading factor in project success (Kloppenborg and Tesch, 2015; Project Management Institute, 2017).

Change Management Challenges for Business Process Reengineering, Enterprise Applications, and Mergers and Acquisitions

Given the challenges of innovation and implementation, it is not surprising to find a very high failure rate among enterprise application and business process reengineering (BPR) projects, which typically require extensive organizational change and which may require replacing old technologies and legacy systems that are deeply rooted in many interrelated business processes. A number of studies have indicated that 70 percent of all business process reengineering projects fail to deliver promised benefits. Likewise, a high percentage of enterprise applications fail to be fully implemented or to meet the goals of their users even after three years of work.

Many enterprise application and reengineering projects have been undermined by poor implementation and change management practices that failed to address employees' concerns about change. Dealing with fear and anxiety throughout the organization, overcoming resistance by key managers, and changing job functions, career paths, and recruitment practices have posed greater threats to reengineering than the difficulties companies faced visualizing and designing breakthrough changes to business processes. All of the enterprise applications require tighter coordination among different functional groups as well as extensive business process change (see Chapter 9).

Projects related to mergers and acquisitions have a similar failure rate. Mergers and acquisitions are deeply affected by the organizational characteristics of the merging companies as well as by their IT infrastructures. Combining the information systems of two different companies usually requires considerable organizational change and complex systems projects to manage. If the integration is not properly managed, firms can emerge with a tangled hodgepodge of inherited legacy systems built by aggregating the systems of one firm after another. Without a successful systems integration, the benefits anticipated from the merger cannot be realized, or, worse, the merged entity cannot execute its business processes effectively.

Controlling Risk Factors

Various project management, requirements gathering, and planning methodologies have been developed for specific categories of implementation problems. Strategies have also been devised for ensuring that users play appropriate roles throughout the implementation period and for managing the organizational change process. Not all aspects of the implementation process can be easily controlled or planned. However, anticipating potential implementation problems and applying appropriate corrective strategies can increase the chances for system success.

The first step in managing project risk involves identifying the nature and level of risk confronting the project. Implementers can then handle each project with the tools and risk management approaches geared to its level of risk. Not all risks are identifiable in advance, but with skillful project management, most are. Frequent communication and a culture of collaboration will help project teams adapt to unforeseen problems that arise (Browning and Ramasesh, 2015; Laufer et al., 2015; McFarlan, 1981).

Managing Technical Complexity

Projects with challenging and complex technology to master benefit from **internal integration tools**. The success of such projects depends on how well their technical complexity can be managed. Project leaders need both heavy technical and administrative experience. They must be able to anticipate problems and develop smooth working relationships among a predominantly technical team. The team should be under the leadership of a manager with a strong technical and project management background, and team members should be highly experienced. Team meetings should take place frequently. Essential technical skills or expertise not available internally should be secured from outside the organization.

Formal Planning and Control Tools

Large projects benefit from appropriate use of **formal planning tools** and **formal control tools** for documenting and monitoring project plans. The two most commonly used methods for documenting project plans are Gantt charts and PERT charts. A **Gantt chart** lists project activities and their corresponding start and completion dates. The Gantt chart visually represents the timing and duration of different tasks in a development project as well as their human resource requirements (see Figure 14.4). It shows each task as a horizontal bar whose length is proportional to the time required to complete it.

Although Gantt charts show when project activities begin and end, they don't depict task dependencies, how one task is affected if another is behind schedule, or how tasks should be ordered. That is where **PERT charts** are useful. *PERT* stands for "Program Evaluation and Review Technique," a methodology developed by the U.S. Navy during the 1950s to manage the Polaris submarine missile program. A PERT chart graphically depicts project tasks and their interrelationships. The PERT chart lists the specific activities that make up a project and the activities that must be completed before a specific activity can start, as illustrated in Figure 14.5.

The PERT chart portrays a project as a network diagram consisting of numbered nodes (either circles or rectangles) representing project tasks. Each node is numbered and shows the task, its duration, the starting date, and the completion date. The direction of the arrows on the lines indicates the sequence of tasks and shows which activities must be completed before the commencement of another activity. In Figure 14.5, the tasks in nodes 2, 3, and 4 are not dependent on each other and can be undertaken simultaneously, but each is dependent on completion of the first task. PERT charts for complex projects can be difficult to interpret, and project managers often use both techniques.

These project management techniques can help managers identify bottlenecks and determine the impact that problems will have on project completion times. They can also help systems developers partition projects into smaller, more manageable segments with defined, measurable business results. Standard control techniques can successfully chart the progress of the project against budgets and target dates, so deviations from the plan can be spotted.

Increasing User Involvement and Overcoming User Resistance

Projects with relatively little structure and many undefined requirements must involve users fully at all stages. Users must be mobilized to support one of many possible design options and to remain committed to a single design. **External integration tools** consist of ways to link the work of the implementation team to users at all organizational levels. For instance, users can become active members of the project team, take on leadership roles, and take charge of installation and training. The implementation team can demonstrate its responsiveness to users, promptly answering questions, incorporating user feedback, and showing their willingness to help.

Participation in implementation activities may not be enough to overcome the problem of user resistance to organizational change. Different users may be affected by the system in different ways. Whereas some users may welcome a new system because it brings changes they perceive as beneficial to them, others may resist these changes because they believe the shifts are detrimental to their interests.

FIGURE 14.4 A GANTT CHART

The Gantt chart in this figure shows the task, person-days, and initials of each responsible person as well as the start and finish dates for each task. The resource summary provides a good manager with the total person-days for each month and for each person working on the project to manage the project successfully. The project described here is a data administration project.

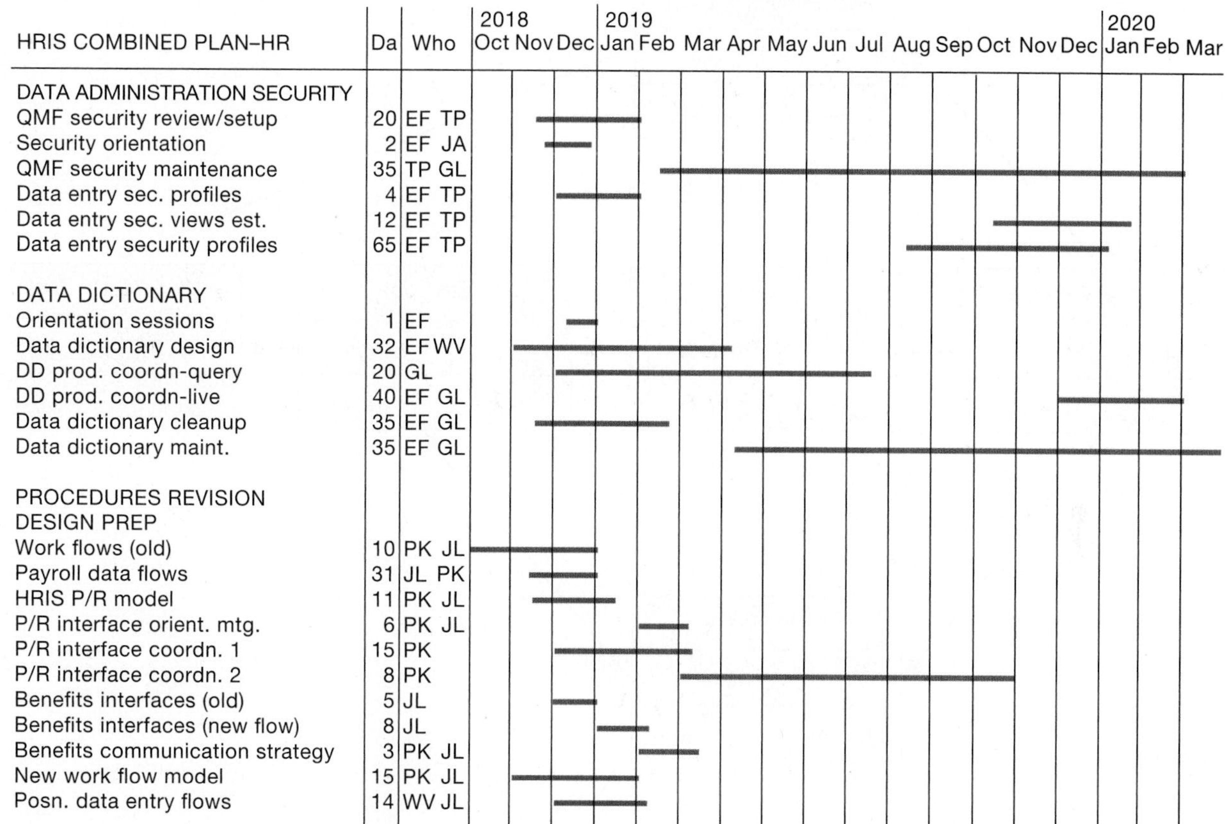
HRIS COMBINED PLAN–HR
Da
Who
2018
Oct Nov Dec
2019
Jan Feb Mar Apr May Jun Jul Aug Sep Oct Nov Dec
2020
Jan Feb Mar
DATA ADMINISTRATION SECURITY
QMF security review/setup 20 EF TP
Security orientation 2 EF JA
QMF security maintenance 35 TP GL
Data entry sec. profiles 4 EF TP
Data entry sec. views est. 12 EF TP
Data entry security profiles 65 EF TP
DATA DICTIONARY
Orientation sessions 1 EF
Data dictionary design 32 EF WV
DD prod. coordn-query 20 GL
DD prod. coordn-live 40 EF GL
Data dictionary cleanup 35 EF GL
Data dictionary maint. 35 EF GL
PROCEDURES REVISION
DESIGN PREP
Work flows (old) 10 PK JL
Payroll data flows 31 JL PK
HRIS P/R model 11 PK JL
P/R interface orient. mtg. 6 PK JL
P/R interface coordn. 1 15 PK
P/R interface coordn. 2 8 PK
Benefits interfaces (old) 5 JL
Benefits interfaces (new flow) 8 JL
Benefits communication strategy 3 PK JL
New work flow model 15 PK JL
Posn. data entry flows 14 WV JL

RESOURCE SUMMARY			Oct 2018	Nov	Dec	Jan 2019	Feb	Mar	Apr	May	Jun	Jul	Aug	Sep	Oct	Nov	Dec	Jan 2020	Feb	Mar
Edith Farrell	5.0	EF	2	21	24	24	23	22	22	27	34	34	29	26	28	19	14			
Woody Vinton	5.0	WV	5	17	20	19	12	10	14	10	2							4	3	
Charles Pierce	5.0	CP		5	11	20	13	9	10	7	6	8	4	4	4	4	4			
Ted Leurs	5.0	TL		12	17	17	19	17	14	12	15	16	2	1	1	1	1			
Toni Cox	5.0	TC	1	11	10	11	11	12	19	19	21	21	21	17	17	12	9			
Patricia Knopp	5.0	PC	7	23	30	34	27	25	15	24	25	16	11	13	17	10	3	3	2	
Jane Lawton	5.0	JL	1	9	16	21	19	21	21	20	17	15	14	12	14	8	5			
David Holloway	5.0	DH	4	4	5	5	5	2	7	5	4	16	2							
Diane O'Neill	5.0	DO	6	14	17	16	13	11	9	4										
Joan Albert	5.0	JA	5	6			7	6	2	1				5	5	1				
Marie Marcus	5.0	MM	15	7	2	1	1													
Don Stevens	5.0	DS	4	4	5	4	5	1												
Casual	5.0	CASL		3	4	3			4	7	9	5	3	2						
Kathy Mendez	5.0	KM		1	5	16	20	19	22	19	20	18	20	11	2					
Anna Borden	5.0	AB					9	10	16	15	11	12	19	10	7	1				
Gail Loring	5.0	GL		3	6	5	9	10	17	18	17	10	13	10	10	7	17			
UNASSIGNED	0.0	X										9			236	225	230	14	13	
Co-op	5.0	CO		6	4				2	3	4	4	2	4	16			216	178	
Casual	5.0	CAUL								3	3	3								
TOTAL DAYS			49	147	176	196	194	174	193	195	190	181	140	125	358	288	284	237	196	12

If the use of a system is voluntary, users may choose to avoid it; if use is mandatory, resistance will take the form of increased error rates, disruptions, turnover, and even sabotage. Therefore, the implementation strategy must not only encourage user participation and involvement, but it must also address the issue of counterimplementation. **Counterimplementation** is a deliberate

FIGURE 14.5 A PERT CHART

This is a simplified PERT chart for creating a small website. It shows the ordering of project tasks and the relationship of a task with preceding and succeeding tasks.

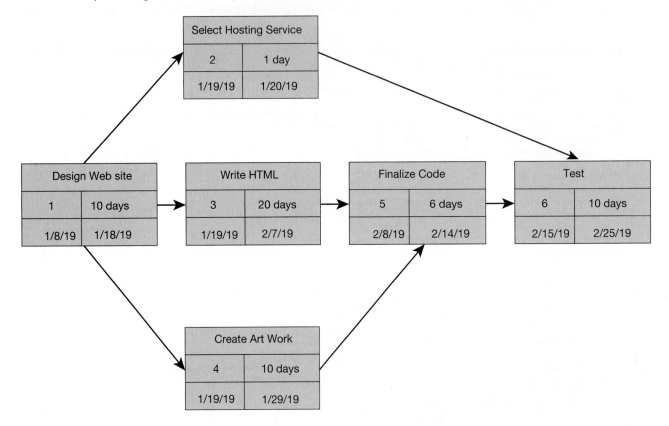

strategy to thwart the implementation of an information system or an innovation in an organization.

Strategies to overcome user resistance include user participation (to elicit commitment as well as to improve design), user education and training, management edicts and policies, and better incentives for users who cooperate. The new system can be made more user-friendly by improving the end-user interface. Users will be more cooperative if organizational problems are solved prior to introducing the new system.

Designing for the Organization

Because the purpose of a new system is to improve the organization's performance, information systems projects must explicitly address the ways in which the organization will change when the new system is installed, including installation of mobile and web applications. In addition to procedural changes, transformations in job functions, organizational structure, power relationships, and the work environment should be carefully planned.

Areas where users interface with the system require special attention, with sensitivity to ergonomics issues. **Ergonomics** refers to the interaction of people and machines in the work environment. It considers the design of jobs, health issues, and the end-user interface of information systems. Table 14.5 lists the organizational dimensions that must be addressed when planning and implementing information systems.

TABLE 14.5 ORGANIZATIONAL FACTORS IN SYSTEMS PLANNING AND IMPLEMENTATION

Employee participation and involvement

Job design

Standards and performance monitoring

Ergonomics (including equipment, user interfaces, and the work environment)

Employee grievance resolution procedures

Health and safety

Government regulatory compliance

Although systems analysis and design activities are supposed to include an organizational impact analysis, this area has traditionally been neglected. An **organizational impact analysis** explains how a proposed system will affect organizational structure, attitudes, decision making, and operations. To integrate information systems successfully with the organization, thorough and fully documented organizational impact assessments must be given more attention in the development effort.

Sociotechnical Design

One way of addressing human and organizational issues is to incorporate **sociotechnical design** practices into information systems projects. Designers set forth separate sets of technical and social design solutions. The social design plans explore different workgroup structures, allocation of tasks, and the design of individual jobs. The proposed technical solutions are compared with the proposed social solutions. The solution that best meets both social and technical objectives is selected for the final design. The resulting sociotechnical design is expected to produce an information system that blends technical efficiency with sensitivity to organizational and human needs, leading to higher job satisfaction and productivity.

You can see some of these project management strategies at work in the Interactive Session on Management, which describes how ConocoPhillips implemented a new access control system.

Project Management Software Tools

Commercial software tools that automate many aspects of project management facilitate the project management process. Project management software typically features capabilities for defining and ordering tasks, assigning resources to tasks, establishing starting and ending dates to tasks, tracking progress at both individual and team levels, and facilitating modifications to tasks and resources. Many automate the creation of Gantt and PERT charts and provide communication, collaboration, and social tools.

Some of these tools are large sophisticated programs for managing very large projects, dispersed work groups, and enterprise functions. These high-end tools can manage very large numbers of tasks and activities and complex relationships. The most widely used project management tool today is Microsoft Project, but there are also lower-cost tools for smaller projects and small businesses. Many project management applications are now cloud-based to enable project team members to access project management

INTERACTIVE SESSION   MANAGEMENT

ConocoPhillips Implements a New System for Access Control

ConocoPhillips Co. is an American multinational energy corporation headquartered in Houston, Texas. It is the world's largest independent oil and natural gas exploration and production company, with $88 billion in total assets as of March 2017. It has 11,600 employees and operations in 17 countries to find and produce oil and natural gas. Information systems are an important tool for managing exploration and production operations, fostering collaboration across functions and business units, recruiting and developing highly talented scientists and engineers, managing risks, and making sound investments.

ConocoPhillips has a large and complex network of global users requiring access to its systems. Consequently, managing access control for the company's information systems is very challenging and the enterprise must work especially hard to meet governance, risk, and compliance (GRC) requirements such as access control and segregation of duties (SoD). (Review the discussion of both of these topics in Chapter 8).

In 2009, ConocoPhillips began using SAP Access Control for this purpose. Access Control is a SAP product for streamlining the process of managing and validating user access to applications and data. SAP Access Control works with SAP and non-SAP applications, including SAP Finance, SAP Sales & Distribution, and Oracle software tools. It automates user access assignments and can automatically review user access and role authorizations and detect and remediate risk violations. The software supports policies regarding the segregation of duties so that people don't have conflicting activities or rights.

SAP has made many improvements to the software, including greater stability and customization features. ConocoPhillips has continuously implemented new releases of the application, the most recent being the upgrade from version 10.0 to 10.1. Every time SAP upgraded the software, certain things that were working previously were affected in moving to the latest release. It might take months to get all processes back to the way ConocoPhillips expected them to run. The latest upgrade to SAP Access Control required a year-long stabilization project.

Throughout this upgrade project and stabilization, SAP and ConocoPhillips worked to keep lines of communication open. ConocoPhillips works closely with SAP and receives a direct line to SAP experts. In turn, the company provides SAP with ideas and suggestions for improving future releases of Access Control. By collaborating with SAP experts and experimenting with different approaches, ConocoPhillips was able to configure the system to suit the enterprise's exact needs. ConocoPhillips improved its ability to schedule necessary jobs, enable emergency access management, and evaluate SoD risks.

SAP Access Control 10.1 had a new capability for customizing user interfaces, which was one of the main selling points for ConocoPhillips to move to this new release. In configuring the user interface, the company removed data fields it didn't use and showed users only what they actually needed to see. ConocoPhillips also added more additional help features. The resulting user interface made it significantly easier for end users to submit or process requests.

The project also increased system usability by minimizing workflows. ConocoPhillips GRC Administrator Trevor Wyatt tried to keep workflows at a controllable number, both to streamline the project as well to make the system solution easier to use. Although other organizations might set up SAP Access Control with hundreds of workflows, ConocoPhillips only has a handful. According to Wyatt, the more workflows you have, the harder it is to troubleshoot and the more things could go wrong. Having simpler workflows for end users means less risk. Instead of taking months to obtain approvals, it takes minutes. Keeping workflows simple minimizes complexity, which causes risk in the workflow.

ConocoPhillips was highly attentive to the needs of the end users throughout the entire upgrade and stabilization project and thereafter. The company provides users with job aids, hands-on training, and in-class training, depending on their needs. Wyatt also believes continuous training is very important, especially when users don't have a background in the technology. ConocoPhillips tries to train and train again. By training thoroughly, ConocoPhillips was able to get thousands of users accustomed to the functionality the newly con-figured SAP Access Control 10.1 offered with few complaints.

Once fully implemented, SAP Access Control 10.1 has working seamlessly at ConocoPhillips, with very few workflow issues. The access control solution is heavily scrutinized by both internal and external auditors to ensure it's working properly. Due to that scrutiny and the success of the SAP Access Control upgrade, there's less work that has to be done dur-ing audit season. As SAP Access Control became more stable, auditors have more confidence in the system and don't have to dig as deep. Additionally, auditors can pull information directly from the sys-tem instead of having to request that information

from the company's GRC team. This saves time and streamlines processes for both auditors and GRC professionals.

After such a careful process of removing issues from the system and configuring it in the way that's best for the business, ConocoPhillips is reaping the benefits of very trustworthy access control processes. It doesn't have to second-guess the system, and has full confidence that it is performing exactly as expected.

Sources: www.sap.com, accessed January 7, 2018; Nicole D'Angelo, "ConocoPhillips Drills Down into Access Control," *SAP Insider Profiles,* July 12, 2017; and www.conocophillips.com, accessed January 7, 2018.

CASE STUDY QUESTIONS

1. How important was this project for ConocoPhillips? Why?

2. What project management techniques described in this chapter were used to implement the new version of SAP Access Control?

3. Why was the project so successful? What manage-ment, organization, and technology issues were addressed?

---

tools and their data wherever they are working. The Interactive Session on Technology describes some capabilities of cloud-based Microsoft Project Online.

While project management software helps organizations track individual projects, the resources allocated to them, and their costs, **project portfolio management** software helps organizations manage portfolios of projects and dependencies among them. Project portfolio management software helps man-agers compare proposals and projects against budgets and resource capacity lev-els to determine the optimal mix and sequencing of projects that best achieves the organization's strategic goals.

14-5 How will MIS help my career?

Here is how Chapter 14 and this book will help you find an entry-level job as an IT project management assistant.

The Company

XYZ Multimedia Entertainment, a large multinational mass media and enter-tainment company headquartered in Los Angeles, is looking for an entry-level IT project management assistant. XYZ Multimedia creates films, TV shows, recordings, streaming Internet content, interactive games, and consumer products for a worldwide audience. It is an intensive user of leading-edge in-formation technology in its products, services, and operations.

INTERACTIVE SESSION   TECHNOLOGY

Arup Moves Project Management to the Cloud

Arup Group Limited is a multinational professional services firm headquartered in London that provides engineering, design, planning, project management, and consulting services for all aspects of structures and environments of human construction. Founded in 1946, Arup now has over 13,000 staff based in 85 offices across 35 countries throughout the globe. The company defines itself as one where professionals of diverse disciplines—engineers, planners, designers, financial experts, consulting specialists, and sustainability professionals—can work together to deliver projects and services of greater quality than by working in isolation. Arup has worked on projects in over 160 countries, including the Pompidou Center in Paris, the Sydney Opera House, the high-speed railway between London and Paris, and the National Aquatics Center for the 2008 Beijing Olympics.

Arup is an intensive user of information technology in all aspects of its work, including working with clients, designing buildings, running structural simulations, and coordinating projects. Its management wants to ensure that Arup's information systems group is working on all the right IT projects for furthering the business and is doing so in the right way. Arup's systems have to be stable, leading edge, and available at all times, with employees able to access the information they need at any time and any place.

Until recently Arup's IT staff relied on Microsoft Excel spreadsheets or Microsoft Word documents as their project management tools. Reports were sporadic and in diverse formats, collaboration was very limited, project delivery styles were inconsistent, and there was no central visibility into what was happening with each project. Arup set up a Global IT Portfolio Management Office to oversee its entire portfolio of IT projects, but it was hampered by having to manually create reports using spreadsheets and e-mail updates from regional offices.

Working with Program Framework consultants who specialize in project portfolio management, Arup decided to adopt Microsoft Project Online to improve project management. Project Online is Microsoft's cloud-based project management tool, and it helps organizations efficiently plan projects, track status, and collaborate with others from any location and any device. Members of Arup's global

workforce have immediate access to project data at any time wherever they are working. The cloud solution also makes it possible to report on projects using live data, with the system able to tie in to other processes such as service and change management. Program Framework consultants helped Arup implement Project Online and train employees. They also developed a customized Project and Program Status Reporting capability for Project Online.

In the past, Arup's Global IT Portfolio Management Office had to spend 40 hours per month compiling reports manually. By the time it created a status report, the report was already out of date. Project Online gives Arup instant views into the status of all of its IT projects. Regional employees can view their own portfolios of projects, while Arup's Global IT Portfolio Management Office has immediate views of all global projects. Arup's management can examine and classify projects throughout the entire enterprise based on their red, green, and amber status indicators. (Red designates projects with critical status, while amber designates those at risk.) The ability to see Arup's entire project portfolio gives management better insight into project delivery. The Global IT Portfolio Management Office can obtain key project status summaries, and highlight reporting of individual projects where it can drill down for further detail, enabling it to make better decisions based on up-to-date data. Project Online has become essential for supporting a common approach to Arup's project management across the globe. There is less duplication of effort and more strategic value in Arup's overall project portfolio.

Project Online is part of Microsoft's cloud-based Office 365 software suite, so it works seamlessly with other Microsoft productivity and communication tools such as OneDrive for Business (cloud storage), Skype for Business (voice, video, chat), Yammer (enterprise social networking), and Visual Studio Team Foundation Server, which Arup uses for software development projects. Arup also plans to implement additional Project Online capabilities for demand and capacity planning, portfolio prioritization, and portfolio balancing. Users can easily copy information from Project and paste it into Office applications like PowerPoint and Word.

Arup uses Project Online for its IT Project Pipeline, a central repository of ideas for future development. Each idea recorded in the Pipeline requires that the initiator furnish information such as project description, budget, and resource needs. Arup's Global IT Portfolio Management Office sends this information to Arup's management committee members to review and prioritize for new initiatives.

When ideas are approved, their Project Pipeline information can easily be transferred to active projects. It only takes a few minutes for Project Pipeline to create a project or program within Project Online. Each has its own Project Details Pages, which include a built-in schedule template and a connected Microsoft SharePoint Server site with document repository and status reporting. This capability saves Arup's Global IT Portfolio Management Office manager Carolyn Bundey several days of work for each new project, creating significant time savings for an annual portfolio of approximately 180 IT projects.

Several years ago, Project Online had about 150 users, but Arup is thinking about providing the tool for all of its employees. Arup licenses three different versions of Project Online. Project managers, owners, and administrators use Project Online with Project Professional for Office 365, enabling them to create and edit project plans inside or outside a web browser. Arup executives use Project Online to review project status. Project team members can view assignments or collaborate with other team members using the lower-cost Project Lite version.

Sources: "Engineering Firm Uses Cloud-Based Solution to Generate, Execute, and Monitor IT Projects," www.microsoft.com, accessed January 2, 2018; "Leading Arup at the Forefront of Innovation in Today's Built Environment," www.gineersnow.com, accessed January 3, 2018; and www.arup.com, accessed January 2, 2018.

CASE STUDY QUESTIONS

1. What is the relationship between information technology, project management, and Arup's business model and business strategy?

2. How does Microsoft Project Online support Arup's business strategy? How did it change the way the company works?

3. What management, organization, and technology issues did Arup have to address when selecting Project Online as its global project portfolio management tool?

Position Description

The IT project management assistant will help IT project managers with planning, budgeting, and overseeing all aspects of information technology projects for the firm. Job responsibilities include:

- Performing tasks designed to enhance the functions and services provided by the firm's centralized Project Management Office. This might include identifying and documenting best practices, investigating available tools, and making recommendations for improving processes and procedures.
- Collaborating with project managers to ensure that the scope and direction of each technical project is on schedule.
- Working with other project stakeholders for support.

Job Requirements

- Bachelor's degree in Computer Science, Computer Engineering, Management Information Systems, Project Management, or a related field
- Knowledge of project management (PMI) teachings
- Knowledge of process documentation (process flow charting)

- Proficiency with Microsoft Word, Excel, PowerPoint
- Strong interviewing and research skills
- Experience with SharePoint and/or Microsoft Project desirable

Interview Questions

1. Have you ever worked on an IT project? What did you do? Did you work with any project management tools such as Microsoft Project?
2. Did you ever work on a non-IT project? What were your responsibilities? Did you use project management software for your work?
3. Have you taken course work in project management? What do you know about process documentation?
4. What is your proficiency level with Microsoft Office tools and with Microsoft Project and SharePoint?

Author Tips

1. Review this chapter and also Chapter 13 on building information systems to familiarize yourself with project management and systems development techniques and methodologies.
2. Use the web to do more research on project management methodologies and tools. Explore the Project Management Institute (PMI) website or review the Project Management Institute's book, *A Guide to the Project Management Body of Knowledge.*
3. Try to find information on how projects are managed at XYZ Multimedia. Inquire what project management methodologies and tools are used at this company. If possible, show you are familiar with these tools and approaches.
4. Provide examples of any project management work you have done in your courses or on a job. Alternatively, provide examples of your writing and verbal communication skills.

REVIEW **SUMMARY**

14-1 What are the objectives of project management, and why is it so essential in developing information systems?

Good project management is essential for ensuring that systems are delivered on time and on budget and provide genuine business benefits. Project management activities include planning the work, assessing the risk, estimating and acquiring resources required to accomplish the work, organizing the work, directing execution, and analyzing the results. Project management must deal with five major variables: scope, time, cost, quality, and risk.

14-2 What methods can be used for selecting and evaluating information systems projects and aligning them with the firm's business goals?

Organizations need an information systems plan that describes how information technology supports the attainment of their business goals and documents all their system applications and IT infrastructure components. Large corporations will have a management structure to ensure the most important systems projects receive priority. Portfolio analysis and scoring models can be used to identify and evaluate alternative information systems projects.

14-3 How can firms assess the business value of information systems?

To determine whether an information systems project is a good investment, one must calculate its costs and benefits. Tangible benefits are quantifiable, and intangible benefits that cannot be immediately quantified may provide quantifiable benefits in the future. Benefits that exceed costs should be analyzed using capital budgeting methods to make sure a project represents a good return on the firm's invested capital.

14-4   What are the principal risk factors in information systems projects, and how can they be managed?

The level of risk in a systems development project is determined by (1) project size, (2) project structure, and (3) experience with technology. IS projects are more likely to fail when there is insufficient or improper user participation in the systems development process, lack of management support, and poor management of the implementation process. There is a very high failure rate among projects involving business process reengineering, enterprise applications, and mergers and acquisitions because they require extensive organizational change.

Implementation refers to the entire process of organizational change surrounding the introduction of a new information system. User support and involvement and management support and control of the implementation process are essential, as are mechanisms for dealing with the level of risk in each new systems project. Project risk factors can be brought under some control by a contingency approach to project management. The risk level of each project determines the appropriate mix of external integration tools, internal integration tools, formal planning tools, and formal control tools to be applied. Project management software helps organizations track individual projects and project portfolio management software helps them manage portfolios of projects and dependencies among them.

Key Terms

Capital budgeting, 542
Change agent, 545
Change management, 545
Counterimplementation, 549
Ergonomics, 550
External integration tools, 548
Formal control tools, 548
Formal planning tools, 548
Gantt chart, 548
Implementation, 545
Information systems plan, 538
Intangible benefits, 542
Internal integration tools, 547

Organizational impact analysis, 551
PERT chart, 548
Portfolio analysis, 540
Project, 536
Project management, 536
Project portfolio management, 553
Scope, 537
Scoring model, 541
Sociotechnical design, 551
Tangible benefits, 542
User-designer communications gap, 545
User interface, 536

MyLab MIS

To complete the problems with MyLab MIS, go to the EOC Discussion Questions in MyLab MIS.

Review Questions

14-1   What are the objectives of project management, and why is it so essential in developing information systems?

- Describe information system problems resulting from poor project management.

- Define project management. List and describe the project management activities and variables addressed by project management.

14-2   What methods can be used for selecting and evaluating information systems projects and aligning them with the firm's business goals?

- Name and describe the groups responsible for the management of information systems projects.

- Describe the purpose of an information systems plan and list the major categories in the plan.

- Explain how portfolio analysis and scoring models can be used to select information systems projects.

14-3 How can firms assess the business value of information systems?

- List and describe the major costs and benefits of information systems.

- Distinguish between tangible and intangible benefits.

14-4 What are the principal risk factors in information systems projects, and how can they be managed?

- Identify and describe each of the principal risk factors in information systems projects.

- Explain why builders of new information systems need to address implementation and change management.

- Explain why eliciting support of management and end users is so essential for successful implementation of information systems projects.

- Explain why there is such a high failure rate for implementations involving enterprise applications, business process reengineering, and mergers and acquisitions.

- Identify and describe the strategies for controlling project risk.

- Identify the organizational considerations that should be addressed by project planning and implementation.

- Explain how project management software tools contribute to successful project management.

Discussion Questions

14-5 How much does project management impact
MyLab MIS the success of a new information system?

14-6 It has been said that most systems
MyLab MIS fail because systems builders ignore organizational behavior problems. Why might this be so?

14-7 What is the role of end users in information
MyLab MIS systems project management?

Hands-On MIS Projects

The projects in this section give you hands-on experience evaluating information systems projects, using spreadsheet software to perform capital budgeting analyses for new information systems investments, and using web tools to analyze the financing for a new home. Visit the MyLab MIS Multimedia Library to access this chapter's Hands-on MIS Projects.

Management Decision Problems

14-8 The U.S. Census launched an IT project to arm its census takers in the field with high-tech handheld devices that would save taxpayer money by directly beaming population data to headquarters from census takers in the field. Census officials signed a $600 million contract with Harris Corporation in 2006 to build 500,000 devices but still weren't sure which features they wanted included in the units. Census officials did not specify the testing process to measure the performance of the handheld devices. As the project progressed, 400 change requests to project requirements were added. Two years and hundreds of millions of taxpayer dollars later, the handhelds were far too slow and unreliable to be used for the 2010 U.S. census. What could Census Bureau management and the Harris Corporation have done to prevent this outcome?

14-9 Caterpillar is the world's leading maker of earth-moving machinery and supplier of agricultural equipment. Caterpillar wants to end its support for its Dealer Business System (DBS), which it licenses to its dealers to help them run their businesses. The software in this system is becoming outdated, and senior management wants to transfer support for the hosted version of the software to Accenture Consultants so it can concentrate on its core business. Caterpillar never required its dealers to use DBS, but the system had become a de facto standard for doing business with the company. The majority of the 50 Cat dealers in North America use some version of DBS, as do about half of the 200 or so Cat dealers in the rest of the world. Before Caterpillar turns the product over to Accenture, what factors and issues should it consider? What questions should it ask? What questions should its dealers ask?

Improving Decision Making: Using Spreadsheet Software for Capital Budgeting for a New CAD System

Software skills: Spreadsheet formulas and functions
Business skills: Capital budgeting

14-10 This project provides you with an opportunity to use spreadsheet software to use the capital budgeting models discussed in this chapter and its Learning Tracks to analyze the return on an investment for a new computer-aided design (CAD) system.

Your company would like to invest in a CAD system that requires purchasing hardware, software, and networking technology as well as expenditures for installation, training, and support. MyLab MIS contains tables showing each cost component for the new system as well as annual maintenance costs over a five-year period, along with a Learning Track on capital budgeting models. You believe the new system will reduce the amount of labor required to generate designs and design specifications, thereby increasing your firm's annual cash flow.

- Using the data provided in these tables, create a worksheet that calculates the costs and benefits of the investment over a five-year period and analyzes the investment using the four capital budgeting models presented in this chapter's Learning Track.

- Is this investment worthwhile? Why or why not?

Improving Decision Making: Using Web Tools for Buying and Financing a Home

Software skills: Internet-based software
Business skills: Financial planning

14-11 This project will develop your skills using web-based software for searching for a home and calculating mortgage financing for that home.

You would like to purchase a home in Fort Collins, Colorado. Ideally, it should be a single-family house with at least three bedrooms and one bathroom that costs between $170,000 and $300,000 and can be financed with a 30-year fixed rate mortgage. You can afford a down payment that is 20 percent of the value of the house. Before you purchase a house, you would like to find out what homes are available in your price range, find a mortgage, and determine the amount of your monthly payment. Use the Realtor.com site to help you with the following tasks:

- Locate homes in Fort Collins, Colorado, that meet your specifications.

- Find a mortgage for 80 percent of the list price of the home. Compare rates from at least three sites (use search engines to find sites other than Yahoo).

- After selecting a mortgage, calculate your closing costs and the monthly payment.

When you are finished, evaluate the whole process. For example, assess the ease of use of the site and your ability to find information about houses and mortgages, the accuracy of the information you found, and the breadth of choice of homes and mortgages.

Collaboration and Teamwork Project

Identifying Implementation Problems

14-12 Form a group with three or four other students. Write a description of the implementation problems you might expect to encounter in one of the systems described in the Interactive Sessions or chapter-ending cases in this text. Write an analysis of the steps you would take to solve or prevent these problems. If possible, use Google Docs and Google Drive or Google Sites to brainstorm, organize, and develop a presentation of your findings for the class.

Pennsylvania's Unemployment Compensation Modernization System: Unfinished Business

CASE STUDY

The Pennsylvania Department of Labor and Industry (DLI) is responsible for the administration and operation of the state's unemployment compensation program, which provides temporary income to replace lost wages for qualified workers. DLI employs over 500 people and has approximately 200 offices statewide to serve Pennsylvania's 6.4 million workers and nearly 300,000 employers. Unemployment compensation (UC) claims are usually filed online or by telephone or mailed to a UC service center.

DLI had a legacy mainframe system for processing unemployment benefits that was over 40 years old. However, it became increasingly expensive to maintain and difficult to modify, with limited functionality for case management and integrating newer tools and technologies to enhance productivity.

In June 2006, DLI awarded IBM a fixed price contract totaling $109.9 million for the Unemployment Compensation Modernization System (UCMS), which would replace the antiquated mainframe system. The initial contract with IBM called for more modern and efficient technology and business processes for (1) maintaining wage records, (2) processing employer taxes, and (3) claims processing, payment, and appeals, to be completed by February 2010. IBM won the UCMS contract after a three-year bidding process, claiming to be the only vendor with the type of proprietary databases capable of supporting a totally integrated computer system.

However, this project experienced significant delays and cost overruns, ultimately costing nearly $180 million, with much of the system never completed when the contract expired in September 2013. By that time, the project was 45 months behind schedule and $60 million over budget. Pennsylvania taxpayers had paid IBM nearly $170 million for what was supposed to be a comprehensive, integrated, and modern system that it never got. IBM's contract was not renewed. In March 2017, Pennsylvania sued IBM for breach of contract, fraudulent and negligent misrepresentation, and charging taxpayers for services it did not provide. IBM said Pennsylvania's claims had no merit and that it would fight the lawsuit. A spokesman for the company laid some of the blame for the project's problems on the state, saying that

there was responsibility on both sides for system performance and service delivery. How did all of this happen?

Phase 1 of UCMS (wage records) was implemented in May 2008. Phase 2, which included the employer tax portion of the system, went live in March 2011 but required additional work, which took years to fix. Phase 3 for benefit claims processing, payment, and appeals continued to lag behind with problems and ultimately never went live.

In 2012, DLI enlisted the Carnegie Mellon Software Engineering Insitute to conduct an independent assessment of the UCMS. The study was completed in July 2013, and recommended continuing work on remaining Phase 2 problems, but stopping work on Phase 3. Many of the problems it identified for Phase 3 could not be solved.

The Carnegie Mellon study found many flaws in the systems development process. IBM had extensive systems experience and technology knowledge but its proposal underestimated the project's scope and complexity. DLI lacked sufficient staffing and experience for effective oversight and management of the contract and project. There was no formal delegation of roles and responsibilities for managing the project. No one at DLI was held accountable. DLI essentially relied on the contractor to self-manage.

UCMS was considered a large-scale software project due to its complexity, large number of information requirements and business rules, and its cost. DLI's solicitation for vendor proposals for UCMS exhibited ambiguity in communicating all of these requirements, and also neglected to define and describe quantitative and qualitative performance measures and metrics for the proposed system.

A large-scale software-intensive system such as UCMS requires a rigorous and disciplined testing strategy, but this was not implemented. IBM decided to use DLI users to help develop test scripts. They provided the business expertise, but IBM did not use IT test experts on its end. User acceptance testing was initiated before completing system tests for Phase 2 and Phase 3. Rigorous testing came too late in the project. DLI did not specify a minimum of metrics for UCMS system performance so that there were no identifiable criteria and evidence for determining that Phase 2 and Phase 3 application releases were stable.

DLI staff had approved IBM's representation of business system requirements without fully understanding what they were approving. IBM's software development and testing program for this project lacked rigor. This resulted in a higher number of software defects than industry norms, software code that was excessively complex (which makes testing too difficult), and late discovery of missing business requirements.

The vast majority of the software defects were serious, and 50 percent were not discovered until the User Acceptance test, very late in the system development cycle. Without thorough and complete testing throughout the development process, there is no way to know how many of the total defects residing in software will be discovered as a system is being used. Carnegie Mellon also found that IBM had not performed a stress test to determine the performance limits of the UCMS system.

IBM's software development plan was supposed to use industry and company standards and practices, but there was no ongoing discipline to execute these standards and practices during the project. DLI accepted Phase 2 prematurely for production in March 2011 with known defects impacting system performance, including software defects, unresolved data conversion issues, and problems with batch processing operations.

A project of this complexity and magnitude requires a high degree of continuity in knowledge throughout the system development cycle, but this was never achieved. During requirements determination, DLI didn't have enough user subject matter experts to participate in joint application design (JAD; see Chapter 13) sessions with technical members of the project team. Thirty-six JAD subcontractors were prematurely removed from the project, leaving IBM with incomplete understanding of unemployment claims processing business requirements. System design and testing staff were not included in the JAD process, running counter to sound business practice. Including them was essential to ensure UC business requirements were defined in sufficient detail to be testable. DLI staff often approved JAD requirements documents and Detailed System Design documents under pressure to meet short deadlines for approval.

Ineffective project management and constant changes in the contractor's workforce prevented transfer of essential knowledge for the entire project, a loss of "project memory." Since the UCMS project's start, 638 different contractors and staff members worked on the project. The majority of the project workforce spent less than one year on the project and 75 percent spent less than 2 years. All of these discontinuities and workforce churn most likely contributed to IBM's schedule delays and inability to provide an accurate picture of the state of the project.

Work on Pennsylvania's UC system continued without IBM. In 2013, the Pennsylvania Legislature passed Act 34, which created a Services Infrastructure Improvement Fund (SIIF) as a temporary supplemental funding source to improve UC services and systems. A total of $178.4 million was authorized and spent during calendar years 2013 through 2016. Even then the project stumbled. Pennsylvania Auditor General Eugene A. DePasquale initiated an audit in January 2017 to determine how the $178 million in SIIF funds were spent. The auditors found that DLI did not use proper accounting methods to record specific SIIF expenditures. DLI comingled unemployment compensation administrative funds from all sources, including federal funds for unemployment compensation administration and interest on unemployment compensation tax money as well as outlays from SIIF.

On a more positive note, there were noticeable improvements and efficiencies from 2013 through 2016 in services provided to UC claimants and in UC system infrastructure. For example, the percentage of first payments paid promptly increased from 81.6 percent to 93.4 percent. However, DLI was unable to show how exactly the SIIF expenditures contributed to these outcomes.

When SIIF funding was not reauthorized and supplemental funding ended in December 2016, DLI was forced to cut $57.5 million from its UC administrative budget for 2017, causing the immediate closure of three of the state's eight UC service centers in December 2016 and the elimination of 521 positions. Customer service declined significantly with claimants not being able to get through on the phone lines and delays in processing claims.

Despite earlier setbacks, DLI is determined to complete the modernization of its unemployment compensation benefits delivery system. In June 2017, DLI signed a $35 million contract with Florida-based Geographic Solutions to create a system that enhances customer service, improves quality, is more operationally efficient, and is sustainable into the future. Geographic Solutions specializes in designing, developing, and maintaining web-based systems for the workforce development and unemployment insurance industries and has developed over 80 workforce systems for state and local agencies across the United States. Geographic Solutions was scheduled to begin work on the system on August 1, 2017 with a projected 18 to 24 months for completion.

In 2015, DLI had hired Chicago-based CSG Government Solutions for $6.1 million to assist with planning for and monitoring this project. CSG specializes in planning, managing, and supporting complex projects that modernize the information technology and business processes of large government programs. CSG analyzed existing systems and workflows, developed the project strategy and technology roadmap, and gathered business and technical requirements to develop an RFP. CSG also established a full-service Project Management Office to monitor project progress, and is providing technical oversight, UC subject matter expertise, requirements management, and testing support throughout the system modernization. Once the new system has been fully implemented, cost savings from benefit modernization are estimated to range from 5 to 10 percent of total UC administrative costs.

Sources: www.geographicsolutions.com, accessed January 3, 2018; www.csgdelivers.com, accessed January 3, 2018; Jan Murphy, "Take Two: Labor & Industry Tries Again to Modernize Jobless Benefits Computer System," *Penn Live*, June 23, 2017; Commonwealth of Pennsylvania Department of the Auditor General, "Performance Audit Report: Pennsylvania Department of Labor and Industry Service and Infrastructure Improvement Fund (SIIF)," April 2017; and Constance Bennett, Nanette Brown, Julie Cohen, Dr. Betsy Clark, Jeff Davenport, Eric Ferguson, John Gross, Michael H. McLendon, and Gregory Such, "Independent Assessment of the Commonwealth of Pennsylvania Unemployment Compensation Modernization System Program (UCMS)," Carnegie Mellon University Software Engineering Institute, July 2013.

CASE STUDY QUESTIONS

14-13 Assess the importance of the Unemployment Compensation Modernization System project for the state of Pennsylvania.

14-14 Why was unemployment compensation modernization a risky project in Pennsylvania? Identify the key risk factors.

14-15 Classify and describe the problems encountered by the UCMS projects. What management, organization, and technology factors were responsible for these problems?

14-16 What could have been done to mitigate the risks of these projects?

MyLab MIS

Go to the Assignments section of MyLab MIS to complete these writing exercises.

14-17 Identify and describe two methods for helping managers select information systems projects.

14-18 Compare the two major types of planning and control tools.

Chapter 14 References

Appan, Radha, and Glenn J. Browne. "The Impact of Analyst-Induced Misinformation on the Requirements Elicitation Process." *MIS Quarterly* 36, No 1 (March 2012).

Ariel Avgar, Prasanna Tambe, and Lorin M. Hitt. "Built to Learn: How Work Practices Affect Employee Learning During Healthcare Information Technology Implementation." *MIS Quarterly* 42, No. 2 (June 2018).

Baird, Aaron, Elizabeth Davidson, and Lars Mathiassen. "Reflective Technology Assimilation: Facilitating Electronic Health Record Assimilation in Small Physician Practices." *Journal of Management Information Systems* 34, No. 3 (2017).

Balaji, Arjun, Raghavan Janardhanan, Shannon Johnston, and Noshir Kaka. "How Predictive Analytics Can Boost Product Development." McKinsey & Company (August 2018).

Bloch, Michael, Sen Blumberg, and Jurgen Laartz. "Delivering Large-Scale IT Projects on Time, on Budget, and on Value." *McKinsey Quarterly* (October 2012).

Brock, Jon, Tamim Saleh, and Sesh Iyer. "Large-Scale IT Projects: From Nightmare to Value Creation." Boston Consulting Group (May 20, 2015).

Browning, Tyson, R., and Ranga V. Ramasesh. "Reducing Unwelcome Surprises in Project Management." *MIT Sloan Management Review* (Spring 2015).

Brynjolfsson, Erik, and Lorin M. Hitt. "Information Technology and Organizational Design: Evidence from Micro Data." (January 1998).

Chandrasekaran, Sriram, Sauri Gudlavalleti, and Sanjay Kaniyar. "Achieving Success in Large Complex Software Projects." *McKinsey Quarterly* (July 2014).

Clement, Andrew, and Peter Van den Besselaar. "A Retrospective Look at PD Projects." *Communications of the ACM* 36, No. 4 (June 1993).

Davies, Andrew, Mark Dodgson, David M. Gann, and Samuel C. MacAulay. "Five Rules for Managing Large Complex Projects. *MIT Sloan Management Review* (Fall 2017).

Dubravka Cecez-Kecmanovic, Karlheinz Kautz, and Rebecca Abrahall. "Reframing Success and Failure of Information Systems: A Performative Perspective." *MIS Quarterly* 38, No. 2 (June 2014).

Florentine, Sharon. "More Than Half of IT Projects Are Still Failing." *CIO* (May 11, 2016).

Flyvbjerg, Bent, and Alexander Budzier. "Why Your IT Project May Be Riskier Than You Think." *Harvard Business Review* (September 2011).

He, Jun, and William R. King. "The Role of User Participation In Information Systems Development: Implications from a Meta-Analysis." *Journal of Management Information Systems* 25, No. 1 (Summer 2008).

Hu, Paul Jen-Hwa, Han-fen Hu, and Xiao Fang. "Examining the Mediating Roles of Cognitive Load and Performance Outcomes in User Satisfaction with a Website: A Field Quasi-Experiment." *MIS Quarterly* 41, No. 3 (September 2017).

Jeffrey, Mark and Ingmar Leliveld. "Best Practices in IT Portfolio Management." *MIT Sloan Management Review* 45, No. 3 (Spring 2004).

Karhade, Prasanna, Michael J. Shaw, and Ramanath Subramanyam. "Patterns in Information Systems Portfolio Prioritization: Evidence from Decision Tree Induction." *MIS Quarterly* 39, No.2 (June 2015).

Keen, Peter W. "Information Systems and Organizational Change." *Communications of the ACM* 24 (January 1981).

Keil, Mark, H. Jeff Smith, Charalambos L. Iacovou, and Ronald L. Thompson. "The Pitfalls of Project Status Reporting." *MIT Sloan Management Review* 55, No. 3 (Spring 2014).

Keil, Mark, Joan Mann, and Arun Rai. "Why Software Projects Escalate: An Empirical Analysis and Test of Four Theoretical Models." *MIS Quarterly* 24, No. 4 (December 2000).

Kim, Hee Woo, and Atreyi Kankanhalli. "Investigating User Resistance to Information Systems Implementation: A Status Quo Bias Perspective." *MIS Quarterly* 33, No. 3 (September 2009).

Kloppenborg, Timothy J., and Debbie Tesch. "How Executive Sponsors Influence Project Success." *MIT Sloan Management Review* (Spring 2015).

Kolb, D. A., and A. L. Frohman. "An Organization Development Approach to Consulting." *Sloan Management Review* 12 (Fall 1970).

Lapointe, Liette, and Suzanne Rivard. "A Multilevel Model of Resistance to Information Technology Implementation." *MIS Quarterly* 29, No. 3 (September 2005).

Laudon, Kenneth C. "CIOs Beware: Very Large Scale Systems." Center for Research on Information Systems, New York University Stern School of Business, working paper (1989).

Laufer, Alexander, Edward J. Hoffman, Jeffrey S. Russell, and W. Scott Cameron. "What Successful Project Managers Do." *MIT Sloan Management Review* (Spring 2015).

Lee, Jong Seok, Mark Keil, and Vijay Kasi. "The Effect of an Initial Budget and Schedule Goal on Software Project Escalation." *Journal of Management Information Systems* 29, No. 1 (Summer 2012).

Li, Xitong, and Stuart E. Madnick. "Understanding the Dynamics of Service-Oriented Architecture Implementation." *Journal of Management Information Systems* 32, No. 2 (2015).

Liang, Huigang, Zeyu Peng, Xue Zeyu, Guo Yajiong, and Wang Xitong. "Employees' Exploration of Complex Systems: An Integrative View." *Journal of Management Information Systems* 32 No. 1 (2015).

Liang, Huigang, Nilesh Sharaf, Qing Hu, and Yajiong Xue. "Assimilation of Enterprise Systems: The Effect of Institutional Pressures and the Mediating Role of Top Management." *MIS Quarterly* 31, No. 1 (March 2007).

McFarlan, F. Warren. "Portfolio Approach to Information Systems." *Harvard Business Review* (September–October 1981).

Mumford, Enid, and Mary Weir. *Computer Systems in Work Design: The ETHICS Method*. New York: John Wiley (1979).

Polites, Greta L., and Elena Karahanna. "Shackled to the Status Quo: The Inhibiting Effects of Incumbent System Habit, Switching Costs, and Inertia on New System Acceptance." *MIS Quarterly* 36, No. 1 (March 2012).

Pratt, Mary K. "Why IT Projects Still Fail." *CIO* (August 1, 2017).

Project Management Institute. *A Guide to the Project Management Body of Knowledge* (6th ed.). Newtown Square, PA: Project Management Institute (2017).

Ramasubbu, Narayan, Anandhi Bharadwaj, and Giri Kumar Tayi. "Software Process Diversity: Conceptualization, Measurement, and Analysis of Impact on Project Performance." *MIS Quarterly* 39, No. 4 (December 2015).

Rivard, Suzanne, and Liette Lapointe. "Information Technology Implementers' Responses to User Resistance: Nature and Effects." *MIS Quarterly* 36, No. 3 (September 2012).

Ryan, Sherry D., David A. Harrison, and Lawrence L. Schkade. "Information Technology Investment Decisions: When Do Cost and Benefits in the Social Subsystem Matter?" *Journal of Management Information Systems* 19, No. 2 (Fall 2002).

Schwalbe, Kathy. An *Introduction to Project Management* (6th ed.). Cengage (2017).

Sharma, Rajeev, and Philip Yetton. "The Contingent Effects of Training, Technical Complexity, and Task Interdependence on Successful Information Systems Implementation." *MIS Quarterly* 31, No. 2 (June 2007).

Swanson, E. Burton. *Information System Implementation*. Homewood, IL: Richard D. Irwin (1988).

Sykes, Tracy Ann. "Support Structures and Their Impacts on Employee Outcomes: A Longitudinal Field Study of an Enterprise System Implementation." *MIS Quarterly* 39, No. 2 (June 2015).

Sykes, Tracy Ann, and Viswanath Venkatesh. "Explaining Post-Implementation Employee System Use and Job Performance: Impacts of the Content and Source of Social Network Ties." *MIS Quarterly* 41, No. 3 (September 2017).

Tornatsky, Louis G., J. D. Eveland, M. G. Boylan, W. A. Hetzner, E. C. Johnson, D. Roitman, and J. Schneider. *The Process of Technological Innovation: Reviewing the Literature*. Washington, DC: National Science Foundation (1983).

Weinnschenk, Carl. "How Project Management Software Increases IT Efficiency." *IT Business Edge* (January 18, 2018).

Yin, Robert K. "Life Histories of Innovations: How New Practices Become Routinized." *Public Administration Review* (January–February 1981).

Zhang, Xiaojun. "Knowledge Management System Use and Job Performance: A Multilevel Contingency Model." *MIS Quarterly* 41, No. 3 (September 2017).

15

Managing Global Systems

LEARNING OBJECTIVES

After reading this chapter, you will be able to answer the following questions:

15-1 What major factors are driving the internationalization of business?

15-2 What are the alternative strategies for developing global businesses?

15-3 What are the challenges posed by global information systems and management solutions for these challenges?

15-4 What are the issues and technical alternatives to be considered when developing international information systems?

15-5 How will MIS help my career?

CHAPTER CASES

New Systems Help Eli Lilly Standardize as a Global Company

The Global Internet Goes Multimedia

AbbVie Builds a Global Systems Infrastructure

E-commerce in China: Opportunities and Obstacles

VIDEO CASES

Daum Runs Oracle Apps on Linux

Lean Manufacturing and Global ERP: Humanetics and Global Shop

---

MyLab MIS

Discussion Questions: 15-5, 15-6; **Hands-on MIS Projects:** 15-7, 15-8, 15-9, 15-10; **Writing Assignments:** 15-15, 15-16; **eText with Conceptual Animations**

New Systems Help Eli Lilly Standardize as a Global Company

Eli Lilly and Company is one of the world's leading pharmaceutical manufacturers, marketing its pharmaceutical and animal health care products in 120 countries. Headquartered in Indianapolis, Indiana, Lilly has 41,000 employees throughout the United States and 73 other countries, 2017 revenue of $22.9 billion, and 13 manufacturing and 6 research and development (R&D) locations around the globe.

As a far-flung global company, Lilly had dozens of disparate local and regional information systems customized to support local business processes, and they were very difficult to coordinate. Imagine the data redundancies and inefficiencies when 40 different local controllers executed the month-end financial closing process on 40 different systems with different data standards!

In order to manage Lilly as a global enterprise and reduce costs, Lilly moved to a shared services model in which common processes are centralized at a regional level or outsourced completely. The company set up four regional shared service centers in Indiana, Ireland, Mexico, and Malaysia. The shared service model helps eliminate redundancies and trim costs by pulling business processes away from local units and regionalizing them at the shared service centers.

© Docstockmedia/Shutterstock

These systems needed to be retired and replaced by a common IT platform—in this case, a single enterprise-wide ERP system. Starting in 2010, Lilly began rolling out a single global instance of SAP to all its locations. Today, essentially all of Lilly's global business runs on SAP ERP and 17 other SAP software solutions, including systems for governance, risk management, and compliance (GRC).

Of special importance was Lilly's adoption in 2013 of SAP GRC Process Control for process automation. Previously, Lilly's financial control group tried to manage the control structure regionally by using individual spreadsheets that identified controls for different locations. The company's master control matrix was a large workbook incorporating data from individual spreadsheets with color coding to manage changes to the file. It was both frustrating and time-consuming to identify which controls were in place at any point in time throughout Lilly's global organization.

SAP GRC Process Controls is a tool that provides organizations with a continuous view of their key compliance activities across all business processes, such as compliance with Sarbanes-Oxley (SOX), segregation of duties (SoD), and operational controls for managing the business. (SOX controls the accuracy and security of data reported within financial statements, and SoD assigns more than one individual to perform a single task to prevent fraud and error.) SAP GRC Process Control serves as a central repository to store data from a global control matrix for Lilly's entire enterprise and improves management of those controls with automated monitoring. The Process Control tool can issue alerts when controls need to be tested, store testing and sign-off documentation, create and delegate remediation plans, and keep an audit trail of changes to controls. By standardizing and streamlining execution of its process controls and business rules throughout the enterprise, Eli Lilly has become even more efficient and effective as a global company.

Sources: www.sap.com, accessed January 9, 2018; Lauren Bonneau, "Eli Lilly and Company Continues Its Global Standardization and Automation Initiative with a rollout of SAP Process Control," *SAP Insider Profiles*, August 10, 2017; www.lilly.com, accessed January 9, 2018; and Dave Hannon, "Lilly Brings Process Consistency to a Diversified Global Organization," *SAP Insider Profiles*, April 1, 2011.

Eli Lilly's efforts to create global reporting systems and a regional shared services model identify some of the issues that truly global organizations need to consider if they want to operate worldwide. Like many large, multinational firms, Eli Lilly has numerous operating units in many different countries. These units had their own systems, business processes, and reporting standards. As a result, Eli Lilly was unable to effectively coordinate global operations or manage its financial reporting controls across multiple countries and regions. Management was unable to see how Lilly was meeting governance, risk, and compliance standards enterprise-wide.

The chapter-opening diagram calls attention to important points raised by this case and this chapter. To solve its global management and business challenges, Eli Lilly moved to a shared services model and standardized and streamlined its business processes on a global level. The company implemented a single instance of the SAP ERP software worldwide. Lilly also implemented SAP Process Control to create a global framework for governance, risk management, and compliance (GRC). Eli Lilly's global systems provide the firm with enterprise-wide information on firm operations and financial performance so that the company can be more easily managed and coordinated from a global perspective.

Here are some questions to think about: How did information technology improve operations and management decision making at Eli Lilly? How did Lilly's new ERP and Process Control systems help Lilly become a more global organization?

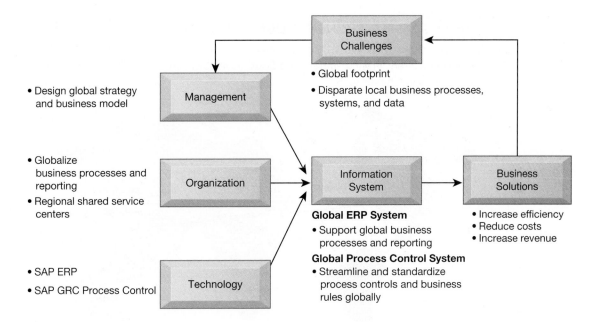

15-1 What major factors are driving the internationalization of business?

In earlier chapters, we describe the emergence of a global economic system and global world order driven by advanced networks and information systems. The new world order is sweeping away many national corporations, national industries, and national economies controlled by domestic politicians. Many localized firms will be replaced by fast-moving networked corporations that transcend national boundaries. The growth of international trade has radically altered domestic economies around the globe.

Consider the path to market for an iPhone, which is illustrated in Figure 15.1. The iPhone was designed by Apple engineers in the United States, sourced with more than 200 high-tech components from around the world, and assembled in China. Companies in Taiwan, South Korea, Japan, France, Italy, Germany, and the United States provided components such as the case, camera, processor, accelerator, gyroscope, electronic compass, power management chip, touch screen controller, and high-definition display screen. Foxconn, a Chinese division of Taiwan's Hon Hai Group, is in charge of manufacturing and assembly.

Developing an International Information Systems Architecture

This chapter describes how to go about building an international information systems architecture suitable for your international strategy. An **international information systems architecture** consists of the basic information systems required by organizations to coordinate worldwide trade and other activities. Figure 15.2 illustrates the reasoning we follow throughout the chapter and

FIGURE 15.1 APPLE IPHONE'S GLOBAL SUPPLY CHAIN

Apple designs the iPhone in the United States and relies on suppliers in the United States, Germany, Italy, France, Japan, and South Korea for other parts. Much of the final assembly occurs in China.

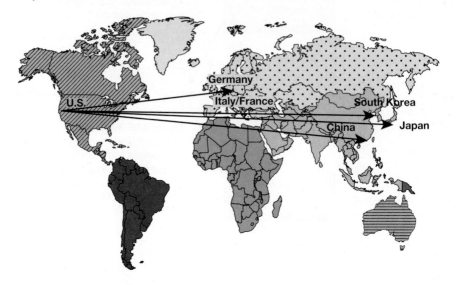

depicts the major dimensions of an international information systems architectue.

The basic strategy to follow when building an international system is to understand the global environment in which your firm is operating. This means understanding the overall market forces, or business drivers, that are pushing your industry toward global competition. A **business driver** is a force in the environment to which businesses must respond and that influences the direction of the business. Likewise, examine carefully the inhibitors or negative factors that create *management challenges*—factors that could scuttle the development

FIGURE 15.2 INTERNATIONAL INFORMATION SYSTEMS ARCHITECTURE

The major dimensions for developing an international information systems architecture are the global environment, the corporate global strategies, the structure of the organization, the management and business processes, and the technology platform.

of a global business. Once you have examined the global environment, you will need to consider a corporate strategy for competing in that environment. How will your firm respond? You could ignore the global market and focus on domestic competition only, sell to the globe from a domestic base, or organize production and distribution around the globe. There are many in-between choices.

After you have developed a strategy, it is time to consider how to structure your organization so it can pursue the strategy. How will you accomplish a division of labor across a global environment? Where will production, administration, accounting, marketing, and human resource functions be located? Who will handle the systems function?

Next, you must consider the management issues in implementing your strategy and making the organization design come alive. Key here will be the design of business processes. How can you discover and manage user requirements? How can you induce change in local units to conform to international requirements? How can you reengineer on a global scale, and how can you coordinate systems development?

The last issue to consider is the technology platform. Although changing technology is a key driving factor leading toward global markets, you need to have a corporate strategy and structure before you can rationally choose the right technology.

After you have completed this process of reasoning, you will be well on your way toward an appropriate international information systems portfolio capable of achieving your corporate goals. Let's begin by looking at the overall global environment.

The Global Environment: Business Drivers and Challenges

Table 15.1 lists the business drivers in the global environment that are leading all industries toward global markets and competition.

The global business drivers can be divided into two groups: general cultural factors and specific business factors. Easily recognized general cultural factors have driven internationalization since World War II. Information, communication, and transportation technologies have created a *global village* in which communication (by telephone, television, radio, or computer network) around the globe is no more difficult than communication down the block. The cost of moving goods and services to and from geographically dispersed locations has fallen dramatically.

The development of global communications has created a global village in a second sense: A **global culture** created by television, the Internet, and other globally shared media such as movies now permits different cultures and

TABLE 15.1 THE GLOBAL ENVIRONMENT: BUSINESS DRIVERS AND CHALLENGES

GENERAL CULTURAL FACTORS	SPECIFIC BUSINESS FACTORS
Global communication and transportation technologies	Global markets
Development of global culture	Global production and operations
Emergence of global social norms	Global coordination
Political stability	Global workforce
Global knowledge base	Global economies of scale

peoples to develop common expectations about right and wrong, desirable and undesirable, heroic and cowardly.

A last factor to consider is the growth of a global knowledge base. At the end of World War II, knowledge, education, science, and industrial skills were highly concentrated in North America, Western Europe, and Japan, with the rest of the world euphemistically called the *Third World*. This is no longer true. Latin America, China, southern Asia, and Eastern Europe have developed powerful educational, industrial, and scientific centers, resulting in a much more democratically and widely dispersed knowledge base.

These general cultural factors leading toward internationalization result in specific business globalization factors that affect most industries. The growth of powerful communications technologies and the emergence of world cultures lay the groundwork for *global markets*—global consumers interested in consuming similar products that are culturally approved. Coca-Cola, American sneakers (made in Korea but designed in Los Angeles), and Cable News Network (CNN) programming can now be sold in Latin America, Africa, and Asia.

Responding to this demand, global production and operations have emerged with precise online coordination between far-flung production facilities and central headquarters thousands of miles away. At Maersk, a major global shipping company based in Copenhagen, Denmark, shipping managers at Copenhagen and other locations can watch the loading of ships in Rotterdam online, check trim and ballast, and trace packages to specific ship locations as the activity proceeds. This is all possible through an international satellite link.

The new global markets and pressure toward global production and operation have called forth whole new capabilities for global coordination. Production, accounting, marketing and sales, human resources, and systems development (all the major business functions) can be coordinated on a global scale.

Frito-Lay, for instance, can develop a marketing sales force automation system in the United States and, once provided, may try the same techniques and technologies in Spain. Micromarketing—marketing to very small geographic and social units—no longer means marketing to neighborhoods in the United States but to neighborhoods throughout the world! Internet-based marketing means marketing to individuals and social networks across the globe. These new levels of global coordination permit, for the first time in history, the location of business activity according to comparative advantage. Design should be located where it is best accomplished, as should marketing, production, and finance.

Finally, global markets, production, and administration create the conditions for powerful, sustained global economies of scale. Production driven by worldwide global demand can be concentrated where it can best be accomplished, fixed resources can be allocated over larger production runs, and production runs in larger plants can be scheduled more efficiently and precisely estimated. Lower-cost factors of production can be exploited wherever they emerge. The result is a powerful strategic advantage to firms that can organize globally. These general and specific business drivers have greatly enlarged world trade and commerce.

Not all industries are similarly affected by these trends. Clearly, manufacturing has been much more affected than services that still tend to be domestic and highly inefficient. However, the localism of services is breaking down in telecommunications, entertainment, transportation, finance, law, and general business. Clearly, those firms that can understand the internationalization of their own industry and respond appropriately will reap enormous gains in productivity and stability.

TABLE 15.2 CHALLENGES AND OBSTACLES TO GLOBAL BUSINESS SYSTEMS	
GLOBAL	SPECIFIC
Cultural particularism: Regionalism, nationalism, language differences	Standards: Different Electronic Data Interchange (EDI), email, telecommunications standards
Social expectations: Brand-name expectations, work hours	Reliability: Phone networks not uniformly reliable
Political laws: Transborder data and privacy laws, commercial regulations	Speed: Different data transfer speeds, many slower than United States
	Personnel: Shortages of skilled consultants

Business Challenges

Although the possibilities of globalization for business success are significant, fundamental forces are operating to inhibit a global economy and to disrupt international business. Table 15.2 lists the most common and powerful challenges to the development of global systems.

At a cultural level, **particularism**, making judgments and taking action on the basis of narrow or personal characteristics, in all its forms (religious, nationalistic, ethnic, regionalism, geopolitical position) rejects the very concept of a shared global culture and rejects the penetration of domestic markets by foreign goods and services. Differences among cultures produce differences in social expectations, politics, and ultimately legal rules. In certain countries, such as the United States, consumers expect domestic name-brand products to be built domestically and are disappointed to learn that much of what they thought of as domestically produced is in fact foreign made.

Different cultures produce different political regimes. Among the many different countries of the world are different laws governing the movement of information, information privacy of their citizens, origins of software and hardware in systems, and radio and satellite telecommunications. Even the hours of business and the terms of business trade vary greatly across political cultures. These different legal regimes complicate global business and must be considered when building global systems.

For instance, European countries have different laws concerning transborder data flow and privacy from those in the United States. **Transborder data flow** is defined as the movement of information across international boundaries in any form. In 1998, the European Union adopted a Data Protection Directive that broadened and standardized privacy protection in E.U. nations, and allowed for the transfer of personal data to systems located in the United States and other nations where these systems met European privacy standards. The General Data Protection Regulation (GDPR), which went into effect in May 2018, provides additional privacy protection for European citizens and applies to all data produced by EU citizens, whether or not the company collecting the data in question is located within the EU, as well as all people whose data is stored within the EU, whether or not they are actually EU citizens. (Review the discussion of GDPR in Chapter 4.)

Cultural and political differences profoundly affect organizations' business processes and applications of information technology. A host of specific barriers arise from the general cultural differences, everything from different reliability of phone networks to the shortage of skilled consultants.

National laws and traditions have created disparate accounting practices in various countries, which affects the ways profits and losses are analyzed. German companies generally do not recognize the profit from a venture until the project is completely finished and they have been paid. Conversely, British firms begin posting profits before a project is completed, when they are reasonably certain they will get the money.

These accounting practices are tightly intertwined with each country's legal system, business philosophy, and tax code. British, U.S., and Dutch firms share a predominantly Anglo-Saxon outlook that separates tax calculations from reports to shareholders to focus on showing shareholders how fast profits are growing. Continental European accounting practices are less oriented toward impressing investors, focusing rather on demonstrating compliance with strict rules and minimizing tax liabilities. These diverging accounting practices make it difficult for large international companies with units in different countries to evaluate their performance.

Language remains a significant barrier. Although English has become a kind of standard business language, this is truer at higher levels of companies and not throughout the middle and lower ranks. Software may have to be built with local language interfaces before a new information system can be successfully implemented.

Currency fluctuations can play havoc with planning models and projections. A product that appears profitable in Mexico or Japan may actually produce a loss because of changes in foreign exchange rates.

These inhibiting factors must be taken into account when you are designing and building international systems for your business. For example, companies trying to implement "lean production" systems spanning national boundaries typically underestimate the time, expense, and logistical difficulties of making goods and information flow freely across different countries.

State of the Art

One might think, given the opportunities for achieving competitive advantages as outlined previously and the interest in future applications, that most international companies have rationally developed marvelous international systems architectures. Nothing could be further from the truth. Most companies have inherited patchwork international systems from the distant past, often based on outdated concepts of information processing, with reporting from independent foreign divisions to corporate headquarters, manual entry of data from one legacy system to another, and little online control and communication. Corporations in this situation increasingly face powerful competitive challenges in the marketplace from firms that have rationally designed truly international systems. Still other companies have recently built technology platforms for international systems but have nowhere to go because they lack global strategy.

As it turns out, there are significant difficulties in building appropriate international architectures. The difficulties involve planning a system appropriate to the firm's global strategy, structuring the organization of systems and business units, solving implementation issues, and choosing the right technical platform. Let's examine these problems in greater detail.

15-2 What are the alternative strategies for developing global businesses?

Three organizational issues face corporations seeking a global position: choosing a strategy, organizing the business, and organizing the systems management area. The first two are closely connected, so we discuss them together.

TABLE 15.3 GLOBAL BUSINESS STRATEGY AND STRUCTURE

BUSINESS FUNCTION	DOMESTIC EXPORTER	MULTINATIONAL	FRANCHISER	TRANSNATIONAL
Production	Centralized	Dispersed	Coordinated	Coordinated
Finance/accounting	Centralized	Centralized	Centralized	Coordinated
Sales/marketing	Mixed	Dispersed	Coordinated	Coordinated
Human resources	Centralized	Centralized	Coordinated	Coordinated
Strategic management	Centralized	Centralized	Centralized	Coordinated

Global Strategies and Business Organization

Four main global strategies form the basis for global firms' organizational structure. These are domestic exporter, multinational, franchiser, and transnational. Each of these strategies is pursued with a specific business organizational structure (see Table 15.3). For simplicity's sake, we describe three kinds of organizational structure or governance: centralized (in the home country), decentralized (to local foreign units), and coordinated (all units participate as equals). Other types of governance patterns can be observed in specific companies (e.g., authoritarian dominance by one unit, a confederacy of equals, a federal structure balancing power among strategic units, and so forth).

The **domestic exporter** strategy is characterized by heavy centralization of corporate activities in the home country of origin. Nearly all international companies begin this way, and some move on to other forms. Production, finance/accounting, sales/marketing, human resources, and strategic management are set up to optimize resources in the home country. International sales are sometimes dispersed using agency agreements or subsidiaries, but even here, foreign marketing relies on the domestic home base for marketing themes and strategies. Caterpillar Corporation and other heavy capital-equipment manufacturers fall into this category of firm.

The **multinational** strategy concentrates financial management and control out of a central home base while decentralizing production, sales, and marketing operations to units in other countries. The products and services on sale in different countries are adapted to suit local market conditions. The organization becomes a far-flung confederation of production and marketing facilities in different countries. Many financial service firms, along with a host of manufacturers, such as General Motors and Intel, fit this pattern.

Franchisers are an interesting mix of old and new. On the one hand, the product is created, designed, financed, and initially produced in the home country but for product-specific reasons must rely heavily on foreign personnel for further production, marketing, and human resources. Food franchisers such as McDonald's and KFC fit this pattern. McDonald's created a new form of fast-food chain in the United States and continues to rely largely on the United States for inspiration of new products, strategic management, and financing. Nevertheless, because the product must be produced locally—it is perishable—extensive coordination and dispersal of production, local marketing, and local recruitment of personnel are required.

Generally, foreign franchisees are clones of the mother country units, but fully coordinated worldwide production that could optimize factors of production is not possible. For instance, potatoes and beef can generally not be bought where they are cheapest on world markets but must be produced reasonably close to the area of consumption.

Transnational firms are the stateless, truly globally managed firms that may represent a larger part of international business in the future. Transnational firms have no single national headquarters but instead have many regional headquarters and perhaps a world headquarters. In a **transnational** strategy, nearly all the value-adding activities are managed from a global perspective without reference to national borders, optimizing sources of supply and demand wherever they appear, and taking advantage of any local competitive advantages. Transnational firms take the globe, not the home country, as their management frame of reference. The governance of these firms has been likened to a federal structure in which there is a strong central management core of decision making but considerable dispersal of power and financial muscle throughout the global divisions. Few companies have actually attained transnational status.

Information technology and improvements in global telecommunications are giving international firms more flexibility to shape their global strategies. Protectionism and a need to serve local markets better encourage companies to disperse production facilities and at least become multinational. At the same time, the drive to achieve economies of scale and take advantage of short-term local advantage moves transnationals toward a global management perspective and a concentration of power and authority. Hence, there are forces of decentralization and dispersal as well as forces of centralization and global coordination.

Global Systems to Fit the Strategy

Information technology and improvements in global telecommunications are giving international firms more flexibility to shape their global strategies. The configuration, management, and development of systems tend to follow the global strategy chosen. Figure 15.3 depicts the typical arrangements. By *systems* we mean the full range of activities involved in building and operating information systems: conception and alignment with the strategic business plan, systems development, and ongoing operation and maintenance. For the sake of simplicity, we consider four types of systems configuration. *Centralized systems* are those in which systems development and operation occur totally at the domestic home base. *Duplicated systems* are those in which development occurs at the home base but operations are handed over to autonomous units in foreign locations. *Decentralized systems* are those in which each foreign unit designs its own unique solutions and systems. *Networked systems* are those in which systems development and operations occur in an integrated and coordinated fashion across all units.

FIGURE 15.3 **GLOBAL STRATEGY AND SYSTEMS CONFIGURATIONS**

The large X's show the dominant patterns, and the small x's show the emerging patterns. For instance, domestic exporters rely predominantly on centralized systems, but there is some development of decentralized systems in local marketing regions.

SYSTEM CONFIGURATION	Strategy			
	Domestic Exporter	Multinational	Franchiser	Transnational
Centralized	X			
Duplicated			X	
Decentralized	x	X	x	
Networked		x		X

As can be seen in Figure 15.3, domestic exporters tend to have highly centralized systems in which a single domestic systems development staff develops worldwide applications. Multinationals offer a direct and striking contrast: Here, foreign units devise their own systems solutions based on local needs with few if any applications in common with headquarters (the exceptions being financial reporting and some telecommunications applications). Franchisers have the simplest systems structure: Like the products they sell, franchisers develop a single system usually at the home base and then replicate it around the world. Each unit, no matter where it is located, has identical applications. Last, the most ambitious form of systems development is found in transnational firms: Networked systems are those in which there is a solid, singular global environment for developing and operating systems. This usually presupposes a powerful telecommunications backbone, a culture of shared applications development, and a shared management culture that crosses cultural barriers. The networked systems structure is the most visible in financial services where the homogeneity of the product—money and money instruments—seems to overcome cultural barriers.

Reorganizing the Business

How should a firm organize itself for doing business on an international scale? To develop a global company and information systems support structure, a firm needs to follow these principles:

1. Organize value-adding activities along lines of comparative advantage. For instance, marketing/sales functions should be located where they can best be performed for least cost and maximum impact; likewise with production, finance, human resources, and information systems.

2. Develop and operate systems units at each level of corporate activity—regional, national, and international. To serve local needs, there should be *host country systems units* of some magnitude. *Regional systems units* should handle telecommunications and systems development across national boundaries that take place within major geographic regions (European, Asian, American). *Transnational systems units* should be established to create the linkages across major regional areas and coordinate the development and operation of international telecommunications and systems development (Roche, 1992).

3. Establish at world headquarters a single office responsible for development of international systems—a global chief information officer (CIO) position.

Many successful companies have devised organizational systems structures along these principles. The success of these companies relies not only on the proper organization of activities but also on a key ingredient—a management team that can understand the risks and benefits of international systems and that can devise strategies for overcoming the risks. We turn to these management topics next.

15-3 What are the challenges posed by global information systems and management solutions for these challenges?

Table 15.4 lists the principal management problems posed by developing international systems. It is interesting to note that these problems are the chief difficulties managers experience in developing ordinary domestic systems as well. But these are enormously complicated in the international environment.

A Typical Scenario: Disorganization on a Global Scale

Let's look at a common scenario. A traditional multinational consumer-goods company based in the United States and operating in Europe would like to expand into Asian markets and knows that it must develop a transnational strategy and a supportive information systems structure. Like most multinationals, it has dispersed production and marketing to regional and national centers while maintaining a world headquarters and strategic management in the United States. Historically, it has allowed each of the subsidiary foreign divisions to develop its own systems. The only centrally coordinated system is financial controls and reporting. The central systems group in the United States focuses only on domestic functions and production.

The result is a hodgepodge of hardware, software, and telecommunications. The email systems between Europe and the United States are incompatible. Each production facility uses a different manufacturing resources planning system (or a different version of the same ERP system) and different marketing, sales, and human resource systems. Hardware and database platforms are wildly different. Communications between different sites are poor, given the high cost of European intercountry communications.

What do you recommend to the senior management leaders of this company, who now want to pursue a transnational strategy and develop an information systems architecture to support a highly coordinated global systems environment? Consider the problems you face by reexamining Table 15.4. The foreign divisions will resist efforts to agree on common user requirements; they have never thought about much other than their own units' needs. The systems groups in U.S. local sites, which have been enlarged recently and told to focus on local needs, will not easily accept guidance from anyone recommending a transnational strategy. It will be difficult to convince local managers anywhere in the world that they should change their business procedures to align with other units in the world, especially if this might interfere with their local performance. After all, local managers are rewarded in this company for meeting local objectives of their division or plant. Finally, it will be difficult to coordinate development of projects around the world in the absence of a powerful telecommunications network and, therefore, difficult to encourage local users to take on ownership in the systems developed.

Global Systems Strategy

Figure 15.4 lays out the main dimensions of a solution. First, consider that not all systems should be coordinated on a transnational basis; only some core systems are truly worth sharing from a cost and feasibility point of view. **Core systems** support functions that are absolutely critical to the organization. Other systems should be partially coordinated because they share key

TABLE 15.4 **MANAGEMENT CHALLENGES IN DEVELOPING GLOBAL SYSTEMS**

Agreeing on common user requirements
Introducing changes in business processes
Coordinating applications development
Coordinating software releases
Encouraging local users to support global systems

| FIGURE 15.4 LOCAL, REGIONAL, AND GLOBAL SYSTEMS

Agency and other coordination costs increase as the firm moves from local option systems toward regional and global systems. However, transaction costs of participating in global markets probably decrease as firms develop global systems. A sensible strategy is to reduce agency costs by developing only a few core global systems that are vital for global operations, leaving other systems in the hands of regional and local units.

Source: From *Managing Information Technology in Multinational Corporations* by Edward M. Roche, © 1992. Adapted by permission of Prentice Hall, Inc., Upper Saddle River, NJ.

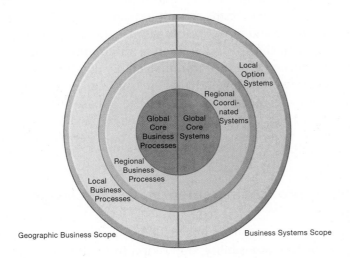

elements, but they do not have to be totally common across national boundaries. For such systems, a good deal of local variation is possible and desirable. A final group of systems is peripheral, truly provincial, and needed to suit local requirements only.

Define the Core Business Processes

How do you identify core systems? The first step is to define a short list of critical core business processes. Business processes are defined and described in Chapter 2, which you should review. Briefly, business processes are sets of logically related tasks to produce specific business results, such as shipping out correct orders to customers or delivering innovative products to the market. Each business process typically involves many functional areas, communicating and coordinating work, information, and knowledge.

The way to identify these core business processes is to conduct a business process analysis. How are customer orders taken, what happens to them once they are taken, who fills the orders, and how are they shipped to the customers? What about suppliers? Do they have access to manufacturing resource planning systems so that supply is automatic? You should be able to identify and set priorities in a short list of 10 business processes that are absolutely critical for the firm.

Next, can you identify centers of excellence for these processes? Is the customer order fulfillment superior in the United States, manufacturing process control superior in Germany, and human resources superior in Asia? You should be able to identify some areas of the company, for some lines of business, where a division or unit stands out in the performance of one or several business functions.

When you understand the business processes of a firm, you can rank-order them. You then can decide which processes should be core applications, centrally coordinated, designed, and implemented around the globe and which should be regional and local. At the same time, by identifying the critical business processes, the really important ones, you have gone a long way to defining a vision of the future that you should be working toward.

Identify the Core Systems to Coordinate Centrally

By identifying the critical core business processes, you begin to see opportunities for transnational systems. The second strategic step is to conquer the core systems and define these systems as truly transnational. The financial and political costs of defining and implementing transnational systems are extremely high. Therefore, keep the list to an absolute minimum, letting experience be the guide and erring on the side of minimalism. By dividing off a small group of systems as absolutely critical, you divide opposition to a transnational strategy. At the same time, you can appease those who oppose the central worldwide coordination implied by transnational systems by permitting peripheral systems development to progress unabated with the exception of some technical platform requirements.

Choose an Approach: Incremental, Grand Design, Evolutionary

A third step is to choose an approach. Avoid piecemeal approaches. These surely will fail for lack of visibility, opposition from all who stand to lose from transnational development, and lack of power to convince senior management that the transnational systems are worth it. Likewise, avoid grand design approaches that try to do everything at once. These also tend to fail because of an inability to focus resources. Nothing gets done properly, and opposition to organizational change is needlessly strengthened because the effort requires extraordinary resources. An alternative approach is to evolve transnational applications incrementally from existing applications with a precise and clear vision of the transnational capabilities the organization should have in five years. This is sometimes referred to as the "salami strategy," or one slice at a time.

Make the Benefits Clear

What is in it for the company? One of the worst situations to avoid is to build global systems for the sake of building global systems. From the beginning, it is crucial that senior management at headquarters and foreign division managers clearly understand the benefits that will come to the company as well as to individual units. Although each system offers unique benefits to a particular budget, the overall contribution of global systems lies in four areas.

Global systems—truly integrated, distributed, and transnational systems—contribute to superior management and coordination. A simple price tag cannot be put on the value of this contribution, and the benefit will not show up in any capital budgeting model. It is the ability to switch suppliers on a moment's notice from one region to another in a crisis, the ability to move production in response to natural disasters, and the ability to use excess capacity in one region to meet raging demand in another.

A second major contribution is vast improvement in production, operation, and supply and distribution. Imagine a global value chain with global suppliers and a global distribution network. For the first time, senior managers can locate value-adding activities in regions where they are most economically performed.

Third, global systems mean global customers and global marketing. Fixed costs around the world can be amortized over a much larger customer base. This will unleash new economies of scale at production facilities.

Last, global systems mean the ability to optimize the use of corporate funds over a much larger capital base. This means, for instance, that capital in a surplus region can be moved efficiently to expand production of capital-starved regions; that cash can be managed more effectively within the company and put to use more effectively.

These strategies will not by themselves create global systems. You will have to implement what you strategize.

The Management Solution: Implementation

We now can reconsider how to handle the most vexing problems facing managers developing the global information systems architectures that were described in Table 15.4.

Agreeing on Common User Requirements

Establishing a short list of the core business processes and core support systems will begin a process of rational comparison across the many divisions of the company, develop a common language for discussing the business, and naturally lead to an understanding of common elements (as well as the unique qualities that must remain local).

Introducing Changes in Business Processes

Your success as a change agent will depend on your legitimacy, your authority, and your ability to involve users in the change design process. **Legitimacy** is defined as the extent to which your authority is accepted on grounds of competence, vision, or other qualities. The selection of a viable change strategy, which we have defined as evolutionary but with a vision, should assist you in convincing others that change is feasible and desirable. Involving people in change, assuring them that change is in the best interests of the company and their local units, is a key tactic.

Coordinating Applications Development

Choice of change strategy is critical for this problem. At the global level there is far too much complexity to attempt a grand design strategy of change. It is far easier to coordinate change by making small incremental steps toward a larger vision. Imagine a five-year plan of action rather than a two-year plan of action, and reduce the set of transnational systems to a bare minimum to reduce coordination costs.

Coordinating Software Releases

Firms can institute procedures to ensure that all operating units convert to new software updates at the same time so that everyone's software is compatible.

Encouraging Local Users to Support Global Systems

The key to this problem is to involve users in the creation of the design without giving up control over the development of the project to parochial interests. The overall tactic for dealing with resistant local units in a transnational company is cooptation. **Cooptation** is defined as bringing the opposition into the process of designing and implementing the solution without giving up control over the direction and nature of the change. As much as possible, raw power should be avoided. Minimally, however, local units must agree on a short list of transnational systems, and raw power may be required to solidify the idea that transnational systems of some sort are truly required.

How should cooptation proceed? Several alternatives are possible. One alternative is to permit each country unit the opportunity to develop one transnational application first in its home territory and then throughout the world. In this manner, each major country systems group is given a piece of the action in developing a transnational system, and local units feel a sense of ownership in the transnational effort. On the downside, this assumes the ability to develop high-quality systems is widely distributed and that a German team, for example, can successfully implement systems in France and Italy. This will not always be the case.

A second tactic is to develop new transnational centers of excellence, or a single center of excellence. There may be several centers around the globe that focus on specific business processes. These centers draw heavily from local national units, are based on multinational teams, and must report to worldwide management. Centers of excellence perform the initial identification and specification of business processes, define the information requirements, perform the business and systems analysis, and accomplish all design and testing. Implementation, however, and pilot testing are rolled out to other parts of the globe. Recruiting a wide range of local groups to transnational centers of excellence helps send the message that all significant groups are involved in the design and will have an influence.

Even with the proper organizational structure and appropriate management choices, it is still possible to stumble over technology issues. Choices of technology platforms, networks, hardware, and software are the final element in building transnational information systems architectures.

15-4 What are the issues and technical alternatives to be considered when developing international information systems?

Once firms have defined a global business model and systems strategy, they must select hardware, software, and networking standards along with key system applications to support global business processes. Hardware, software, and networking pose special technical challenges in an international setting.

One major challenge is finding some way to standardize a global computing platform when there is so much variation from operating unit to operating unit and from country to country. Another major challenge is finding specific software applications that are user-friendly and that truly enhance the productivity of international work teams. The universal acceptance of the Internet around the globe has greatly reduced networking problems. But the mere presence of the Internet does not guarantee that information will flow seamlessly throughout the global organization because not all business units use the same applications, and the quality of Internet service can be highly variable (just as with the telephone service). For instance, German business units may use an open source collaboration tool to share documents and communicate, which is incompatible with American headquarters teams, which use Microsoft solutions.

Overcoming these challenges requires systems integration and connectivity on a global basis.

Computing Platforms and Systems Integration

The development of a transnational information systems architecture based on the concept of core systems raises questions about how the new core systems will fit in with the existing suite of applications developed around the globe by different divisions and different people and for different kinds of computing hardware. The goal is to develop global, distributed, and integrated systems to support digital business processes spanning national boundaries. Briefly, these are the same problems faced by any large domestic systems development effort. However, the problems are magnified in an international environment. Just imagine the challenge of integrating systems based on the Windows, Linux, Unix, or proprietary operating systems running on IBM, Oracle, HP, and other hardware in many different operating units in many different countries!

Moreover, having all sites use the same hardware and operating system does not guarantee integration. Some central authority in the firm must establish data standards as well as other technical standards with which sites are to comply. For instance, technical accounting terms such as the beginning and end of the fiscal year must be standardized (review the earlier discussion of the cultural challenges to building global businesses) as well as the acceptable interfaces between systems, communication speeds and architectures, and network software.

Connectivity

Truly integrated global systems must have connectivity—the ability to link together the systems and people of a global firm into a single integrated network just like the phone system but capable of voice, data, and image transmissions. The Internet has provided an enormously powerful foundation for providing connectivity among the dispersed units of global firms. However, many issues remain. The public Internet does not guarantee any level of service (even in the United States). Few global corporations trust the security of the public Internet and generally use private networks to communicate sensitive data and Internet virtual private networks (VPNs) for communications that require less security. Not all countries support even basic Internet service that requires obtaining reliable circuits, coordinating among different carriers and the regional telecommunications authority, and obtaining standard agreements for the level of telecommunications service provided. Table 15.5 lists the major challenges posed by international networks.

TABLE 15.5   **CHALLENGES OF INTERNATIONAL NETWORKS**
Quality of service
Security
Costs and tariffs
Network management
Installation delays
Poor quality of international service
Regulatory constraints
Network capacity

FIGURE 15.5 INTERNET POPULATION IN SELECTED COUNTRIES

The percentage of the total population using the Internet in developing countries is much smaller than in the United States and Europe, but it is growing rapidly.

Source: Based on data from Internetworldstats.com, 2017 and authors.

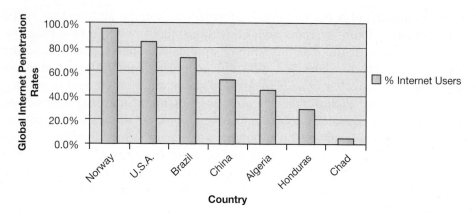

While private networks have guaranteed service levels and better security than the Internet, the Internet is the primary foundation for global corporate networks when lower security and service levels are acceptable. Companies can create global intranets for internal communication or extranets to exchange information more rapidly with business partners in their supply chains. They can use the public Internet to create global networks using VPNs from Internet service providers, which provide many features of a private network using the public Internet (see Chapter 7). However, VPNs may not provide the same level of quick and predictable response as private networks, especially during times of the day when Internet traffic is very congested, and they may not be able to support large numbers of remote users.

Access to Internet service is limited in many developing countries (see Figure 15.5). Where an Internet infrastructure exists in less-developed countries, it often lacks bandwidth capacity and is unreliable in part due to power grid issues. The purchasing power of most people in developing countries makes access to Internet services very expensive in local currencies, although inexpensive mobile devices and low-cost data plans are becoming more widely available.

In addition, many countries monitor transmissions. Governments in China, Iran, and Saudi Arabia monitor Internet traffic and block access to websites considered morally or politically offensive. On the other hand, the rate of growth in the Internet population has been faster in Asia, Africa, and the Middle East than in North America and Europe. Therefore, in the future, Internet connectivity will be much more widely available and reliable in less-developed regions of the world, and it will play a significant role in integrating these economies with the world economy.

Software Localization

The development of core systems poses unique challenges for application software: How will the old systems interface with the new? Entirely new interfaces must be built and tested if old systems are kept in local areas (which is common). These interfaces can be costly and messy to build. If new software must be created, another challenge is to build software that can be realistically used by multiple business units from different countries given that business units are accustomed to their unique business processes and definitions of data.

Aside from integrating the new with the old systems, there are problems of human interface design and functionality of systems. For instance, to be truly useful for enhancing productivity of a global workforce, software interfaces must be easily understood and mastered quickly. When international systems involve knowledge workers only, English may be the assumed international standard. But as international systems penetrate deeper into management and clerical groups, a common language may not be assumed and human interfaces must be built to accommodate different languages and even conventions. The entire process of converting software to operate in a second language is called **software localization**.

Most of the world's population accesses the Internet using a mobile device, so apps must be built for mobile platforms, tiny screens, and low bandwidth. Since many mobile Internet users cannot read or write, special interfaces using video and audio need to be built to serve this group. The Interactive Session on Technology addresses this issue.

What are the most important software applications? Many international systems focus on basic transaction and management reporting systems. Increasingly, firms are turning to supply chain management and enterprise resource planning systems to standardize their business processes on a global basis and to create coordinated global supply chains and workforces (see the Interactive Session on Management). However, these cross-functional systems are not always compatible with differences in languages, cultural heritages, and business processes in other countries. Company units in countries that are not technically sophisticated may also encounter problems trying to manage the technical complexities of enterprise applications.

Electronic Data Interchange (EDI) systems and supply chain management systems are widely used by manufacturing and distribution firms to connect to suppliers on a global basis. Collaboration and enterprise social networking systems, email, and videoconferencing are especially important worldwide tools for knowledge- and data-based firms, such as advertising firms, research-based firms in medicine and engineering, and graphics and publishing firms.

15-5 How will MIS help my career?

Here is how Chapter 15 and this book can help you find a job as an entry-level sales and marketing trainee for a global data services company.

The Company

Global Online Stats, a leading global provider of quantitative data, statistics, and market research products, has an open position for an entry-level sales and marketing trainee. The company has more than 500 employees and offices in Boston, London, and Paris. The company provides tools and services for accessing an online quantitative database aimed at business firms of all sizes, including consulting firms, media agencies, and marketing departments in large corporations from a variety of industries and countries.

INTERACTIVE SESSION   TECHNOLOGY

The Global Internet Goes Multimedia

Megh Singh is a porter in India's New Delhi railroad station, earning less than $8 per day. From time to time throughout the day he can be found under the station stairwell whispering into his smartphone. Singh is using speech recognition software to access the Internet using the station's free Wi-Fi system. His smartphone is a no-frills Sony Corp. model with pared-down storage (4 gigabytes, compared to 32 gigabytes, which is prevalent in developed countries). Singh's smartphone has Google search Facebook's What's App but Singh also uses apps, such as JC Browser, MX Player, and SHAREit, that have been explicitly designed for slow connections and minimal data storage.

Most Indian porters still believe smartphones are only for the rich and literate, but a growing minority have been using cheap smartphones to go online since the railroad station started providing free Wi-Fi service in 2015. Singh likes to use his smartphone to check train schedules, message his family, and download movies. He arrives at the station early each morning to send his family and friends recorded messages via WhatsApp. He receives recorded replies from them throughout the day. Singh also uses YouTube, Google, and MX Player to search the Internet for shows and clips. He uses voice search on YouTube, downloading 20 clips per day to watch at night when he returns to the room he shares with five other porters.

Singh is not comfortable reading or using a keyboard. He doesn't know anything about email or how to send it. However, he claims he can enjoy the Internet to its fullest by relying on video and voice. Singh represents the new wave of new Internet users around the world. Instead of typing searches and emails, the "next billion" Internet newcomers will be primarily using voice activation and communicating with images.

Text is not disappearing entirely from the Internet, and it still has its uses. But instead of typing searches and reading text-based web pages, Internet users will be increasingly using audio and video. Influential communicators will rely more and more on podcasts, Instagram, YouTube videos, and apps such as HHQ Trivia. This is true in wealthy advanced countries such as the United States and Germany as well as in poorer countries with low per capita income and Internet penetration.

During the early years of the Internet, text used to be the only format with which computers could easily work. Today, with more powerful and sophisticated hardware and software, computers can decipher and manipulate multimedia. For many people, including those who cannot read and write, it has become much easier to communicate through images and sounds than through text.

Only 400 million of India's 1.3 billion people are online, and the vast majority access the Internet via a mobile device. Thanks to a price war and vendors' efforts to court low-income users, these numbers are rising. Vodafone India, a subsidiary of Vodafone PLC, found that new users didn't understand data limits. It decided to offer a new option to buy as much data as they wanted at a cost of less than 25 cents per hour. Facebook has sponsored free Wi-Fi hotspots across India, where it has 200 million active users. Developers at the company's Menlo Park, California headquarters stage "2G Tuesdays" when they can experience how Facebook works on slow Internet connections. Facebook has built a lighter, less data-consuming version for emerging markets as has LinkedIn. LinkedIn Lite is a less data-heavy app that works on 2G phones and will help blue-collar workers find jobs.

New companies are springing up to provide apps and services tailored to less-affluent, less-educated Internet users. The apps on Mr. Singh's phone are a good example. UC Browser from Alibaba Holding Group's UCWeb is optimized to use less data for low-speed connections. UC Browser accounts for over 40 percent of India's mobile browser market. Lenovo Group's SHAREit enables users to send files, photos, videos, and apps from one device to another using direct Wi-Fi connections. YouTube apps created for India make it easier to work with slow Internet speeds, save videos to watch offline, and monitor their data use.

Google changed the way certain searches from India appear on the Internet. For example, if a user is searching for a local cricket star, the top of the search will display videos and photos instead of long text lists of links.

In 2016 Indian banks launched a mobile payment system to help people who were not very tech-literate use their phones to make payments and transfer money. The sign-up process was simplified. Paytm is the largest mobile money app in India, with over 200 million users, far more than the number of Indians owning credit cards.

Sources: Farhad Manjoo, "Welcome to the Post-Text Future," *New York Times*, February 14, 2018; www.shareit.com, accessed February 16, 2018; Eric Ballman, "The End of Typing: The Next Billion Mobile Users Will Rely on Voice and Video," *Wall Street Journal*, August 7, 2017; and Julia Love, "YouTube Unveils India Mobile App for Spotty Internet Signals," Reuters, April 4, 2017.

CASE STUDY QUESTIONS

1. Why are voice and video becoming the primary means of communication over the Internet?

2. How will this trend impact companies trying to do business worldwide? How will it affect the way they run their businesses and interact with customers?

3. What kinds of companies are likely to benefit from a more multimedia Internet? Explain.

Position Description

This position works closely with the Managing Director and Head of Global Sales to develop and maintain sales leads and new accounts. Job responsibilities include:

- Developing new accounts with leads generated by existing customers and relationships with media and industry associations as well as through cold calling, emailing, and online prospecting.
- Developing account relationships to turn sporadic customers into long-term business accounts.
- Developing sales opportunities for various categories of products and lines of business.
- Finding and scheduling appointments with new prospective clients.
- Updating customer and client profiles.

Job Requirements

- Four-year college degree
- Very strong verbal and written communication skills
- Microsoft Office skills
- Experience at a sales or marketing internship or in cold calling desirable
- Outgoing, competitive, proactive sales personality

Interview Questions

1. Did you work with quantitative data in your college courses or at a prior job? What did you do with the data?
2. Have you ever worked with online databases or database software? Exactly what did you do with these databases? Did you ever take a database course?

INTERACTIVE SESSION   MANAGEMENT

AbbVie Builds a Global Systems Infrastructure

AbbVie, headquartered in Chicago, Illinois, is a global research-based biopharmaceutical company that was spun off from Abbott Laboratories in January 2013. As a separate entity, AbbVie is still a very large company, with more than 29,000 employees in over 70 countries and 19 research and manufacturing sites across the globe. In 2017, AbbVie produced $28.2 billion in revenue. Humira for treating rheumatoid arthritis and Crohn's disease is among its top-selling global products.

When AbbVie separated from Abbott Laboratories, the company had inherited 50 or 60 disparate legacy systems that were supporting mission-critical processes in over 100 worldwide locations. The legacy systems were supported by Abbott under a transitional services agreement (TSA) and were due to be terminated at the end of 2015. AbbVie's management had to make a choice: Should the company continue to run these legacy systems on its own or should it invest in a more up-to-date platform for supporting business processes across all of its global affiliates and manufacturing locations?

Complicating the decision were time pressures: AbbVie had only until the end of 2015 (three years) to implement a solution and slightly over two years to establish an infrastructure stipulated by the TSA. AbbVie decided to create standard business processes for all its affiliates and manufacturing facilities and to support these processes with a single instance of SAP ERP across the globe. The project was very ambitious: The new system had to be globally operational in more than 150 countries within 3 years. AbbVie designed a new operating model that included many organizational changes, including business process outsourcing, centers of excellence, and regional shared services.

AbbVie didn't waste any time. It selected IBM Global Business Services consultants to guide the global SAP deployment. Starting in August 2013, AbbVie rolled out SAP ERP to 110 affiliates and manufacturing sites within 18 months. The company standardized end-to-end processes using a global SAP template, and allowed the software to be customized only for country-specific requirements. These requirements were identified in advance by teams creating local implementation guides.

AbbVie business process teams hammered out standard definitions for end-to-end processes such as procure-to-pay, order-to-cash, record-to-report, and warehouse management. AbbVie made the template usable globally by extending the functionality for multiple currencies and languages and updating it on a country-by-country basis depending on local regulations or legal requirements.

Each time an affiliate requested a customization, the AbbVie project team reviewed it against the list of local legal requirements it had collected. AbbVie then determined if the customization was required by other countries or was for only one, and it pushed back on one-of-a-kind requests. Testing and confirming with several affiliates helped ensure that the template met the requirements of most countries, so the need for future customization was minimal.

AbbVie tested the effectiveness of its global template during development, capturing metrics around adoption—number of adoptions, adaptations, additions, and abstentions. The project team compared the percentages of those metrics from country to country and reported the results to AbbVie's business unit leaders. If, for instance, the metrics showed that Germany had adopted 82 percent of the template and France 70 percent, business support could investigate to see if there was a process that needed to be changed in France. This was key to deploying the entire global instance of SAP ERP in 18 months.

The project team was also tasked with migrating data from different legacy applications to the data structure for the global SAP ERP system. For each stand-alone legacy system, the team extracted raw data, stored them in a secure data warehouse, and then identified any missing or inaccurate fields and other data cleansing requirements. While the team was consolidating and cleansing the data, it taught business users about SAP-specific data fields, how the fields were used, and how they changed previous business processes. The team would obtain data from the business, put it in a data mapping template, and load the data in various test environments. Once business users verified the accuracy of data, it would be ready to go live in production.

These activities facilitated change management by placing a high value on both system transparency and training. About six months before rolling out a new location, country-specific transition leaders would train users on the template and familiarize them with any process changes. The transition leaders were liaisons between AbbVie's technology team and its business process team, helping the company to quickly address change management issues as they arose.

AbbVie also took the time during implementation to verify it was in compliance with all local data privacy regulations. In May 2015, the company completed the global rollout of SAP ERP. The company was thus able to successfully standardize global processes and meet the TSA. Other major benefits of the new global system were unprecedented levels of agility and transparency.

AbbVie now has a set of key metrics that are measured at the end of every month, such as the length of time to create new customers, vendor payments, payment terms, or order fulfillments. The global system features dashboards for managers to look at every country, measure results, find the root cause of problems, and take corrective action more easily. Reporting from the system is more accurate.

AbbVie was able to pull off a major global system implementation because it was far-sighted and well organized and did the difficult work of streamlining processes on a global scale at the project outset. The global SAP project team questioned existing processes and found it could streamline many of them, making the enterprise much more agile. AbbVie's business efficiency also improved because corrective actions often led to additional process improvements. By looking at the metrics, the project team can suggest measures to improve a process to get more out of the company's investment. AbbVie can now operate as a single business across countries.

Sources: "AbbVie Builds a Global Pharmaceuticals Company on New Foundations with SAP and IBM," https://www-01.ibm.com, accessed January 6, 2018; Ken Murphy, "Biopharmaceutical Startup AbbVie Receives Healthy Long-Term Prognosis," *SAP Insider Profiles*, September 19, 2017; and www.abbvie.com, accessed January 6, 2018.

CASE STUDY QUESTIONS

1. What management problems typical of global systems was AbbVie experiencing? What management, organization, and technology factors were responsible for those problems?

2. What elements of the global systems strategy described in this chapter did AbbVie pursue?

3. How did AbbVie's new SAP ERP system support its global business strategy?

4. How did AbbVie's new system improve operations and management decision making?

3. What is your level of expertise with Microsoft Office tools—Word, Excel, PowerPoint, Access?

4. What sales experience have you had?

5. Do you have any foreign language proficiency?

6. What challenges would you anticipate in trying to sell our products and services to non-U.S. organizations?

Author Tips

1. Review Sections 15-1, 15-3, and 15-4 of this chapter, Chapter 6 on data management, and the Chapter 12 discussion of business intelligence and analytics.

2. Use the web to research the company, its products, services, and customers, and the way it operates. Think about what the company needs to do to expand sales globally.

3. Ask exactly how you would be using Microsoft Office tools in your job.

4. Ask about how much training you would receive in how to use the company's data products.

REVIEW SUMMARY

15-1 What major factors are driving the internationalization of business?

The growth of inexpensive international communication and transportation has created a world culture with stable expectations or norms. Political stability and a growing global knowledge base that is widely shared also contribute to the world culture. These general factors create the conditions for global markets, global production, coordination, distribution, and global economies of scale.

15-2 What are the alternative strategies for developing global businesses?

There are four basic international strategies: domestic exporter, multinational, franchiser, and transnational. In a transnational strategy, all factors of production are coordinated on a global scale. However, the choice of strategy is a function of the type of business and product.

There is a connection between firm strategy and information systems design. Transnational firms must develop networked system configurations and permit considerable decentralization of development and operations. Franchisers almost always duplicate systems across many countries and use centralized financial controls. Multinationals typically rely on decentralized independence among foreign units with some movement toward development of networks. Domestic exporters typically are centralized in domestic headquarters with some decentralized operations permitted.

15-3 What are the challenges posed by global information systems and management solutions for these challenges?

Global information systems pose challenges because cultural, political, and language diversity magnifies differences in organizational culture and business processes and encourages proliferation of disparate local information systems that are difficult to integrate. Typically, international systems have evolved without a conscious plan. The remedy is to define a small subset of core business processes and focus on building systems to support these processes. Tactically, managers will have to co-opt widely dispersed foreign units to participate in the development and operation of these systems, being careful to maintain overall control.

15-4 What are the issues and technical alternatives to be considered when developing international information systems?

Implementing a global system requires an implementation strategy that considers both business design and technology platforms. The main hardware and telecommunications issues are systems integration and connectivity. The choices for integration are to go either with a proprietary architecture or with open systems technology. Global networks are extremely difficult to build and operate. Firms can build their own global networks or they can create global networks based on the Internet (intranets or virtual private networks). The main software issues concern building interfaces to existing systems and selecting applications that can work with multiple cultural, language, and organizational frameworks.

Key Terms

Business driver, 568
Cooptation, 579
Core systems, 576
Domestic exporter, 573
Franchisers, 573
Global culture, 569
International information systems architecture, 567

Legitimacy, 579
Multinational, 573
Particularism, 571
Software localization, 583
Transborder data flow, 571
Transnational, 574

MyLab MIS

To complete the problems with MyLab MIS, go to EOC Discussion Questions in MyLab MIS.

Review Questions

15-1 What major factors are driving the internationalization of business?

- List and describe the five major dimensions for developing an international information systems architecture.
- Describe the five general cultural factors leading toward growth in global business and the four specific business factors. Describe the interconnection among these factors.
- List and describe the major challenges to the development of global systems.
- Explain why some firms have not planned for the development of international systems.

15-2 What are the alternative strategies for developing global businesses?

- Describe the four main strategies for global business and organizational structure.
- Describe the four different system configurations that can be used to support different global strategies.

15-3 What are the challenges posed by global information systems and management solutions for these challenges?

- List and describe the major management issues in developing international systems.
- Identify and describe three principles to follow when organizing the firm for global business.
- Identify and describe three steps of a management strategy for developing and implementing global systems.
- Define cooptation and explain how it can be used in building global systems.

15-4 What are the issues and technical alternatives to be considered when developing international information systems?

- Describe the main technical issues facing global systems.
- Identify some technologies that will help firms develop global systems.

Discussion Questions

15-5 If you were a manager in a company that
MyLab MIS operates in many countries, what criteria would you use to determine whether an application should be developed as a global application or as a local application?

15-6 Describe ways the Internet can be used in
MyLab MIS international information systems.

Hands-On MIS Projects

The projects in this section give you hands-on experience conducting international market research, analyzing international systems issues for an expanding business, and building a job posting database and web page for an international company. Visit MyLab MIS to access this chapter's Hands-on MIS Projects.

Management Decision Problems

15-7 United Parcel Service (UPS) has been expanding its package delivery and logistics services in China, serving both multinational companies and local businesses. UPS drivers in China need to use UPS systems and tools such as its handheld Delivery Information Acquisition Device for capturing package delivery data. UPS wants to make its WorldShip and other shipping-management services accessible to Chinese and multinational customers via the web. What are some of the international systems issues UPS must consider in order to operate successfully in China?

15-8 Your company manufactures and sells tennis racquets and would like to start selling outside the United States. You are in charge of developing a global web strategy, and the first countries you are thinking of targeting are Brazil, China, Germany, Italy, and Japan. Using the statistics in the *CIA World Factbook* and other online sources, which of these countries would you target first? What criteria did you use? What other considerations should you address in your web strategy? What features would you put on your website to attract buyers from the countries you target?

Achieving Operational Excellence: Building a Job Database and Web Page for an International Consulting Firm

Software skills: Database and web page design
Business skills: Human resources internal job postings

15-9 Companies with many overseas locations need a way to inform employees about available job openings in these locations. In this project you'll use database software to design a database for posting internal job openings and a web page for displaying this information.

KTP Consulting operates in various locations around the world. KTP specializes in designing, developing, and implementing enterprise systems for medium- to large-size companies. KTP offers its employees opportunities to travel, live, and work in various locations throughout the United States, Europe, and Asia. The firm's human resources department has a simple database that enables its staff to track job vacancies. When an employee is interested in relocating, she or he contacts the human resources department for a list of KTP job vacancies. KTP also posts its employment opportunities on the company website.

What type of data should be included in the KTP job vacancies database? What information should not be included in this database? Based on your answers to these questions, build a job vacancies database for KTP. Populate the database with at least 20 records. You should also build a simple web page that incorporates job vacancy data from your newly created database. Submit a copy of the KTP database and web page to your professor.

Improving Decision Making: Conducting International Marketing and Pricing Research

Software skills: Internet-based software
Business skills: International pricing and marketing

15-10 In this project you'll use the web to research overseas distributors and customs regulations and use Internet-based software to calculate prices in foreign currencies.

You are in charge of marketing for a U.S. manufacturer of furniture that has decided to enter the international market. You want to test the market by contacting a European office furniture retailer to offer it a specific desk that you have to sell at about $165. Using the web, locate the information needed to locate and contact this firm and to find out how many euros you would get for the chair in the current market. In addition, consider using a universal currency converter website, which determines the value of one currency expressed in other currencies. Obtain both the information needed to contact the firm and the price of your chair in its local currency. Then locate and obtain customs and legal restrictions on the products you will export from the United States and import into the country of the retailer you have selected. Finally, locate a company that will represent you as a customs agent and gather information on shipping costs.

Collaboration and Teamwork Project

Identifying Technologies for Global Business Strategies

15-11 With a group of students, identify an area of information technology and explore how this technology might be useful for supporting global business strategies. For instance, you might choose email, smartphones, virtual private networks, enterprise systems, collaboration software, or the web. It will be necessary to identify a business scenario to discuss the technology. You might choose an automobile parts franchise or a clothing franchise, such as Express, as example businesses. Which applications would you make global, which core business processes would you choose, and how would the technology be helpful? If possible, use Google Docs and Google Drive or Google Sites to brainstorm, organize, and develop a presentation of your findings for the class.

E-Commerce in China: Opportunities and Obstacles

CASE STUDY

What's the world's largest and fastest-growing e-commerce market? It's China, with over 800 million Internet users, and accounting for over 50 percent of global retail e-commerce sales (projected to be nearly 60% by 2021). China's mobile payment market is a whopping 11 times the size of the U.S. market. The volume of online sales in China now exceeds that in the United States. E-commerce is predicted to account for 40.8 percent of all retail sales in China by 2021.

Chinese e-commerce is very mobile: By the end of 2018, more than 75 percent of ecommerce sales in China—over $1 trillion worth—were transacted via a mobile device. M-commerce accounted for 81.6 percent of Chinese e-commerce sales in 2017. Payment for both online and in-store sales via mobile phone services such as WeChat is sweeping the country. According to iResearch Consulting Group, a Chinese firm, mobile payments in China totaled $9 trillion in 2016, compared to $112 billion in mobile payments that same year in the United States. China has also become the world's largest mobile-payment market.

Tencent's WeChat, with over 900 million active users, is the dominant mobile platform in China. Retailers and brands have found that capturing the consumer's attention typically requires operating within the WeChat environment on the WeChat platform, as opposed to building a direct-to-consumer mobile app. Retailers such as Estee Lauder, Coach, and Gap run their loyalty programs within the WeChat app, and conduct customer relationship management (CRM) on the WeChat platform itself. Max Factor built a new social CRM system on the WeChat platform. It created a detailed customer database with 36 categories of tags using online and offline data. Max Factor built now use real-time data to send personalized messages based on different stages of the customer life cycle via the WeChat platform.

Credit cards never became widely used in China. Until recently, discretionary spending was not really possible for many Chinese, and there has been a long-standing cultural aversion to debt. On top of that, the government made it difficult for companies such as Visa Inc. and Mastercard Inc. to set up shop.

E-commerce has given China's digital consumers access to products from overseas, and a notable share of consumers appears to be taking advantage. Cross-border shoppers appear to prefer items that are either too expensive or too scarce domestically.

The most popular categories of goods Chinese purchased online include apparel, food and beverages, household products, consumer electronics, appliances, and personal care products. Food, luxury, and sports and wellness products are key categories for future growth. Chinese online shoppers tend to be young, urban, and highly educated. They are much more consumption-oriented than older generations, which were shaped as savers by different political and economic circumstances. Younger shoppers are more willing to spend.

Social media is an important channel for initiating online purchases. About 45 percent of Chinese consumers use social media to discover new products, 54 percent to review and comment on products, and 25 percent to purchase directly through a social channel. Retailers and brands need to build and participate in social communities and engage with customers on social platforms.

To some extent, e-commerce is replacing shopping in physical marketplaces in China, and will comprise 42 percent of growth in private consumption by 2020, according to Boston Consulting and AliResearch. For this reason, superstores such as Walmart and Carrefour have shut down a number of stores.

It sounds like there are opportunities galore for global companies that want to sell into the Chinese e-commerce market. Not so easy. China may be the world's largest and fastest-growing e-commerce market, but it is also one of the most difficult for foreign firms to penetrate. E-commerce in China is crowded and hyper-competitive, and the country is not entirely open for online business.

First, there's what's called the Great Firewall of China—a combination of legislation and technologies to regulate the Internet domestically in China. China blocks access to select foreign websites (such as Google, Snapchat, Facebook, Twitter, and the New York Times) and can slow down cross-border Internet traffic. China limits access to foreign information sources, blocks foreign Internet tools such as Google search and mobile apps), and requires foreign companies to adapt to domestic regulations. A new cybersecurity law that went into effect in June 2017 requires security checks on foreign companies and forces firms to store key data in China. For example, Apple works with a local Chinese company to store Chinese data from its iCloud service at a data center in southwest China.

The Great Firewall has also impacted China's internal Internet economy by nurturing domestic companies and reducing the appeal of products from foreign Internet companies. The Great Firewall fosters trade protectionism that has allowed China to grow its own Internet giants: Tencent, Alibaba, and Baidu. Tencent is one of the world's largest Internet and technology companies, as well as its largest and most valuable gaming and social media company. It also owns the majority of China's music services. Alibaba Group Holding is a multinational e-commerce, retail, Internet, AI, and technology conglomerate that provides consumer-to-consumer, business-to-consumer, and business-to-business sales services via web portals, as well as electronic payment services, shopping search engines, and data-centric cloud computing services. Baidu provides Internet search services in China and internationally along with transaction services, such as Baidu Deliveries, Baidu Mobile Game, Baidu Wallet, and Baidu Maps.

China has its own version of many popular foreign e-commerce businesses, such as weibo.com (Twitter), Youku Tudou (YouTube), WeChat (Facebook), and Ctrip (Orbitz and others). Alibaba has outmaneuvered eBay, and Uber had to sell its Chinese business to a local rival. The Internet behind the Great Firewall can be considered a "parallel universe" to the Internet that exists outside. According to a report on Internet freedom published by Freedom House, a U.S. pro-democracy group, China ranked last among the countries of the world for Internet openness.

There are costs for gaining entry to the Chinese market. Initial deposits can range from $8,000 to $25,000, annual service fees from $5,000–$10,000, and commissions on sales revenue around 5%. Other costs can include being required to use approved agencies in the production of storefronts and sales information as well as guaranteed stock availability and stock location. Agency fees alone can run into many thousands of dollars. Technical requirements of Chinese Internet filters can make operating difficult, and may force firms to find alternatives to the services technology companies rely on outside China.

It is possible to work with businesses that allow Chinese consumers to purchase from international brands, without the brand having to have a Chinese presence. For example, Xiaoshongshu (Little Red Book) features a mobile app that allows customers to select products from key foreign markets and pay the company for them. Xiaoshongshu then sources these products for the customer.

Some other points to keep in mind: Although China heavily regulates the Internet, most Chinese are not that interested in bypassing government filters to visit foreign websites such as Google or Facebook. China has an array of domestic websites to fill the void. Even when foreign websites aren't blocked, Chinese competitors usually prevail because so many people are using their products that they become indispensable. Internet calling and messaging apps such as Skype and WhatsApp are accessible in China, but they're often no substitute for Chinese products in the Chinese market. In China, Tencent's WeChat app is far more popular than Skype, WhatsApp, and Slack.

Once a new technology or business model appears, the Chinese can quickly adapt it to the local market. Oppo and Vivo, China's first and third smartphone brands by market share in 2016, appeal to young people and residents in smaller, less-wealthy cities. Their phones look like iPhones and have many of the same features, but they cost less than half the price of an iPhone. While Oppo and Vivo have doubled their Chinese market share, Apple's has fallen by 13 percent to the fourth position.

To keep up with increasing demand from smaller urban and rural areas, online retailers are seeking to expand logistics infrastructure and services. For example, Cainiao, the logistics arm of Alibaba, owns 180,000 express delivery stations for the shipment of products and has recently expanded its fresh food distribution centers across China. Logistics remains a major challenge as Chinese e-commerce players attempt to reach more customers over wider geographic regions. China's logistics system is far from efficient, with insufficient warehouse space and trucking routes throughout the country. China's package-delivery business has been growing 30 percent annually, but that's not fast enough to keep up with demand. The scarcity of high-quality logistics providers in China often burdens e-commerce firms with late deliveries, damaged and lost parcels, slow collect-on-delivery (COD) processes, poor return procedures, and no special services such as installation or the ability to try on purchases. These inefficiencies add considerably to e-commerce operating costs and erode profit margins.

Sources: "Overview of China Ecommerce Market," ecommerceworldwide.com, accessed February 1, 2018; Paul Mozur, "China Presses Its Internet Censorship Issues Across the Globe," *New York Times*, March 2, 2018; "China E-commerce Market (B2B, B2C, Mobile) in Q3 2017," *China Internet Watch*, January 25, 2018; Corey McNair, "Worldwide Retail and Ecommerce Sales," eMarketer, January 2018; Paul Mozur and Carolyn Zhang, "In China, Silicon Valley Giants Confront New Walls," *New York Times*, July 22, 2017; "Retail Ecommerce Sales in China 2016–2021," eMarketer, June 2017; "New eMarketer Forecast Sees Mobile Driving Retail Ecommerce in China," July 5, 2017; "eCommerce in China—the Future Is Already

Here," Pricewaterhouse Coopers, 2017; McKinsey & Company, "How Savvy Social Shoppers Are Transforming E-Commerce," *McKinsey Digital*, April 2016; and Alan Lau and Min Su, "China's E-commerce Soft Spot: Logistics," *McKinsey Quarterly*, April 2016.

CASE STUDY QUESTIONS

15-12 Describe the political, cultural, and organizational obstacles for foreign companies that want to do business online in China.

15-13 How do these factors impede companies from setting up e-commerce businesses in China?

15-14 What would your company need to do to create a successful e-commerce presence in China? Explain.

MyLab MIS

Go to the Assignments section of MyLab MIS to complete these writing exercises.

15-15 Identify and describe solutions to the five management challenges of developing global systems.

15-16 Identify and describe five problems of international networks that prevent companies from developing effective global systems.

Chapter 15 References

Accenture. "Technology Not Widely Used in Global Companies' Emerging Market Supply Chains, Study Says." (September 16, 2014).

Bisson, Peter, Elizabeth Stephenson, and S. Patrick Viguerie. "Global Forces: An Introduction." *McKinsey Quarterly* (June 2010).

Burtch, Gordon, Anindya Ghose, and Sunil Watta. "Cultural Differences and Geography as Determinants of Online Prosocial Lending." *MIS Quarterly* 38, No. 3 (September 2014).

Chakravorti, Bhaskar, Ajay Bhalla, and Ravi Shankar Chaturved. "The 4 Dimensions of Digital Trust, Charted Across 42 Countries." *Harvard Business Review* (February 19, 2018).

Davison, Robert. "Cultural Complications of ERP." *Communications of the ACM* 45, No. 7 (July 2002).

Deans, Candace P., and Michael J. Kane. *International Dimensions of Information Systems and Technology*. Boston, MA: PWS-Kent (1992).

Dewhurst, Martin, Jonathan Harris, and Suzanne Heywood. "The Global Company's Challenge." *McKinsey Quarterly* (June 2012).

Ghislanzoni, Giancarlo, Risto Penttinen, and David Turnbull. "The Multilocal Challenge: Managing Cross-Border Functions." *McKinsey Quarterly* (March 2008).

Gulati, Ranjay. "GE's Global Growth Experiment." *Harvard Business Review* (September–October 2017).

Ives, Blake, and Sirkka Jarvenpaa. "Applications of Global Information Technology: Key Issues for Management." *MIS Quarterly* 15, No. 1 (March 1991).

Ives, Blake, S. L. Jarvenpaa, and R. O. Mason. "Global Business Drivers: Aligning Information Technology to Global Business Strategy." *IBM Systems Journal* 32, No. 1 (1993).

King, William R., and Vikram Sethi. "An Empirical Analysis of the Organization of Transnational Information Systems." *Journal of Management Information Systems* 15, No. 4 (Spring 1999).

Kirsch, Laurie J. "Deploying Common Systems Globally: The Dynamic of Control." *Information Systems Research* 15, No. 4 (December 2004).

Martinsons, Maris G. "ERP In China: One Package Two Profiles." *Communications of the ACM* 47, No. 7 (July 2004).

Meyer, Erin. "When Culture Doesn't Translate." *Harvard Business Review* (October 2015).

McKinsey & Company. "Lions Go Digital: The Internet's Transformative Potential in Africa." (November 2013).

Mouchawar, Ronaldo. "Souq.com's CEO on Building an E-Commerce Powerhouse in the Middle East." *Harvard Business Review* (September–October 2017).

Naím, Moises, and Philip Bennett. "The Anti-Information Age." *The Atlantic* (February 16, 2016).

Roche, Edward M. *Managing Information Technology in Multinational Corporations*. New York: Macmillan (1992).

Su, Ning. "Cultural Sensemaking in Offshore Information Technology Service Suppliers: A Cultural Frame Perspective." *MIS Quarterly* 39, No. 4 (December 2015).

The Guardian. "Internet Censorship Listed: How Does Each Country Compare?" theguardian.com, accessed February 23, 2018.

Tractinsky, Noam, and Sirkka L. Jarvenpaa. "Information Systems Design Decisions in a Global Versus Domestic Context." *MIS Quarterly* 19, No. 4 (December 1995).

3-D printing   Uses machines to make solid objects, layer by layer, from specifications in a digital file. Also known as additive manufacturing.

3G networks   Cellular networks based on packet-switched technology with speeds ranging from 144 Kbps for mobile users to more than 2 Mbps for stationary users, enabling users to transmit video, graphics, and other rich media in addition to voice.

4G networks   Recent wireless communication technology capable of providing between 1 Mbps and 1 Gbps speeds; up to 10 times faster than 3G networks.

5G networks   Next wireless technology evolution, supporting transmission of huge amounts of data in the gigabit range, with fewer transmission delays and the ability to connect many more devices (such as sensors and smart devices) at once than existing cellular systems.

acceptable use policy (AUP)   Defines acceptable uses of the firm's information resources and computing equipment, including desktop and laptop computers, wireless devices, telephones, and the Internet, and specifies consequences for noncompliance.

acceptance testing   Provides the final certification that the system is ready to be used in a production setting.

accountability   The mechanisms for assessing responsibility for decisions made and actions taken.

advertising revenue model   Website generating revenue by attracting a large audience.

affiliate revenue model   An e-commerce revenue model in which websites are paid as "affiliates" for sending their visitors to other sites in return for a referral fee.

agency theory   Economic theory that views the firm as a nexus of contracts among self-interested individuals who must be supervised and managed.

agent-based modeling   Modeling complex phenomena as systems of autonomous agents that follow relatively simple rules for interaction.

agile development   Rapid delivery of working software by breaking a large project into a series of small sub-projects that are completed in short periods of time using iteration and continuous feedback.

analytic platform   Preconfigured hardware-software system that is specifically designed for high-speed analysis of large datasets.

analytical CRM   Customer relationship management applications dealing with the analysis of customer data to provide information for improving business performance.

Android   A mobile operating system developed by Android, Inc. (purchased by Google) and later the Open Handset Alliance as a flexible, upgradeable mobile device platform.

anti-malware software   Software designed to detect, and often eliminate, malware from an information system.

application controls   Specific controls unique to each computerized application that ensure that only authorized data are completely and accurately processed by that application.

application server   Software that handles all application operations between browser-based computers and a company's back-end business applications or databases.

apps   Small pieces of software that run on the Internet, on your computer, or on your cell phone and are generally delivered over the Internet.

artificial intelligence (AI)   Effort to develop computer-based systems that can think and behave like humans.

attribute   A piece of information describing a particular entity.

augmented reality (AR)   A technology for enhancing visualization. Provides a live direct or indirect view of a physical real-world environment whose elements are augmented by virtual computer-generated imagery.

authentication   The ability of each party in a transaction to ascertain the identity of the other party.

automation   Using the computer to speed up the performance of existing tasks.

backward chaining   A strategy for searching the rule base in an expert system that acts like a problem solver by beginning with a hypothesis and seeking out more information until the hypothesis is either proved or disproved.

balanced scorecard method   Framework for operationalizing a firm's strategic plan by focusing on measurable financial, business process, customer, and learning and growth outcomes of firm performance.

bandwidth   The capacity of a communications channel as measured by the difference between the highest and lowest frequencies that can be transmitted by that channel.

behavioral models   Descriptions of management based on behavioral scientists' observations of what managers actually do in their jobs.

behavioral targeting   Tracking the click-streams (history of clicking behavior) of individuals across multiple websites for the purpose of understanding their interests and intentions, and exposing them to advertisements that are uniquely suited to their interests.

benchmarking   Setting strict standards for products, services, or activities and measuring organizational performance against those standards.

best practices   The most successful solutions or problem-solving methods that have been developed by a specific organization or industry.

big data   Data sets with volumes so huge that they are beyond the ability of typical relational DBMS to capture, store, and analyze. The data are often unstructured or semi-structured.

biometric authentication   Technology for authenticating system users that compares a person's unique characteristics such as fingerprints, face, or retinal image against a stored set profile of these characteristics.

bit   A binary digit representing the smallest unit of data in a computer system. It can only have one of two states, representing 0 or 1.

blockchain   Distributed ledger system that stores permanent and tamper-proof records of transactions and shares them among a distributed network of computers.

blog   Popular term for "weblog," designating an informal yet structured website where individuals can publish stories, opinions, and links to other websites of interest.

blogosphere   Totality of blog-related websites.

Bluetooth   Standard for wireless personal area networks that can transmit up to 722 Kbps within a 10-meter area.

botnet   A group of computers that have been infected with bot malware without users' knowledge, enabling a hacker to use the amassed resources of the computers to launch distributed denial-of-service attacks, phishing campaigns, or spam.

broadband   High-speed transmission technology. Also designates a single communications medium that can transmit multiple channels of data simultaneously.

bugs   Software program code defects.

bullwhip effect   Distortion of information about the demand for a product as it passes from one entity to the next across the supply chain.

business continuity planning   Planning that focuses on how the company can restore business operations after a disaster strikes.

business driver   A force in the environment to which businesses must respond and that influences the direction of business.

business ecosystem   Loosely coupled but interdependent networks of suppliers, distributors, outsourcing firms, transportation service firms, and technology manufacturers.

business functions   Specialized tasks performed in a business organization, including manufacturing and production, sales and marketing, finance and accounting, and human resources.

business intelligence   Applications and technologies to help users make better business decisions.

business model   An abstraction of what an enterprise is and how the enterprise delivers a product or service, showing how the enterprise creates wealth.

business performance management (BPM)   Attempts to systematically translate a firm's strategies (e.g., differentiation, low-cost producer, market share growth, and scope of operation) into operational targets.

business process management (BPM)   An approach to business that aims to continuously improve and manage business processes.

business process redesign   Type of organizational change in which business processes are analyzed, simplified, and redesigned.

business processes   The unique ways in which organizations coordinate and organize work activities, information, and knowledge to produce a product or service.

business-to-business (B2B) electronic commerce   Electronic sales of goods and services among businesses.

business-to-consumer (B2C) electronic commerce   Electronic retailing of products and services directly to individual consumers.

BYOD   Stands for "bring your own device," and refers to employees using their own computing devices in the workplace.

byte   A string of bits, usually eight, used to store one number or character in a computer system.

cable Internet connections   Internet connections that use digital cable lines to deliver high-speed Internet access to homes and businesses.

capital budgeting   The process of analyzing and selecting various proposals for capital expenditures.

carpal tunnel syndrome (CTS)   Type of RSI in which pressure on the median nerve through the wrist's bony carpal tunnel structure produces pain.

change agent   In the context of implementation, the individual acting as the catalyst during the change process to ensure successful organizational adaptation to a new system or innovation.

change management   Managing the impact of organizational change associated with an innovation, such as a new information system.

chat   Live, interactive conversations over a public network.

chatbot   Software agent designed to simulate a conversation with one or more human users via textual or auditory methods.

chief data officer (CDO)   Responsible for enterprise-wide governance and utilization of information to maximize the value the organization can realize from its data.

chief information officer (CIO)   Senior manager in charge of the information systems function in the firm.

chief knowledge officer (CKO)   Senior executive in charge of the organization's knowledge management program.

chief privacy officer (CPO)   Responsible for ensuring the company complies with existing data privacy laws.

chief security officer (CSO)   Heads a formal security function for the organization and is responsible for enforcing the firm's security policy.

choice   Simon's third stage of decision making, when the individual selects among the various solution alternatives.

Chrome OS   Google's lightweight computer operating system for users who do most of their computing on the Internet; runs on computers ranging from netbooks to desktop computers.

churn rate   Measurement of the number of customers who stop using or purchasing products or services from a company. Used as an indicator of the growth or decline of a firm's customer base.

classical model of management   Traditional description of management that focused on its formal functions of planning, organizing, coordinating, deciding, and controlling.

click fraud   Fraudulently clicking on an online ad in pay per click advertising to generate an improper charge per click.

client   The user point-of-entry for the required function in client/server computing. Normally a desktop computer, workstation, or laptop computer.

client/server computing   A model for computing that splits processing between clients and servers on a network, assigning functions to the machine most able to perform the function.

cloud computing   Model of computing in which computer processing, storage, software, and other services are provided as a shared pool of virtualized resources over a network, primarily the Internet.

collaboration   Working with others to achieve shared and explicit goals.

communities of practice (COPs)   Informal social networks of professionals and employees within and outside the firm who have similar work-related activities and interests and share their knowledge.

community provider   A website business model that creates a digital online environment where people with similar interests can transact (buy and sell goods); share interests, photos, videos; communicate with like-minded people; receive interest-related information; and even play out fantasies by adopting online personalities called avatars.

competitive forces model   Model used to describe the interaction of external influences, specifically threats and opportunities, that affect an organization's strategy and ability to compete.

complementary assets   Additional assets required to derive value from a primary investment.

component-based development   Building large software systems by combining preexisting software components.

computer abuse   The commission of acts involving a computer that may not be illegal but are considered unethical.

computer crime   The commission of illegal acts through the use of a computer or against a computer system.

computer forensics   The scientific collection, examination, authentication, preservation, and analysis of data held on or retrieved from computer storage media in such a way that the information can be used as evidence in a court of law.

computer hardware   Physical equipment used for input, processing, and output activities in an information system.

computer literacy   Knowledge about information technology, focusing on understanding of how computer-based technologies work.

computer software   Detailed, preprogrammed instructions that control and coordinate the work of computer hardware components in an information system.

computer virus   Rogue software program that attaches itself to other software programs or data files in order to be executed, often causing hardware and software malfunctions.

computer vision syndrome (CVS)   Eyestrain condition related to computer display screen use; symptoms include headaches, blurred vision, and dry and irritated eyes.

computer vision systems   Systems that try to emulate the human visual system to view and extract information from real-world images.

computer-aided design (CAD)   Information system that automates the creation and revision of designs using sophisticated graphics software.

computer-aided software engineering (CASE)   Automation of step-by-step methodologies for software and systems development to reduce the amounts of repetitive work the developer needs to do.

consumer-to-consumer (C2C)   Consumers selling goods and services electronically to other consumers.

consumerization of IT   New information technology originating in the consumer market that spreads to business organizations.

controls   All of the methods, policies, and procedures that ensure protection of the organization's assets, accuracy and reliability of its records, and operational adherence to management standards.

conversion   The process of changing from the old system to the new system.

cookies   Tiny file deposited on a computer hard drive when an individual visits certain websites. Used to identify the visitor and track visits to the website.

cooptation   Bringing the opposition into the process of designing and implementing a solution without giving up control of the direction and nature of the change.

copyright   A statutory grant that protects creators of intellectual property against copying by others for any purpose for a minimum of 70 years.

core competency   Activity at which a firm excels as a world-class leader.

core systems   Systems that support functions that are absolutely critical to the organization.

cost transparency   The ability of consumers to discover the actual costs merchants pay for products.

counterimplementation   A deliberate strategy to thwart the implementation of an information system or an innovation in an organization.

cross-selling   Marketing complementary products to customers.

crowdsourcing   Using large Internet audiences for advice, market feedback, new ideas, and solutions to business problems. Related to the "wisdom of crowds" theory.

culture   The set of fundamental assumptions about what products the organization should produce, how and where it should produce them, and for whom they should be produced.

customer lifetime value (CLTV)   Difference between revenues produced by a specific customer and the expenses for acquiring and servicing that customer minus the cost of promotional marketing over the lifetime of the customer relationship, expressed in today's dollars.

customer relationship management (CRM)   Business and technology discipline that uses information systems to coordinate all of the business processes surrounding the firm's interactions with its customers in sales, marketing, and service.

customer relationship management systems   Information systems that track all the ways in which a company interacts with its customers and analyze these interactions to optimize revenue, profitability, customer satisfaction, and customer retention.

customization   The modification of a software package to meet an organization's unique requirements without destroying the package software's integrity.

customization   In e-commerce, changing a delivered product or service based on a user's preferences or prior behavior.

cybervandalism   Intentional disruption, defacement, or destruction of a website or corporate information system.

cyberwarfare   State-sponsored activity designed to cripple and defeat another state or nation by damaging or disrupting its computers or networks.

data   Streams of raw facts representing events occurring in organizations or the physical environment before they have been organized and arranged into a form that people can understand and use.

data administration   A special organizational function for managing the organization's data resources, concerned with information policy, data planning, maintenance of data dictionaries, and data quality standards.

data cleansing   Activities for detecting and correcting data in a database or file that are incorrect, incomplete, improperly formatted, or redundant. Also known as data scrubbing.

data definition   DBMS capability that specifies the structure and content of the database.

data dictionary   An automated or manual tool for storing and organizing information about the data maintained in a database.

data element   A field.

data flow diagram (DFD)   Primary tool for structured analysis that graphically illustrates a system's component process and the flow of data between them.

data governance   Policies and processes for managing the availability, usability, integrity, and security of the firm's data.

data inconsistency   The presence of different values for same attribute when the same data are stored in multiple locations.

data lake   Repository for raw unstructured data or structured data that for the most part have not yet been analyzed.

data management technology   Software governing the organization of data on physical storage media.

data manipulation language   A language associated with a database management system that end users and programmers use to manipulate data in the database.

data mart   A small data warehouse containing only a portion of the organization's data for a specified function or population of users.

data mining   Analysis of large pools of data to find patterns and rules that can be used to guide decision making and predict future behavior.

data quality audit   A survey and/or sample of files to determine accuracy and completeness of data in an information system.

data redundancy   The presence of duplicate data in multiple data files.

data visualization   Technology for helping users see patterns and relationships in large amounts of data by presenting the data in graphical form.

data warehouse   A database, with reporting and query tools, that stores current and historical data extracted from various operational systems and consolidated for management reporting and analysis.

data workers   People such as secretaries or bookkeepers who process the organization's paperwork.

database   A group of related files.

database (rigorous definition)   A collection of data organized to service many applications at the same time by storing and managing data so that they appear to be in one location.

database administration   Refers to the more technical and operational aspects of managing data, including physical database design and maintenance.

database management system (DBMS)   Special software to create and maintain a database and enable individual business applications to extract the data they need without having to create separate files or data definitions in their computer programs.

database server   A computer in a client/server environment that is responsible for running a DBMS to process SQL statements and perform database management tasks.

decisional roles   Mintzberg's classification for managerial roles where managers initiate activities, handle disturbances, allocate resources, and negotiate conflicts.

decision-support systems (DSS)   Information systems at the organization's management level that combine data and sophisticated analytical models or data analysis tools to support semi-structured and unstructured decision making.

"deep learning"   Using multiple layers of neural networks to reveal the underlying patterns in data, and in some limited cases identify patterns without human training.

deep packet inspection (DPI)   Technology for managing network traffic by examining data packets, sorting out low-priority data from higher priority business-critical data, and sending packets in order of priority.

demand planning   Determining how much product a business needs to make to satisfy all its customers' demands.

denial-of-service (DoS) attack   Flooding a network server or web server with false communications or requests for services in order to crash the network.

design   Simon's second stage of decision making, when the individual conceives of possible alternative solutions to a problem.

DevOps Organizational strategy to create a culture and environment to promote rapid and agile development practices by emphasizing close collaboration between software developers and the IT operational staff.

digital asset management systems Classify, store, and distribute digital objects such as photographs, graphic images, video, and audio content.

digital certificate An attachment to an electronic message to verify the identity of the sender and to provide the receiver with the means to encode a reply.

digital dashboard Displays all of a firm's key performance indicators as graphs and charts on a single screen to provide one-page overview of all the critical measurements necessary to make key executive decisions.

digital divide Large disparities in access to computers and the Internet among different social groups and different locations.

digital firm Organization where nearly all significant business processes and relationships with customers, suppliers, and employees are digitally enabled, and key corporate assets are managed through digital means.

digital goods Goods that can be delivered over a digital network.

Digital Millennium Copyright Act (DMCA) Adjusts copyright laws to the Internet Age by making it illegal to make, distribute, or use devices that circumvent technology-based protections of copyrighted materials.

digital subscriber line (DSL) A group of technologies providing high-capacity transmission over existing copper telephone lines.

direct cutover strategy A risky conversion approach where the new system completely replaces the old one on an appointed day.

direct goods Goods used in a production process.

disaster recovery planning Planning for the restoration of computing and communications services after they have been disrupted.

disintermediation The removal of organizations or business process layers responsible for certain intermediary steps in a value chain.

disruptive technologies Technologies with disruptive impact on industries and businesses, rendering existing products, services, and business models obsolete.

distributed database Database stored in multiple physical locations.

distributed denial-of-service (DDoS) attack Numerous computers inundating and overwhelming a network from numerous launch points.

documentation Descriptions of how an information system works from either a technical or end-user standpoint.

domain name English-like name that corresponds to the unique 32-bit numeric Internet Protocol (IP) address for each computer connected to the Internet.

Domain Name System (DNS) A hierarchical system of servers maintaining a database enabling the conversion of domain names to their numeric IP addresses.

domestic exporter Form of business organization characterized by heavy centralization of corporate activities in the home county of origin.

downtime Period of time in which an information system is not operational.

drill down The ability to move from summary data to lower and lower levels of detail.

drive-by download Malware that comes with a downloaded file a user intentionally or unintentionally requests.

due process A process in which laws are well-known and understood and there is an ability to appeal to higher authorities to ensure that laws are applied correctly.

dynamic pricing Pricing of items based on real-time interactions between buyers and sellers that determine what a item is worth at any particular moment.

e-government Use of the Internet and related technologies to digitally enable government and public sector agencies' relationships with citizens, businesses, and other arms of government.

edge computing Method of optimizing cloud computing systems by performing some data processing on a set of linked servers at the edge of the network, near the source of the data.

efficient customer response system System that directly links consumer behavior back to distribution, production, and supply chains.

electronic business (e-business) The use of the Internet and digital technology to execute all the business processes in the enterprise. Includes e-commerce as well as processes for the internal management of the firm and for coordination with suppliers and other business partners.

electronic commerce (e-commerce) The process of buying and selling goods and services electronically involving transactions using the Internet, networks, and other digital technologies.

electronic data interchange (EDI) The direct computer-to-computer exchange between two organizations of standard business transactions, such as orders, shipment instructions, or payments.

email The computer-to-computer exchange of messages.

employee relationship management (ERM) Software dealing with employee issues that are closely related to CRM, such as setting objectives, employee performance management, performance-based compensation, and employee training.

encryption The coding and scrambling of messages to prevent their being read or accessed without authorization.

end-user development The development of information systems by end users with little or no formal assistance from technical specialists.

end-user interface The part of an information system through which the end user interacts with the system, such as online screens and commands.

end users Representatives of departments outside the information systems group for whom applications are developed.

enterprise applications Systems that can coordinate activities, decisions, and knowledge across many different functions, levels, and business units in a firm. Include enterprise systems, supply chain management systems, and knowledge management systems.

enterprise content management (ECM) Help organizations manage structured and semi-structured knowledge, providing corporate repositories of documents, reports, presentations, and best practices and capabilities for collecting and organizing email and graphic objects.

enterprise software Set of integrated modules for applications such as sales and distribution, financial accounting, investment management, materials management, production planning, plant maintenance, and human resources that allow data to be used by multiple functions and business processes.

enterprise systems Integrated enterprise-wide information systems that coordinate key internal processes of the firm.

enterprise-wide knowledge management systems General-purpose, firmwide systems that collect, store, distribute, and apply digital content and knowledge.

entity A person, place, thing, or event about which information must be kept.

entity-relationship diagram A methodology for documenting databases illustrating the relationship between various entities in the database.

ergonomics The interaction of people and machines in the work environment, including the design of jobs, health issues, and the end-user interface of information systems.

e-tailer Online retail stores from the giant Amazon to tiny local stores that have websites where retail goods are sold.

ethical no-free-lunch rule Assumption that all tangible and intangible objects are owned by someone else, unless there is a specific declaration otherwise, and that the creator wants compensation for this work.

ethics Principles of right and wrong that can be used by individuals acting as free moral agents to make choices to guide their behavior.

evil twins Wireless networks that pretend to be legitimate to entice participants to log on and reveal passwords or credit card numbers.

exchange Third-party Net marketplace that is primarily transaction oriented and that connects many buyers and suppliers for spot purchasing.

executive support systems (ESS) Information systems at the organization's strategic level designed to address unstructured decision making through advanced graphics and communications.

expert system Knowledge-intensive computer program that captures the expertise of a human in limited domains of knowledge.

explicit knowledge Knowledge that has been documented.

external integration tools Project management technique that links the work of the implementation team to that of users at all organizational levels.

extranet Private intranet that is accessible to authorized outsiders.

Fair Information Practices (FIP) A set of principles originally set forth in 1973 that governs the collection and use of information about individuals and forms the basis of most U.S. and European privacy laws.

fault-tolerant computer systems Systems that contain extra hardware, software, and power supply components that can back a system up and keep it running to prevent system failure.

feasibility study As part of the systems analysis process, the way to determine whether the solution is achievable, given the organization's resources and constraints.

feedback Output that is returned to the appropriate members of the organization to help them evaluate or correct input.

field A grouping of characters into a word, a group of words, or a complete number, such as a person's name or age.

file A group of records of the same type.

File Transfer Protocol (FTP) Tool for retrieving and transferring files from a remote computer.

FinTech Start-up innovative financial technology firms and services.

firewall Hardware and software placed between an organization's internal network and an external network to prevent outsiders from invading private networks.

foreign key Field in a database table that enables users find related information in another database table.

formal control tools Project management technique that helps monitor the progress toward completion of a task and fulfillment of goals.

formal planning tools Project management technique that structures and sequences tasks, budgeting time, money, and technical resources required to complete the tasks.

forward chaining A strategy for searching the rule base in an expert system that begins with the information entered by the user and searches the rule base to arrive at a conclusion.

franchiser Form of business organization in which a product is created, designed, financed, and initially produced in the home country, but for product-specific reasons relies heavily on foreign personnel for further production, marketing, and human resources.

free/freemium revenue model An e-commerce revenue model in which a firm offers basic services or content for free while charging a premium for advanced or high-value features.

Gantt chart Visually represents the timing, duration, and resource requirements of project tasks.

general controls Overall control environment governing the design, security, and use of computer programs and the security of data files in general throughout the organization's information technology infrastructure.

General Data Protection Regulation (GDPR) Legislation effective May 25, 2018 that updates and unifies data privacy laws across the European Union, focusing on making businesses more transparent and expanding the privacy rights of data subjects.

genetic algorithms Problem-solving methods that promote the evolution of solutions to specified problems using the model of living organisms adapting to their environment.

geoadvertising services Delivering ads to users based on their GPS location.

geographic information system (GIS) System with software that can analyze and display data using digitized maps to enhance planning and decision-making.

geoinformation services Information on local places and things based on the GPS position of the user.

geosocial services Social networking based on the GPS location of users.

global culture The development of common expectations, shared artifacts, and social norms among different cultures and peoples.

Golden Rule Putting oneself in the place of others as the object of a decision.

Gramm-Leach-Bliley Act Requires financial institutions to ensure the security and confidentiality of customer data.

green computing (green IT) Refers to practices and technologies for designing, manufacturing, using, and disposing of computers, servers, and associated devices such as monitors, printers, storage devices, and networking and communications systems to minimize impact on the environment.

group decision-support system (GDSS) An interactive computer-based system to facilitate the solution to unstructured problems by a set of decision makers working together as a group.

hacker A person who gains unauthorized access to a computer network for profit, criminal mischief, or personal pleasure.

Hadoop Open source software framework that enables distributed parallel processing of huge amounts of data across many inexpensive computers.

hertz Measure of frequency of electrical impulses per second, with 1 Hertz equivalent to 1 cycle per second.

HIPAA Law outlining rules for medical security, privacy, and the management of healthcare records.

hotspot A specific geographic location in which an access point provides public Wi-Fi network service.

HTML5 Next evolution of HTML, which makes it possible to embed images, video, and audio directly into a document without add-on software.

hubs Very simple devices that connect network components, sending a packet of data to all other connected devices.

hybrid cloud Computing model where firms use both their own IT infrastructure and also public cloud computing services.

Hypertext Markup Language (HTML) Page description language for creating web pages.

Hypertext Transfer Protocol (HTTP) The communications standard used to transfer pages on the web. Defines how messages are formatted and transmitted.

identity management Business processes and software tools for identifying the valid users of a system and controlling their access to system resources.

identity theft Theft of key pieces of personal information, such as credit card or Social Security numbers, in order to obtain merchandise and services in the name of the victim or to obtain false credentials.

Immanuel Kant's categorical imperative A principle that states that if an action is not right for everyone to take it is not right for anyone.

implementation All the organizational activities surrounding the adoption, management, and routinization of an innovation, such as a new information system.

in-memory computing Technology for very rapid analysis and processing of large quantities of data by storing the data in the computer's main memory rather than in secondary storage.

indirect goods Goods not directly used in the production process, such as office supplies.

inference engine The strategy used to search through the rule base in an expert system; can be forward or backward chaining.

information Data that have been shaped into a form that is meaningful and useful to human beings.

information asymmetry Situation where the relative bargaining power of two parties in a transaction is determined by one party in the transaction possessing more information essential to the transaction than the other party.

information density The total amount and quality of information available to all market participants, consumers, and merchants.

information policy Formal rules governing the maintenance, distribution, and use of information in an organization.

information requirements A detailed statement of the information needs that a new system must satisfy; identifies who needs what information, and when, where, and how the information is needed.

information rights The rights that individuals and organizations have with respect to information that pertains to themselves.

information system Interrelated components working together to collect, process, store, and disseminate information to support decision making, coordination, control, analysis, and visualization in an organization.

information systems audit Identifies all the controls that govern individual information systems and assesses their effectiveness.

information systems department The formal organizational unit that is responsible for the information systems function in the organization.

information systems literacy Broad-based understanding of information systems that includes behavioral knowledge about organizations and individuals using information systems as well as technical knowledge about computers.

information systems managers Leaders of the various specialists in the information systems department.

information systems plan A road map indicating the direction of systems development: the rationale, the current situation, the management strategy, the implementation plan, and the budget.

information technology (IT) All the hardware and software technologies a firm needs to achieve its business objectives.

information technology (IT) infrastructure Computer hardware, software, data, storage technology, and networks providing a portfolio of shared IT resources for the organization.

informational roles Mintzberg's classification for managerial roles where managers act as the nerve centers of their organizations, receiving and disseminating critical information.

informed consent Consent given with knowledge of all the facts needed to make a rational decision.

input The capture or collection of raw data from within the organization or from its external environment for processing in an information system.

instant messaging Chat service that allows participants to create their own private chat channels so that a person can be alerted whenever someone on his or her private list is online to initiate a chat session with that particular individual.

intangible benefits Benefits that are not easily quantified; they include more efficient customer service or enhanced decision making.

intellectual property Intangible property created by individuals or corporations that is subject to protections under trade secret, copyright, and patent law.

intelligence The first of Simon's four stages of decision making, when the individual collects information to identify problems occurring in the organization.

intelligent agent Software program that uses a built-in or learned knowledge base to carry out specific, repetitive, and predictable tasks for an individual user, business process, or software application.

intelligent techniques Technologies that aid human decision makers by capturing individual and collective knowledge, discovering patterns and behaviors in large quantities of data, and generating solutions to problems that are too large and complex for human beings to solve on their own.

internal integration tools Project management technique that ensures that the implementation team operates as a cohesive unit.

international information systems architecture The basic information systems required by organizations to coordinate worldwide trade and other activities.

Internet Global network of networks using universal standards to connect millions of different networks.

Internet of Things Pervasive web in which each object or machine has a unique identity and is able to use the Internet to link with other machines or send data. Also known as the Industrial Internet.

Internet Protocol (IP) address Four-part numeric address indicating a unique computer location on the Internet.

Internet service provider (ISP) A commercial organization with a permanent connection to the Internet that sells temporary connections to subscribers.

Internet2 Research network with new protocols and transmission speeds that provides an infrastructure for supporting high-bandwidth Internet applications.

interorganizational systems Information systems that automate the flow of information across organizational boundaries and link a company to its customers, distributors, or suppliers.

interpersonal roles Mintzberg's classification for managerial roles where managers act as figureheads and leaders for the organization.

intranet An internal network based on Internet and World Wide Web technology and standards.

intrusion detection system Tools to monitor the most vulnerable points in a network to detect and deter unauthorized intruders.

iOS Operating system for the Apple iPad, iPhone, and iPod Touch.

IPv6 New IP addressing system using 128-bit IP addresses. Stands for Internet Protocol version 6.

IT governance Strategy and policies for using information technology within an organization, specifying the decision rights and accountabilities to ensure that information technology supports the organization's strategies and objectives.

iterative A process of repeating over and over again the steps to build a system.

Java Programming language that can deliver only the software functionality needed for a particular task, such as a small applet downloaded from a network; can run on any computer and operating system.

joint application design (JAD) Process to accelerate the generation of information requirements by having end users and information systems specialists work together in intensive interactive design sessions.

just-in-time strategy Scheduling system for minimizing inventory by having components arrive exactly at the moment they are needed and finished goods shipped as soon as they leave the assembly line.

key field A field in a record that uniquely identifies instances of that record so that it can be retrieved, updated, or sorted.

key performance indicators Measures proposed by senior management for understanding how well the firm is performing along specified dimensions.

keylogger Spyware that records every keystroke made on a computer to steal personal information or passwords or to launch Internet attacks.

knowledge Concepts, experience, and insight that provide a framework for creating, evaluating, and using information.

knowledge base Model of human knowledge that is used by expert systems.

knowledge discovery Identification of novel and valuable patterns in large databases.

knowledge management The set of processes developed in an organization to create, gather, store, maintain, and disseminate the firm's knowledge.

knowledge management systems Systems that support the creation, capture, storage, and dissemination of firm expertise and knowledge.

knowledge workers People such as engineers or architects who design products or services and create knowledge for the organization.

knowledge work systems Information systems that aid knowledge workers in the creation and integration of new knowledge into the organization.

learning management system (LMS) Tools for the management, delivery, tracking, and assessment of various types of employee learning.

legacy system A system that has been in existence for a long time and that continues to be used to avoid the high cost of replacing or redesigning it.

legitimacy The extent to which one's authority is accepted on grounds of competence, vision, or other qualities.

liability The existence of laws that permit individuals to recover the damages done to them by other actors, systems, or organizations.

Linux Reliable and compactly designed operating system that is an offshoot of UNIX and that can run on many different hardware platforms and is available free or at very low cost. Used as alternative to UNIX.

local area network (LAN) A telecommunications network that requires its own dedicated channels and that encompasses a limited distance, usually one building or several buildings in close proximity.

location-based services GPS map services available on smartphones.

location analytics Ability to gain insights from the location (geographic) component of data, including location data from mobile phones, output from sensors or scanning devices, and data from maps.

long tail marketing Refers to the ability of firms to profitably market goods to very small online audiences, largely because of the lower costs of reaching very small market segments (people who fall into the long tail ends of a Bell curve).

machine learning Software that can identify patterns and relationships in very large data sets without explicit programming although with significant human training.

mainframe Largest category of computer, used for major business processing.

maintenance Changes in hardware, software, documentation, or procedures to a production system to correct errors, meet new requirements, or improve processing efficiency.

malware Malicious software programs such as computer viruses, worms, and Trojan horses.

managed security service provider (MSSP) Company that provides security management services for subscribing clients.

management information systems (MIS) Specific category of information system providing reports on organizational performance to help middle management monitor and control the business.

management information systems (MIS) The study of information systems focusing on their use in business and management.

managerial roles Expectations of the activities that managers should perform in an organization.

market creator An e-commerce business model in which firms provide a digital online environment where buyers and sellers can meet, search for products, and engage in transactions.

market entry costs The cost merchants must pay to bring their goods to market.

marketspace A marketplace extended beyond traditional boundaries and removed from a temporal and geographic location.

mashups Composite software applications that depend on high-speed networks, universal communication standards, and open source code.

mass customization The capacity to offer individually tailored products or services using mass production resources.

massive open online course (MOOC) Online course made available via the web to very large numbers of participants.

menu costs Merchants' costs of changing prices.

metropolitan area network (MAN) Network that spans a metropolitan area, usually a city and its major suburbs. Its geographic scope falls between a WAN and a LAN.

microblogging Blogging featuring very short posts, such as using Twitter.

micropayment systems Payment for a very small sum of money, often less than $10.

middle management People in the middle of the organizational hierarchy who are responsible for carrying out the plans and goals of senior management.

minicomputer Middle-range computer used in systems for universities, factories, or research laboratories.

mobile commerce (m-commerce) The use of wireless devices, such as smartphones or tablets to conduct both business-to-consumer and business-to-business e-commerce transactions over the Internet.

mobile device management (MDM) Software that monitors, manages, and secures mobile devices that are deployed across multiple mobile service providers and multiple mobile operating systems used in the organization.

mobile web app Internet-enabled app with specific functionality for mobile devices that is accessed through a mobile device's web browser.

mobile website Version of a regular website that is scaled down in content and navigation for easy access and search on a small mobile screen.

modem A device for translating a computer's digital signals into analog form for transmission over analog networks or for translating analog signals back into digital form for reception by a computer.

Moore's Law Assertion that the number of components on a chip doubles each year.

multicore processor Integrated circuit to which two or more processors have been attached for enhanced performance, reduced power consumption, and more efficient simultaneous processing of multiple tasks.

multinational Form of business organization that concentrates financial management, and control out of a central home base while decentralizing production, sales, and marketing.

multitiered (N-tier) client/server architecture Client/server network in which the work of the entire network is balanced over several different levels of servers.

multitouch Interface that features the use of one or more finger gestures to manipulate lists or objects on a screen without using a mouse or keyboard.

nanotechnology Technology that builds structures and processes based on the manipulation of individual atoms and molecules.

native advertising Placing ads within social network newsfeeds or traditional editorial content, such as a newspaper article.

native app Standalone application designed to run on a specific platform and device and installed directly on the mobile device

natural language processing (NLP) AI technique for enabling a computer to understand and analyze natural language as opposed to language formatted to be understood by computers.

near field communication (NFC) Short-range wireless connectivity standard that uses electromagnetic radio fields to enable two compatible devices to exchange data when brought within a few centimeters of each other.

net marketplace A single digital marketplace based on Internet technology linking many buyers to many sellers.

network The linking of two or more computers to share data or resources, such as a printer.

network economics Model of strategic systems at the industry level based on the concept of a network where adding another participant entails zero marginal costs but can create much larger marginal gains.

network operating system (NOS)   Special software that routes and manages communications on the network and coordinates network resources.

networking and telecommunications technology   Physical devices and software that link various computer hardware components and transfer data from one physical location to another.

neural network   Algorithms loosely based on the processing patterns of the biological brain that can be trained to classify objects into known categories based on data inputs.

non-relational database management system   Database management system for working with large quantities of structured and unstructured data that would be difficult to analyze with a relational model.

nonobvious relationship awareness (NORA)   Technology that can find obscure hidden connections between people or other entities by analyzing information from many different sources to correlate relationships.

normalization   The process of creating small stable data structures from complex groups of data when designing a relational database.

object   Software building block that combines data and the procedures acting on the data.

object-oriented development   Approach to systems development that uses the object as the basic unit of systems analysis and design. The system is modeled as a collection of objects and the relationship between them.

Office 365   Hosted cloud version of Microsoft Office productivity and collaboration tools as a subscription service.

offshore outsourcing   Outsourcing systems development work or maintenance of existing systems to external vendors in another country.

on-demand computing   Firms off-loading peak demand for computing power to remote, large-scale data processing centers, investing just enough to handle average processing loads and paying for only as much additional computing power as the market demands. Also called utility computing.

online analytical processing (OLAP)   Capability for manipulating and analyzing large volumes of data from multiple perspectives.

online transaction processing   Transaction processing mode in which transactions entered online are immediately processed by the computer.

open source software   Software that provides free access to its program code, allowing users to modify the program code to make improvements or fix errors.

operating system   Software that manages the resources and activities of the computer.

operational CRM   Customer-facing applications, such as sales force automation, call center and customer service support, and marketing automation.

operational intelligence   Business analytics that delivers insight into data, streaming events, and business operations.

operational management   People who monitor the day-to-day activities of the organization.

opt-in   Model of informed consent permitting prohibiting an organization from collecting any personal information unless the individual specifically takes action to approve information collection and use.

opt-out   Model of informed consent permitting the collection of personal information until the consumer specifically requests that the data not be collected.

organization (behavioral definition)   A collection of rights, privileges, obligations, and responsibilities that are delicately balanced over a period of time through conflict and conflict resolution.

organization (technical definition)   A stable, formal, social structure that takes resources from the environment and processes them to produce outputs.

organizational and management capital   Investments in organization and management such as new business processes, management behavior, organizational culture, or training.

organizational impact analysis   Study of the way a proposed system will affect organizational structure, attitudes, decision making, and operations.

organizational learning   Creation of new standard operating procedures and business processes that reflect organizations' experience.

output   The distribution of processed information to the people who will use it or to the activities for which it will be used.

outsourcing   The practice of contracting computer center operations, telecommunications networks, or applications development to external vendors.

packet switching   Technology that breaks messages into small, fixed bundles of data and routes them in the most economical way through any available communications channel.

paradigm shift   Radical reconceptualization of the nature of the business and the nature of the organization.

parallel strategy   A safe and conservative conversion approach where both the old system and its potential replacement are run together for a time until everyone is assured that the new one functions correctly.

particularism   Making judgments and taking action on the basis of narrow or personal characteristics, in all its forms (religious, nationalistic, ethnic, regionalism, geopolitical position).

partner relationship management (PRM)   Automation of the firm's relationships with its selling partners using customer data and analytical tools to improve coordination and customer sales.

password   Secret word or string of characters for authenticating users so they can access a resource such as a computer system.

patch   Small pieces of software to repair the software flaws without disturbing the proper operation of the software.

patent   A legal document that grants the owner an exclusive monopoly on the ideas behind an invention for 20 years; designed to ensure that inventors of new machines or methods are rewarded for their labor while making widespread use of their inventions.

peer-to-peer   Network architecture that gives equal power to all computers on the network; used primarily in small networks.

personal area network (PAN)   Computer network used for communication among digital devices that are close to one person.

personalization   Ability of merchants to target marketing messages to specific individuals by adjusting the message for a person's name, interests, and past purchases.

PERT chart   Network diagram depicting project tasks and their interrelationships.

pharming   Phishing technique that redirects users to a bogus web page, even when an individual enters the correct web page address.

phased approach   Introduces the new system in stages either by functions or by organizational units.

phishing   Form of spoofing involving setting up fake websites or sending email messages that resemble those of legitimate businesses that ask users for confidential personal data.

pilot study strategy   A strategy to introduce the new system to a limited area of the organization until it is proven to be fully functional; only then can the conversion to the new system across the entire organization take place.

pivot table   Spreadsheet tool for reorganizing and summarizing two or more dimensions of data in a tabular format.

platform   Business providing information systems, technologies, and services that thousands of other firms in different industries use to enhance their own capabilities.

podcasting   Publishing audio broadcasts via the Internet so that subscribing users can download audio files onto their personal computers or portable music players.

portal   Web interface for presenting integrated personalized content from a variety of sources. Also refers to a website service that provides an initial point of entry to the web.

portfolio analysis   An analysis of the portfolio of potential applications within a firm to determine the risks and benefits, and to select among alternatives for information systems.

post-implementation audit Formal review process conducted after a system has been placed in production to determine how well the system has met its original objectives.

predictive analytics The use of data mining techniques, historical data, and assumptions about future conditions to predict outcomes of events, such as the probability a customer will respond to an offer or purchase a specific product.

predictive search Part of a search alogrithm that predicts what a user query is looking as it is entered based on popular searches.

price discrimination Selling the same goods, or nearly the same goods, to different targeted groups at different prices.

price transparency The ease with which consumers can find out the variety of prices in a market.

primary activities Activities most directly related to the production and distribution of a firm's products or services.

primary key Unique identifier for all the information in any row of a database table.

privacy The claim of individuals to be left alone, free from surveillance or interference from other individuals, organizations, or the state.

private cloud A proprietary network or a data center that ties together servers, storage, networks, data, and applications as a set of virtualized services that are shared by users inside a company.

private exchange Another term for a private industrial network.

private industrial networks Web-enabled networks linking systems of multiple firms in an industry for the coordination of trans-organizational business processes.

process specifications Describe the logic of the processes occurring within the lowest levels of a data flow diagram.

processing The conversion, manipulation, and analysis of raw input into a form that is more meaningful to humans.

product differentiation Competitive strategy for creating brand loyalty by developing new and unique products and services that are not easily duplicated by competitors.

production The stage after the new system is installed and the conversion is complete; during this time the system is reviewed by users and technical specialists to determine how well it has met its original goals.

production or service workers People who actually produce the products or services of the organization.

profiling The use of computers to combine data from multiple sources and create electronic dossiers of detailed information on individuals.

program-data dependence The close relationship between data stored in files and the software programs that update and maintain those files. Any change in data organization or format requires a change in all the programs associated with those files.

programmers Highly trained technical specialists who write computer software instructions.

programming The process of translating the system specifications prepared during the design stage into program code.

project Planned series of related activities for achieving a specific business objective.

project management Application of knowledge, tools, and techniques to achieve specific targets within a specified budget and time period.

project portfolio management Helps organizations evaluate and manage portfolios of projects and dependencies among them.

protocol A set of rules and procedures that govern transmission between the components in a network.

prototype The preliminary working version of an information system for demonstration and evaluation purposes.

prototyping The process of building an experimental system quickly and inexpensively for demonstration and evaluation so that users can better determine information requirements.

public cloud A cloud maintained by an external service provider, accessed through the Internet, and available to the general public.

public key encryption Uses two keys: one shared (or public) and one private.

public key infrastructure (PKI) System for creating public and private keys using a certificate authority (CA) and digital certificates for authentication.

pull-based model Supply chain driven by actual customer orders or purchases so that members of the supply chain produce and deliver only what customers have ordered.

push-based model Supply chain driven by production master schedules based on forecasts or best guesses of demand for products, and products are "pushed" to customers.

quantum computing Use of principles of quantum physics to represent data and perform operations on the data, with the ability to be in many different states at once and to perform many different computations simultaneously.

query language Software tool that provides immediate online answers to requests for information that are not predefined.

radio frequency identification (RFID) Technology using tiny tags with embedded microchips containing data about an item and its location to transmit short-distance radio signals to special RFID readers that then pass the data on to a computer for processing.

ransomware Malware that extorts money from users by taking control of their computers or displaying annoying pop-up messages.

Rapid Application Development (RAD) Process for developing systems in a very short time period by using prototyping, state-of-the-art software tools, and close teamwork among users and systems specialists.

rationalization of procedures The streamlining of standard operating procedures, eliminating obvious bottlenecks, so that automation makes operating procedures more efficient.

record A group of related fields.

referential integrity Rules to ensure that relationships between coupled database tables remain consistent.

relational DBMS A type of logical database model that treats data as if they were stored in two-dimensional tables. It can relate data stored in one table to data in another as long as the two tables share a common data element.

repetitive stress injury (RSI) Occupational disease that occurs when muscle groups are forced through repetitive actions with high-impact loads or thousands of repetitions with low-impact loads.

request for proposal (RFP) A detailed list of questions submitted to vendors of software or other services to determine how well the vendor's product can meet the organization's specific requirements.

responsibility Accepting the potential costs, duties, and obligations for the decisions one makes.

responsive web design Ability of a website to automatically change screen resolution and image size as a user switches to devices of different sizes, such as a laptop, tablet computer, or smartphone. Eliminates the need for separate design and development work for each new device.

revenue model A description of how a firm will earn revenue, generate profits, and produce a return on investment.

richness Measurement of the depth and detail of information that a business can supply to the customer as well as information the business collects about the customer.

risk assessment Determining the potential frequency of the occurrence of a problem and the potential damage if the problem were to occur. Used to determine the cost/benefit of a control.

risk aversion principle Principle that one should take the action that produces the least harm or incurs the least cost.

robotics Use of machines that can substitute for human movements as well as computer systems for their control, sensory feedback, and information processing.

router Specialized communications processor that forwards packets of data from one network to another network.

routines Precise rules, procedures, and practices that have been developed to cope with expected situations.

RSS Technology using aggregator software to pull content from websites and feed it automatically to subscribers' computers.

safe harbor Private self-regulating policy and enforcement mechanism that meets the objectives of government regulations but does not involve government regulation or enforcement.

sales revenue model Selling goods, information, or services to customers as the main source of revenue for a company.

Sarbanes-Oxley Act Law passed in 2002 that imposes responsibility on companies and their management to protect investors by safeguarding the accuracy and integrity of financial information that is used internally and released externally.

scalability The ability of a computer, product, or system to expand to serve a larger number of users without breaking down.

scope Defines what work is and is not included in a project.

scoring model A quick method for deciding among alternative systems based on a system of ratings for selected objectives.

search costs The time and money spent locating a suitable product and determining the best price for that product.

search engine A tool for locating specific sites or information on the Internet.

search engine marketing Use of search engines to deliver in their results sponsored links, for which advertisers have paid.

search engine optimization (SEO) The process of changing a website's content, layout, and format in order to increase the ranking of the site on popular search engines and to generate more site visitors.

Secure Hypertext Transfer Protocol (S-HTTP) Protocol used for encrypting data flowing over the Internet; limited to individual messages.

Secure Sockets Layer (SSL) Enables client and server computers to manage encryption and decryption activities as they communicate with each other during a secure web session.

security Policies, procedures, and technical measures used to prevent unauthorized access, alteration, theft, or physical damage to information systems.

security policy Statements ranking information risks, identifying acceptable security goals, and identifying the mechanisms for achieving these goals.

semantic search Search technology capable of understanding human language and behavior.

semi-structured decisions Decisions in which only part of the problem has a clear-cut answer provided by an accepted procedure.

senior management People occupying the topmost hierarchy in an organization who are responsible for making long-range decisions.

sensitivity analysis Models that ask "what-if" questions repeatedly to determine the impact of changes in one or more factors on the outcomes.

sentiment analysis Mining text comments in an email message, blog, social media conversation, or survey form to detect favorable and unfavorable opinions about specific subjects.

server Computer specifically optimized to provide software and other resources to other computers over a network.

service level agreement (SLA) Formal contract between customers and their service providers that defines the specific responsibilities of the service provider and the level of service expected by the customer.

service-oriented architecture (SOA) Software architecture of a firm built on a collection of software programs that communicate with each other to perform assigned tasks to create a working software application

shopping bot Software with varying levels of built-in intelligence to help electronic commerce shoppers locate and evaluate products or service they might wish to purchase.

Six Sigma A specific measure of quality, representing 3.4 defects per million opportunities; used to designate a set of methodologies and techniques for improving quality and reducing costs.

smart card A credit-card-size plastic card that stores digital information and that can be used for electronic payments in place of cash.

smartphone Wireless phone with voice, text, and Internet capabilities.

sniffer Type of eavesdropping program that monitors information traveling over a network.

social business Use of social networking platforms, including Facebook, Twitter, and internal corporate social tools, to engage employees, customers, and suppliers.

social CRM Tools enabling a business to link customer conversations, data, and relationships from social networking sites to CRM processes.

social engineering Tricking people into revealing their passwords by pretending to be legitimate users or members of a company in need of information.

social graph Map of all significant online social relationships, comparable to a social network describing offline relationships.

social networking sites Online community for expanding users' business or social contacts by making connections through their mutual business or personal connections.

social search Effort to provide more relevant and trustworthy search results based on a person's network of social contacts.

social shopping Use of websites featuring user-created web pages to share knowledge about items of interest to other shoppers.

sociotechnical design Design to produce information systems that blend technical efficiency with sensitivity to organizational and human needs.

sociotechnical view Seeing systems as composed of both technical and social elements.

software as a service (SaaS) Services for delivering and providing access to software remotely as a web-based service.

software-defined networking (SDN) Using a central control program separate from network devices to manage the flow of data on a network.

software-defined storage (SDS) Software to manage provisioning and management of data storage independent of the underlying hardware.

software localization Process of converting software to operate in a second language.

software package A prewritten, precoded, commercially available set of programs that eliminates the need to write software programs for certain functions.

spam Unsolicited commercial email.

spoofing Tricking or deceiving computer systems or other computer users by hiding one's identity or faking the identity of another user on the Internet.

spyware Technology that aids in gathering information about a person or organization without their knowledge.

SQL injection attack Attacks against a website that take advantage of vulnerabilities in poorly coded SQL (a standard and common database software application) applications in order to introduce malicious program code into a company's systems and networks.

strategic transitions A movement from one level of sociotechnical system to another. Often required when adopting strategic systems that demand changes in the social and technical elements of an organization.

streaming A publishing method for music and video files that flows a continuous stream of content to a user's device without being stored locally on the device.

structure chart System documentation showing each level of design, the relationship among the levels, and the overall place in the design structure; can document one program, one system, or part of one program.

structured Refers to the fact that techniques are carefully drawn up, step by step, with each step building on a previous one.

structured decisions Decisions that are repetitive and routine and have a definite procedure for handling them.

structured knowledge   Knowledge in the form of structured documents and reports.

Structured Query Language (SQL)   The standard data manipulation language for relational database management systems.

subscription revenue model   Website charging a subscription fee for access to some or all of its content or services on an ongoing basis.

supervised learning   Machine learning algorithm trained by providing specific examples of desired inputs and outputs classified by humans in advance.

supply chain   Network of organizations and business processes for procuring materials, transforming raw materials into intermediate and finished products, and distributing the finished products to customers.

supply chain execution systems   Systems to manage the flow of products through distribution centers and warehouses to ensure that products are delivered to the right locations in the most efficient manner.

supply chain management systems   Information systems that automate the flow of information between a firm and its suppliers in order to optimize the planning, sourcing, manufacturing, and delivery of products and services.

supply chain planning systems   Systems that enable a firm to generate demand forecasts for a product and to develop sourcing and manufacturing plans for that product.

support activities   Activities that make the delivery of a firm's primary activities possible. Consist of the organization's infrastructure, human resources, technology, and procurement.

switch   Device to connect network components that has more intelligence than a hub and can filter and forward data to a specified destination.

switching costs   The expense a customer or company incurs in lost time and expenditure of resources when changing from one supplier or system to a competing supplier or system.

system testing   Tests the functioning of the information system as a whole in order to determine if discrete modules will function together as planned.

systems analysis   The analysis of a problem that the organization will try to solve with an information system.

systems analysts   Specialists who translate business problems and requirements into information requirements and systems, acting as liaison between the information systems department and the rest of the organization.

systems design   Details how a system will meet the information requirements as determined by the systems analysis.

systems development   The activities that go into producing an information systems solution to an organizational problem or opportunity.

systems life cycle   A traditional methodology for developing an information system that partitions the systems development process into formal stages that must be completed sequentially with a very formal division of labor between end users and information systems specialists.

T lines   High-speed guaranteed service level data lines leased from communications providers, such as T-1 lines (with a transmission capacity of 1.544 Mbps).

tablet computer   Mobile handheld computer that is larger than a mobile phone and operated primarily by touching a flat screen.

tacit knowledge   Expertise and experience of organizational members that has not been formally documented.

tangible benefits   Benefits that can be quantified and assigned a monetary value; they include lower operational costs and increased cash flows.

taxonomy   Method of classifying things according to a predetermined system.

teams   Formal groups whose members collaborate to achieve specific goals.

teamware   Group collaboration software that is customized for teamwork.

technology standards   Specifications that establish the compatibility of products and the ability to communicate in a network.

telepresence   Telepresence is a technology that allows a person to give the appearance of being present at a location other than his or her true physical location.

Telnet   Network tool that allows someone to log on to one computer system while doing work on another.

test plan   Prepared by the development team in conjunction with the users; it includes all of the preparations for the series of tests to be performed on the system.

testing   The exhaustive and thorough process that determines whether the system produces the desired results under known conditions.

text mining   Discovery of patterns and relationships from large sets of unstructured data.

token   Physical device similar to an identification card that is designed to prove the identity of a single user.

total cost of ownership (TCO)   Designates the total cost of owning technology resources, including initial purchase costs, the cost of hardware and software upgrades, maintenance, technical support, and training.

total quality management (TQM)   A concept that makes quality control a responsibility to be shared by all people in an organization.

touch point   Method of firm interaction with a customer, such as telephone, email, customer service desk, conventional mail, or point-of-purchase.

trade secret   Any intellectual work or product used for a business purpose that can be classified as belonging to that business, provided it is not based on information in the public domain.

transaction costs   Costs incurred when a firm buys on the marketplace what it cannot make itself.

transaction cost theory   Economic theory stating that firms grow larger because they can conduct marketplace transactions internally more cheaply than they can with external firms in the marketplace.

transaction fee revenue model   An online e-commerce revenue model where the firm receives a fee for enabling or executing transactions.

transaction processing systems (TPS)   Computerized systems that perform and record the daily routine transactions necessary to conduct the business; they serve the organization's operational level.

transborder data flow   The movement of information across international boundaries in any form.

Transmission Control Protocol/Internet Protocol (TCP/IP)   Dominant model for achieving connectivity among different networks. Provides a universally agreed-on method for breaking up digital messages into packets, routing them to the proper addresses, and then reassembling them into coherent messages.

transnational   Truly global form of business organization with no national headquarters; value-added activities are managed from a global perspective without reference to national borders, optimizing sources of supply and demand and local competitive advantage.

Trojan horse   A software program that appears legitimate but contains a second hidden function that may cause damage.

tuple   A row or record in a relational database.

two-factor authentication   Validating user identity with two means of identification, one of which is typically a physical token, and the other of which is typically data.

unified communications   Integrates disparate channels for voice communications, data communications, instant messaging, email, and electronic conferencing into a single experience where users can seamlessly switch back and forth between different communication modes.

unified threat management (UTM)   Comprehensive security management tool that combines multiple security tools, including firewalls, virtual private networks, intrusion detection systems, and web content filtering and anti-spam software.

uniform resource locator (URL) The address of a specific resource on the Internet.

unit testing The process of testing each program separately in the system. Sometimes called program testing.

Unix Operating system for all types of computers, which is machine independent and supports multiuser processing, multitasking, and networking. Used in high-end workstations and servers.

unstructured decisions Nonroutine decisions in which the decision maker must provide judgment, evaluation, and insights into the problem definition; there is no agreed-upon procedure for making such decisions.

unsupervised learning Machine learning algorithm trained to use information that is neither classified nor labeled in advance and to find patterns in that information without explicit human guidance.

user interface The part of the information system through which the end user interacts with the system; type of hardware and the series of on-screen commands and responses required for a user to work with the system.

user-designer communications gap The difference in backgrounds, interests, and priorities that impede communication and problem solving among end users and information systems specialists.

utilitarian principle Principle that assumes one can put values in rank order of utility and understand the consequences of various courses of action.

value chain model Model that highlights the primary or support activities that add a margin of value to a firm's products or services where information systems can best be applied to achieve a competitive advantage.

value web Customer-driven network of independent firms who use information technology to coordinate their value chains to collectively produce a product or service for a market.

virtual company Organization using networks to link people, assets, and ideas to create and distribute products and services without being limited to traditional organizational boundaries or physical location.

virtual private network (VPN) A secure connection between two points across the Internet to transmit corporate data. Provides a low-cost alternative to a private network.

virtual reality systems Interactive graphics software and hardware that create computer-generated simulations that provide sensations that emulate real-world activities.

virtualization Presenting a set of computing resources so that they can all be accessed in ways that are not restricted by physical configuration or geographic location.

visual web Refers to web linking visual sites such as Pinterest where pictures replace text documents and where users search on pictures and visual characteristics.

Voice over IP (VoIP) Facilities for managing the delivery of voice information using the Internet Protocol (IP).

war driving Technique in which eavesdroppers drive by buildings or park outside and try to intercept wireless network traffic.

web beacons Tiny objects invisibly embedded in email messages and web pages that are designed to monitor the behavior of the user visiting a website or sending email.

web browser An easy-to-use software tool for accessing the World Wide Web and the Internet.

web hosting service Company with large web server computers to maintain the websites of fee-paying subscribers.

web mining Discovery and analysis of useful patterns and information from the World Wide Web.

web server Software that manages requests for web pages on the computer where they are stored and that delivers the page to the user's computer.

web services Set of universal standards using Internet technology for integrating different applications from different sources without time-consuming custom coding. Used for linking systems of different organizations or for linking disparate systems within the same organization.

website All of the World Wide Web pages maintained by an organization or an individual.

Wi-Fi Stands for "wireless fidelity" and refers to the 802.11 family of wireless networking standards.

wide area network (WAN) Telecommunications network that spans a large geographical distance. May consist of a variety of cable, satellite, and microwave technologies.

wiki Collaborative website where visitors can add, delete, or modify content, including the work of previous authors.

WiMax Popular term for IEEE Standard 802.16 for wireless networking over a range of up to 31 miles with a data transfer rate of up to 75 Mbps. Stands for Worldwide Interoperability for Microwave Access.

Windows Microsoft family of operating systems for both network servers and client computers.

Windows 10 Most recent Microsoft Windows client operating system.

Wintel PC Any computer that uses Intel microprocessors (or compatible processors) and a Windows operating system.

wireless sensor networks (WSNs) Networks of interconnected wireless devices with built-in processing, storage, and radio frequency sensors and antennas that are embedded into the physical environment to provide measurements of many points over large spaces.

wisdom The collective and individual experience of applying knowledge to the solution of problems.

wisdom of crowds The belief that large numbers of people can make better decisions about a wide range of topics or products than a single person or even a small committee of experts.

World Wide Web A system with universally accepted standards for storing, retrieving, formatting, and displaying information in a networked environment.

worms Independent software programs that propagate themselves to disrupt the operation of computer networks or destroy data and other programs.

XML (Extensible Markup Language) General-purpose language that describes the structure of a document and can perform presentation, communication, and storage of data, allowing data to be manipulated by the computer.

zero-day vulnerabilities Security vulnerabilities in software, unknown to the creator, that hackers can exploit before the vendor becomes aware of the problem.

INDEXES

Name Index

Organizations Index

Subject Index

OTHER MIS TITLES OF INTEREST

Introductory MIS

Experiencing MIS, 8/e
Kroenke & Boyle ©2019

Using MIS, 11/e
Kroenke & Boyle ©2020

Management Information Systems, 16/e
Laudon & Laudon ©2020

Essentials of MIS, 13/e
Laudon & Laudon ©2019

Processes, Systems, and Information: An Introduction to MIS, 3/e
McKinney & Kroenke ©2019

Information Systems Today, 8/e
Valacich & Schneider ©2018

Introduction to Information Systems, 3/e
Wallace ©2018

Database

Hands-on Database, 2/e
Conger ©2014

Modern Database Management, 13/e
Hoffer, Ramesh, & Topi ©2019

Database Concepts, 9/e
Kroenke, Auer, Vandenberg, Yoder ©2020

Database Processing, 15/e
Kroenke, Auer, Vandenberg, Yoder ©2019

Systems Analysis and Design

Modern Systems Analysis and Design, 9/e
Valacich & George ©2020

Systems Analysis and Design, 10/e
Kendall & Kendall ©2019

Decision Support Systems

Business Intelligence, Analytics, and Data Science, 4/e
Sharda, Delen & Turban ©2018

Analytics, Data Science, and Artificial Intelligence: Systems for Decision Support, 11/e
Sharda, Delen & Turban ©2020

Networking & Security

Business Data Networks and Security, 11/e
Panko & Panko ©2019

Corporate Computer Security, 4/e
Boyle & Panko ©2015

Electronic Commerce

E-commerce 2019: Business, Technology, Society, 15/e
Laudon & Traver ©2020

Project Management

Project Management: Process, Technology and Practice
Vaidyanathan ©2013

INTEGRATING BUSINESS WITH TECHNOLOGY

By completing the projects in this text, students will be able to demonstrate business knowledge, application software proficiency, and Internet skills. These projects can be used by instructors as learning assessment tools and by students as demonstrations of business, software, and problem-solving skills to future employers. Here are some of the skills and competencies students using this text will be able to demonstrate:

Business Application skills: Use of both business and software skills in real-world business applications. Demonstrates both business knowledge and proficiency in spreadsheet, database, and web page/blog creation tools.

Internet skills: Ability to use Internet tools to access information, conduct research, or perform online calculations and analysis.

Analytical, writing and presentation skills: Ability to research a specific topic, analyze a problem, think creatively, suggest a solution, and prepare a clear written or oral presentation of the solution, working either individually or with others in a group.

Business Application Skills

BUSINESS SKILLS	SOFTWARE SKILLS	CHAPTER
Finance and Accounting		
Financial statement analysis	Spreadsheet charts	Chapter 2*
	Spreadsheet formulas	Chapter 10
	Spreadsheet downloading and formatting	
Pricing hardware and software	Spreadsheet formulas	Chapter 5
Technology rent vs. buy decision	Spreadsheet formulas	Chapter 5*
Total Cost of Ownership (TCO) analysis		
Analyzing telecommunications services and costs	Spreadsheet formulas	Chapter 7
Risk assessment	Spreadsheet charts and formulas	Chapter 8
Retirement planning	Spreadsheet formulas and logical functions	Chapter 11
Capital budgeting	Spreadsheet formulas	Chapter 14
		Chapter 14*
Human Resources		
Employee training and skills tracking	Database design	Chapter 13*
	Database querying and reporting	
Job posting database and Web page	Database design	Chapter 15
	Web page design and creation	
Manufacturing and Production		
Analyzing supplier performance and pricing	Spreadsheet date functions	Chapter 2
	Database functions	
	Data filtering	
Inventory management	Importing data into a database	Chapter 6
	Database querying and reporting	
Bill of materials cost sensitivity analysis	Spreadsheet data tables	Chapter 12*
	Spreadsheet formulas	
Sales and Marketing		
Sales trend analysis	Database querying and reporting	Chapter 1
Customer reservation system	Database querying and reporting	Chapter 3

Internet Skills

Analytical, Writing and Presentation Skills*

*Dirt Bikes Running Case on MyLab MIS